Bolivia

Amazon Basin
p286

**The Cordilleras
& Yungas**
p107

Lake Titicaca
p88

**La Paz
& Around**
p46

**Santa Cruz &
Gran Chiquitania**
p253

**Central
Highlands**
p179

**Southern
Altiplano**
p142

**South Central
Bolivia &
the Chaco**
p232

Isabel Albiston, Michael Grosberg, Mark Johanson

Contents

LAKE TITICACA P88

LAGUNA HEDIONDA P170

Contents

UNDERSTAND

SURVIVAL GUIDE

SPECIAL FEATURES

Welcome to Bolivia

Superlative in its natural beauty, rugged, vexing, complex and slightly nerve-racking, Bolivia is one of South America's most diverse and intriguing nations.

Adventure

Bolivia is not for the faint of heart: rattling down the World's Most Dangerous Road into sultry Yungas; soaring breathless above verdant La Paz valleys in a paraglider; jumping on a horse for a Wild West adventure near Tupiza; pulling a catfish that outweighs you out of an Amazon river (and maybe cooking it for dinner!). Whether your tools are crampons and an ice axe for scaling 6000m Andean peaks, or a helmet and bravado for jumping into the abyss on a glider, Bolivia's rocks, rivers and ravines will challenge – nay, provoke – you into pushing your own personal limits.

Culture

Bolivians love a parade, and hardly a month passes without a procession of brightly costumed celebrants honoring an important historical date or deity. You'll hear them from blocks away before the brass bands and whirligigging dancers approach and envelop you (you may even get to join in). Learn about the history and culture of the country's indigenous peoples at excellent museums, and through the continued presence of traditions and customs in everyday life. Bolivia has South America's largest percentage of indigenous people – get to know them better by participating in community-based tourism and hiring local guides.

Nature

Bolivia is so biodioverse that unique species are being discovered to this day. Tiptoe into caves of tube-lipped nectar bats, their tongues probing the darkness. Tread lightly on the terrain of the poisonous annellated coral snake, deadly in look and effect. Listen for the cackling call and response of a dozen different macaw species (among 1000 bird species) including the world's rarest, the bluebeard, which can only be found here. Multihued butterflies and moths flit at your feet in the jungle; lithe alpacas and vicuñas stand out in the stark altiplano. Deep in the forest live jaguars, pumas and bears.

Food & Drink

Ever had a llama tenderloin? Here's your chance, maybe with a glass of Tarija wine. Bolivia's food is as diverse as its peoples and you'll find new delicacies to sample in every town. Markets are a good place to start, though the steaming pots of unfamiliar concoctions might test your nerve. Freshly blended fruit juices will no doubt become a daily habit, and Yungas coffee can be found in a number of new cafes that are popping up around Bolivia. La Paz, Cochabamba and Santa Cruz have thriving restaurant scenes where you can sample contemporary takes on traditional local dishes.

Why I Love Bolivia

By Isabel Albiston, Writer

My first impressions of La Paz are imprinted on my mind: steep narrow streets, piercing blue skies, colorful textiles, popcorn vendors in pigeon-filled squares. What I took to be a parade (people in traditional Andean dress with drums) turned out to be a political protest. I was hooked! In Bolivia, traditional life is interspersed with 21st-century modernity like a mixed-up pack of photographs. It's a country of sublime landscapes, where true adventures are possible in a way that often eludes travelers. The swaths of wildlife-filled forests and the immensity of the mountains always draw me back.

For more about our writers, see p384

Above: Traditional dance performance on Isla del Sol (p100)

Bolivia

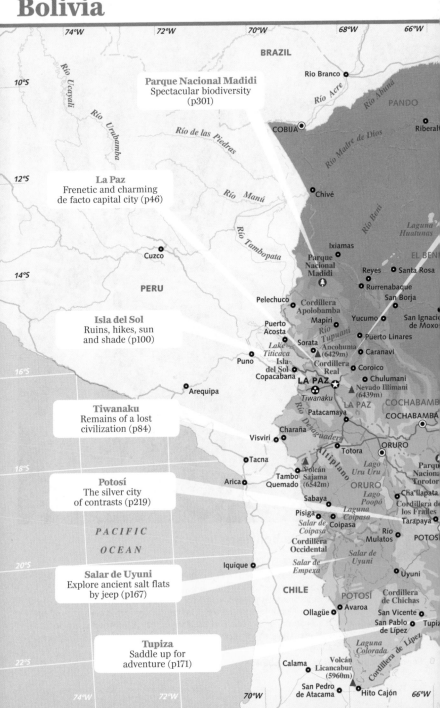

Parque Nacional Madidi
Spectacular biodiversity
(p301)

La Paz
Frenetic and charming
de facto capital city (p46)

Isla del Sol
Ruins, hikes, sun
and shade (p100)

Tiwanaku
Remains of a lost
civilization (p84)

Potosí
The silver city
of contrasts (p219)

Salar de Uyuni
Explore ancient salt flats
by jeep (p167)

Tupiza
Saddle up for
adventure (p171)

BRAZIL

PERU

CHILE

PACIFIC

OCEAN

PANDO

EL BENI

LA PAZ

COCHABAMBA

ORURO

POTOSÍ

Rio Branco

Río Acre

Río Abuná

COBIJA

Riberal

Río Madre de Dios

Río de las Piedras

Chivé

Río Manú

Río Beni

Laguna
Huatunas

Ixiamas

Parque
Nacional
Madidi

Reyes   Santa Rosa

Rurrenabaque

San Borja

San Ignacio
de Moxo

Cuzco

Pelechuco   Cordillera
Apolobamba

Mapiri   Yucumo

Puerto
Acosta   Río
Tupuani   Puerto Linares

Sorata   Ancohuma
(6429m)   Caranavi

Puno   Isla
del Sol   Cordillera
Real   Coroico

Copacabana   LA PAZ   Chulumani
Nevado Illimani
(6439m)

Arequipa   Tiwanaku
Patacamaya   COCHABAMBA

Charaña   Río Desaguadero

Visviri   Totora   ORURO

Tacna   Altiplano   Lago
Uru Uru   Parqu
Nacional
Tororot

Arica   Tambo
Quemado   Volcán
Sajama
(6542m)   ORURO   Cha'lapata

Sabaya   Lago
Poopó   Cordillera de
los Frailes

Pisiga   Laguna
Coipasa   Tarapaya

Salar de
Coipasa   Coipasa   Río
Mulatos   POTOSÍ

Cordillera
Occidental   Salar de
Uyuni

Iquique   Salar de
Empexa   Uyuni

POTOSÍ   Cordillera
de Chichas

Ollagüe   Avaroa   San Vicente

San Pablo   Tupi
de Lípez

Laguna
Colorada

Calama   Volcán
Licancabur
(5960m)   Cordillera de Lípez

San Pedro
de Atacama   Hito Cajón

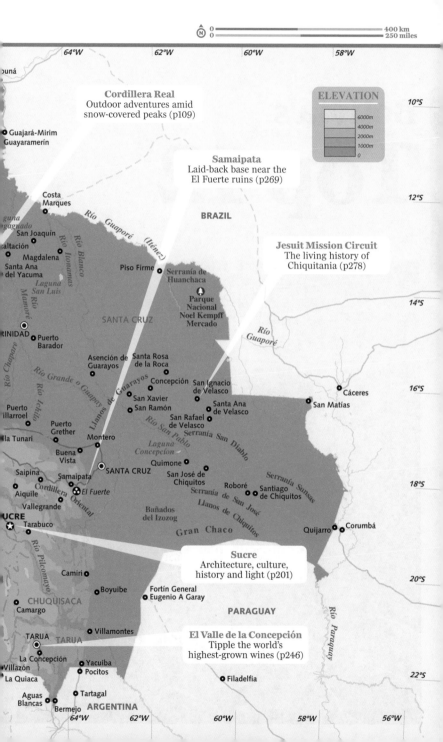

Cordillera Real
Outdoor adventures amid
snow-covered peaks (p109)

Samaipata
Laid-back base near the
El Fuerte ruins (p269)

Jesuit Mission Circuit
The living history of
Chiquitania (p278)

Sucre
Architecture, culture,
history and light (p201)

El Valle de la Concepción
Tipple the world's
highest-grown wines (p246)

ELEVATION

6000m
4000m
2000m
1000m
0

N

0
0
400 km
250 miles

64°W   62°W   60°W   58°W

10°S

buná

Guajará-Mirim
Guayaramerín

Costa
Marques

BRAZIL

12°S

guna
agagnado
San Joaquín

altación

Magdalena

Santa Ana
del Yacuma

Laguna
San Luis

Río Iténez

Río Guaporé (Iénez)

Piso Firme

Serranía de
Huanchaca

Parque
Nacional
Noel Kempff
Mercado

14°S

Río Blanco

Río Mamoré

TRINIDAD   Puerto
Barador

SANTA CRUZ

Río
Guaporé

Río Chapare

Río Grande o Guapay

Asención de
Guarayos

Santa Rosa
de la Roca

Concepción

San Ignacio
de Velasco

Cáceres

16°S

San Matías

Puerto
Villarroel

Río Ichilo

Puerto
Grether

lla Tunari

Buena
Vista

Montero

San Xavier

San Ramón

San Rafael
de Velasco

Santa Ana
de Velasco

Llanos de Guarayos

Río San Pablo

Serranía San Diablo

Saipina

Aiquile

Samaipata

SANTA CRUZ

Laguna
Concepción

Quimone

Cordillera Oriental

El Fuerte

San José de
Chiquitos

Roboré

Santiago
de Chiquitos

Serranía Sansas

18°S

Vallegrande

Bañados
del Izozog

Serranía de San José

Llanos de Chiquitos

SUCRE   Tarabuco

Gran Chaco

Quijarro   Corumbá

Río Pilcomayo

Camiri

Boyuibe

Fortín General
Eugenio A Garay

20°S

CHUQUISACA
Camargo

PARAGUAY

Río Paraguay

TARIJA   TARIJA

Villamontes

La Concepción

Villazón

La Quiaca

Yacuiba

Pocitos

Filadelfia

22°S

Aguas
Blancas

Bermejo

Tartagal

ARGENTINA

64°W   62°W   60°W   58°W   56°W

Bolivia's
Top 12

Salar de Uyuni

1 Who knew feeling this cold could feel so good? While a three- to four-day jeep tour through the world's largest salt flat (p167) will leave your bones chattering, it could quite possibly be the defining experience of your Bolivian adventure. The vastness, austerity and crystalline perfection of the salt flat will inspire you. An early-morning exploration of rock gardens, geyser fields and piping-hot springs along with the camaraderie of three days on the road with your fellow 'Salterians' will create a lasting memory.

Parque Nacional Madidi

2 Perhaps the most biodiverse area on the planet, Parque Nacional Madidi (p301) encompasses a spellbinding range of habitats, from Andean mountains to steamy lowland rainforests, home to an astonishing array of wildlife. Take it all in on guided rainforest walks and boat trips on the river before bedding down for the night at one of several community-run eco-lodges. Here the cinematic beauty of the surroundings is enhanced by a soundtrack of birdsong at dawn, the buzzing of insects, the call of the howler monkey and the croaking of frogs.

SERGIO PESSOLANO/GETTY IMAGES ©

JESS KRAFT/SHUTTERSTOCK ©

Trekking in the Cordillera Real

3 Walk in the path of the Incas along the many trekking routes that weave their way from the Andes into the Amazon Basin, through the remarkable skyward-bound wilderness of the Cordillera Real (p109). These four- to 14-day treks are no small undertaking, but it will be worth every step, every drop of sweat and every blister. Along the way, you'll have the chance to dine with locals, cool off beside cascading waterfalls and connect with Pachamama (Mother Earth) deep within her potent green realm.

Isla del Sol, Lake Titicaca

4 Plopped onto sprawling Lake Titicaca like the cherry on an ice-cream sundae, Isla del Sol (p100) is considered the birthplace of Andean civilization. You can easily spend four days here, tracking down forgotten Inca roads to small archaeological sites, remote coves and intact indigenous communities. At the end of the day, take in the sunset with a *cerveza* (beer) from your ridgetop lodge. The lake itself has a magnetism, power and energy unique to this world – no wonder many claim the ancient civilization of Atlantis was found here.

ALEJANDRO ZEBALLOS/500PX ©

ELISA LOCCI/SHUTTERSTOCK ©

La Paz Markets

5 The whirling engine that feeds and fuels a nation, the markets (p62) of La Paz are so crazy, so disjointed, so colorful and mad and stinky and remarkable that you'll end up spending at least a few afternoons wandering from stall to stall. There are sections for food, sections for sorcery, sections where you can buy back your stolen camera, sections for pipes and Styrofoam – in every shape and form imaginable – and sections packed with fruits, flowers and rotting fish that will push you to olfactory overload.

Sucre

6 Glistening in the Andean sun, the white city of Sucre (p201) is the birthplace of the nation and a must-see for any visitor to Bolivia. Occupying a lush valley, surrounded by mountains, it's an eclectic mix of the old and the new. Here you can while away your days perusing historic buildings and museums, and spend your nights enjoying the city's famous nightlife. Visitors to Sucre invariably fall in love with the place. Universidad San Francisco Xavier, home to the Museos Universitarios (p205)

Samaipata

7 Cosmopolitan Samaipata (p269) manages to retain the air of a relaxing mountain village, despite becoming an increasingly unmissable stop on the Bolivian tourist trail. But it's not just the rolling valley views, pleasant climate, great-value accommodations and top-class restaurants that bring in the visitors. Samaipata's proximity to the mystical El Fuerte ruins (p270; pictured) and a series of worthy day trips to nearby areas of outstanding natural beauty mean that many visitors find themselves staying for a lot longer than they planned.

JESS KRAFT/500PX ©

Tupiza

8 Cut from the pages of a Wild West novel, the canyon country around Tupiza (p171) is an awesome place for heading off into the sunset (in a saddle, atop a mountain bike, on foot or in a 4WD). From town you can ramble out into the polychromatic desert wonderlands and canyons, visiting hard-cut mining villages and the town where Butch Cassidy and the Sundance Kid met their end. The pleasant weather and lyrical feel of the town make it a welcome retreat after a bit of hardship in the highlands.

Wine Tasting near Tarija

9 Take a deep breath of the thin mountain air and prepare to get dizzy sampling wine from the world's highest vineyards, in Tarija (p234). Produced in a Mediterranean climate at altitudes of up to 2400m, these wines are sold throughout Bolivia and have received international plaudits for their fresh, aromatic taste. Whether you prefer *tinto*, *rosado* or *blanco* (red, rosé or white), you are likely to be pleasantly surprised by the quality on offer and may find yourself taking a bottle or two home for your friends.

Tiwanaku

10 Bolivia's hallmark archaeological site (p84) sets your imagination on fire. Despite lacking the power and prestige of other ruins in Latin America – those who have visited Machu Picchu or Tikal will be hard pressed not to strike comparisons – for history buffs this pre-Inca site has a lot to offer. A massive celebration is held on the solstices, and the on-site museum provides a thought-provoking glimpse into life in this religious and astronomical center. An easy day trip from La Paz, Tiwanaku is a good place to start your Andean odyssey.

Potosí

11 Said to be the highest city in the world, Potosí (p219) once sat upon a land laden with silver that funded the Spanish empire for centuries. Though the silver mines lie barren, the remnants of the wealthy past can still be seen through the cracked brickwork of the ornate colonial-era buildings and wonderfully preserved churches. Potosí's most famous museum, the Casa Nacional de la Moneda (p221; pictured), was once Bolivia's national mint and offers a fascinating insight into the rise and fall of a city that once described itself as 'the envy of kings.'

Jesuit Mission Circuit

12 Though traveling around the mission circuit (p278) is a challenge in itself, the fantastically ornate reconstructions of Jesuit churches that are the centerpieces of the villages along the route make it well worth the effort. Lovingly restored by professional artisans and historians to offer a glimpse of their former glory, the churches of the mission circuit are testimony to the efforts of the missionaries who, against all odds, managed to establish communities in remote Chiquitania before being expelled from the Spanish colonies in 1767. San José de Chiquitos (p284)

Need to Know

For more information, see Survival Guide (p343)

Currency
Boliviano (B$)

Languages
Spanish, Quechua
and Aymará

Visas
US citizens need a visa
to visit Bolivia. Citizens
of Australia, Canada,
New Zealand and most
European countries do
not need a visa.

Money
Cash is king, dollars
are better than euros;
watch for counterfeits.
ATMs and credit cards
accepted in cities and
many towns.

Time
One hour ahead of US
Eastern Standard Time
(GMT/UTC minus four
hours)

Cell Phones
Cellular SIM cards are
cheap, include credit
and are available from
larger carrier outlets
as well as small private
phone shops.
    Make sure your
phone has triband
network capabilities.

When to Go

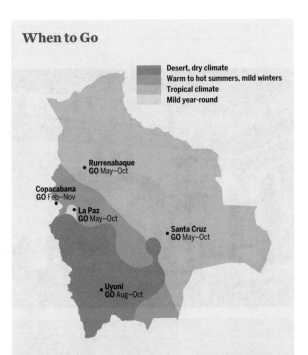

Desert, dry climate
Warm to hot summers, mild winters
Tropical climate
Mild year-round

Rurrenabaque
GO May–Oct

Copacabana
GO Feb–Nov

La Paz
GO May–Oct

Santa Cruz
GO May–Oct

Uyuni
GO Aug–Oct

High Season
(May–Oct)

➡ Mostly sunny days
throughout Bolivia
but cooler in the
altiplano.

➡ Reliable weather
means easier
transit, and better
climbing, trekking
and mountain
biking.

➡ Higher prices
for tours and
accommodations.

Shoulder
(Oct–Nov)

➡ Spring draws in
and temperatures
begin to rise,
though the
weather is
mostly dry.

➡ A great time to
visit the Salar de
Uyuni.

➡ Crowds begin to
disperse; a good
time for budget
hunters.

Low Season
(Nov–Apr)

➡ Summer is rainy
season; it can be
miserable in the
lowlands.

➡ Overland
transportation
becomes difficult
where the roads
are unpaved.

➡ Climbing is
dangerous, and
trekking and
biking tedious.

Useful Websites

Bolivia.com (www.bolivia.com, in Spanish) News and cultural information.

Bolivian Express (www.bolivianexpress.org) English magazine focusing on cultural coverage.

Bolivia Online (www.bolivia-online.net) Solid portal in English, Spanish and German.

Bolivia en Tus Manos (Bolivia in Your Hands, www.boliviaentusmanos.com, in Spanish) News, culture and tourism site.

Lonely Planet (www.lonelyplanet.com/bolivia) Destination information, hotel bookings, traveler forum and more.

Important Numbers

Country Code	📞591
International Access Code	📞00
Ambulance	📞118
Fire	📞119
Operator	📞104

Exchange Rates

Australia	A$1	B$5.03
Canada	C$1	B$5.22
Europe	€1	B$7.86
Japan	¥100	B$6.25
New Zealand	NZ$1	B$4.55
UK	£1	B$8.81
US	US$1	B$6.91

For current exchange rates, see www.xe.com.

Daily Costs

Budget: less than B$200

➡ Dorm/budget beds: B$40–70

➡ Bread for breakfast, set lunch, dinner supplies bought in local market: B$50

➡ Museum admission, limited tours: B$125

➡ 2nd-class transit: B$70–100

Midrange: B$200–650

➡ Midrange hotel: B$160–400

➡ Hotel breakfast, lunch and dinner in a restaurant: B$200

➡ Extra cash for beers, guided trips, excursions: B$300

➡ 1st-class transit: B$150–200

Top end: more than B$650

➡ Top-end hotel: B$400

➡ Breakfast buffet, lunch and dinner at high-end restaurant: B$250

➡ Plenty of extra cash for guided trips: B$300–400

➡ 1st-class transit and air transfers: B$300–500

Opening Hours

Banks Standard hours 9am–4pm or 6pm Monday to Friday, and 10am–noon or 5pm Saturday.

Shops Weekdays 10am–7pm but sometimes close for lunch noon–2pm. Open 10am–noon or 5pm Saturdays.

Restaurants Hours vary, but are generally open for breakfast (8am–10am), lunch (noon–3pm) and dinner (6pm–10pm or 11pm) daily.

Arriving in Bolivia

El Alto International Airport, La Paz (p352) A taxi costs B$70 (US$10) to the city center. Minibuses charge B$3.80 (US$0.50) during the day. Note that the airport is at a high altitude (4050m).

Viru-Viru International, Santa Cruz (p352) A taxi costs B$70 (US$10) to the city center. Alternatively take the minibus, which charges B$6 (US$1) to the city center.

Jorge Wilstermann International Airport, Cochabamba (p352) Micro B (B$2) shuttles between the airport and the main plaza. Taxis to or from the center cost B$25 to B$30.

Getting Around

Air Air travel is the quickest and most reliable way to reach out-of-the-way places, and it's reasonably inexpensive.

Bus The most popular form of transport; it can be uncomfortable and at times nerve-racking, but it's cheap and relatively safe.

Tours Popular and hassle-free way to get to remote locations like the Salar de Uyuni.

Train Around the same price as the bus, but much slower. It does, however, offer heating and air-conditioning.

For much more on **getting around**, see p353

First Time Bolivia

For more information, see Survival Guide (p343)

Checklist

➡ Check the up-to-date visa requirements for your country

➡ Get any vaccinations you might need

➡ Make sure your passport is valid for at least six months past your arrival date

➡ Check the airline baggage restrictions

➡ Arrange for appropriate travel insurance

➡ Check your debit and credit card will work abroad

What to Pack

➡ Proof of vaccination for yellow fever

➡ Copy of your passport

➡ Plug adapter

➡ Binoculars for wildlife watching

➡ Headlamp

➡ Sleeping bag for the altiplano

➡ Sunscreen and a hat

➡ First-aid kit and bug spray

➡ Ear plugs

➡ Small padlock

Top Tips for Your Trip

➡ Allow yourself plenty of time to acclimatize to the altitude. Go up slowly and take it easy when you reach new heights.

➡ Even a little Spanish will be a huge help in Bolivia. If you can, take some classes before you travel.

➡ Prepare yourself for sometimes challenging but always rewarding travel experiences. Your trip will go more smoothly if you are patient and flexible.

➡ Allow time in your schedule for unexpected delays. Keep an eye on the news and ask locals about potential *bloqueos* (road closures caused by protesters) that might affect your travel plans.

➡ Stay away from political protests. They might pique your interest, but clashes could happen at any time.

➡ Be respectful of local people and don't take photographs without asking permission, no matter how tempting it is to take a snap of someone in traditional dress.

What to Wear

Bolivia is a tough travel destination with a climate that can swing from extremely cold to extremely hot to extremely wet in just a few hours or kilometers. It's best to be practical when deciding on clothes, and wear whatever will make you most comfortable and keep you warm/cool/dry as necessary. Clothes should be hard-wearing and able to withstand getting on and off dusty vehicles and the odd rough surface. If you are going to the altiplano, wear thermals and warm clothes. You'll need a rain jacket (year-round) as well as sunglasses. Bring sturdy shoes.

Sleeping

Bolivian accommodations are among South America's cheapest, though price and value are hardly uniform. In the altiplano, having heat and hot water often makes the difference in price, while in lowland areas, air-con and fans are common delimiters.

Yellow-Fever Vaccination Certificates

Border agents may or may not request a yellow-fever vaccination certificate, but there are occasional checkpoints heading into the lowlands, where you will need to produce a certificate. Some neighboring countries, including Brazil, require anyone entering from Bolivia to have proof of a yellow-fever vaccination. If necessary, a jab can often be administered at the border but it is preferable to take care of this at home.

Bargaining

Gentle haggling is usually fine at markets, and some negotiation is common if arranging a service such as renting a taxi for a day. Use your judgement and decide if the price seems fair; attempts to bargain hard may become uncomfortable. Bear in mind that many Bolivians have very little money, and arguing over a dollar or two probably isn't worth it.

Tipping

Restaurants Service is not usually included in the bill; leave 10% to 15%.

Tours Guides are grateful for tips (10% to 20% is the norm); remember that their wage is often much lower than the tour price.

Taxis Tipping is not expected, though it's common to round up.

At the Mercado Negro (p62) in La Paz

Etiquette

Greetings A handshake is the most usual form of greeting. When meeting, people will usually say *buenos días* (good morning), *buenas tardes* (good afternoon) or *buenas noches* (good evening).

Forms of Address It is common to use *señor/señora* and the *usted* form of address (using *usted* and the corresponding verb forms rather than *tú* for the word 'you') with people you don't know well. On the altiplano, some locals will use *amigo/amiga*, which is intended to show friendliness.

Photographs Ask permission to take photographs of people, especially in rural areas.

Politics It's fine to express well-informed opinions, and Bolivians are generally happy to talk about their political views. Naturally, you should be tactful and avoid being overtly critical of the country.

Eating When passing a table of diners who are seated in a restaurant, it's common to say *buen provecho* (enjoy your meal).

Eating

Long dismissed as the poor relation of South American cuisine, Bolivia is emerging as a foodie destination, with a string of highly-rated restaurants attracting acclaim. Variety adds to the appeal: Bolivia's culinary scene is as diverse as its peoples and landscapes. Many traditional recipes used today have been passed down over generations, and fresh market produce, free-range livestock and local grains have long been in fashion here.

If You Like...

Adventure Sports
This Andean nation has kick-ass mountain biking, lost summits that have only seen a handful of ascents, 'easy' 6000m climbs for beginners, plus adrenaline-charged activities.

Climbing Step into this mountaineer's dreamland with steep, glaciated peaks that see little traffic. (p29)

Mountain biking With elevation drops of 4000m, Bolivia offers some of the best mountain-bike descents in the world. (p31)

Paragliding Paragliding in Cordillera Real and Central Highlands (La Paz and Cochabamba) is as good as it gets. (p34)

Boating Take a flat-water Amazon cruise, troll Titicaca in a *totora* (reed) boat or power your way through white-water rock gardens. (p32)

History
History buffs will be spoiled for choice, with archaeological sites, well-preserved colonial cities, mystical cathedrals and missions to explore.

Sucre Bolivia's white city is home to some of the nation's best museums. (p201)

Potosí This colonial city fueled Bolivia's economy for hundreds of years. (p219)

La Paz A wealth of museums are located in the country's capital. (p48)

Tiwanaku Bolivia's best-known pre-Inca ceremonial site has large ritual platforms, monoliths and a mysterious arch. (p85)

El Fuerte Hilltop ruins that hold the secrets of a number of peoples and cultures. (p270)

Jesuit Mission Circuit There's a mystical air to the missions of the Chiquitania region outside Santa Cruz. (p278)

Wildlife Watching
Bolivia is a hands-down favorite for nature lovers and bird-watchers.

Parque Nacional Madidi The Amazon comes to you in Bolivia's most well-known national park. (p301)

Parque Nacional Tunari Easily accessed wilderness area just outside Cochabamba. (p194)

Parque Nacional Amboró This national park is home to rare species, such as the spectacled bear, and is a bird-watcher's paradise. (p267)

Parque Nacional Sajama The bleak landscape of Sajama is home to rheas, vicuñas and even some Andean wildcats. (p154)

Parque Nacional Carrasco Explore the cloud forest of this isolated park that's full of mammals, reptiles and birds. (p292)

Valle de los Condores Spot condors gliding over and around high-altitude cliffs. (p238)

Trekking
For long-distance hauls and shorter day trips along ancient Inca paving, down cloud-encased valleys and through vast swaths of untamed wilderness, you can't beat Bolivia's treks.

El Choro Traversing Parque Nacional Cotopata, the Choro trek is the most popular trip around. (p120)

Takesi Unique cultural experiences await in the remote rural villages along this easily accessible option. (p122)

Yunga Cruz The most demanding of the Inca treks, this trip takes you over the shoulder of Illimani down into the warm climes of the Yungas. (p123)

Cordillera de los Frailes Immerse yourself in Jalq'a culture on this fun village-to-village trek outside Sucre. (p214)

Artisan Crafts
Take a little piece of Bolivia home with you: intricate textiles, witch's talismans, high-quality silver, baskets, scarves, shawls and more.

Musical instruments For *charangos* (ukulele-like instruments) and those famous

panpipes, head to La Paz's Calle Sagárnaga. (p75)

Silver One of the country's prime exports takes artistic form in the crafts shops of Potosí. (p229)

Ceramics Towns such as Huay-culli specialize in unique ceramics, often with an Andean twist. (p194)

Weaving Head out to off-the-beaten-path villages like Cande-laria and see some of the finest woven rugs around. (p207)

Woolen goods Scour the alti-plano for scarves and sweaters made from alpaca, llama and even vicuña wool. (p157)

Art

Bolivia's rich cultural herit-age is evident in its diverse artworks.

Museo de Arte Indígena Dis-plays art by indigenous groups in the Sucre area. (p201)

Museo Nacional del Arte This museum in La Paz focuses on religious themes. (p53)

Museos Universitarios Three separate halls housing colonial relics, anthropological artifacts and modern art. (p205)

Museo Casa Arte Taller Cardozo Velasquez The unique sculptures of this talented artist are displayed in his Oruro home. (p147)

La Capilla Sixtina del Altiplano The painted interior of this remote church has earned it the moniker: the 'Sistine Chapel of the Andes.' (p153)

Salar Galería de Arte Bolivia's top contemporary artists show-case their work here. (p49)

Mamani Mamani Gallery The colorful work of Roberto Mamani Mamani is displayed and sold in this gallery. (p53)

Santuario Mariano de la Torre Intricately carved wooden pillars, and a moving memorial. (p283)

Top: Illimani (p112)

Bottom: Charangos

Month by Month

January

Although part of summer, this is the rainiest month of the year, making getting around tough. Climbing is basically out of the question, but you could rough it on hikes and other outdoor activities.

🎊 Día de los Reyes Magos

'Kings' Day' (Epiphany) is celebrated on January 6 as the day the three wise kings visited baby Jesus after his birth. The largest celebrations are in Reyes (in the Beni region), Sucre, Tarija, and rural villages in the departments of Oruro, Cochabamba and Potosí.

🎊 Alasitas

Taking place in La Paz and Copacabana on January 24 and for two weeks after, this giant fair celebrates Ekeko, the Aymará god of abundance, with stalls and street vendors selling miniatures of items people are longing for – tiny houses, cars, banknotes etc. (p61)

February

This wet and warm month sees important celebrations for Pachamama (Mother Earth), especially in traditional communities, with ceremonies and rituals taking place in her honor.

🎊 Fiesta de La Virgen de Candelaria

This week-long festival is held during the first week of February in Aiquile (Cochabamba), Samaipata (Santa Cruz), Angostura (Tarija) and Cha'llapampa (Oruro). The biggest celebration kicks off on February 2 in Copacabana. (p93)

🎊 Carnaval

Celebrations are held nationwide the week before Lent. Oruro is known for having the most colorful Carnaval fiesta; Santa Cruz, Sucre and Tarija follow suit. Carnaval dates change each year, depending on when Lent falls, so check your calendar.

March

The rain starts to taper off, making it slightly easier to get around. You could consider heading out for a trek or on a mountain bike. River rafting is getting good.

🎊 Semana Santa

One of the most impressive of the Holy Week activities is the Good Friday fiesta in Copacabana, when hundreds of pilgrims arrive on foot. It's a fun time across the country. (p93)

🎊 Pujllay

Celebrated in Tarabuco on the second Sunday in March, indigenous people gather to mark the 1816 victory of local armies over Spanish troops with ritual dancing, song, music and *chicha* (fermented corn) drinking. (p213)

May

Winter is here! The weather is nice in the lowlands, but transit can still be a mess. The rains are nearly gone, and outdoor activity begins.

🎊 Fiesta de la Cruz

The Festival of the Cross (May 3) brings revelry to Vallegrande (Santa Cruz), Cochabamba and Copacabana. Tinku ritual combats take place in rural communities around Potosí.

⭐ Gran Poder

Held in late May or early June, La Festividad de Nuestro Señor Jesús del Gran Poder in Laz Paz involves candle processions, elaborate costumes and dancing. (p61)

June

It's getting a little too cold for comfort in the altiplano, but the rains are basically gone. Transport in the lowlands should be getting easier and temperatures are cooling off.

⭐ Willkakuti

On June 21, the Aymará celebrate the winter solstice – the return of the new sun – and their New Year. The biggest ceremony takes place overnight in Tiwanaku. (p87)

⭐ San Juan

This Christian holiday is held nationwide (June 24), with bonfires, fireworks and traditional burning of wood. The largest celebrations take place around Santa Cruz, with firewalkers in the village of Porongo.

July

High season is in full swing. It's dry and cold in the altiplano, cooler and drier in the lowlands, and just nice in the areas in between.

⭐ Fiesta del Santo Patrono de Moxos

Running from July 22 to the end of the month, this

kick-ass festival is the biggest in Beni. Expect outrageous costumes, plenty of drinking and some hard partying. (p305)

⭐ Fiesta del Señor Santiago

In Parque National Torotoro, villages celebrate the Fiesta del Señor Santiago with sheep sacrifices, dynamite explosions, colorful costumes and plenty of *chicha*. (p199)

August

It's the height of the tourist season and starting to warm up a little in the altiplano, making it a good time to visit the Salar de Uyuni. Important religious and indigenous festivals also take place.

⭐ Independence Day

This lively public holiday (August 6) sees lots of gunfire in the air and parades galore. It's celebrated everywhere, but is especially boisterous in Copacabana. (p94)

⭐ Fiesta de la Virgen de Urkupiña

Folkloric musicians and dancers from around the country gather in Quillacollo near Cochabamba to perform in front of cheering, intoxicated crowds. (p186)

September

Some tourists head home, making this cool, dry time perfect to pick up deals. Conditions for adventure sports continue to be excellent, though expect a slight increase in rain.

⭐ Fiesta de San Roque

One of Tarija's biggest celebrations, San Roque marks the end of the plague and leprosy in the area. It kicks off on August 16, but most of the celebrations begin on the first Sunday of September, lasting eight days. (p240)

October

At the end of winter (and the high season), rainfall spikes in the lowlands, while it's still relatively tolerable in the altiplano. Deals can be had, but it's getting tougher to climb, trek and generally be outdoors. It'll stay rainy until April.

☆ Feria del Charango

For over 30 years, *charanguistas* (people who play the *charango*) from around the globe have come by the thousands to the little burg of Aiquile, four hours from Cochabamba, to get their 10-string groove on.

December

One of the hottest months of the year in the lowlands, with humid days and warm nights. The rain continues in the altiplano and tours may not be possible.

⭐ New Year's Eve

Street vendors sell underwear before January 1. Red will help your love life, with yellow for money and pink for health. When the gongs chime at midnight, 12 grapes are swallowed for good luck. Fake money is counted to signal wealth in the new year.

Itineraries

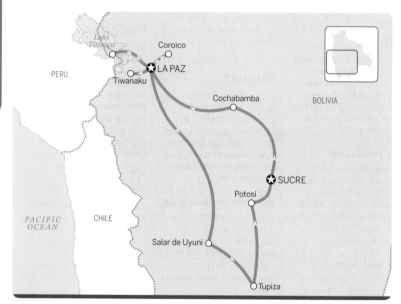

 2 WEEKS Best of Bolivia

This bare-bones itinerary will take you to the best of Bolivia – from colorful markets to stark salt plains to a city in the sky – at a head-rattling pace.

Start with a day of acclimatization in **La Paz**, visiting the markets. History buffs can take a side trip to **Tiwanaku**. From La Paz, head to **Lake Titicaca**. Allow up to three days on the lake to take in the sites of Copacabana and Isla del Sol and continue acclimatization. From there, circle down the altiplano (via La Paz) to the **Salar de Uyuni** for a bone-chatteringly cold three-day jeep tour. Extend your trip to the former territory of Butch Cassidy in the pleasant cowboy town of **Tupiza**.

Swing up to **Potosí**, a starkly beautiful Unesco World Heritage city, situated at 4070m, where you can visit the mint and mines. After a day or two, head to the white city of **Sucre** to hang out with students in grand plazas. Return to La Paz via **Cochabamba**, taking in the views along the way. On your last day in La Paz, consider a day of museum-hopping or take a mountain-bike ride down the World's Most Dangerous Road to **Coroico**.

Top: Parque Nacional Sajama (p154)

Bottom: At the Fiesta de la Virgen de Guadalupe (p207)

RAFAL CICHAWA/SHUTTERSTOCK ©

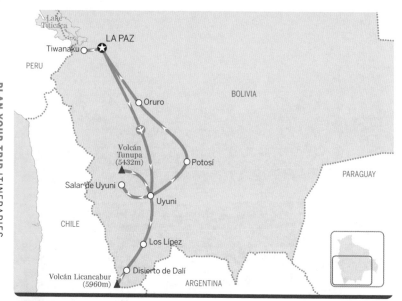

Altiplano Highlights

With one week to play with, this itinerary allows time to get a taste of life in an Andean city and take in the awe-inspiring scenery of the Salar de Uyuni.

Fly into **La Paz** and spend two days exploring the city's museums and galleries while you acclimatize. Soak in the atmosphere of the Andean markets, dine at La Paz's excellent restaurants, and dip into the city's coffee and bar scene. Zip up in the *teleférico* to see the unusual architecture of the neighborhood of El Alto, then visit a *peña* (folk-music venue) in La Paz's *Casco Viejo* neighborhood. If you have time, consider a day trip to see the ruins at **Tiwanaku**, where you'll find carved monoliths, archways and arcades, and two museums. From La Paz, take a flight to **Uyuni** to pick up a three-day jeep tour to the *salar* (salt desert). Get your camera and your plastic dinosaur ready for photos that play with perspective on the endless white crusty surface of the salt flats, and for snaps of spectacular sunsets. Brave the cold to gaze at the stars in the dark night sky.

Continue via the colored lakes of **Los Lípez**, with stops to spot flighty flamingos and geysers, and to take a dip in some thermal springs, before looping back through the otherworldly landscape of the **Desierto de Dalí** to Uyuni. If you can cope with the altitude, consider adding a volcano climb to your itinerary; custom tours can include a hike up **Volcán Licancabur** (5960m) or **Volcán Tunupa** (5432m). Spend a night in Uyuni to rest after the tour, before catching a bus to **Potosí**. Take a day or two to wander the streets and check out the city's museums and mines. If you have time, take the bus back to La Paz, breaking the journey in **Oruro**. This gritty mining city has some quirky museums and there are opportunities for day trips to neighboring villages. Alternatively, catch a flight from Potosí to La Paz.

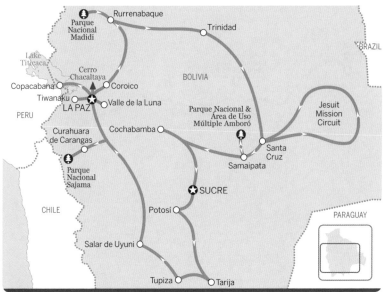

 The Whole Country

Set aside five weeks to acclimatize to the high altitude, take in one of Bolivia's signature treks, climb a peak, do a mountain-bike trip or simply dive into Bolivian culture.

From **La Paz** you can choose from a variety of day trips, including a visit to **Tiwanaku** or hiking in nearby **Chacaltaya** or **Valle de la Luna**. The adventurous can take on the Takesi or Choro treks, or ride a bike (or bus) down the World's Most Dangerous Road to **Coroico** in the Yungas. Next head north to **Rurrenabaque** and the famous **Parque Nacional Madidi** – depending on your time and budget you can get here by land, air or boat. Take the time to explore this wild, little-trodden utopia. From 'Rurre,' take a bus to **Trinidad**, where you can kick back for a few days, eating river fish and seeing a museum or two, before heading by plane or bus to **Santa Cruz**. From here you'll kick off a multiday road trip through the **Jesuit Mission Circuit**, curling back around via Santa Cruz to the unique ruins near the hippie village of **Samaipata** and the spectacular **Parque Nacional & Área de Uso Múltiple Amboró**. Head up to **Cochabamba** for good market buys. From there you'll start gaining some altitude as you pass through the culturally charged towns of **Sucre** and **Potosí**. After you've had your fill of these colonial masterpieces, cruise down to wine country near **Tarija** for a few days of warm weather, wine and chilled-to-perfection zen. You can then loop across to **Tupiza** for a day or two of mountain biking, while you arrange your four-day **Salar de Uyuni** trip, going the back way to avoid the crowds. On the way back toward La Paz, adventurous spirits may wish to stop near **Curahuara de Carangas**, before heading on to the high-plains wonderland of **Parque Nacional Sajama**, where hot springs and wildlife watching await.

If you still have time, continue through La Paz to **Copacabana** for a day or two of beachfront fun on **Lake Titicaca**. Cruise over on the ferry, stopping at Isla de la Luna for an afternoon on your way to Isla del Sol. It'd be easy to spend five days here, trekking to lost valleys, ruins and small indigenous villages.

PLAN YOUR TRIP ITINERARIES

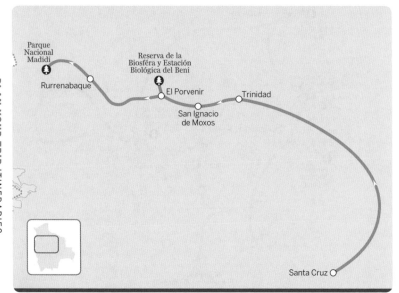

4 WEEKS: Exploring the Amazon

More than half of Bolivia's territory lies in the Amazon, and yet this is one of the least visited parts of the country. Waterway adventures here are good (and wet) in the rainy season, but if you plan on any type of road travel you should stick with the dry months.

Start in **Santa Cruz**, a sophisticated and cosmopolitan city with a dreamy (sometimes steamy) climate and tropical atmosphere. Dip into the urban culture for a while and party with the rich kids in the *discotecas,* or take a day trip to nearby gardens or waterfalls. From here fly or catch the overnight bus to **Trinidad**, a growing town with a pretty plaza. Stay in town for a bit, whirl around on a motorcycle for a local fish meal, take a visit to a museum or two and have a much-needed siesta or three – it gets hot.

A three-hour bus ride will take you to the Jesuit mission village of **San Ignacio de Moxos** – if possible, plan your trip around the town's colorful, not-to-be-missed festival in July. From here, wildlife watchers should make a detour via **El Porvenir** into **Reserva de la Biosféra Estación Biológica del Beni**, where the trained eye can spot up to 500 unique species of birds, including a cornucopia of herons and egrets, along with prayerful cormorants, with wings spread in apparent supplication. There are around 100 different mammals in the reserve, which is also home to the Chimane tribe.

It's a long slog from here via San Borja to **Rurrenabaque**, hammock country, from where you can set out for a couple of days on a jungle or pampas tour. One option is to get your jungle fill at the San Miguel del Bala ecoresort, just upriver from Rurrenabaque. Whatever you do, don't miss a trip to **Parque Nacional Madidi**. Bolivia's best-known national park offers a week's- or a lifetime's-worth of adventures in over 1.8 million hectares. The park's remarkable biodiversity is best enjoyed at a slow pace and you should leave enough time to stay in the highly regarded, community-run Chalalán Ecolodge.

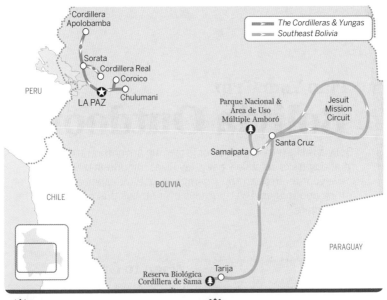

Cordillera Apolobamba
Sorata
Cordillera Real
Coroico
PERU
LA PAZ
Chulumani
Parque Nacional & Área de Uso Múltiple Amboró
Jesuit Mission Circuit
Santa Cruz
Samaipata
BOLIVIA
CHILE
PARAGUAY
Reserva Biológica Cordillera de Sama
Tarija

The Cordilleras & Yungas
Southeast Bolivia

2 WEEKS — The Cordilleras & Yungas

Trapped between the heights of the Andes and the Amazon, this fascinating area is a trekking, climbing, hiking and biking wonderland.

Getting here is half the fun. Trekkers can start from outside **La Paz**, traveling by foot via the Takesi or Choro treks into the heart of the Yungas. You can also get into the Southern Yungas on a butt-busting daylong mountain-bike ride down the World's Most Dangerous Road. Be sure to spend a few days at the end of your descent in the pleasant Yungas villages of **Coroico** or **Chulumani**, both of which offer plenty of day hikes, swimming options and a chilled-out traveler vibe. From there, it's back to the capital and on to climbing and trekking in the **Cordillera Real**, stopping in the cool-air, soft-spirited Andean town of **Sorata**. Adventurers could take on any number of treks from Sorata. There are also good mountain-bike adventures or you can head up to the glaciated peaks of the Cordillera. If you have the time, extend your journey to the seldom-visited **Cordillera Apolobamba** for visits with lost tribes, wildcat miners and loads of deep wilderness trekking.

3 WEEKS — Southeast Bolivia

This trip will get you away from the main tourist track and into Bolivia's warm southern comforts. Along the way, there are a few hiking options, interesting cultural centers and energetic cityscapes.

Start with a few days of partying in **Santa Cruz**, Bolivia's second city. It's great fun just wandering around the streets as you soak up *camba* (lowland) culture. Next make your way out of the city for a week-long dusty adventure through the **Jesuit Mission Circuit**, a series of beautiful missions where baroque music and faith meld with the chilled-out culture of the Guaraní. Cruise back through Santa Cruz on your way to the pre-Inca ruins at **Samaipata** and wildlife watching at **Parque Nacional & Área de Uso Múltiple Amboró**. From the park (backtracking via Samaipata and Santa Cruz), make your way down to the relaxed wine-country town of **Tarija**. After a few days in town, you can customize the tail end of your adventure, with hikes along the Inca Trail in the **Reserva Biológica Cordillera de Sama** or in any of the numerous national parks and reserves unique to the Chaco region.

Plan Your Trip
Bolivia Outdoors

Bolivia is like a theme park for grown-up adventurers. It offers multiday treks, relatively easy day hikes, mountain biking that'll leave your teeth chattering, climbs to lost Andean peaks, rivers for rafting and rugged 4WD journeys over stones that once paved the Inca empire.

Bolivia's Best...

Trekking

El Choro (p120) Two- or three-day classic through the Cordillera Real.

Takesi (p122) Bolivia's Inca Trail passes small villages on a two-day journey.

Yunga Cruz (p123) Five- or six-day thigh buster in the Yungas.

Valle de los Condores (p238) Two- to four-day treks near Tarija.

Biking

World's Most Dangerous Road (p117) Classic mountain-biking adventure.

Zongo Valley (p84) Experts only at this downhill mecca.

Sorata (p131) Less traveled, with more single track.

La Paz (p57) Get steep near Chacaltaya and the Zona Sur.

Climbing

Huayna Potosí (p110) Good for beginners, but certainly no cakewalk.

Volcán Sajama (p154) A popular climb, but altitude and ice pose challenges.

Cordillera Apolobamba (p135) Far from civilization, this is where adventure begins.

When to Go

Dry season (May through October) makes for safer climbs, drier bike trails and easier hikes. Plan to get wet (and muddy) the rest of the year.

Hiking & Trekking

Hiking and trekking are arguably the most rewarding Andean activities. Add a porter, llama train and experienced guide, and you have all the makings for a grand adventure. Some of the most popular hikes and treks begin near La Paz, traverse the Cordillera Real along ancient Inca routes and end in the Yungas, including the well-known El Choro (p120), Takesi (p122) and Yunga Cruz (p123) treks.

Sorata is a hiker's dream come true, offering a variety of options from don't-leave-home-without-a-machete-type hikes to more pleasant walks on Inca trails surrounding the Illampu Massif. The Área Natural de Manejo Integrado Nacional (Anmin) Apolobamba (p139), which includes the four- to five-day Lagunillas to Agua Blanca (p139) trek, is becoming more popular, but is best visited with a local guide.

Near Tarija, two- to four-day treks through the Valle de los Condores (p238) offer spectacular bird-watching as well as walking.

National parks are also paradise for hikers, with hiking opportunities in Parque Nacional & Área de Uso Múltiple Amboró (p267) and Parque Nacional Sajama (p154). A few hikes outside Charazani (p135) are worth checking out.

For a shorter jaunt, hire a guide and cruise the cultural and historic sites and hot springs around Cordillera de los Frailes (p214) outside Sucre or visit Refugio los Volcánes (p269) near Samaipata.

Many treks can be done by experienced outdoors travelers without a guide (you should know how to use a map, compass and GPS, how to build a fire – even in the rain – and how to open a bottle of wine with a pocket knife). Nevertheless, hiring a guide provides an added level of security. No matter what, check out the security situation before heading out.

Mountaineering & Climbing

Staying Safe

Dangers include getting lost, avalanches, crevasses, snow blindness, dehydration, altitude sickness and occasional muggings on the way up. Be careful in hiring your guide, buy mountaineering insurance, drink lots of water, protect your skin, dress properly and wear sunglasses. Altitude sickness is a very real thing – watch for signs of fatigue, dizziness and nausea. Proper acclimatization and hydration will help. If you think you are getting sick, head down.

Socorro Andino Bolivia (p111) provides rescue assistance if you need help.

Hiring a Guide

Many travel agencies in La Paz and larger cities organize climbing and trekking trips in the Cordillera Real and other areas. Not all, however, are everything they claim to be. Some guides have gotten lost, several have died, and others have practiced less-than-professional tactics, such as stringing 10 or more climbers on the same rope. Always do your research and go with professionally accredited guides such as those registered with the Asociación de Guias de Montaña (www.agmtb.org), an internationally certified association of registered mountain guides. They're more expensive, but it's worth the cost.

In choosing an agency, ask to see the equipment you will be using and meet the guide. If harnesses are worn, double boots are broken down or the ropes are frayed, demand they be replaced. Talk with the guide and make sure you feel comfortable with him or her. When you hit the mountain, the guide should teach you how to travel on a rope (two people and a guide per rope, no more) and self-arrest with your ice axe.

Agencies can provide almost everything you will need – from just organizing transportation to a full service with guide, cook, mules, porters, an itinerary and so forth – but you should bring warm clothes (avoid cotton and stick to wool or synthetics), a headlamp and extra batteries, plenty of water and snacks. The guides will generally prepare three meals a day.

Professional trekking guides generally charge US$60 to US$80 per day (plus food).

Maps

Historically, maps of Bolivian climbing areas have been poor in quality and difficult to obtain. Even now, elevations of peaks are murky, with reported altitudes varying as much as 600m – it seems the rumor that Ancohuma is taller than Argentina's Aconcagua won't die.

Maps are available from Los Amigos del Libro (p347) in La Paz and Santa Cruz, and from some bookstores. In La Paz try the trekking agents and tourist shops along Sagárnaga.

The *Travel Map of Bolivia,* one of the best country maps, and *New Map of the Cordillera Real,* which shows mountains, roads and precolonial routes, are published by O'Brien Cartographics. They are out of print, but still available at various tourist hangouts, including the postcard kiosks within La Paz's Central Post Office (p78).

Government 1:50,000 topographical and specialty sheets are available from the Instituto Geográfico Militar (IGM), which has offices in most major cities, including a branch in La Paz (p347).

Walter Guzmán Córdova has produced 1:50,000 colorful contour maps of El Choro–Takesi–Yunga Cruz,

DMITRY BURLAKOV/SHUTTERSTOCK ©

Top: Termas de Polques hot springs (p170)

Bottom: Salar de Uyuni (p167)

RESPONSIBLE TREKKING

To help preserve the ecology and beauty of Bolivia, consider the following tips when trekking.

Carry out your rubbish OK, so many tracks in Bolivia are already littered, but this doesn't mean that you should add to the problem.

Never bury your rubbish Digging disturbs soil and ground cover, and causes erosion; foreign matter affects local wildlife and may take years to rot.

Keep water sources clean Contamination of water sources by human feces can lead to the transmission of all sorts of nasties. Where there is a toilet, use it; where there is none, best practice is to carry waste out. If you decide to bury it, dig a deep hole away from water sources. Additionally, don't use detergents or toothpaste in or near watercourses.

Stick to existing trails Avoid cutting corners – it contributes to erosion.

Don't depend on open fires for cooking Cook on a lightweight kerosene, alcohol or Shellite (white-gas) stove and avoid those powered by disposable butane-gas canisters. Continuous cutting of wood by local communities and trekkers can cause deforestation, plus wildfire risks.

Do not feed the wildlife It can lead to animals becoming dependent on handouts, unbalanced populations and disease.

Always seek permission to camp Ask in the village where you can camp overnight.

Mururata–Illimani, Huayna Potosí–Condoriri and Sajama, but those other than El Choro–Takesi–Yunga Cruz map are in short supply. The Deutscher Alpenverein (German Alpine Club) produces the excellent and accurate 1:50,000 maps *Alpenvereinskarte Cordillera Real Nord (Illampu)*, which includes the Sorata area, and *Alpenvereinskarte Cordillera Real Süd (Illimani)*, which centers on Illimani.

Guidebooks

The best mountaineering guide is *Bolivia: A Climbing Guide* by Yossi Brain; the late author worked as a climbing guide in La Paz and also served as secretary of the Club Andino Boliviano. *The Andes of Bolivia* by Alain Mesili is available in English.

Mountain Biking

Bolivia is blessed with some of the most dramatic mountain-biking terrain in the world, and offers seven months every year of near-perfect weather and relatively easy access to mountain ranges, magnificent lakes, precolonial ruins and trails, and myriad eco-zones connected by an extensive network of footpaths and jeep roads.

The Bolivian Andes are full of long and thrilling descents, as well as challenging touring possibilities – though most people opt for downhill rides because of the altitude. One of the world's longest downhill rides will take you from Parque Nacional Sajama (p154) down to the Chilean coast at Arica. In the dry season you can even tackle the mostly level roads of the vast Amazon lowlands.

Some rides from La Paz can be done by riders of any experience level. There are more combinations than a bike lock as trails lead through Inca roads, tropical tracks, jeep roads and scree chutes. The best known (but not necessarily the best for serious riders) is the thrilling 3600m trip down the World's Most Dangerous Road (p117) from La Cumbre to Coroico. Another popular route near La Paz is the lush Zongo Valley ride, which can be started from Chacaltaya (p84) at 5395m.

The town of Sorata (p131) has cemented its position as the mountain-bike mecca of Bolivia, with scores of downhill single-track trails and jeep roads near town, including a combination bike-and-boat trip from Sorata to Rurrenabaque. For the hardcore rider, scree chutes to biker-built single track and jump zones abound.

GO WITH THE FLOW

Numerous tour operators combine rafting, biking, hiking and 4WD trips. These trips can be costly, but it's great fun to mix things up a bit.

Sorata to Rurrenabaque A double-action trip including a five-day ride-and-river jaunt. This full-on adventure includes a two-day biking trip, which culminates in an exciting 4000m descent on single track via Consata and Mapiri, followed by three days of floating down the Río Beni on a riveting expedition in a motorized dugout canoe, with side hikes to waterfalls and to Parque Nacional Madidi for wildlife watching. It's offered by Gravity tours (p132).

Coroico You can custom-build trips with guides from Coroico that will take you to waterfalls at dawn, in an all-terrain vehicle (ATV) at noon and to visit canyons at sunset.

Tupiza (p173) Travel by horse, ATV and mountain bike on innovative triathlons.

Copacabana Paddle a swan boat across the bay, cycle to Yampupata, row to Isla del Sol, run across the island, then take the boat back. It's never been done in one day (according to legend).

Every year, typically in October, Sorata is host to the longest downhill race on a hand-built course, the Jach'a Avalancha (Grand Avalanche) Mountain Bike Race (p131). Other epic descents begin in Sorata and head into the hinterland of the Cordillera Muñecas, or start in Copacabana and La Paz and head to Sorata.

More and more travelers are taking up the cycling challenge and heading on two wheels from the north of the country to the south, or vice versa. Those with their own bikes need to consider several factors. During part of the rainy season, particularly December to February, some roads become mired in muck and heavy rain can greatly reduce visibility, creating dangerous conditions. Also worth noting is Bolivia's lack of spare parts. Comprehensive repair kits are essential. In the Southern Altiplano and Uyuni regions, water is very scarce; you must be able to carry at least two days' worth of water in some places.

Four-Wheel Driving

Heading out in a 4WD is becoming an increasingly popular activity. It allows you access to places that are tricky to get to and, although sometimes on the pricier side, may be the only feasible way of visiting a region. As well as the standard Southwest Circuit (p162) tours (setting off from Uyuni, Tupiza or La Paz), you can cruise out to the *quebradas* (ravines or

washes, usually dry) beyond Tupiza, visit the Tarabuco market (p206) on a tour from Sucre or the Incallajta (p195) Inca ruins near Cochabamba.

Tours in 4WDs are a great way to enter some of the country's national parks. Current trips include those around Parque Nacional Torotoro (p197; from Cochabamba) and Parque Nacional Sajama (p154; from La Paz), or into the Cordillera de los Frailes (p214; from Sucre).

For those keen to arrange trips themselves, consider hiring a driver. This can be an efficient and good-value way of seeing specific areas, especially if you are in a group.

Whitewater Rafting & Kayaking

One of Bolivia's greatest secrets is the number of white-water rivers that drain the eastern slopes of the Andes between the Cordillera Apolobamba and the Chapare. Here, avid rafters and kayakers can enjoy thrilling descents. While access will normally require long drives and/or treks – and considerable expense if done independently – there are a few fine rivers that are relatively accessible.

Some La Paz tour agencies can organize day trips on the Río Coroico (p116). Other options include the Río Unduavi and numerous wild Chapare rivers.

Top: Cycling the World's Most Dangerous Road (p117)

Bottom: Church in Tomarapi, near Parque Nacional Sajama (p154)

JOSE ARCOS AGUILAR/SHUTTERSTOCK ©

JERRY DODRILL/SHUTTERSTOCK ©

Mountaineering in the Andes

A more gentle but fun rush in the Chuquisaca region is a float downriver in rubber inner tubes. This trip is often coupled with mountain biking. One of the greatest thrills along the same biathlon idea is to cruise 4000m downhill on mountain bike to Mapiri and then raft your way for several days, camping en route, to Rurrenabaque. Amazon canoe tours along the Río Beni (p295) are unforgettable, as are the trips along the Río Mamoré (p311) from Trinidad.

Horseback Riding

For some, a horse saddle sure beats a bus seat, and it's a great way to absorb the sights, sounds and smells of a country. Horseback-riding trips are a new and increasingly popular way to reach otherwise inaccessible wilderness areas. The best place to try it is in Tupiza (p173), former territory of Butch Cassidy and the Sundance Kid. You get to see the multi-colored desert landscape, *quebradas* and cacti-dotted countryside.

Wildlife Watching

Flora and fauna fanatics are spoilt for choice in this extraordinary country where world-class wildlife watching abounds. The diversity of intact habitats throughout the country accounts for the huge number of surviving species.

The Parque Nacional Madidi (p301), for example, home to over 1000 bird species as well as wildlife endemic to the majority of Bolivia's ecosystems, from tropical rainforest and savanna to cloud forest and alpine tundra, is arguably one of the most biodiverse places on the planet. Agencies, often run by scientists or environmentalists, run nature trips out of Santa Cruz, Cochabamba and Samaipata, and, to a lesser extent, La Paz.

Hot spots for bird-watching include the highlands around La Paz and Cochabamba, Parque Nacional & Área de Uso Múltiple Amboró and the Reserva Biosférica del Beni. Contact Asociación Armonía (www.armonia-bo.org), the Bolivian partner of BirdLife International, for further bird-watching information. Other organizations with bird knowledge include Bird Bolivia (p358), Fundación Amigos de la Naturaleza (p264) and Michael Blendinger Tours (p272).

Other Activities

Paragliding is an up-and-coming activity, but ask carefully about your pilot's experience. One great view is just south of La Paz (p57), and Sucre is a popular spot for it too (p206).

More relaxing hot spots are the many *termas* (hot springs) that bubble away in various parts of the country. You don't have to go to the ends of the earth to immerse yourself in this less energetic activity – there are springs in Tarapaya (p226) just outside Potosí, Talula (p217), San Xavier (p279) and Sajama (p155).

Ziplining and canopy tours are just starting up, with ziplines near Coroico (p114) and a community-run endeavor near Rurrenabaque (p294). You can also fish, canyoneer, drive an ATV (noise and pollution pots that they are), and even rappel off buildings in La Paz (p57).

Plan Your Trip

Eat & Drink Like a Local

Bolivia's cuisine is as varied as its topography. And while there are traditional delicacies to be discovered in every town, Bolivia's food scene is evolving. Exciting young chefs are causing a buzz in La Paz, where restaurants serve coffee from the Yungas and wine from the vineyards of Tarija.

Food Experiences

Meals of a Lifetime

Gustu (p71) Top of every foodie's to-do list should be a visit to the groundbreaking restaurant at the center of La Paz's food boom.

Visiting Tarija's wineries (p246) Tap into Tarija's burgeoning wine industry on a tour of the vineyards in nearby Valle de la Concepción.

Mercado Central (p209) A floor of vendors with blenders whiz up fresh fruit juices at Sucre's central market.

Cafe Munaipata (p116) Coffee-bean picking, roasting and taste-tasting are all covered on tours of this pretty plantation in the Yungas, one of several in the area.

Cochabamba's ice-cream parlors (p192) Join the crowds screaming for ice cream (and cake) at Cochabamba's multistory *heladerías* (ice-cream parlors).

El Puente Night Market (p242) This Tarija market is the place to sample local specialties.

Andean Culture Distillery (p72) Liquor lovers can take a tour of Bolivia's first craft distillery, in La Paz, where Killa Andean Moonshine is made from corn. Like *chicha,* only stronger!

The Year in Food

Bolivia's culinary habits are dictated more by altitude and climate, and by cultural traditions, than by season.

Easter (March/April)

During Easter week, Bolivians eat *sopa de te'qo* (vegetable soup) and *biscocho de Semana Santa* (round, flat biscuits).

August

In the first week of August, Villa Tunari in the Chapare region of the Amazon Basin celebrates Amazonian fish dishes in the Feria Regional del Pescado (p291).

December

Bolivians celebrate *Noche Buena* (Christmas Eve) with a family feast. Traditionally, the meal includes *picana,* a stew made with chicken, beef, lamb, vegetables and potatoes, and *lechón al horno* (roast pork). On Christmas morning, a popular breakfast is *buñuelos con chocolate* (a sweet, soft doughnut with chocolate dipping sauce).

Tomatitas riverfront restaurants (p240) Informal open-air dining at a row of local restaurants serving *cangreitos* (soft-shelled freshwater crabs), near Tarija.

Santa Cruz's international dining scene (p260) With fusion food at Jardín de Asia and Peruvian at Sach'a Rest, as well as Swiss-style fine dining, Argentinian steakhouses and Japanese restaurants, Santa Cruz excels in international cuisine.

Cheap Treats

Salteñas The ubiquitous yellow-orange empanada of La Paz and beyond leaves a tasty film on your fingers and a warm glow in your stomach. A good place to try them is Salteñas Especiales Marianita (p175) in Tupiza.

Charque-filled tamales Cornmeal dough filled with llama meat; look for them at Tupiza's Mercado de Ferias (p176).

Cuñapé These cheesy bread rolls can be found in Chiquitos close to the border with Paraguay, where they're known as *chipá*.

Sonso de yuca Grilled mashed yucca with cheese; try it at El Puente Night Market (p242) in Tarija.

Api de maíz morado This hot drink made with ground purple corn, cinnamon, sugar and cloves is popular in the altiplano; look for it in the markets of La Paz, Oruro, Potosí and Cochabamba.

Pan de arroz In Santa Cruz, look out for these tasty rolls made with rice flour, tapioca and cheese, and baked in a banana leaf.

Dare to Try

Sopa la Poderosa A 'powerful soup' from Tarija made with vegetables, rice...and bull's penis.

Anticuchos Grilled cow's heart on skewers, served at markets or street stalls – look for them in the streets of La Paz.

Chuño This traditional altiplano staple is made by laying potatoes out overnight to freeze, allowing them to thaw the next day and repeating the process over several days. The potatoes are then crushed underfoot to remove the skin and the liquid. The technique was developed by the Incas some 800 years ago; the freeze-dried potatoes could then be transported by llama caravans like modern-day packets of chips on a bus. If you are in the highlands in June you may see potatoes being left out to freeze; the technique is still common in rural areas close to Oruro.

WHAT TO DRINK

It gets cold in the altiplano, and hot drinks are popular.

➡ *mate de coca* – an infusion of water and dried coca leaves

➡ *trimate* – a combination of chamomile, coca and anise

Juices are fantastic, and there are a whole host of strange and inventive concoctions on offer at ubiquitous juice stalls. Hand over your cash, swig it down and hand your glass back before going on your merry way.

➡ *api* – made from a ground purple corn

➡ *mocochinche* – sugary peach drink made from boiled cane sugar, cinnamon sticks and featuring a floating dried peach (another Andean food-preservation marvel)

➡ *tostada* – sweet and nutty

➡ *horchata* – a corn-based drink

➡ *licuados* – fruit shakes blended with water or milk

And of course there are plenty of alcoholic drinks to choose from.

➡ Top *cervezas* (beers) include Paceña, Huari, Sureña, Taquiña, Potosina and Tropical Extra

➡ *Vino* (wine) is good, especially around Tarija

➡ *Singani* is a white grape brandy, popular in a *chufflay* (mixed drink with soda or lemonade)

➡ *Chicha* is a fermented-corn drink popular in the countryside

Top: Mercado Central (p228), Potosí

Bottom: *Sopa de maní*

ALEXANDR VOROBEV/SHUTTERSTOCK ©

BOLIVIAN FRUITS

Many deliciously juicy South American fruits are cultivated in Bolivia. Most notable are the following.

➡ *chirimoya* (custard apple)

➡ *tuna* prickly (pear cactus)

➡ *maracuya* and *tumbo* (passion fruits)

In the lowlands, the range of exotic tropical fruits defies middle-latitude expectations.

➡ hand-shaped *ambaiba*

➡ small, round, green and purple *guaypurú*

➡ spiny yellow *ocoro*

➡ lemon-like *guapomo*

➡ bean-like *cupesi*

➡ *marayau*, which resembles a bunch of giant grapes

➡ currant-like *nui*

➡ scaly, onion-looking *sinini*

➡ stomach-shaped *paquio*

Local Specialties

Bolivia's food scene is as diverse as its peoples, and there's even a 'traveling chef' show on TV to showcase regional culinary styles.

The Altiplano

Until recently La Paz wasn't known for its fine dining, but these days the city's culinary scene is flourishing. In 2013, Danish food entrepreneur Claus Meyer (of Copenhagen restaurant Noma, which hovers near the top of the world's best restaurant list) opened Gustu in the Calacoto neighborhood. The restaurant's philosophy is to use only Bolivian ingredients, and employ chefs trained at Melting Pot, a culinary school set up by Meyer for disadvantaged youths. The graduates have now started opening their own restaurants, including Ali Pacha (p69).

The most typical Andean foods are found in the markets. Look for *salteñas* (hot pastry pies filled with mince-meat or chicken) and *api de maíz morado* (a hot drink made with purple corn). To combat the effects of the altitude, try drinking *mate de coca,* an infusion of water and dried coca leaves.

In Oruro, grilled meat is king. A typical local dish is *charquekan* made with dried llama meat and served with egg, corn, cheese and hot sauce, but there are also plenty of restaurants serving grilled steaks and other beef dishes.

The most deservedly popular fish in the altiplano are *trucha* (trout) and *pejerrey* (kingfish), introduced species from Lake Titicaca. A novel dish from Potosí is *k'alaphurka,* a gurgling corn and bacon soup heated by dropping a hot volcanic stone in the bowl.

The Valleys

Los Valles (the Valleys) refers to the strip of land running from north to south, sandwiched between the altiplano and the Amazon Basin, at an altitude of about 2000m.

Cochabamba has a thriving restaurant scene and offers some of the best food in the country. There's great dining here, from high-end restaurants to street food. Local specialties include *silpancho* (schnitzel-style meat on rice and potatoes), *lomo borracho* (beef with egg in a beer soup) and *picante de pollo* (chicken in a spicy sauce). Look out, too, for *ranga-ranga* (minced beef with onions and yellow peppers).

At Tarija's markets you can try *falso conejo* (ground meat with vegetables, onions and rice), *saice* (spicy diced beef and vegetables) and *sonso* (grilled mashed yucca with cheese).

A dish that's popular all over Bolivia is *pique a lo macho*. This hangover killer is a heaping mess of beef, sausage, boiled eggs, gravy, peppers and onions over french fries. Waiter!

The Lowlands

Head east toward Santa Cruz and Bolivia's culinary landscape transforms with the changing vegetation. The city's best restaurants serve food from outside Bolivia and include some excellent places to eat Japanese, Peruvian and even Swiss food.

Outside the city, international cuisine all but disappears. Regional specialties in Santa Cruz province and Chiquitos include *majadito de charque* (a dish made with rice and dried meat), *sopa de maní* (soup made with ground peanuts), *cuñapé* (cheesy bread rolls) and *pan de arroz* (rolls made with rice flour and tapioca).

Further north, the Amazon Basin has an abundance of river fish and fruits, perfect for smoothies. In Beni, beef may be served as *pacumutus,* enormous chunks of grilled meat accompanied by yucca, onions and other trimmings.

Salteñas

How to Eat & Drink

When to Eat

➡ *Desayuno* (breakfast) consists of little more than coffee and a bread roll, and is often followed by a midmorning street snack such as a *salteña* (meat and vegetable pasty), *tucumana* (an empanada-like pastry) or an empanada. Better hotels will serve a bountiful buffet breakfast.

➡ *Almuerzo* (lunch) is the main meal of the day, though when advertised by restaurants *almuerzo* usually refers to a no-frills set meal, with a starter (sometimes), main course and dessert (usually between B$15 and B$40). Some also throw in a drink.

➡ *Cena,* the evening meal, is mostly served à la carte. Many highlanders prefer a light *te* (tea) instead of an evening meal.

Where to Eat

Outside major cities, your choice of restaurant is likely to be limited to pizzerias or local restaurants serving the typical food of the area.

Meat invariably dominates most meals and is usually accompanied by rice, a starchy tuber (usually potato) and shredded lettuce or cabbage. Altiplano fare tends to be starchy, fried and loaded with carbohydrates. In the lowlands, fish, fruit and vegetables feature more prominently.

Vegetarian options are on the rise, but overcooked vegetables, rice, potatoes, pizza and pasta may be something you tire of. Quinoa is a supergrain, perfect for vegetarians.

Menu Decoder

➡ A large bowl of *sopa* (soup) – whether vegetarian or meat based – is the start of every great Bolivian meal.

➡ Beef is typically *asado* (barbecued) or *parrillada* (grilled) in various cuts, including *lomo* (filet), *brazuelo* (shank) and *churrasco* (skirt steak).

➡ Jerked beef, llama or other red meat is called *charque.*

➡ On the altiplano, beef is often served with *choclo* (corn), corn on the cob, or *mote* (rehydrated dried corn kernels); in the lowlands it's served with yucca or mashed plantain.

➡ *Pollo* (chicken) is either *frito* (fried), *al spiedo* or *a la broaster* (cooked on a spit), *asado* or *dorado* (broiled). Cheap chicken restaurants are ubiquitous in Bolivia, where a meal of chicken and potatoes can be extremely cheap.

➡ Do you have a nut allergy? *Maní* means peanut, and is a popular ingredient, especially in soups.

Plan Your Trip
Travel with Children

From llama-dotted mountains and lunar-like landscapes to boat trips through steamy jungles, Bolivia offers adventures that will leave an imprint on young travelers. Visiting Bolivia is a one-of-a-kind cultural experience, and while traveling with children poses some challenges, the rewards are great.

Best Regions for Kids

Amazon Basin
Wildlife spotting and riverboat trips in Parque Nacional Madidi, with accommodations in family-friendly ecolodges.

Sucre
A great central plaza, and mild and comfortable climate, plus dinosaur footprints and excursions to the surrounding countryside.

Tupiza
There are Wild West adventures to be had in the countryside surrounding this laid-back town, with plenty of options for day-trip excursions by horseback, bicycle or jeep. At 2850m, the altitude is manageable.

Santa Cruz
Kid-friendly outings abound, with botanical gardens, butterfly farms and zoos within easy reach of the city center. There are plenty of eating options for fussy diners as well as malls selling any items you might need.

Samaipata
Day trips to El Fuerte ruins, a pleasant climate and plenty of choice of accommodations, from campsites to hotels.

La Paz
Kids will love the children's museum and cable cars, but be sure to acclimatize carefully – it's high up here!

Bolivia for Kids

Bolivians love children, and bringing your kids will do wonders for breaking down cultural barriers. But while families can and do visit Bolivia, be prepared to grapple with a number of potential obstacles, including the altitude of the altiplano, the sometimes inhospitable climate, poor levels of hygiene and a general lack of predictability – floods, snow and *bloqueos* (road blocks caused by political protests) might force you to change your plans. Be prepared to be flexible.

Children's Highlights
Outdoor Attractions

Biocentro Güembé (p261) Outdoor center near Santa Cruz with a butterfly farm, orchid exhibitions and natural pools.

Mi Teleférico (p78) Swing high on La Paz's 30km-long cable-car system.

Parque Cretacico (p204) Follow in the footsteps of dinosaurs at this park near Sucre.

Jardín Botánico (p261) These gardens are an easy day trip from Santa Cruz.

El Fuerte (p270) Pre-Inca ruins with plenty of space to run around.

Animal Encounters

Parque Nacional Madidi (p301) Wildlife watching in the Amazon Basin.

Parque Nacional Sajama (p154) Llamas, alpacas and vicuñas are among the animals found in this national park, but be sure to acclimatize.

Senda Verde Wildlife Sanctuary (p114) Fun sanctuary where humans are 'caged' and monkeys run free.

Zoológico Municipal Fauna Sudamericana (p258) Santa Cruz's zoo, near the city center.

Zoo El Refugio (p271) This refuge for rescued animals is near Samaipata.

Rainy-Day Activities

Pipiripi (p55) La Paz's children's museum, with interactive exhibits.

Museo Antropológico Eduardo López Rivas (p147) Dry but educational museum in Oruro.

Ventura Mall (p263) Modern mall with a food court, cinema and occasional kids' activities.

Family-Friendly Hotels

El Pueblito (p272) Kids will love this minivillage with a playground in Samaipata.

Hotel Los Tajibos (p260) Plush resort with a children's pool.

El Jardín (p272) Chilled-out gardens and space to camp in Samaipata.

Chalalán Ecolodge (p301) Memorable jungle experience in Parque Nacional Madidi.

AGATHA KADAR/SHUTTERSTOCK ©

PLAN YOUR TRIP TRAVEL WITH CHILDREN

Planning

There are a few things to consider before bringing your children to Bolivia. Think carefully about what you might need, as clothing and equipment can be difficult to find outside the main cities, and are certainly more expensive.

For all-round information and advice, check out Lonely Planet's *Travel with Children*.

Accommodations

➡ Many hotels have family rooms with three or four beds.

➡ The most family-friendly hotels are resorts, with playgrounds and pools.

➡ Remember that nights at high altitude are bitterly cold, and not all hotels are heated; be sure to check.

➡ In warmer, lowland areas, consider camping; many hostels have space to pitch a tent and allow use of their facilities.

➡ Cribs, diaper-changing facilities and childcare services are only available in the finest hotels in big cities.

What to Pack

➡ First-aid kit including diarrhea tablets, rehydration salts, sunscreen, bug spray, adhesive plasters, thermometer and any medicines your child might need

➡ High-factor sun protection

➡ Required vaccination certificates, passports and visas

➡ Snacks and favorite foods from home

➡ Clothes for all weather and sunhat

➡ Parental permission note if traveling solo

➡ Baby carrier, as strollers are basically pointless

➡ Favorite toys

➡ Wipes

➡ If you plan on driving, bring your car seat from home

Regions at a Glance

La Paz & Around

Food & Drink
Shopping
Nightlife

Gastronomic Boom

With the opening of a spate of top-rated places, the city's restaurant scene is booming. If fine dining's not your thing, hit the city's stalls for lip-smackingly good street food. More of a java head? Cool new coffee bars are the place to get your caffeine fix.

Artisan Crafts

In the tangle of open-air stalls, covered malls, crafts kiosks and witches' markets you can find just about everything under the sun, including crafts and textiles from throughout Bolivia, aphrodisiacs, wood carvings, metal pipes and tin pans.

Party in Peace

La Paz loves to party. And at 3660m, just about everybody's a lightweight. Diverse religious and civic festivals bring plenty of daytime pageantry. Come sunset, a parade of different sorts takes hold in the discos and bars of Sopocachi.

p46

Lake Titicaca

History
Hiking
Scenery

Birthplace of the Sun

The Tiwanaku and Inca believed the sun and their civilization were born from this remarkable body of water and this mystical place remains a great spot to explore pre-Columbian history.

Island Walks

On Isla del Sol you'll encounter numerous ruins that date to before the Conquest, as well as intact indigenous villages. But be sure to check for the latest updates on an in-island conflict that has left much of Isla del Sol out of bounds to travelers.

Water & Ice

There are no bad views over Lake Titicaca. Crossing between islands, you'll be entranced by mirrored reflections of the nearby Cordillera Real, while the sunsets and sunrises will burn their imprint into your soul.

p88

The Cordilleras & Yungas

Trekking
Climbing
Biking

Inca Trails

Ancient Inca trails lead from the high Andes to the edge of the Amazon, taking you through diverse ecosystems, past squawking riots of tropical birds, indigenous villages, waterfalls and impressively sheer cliffs. From well-trodden trails to lesser-followed paths, there are many options to choose from.

Step into Vertical

Strap on your crampons and ice axe for an ascent of the peaks of the Cordilleras Real, Apolobamba and Quimsa Cruz. There are peaks that have only been summited a handful of times and trade routes good for novice climbers.

Downhill Biking

With elevation drops of more than 3000m, this is one of the best downhill mountain-biking spots in the world. Push the envelope on arm-busting descents of the World's Most Dangerous Road, past waterfalls near Sorata or down seldom-visited single tracks.

p107

Southern Altiplano

Wildlife
Adventure
Scenery

High-Plains Fauna

Bolivia's altiplano is a wilderness of bleak and vast proportions. Up here, under the sheltering sun, wild herds of vicuñas are on the rise. Lucky visitors will also spot South America's aloof version of the ostrich, the rhea, plus any number of Andean camelids.

Salar de Uyuni

Adventure abounds on a three- or four-day jeep tour of the Salar de Uyuni. There are mountain-bike trips, horseback adventures and ATV tours from nearby Tupiza, as well as climbs up massive volcanic peaks and descents into centuries-old mines.

The View

As you make your way across this remarkable and remote wilderness, you'll marvel at the world's largest salt flat, whimsical rock formations, cacti-filled valleys straight out of the Old West, volcanic peaks, Technicolor lakes and a sky that seems to stretch forever.

p142

Central Highlands

Climate
History
Mines

Cool Breezes

Cochabambinos (Cochabamba residents) say their year-round spring-like climate makes it the ideal place to live. Whether coming from sultry lowlands or freezing highlands, you might just agree. If you're heading down from mountains, the air will feel heady with oxygen. It's a good acclimatizing spot heading the other way.

Colonial Architecture

There is nowhere in Bolivia that can match the majesty of Sucre, a wonderfully understated town in the foothills of the Andes that gave birth to the nation's independence. The museums, cathedrals and plazas make this one of Bolivia's most historic cities.

Silvery Past

A visit to the silver mines of Potosí offers an evocative, haunting and daunting journey into the region's past. The ornate colonial architecture of the city the mine funded are also worthy of your time.

p179

South Central Bolivia & the Chaco

Scenery
Wine
Food

Windswept Highlands

The arid, thorny hills of the baking-hot Chaco give way to a windswept highland landscape peppered with pink-flamingo lakes. There's a delightful vibe around Tarija's wine country, and plenty of wild national parks and reserves.

Oenophilia

Though its reputation is growing, Bolivian wine doesn't often get the credit it deserves. A few days sampling the goods in the Valle de la Concepción near Tarija will quickly turn you into a convert, as will the friendly folks who call this land of wine and honey home.

Local Delicacies

Chapaco (local to Tarija) cuisine is unique and inventive. While some of the dishes sound more appealing than others, you won't find a similar menu elsewhere in the country. Try it at the night market or at one of the city's welcoming restaurants.

p232

Santa Cruz & Gran Chiquitania

Food
History
Missions

International Dining

Santa Cruz is big on eats, and its cosmopolitan population offers a variety of culinary options that will whet the appetite of even the fussiest eater. From Peruvian ceviche to US-style chicken wings, you're sure to leave town well-fed.

Revolutionary Trail

Che pilgrims will make a beeline for La Higuera, where the revolutionary's Bolivian project finally came to an end. He was executed by troops, and taken to nearby Vallegrande, where his body was displayed. A series of sights in both towns commemorate the revolutionary; local guides offer fascinating tours of the Che Trail.

Jesuit Missions

Wonderfully ornate churches that have been reconstructed in their original style are the centerpieces of the remote towns that make up the Jesuit Mission Circuit, one of the country's most surprising and entrancing highlights.

p253

Amazon Basin

Adventure
Culture
Wildlife

Outdoor Adventure

The very word Amazon is synonymous with adventure. Progress is slow and the insects can be a distraction, but this is a land where nature rules and you are just a guest. Float down the river on a jungle journey you'll never forget; your inner 10-year-old will thank you.

Festivals Unfettered

Exuberant festivals in Trinidad and San Ignacio de Moxos are famous nationwide for their color and chaos, and will leave you in no doubt that you are in the heart of the Amazon.

Wild Explorer

Hands down the most biodiverse region on the planet, the Amazon has almost mythical status among ecotourists, who are tempted by the possibility of a fleeting glimpse of a jaguar or the world's rarest macaw, and wooed by the morning chorus of howler monkeys.

p286

On the Road

La Paz & Around

Why Go?

Bolivia's diverse cultural currents collide together in and around the de facto capital of La Paz, where some 800,000 people all fight for space within the tight contours of a stark river valley. A mad carnival of jostling pedestrians, honking, diesel-spewing minivans, street marches and cavalcades of vendors, La Paz surrounds you: you'll love it, you'll hate it, but you can't ignore it. Sharp-suited business-men flank machine-gun-toting bank guards and balaclava-camouflaged shoeshine boys. Lung-busting inclines terminate in peaceful plazas.

Look up toward the Altiplano, and you'll find a million more Bolivians reaching for the sky from the dusty satellite city of El Alto, the launchpad for high-altitude destinations (including the enigmatic ruins of Tiwanaku), while the affluent Zona Sur neighborhood of La Paz ushers visitors into the grand canyons and verdant valleys of the greener altitudes down below.

Best Places to Eat

➡ Gustu (p71)
➡ Ali Pacha (p69)
➡ Popular Cocina Boliviana (p69)
➡ Namas Té (p69)
➡ Los Qñapes (p71)

Best Places to Stay

➡ Atix Hotel (p67)
➡ Hotel Rosario (p66)
➡ Onkel Inn (p64)
➡ Loki Hostel (p66)
➡ Ananay Hostal (p67)

When to Go
La Paz

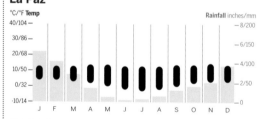

Nov–Apr Rain most afternoons turns the steep streets into torrents.

May–Oct Winter days are cool but sunny, making this La Paz's high season.

Jan–Jun Festival season includes Alasitas, Gran Poder, Carnaval and Aymará New Year.

Map labels (as they appear):

Villa Fátima Bus Terminal

(11km); El Alto (11km);
Tiwanaku Ruins (70km)

Museo de la Revolución Nacional
Gal Monje

Cancha Ferroviaria

VILLA DE LA CRUZ

NORTE

VILLA PABÓN

Av Busch

VILLA VICTORIA

CHALLAPAMPA

Río Achachicala
Autopista El Alto

Former Train Station

Av Ismael Montes

Av Armentia

Calle Jaén Museums

Casco Viejo

Museo de Textiles Andinos Bolivianos

Av República

SAN SEBASTIÁN

Av América

Jallalla

Plaza San Francisco

Ingavi

Junín

SAN JUAN

MIRAFLORES

Tejada Sorzano

Cemetery Bus Terminal

Tumusla

Mercado de las Brujas

Potosí

Ballivián

Comercio

Sucre

Héroes del Pacífico

La Paz Cemetery

Max Paredes

Sagárnaga

Illampu

14 DE SEPTIEMBRE

Los Andes

Entre Ríos

LOS ANDES

See Central La Paz Map (p50)

Max Paredes

Illimani

Av Simón Bolívar

Av 16 de Julio (El Prado)

Murillo

Parque Urbano Central

Río Choqueyapu

Estadio Andrade

Colombia

Boquerón

Av 20 de Octubre

Plaza del Estudiante

Zapata

Zuazo

Capitán Ravelo

Av del Poeta

Av Buenos Aires

BELLO HORIZONTE

Av Arce

Av 6 de Agosto

Plaza Isabel la Católica

Estadio Bolívar

Ecuador

Gutiérrez

Belisario Salinas

Monticulo

Gustu (6km);
Zona Sur (6km);

Cañón de Palca (35km)

Mi Teleférico

Victor Sanjinés

Plaza España

KANTUTANI

See Sopocachi Map (p54)

Av Buenos Aires

N
0   1 km
0   0.5 miles

La Paz & Around Highlights

1 Mi Teleférico (p78)
Gliding above the city on the world's longest cable-car system.

2 Mercado de las Brujas (p63) Buying aphrodisiacs as you have your fortune told.

3 Calle Jaén Museums (p53) Getting cultured while strolling down the city's most atmospheric street.

4 Gustu (p71) Dining at the restaurant that sparked a citywide gastronomy movement.

5 El Alto (p76) Experiencing sensory overload in the prismatic *cholets* (New Andean mansions) of Aymará architect Freddy Mamani.

6 Cañón de Palca (p83) Escaping into the badlands

on a hike through this starkly beautiful canyon.

7 Jallalla (p73) Eating to the beat of folkloric music at the newest – and best – *peña* (folk-music venue) in town.

8 Tiwanaku (p84) Diving into the history of a lost civilization at these mysterious ruins.

LA PAZ

🎵 2 / POP 1.7 MILLION / ELEV 3660M (12,007FT)

Coming from the Bolivian countryside, you'll be struck by the gritty city reality of La Paz. It's the urban jungle, baby: diesel, dust and detritus; blinding altiplano sun, cold cavernous corners of Dickensian darkness. The city seems to reinvent itself at every turn – a jaw-dropping subway in the sky brings you from the heights of El Alto to the depths of Zona Sur in the blink of an eye. Standing hotels are remodeled at a manic pace, and new boutique hotels are springing up like rows of altiplano corn. A maze of contradictions, where cobblestones hit concrete, and Gothic spires vie with glossy hotels, La Paz amazes and appalls all who enter.

History

La Ciudad de Nuestra Señora de La Paz (the City of Our Lady of Peace) was founded on October 20, 1548, by a Spaniard, Captain Alonzo de Mendoza, at present-day Laja situated on the Tiwanaku road. Soon after, La Paz was shifted to its present location, the valley of the Chuquiago Marka (now called the Río Choqueyapu), which had been occupied by a community of Aymará miners.

The Spaniards didn't waste any time in seizing the gold mines, and Captain Mendoza was installed as the new city's first mayor. Unions between Spanish men and indigenous women eventually gave rise to a primarily mestizo population.

If the founding of La Paz had been based on anything other than gold, its position in the depths of a rugged canyon probably would have dictated an unpromising future. However, the protection this setting provided from the fierce altiplano climate and the city's convenient location on the main trade route between Lima and Potosí – much of the Potosí silver bound for Pacific ports passed through La Paz – offered the city some hope of prosperity once the gold ran out. And by the time the railway was built, the city was well established enough to continue commanding attention.

In spite of its name, the City of Our Lady of Peace has seen a good deal of violence. Since Bolivian independence in 1825, the republic has endured more than 190 changes of leadership. An abnormally high mortality rate once accompanied high office in Bolivia. In fact, the presidential palace on the plaza is now known as the Palacio Quemado (Burned Palace), owing to its repeated gutting by fire. As recently as 1946 then-president Gualberto Villarroel was publicly hanged in Plaza Murillo.

Today La Paz is Bolivia's de-facto capital (Sucre remains the constitutional capital).

⊙ Sights

La Paz has a decent collection of museums and notable buildings, but the main attraction here is getting lost in its bustling markets, frenetic commercial streets and stunning hilltop lookouts. Most official sights, including museums, are closed during the Christmas holiday period (December 25 to January 6).

LA PAZ IN...

Two Days

Given the altitude and hills, La Paz is best explored at a leisurely pace. On your first morning, stroll the historic cobblestone streets around Iglesia de San Francisco (p49) and Calle Jaén, home to the wonderful Calle Jaén Museums (p53). Tie some cultural threads together at the Museo de Textiles Andinos Bolivianos (p53), or wander through the interesting (if slightly over-the-top) *artesanía* (handcraft) alley leading to Mercado de las Brujas (p63), the Witches' Market. Head to the posh Zona Sur neighborhood in the evening to try the award-winning Bolivian fare of Gustu (p71).

On the second day, hop aboard Mi Teleférico (p78) and glide up to El Alto to check out the psychedelic 'New Andean' architecture of Freddy Mamani. Catch a ride back down into the upmarket Sopocachi (Map p54) neighborhood for dinner and drinks before settling in for some traditional music at a peña (p73).

Four Days

Follow the two-day itinerary, then on your third day visit the wild rock gardens that surround the city in the Valle de la Luna (p81) or Muela del Diablo (p81). It's always fun to bring a picnic of fresh foods from the markets. On the fourth day take a day trip out to Tiwanaku (p84) to explore the ruins or do a day's bike trip (p57) on the outskirts of La Paz.

⊙ West of El Prado

The areas west of El Prado include the fascinating markets around Rosario, Belén and San Pedro, the cemetery and the sophisticated Sopocachi neighborhood, with some of La Paz's best nightspots. You can spend a few hours people-watching on **Plaza Eduardo Avaroa**, before hoofing up to the wonderful views from **Montículo Park**.

Iglesia de San Francisco CHURCH
(Map p50; Plaza San Francisco, Rosario) The hewed stone basilica of San Francisco was founded in 1548 by Fray Francisco de los Ángeles. The original structure collapsed under heavy snowfall around 1610, but it was rebuilt between 1743 and 1772. The second building is made of stone quarried at nearby Viacha. The facade is decorated with carvings of natural themes such as *chirimoyas* (custard apples), pine cones and tropical birds.

The mass of rock pillars and stone faces in the upper portion of Plaza San Francisco is intended to represent Bolivia's three great cultures – Tiwanaku, Inca and Aymará.

The cloisters and garden of **Museo San Francisco** (Map p50; ☑ 231-8472; Plaza San Francisco, Rosario; B$20; ⊙ 9am-6pm Mon-Sat), adjacent to the basilica, beautifully revive the history and art of the city's landmark. There are heavenly religious paintings, historical artifacts, an interesting anteroom and a God-like, if quirky, view from the roof.

The **plaza** is often the staging ground for rallies and protests.

La Paz Cemetery CEMETERY
(http://cementerio.lapaz.bo; Av Baptista, Tacagua; ⊙ 8:30am-5pm) As in many Latin American cemeteries, bodies are first buried in the Western way or are placed in a crypt. Then, within 10 years, they are disinterred and cremated. After cremation, families purchase or rent glass-fronted spaces in the cemetery walls for the ashes, they affix plaques and mementos of the deceased, and place flowers behind the glass door.

Each wall has hundreds of these doors, and some of the walls have been expanded upward to such an extent that they resemble three- or four-story apartment blocks. As a result the cemetery is an active place, full of people passing through to visit relatives and leave or water fresh flowers.

It's possibly most interesting on November 2, the Día de los Muertos (Day of the Dead; p64), when half the city turns out to honor their ancestors.

Be aware that the area around the cemetery is a little unsavory. And don't come here at night.

Salar Galería de Arte GALLERY
(Map p54; www.salart.org; Av Ecuador 2534, Sopocachi; ⊙ 10am-6pm Tue-Fri, weekend by appointment) Bolivia's top contemporary artists showcase their work at this whimsical three-story gallery.

Museo de la Coca MUSEUM
(Map p50; ☑ 231-1998; www.cocamuseum.com; Linares 906, Rosario; B$15; ⊙ 10am-7pm Mon-Sat) Chew on some facts inside the small, slightly tired Coca Museum, which explores the sacred leaf's role in traditional societies, its use by the soft-drink and pharmaceutical industries, and the growth of cocaine as a party drug. The displays (ask for a translation in your language) are educational, provocative and evenhanded.

The on-site cafe serves cocktails, sweets and even nachos, all made with coca.

Museo Elsa Paredes de Salazar MUSEUM
(Muñecas del Bolivia y el Mundo, Dolls of the World; Map p54; ☑ 7620-1981; www.facebook.com/MuseodeMunecasElsaParedes; Guitiérrez 550, Sopocachi; B$10; ⊙ by appointment Tue & Thu 4-7pm) An intriguing collection of more than 800 dolls from around the world, most dressed in traditional Bolivian costumes, but some from other continents and cultures. Look for the Evo Morales bobblehead.

Fundación Solón GALLERY
(Walter Solón Romero Art Gallery; Map p54; ☑ 241-7057; www.fundacionsolon.org; Av Ecuador 2519, Sopocachi; suggested donation B$5; ⊙ 9am-1pm & 3-7pm Mon-Fri) This building was once home to Walter Solón Romero, one of the nation's most important and politically active artists. Known for his elaborate murals and fascination with Don Quijote, Solón paid a high price when his son died in prison during the repressive 1970s. A sense of humor only slightly shades the visceral cry for justice in the maestro's works.

Museo Tambo Quirquincho MUSEUM
(Map p50; ☑ 239-0969; Plaza Alonso de Mendoza, Rosario; B$8; ⊙ 9am-12:30pm & 3-7pm Tue-Fri, to 1pm Sat & Sun) This intriguing museum, a former *tambo* (wayside market and inn), houses 10 rooms of temporary art exhibitions that change monthly. Past exhibitions

Central La Paz

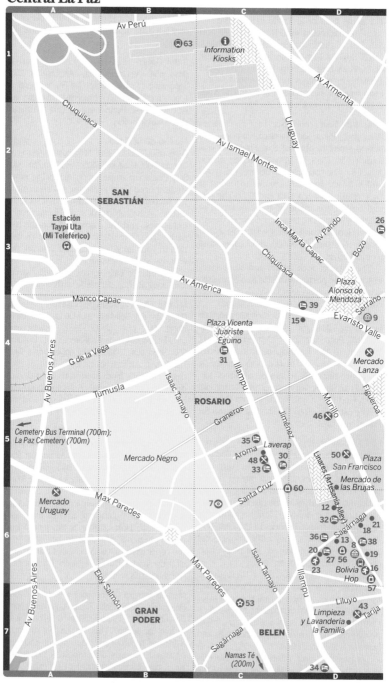

Av Perú

63

Information
Kiosks

Av Armentia

Chuquisaca

Av Ismael Montes

Uruguay

SAN
SEBASTIÁN

Inca Mayta Capac

Av Pando

26

Bozo

Estación
Taypi Uta
(Mi Teleférico)

Chiquisaca

Av América

Plaza
Alonso de
Mendoza

Serrano

Manco Capac

39

Evaristo Valle

15

9

Plaza Vicenta
Juariste
Eguino

Mercado
Lanza

Av Buenos Aires

G de la Vega

31

Illampu

Tumusla

ROSARIO

Figueroa

Isaac Tamayo

Graneros

Murillo

46

Cemetery Bus Terminal (700m);
La Paz Cemetery (700m)

Mercado Negro

Jiménez

35

50

Plaza
San Francisco

Aroma

Laverap

Mercado de
las Brujas

48

30

Mercado
Uruguay

Max Paredes

33

Santa Cruz

60

12

7

32

18

21

Av Buenos Aires

Isaac Tamayo

36

Sagárnaga

13

38

20

8

19

Eloy Salmón

Max Paredes

27

56

23

Bolivia
Hop

16

57

Illampu

Liluyo

53

43

GRAN
PODER

Limpieza
y Lavandería
la Familia

Tarija

Sagárnaga

BELEN

Namas Té
(200m)

34

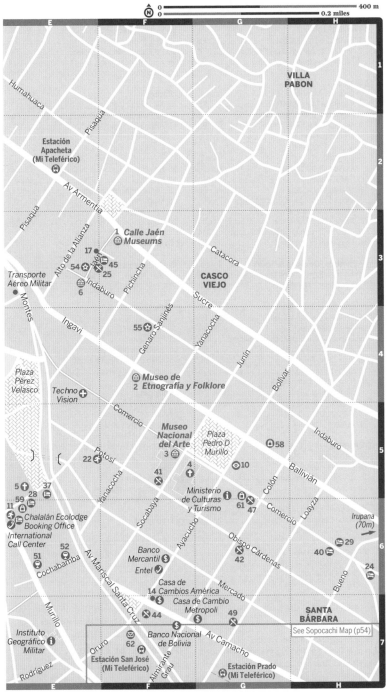

0   400 m
0   0.2 miles

VILLA PABON

Humahuaca

Pisaqua

Estación Apacheta (Mi Teleférico)

Av Armentia

Pisaqua

1 Calle Jaén Museums

17

Alto de la Alianza

54   45
25

Catacora

CASCO VIEJO

6   Indaburo

Transporte Aéreo Militar

Montes

Pichincha

Sucre

Ingavi

55   Genaro Sanjinés

Yanacocha

2 Museo de Etnografía y Folklore

Junín

Bolívar

Plaza Pérez Velasco

Techno Vision

Comercio

Indaburo

Museo Nacional del Arte

Plaza Pedro D Murillo

58

22   3   Potosí

Yanacocha

41   4   10   Ballivián

5   37

28

59   Ministerio de Culturas y Turismo   61   47   Colón   Comercio   Loayza

11   Socabaya

Chalalán Ecolodge Booking Office

International Call Center

52   Ayacucho   Obispo Cárdenas   Irupana (70m)

51   Cochabamba   42   40   29

Av Mariscal Santa Cruz

Banco Mercantil   Mercado   24

Entel   Bueno

Casa de 14 Cambios América   Casa de Cambio Metropoli   49   SANTA BÁRBARA

44   Av Camacho   See Sopocachi Map (p54)

Murillo

Instituto Geográfico Militar   62   Banco Nacional de Bolivia

Oruro   Almirante Grau   Estación Prado (Mi Teleférico)

Estación San José (Mi Teleférico)

Rodríguez

Central La Paz

have often included the work of rising Bolivian artists.

Iglesia Indígena de San Pedro CHURCH
(Map p54; Plaza San Pedro, San Pedro) Founded in 1549 and finished at the end of the 18th century after the siege of La Paz by Tupac Katari, the 'Indigenous Church of San Pedro' has baroque and neoclassic touches.

◎ East of El Prado

East of El Prado you'll find most of the city's museums, as well as the presidential palace.

★**Museo Nacional del Arte**   MUSEUM
(National Art Museum; Map p50; www.face
book.com/museonacionaldeartebolivia; cnr Com
ercio & Socabaya, Casco Viejo; B$20; ⊙9:30am-
12:30pm & 3-7pm Tue-Fri, 10am-5:30pm Sat,
10am-1:30pm Sun) This colonial building was
constructed in 1775 of pink sandstone and
has been restored to its original grandeur,
in mestizo (mixed) baroque and Andino
baroque styles. In the center of a huge
courtyard, surrounded by three stories
of pillared corridors, is a lovely alabaster
fountain. The various levels are dedicated
to different eras, with an emphasis on religious themes.

Highlights include works by former
paceño (La Paz native) Marina Núñez del
Prado (p73). Ask for a free guided tour (minimum of five people).

Next door is a gorgeous new space for
rotating exhibitions of contemporary Bolivian art. Unlike the main museum, entrance
to these galleries is free.

★**Museo de Etnografía
y Folklore**   MUSEUM
(Ethnography & Folklore Museum; Map p50;
☑240-8640; www.musef.org.bo; cnr Ingavi & Sanjinés, Casco Viejo; B$20, with photography B$40;
⊙9am-12:30pm & 3-7pm Mon-Fri, 9am-4:30 Sat,
9am-12:30pm Sun) Anthropology buffs should
check out this museum, one of the city's
best. The building, itself a real treasure,
was constructed in 1720 and was once the
home of the Marqués de Villaverde. Highlights include an awe-inspiring collection of
ritualistic masks and an exhibition of stunning weavings from around the country. A
guided tour is available by calling ahead.

★**Museo de Textiles
Andinos Bolivianos**   MUSEUM
(MUTAB; ☑224-3601; www.museodetextiles.
org; Plaza Benito Juárez 488, Miraflores; B$15;
⊙9:30am-noon & 3-6:30pm Mon-Sat) Fans of
Bolivia's lovely traditional weaving consider this small textile museum a must-see.
Examples of the country's finest traditional
textiles (including pieces from the Cordillera Apolobamba, and the Jal'qa and Candelaria regions of the Central Highlands)
are grouped by region and described in
Spanish and English. The creative process
is explained from fiber to finished product. The gift shop sells museum-quality
originals; 90% of the sale price goes to the
artists.

Walk 20 minutes northeast from El Prado
or catch *micros* (small buses) 131 or 135, or
minibuses marked 'Av Busch.'

The sister Museum of the Poncho (p91) is
located in Copacabana.

★**Calle Jaén Museums**   MUSEUM
(Map p50; Calle Jaén, Casco Viejo; 4 museums
B$20; ⊙9am-12:30pm & 3-7pm Tue-Fri, 9am-1pm
Sat & Sun) La Paz's best-preserved colonial
street is home to four small museums. They
are all clustered together and can gener-
ally be bundled into one visit. Buy tickets
at the **Museo Costumbrista** (Map p50; cnr
Jaén & Sucre) and continue to the **Museo de
Metales Preciosos** (Museum of Precious Met-
als; Map p50; Calle Jaén 777), **Museo del Lito-
ral** (Museo de la Guerra del Pacífico; Map p50; Calle
Jaén 798) and **Casa de Murillo** (Map p50; Calle
Jaén 790).

The Museo Costumbrista Juan de Vargas
contains art and photos, as well as some
superb ceramic figurine dioramas of old La
Paz: a representation of *akulliko*, the hour
of coca-chewing; the festivities surrounding
St John the Baptist's Day, and the hanging
of Murillo in 1810. Also on display are colonial artifacts and colorful dolls wearing traditional costumes.

Also known as Museo del Oro (Gold
Museum), the Museo de Metales Preciosos
houses four impressively presented salons
of pre-Columbian silver, gold and copper
works and pieces from Tiwanaku.

The diminutive Museo del Litoral con-
sists mainly of historical maps that defend
Bolivia's emotionally charged claims to
Antofagasta and Chile's Segunda Región.

Once the home of Pedro Domingo Murillo, a leader in the La Paz Revolution of
July 16, 1809, the Casa de Murillo displays
collections of colonial art, furniture and
household items of glass and silver that once
belonged to Bolivian aristocracy.

Mamani Mamani Gallery   GALLERY
(Fundación Mamani Mamani; Map p50; ☑290-
6294; www.mamani.com; Indaburo 710, cnr Jaén,
Casco Viejo) A gallery of art, yes, but also a
collection of saleable artwork, including
notecards and posters of Bolivia's most
colorful and well-known modern artist,
cochabambino Roberto Mamani Mamani
(aka Roberto Aguilar Quisbert). You need to
see his vibrant interpretations of his Aymará
heritage, and you might need to bring some
of it home! The cultural center has dance
and painting classes.

Sopocachi

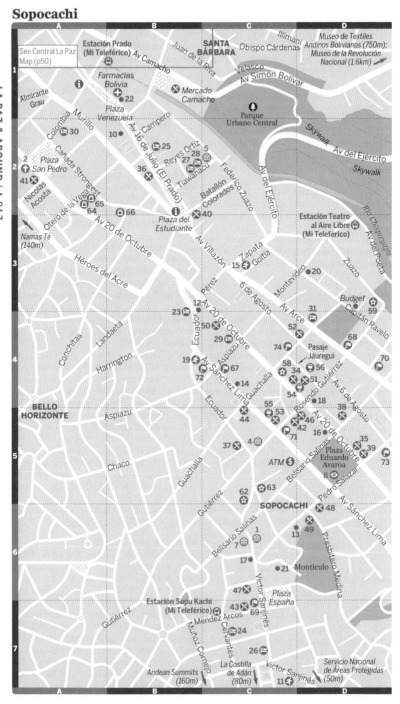

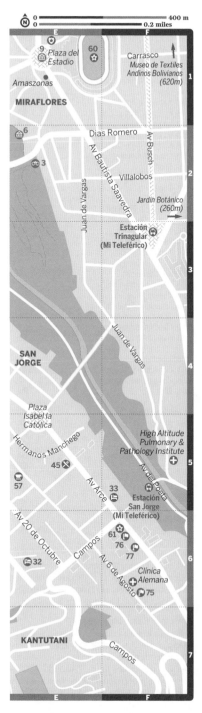

Catedral Metropolitana
CATHEDRAL

(Map p50; Plaza Murillo, Casco Viejo) Although it's a relatively recent addition to La Paz's religious structures, the 1835 cathedral is impressive – mostly because it is built on a steep hillside. The main entrance is 12m higher than its base on Calle Potosí. The cathedral's sheer immensity, with its high dome, hulking columns, thick stone walls and high ceilings, is overpowering, but the altar is relatively simple.

Inside, the main attraction is the profusion of stained-glass work; the windows behind the altar depict a gathering of Bolivian politicos being blessed from above by a flock of heavenly admirers.

Beside the cathedral is the **Presidential Palace** (Map p50), a mustard-yellow building that is the official residence of the President of Bolivia. It earned its nickname, the 'Burnt Palace,' in an 1875 uprising when it was set aflame and badly damaged.

Museo de Instrumentos Musicales
MUSEUM

(Museum of Musical Instruments; Map p50; Jaén 711, Casco Viejo; B$5; ⊙9:30am-1:30pm & 2:30-6:30pm) A must for musicians. The brainchild of *charango* master Ernesto Cavour Aramayo displays all possible incarnations of the *charango* (a traditional Bolivian ukulele-type instrument) and other Bolivian folk instruments. You can also arrange *charango* and wind instrument lessons here for around B$50 per hour.

Pipiripi
MUSEUM

(Map p54; Av del Ejército, Miraflores; B$3; ⊙9:30am-12:30pm & 3-6:30pm Wed-Fri, 10am-6:30pm Sat & Sun; 🛝) La Paz's children's museum has interactive exhibits and plenty of stickiness and stinky-sock smells over four rambling levels. The views are awesome, and exhibits include a word forest (English words count), textile and market areas, and a giant Scrabble game.

Mirador Laikakota
VIEWPOINT

(Map p54; Av del Ejército, Miraflores; B$3; ⊙8am-5pm; 🛝) The Mirador Laikakota – part of the children's museum – is in a tranquil park setting and is perfect for kids.

Museo de la Revolución Nacional
MUSEUM

(Museum of the National Revolution; Plaza Villarroel, Miraflores; B$5; ⊙9:30am-12:30pm & 3-7pm Tue-Fri, 9am-1pm Sat & Sun) The first question to ask is 'Which Revolution?'

Sopocachi

(Bolivia has had more than 100 of them). The answer is that of April 1952, the popular revolt of armed miners that resulted in the nationalization of Bolivian mining interests. It displays photos and paintings from the era.

Museo Nacional de Arqueología Tiwanaku   MUSEUM
(National Archaeology Museum; Map p54; ☑ 233-1633; Tiawanacu 93, Prado; B$14; ☺ 9am-12:30pm & 3-7pm Tue-Fri, 9am-1pm Sat & Sun) Two blocks east of El Prado, this small but well-sorted collection of artifacts illustrates the most interesting aspects of Tiwanaku culture – those that weren't appropriated, anyway.

Templete Semisubterráneo & Museo al Aire Libre   MUSEUM
(Map p54; Stadium, Miraflores) FREE The open-pit museum opposite the stadium contains replicas of statues from Tiwanaku's Templete Semisubterráneo. Only worth seeing if you can't visit Tiwanaku itself. If you

have some time while you're here, hoof your way up to the **Killi Killi** lookout for breathtaking views.

⊙ Zona Sur

A lovely spot to escape from the chaos of the rest of La Paz, with fantastic opportunities for shopping, dining and gallery-hopping. Just outside of the Zona Sur, there are several good hiking spots.

⊙ El Alto

La Ceja   AREA

In the lively La Ceja (Eyebrow) district, which commands one of the highest real-estate prices in El Alto for its commercial value, you'll find a variety of electronic gadgets and mercantile goods. For an excellent market experience, don't miss the massive Mercado 16 de Julio (p63), which stretches for many blocks along the main thoroughfare and across Plaza 16 de Julio. This shopaholic's paradise has absolutely everything, from food and electronics, to vehicles and animals, all at reasonable prices. Heads up: watch your wallet in both senses of the phrase.

Tupac Katari Mirador   VIEWPOINT

(Pasankeri) For a great view of La Paz, head in a taxi to the Tupac Katari Mirador, situated right on the edge of the rim that plunges down the valley to La Paz. It was – and is – a sacred Inca site and ritual altar where Tupac Katari is believed to have been drawn and quartered by colonialists.

The colonialists constructed and interred a statue of Christ on the same site, but that didn't stop locals from performing spiritual rituals here. Around the *mirador* (lookout) is a long line of small identical blue booths. These house *curanderos* (healers) or *yatiris*, who provide sage advice. Note: the counsel of a *yatiri* is taken extremely seriously – both photos and tourist appointments are considered inappropriate.

🏃 Activities

You'll get plenty of exercise hoofing up and down El Prado but you don't have to head far out of town for a real adrenaline rush. Note that the **Asociación de Guías de Montaña** (www.agmtb.org, in Spanish) certifies guides in Bolivia, and it's worth checking out their information before deciding on an operation.

★**AndesXtremo**   PARAGLIDING

(Map p54; ☑ 7358-3349; www.andesxtremo.com; Francisco Bedregal 2962, Sopocachi; ⊙ 8:30am-12:30pm & 2:30-6:30pm Mon-Fri, to 12:30pm Sat)

If the teleférico (p78) wasn't enough for you, then these guys will get you higher than you've ever been in La Paz on a tandem-paragliding adventure. They also offer rock climbing, mountaineering, canyoning and caving.

Urban Rush   RAPPELLING

(Map p50; ☑ 231-0218; www.urbanrushbolivia.com; Potosí 920, Casco Viejo; ⊙ noon-6pm) Run by Gravity Assisted Mountain Biking, this company offers an urban rappel down the Hotel Presidente (the big blue building across the street from Iglesia de San Francisco).

Casa del Sol   YOGA

(Map p54; ☑ 244-0928; Goitia 127, Prado; 2hr class B$35; ⊙ 6am-11pm) Casa del Sol offers Hatha yoga classes four times daily to get the kinks out. Enjoy a nice veggie breakfast or lunch after at the attached cafe.

Sabor Clandestino   FOOD

(☑ 7054-8279; www.facebook.com/Sabor-Clandestino-337274726662632/) Join Chef Marco Quelca on a trip into nature near La Paz for a multi-course gourmet meal in the open air. Events typically take place on Saturdays or Sundays and are always reachable by public transportation. Check Facebook for upcoming dates.

Mountain Biking

There are tons of mountain-biking options just outside of La Paz. Intermediate riders can take on a thrilling downhill ride on the World's Most Dangerous Road (p117), while advanced riders may wish to go for the less-traveled Chacaltaya to Zongo (p84) route or the rides near Sorata (p131). Beginners not quite ready for the death road may want to check out the **Balcón Andino** descent near the Zona Sur, a 2400m roller coaster on a wide dirt road.

★**Gravity Assisted**
Mountain Biking   MOUNTAIN BIKING

(Map p50; ☑ 231-0218, mobile 7721-9634; www.gravitybolivia.com; Linares 940, Rosario; ⊙ 9am-7pm Mon-Fri, 10am-3pm Sat, 2-6pm Sun) This knowledgeable, highly regarded and professional outfit has an excellent reputation among travelers and tip-top Kona downhill bikes. Their Dangerous Road Trip (B$850 per person) ends with hot showers, an all-you-can-eat buffet and an optional tour of the Senda Verde animal refuge (p114).

Xtreme Downhill CYCLING
(Map p50; ☑ mobile 7775-1587; www.xtreme downhill.com; Sagárnaga 392, Rosario; ☺ 10am-8pm) A recommended and safety-focused outfitter for Death Road cycle trips (B$400 to B$600, depending on the bike).

Climbing

La Paz is the staging ground for most of the climbs in the Cordilleras. From here novice climbers can arrange trips to Huayna Potosí (p110), two to three days for B$900 to B$1200. More experienced climbers may look to climb Illimani or Sajama (p154), each about four to five days for roughly US$485.

Andean Expeditions Dirninger CLIMBING, HIKING
(Map p50; ☑ 241-4235, mobile 7755-0226; www.andean-expeditions.com; Sagárnaga 189, Galería Doryan, 3rd fl, Oficina 32, Rosario; ☺ 9am-12:30pm & 2-5:30pm Mon-Fri) An Austrian-founded company that offers mountain treks in Bolivia and neighboring countries, and uses guides certified by the International Federation of Mountain Guides Associations (IFMGA). More than 10 years in Bolivia, and not the same old run-of-the-mill tours.

Andean Summits CLIMBING
(☑ 242-2106; www.andeansummits.com; Muñoz Cornejo 1009, Sopocachi; ☺ 9am-noon & 3-7pm Mon-Fri, 9am-12:30pm Sat) Offers a variety of outdoor activities from mountaineering and trekking to 4WD tours in Bolivia and beyond. The owners are professional IFMGA mountain guides.

Hiking

Except for the altitude, La Paz and its environs are made for hiking. Many La Paz tour agencies offer daily 'hiking' tours to Chacaltaya (p84), a rough 30km drive north of La Paz, and an easy way to bag a high peak without having to do any really hard-core hiking. Head to Valle de la Luna (p81), Valle de las Ánimas (p83) or Muela del Diablo (p81) for do-it-yourself day hikes from La Paz.

★ **La Paz on Foot** ECOTOUR
(Map p54; ☑ mobile 7154-3918; www.lapazon foot.com; Av Ecuador 2022, Sopocachi; ☺ 10:30am-6:30pm Mon-Fri) This tip-top operation, run by the passionate English-speaking ecologist Stephen Taranto, offers a range of activities, including walks in and

around La Paz, Apolobamba, the Yungas, Chulumani, Madidi and Titicaca. The interactive La Paz urban treks (half-day or full-day, fee depending on group size) venture from the heights of El Alto to the depths of the historic center.

Other tours include art and architecture, living history, textiles, stimulants (think coca, cocoa and coffee) and community-based activities. Multilingual guides are available.

🎓 Courses

For musical instruction (in Spanish) on traditional Andean instruments (such as the *zampoña*, *quena* or *charango*), inquire at the Museo de Instrumentos Musicales (p55).

Note that not everyone advertising language instruction is accredited or even capable of teaching Spanish, however well they speak it, so seek local recommendations and examine credentials before signing up. Plan on paying around B$60 to B$80 per hour for individual instruction and B$30 to B$50 for group lessons. Many schools can also offer homestays.

Ayni Spanish Institute LANGUAGE
(Map p50; ☑ mobile 7199-3790; http://spanish bolivia.com; Linares 880, Oficina 14, Rosario; 1hr class from B$50; ☺ 9:30am-12:30pm & 2:30-6:30pm Mon-Fri) Highly qualified linguists teach Spanish classes with a focus on the language's everyday use.

Asociación Hastinapura Bolivia YOGA
(Map p54; ☑ 242-4145; www.facebook.com/has tinapuraLaPazBolivia; Av Ecuador 1999, Sopocachi; 1½hr yoga session B$20) This serene and oh-so-friendly spot offers Hatha yoga and meditation courses, as well as workshops on mystic philosophy and spiritual growth (all in Spanish). Check Facebook for the latest schedules.

ie Instituto Exclusivo LANGUAGE
(Map p54; ☑ 242-1072; www.instituto-exclusivo. com; Av 20 de Octubre 2315, Sopocachi; courses per hour B$85; ☺ 8am-9pm Mon-Fri) Specialized Spanish-language courses for travelers and professionals. Also offers Aymará and Quechua lessons with native speakers.

Pico Verde Languages LANGUAGE
(Map p50; ☑ 231-8328; www.pico-verde.com; Sagárnaga 363, 2nd fl, Rosario; group lessons from per hour B$35) Offers flexible schedules for Spanish classes and can set you up with a homestay.

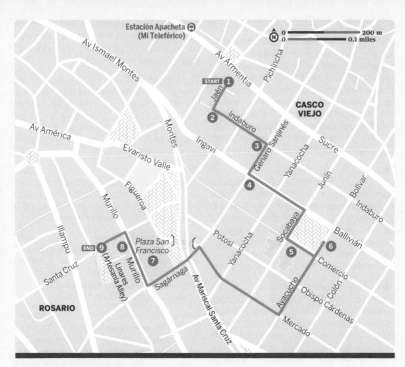

City Walk
Historic Center

START CALLE JAÉN
END MERCADO DE LAS BRUJAS
LENGTH 2KM; FOUR HOURS

Begin the walk on La Paz's best-preserved colonial street, **1 Calle Jaén** (p53), which is home to four small museums exploring Bolivian art, culture and history. At the southern end of the street, be sure to pop in to the **2 Mamani Mamani Gallery** (p53) to see the colorful works of one of Bolivia's most prominent modern artists. Walk down Indaburo to the banana-yellow **3 Teatro Municipal Alberto Saavedra Pérez** (p74), a grand performance hall, then turn one block south to the **4 Museo de Etnografía y Folklore** (p53), one of the city's finest museums and a must for anthropology buffs.

From here, follow Ingavi over to the pigeon-filled Plaza Murillo, home to the immense and impressive **5 Catedral Metropolitana** (p55). Beside the cathedral is the storied **6 Presidential Palace** (p55), in front of which stands a bust of President Gualberto Villarroel. In 1946, he was tossed out of the palace by vigilantes and hanged from a lamppost in the square. Interestingly enough, Pedro Domingo Murillo, for whom the plaza was named, met a similar fate here in 1810.

Follow the businessmen downhill to Calle Mercado, walking past historic bank buildings and government offices over to Plaza San Francisco. This iconic square, one of the city's focal points, is filled with artists, activists and *lustrabotas* (shoeshiners), and is a great place to check the pulse of the nation. The cloisters and garden of **7 Museo San Francisco** (p49) lie adjacent to the plaza's namesake basilica, which in its current form was built between 1743 and 1772.

Walk uphill past the tourist shops and adventure outfitters of Calle Sagárnaga over to **8 Popular Cocina Boliviana** (p69), where you can rest your legs (and catch your breath!). The cheap and seasonal three-course tasting menus here are inspired by the city's humble lunch spots. After your meal, finish the tour in the **9 Mercado de las Brujas** (p63). This so-called Witches' Market is full of herbal folk remedies, baby llama fetuses and wandering *yatiris* (traditional healers). Be careful what you wish for!

👉 Tours

Many of Bolivia's tour agencies are based in La Paz, including international operators. Some are clearly better than others (many are not formally registered; check carefully if choosing between those on Sagárnaga), and many specialize in particular interests or areas. Most agencies run day tours (B$70 to B$500 per person) in and around La Paz, to Lake Titicaca, Tiwanaku, Zongo Valley, Chacaltaya, Valle de la Luna and other sites.

★ HanaqPacha Travel — TOURS
(Map p50; ☑ mobile 6980-3602; www.hanaqpachatravel.com; Jaén 765, Casco Viejo; ⊙ 9am-6:30pm) Runs recommended daily tours to El Alto (B$140) to see the prismatic *cholets* of Aymará architect Freddy Mamani. Also has a daily Tastes of Bolivia tour (B$140) to learn about typical food. Uyuni, Tiwanaku and Rurrenabaque are the focus of longer tours.

★ Climbing South America — CLIMBING
(Map p50; ☑ mobile 7190-3534; www.climbingsouthamerica.com; Linares 940, 2nd fl, Rosario; ⊙ 9am-6:30pm Mon-Fri, 10am-3pm Sat) A reputable English-speaking operator for climbing, mountaineering and trekking in the nearby mountains. Also sells great maps.

Banjo Tours — ADVENTURE
(Map p54; ☑ mobile 6716-5394; www.banjotours.com; Pedro Salazar 623, Oficina 2, Sopocachi; ⊙ 8am-noon & 2-6pm Mon-Fri, to noon Sat) Banjo doesn't offer the same cookie-cutter tours as its competitors; it's a highly-recommended outfit for quality small-group adventures off the beaten path.

Madidi Travel — ECOTOUR
(Map p50; ☑ 231-8313; www.madidi-travel.com; Linares 947, Rosario; ⊙ 9am-7pm Mon-Fri, to 5pm Sat & Sun) Specializing in trips to Madidi, this tour operator's 4000-hectare private reserve east of the park (Eco Reserve Serere) adds another layer of protection.

Hormigón Armado — WALKING
(Map p54; ☑ mobile 7655-8885; http://hormigonarmado.wix.com/lustrabotas; Av Ecuador 2582, Sopocachi) Walking tours of La Paz run by the people who know its streets best: the *lustrabotas* (shoe-shiners). Reserve at least two days in advance.

Tusoco Travel — CULTURAL
(Map p50; ☑ mobile 7220-7682; www.tusoco.com; Sagárnaga 227, Rosario; ⊙ 9:30am-1:30pm & 3:30-7:30pm Mon-Fri, 10am-2pm Sun) 🌿 Supports 22 indigenous communities across Bolivia by offering tours that provide them a sustainable income while promising travelers meaningful cultural interactions.

Deep Rainforest — BOATING
(Map p50; http://deep-rainforest.com; Av América 121, Oficina 1, Rosario; ⊙ 2-7pm Mon-Sat) Specialists in the four-day, three-night boat trips and six-day, five-night rafting trips from Guanay to Rurrenabaque. There are regular departures from La Paz.

Terra Andina — TOURS
(Map p54; ☑ 241-9932; www.bolivia-travels.com; Av Ecuador 2682, Sopocachi; ⊙ 9am-6:30pm Mon-Fri) Tailor-made trekking, climbing and 4WD tours in English, French or German.

Magri Turismo — TOURS
(Map p54; ☑ 244-2727; www.magriturismo.com; Capitán Ravelo 2101, Sopocachi; ⊙ 8:30am-12:30pm & 2:30-6:30pm Mon-Fri, 9am-noon Sat) A large, well-established agency with a range of tours organized around Bolivia.

Bolivian Journeys — ADVENTURE
(Map p50; www.bolivianjourneys.org; Sagárnaga 363, Rosario; ⊙ 9am-7pm Mon-Fri, to noon Sat) This company specialising in climbing, mountaineering and trekking organizes guided climbs to Huayna Potosí. Equipment rental is available, with maps and gas for MSR stoves for sale.

Fremen Tours — TOURS
(Map p54; ☑ 242-1258; www.andes-amazonia.com; Av 20 de Octubre 2396, Sopocachi; ⊙ 9am-noon & 2:30-6pm Mon-Fri) Upmarket agency specializing in soft adventure in the Amazon and Chapare.

Andesuma — TOURS
(☑ 242-7146; www.andesuma.com) A German-run agency offering personalized tours all over Bolivia with a focus on adventure, culture, trekking and climbing. It specializes in off-the-beaten-path destinations such as Cordillera Apolobamba, Cordillera Quimsa Cruz and Torotoro.

Bolivia Millenaria — CULTURAL
(Map p54; ☑ 241-4753; www.millenariantours.com; Av Sánchez Lima 2193, Sopocachi; ⊙ 9am-3pm Mon-Fri) This agency offers tailor-made tours around Bolivia with a focus on remote parks and cultural interactions.

America Tours — TOURS
(Map p54; ☑ 237-4204; www.america-ecotours.com; Av 16 de Julio 1490, Oficina No 9, Prado;

Zona Sur

9am-5pm Mon-Fri) This warmly recommended English-speaking agency offers a wide range of community-based ecotourism projects and tailor-made tours around La Paz and Bolivia.

Inca Land Tours CULTURAL
(Map p50; 231-6760; www.incalandtours.com; Sagárnaga 233, Oficina No 3, Rosario; 7:30am-8pm) An established Peruvian budget operation specializing in tours out of Rurrenabaque and Coroico.

Turisbus TOURS
(Map p50; 279-8786; www.turisbus.com; Hotel Rosario, Illampu 704, Rosario) A large range of day and multiday tours organized for groups and individuals around Bolivia.

☆ Festivals & Events

La Paz is always looking for an excuse to celebrate. Check with Tourist Information (p79) for a complete list of what's on.

Alasitas CULTURAL
(Jan 24) During Inca times the Alasitas (Aymará for 'buy from me') fair coincided with the spring equinox (September 21), and was intended to demonstrate the abundance of the fields. The little god of abundance, Ekeko ('dwarf' in Aymará), made his appearance. Modern Alasitas traditions are now celebrated throughout the city in January.

The date underwent some shifts during the colonial period, which the *campesinos* (subsistence farmers) weren't too happy about, so they turned the celebration into a kitschy mockery of the original. 'Abundance' was redefined to apply not only to crops, but also to homes, tools, cash, clothing, cars, trucks, airplanes and even 12-story buildings.

Zona Sur

La Paz Markets

La Paz's frenetic markets are easily the highlight of any trip, where modern commerce and culture collide in a wonderful riot of honks, shrieks and smells. You'll find open-air markets all across town, though the Rosario neighborhood has a notable concentration. Every day is a de facto market day in La Paz, but Saturdays are particularly fun.

The narrow cobblestone streets off Max Paredes – the **Mercado Negro** (Black Market; Map p50. B5; ☉6am-8pm) – are a good place to start. Especially interesting are the sections near Graneros ('designer' clothes), Tumusla and Isaac Tamayo (everything and anything), and between Santa Cruz and Sagárnaga (tools and building materials). The best place for electronics is along Eloy Salmón. Be especially careful when wandering around this part of town: it's notorious for light fingers. It's best to take a taxi here at night.

North of Plaza San Francisco, on Calle Figueroa, the **Mercado Lanza** (Rosario; Map p50, D4; snacks B$5-25; ☉6am-8pm) is one of La Paz's main food markets. It sells all manner of fruits, vegetables, juices, dairy products, breads and canned foods, and there are numerous stalls where you can pick up a sandwich, soup, *salteña* (filled pastry shells), *api con pastel* (sweet corn drink and fried cheese empanada) or full meal. It also houses the splendid **Flower Market**.

The five-story **Mercado Camacho** (cnr Av Camacho & Bueno, Casco Viejo; Map p54, B1; snacks B$5-25; ☉7am-9pm Mon-Fri,

1. Flower Market
2. Souvenirs at the Mercado de las Brujas
3. *Api con pastel*

to 6pm Sat & Sun), near Parque Urbano Central, makes an ideal lunch stop with untold stands selling empanadas, fruit juices and chorizo sandwiches. **Mercado Uruguay** (off Max Paredes, Rosario; Map p50, A6; snacks B$5-25; ☺7am-8pm), on the far side of El Prado, is purely the domain of adventurous eaters after tiny *ispi* fish from Lake Titicaca or stews made with unidentifiable offal.

Just downhill from here is the famed **Mercado de las Brujas** (Witches' Market; La Hechiceria; Map p50, D5), which is chock-a-block with stores selling mysterious potions for lovemaking, hanging llama fetuses and Aymará good-luck charms, including frogs. Artisan stores in the area sell *oriente* wood carvings and ceramics, and Potosí silver. Others deal in rugs, wall-hangings, woven belts and pouches. Amid the lovely weavings and other items of exquisite craftsmanship, you'll find plenty of tourist kitsch, an art form unto itself: Inca-themed ashtrays, fake Tiwanaku figurines, costume jewelry and mass-produced woolens.

To visit the biggest market in Bolivia – some say it's the largest in South America – you'll need to hop in a cable car and head up to El Alto, where each Thursday and Sunday the massive **Mercado 16 de Julio** (☺6am-3pm Thu & Sun) completely absorbs dozens of city blocks. You can buy everything from new cars to animals, textiles and firearms. For the most part, however, it's a colossal flea market, the likes of which you won't soon forget.

**La Festividad de Nuestro
Señor Jesús del Gran Poder** RELIGIOUS
(☺late May/early Jun) El Gran Poder has developed into a unique La Paz festival, and an elaborate display of economic power; embroiderers prepare lavish costumes and upwards of 25,000 performers practice for weeks in advance. A number of dances are featured, such as the *suri sikuris* (in which the dancers are bedecked in ostrich feathers), the lively *kullawada, morenada, caporales* and the *inkas*, which duplicates Inca ceremonial dances.

It began in 1939 as a candle procession led by an image of Christ through the predominantly *campesino* neighborhoods of upper La Paz. The following year the local union of embroiderers formed a folkloric group to participate, other festival-inspired folkloric groups joined in, and the celebration grew larger and more lively into what it is today.

Fiestas Julianas CULTURAL
(☺Jul 16) The patron saint of the department of La Paz, Santa Juliana, gets her own public holiday, which includes many dances and parades. On the Friday before, people gather at Plaza San Francisco (p49) for a massive *verbena* (nightlong party). There is also a month-long cultural series at the Teatro Municipal (p74) featuring folk music throughout July.

**Entrada Folklórica
de Universitaria** FOLKLORE
(☺last Sat in Jul) With an atmosphere alluding to Carnaval, hundreds of dance groups (made up of students from around the country) perform traditional dances through the streets of La Paz.

Día de los Muertos RELIGIOUS
(☺Nov 1) Families prepare the favorite dishes of their loved ones, along with little sweet breads, with plaster-cast faces, representing their dead relatives. Head to the cemetery (p49) to witness some of the rituals.

🛏 Sleeping

Most backpackers beeline for central La Paz to find a bed. The area around the Mercado de las Brujas (Witches' Market; between Illampu, Av Mariscal Santa Cruz and Sagárnaga) is a true travelers' ghetto. To be closer to a wider array of restaurants and a bar or two, consider Sopocachi. For more upmarket luxury, look along the lower Prado and further south in the Zona Sur.

🛏 West of El Prado

★**Onkel Inn** HOSTEL **$**
(Map p54; ☎249-0456; www.onkelinn.com; Colombia 257, San Pedro; dm/s/d/tr incl breakfast B$77/139/271/299; @☎) A bright, HI-affiliated place in a convenient spot between San Pedro and El Prado. It's less of a scene than the hostels up by the terminal, good for *tranquilo* (quiet) travelers. The dorms are the nicest in town with crisp sheets, orange bedcovers and a bright modern feel. Some bunks will leave you with vertigo; nice common areas and even a sauna!

3600 Hostel HOSTEL **$**
(Map p54; ☎212-0478; www.3600hostel.com; Av Ecuador 1982, Sopocachi; dm incl breakfast B$90-105, d with private bathroom B$300, tr with shared bathroom B$280; ☎) Named for the altitude in which it lies, this lovingly restored 1840s-era home has a stone-floored interior patio, funky furniture and gorgeous stained-glass windows. The dorms are spacious with privacy curtains, though the top bunks are seriously high. It's one of the few places in town with a women-only dorm.

Greenhouse
HOSTEL **$**

(Map p54; ✐ mobile 7962-7775; www.greenhouse bolivia.com; Victor Sanjinés 2866, Sopocachi; dm/d incl breakfast B$70/195; ⊕) This converted house near Plaza España has gorgeously manicured gardens out front, a great patio out back and an extremely chill vibe; we just wish the dorms were a little cleaner.

Hostal Maya Inn
HOTEL **$**

(Map p50; ✐231-1970; www.hostalmaya.com; Sagárnaga 339, Rosario; s/d/tr incl breakfast B$100/180/240, with shared bathroom B$80/140/180; @⊕) This is a friendly, if basic, place. The most appealing rooms have windows (note: a few don't), although rooms at the front can be a little noisy. The electric showers are often rough for hot-water lovers, and the hallways can be spookily dark.

Hotel Continental
HOTEL **$**

(Map p50; ✐245-1176; Illampu 626, Rosario; s/d/tr B$100/150/200, with shared bathroom B$80/120/190; ⊕) This dark and slightly dreary downtown option is popular among thriftsters. The detergent smell can be overpowering, but at least you know somebody is cleaning the place.

Hotel Sagárnaga
HOTEL **$$**

(Map p50; ✐235-0252; www.hotelsagarnaga. com; Sagárnaga 326, Rosario; s/d incl breakfast B$147/270; @⊕) The knight in shining armor at the front desk (and no, we're not talking about the receptionist, although he *is* friendly) welcomes you to this renovated gem in the heart of Sagárnaga. East-facing rooms are the best, though all offer good value for money with safes, TVs and parquet floors.

Rendezvous
GUESTHOUSE **$$**

(Map p54; ✐291-2459; www.rendezvouslapaz.com; Pasaje M Carranza 461, Sopocachi; r incl breakfast from US$30; @) A great mid-range bet for couples in search of privacy, peace and quiet. The 11 rooms are each unique, with local artwork and refurbished antiques. Guests also rave about the on-site **restaurant**.

Hotel Las Brisas
HOTEL **$$**

(Map p50; ✐246-3691; www.lasbrisas-hotel. com; Illampu 742, Rosario; s/d/tr incl breakfast B$188/278/383; @⊕) This is a solid budget bet with a 'Bolivia moderna' style – think neat rooms (some with internal windows), funky murals and crispy sheets coupled with a few shabby bits and external glassy walls. The rooms at the front have excellent views

DON'T MISS

JARDÍN BOTÁNICO

An oasis in the urban jungle, the time you spend at the **Jardín Botánico** (cnr Lucas Jaimes & Nicaragua; B$1; ⊕9am to 5pm, Mon-Fri, to 6pm Sat & Sun) will be the most tranquil during your visit to La Paz. Swan along the palm-shaded pathways that block out the Miraflores traffic. Over 1700 Bolivian native plants coexist peacefully aside exotic imports from New Zealand and beyond. Just chill, *hermano*. It's a 500m walk from Hernando Siles (p74) stadium.

and the staff are friendly, plus there's a nice courtyard and sunny top-floor restaurant.

La Posada de la Abuela
HOTEL **$$**

(Map p50; ✐233-2285; Linares 947, Rosario; d/tr incl breakfast B$340/560; @⊕) Travelers praise this pleasant oasis in the heart of the artisan and tourist center. The rooms are sterile and clean (some have internally facing windows), and the plant-filled courtyard adds a colorful, if potentially noisy, touch.

New management had plans to make renovations at the time of research.

Hostal Naira
HOTEL **$$**

(Map p50; ✐235-5645; www.hostalnaira.com; Sagárnaga 161, Rosario; s/d/tr incl breakfast B$320/465/675; ⊕) You can't get a better location – right at the bottom of Sagárnaga near Plaza San Francisco. The rooms are also quite comfortable with vaulted ceilings and antique furnishings, and no dirt within sight. There's an elegant courtyard, though it can be a touch noisy at night.

Hotel Berlina
HOTEL **$$**

(Map p50; ✐246-1928; www.hotel-berlina. com; Illampu 761, Rosario; s/d/tr/q incl breakfast B$250/350/450/550; P@⊕) A place that has risen in quality in recent times. The triple rooms and apartments are huge, the rooftop **restaurant** has great panoramas, and a recent remodel gives the whole joint an air of spit-and-polish. East-facing rooms on an upper story offer the best views, while road-front views can be noisy.

Hotel Milton
HOTEL **$$**

(Map p50; ✐235-3511; www.hotelmiltonbolivia. com; Illampu 1126-1130, Rosario; s/d/tr incl breakfast B$120/230/330; @⊕) Tune in and drop out! This '70s pad truly is a paradise lost with red vinyl-studded walls, painted murals and

LA PAZ & AROUND LA PAZ

EKEKO

Ekeko is the household god and the keeper and distributor of material possessions. During Alasitas his devotees collect miniatures of those items they'd like to acquire during the following year and heap them onto small plaster images of the god. He's loaded down with household utensils, baskets of coca, wallets full of miniature currency, liquor, chocolate and other luxury goods. The more optimistic devotees buy miniature souped-up *camiones* (trucks), 1st-class airline tickets to Miami and three-story suburban homes! All items must be blessed by a certified *yatiri* (witch doctor) before they can become real.

If this apparent greed seems not to be in keeping with Aymará values – which emphasize the community and balance in all things – it's worth noting that Ekeko is also charged with displaying items that a family is able to share with the community.

funky wallpaper. Darker rooms at the back are a bit dingy, but the higher and lighter front rooms afford stupendous views over La Paz, making this a solid budget bet.

Hotel Fuentes   HOTEL **$$**
(Map p50; ☑ 231-3966; www.hotelfuentes.com. bo; Linares 888, Rosario; s/d/tr incl breakfast B$170/220/290; ☎) This cozy place is just-ever-so-slightly overpriced. Nevertheless, there's friendly service, and the basic rooms with bowed beds and parquet floors, cable TV and hot water are certainly doable. Some rooms on the higher levels have superlative views. A book exchange is a nice bonus.

Hotel Madre Tierra   HOTEL **$$**
(Map p54; ☑ 241-9910; www.hotelmadretierra.com; Av 20 de Octubre, Sopocachi; s/d B$350/450; ☎) This modern, slightly overpriced offering has friendly service and tidy rooms. Unfortunately, some are quite dark, and those facing the road can get noisy. Solid mattresses, cleanliness, minibars and cable TV make up for the drawbacks.

★ **Hotel Rosario**   BOUTIQUE HOTEL **$$$**
(Map p50; ☑ 245-1658; www.hotelrosario.com; Illampu 704, Rosario; d/tr/q incl breakfast US$93/115/148; @☎) The professional, English-speaking staff at La Paz's best

three-star hotel pamper you with five-star treatment. The ultraclean rooms in the well-maintained colonial residence all have solar-powered hot showers, cable TV and heaters. There is free internet and a generous breakfast buffet. Groups love it, so reserve ahead. There's a sister hotel at Copacabana (p96).

La Casona   HISTORIC HOTEL **$$$**
(Map p50; ☑ 290-0505; www.lacasonahotel boutique.com; Av Mariscal Santa Cruz 938, Prado; s/d/ste incl breakfast B$814/975/1383; @☎) A solid bet in the luxury boutique category, La Casona has 47 rooms in a beautifully restored colonial-era building surrounding a small courtyard. The rates have ballooned in recent years, but the rooms with high ceilings, exposed wood beams and thoughtful Andean textile accents are certainly welcome retreats. The rooftop stained-glass cupola is popular for weddings.

Casa Fusión   BOUTIQUE HOTEL **$$$**
(Map p54; ☑ 214-1372; www.casafusion.com.bo; Cervantes 2725, Sopocachi; s/d/tr incl breakfast B$510/600/685; @☎) While it lacks a little personality, this Sopocachi boutique hotel does have modern clean lines, more Scandinavian furnishings than you'll find in your local Ikea store, thick down comforters, blazing-hot showers and friendly service.

The top-story rooms have the best views and you're just a half-block from the teleférico (p78) station.

Real Plaza Hotel   BUSINESS HOTEL **$$$**
(Map p54; ☑ 244-1111; www.realplazabolivia.com; Av Arce 2177, Prado; s/d incl breakfast US$100/120, ste US$150-170; P❋@☎☎) The renamed Radisson has everything you'd expect in an upmarket business hotel, though it's definitely starting to show its age. Rooms are slightly generic, but include giant resort beds, great views and your typical hodgepodge of high-market amenities. Ask for a south-facing room for the best views.

East of El Prado

★**Loki Hostel**   HOSTEL **$**
(Map p50; ☑ 245-7300; www.lokihostel.com/ la-paz; Av América 120, Plaza Alonso de Mendoza; dm B$62-72, d B$205; @☎) This party hostel has a gilded bar, several sunny hangout areas with games and TVs, and more than 180 beds. The rooftop terrace is dope. One of a chain of 'Lokis' throughout Peru and Argentina.

Wild Rover HOSTEL $

(Map p50; ☑ 211-6903; www.wildroverhostel.com; Comercio 1476, Casco Viejo; dm B$57-92, r with shared bathroom B$230; @ 🛜) Your best bet to meet fellow travelers, the Wild Rover has a high-octane, take-no-prisoners vibe that 20-somethings will love and 30-somethings and older will loathe. The rooms at some other hostels are better, and the dorm rooms are too tightly packed, but you'll be spending most of your day at the boisterous Irish pub anyway.

Arthy's Guesthouse GUESTHOUSE $

(Map p50; ☑ 228-1439; arthyshouse@gmail.com; Ismael Montes 693; dm B$76, r per person with shared bathroom B$100; 🛜) This clean and cozy place hidden behind a bright orange door deservedly receives rave reviews as a 'tranquil oasis,' despite its location on one of La Paz's busiest roads. The friendly, English-speaking owners will do all they can do to help you. Kitchen facilities are available. Note, though, that there is a midnight curfew.

★ Ananay Hostal HOSTEL $$

(Map p50; ☑ 290-6507; hostal.ananay@gmail. com; Jaén 710, Casco Viejo; r per person incl breakfast B$145, with shared bathroom B$110; 🛜) A brightly painted courtyard centers this historic home, a former *peña*, in the heart of Jaén's museum district. The place includes rooftop city views and several comfortable common areas, including a beanbag-chair lounge with TV. The name, which fits, means 'how nice' in Quechua.

Casa Prado BOUTIQUE HOTEL $$

(Boutique Hotel; Map p54; ☑ 231-2094; www. casapradolapaz.com.bo; Av 16 de Julio 1615, Prado; r/ste incl breakfast US$60/70/80; 🛜) Another of the boutique options springing up in downtown, this historic home was once owned by the Prado family. All the bells and whistles of modernity (wi-fi and ironing boards) with the whiff of colonial grandeur. The floorboards creak with history, and you're steps from sights and eats.

Hotel El Consulado HISTORIC HOTEL $$

(Map p54; ☑ 211-7706; info@hotel-elconsulado. com; Bravo 299, cnr Tiwanacu, Prado; s/d/q incl breakfast US$58/68/140; @ 🛜) Seven delightful rooms are housed in the converted Panamanian consulate, a stunning colonial building, above the cafe of the same name. This boutique place oozes European style (it's Danish run), with large, airy and spacious rooms in a quiet location. Those with private bathrooms have clawed baths.

Hostal República HOSTEL $$

(Map p50; ☑ 220-2742; www.hostalrepublica.com; Comercio 1455, Casco Viejo; d/apt B$280/420, dm/s with shared bathroom B$70/147; 🛜) Three blocks from the historic heart of the city, this hostel occupies a lovely building that was home to one of Bolivia's first presidents. Its two large courtyards make for a quiet oasis. All the rooms are fairly basic, but pleasant enough. Two apartments sleep five each.

Altu Qala BOUTIQUE HOTEL $$$

(Map p50; www.altuqala.com; Plaza Tomás Frías 1570, Casco Viejo; r from US$300; 🛜) The design concept at this stunning 10-room boutique hotel, opened in late 2018, is mid-century meets neoclassical, and the minutest of details do not go unnoticed (the floor tiles alone are like a mesmerizing optical illusion!). It's located in the same revamped early-1900s building as Hb Bronze Coffeebar (p72) and boasts a rooftop terrace with 360-degree views over the city.

Stannum Boutique Hotel BOUTIQUE HOTEL $$$

(Map p54; ☑ 214-8393; www.stannumhotels.com; Av Arce 263, 12th fl, Multicine Mall, Sopocachi; r incl breakfast from US$110; P ✳ @ 🛜) This flashy Nora Quintana–designed hotel has you wondering if you just stepped into a Turkish opium den – purple couches, heart-shaped chairs and ambient music dominate the lobby-bar, while the 40 unique rooms have vistas of either the mountains or city. There's also a spa, gym and business center; if you tire of that, the cinema is downstairs.

Hotel Europa BUSINESS HOTEL $$$

(Map p54; ☑ 231-5656; www.hoteleuropa.com.bo; Tiawanacu 64, Prado; s/d/ste US$205/225/285; P @ 🛜 ✳) One of the city's sleekest business hotels. While the Europa's rooms aren't quite as nice as some of La Paz's other business hotels, many have been recently renovated and you do get an excellent spa and pool area (open to the public for a daily-use fee). The rooftop restaurant sports a 360-degree view of La Paz.

🍴 Zona Sur

★ Atix Hotel DESIGN HOTEL $$$

(Map p61; ☑ 277-6500; www.atixhotel.com; Calle 16 No 8052, Calacoto; r from US$150; P ✳ @ 🛜) La Paz finally has a world-class design hotel in this Zona Sur stunner. Nearly everything you see – from the specially-commissioned art on the walls to the wooden headboards–comes from Bolivian artisans. The on-site restaurant, **Ona**, also champions Bolivian goods, while the glassed-in rooftop pool and bar offer sweeping views of distant hills.

Casa Grande   BUSINESS HOTEL $$$
(Map p61; ☑277-4000, 279-5511; www.casa-grande.com.bo; Calle 16 No 8009, Calacoto; hotel s/d/f incl breakfast B$1253/1392/2088, suites B$1148/1288/1566; 🅿️❄️@🛜🏊) Amazing rehab job at the existing Casa Grande Suites on Calle 17, and the sleek, well-appointed and newer Casa Grande Hotel two blocks away is a stunner: it looks like Spielberg dropped a spaceship in the middle of Calacoto. You could fit half the Amazon in the atrium, there's a wet and dry sauna...well, you get the picture.

Camino Real   BUSINESS HOTEL $$$
(Map p61; ☑279-2323; www.caminoreal.com.bo; Ballivián 369, cnr Calle 10, Calacoto; s/d with breakfast B$1632/1776; 🅿️❄️@🛜🏊) The towering Camino Real in the Zona Sur has a soaring atrium, and high-end rooms with flatscreens, modern furnishings, work spaces and great views of the neighboring bluffs. It'd be nice if there were better common areas, but the on-site restaurant, sauna and gym will do.

🍴 Eating

La Paz is a real treat if you're looking to spoil yourself after the culinary minefields of rural Bolivia. A newfound gastronomic renaissance means you can now find creative vegan fare, homemade pastas, fresh sushi and, most importantly, inventive takes on traditional fare from the Amazon to the Andes. You won't eat better anywhere else in Bolivia, guaranteed.

 Rosario & Casco Viejo

Cheap lunch spots and bustling street markets make Rosario the most affordable place to eat, though quality is hit or miss. There are plenty of international eateries on **Sagárnaga**, but the better options lie nearby on **Murillo**. Casco Viejo, a culinary backwater for decades, is slowly finding its groove thanks to young forward-thinking chefs.

Hay Pan   CAFE, WINE BAR $
(Map p50; www.facebook.com/haypanlapaz; Murillo 764, Rosario; mains B$20-30; ⊙7-11am

& 7-11pm Mon-Sat) This cozy little cafe with colorful Andean decor does bountiful breakfasts that include strong coffees and fresh-baked breads. It doubles as a vino bar in the evening with soothing tunes spinning on the record player, a wide-ranging Bolivian wine list and make-your-own charcuterie boards.

Antigua Miami   CAFE $
(Map p50; www.facebook.com/antiguamiami; Murillo 826, Rosario; sandwiches B$25-30; ⊙noon-6pm Mon-Sat; 🛜) A hipster-y little cafe with gorgeous floor tiles, strong coffees and belly-pleasing panini sandwiches.

Etno Café Cultural   CAFE $
(Map p50; http://etnocafecultural.blogspot.com; Jaén 772, Casco Viejo; mains B$20-35; ⊙11am-2am Mon-Sat; 🛜) This edgy scarlet cafe makes a great stop after visiting the museums of Calle Jaén (p53) or for an evening nightcap. Come for decent coffees, salads or distinctly Bolivian drinks like quinoa beer or a shot of coca liquor on the rocks. There's often live music and cultural events in the evenings.

Martinni Pizza   PIZZA $
(Map p50; Illampu 738, Rosario; pizza slice B$12; ⊙1-10pm) If you believe the napkin reviewers (one day they'll put Lonely Planet writers out of a job for good), this small pizza joint is the best slice in La Paz. We wouldn't go that far, but this is a damn good pie, with crispy crust, fresh ingredients and plenty of savory thrust in the sauce.

Anticafé Chukuta   CAFE $
(Map p50; www.facebook.com/anticafe.chukuta; Tarija 328, Rosario; mains B$25-30; ⊙2-9pm Tue-Sat, 9:30am-3pm Sun; 🛜) With its exposed stone walls, pallet furniture, hanging basket lamps and colorful art, this new cafe (opened in late 2016) could not be cuter. You can build your own granola, salads and sandwiches, then stick around for an afternoon coffee. There are plenty of board games and books to keep you stimulated!

Paceña La Salteña   FAST FOOD $
(Map p50; www.pacenalasaltena.com; Loayza 233, Casco Viejo; salteña B$5-10; ⊙8:30am-2:30pm; ☑) Eating a *salteña* (a baked pastry stuffed with out-of-this-world meat and vegetable goodness) is a not-to-be-missed local experience. The peach walls, chintz curtains and gold trimmings give the fare a gilded edge at this award-winning *salteñería*. Vegetarian *salteñas* are available, too. How many triangular napkins will *you* need?

★**Popular Cocina Boliviana** BOLIVIAN $$
(Map p50; www.facebook.com/popularlapazbolivia; Murillo 826, Rosario; 3-course lunch B$50; ⊘12:30-2:30pm Mon-Sat) The concept of waiting in line for a restaurant doesn't exist in La Paz, but that's exactly what you'll need to do to get into Popular. Seasonal three-course menus put a gourmet spin on the city's humble lunch spots. Ingredients come fresh from the market, and the plates are true works of art. Did we mention that it's ridiculously affordable?

Km 0 SANDWICHES $$
(Map p50; www.kilometro-0.com; Comercio 1280, Casco Viejo; sandwiches B$30-50; ⊘9am-9pm Mon-Sat; 🛜) Part co-working space, part innovative cafe with Bolivian-inspired sandwiches. It's located in a building (renovated in 2018) near Plaza Murillo whose muted earth tones and antique furnishings make it very inviting.

★**Ali Pacha** VEGETARIAN $$$
(Map p50; 🖰220-2366; www.alipacha.com; Colón 1306, Casco Viejo; 3/5/7 courses B$100/150/200; ⊘noon-3pm Tue-Sat & 7-10pm Wed-Sat; 🛜🍽) Locals thought it absurd on so many levels to open a high-end vegetarian restaurant with degustation menus in La Paz's downtrodden Casco Viejo neighborhood. And it is absurd. Fantastically so! Even carnivores will swoon over the creative plant-based creations and herbaceous cocktails. You're guaranteed to taste the flavors of Bolivia like never before.

La Casona Restaurant BOLIVIAN $$$
(Map p50; www.lacasonahotelboutique.com; Av Mariscal Santa Cruz 938, Prado; mains B$75-95, almuerzo B$45; ⊘9am-9pm; 🛜) The upscale executive *almuerzo* (set lunch) here comes with an extensive salad bar, soup and your choice of mains like chicken in wine sauce or delicately crafted *milanesas* (breaded meat fillets). The atmosphere is quite nice (it's located in an old carriage house), making this one of the best lunch spots in town. They go à la carte at night.

🍴 El Prado

Café Ciudad INTERNATIONAL $
(Map p54; Plaza del Estudiante, Prado; B$20-50; ⊘24hr; 🛜) This La Paz institution serves up warm coffee, surly service, yummy pizzas, hamburgers and other international favorites – plus one of the best *pique a lo machos*, a Bolivian dish with sausages and

EASY EATS

When in doubt, you can can always head to **Alexander Coffee**, with locations in **Prado** (Map p54; Av 16 de Julio 1832; mains B$16-40; ⊘8am-11pm; 🛜), **Casco Viejo** (Map p50; Potosí 1091; mains B$16-40; ⊘8am-11pm; 🛜) and **Sopocachi** (Map p54; Av 20 de Octubre 2463; mains B$16-40; ⊘9am-1am Mon-Sat; 🛜). Popular with La Paz's yuppie set, this chain cafe serves java drinks, good fruit juices and tasty snacks. While they are a bit saccharine, they're good spots if your stomach is easily upset.

french fries in sauce, in town. It's open 24 hours a day, seven days a week.

Confitería Club de La Paz CAFE $$
(Map p50; cnr Avs Camacho & Mariscal Santa Cruz, Prado; mains B$20-50; ⊘8am-midnight Mon-Fri, to 4pm Sat) For a quick coffee or sandwich, join the well-dressed elderly patrons in their daily rituals. The cafe was formerly renowned as a literary cafe and haunt of politicians (and, formerly, of Nazi war criminals); today, it's better known for its strong espresso and cakes.

🍴 San Pedro

★**Namas Té** VEGETARIAN $
(www.namastebolivia.com; Zoilo Flores 1334, San Pedro; mains B$12-30; ⊘8:30am-7pm Mon-Fri, to 4pm Sat; 🍽) Tea lovers take note: the tea menu at this lovable lime-green veggie restaurant is a staggering four pages long! There's also plenty of quinoa in many forms and even a raved-about tofu pad thai. Smoothies, juices and sandwiches round out the well-priced menu.

Helados Splendid ICE CREAM $
(Map p54; cnr Nicolás Acosta & Av 20 de Octubre, San Pedro; ice cream B$13-17; ⊘10:30am-6pm Tue-Sun) Helados Splendid has been scooping up splendid ice cream for nearly 60 years.

🍴 Sopocachi

A great spread of Bolivian and international restaurants at more affordable prices than further south in Zona Sur. To find out the latest and greatest in the local culinary world, look out for the free magazines *La Paz In* and *Azafrán*, which are widely distributed in restaurants near Plaza Eduardo Avaroa.

La Espinita
SEAFOOD $

(Map p54; Quintín Barrios 712, Sopocachi; mains B$20-30; ⊗noon-2:30pm Tue-Sun) Get down to 'the bones' with a hearty Andean lunch of four favorite fried fish in a delicious home-made batter, all served with crisy *ispi* (little sardine-sized dudes) on top, and sides of potato and *mote* (big corn). Wash it down with fresh juices, and it's no wonder locals are flocking to this pint-sized eatery. Don't mind the eyes!

Kuchen Stube
BAKERY $

(Map p54; www.facebook.com/kuchenstube; Gutiérrez 461, Sopocachi; mains B$25-30; ⊗7:30am-10pm; 🕾) A favorite for sweet snacks with decadent German pastries, reasonable coffee, fresh juices and quiche lorraine.

Salteñería Mi Favorita
FAST FOOD $

(Map p54; 6 de Agosto & Guachalla, Sopocachi; salteña B$5-10; ⊗8am-6pm) Locals dig this pint-sized *salteña* joint with five options and five tables.

Mujeres Creando
CAFE $

(Virgen de los Deseos; Map p54; ☑241-3764; www.mujerescreando.org; Av 20 de Octubre 2060, Sopocachi; mains B$12-40; ⊗9am-10pm Mon-Fri) A very basic cafe behind a good cause – it supports a range of women's rights activities around the country, offering a common area to talk, as well as a library and a small crafts store. Also houses a small **hostal**. You can't miss the kissing llamas mural or the hot-pink house.

Armonía
VEGETARIAN $

(Map p54; ☑241-8458; Av Ecuador 2286, Sopocachi; buffet B$34; ⊗noon-2:30pm Mon-Sat; 🗷) 🖉 A recommended all-you-can-eat vegetarian lunch is found above **Librería Armonía** in Sopocachi. Organic products are served when possible.

Toga
ASIAN $$

(Map p54; ☑mobile 7650-4643; Av Sánchez Lima 2235, Sopocachi; 4-course meal B$35; ⊗10am-11pm Mon-Sat) There's no fixed menu here so you'll have to put your trust in chef Rubén Gruñeiro as he takes you on a four-course culinary journey mixing Asian flavors with Bolivian produce. With just four tables and an open kitchen, it's an incredibly intimate experience.

La Huerta
HEALTH FOOD $$

(Map p54; www.facebook.com/lahuerta.mercado; Pedro Salazar 559, Sopocachi; ⊗10:30am-8pm

Mon-Sat; 🗷) 🖉 La Paz's best organic store with soaps, fresh-baked bread, organic snacks and quinoa-infused everything (juices, chocolates, cereal bars). An attached **veggie restaurant** offers a daily lunch buffet (with plenty of vegan and gluten-free options, pay by the kilo) as well as an afternoon tea service.

MagicK Cafe Cultural
INTERNATIONAL $$

(Map p54; www.cafemagick.com; Presbítero Medina 2526, Sopocachi; mains B$30-55; ⊗4-11:30pm Tue-Sat; 🕾🗷) This funky pescetarian restaurant serves up fig-and-blue-cheese pizza, quinoa tabbouleh and pasta with smoked trout in a lovingly converted Sopocachi home. Vegan and gluten-free options abound, as do good tunes and chill vibes.

Horno Camba
SOUTH AMERICAN $$

(Map p54; Méndez Arcos 732, Sopocachi; mains B$20-60; ⊗noon-8:30pm Mon-Fri, to 3pm Sun) If you're missing yummy Santa Cruz breakfast and lunch treats like *sonsos* (wonderful Santa Cruz–style pancake with yucca and cheese melted inside) and *cuñapés* (cheesy pastries), here's your recompense. Some nice set lunches, as well, one block above Plaza España.

Ají Seco
BURGERS $$

(Map p54; ☑241-8657; www.facebook.com/restaurante.aji.seco; Av 20 de Octubre 2247, Sopocachi; B$30-35; ⊗noon-11pm Mon-Sat; 🕾) The house specialty in this Sopocachi dive is the hamburger in all its guises: Spanish burgers stuffed with chorizo, Italian burgers filled with salami and Mexican burgers stuffed with – naturally – avocado. Sides of celery and carrots for you health nuts.

Café Blueberries
CAFE $$

(Map p54; Av 20 de Octubre 2475, Sopocachi; mains B$20-55; ⊗8am-11:30pm Mon-Sat, 1-9pm Sun; 🕾) Tea lovers will enjoy the selection of infusions and accompanying snacks, from salads to cakes. The pleasant front terrace overlooks Plaza Avaroa, and the back sun-room overlooks a pretty rose garden. And blueberries are everywhere – in the pancakes, crepes, yogurts and shakes!

Café Beirut
MIDDLE EASTERN $$

(Map p54; ☑277-4496; Belisario Salinas 380, Sopocachi; B$30-60; ⊗8am-9pm; 🕾) A dash of Arabian flavor in the Andes, you can grab a nice combo plate of hummus, baba ghanoush and labne for a nice price (the side bread isn't exactly right, but...), and top it off with a hit off a fruit-flavored shisha pipe or a flaky baklava. So why the tacos, dude?

Pronto
ITALIAN **$$$**

(Map p54; ☑ 244-1369; http://prontodalicatessen.business.site; Jáuregui 2248, Sopocachi; mains B$70-110; ⏰ 6:30-11pm Mon-Sat) We don't know where (or how) they get their fresh ingredients, but this candlelit underground restaurant has figured it out, offering up dish after dish of thoughtfully prepared, well-structured and delicately balanced antipasti, pasta and mains. The *antipasta della casa* is a remarkable mix of stewed tomatoes, walnuts and other wonderful treats. Call ahead for reservations on the weekends.

🍴 Zona Sur

The vast majority of the city's fine dining is found in this neighborhood, where prices match the quality. **Calle Montenegro** has a good collection of bars, restaurants and shops all within walking distance of each other.

Los Qñapés
BOLIVIAN **$**

(Map p61; www.facebook.com/losqnapes; René Moreno 1283, San Miguel; snacks B$6-15; ⏰ 3:30-10pm) 🍴 Snack on Bolivian favorites like *cuñapé* (a cheesy yuca bread), *humintas* (a steamed corn pie) and *masacos* (plantains or yucca mashed with meat or cheese) at this always-busy cafe. All of the ingredients are organic and come from within the country.

Q'atu Panadería
BAKERY **$**

(Map p61; http://qatupanaderia.com; Av Montenegro 953; B$20-40; ⏰ 10am-7pm Mon-Sat) Leave it to the team behind Gustu to deliver fresh Bolivian products in unique ways at this humble venture into fast food. Part sandwich shop, part bakery, you'll find intriguing juices, flaky croissants and even a few locally inspired salads. We just wish the space was a little less generic.

⭐ Gustu
BOLIVIAN **$$$**

(Map p61; ☑ 211-7491; www.gustu.bo; Calle 10 No 300, Calacoto; almuerzo B$95, dinner tasting menu B$430-560, à la carte mains B$95-130; ⏰ noon-3pm & 6:30-11pm; 🅿 🛜) Credited with sparking La Paz's culinary renaissance, and launched by the Danish culinary entrepreneur Claus Meyer (of Noma fame), this groundbreaking restaurant works to both rescue and showcase underutilized Bolivian

ingredients. It's located in a gorgeous building rich with Andean textiles, and offers everything from Andean grains to caiman from the Amazon. Even the wine pairings come from within Bolivia.

Those looking for a true foodie bargain should stop by for the three-course set lunches, which cost just B$95.

El Vagón del Sur
BOLIVIAN **$$$**

(Map p61; ☑ 297-1944; www.facebook.com/elvagondelsur; Av Los Sauces 248, Calacoto; mains B$80-115; ⏰ 11:30am-3pm & 6:30-10pm Tue-Fri, 11:30am-4:30pm Sat & Sun; 🛜🍴) This posh upmarket eatery puts its gourmet touch on Bolivian classics like *saice* (spicy chopped beef with black Andean potatoes). The waiters – with their crisp white shirts – offer tip-top service as you navigate the list of local wines, beers and spirits.

Propiedad Pública
INTERNATIONAL **$$$**

(Map p61; ☑ 277-6312; Enrique Peñaranda L-29, San Miguel; mains B$60-80; ⏰ 7-10pm Wed-Sat, also noon-3pm Fri-Sun) You can sure taste the freshness of the creative homemade pastas at this trendy San Miguel eatery. The wine and cocktail menu is equally inspired. A bit pricy, but you get what you pay for.

Furusato
JAPANESE **$$$**

(Map p61; ☑ 279-6499; http://furusato.com.bo; Inofuentes 437, Calacoto; mains B$50-150; ⏰ noon-3pm & 7-11pm Wed-Mon, 7-11pm Tue) This place is neater than an origami figure – and fittingly so. It's very formal, with exquisite Japanese fare and jaw-splitting views of the nearby cliff, although friendliness isn't always on the menu.

🍴 Self-Catering

If you don't mind the hectic settings and questionable hygiene, your cheapest and most-interesting food options are found in the markets. The *comedor* (dining hall) at Mercado Uruguay (p63) sells set meals (of varying standards), including tripe and *ispi* (similar to sardines) for less than B$10. Other areas to look for cheap and informal meals include the Mercado Camacho (p62), known for its juice stands, fresh breads and puffy *llauchas* (cheese pastries).

Ketal Supermercado
SUPERMARKET **$**

(Map p54; cnr Av Arce & Pinilla, Sopocachi; items B$5-50; ⏰ 7:30am-10pm) If you're heading off for a picnic, load up here on everything from olives to cheese, crackers and beer.

LUSTRABOTAS

Around La Paz *lustrabotas* (shoeshine men and boys) are a familiar sight and hound everyone with footwear, even those sporting sandals. Many *lustrabotas*, especially the older ones, wear ski masks and baseball caps – it's said that they often do so to avoid social stigma, as many are working hard to support families or pay their way through school.

You can support their cause for between B$2 and B$3 or by buying a local newspaper funded by La Paz businesses called *Hormigón Armado* (Reinforced Concrete, in Spanish only), which spotlights the struggles of their lifestyle, while funding educational and career opportunities. Hormigón Armado also offers tours (p60) to popular neighborhoods, showing the markets, traditions and customs of La Paz.

Irupana SUPERMARKET $
(www.irupanabio.com; Yungas 692, Casco Viejo; items B$5-50; ⊗8:30am-8:30pm) 🍴 Locally made organic produce is sold at this health-food chain. There is another branch in **Sopocachi** (Map p54; cnr Guachalla & Av Sánchez Lima, Sopocachi; items B$5-50; ⊗8:30am-8:30pm) 🍴.

Hiper Maxi SUPERMARKET $
(Map p54; Gutiérrez 469, Sopocachi; items B$5-50; ⊗8:30am-10:30pm) A large supermarket with all your essentials.

🍷 Drinking & Nightlife

While dive bars and flashy clubs are ubiquitous in Casco Viejo, there are also many elegant bars in La Paz. Local, gilded youth mingle with expats at clubs along **20 de Octubre** in Sopocachi and in Zona Sur, where US-style bars and discos are spread along **Av Ballivián** and **Calle 21**. The faux-Irish and British bars in Rosario aren't worth your time.

⭐**Hb Bronze Coffeebar** COFFEE
(Map p50; http://hb-bronze.com; Plaza Tomás Frías 1570, Casco Viejo; ⊗8:30am-midnight Mon-Sat, 1-9pm Sun; 🛜) Sleek, earthy and architecturally inspiring – coffee shops don't get much cooler than Hb Bronze! This sorely needed addition to the Casco Viejo neighborhood offers the strongest brews in the city, and it

doubles as a bar by night with 100% Bolivian cocktails, beers and wines. The food (including bountiful shared plates) is equally memorable.

⭐**La Costilla de Adán** COCKTAIL BAR
(🛜mobile 7207-4518; Armaza 2974, Sopocachi; ⊗9pm-4am Wed-Sat) Take a dive down the rabbit hole into the warped mind of owner Roberto Cazola at this supremely surreal speakeasy. Prepare yourself for hundreds of creepy dolls, a dozen hanging bicycles and a night full of wonder next to the roaring fire. There's no sign out front. Simply ring the bell, wait, and let the magic begin.

⭐**Typica** COFFEE
(Map p54; www.facebook.com/typica.cafe; Av 6 de Agosto 2584, Sopocachi; ⊗7am-10:30pm Mon-Sat, 8am-8pm Sun; 🛜) Pick one of four Bolivian roasts and then choose your brew method (Chemex, V60, AeroPress or siphon) at this delightfully bohemian coffeehouse with mismatched antique furnishings and great tunes. Stick around for cakes, empanadas and sandwiches.

Diesel Nacional BAR
(Map p54; 🛜mobile 7015-5405; Av 20 de Octubre 2271, Sopocachi; ⊗7pm-3am Mon-Sat) Quench your metal fetish with a trip to this dark, smoky and oh-so-industrial steampunk bar. The music is as edgy as the clientele, and the cocktails are as strong as the recycled vehicle, plane and train parts that make up the decor.

Andean Culture Distillery DISTILLERY
(Map p50; 🛜mobile 7655-8691; www.facebook.com/andeanculturedistillery; Murillo 826, Rosario; ⊗tours 4pm Mon-Fri) You've no doubt seen it on menus across town, so why not stop by the first craft distillery in Bolivia to learn more about its Killa Andean Moonshine. Tours include a shot and a cocktail.

Hallwright's WINE BAR
(Map p54; www.facebook.com/hallwrights; Av Sánchez Lima 2235, Sopocachi; ⊗5-11pm Mon-Sat) Want to taste some of Bolivia's high-altitude wines? Make a beeline for this cozy wine bar where the bartender will introduce you to the best local vino. There's a very appetizing selection of tapas, and an unmissable two-for-one happy hour from 6pm to 7:30pm.

Open Mind Club GAY
(Map p50; www.facebook.com/omc.openmindclub; Cochabamba 100, Rosario; ⊗9pm-4am Fri

& Sat) La Paz's best gay club is, predictably, lit in a rainbow of colors and lined in shiny mirrors. Don't even think about going before midnight or you'll be shaking your booty to reggaeton all alone.

Café Sol y Luna PUB
(Map p50; www.solyluna-lapaz.com; cnr Murillo & Cochabamba, Rosario; ⊙4pm-midnight; 🛜) This is a low-key, Dutch-run hangout offering cocktails, good coffee and tasty global cusine. It has three cozy levels with a book exchange and an extensive guidebook reference library (many current Lonely Planet titles), talks, salsa nights, live music and other activities. Try the *chala* (white) Bolivian beer.

Reineke Fuchs BEER HALL
(Map p54; www.reinekefuchs.com; Pasaje Jáuregui 2241, Sopocachi; ⊙noon-3pm & 7pm-late Mon-Fri, 7pm-late Sat) This woodsy Sopocachi *brewhaus* features imported German beers, *schnappsladen* and hearty sausage-based fare. They also make their own lager, pilsener, dunkel and amber ales, based on centuries-old Deutschland traditions – heady concoctions, indeed.

☆ Entertainment

Pick up a copy of the free monthly booklet *Jiwaki* (available in bars and cafes) for a day-by-day rundown of what's on. Otherwise, watch hotel noticeboards for bar and live-music posters, or check the newspapers.

Las Flaviadas CLASSICAL MUSIC
(Fundación Flavio Machicado Viscarra; Map p54; 🗋 241-1791; www.flaviadas.org; Av Ecuador 2448, Sopocachi; by donation; ⊙6:30-8:30pm Sat) Flavio Machicado opened his home to music lovers in 1922 and the *paceña* tradition is continued by his son, Eduardo. Enter the genteel Sopocachi home and listen to two hours of classical music, from Bach to Bolivian artists like Piraí Vaca, while a crackling fire warms you. Start your Saturday *suavamente* (smoothly).

Peñas

Typical of La Paz (and most of Bolivia) are folk-music venues known as *peñas*. Most present traditional Andean music, rendered on *zampoñas* (pan flutes), *quenas* (cane flute) and *charangos* (ukulele-style instrument), but also often include guitar shows and song recitals. Most only have shows on Friday and Saturday nights, starting at 9pm or 10pm and running into the wee hours. Admission ranges from B$25 to B$100 and usually includes the first drink; meals cost extra.

★ Jallalla LIVE MUSIC
(Map p50; Indaburo 710, cnr Jaén, Casco Viejo; cover incl cocktail B$30-70; ⊙9pm-1am Tue, Thu, Fri & Sat) Just above the Mamani Mamani Gallery (p53), and with a veritable Sistine Chapel of Mamani Mamani's art on the ceiling, this is the one *peña* you won't want to miss. Not only is there top-tier live music, but also authentic Bolivian tapas (from ex-Gustu chefs!) and creative local libations

---

MARINA NÚÑEZ DEL PRADO

Bolivia's foremost sculptor, Marina Núñez del Prado, was born on October 17, 1910, in La Paz. From 1927 to 1929 she studied at the Escuela Nacional de Bellas Artes (National School of Fine Arts), and from 1930 to 1938 she worked there as a professor of sculpture and artistic anatomy.

Núñez del Prado's early works were in cedar and walnut, and represented the Andes: indigenous faces, groups and dances. From 1943 to 1945 she lived in New York and turned her attentions to Bolivian social themes, including mining and poverty. She later went through a celebration of Bolivian motherhood with pieces depicting indigenous women, pregnant women and mothers protecting their children. Other works dealt largely with Andean themes, some of which took appealing abstract forms. She once wrote, 'I feel the enormous good fortune to have been born under the tutelage of the Andes...my art expresses the spirit of my Andean homeland and the spirit of my Aymará people.'

During her long career she held more than 160 exhibitions, which garnered her numerous awards, and she received international acclaim from the likes of Pablo Neruda, Gabriela Mistral, Alexander Archipenko and Guillermo Niño de Guzmán. In her later years the artist lived in Lima with her husband, Peruvian writer Jorge Falcón. She died there in September 1995 at the age of 84.

like the Luka Quivo (Vodka 1825, fresh orange juice, ginger and *airampo* cactus).

Peña Jamuy LIVE MUSIC
(Map p50; ☑ mobile 7676-7817; www.facebook. com/jamuybolivia; Max Paredes, near Sagárnaga, Rosario; cover B$25-50; ⊙ 9pm-7am Fri & Sat) While tourists head to Peña Huari, locals flock to nearby Peña Jamuy, which is bigger, brighter and a lot more fun. This two-story Andean-themed venue hosts all-night ragers each weekend with live folk music and no shortage of alcohol.

Peña Huari TRADITIONAL MUSIC
(Map p50; ☑ 231-6225; Sagárnaga 339, Rosario; cover B$105; ⊙ show 8pm) The city's best-known *peña* is aimed at tourists and Bolivian business-people. The attached **restaurant** specializes in Bolivian cuisine, including llama steak, Lake Titicaca trout, *charquekan* (jerky) and salads.

Theater

Teatro Municipal Alberto Saavedra Pérez THEATER
(Map p50; cnr Sanjinés & Indaburo, Casco Viejo; tickets B$20-50) The municipal theater has an ambitious program of folkloric shows, folk-music concerts and foreign theatrical presentations. It's a great old restored building with a round auditorium, elaborate balconies and a vast ceiling mural.

Teatro NUNA THEATER
(Map p61; www.teatronuna.com; Calle 21 No 8509, Calacoto) Since opening its doors in 2013, this intimate theater in Zona Sur has fast become one of the most dynamic and lauded in the city. It hosts shows for many of the city's theater, dance and music festivals.

Teatro del Charango LIVE MUSIC
(Map p50; ☑ 240-8177; Jaén 711, Casco Viejo; ticket B$20; ⊙ 7pm Sat) This intimate theater at the Museo de Instrumentos Musicales (p55) hosts live folk-music shows.

Cultural Centers

Nueva Acrópolis CULTURAL CENTER
(Map p54; ☑ 291-1172; www.acropolis.org.bo; Ecuador 2405, Sopocachi; ⊙ 7:30-10:30pm Mon-Fri) This locally run cultural center offers courses, talks and other intellectual exercises, mostly in Spanish.

Goethe Institute CULTURAL CENTER
(Map p54; ☑ 243-1916; www.goethe.de/lapaz; Av Arce 2708, Sopocachi; ☎) The German cultural center has a library, German-language courses and exhibits. It hosts movie nights on Fridays in the Cinemateca Boliviana.

Alianza Francesa CULTURAL CENTER
(Map p54; ☑ 242-5005; http://lapaz.alianza francesa.org.bo; cnr Guachalla & Av 20 de Octubre, Sopocachi; ⊙ 8:30am-12:30pm & 2-7:30pm Mon-Thu, 8:30am-12:30pm Fri & Sat) This French cultural center has lectures, courses, rotating exhibits and frequent events in French and Spanish.

Cinema

La Paz's cultural centers often show foreign-language films. Most movies are in English with Spanish subtitles and cost around B$30. There are several cinemas along El Prado.

Cinemateca Boliviana CINEMA
(Map p54; ☑ 244-4090; www.cinemateca boliviana.net; Oscar Soria 110 & Gutiérrez, Sopocachi; B$20-30; ⊙ 3pm-midnight Mon-Fri, from 10:30am Sat & Sun) Art films (and Bolivian films) gone wild.

Spectator Sports

★ Estadio Hernando Siles STADIUM
(Estadio Olímpico La Paz; Map p54; Miraflores; tickets B$40-120) The popularity of *fútbol* (soccer) in Bolivia is comparable to that in other Latin American countries. Matches are played at Estadio Hernando Siles. Sundays are the big game days, and there are typically matches on Wednesdays and Saturdays, too. Prices vary according to seats and whether it's a local or international game. Get tickets at www.todotix.com, in Spanish.

You can imagine what sort of advantage the local teams have over mere lowlanders; players from elsewhere (except Potosí!) consider the high-altitude La Paz games a suicide attempt! Bring a hat.

Cholitas Wrestling WRESTLING
(☑ mobile 7729-4590; www.cholitaswrestling. com; Calle 4 Villa Dolores s/n, El Alto; B$95; ⊙ 5:30pm Thu, 4:30pm Sun) Some view these wrestling matches between indigenous women (derogatively called *cholitas*) as empowering. Others find it belittling. You can be the judge. The staged bouts take place in El Alto on Thursday and Sunday afternoons. You can go on your own, but for ease of mind, many choose to get there by booking online or through a Sagárnaga tour agency.

🛍 Shopping

La Paz is a shopper's paradise; not only are prices very reasonable, but the quality of what's offered can be astounding. The main tourist shopping area lies along the very steep and literally breathtaking **Calle Sagárnaga** between **Av Mariscal Santa Cruz** and **Tamayo**, and adjoining streets. Head to the **San Miguel neighborhood** in the Zona Sur for stunning designer goods.

★**Walisuma**   ARTS & CRAFTS
(Map p61; www.facebook.com/walisuma.org; Aliaga 1231, San Miguel; ⊙10am-8pm Mon-Fri, to 7pm Sat) 🖉 For a one-of-a-kind souvenir head to Walisuma, which works with 59 different Bolivian artisans. Star items include gorgeous (and ultrasoft) alpaca and vicuña textiles made with natural dyes. There are also quinoa soaps, flavored Uyuni salts and designer sweaters. Prices match the quality.

The Writer's Coffee   BOOKS
(Map p50; www.thewriterscoffee.com; Comercio 1270, Casco Viejo; ⊙8:30am-7:30pm Mon-Fri, 9am-12:30pm Sat; 🕾) A gorgeous old-school bookstore with floor-to-ceiling shelves and great titles on local art and history. There's a chilled-out **coffee shop** in the front corner where you can dig in to your purchases or catch up on wi-fi.

**Mistura Manifestación
Creativa**   ARTS & CRAFTS
(Map p50; www.misturabolivia.com; Sagárnaga 163, Rosario; ⊙9:30am-8pm Mon-Sat) Stop by this lovely little concept store for silver jewelry, bowler hats, alpaca sweaters or local wine and gin.

El Ceibo   FOOD & DRINKS
(Map p54; www.elceibo.com; cnr Cañada Strongest & Castrillo, San Pedro; ⊙9am-1pm & 2-6:30pm Mon-Fri, 9am-12:30pm Sat) 🖉 Chocoholics mustn't miss El Ceibo, an ecologically friendly producer of fantastic local chocolates.

Artesanía Sorata   ARTS & CRAFTS
(Map p50; www.artesaniasorata.com; Sagárnaga 303, Rosario; ⊙10am-7pm) A community-focused project that specializes in export-quality handmade dolls, original alpaca products and other beautiful items.

Comart Tukuypaj   ARTS & CRAFTS
(Map p50; www.comart-tukuypaj.com; Linares 958, Rosario; ⊙10am-7pm Mon-Fri, to 5pm Sat) Offers export-quality, fair-trade llama, alpaca and

artesanías (handcrafts) from around the country.

Cava de Bodegas   WINE
(Map p54; cnr Cañada Strongest & Otero de la Vega, San Pedro;   ⊙10am-7:30pm Mon-Sat) Award-winning, high-altitude Bolivian vintages are available at this small wine-and-liquor store.

Campos de Solana/Casa Real   WINE
(Map p54; cnr Otero de la Vega & 20 de Octubre, San Pedro; ⊙10am-7:30pm Mon-Sat) Shop at the store of this Tarija winery, best known for its malbec and riesling.

Los Amigos del Libro   BOOKS
(Map p50; Ballivián 1273; ⊙9am-12:30pm & 3-7:30pm Mon-Fri, 9:30am-12:30pm Sat) La Paz's widest selection of foreign-language novels and magazines.

Outdoor Gear

For all kinds of backpack protection – plastic sacks, chains, padlocks etc – check the street stalls along **Calle Isaac Tamayo**. For proper gear, head one block over to the outdoor stores along **Illampu**.

**Sampaya Outdoor
Equipment**   SPORTS & OUTDOORS
(Map p50; www.facebook.com/sampayaoutdoor; Illampu 803, Rosario; ⊙10am-8pm) The best of Illampu's many outdoor stores with backpacks, tents, hiking shoes, coats, pants and other trekking gear.

Musical Instruments

Many La Paz artisans specialize in traditional woodwind instruments such as the *quena* (two-handed cane flute), *zampoña* (pan flute), *tarka* (wooden flute) and *pinquillo* (one-handed cane flute). Several shops sell instruments along **Sagárnaga**, **Linares** and **Illampu**. Be aware, though, that there's a lot of low-quality or merely decorative tourist rubbish around.

ℹ Orientation

The La Paz metropolitan area is divided into three very distinct zones. North of the city center is the separate municipality of **El Alto** (where you arrive if coming by plane). This fast-growing commercial and industrial city is the center for Aymará culture, has fascinating markets and few tourist attractions.

Down from here in the valley is the city of **La Paz**, where most travelers spend their time. On the west side of the valley are the notable commercial districts Rosario, Belen, San Pedro and

DON'T MISS

EL ALTO & THE 'NEW ANDEAN' MANSIONS

A famous billboard in El Alto once announced: 'El Alto is not part of Bolivia's problem. It's part of Bolivia's solution.' Not all would agree, but visiting here is certainly an experience. Having once been a humble melting pot for *campesinos* (subsistence farmers) and people from all around the country, it now boasts a population of 912,900, and a 5% to 6% growth rate per year. A city in its own right, it's considered the Aymará capital of the world.

The recent economic boom in Bolivia has resulted in property values in El Alto often surpassing those in the city below, and building projects are sprouting like new rows of corn. Of particular note are the psychedelic *cholets* of Aymará architect Freddy Mamani, which can cost up to US$600,000.

Mamani has spent the last decade singularly transforming the architectural landscape of El Alto the way Antoni Gaudí once did with Barcelona. The angularly erratic buildings of his 'New Andean' style dazzle like diamonds in the rough, giving this once monochromatic satellite city a sorely needed identity, all while helping the world's highest major metropolis emerge from its Andean shadow. Thanks to the new cable cars (per ride B$3), tourists, too, are finally taking notice of El Alto as they trickle in and discover its chaotic charms.

Taxis to El Alto charge around B$70 from the center of La Paz. *Micros* (small buses) marked 'Ceja' or 'El Alto' will get you here for B$3. For a peek inside one of the *cholets*, book a tour with HanaqPacha Travel (p60) or La Paz on Foot (p58).

Sopocachi. To the east, the action centers on the Casco Viejo and Miraflores neighborhoods. If you get lost in La Paz, head downhill. You'll soon enough find yourself somewhere along the main thoroughfare, El Prado.

Further down the valley to the south is the **Zona Sur**. This is where the city's wealthy live, and there's a good collection of upscale restaurants and hotels.

ℹ Information

DANGERS & ANNOYANCES

La Paz is a big city, and if you're a gringo, you stand out a bit. Especially at night, exercise caution and keep your wits about you. In all likelihood your stay in La Paz will be safe and problem free, but a little common sense goes a long way.

Police Stations

Tourist police (Policía Turística; Map p54; ☑ 800-140-071, 800-140-081; Puerta 22, Plaza del Estadio, Miraflores; ⊙24hr) Next to Disco Love City, and English-speaking. Report thefts to obtain a *denuncia* (affidavit) for insurance purposes – they won't recover any stolen goods. They also have a kiosk in front of the bus terminal (p79). Insist on getting the paperwork!

Scams & Tricks

Fake police officers have been a problem in the past, though there are very few reports of this anymore. Just in case: note that authentic police officers will always be uniformed (undercover police are under strict orders not to hassle foreigners) and will never insist that you show them your passport, get in a taxi with them or allow

them to search you in public. If confronted by an impostor, refuse to show them your valuables, or insist on going to the nearest police station on foot.

The best way to prevent taxi trouble is to take a radio cab; these have a radio in the car and a promo bubble on the roof (do not take the informal cabs, which merely have a 'taxi' sticker). At night, ask the restaurant or hotel to call a cab – the cab's details are recorded at a central base. Don't share cabs with strangers and beware of accepting lifts from drivers who approach you (especially around dodgy bus areas). Uber is now available in La Paz and is a great alternative for those with signal.

Petty theft and pickpocketing are less common in La Paz than many South American cities but you should still keep a close eye on your stuff in restaurants, bus terminals, markets and internet cafes. One scam involves someone spilling a substance on you or spitting a phlegm ball at you. While you or they are wiping it off, another lifts your wallet or slashes your pack; the perpetrator may be an 'innocent' granny or young girl. Similarly, make sure that you don't bend over to pick up a valuable item that has been 'dropped.' You risk being accused of theft, or of being pickpocketed.

Risky Areas

You should avoid El Alto, San Pedro, the cemetery and higher-elevation neighborhoods altogether at night. Use special caution in the bus terminals.

Other Concerns

La Paz is a great city to explore on foot, but take the local advice to *camina lento, toma poco...y duerme solo* (walk slowly, drink little...and sleep by your lonesome) to avoid feeling the effects of *soroche* (altitude sickness). *Soroche* pills are said to be ineffective, and can even increase altitude sickness. Acetaminophen (also known as Tylenol or paracetamol) does work, and drinking lots of water helps, too.

Take care crossing roads and avoid walking in busy streets at peak hours when fumes can be overwhelming.

Protests are not uncommon in La Paz, and they do sometimes turn violent. These center around Plazas San Francisco and Murillo.

INTERNET ACCESS

La Paz has nearly as many cybercafes as shoeshine boys. Charges range from B$2 to B$5 an hour, and connections are generally fastest in the morning or late evening. Most cafes and hotels have wi-fi access.

LAUNDRY

Lavanderías (laundries) are the cheapest and most-efficient way of ensuring clean (and dry) clothes in La Paz. Higher-end hotels charge per piece (10 times the price), while budget digs may charge a fair per-kilo rate.

Illampu, at the top of Sagárnaga, is lined with laundries. For quick, reliable same-day, machine-wash-and-dry services, expect to pay B$10 to B$15 per kilo.

Lavandería Maya (Map p50; Sagárnaga 339, Hostal Maya, Rosario; per kilo B$10; ⊙9am-7pm Mon-Sat)

Laverap (Map p50; Aroma 730, Rosario; per kilo B$10; ⊙9am-1:30pm & 3:30-7:30pm Mon-Sat)

Limpieza y Lavandería la Familia (Map p50; ☑290-0557; Tarija 352; per kilo B$10; ⊙9am-6:30pm Mon-Fri, to 2pm Sat)

MAPS

Free city maps are available at the tourist offices, hostels and traveler-oriented restaurants.

La Paz is the best place to stock up on maps for the rest of your trip.

Climbing South America (p60) One of the largest collections of trekking maps for sale in Bolivia, with a focus on routes in the Cordilleras and Yungas.

Instituto Geográfico Militar (IGM; Map p50; Av Diagonal Juan XXIII No 100, Edificio Murillo, San Pedro; ⊙8:30am-12:30pm & 2:30-6:30pm Mon-Thu, 8:30am-12:30pm Fri) Offers original 1:50,000 topographic maps (B$40) or photocopies (B$35) if a sheet is unavailable.

MEDIA

La Razón (www.la-razon.com), *El Diario* (www.eldiario.net) and *La Prensa* (www.laprensa.com.bo) are La Paz's major daily newspapers. National media chains **ATB** (www.atb.com.bo) and **Radio Fides** (www.radiofides.com) host the most up-to-date online news sites. Each of these sites is in Spanish only.

MEDICAL SERVICES

For serious medical emergency conditions, contact your embassy for doctor recommendations.

Doctors

Dr Ebert Orellana Jordán (☑242-2342, mobile 6516-9407; Clínica Médica Lausanne, cnr Av Los Sargentos & Costanera) English-speaking doctor often recommended by embassies.

Dr Fernando Patiño (Map p61; ☑279-8525, mobile 7722-5625; curare27@gmail.com; Los Manzanos 400 cnr Calle 10, Calacoto) English-speaking doctor. Call the mobile number on weekends for emergencies.

Medical Centers

Clínica Alemana (Map p54; ☑243-3676; www.clinicalemana.com.bo; Av 6 de Agosto 2821; ⊙24hr) Offers German efficiency.

Clínica Médica Lausanne (☑278-5775; assistmedbolivia@hotmail.com; cnr Av Los Sargentos & Costanera; ⊙24hr) Across from Club Hípico. Some travelers have complained of overcharging.

High Altitude Pulmonary & Pathology Institute (Map p54; ☑224-5394, mobile 7325-8026; www.altitudeclinic.com; Av Copacabana Prolongación 55, Miraflores) Offers medical checkups and can help with high-altitude problems. English spoken.

Hope Centro Médico Internacional (CMI; Map p61; ☑277-2118; www.cmihope.com; Las Retamas 8482; ⊙8am-6pm Mon-Fri) English-speaking doctors and top-notch treatment.

Techno Vision (Map p50; ☑240-9637; Comercio 844, Casco Viejo; ⊙10:30am-9:30pm Mon-Fri) Glasses and eye care.

SIMPLE RULES TO KEEP YOU SAFE

➡ Travel in groups.

➡ Take cabs to go longer distances after 9pm. Make sure it's a radio taxi with a bubble on top.

➡ Don't walk down dark alleys.

➡ Carry small amounts of cash, and leave the fancy jewelry and electronics at home or in the hotel safe.

➡ If physically threatened, it is always best to hand over valuables immediately.

➡ Remember that you likely don't know anybody in Bolivia. It's sad to say, but you should be wary of strangers here.

DON'T MISS

MI TELEFÉRICO

Designed by Austrian company Doppelmayr, the **teleférico** (Aerial Cable Car System; www.miteleferico.bo; ticket B$3, plus B$2 per line transfer; ⏰6am-11pm Mon-Sat, 7am-9pm Sun) has been an apple in the eye of Bolivian politicians for decades. Opposition to the project faded under Morales' presidency, and the initial red, green and yellow lines – the colors of the national flag – debuted in May 2014. Seven lines were operating in mid-2018, with four more set to open by the end of 2019.

At 30km-long and growing, Mi Teleférico is easily the world's longest aerial cable-car system. Riders can hop between lines for an additional B$2 per segment (pay in advance), creating endless combinations of ways to travel across the city. One popular trip takes you from the Zona Sur to El Alto via the yellow and green lines.

The thrill of riding above La Paz' swirling traffic and deep canyons is undeniably cool. You'll feel the car gently shudder as it passes through each concrete stanchion, and probably giggle a bit as the enthusiastic teens in their bright vests help you onto the car, ensuring a balanced load. There's more than enough time to cruise down from the center to the Zona Sur for lunch or dinner, and back. Not for the faint of heart – but then again, what in Bolivia is?

Pharmacies

Farmacias Bolivia (Map p54; Av 16 de Julio 1473; ⏰24hr) A good pharmacy on El Prado.

MONEY
ATMs

Cash withdrawals of bolivianos and US dollars are possible at numerous **ATMs** (Map p54; Av Sánchez Lima; ⏰24hr) at major intersections around the city.

Banco Mercantil (Map p50; cnr Mercado & Ayacucho; ⏰24hr)

Banco Nacional de Bolivia (Map p50; cnr Colón & Camacho; ⏰24hr)

Money Changers

Casas de cambio (exchange bureaux) in the city center can be quicker and more convenient than banks. Most places open from 9am to 6pm weekdays, and on Saturday mornings.

Be wary of counterfeit US dollars and bolivianos, especially with *cambistas* (street money changers) who loiter around the intersections of Colón, Camacho and Av Mariscal Santa Cruz. Traveler's checks can be virtually impossible to change, except at money changers and banks.

Casa de Cambio América (Map p50; Camacho 1233, Casco Viejo; ⏰9am-6pm Mon-Fri, 9:30am-noon Sat)

Casa de Cambio Metropoli (Map p50; cnr Colón & Camacho, Casco Viejo; ⏰8:45am-6:30pm Mon-Fri, 9am-1pm Sat)

Money Transfers

Try Western Union/DHL, which has outlets scattered all around town, for urgent international money transfers.

POST

Central Post Office (Ecobol; Map p50; cnr Av Mariscal Santa Cruz & Oruro, Prado; ⏰8:30am-6:30pm) *Lista de correos* (poste restante) mail is held for three months for free here – bring your passport. A downstairs customs desk facilitates international parcel posting. Note that most official post offices beyond La Paz have closed in recent years, with local transport syndicates now running the show. If you need to send something internationally, do it here.

TELEPHONE

You can buy cell-phone SIM cards (known as *chips*) for about B$10 from any carrier outlet. If you plan on heading to more remote areas of Bolivia, **Entel** (Map p50; Ayacucho 267, Casco Viejo; ⏰8am-7:30pm Mon-Fri, 9am-1pm Sat & Sun) is your best bet.

Convenient *puntos* (privately run phone offices) of various carriers – Entel, Tigo, Viva etc – are also scattered throughout the city, and some mobile services now have wandering salesmen who will allow you to make a call from their cell phone. Street kiosks, which are on nearly every corner, also sell phone cards, and offer brief local calls for about B$1 per minute. International calls can be made at low prices from the **international call center** (Map p50; cnr Sagárnaga & Murillo; ⏰8:30am-8pm Mon-Sat).

TOURIST INFORMATION

Information Kiosks (Map p50; Main Bus Terminal, cnr Avs Perú & Uruguay) These kiosks at the main bus terminal have maps and standard bus prices, for reference. The attendants, if they happen to be around, may help you find a hotel.

Ministerio de Culturas y Turismo (Map p50; ☎2-220-0910; www.minculturas.gob.bo; Palacio Chico, cnr Ayacucho & Potosí, La Paz; ⏰8:30am-6:30pm Mon-Fri) Provides a register of official operators in the tourist industry.

Servicio Nacional de Áreas Protegidas
(Sernap; ☑ 242-6272; www.sernap.gob.bo; Francisco Bedregal 2904, 3rd fl, Sopocachi) Provides limited information on Bolivia's 22 protected national areas. There are offices close to all the major parks, but attention is sometimes erratic. That said the website is informative if you read Spanish.

Tourist Information (Map p54; cnr Av Mariscal Santa Cruz & Colombia, Prado; ☉ 8:30am-7pm Mon-Fri) Stop by to grab some maps and get detailed information. English is spoken by some staff.

Tourist Information (Map p54; www.face book.com/GamIpturismo; Plaza del Estudiante, Prado; ☉ 8:30am-7pm Mon-Fri) Maps, flyers and some English-speaking staff.

ⓘ Getting There & Away

AIR

El Alto International Airport (p352) is 10km via toll road from the city center on the altiplano. At 4062m, it's the world's highest international airport.

Airport services include oxygen tanks in the international arrivals area, a newsstand, ATMs, internet, souvenir stores, a small 'sleepbox' hotel with bunkbeds paid by the hour, coffee shops, fast food, a bistro and a duty-free shop in the international terminal. The currency-exchange desk outside the international arrivals area gives poor rates on traveler's checks – if possible, wait until you're in town.

Times and schedules for flights change often. Check your airline's website or call.

Airlines

Amazonas (Map p54; ☑ 222-0848; www. amazonas.com; Av Saavedra 1649, Miraflores; ☉ 8:30am-7pm Mon-Fri, 9am-5pm Sat & Sun) Daily flights to Rurrenabaque, Santa Cruz and Uyuni, as well as Iquique in northern Chile.

Avianca (Map p61; ☑ 215-8204; www.avia nca.com; Capriles 1246, Manzano F, San Miguel; ☉ 9am-6:30pm Mon-Fri, to noon Sat) Major South American airline with flights to Colombia and Peru.

Boliviana de Aviación (BOA; Map p61; ☑ 901-10-5010; www.boa.bo; René Moreno 1367; ☉ 9am-12:30pm & 2:30-6:30pm Mon-Fri, 9am-noon Sat) Flights to Cobija, Cochabamba, Potosí, Sucre, Santa Cruz, Trinidad, Tarija and Uyuni.

EcoJet (Map p61; ☑ 901-105-055; www.eco jet.bo; Av Ballivián 322, Calacoto; ☉ 9am-12:30pm & 2:30-6:30pm Mon-Fri, 9am-noon Sat) Domestic airline with direct flights to Cobija, Cochabamba, Trinidad and Sucre.

LATAM (Map p61; ☑ 277-5677; www.latam. com; Av Montenegro E6, San Miguel; ☉ 9am-

6:30pm Mon-Fri, to noon Sat) International airline with regular flights to Lima and Santiago.

Transporte Aéreo Militar (TAM; Map p50; ☑ 268-1111; www.tam.bo; Montes 734, Rosario; ☉ 8am-6:15pm Mon-Fri, 9am-1pm Sat) Flights to Cobija, Cochabamba, Guayamerín, Riberalta, Rurrenabaque, Santa Cruz, Sucre, Tarija, Trinidad and Yacuiba. Schedules are more erratic than other airlines and planes are older.

Departure Tax

The domestic departure tax is B$15, while the international departure tax is US$20 (payable in cash only in the airport lobby, though most international airlines include it in the ticket price).

BUS

La Paz has three bus terminals/bus areas. You can use the main bus terminal for most national and international destinations. If you are going to the Yungas or Amazon, you'll need to go to Villa Fátima. For Sorata, Titicaca and Tiwanaku, head to the cemetery bus terminal.

Most national destinations are serviced hourly for major cities and daily for less visited spots. International departures generally leave several times a week – check ahead as schedules change. You can get to all the bus areas by *micros* (small buses), but radio taxis are more convenient with luggage.

Main Bus Terminal (Terminal de Buses; Map p50; cnr Avs Perú & Uruguay, Challapampa) This services all domestic destinations south and east of Paz, as well as international destinations. It is a 15-minute uphill walk north of the city center. Fares are relatively uniform among companies. The station was designed by Gustave Eiffel, and has showers, luggage storage and other facilities.

Villa Fátima Bus Terminal (Av Castillo s/n, Villa Fátima) Services Coroico, Chulumani, Guanay and other Yungas and Amazon destinations. In general, the *micros* are more expensive with faster and more-direct service, while the

---

ⓘ USEFUL WEBSITES

Boliviaweb (www.boliviaweb.com) Practical info for pre-trip planning.

Bolivia Online (www.bolivia-online.net) Virtual travel guide and information portal.

Bolivian Express (www.bolivianexpress. org) Arts and cultural events.

La Razón (www.la-razon.com/salimos-hoy.html, in Spanish) Events calendar in Spanish.

Lonely Planet (www.lonelyplanet.com/ bolivia/la-paz) Destination information, hotel bookings, traveler forum and more.

flotas (buses) offer cheaper, longer and more comfortable trips. The terminal is about 2km uphill from Plaza Gualberto Villarroel.

Cemetery Bus Terminal (Av Baptista) Offers cheap buses to Copacabana, Tiwanaku, Titicaca and Sorata, most of which leave when full. This area is especially hairy at night, and you should watch your bags while boarding.

Tourist Services

Tourist services – either from the main bus terminal or by hotel pickup – are offered to Copacabana, Puno, Tiwanaku, Uyuni and Valle de la Luna, among other destinations. These cut down on risk and up your comfort.

Vicuña Travel (Map p50; ☎ 228-0140; http://vicuna-travel.com; Main Bus Terminal, cnr Avs Perú & Uruguay, Challapampa) Daily bus tours to Tiwanaku include pickup from your hotel at 8am and a return to the terminal by 4:30pm (B$70).

Diana Tours (Map p50; www.diana-tours.com; Sagárnaga 326, Rosario; trips from B$80) Round-trip guided trips to Tiwanaku or Chacaltaya and Valle de la Luna, leaving at 8:30am. Also offers transport to Copacabana, Uyuni, Puno and (occasionally) Rurrenabaque.

Bolivia Hop (Map p50; www.boliviahop.com; Linares 940, Rosario; ⌚ office 8:30am-7pm) Seamless hop-on–hop-off tourist buses traveling between La Paz and Copacabana, and stops in Peru such as Puno and Cuzco (or alternatively Arequipa), with optional activities along the way.

Buses from Main Terminal

DESTINATION	COST (B$)	TIME (HR)
Arequipa (Peru)	140	14
Arica (Chile)	80-180	10
Buenos Aires (Argentina)	800-1200	48-50
Camargo	70-100	16
Cochabamba	40-50	8
Copacabana	30	3-4
Cuzco (Peru)	160-180	14
Iquique (Chile)	100-180	13-15
Juliaca	120	7
Lima (Peru)	450-550	28
Oruro	30-40	3½
Potosí	50-90	9
Puno (Peru)	70-120	7-8
Santa Cruz	110	17-18
Sucre	180	12
Tarija	80	18
Tupiza	100-175	17-18
Uyuni	110	11-12
Villazón	90-175	18

Buses from Villa Fátima

DESTINATION	COST (B$)	TIME (HR)
Caranavi	25-60	5-7
Chulumani	30	4
Coroico	20-35	3
Guanay	100	6
Rurrenabaque	70-190	12-16
Yolosita	20-35	3

Buses from Cemetery

DESTINATION	COST (B$)	TIME (HR)
Copacabana	20-25	3-4
Desaguadero	15	2
Huarina (for Cordillera Apolobamba)	15	2
Sorata	20	3½
Tiwanaku	15	1½

TRAIN

Empresa Ferroviaria Andina (FCA; ☎ 212-9774.; www.ferroviaria-andina.com.bo/turismo; Av Arica s/n; tickets B$40-80) runs occasional round-trip tourist trains from El Alto to Tiwanaku (1½-hour stop) and on to Guaqui on Lake Titicaca (2½-hour stop). The train departs El Alto on the second Sunday of each month at 8am. Check the website or call ahead. Trains for the Argentine border, via Uyuni and/or Tupiza, all leave from Oruro.

ⓘ Getting Around

TO/FROM THE AIRPORT

There are two access routes to El Alto International Airport (p352): the *autopista* toll road (B$3), and the sinuous free route, which leads into Plaza Ballivián in El Alto.

Minibus 212 runs frequently between Plaza Isabel la Católica and the airport between around 7am and 8pm (B$3.80). Look for the sign that says 'Minibus Cotranstur' just outside arrivals. Heading into town from the airport, this service will drop you anywhere along El Prado.

Radio taxis (up to four passengers, around B$70) will pick you up at your door; confirm the price with the dispatcher, or ask the driver to verify it. For a fifth person, there is an additional B$10 charge.

CAR & MOTORCYCLE

Driving the steep, winding, frenetic one-way streets of La Paz may be intimidating for the uninitiated, but for longer day trips into the immediate hinterlands, you could consider renting a car (per day US$50 to US$100), but hiring a driver is probably easier and just as economical.

Avis (☏ 211-1870; www.avis.com.bo; cnr Av Costanera & Calle 5/6, Obrajes; ☺ 9am-12:30pm & 2:30-7pm Mon-Fri, 9am-2pm Sat)

Budget (Map p54; www.budget.bo; Capitán Ravelo 2130, Sopocachi; ☺ 8am-7pm Mon-Fri, to 3pm Sat) Branches at the airport and Camino Real hotel (p68). Watch for unexpected extra expenses, like car washes.

Hertz (Map p61; ☏ mobile 7889-7564; www.hertz.com.bo; cnr Calle 17 & Aliaga, Calacoto; ☺ 8:30am-7pm Mon-Fri, 9am-1pm Sat)

PUBLIC TRANSPORTATION
Micro & Minibus

La Paz's sputtering and smoke-spewing *micros*, the older three-quarter-sized buses, charge about B$2 per trip. Minibuses service most places as well, for a slightly higher cost. In addition to a route number or letter, *micros* plainly display their destination and route on a signboard posted in the front window. Minibuses usually have a young tout screaming the stops. Wave to catch the bus. They stop at signed *paradas* (official stops), or, if the cops aren't watching, whenever you wave them down.

Trufi

Trufis are shared cars or minibuses that ply set routes. Destinations are identified on placards on the roof or windscreen. They charge approximately B$3 around town and B$4 to Zona Sur.

Taxi

Radio taxis (with roof bubbles advertising their telephone numbers) are recommended. Charges are a little higher after 11pm. Normal taxi services (with just a taxi sign, no phone number and no bubble) are best avoided as they've been used in the past for (rare) express kidnappings.

Ask your hotel or restaurant to ring for a taxi. Otherwise, taxis can be waved down anywhere, except near intersections or in areas cordoned off by the police. Always confirm the fare before you leave.

A newer solution to safe taxis is to use the **Easy Taxi app** (www.easytaxi.com/bo, in Spanish). **Uber** (www.uber.com) is also available now in La Paz, and you can review the driver's rating before booking a ride.

AROUND LA PAZ

Valle de la Luna

About 10km down the canyon of the Río Choqueyapu from the city center, **Valle de la Luna** (Valley of the Moon; B$25; ☺ dawn to dusk) is a slightly over-hyped place, though it's a pleasant break from urban La Paz. It could be easily visited in a morning or combined with another outing such as a hike to Muela del Diablo (p81) to fill an entire day. It isn't

a valley at all, but a bizarre, eroded hillside maze of canyons and pinnacles technically known as badlands. Unfortunately, urban growth has caught up to the area, making it less of a viewpoint than it otherwise might be. Note: readers have reported muggings in recent years, even while in the site's confines.

Diana Tours (p80) offers round-trip guided visits to Valle de la Luna and Chacaltaya (B$130), with a pickup from your hotel at 8:30am. If on your own, from Av México in La Paz, which parallels the Prado, catch any form of transportation marked 'Mallasa' or 'Zoológico.' These will drop you off near the entrance. For a taxi from the center of La Paz, you'll pay around B$80 for up to three people, and the driver may wait for an hour or so while you look around.

Nearby, **Colibri Camping & Eco Lodge** (☏ mobile 7629-5658; www.colibricamping.com; Calle 4 s/n, Jupapina; campsite/tipi per person B$50/120, cabin per person B$120-250) 🏕 is an excellent glamping spot offering tipis, ecotents, cottages and fully equipped tent sites. It's perfect for those who want access to the big city and the tranquility of the Bolivian countryside. Ask the British–Bolivian family who runs the place about the volunteer program they set up called Up Close Bolivia.

Muela del Diablo

The prominent rock outcrop known as the Devil's Molar (3825m) is actually an extinct volcanic plug that rises between the Río Choqueyapu and the suburban sprawl of

Around La Paz

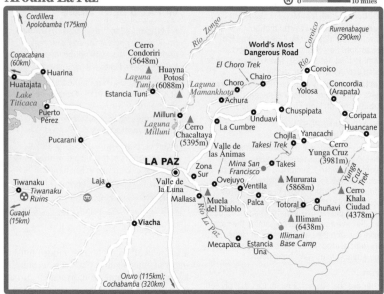

La Paz's Pedregal and Calacoto. A hike to its base makes a pleasant – and easy – half-day walking trip; it offers incredible views of the city and valley, and can be easily combined with a visit to Valle de la Luna (p81).

From the cemetery in **Pedregal**, the trail climbs steeply (several times crossing the new road that provides access to the hamlet near the base of the *muela*). After a breathless hour or so, you'll reach a pleasant grassy swale where the 'tooth' comes into view, as well as some precarious pinnacles further east.

At this point the walking track joins the road and descends through the hamlet. About 300m further along, a side route branches off to the left and climbs toward the *muela*'s base. From the end of this route you can pick your way with extreme caution up to the cleft between the double summit, where there's a large cross. Without technical equipment and expertise, however, it's inadvisable to climb further.

After descending to the main track, you can decide whether to return the way you came, or follow the steep track that circles the *muela* in a counterclockwise direction and descends to the Río Choqueyapu before climbing the other side of the valley to the zoo in Mallasa. The latter option will turn

this hike into a full-day trip, as it takes about six hours between Pedregal and Mallasa.

Inquire locally about safety before heading out and travel in pairs or groups, or with a local guide.

From La Paz the best access to the start of the hike is on minibus 288, marked 'Pedregal,' from the lower Prado. The end of the line is the parking area a couple of hundred meters downhill from Pedregal's cemetery. Returning from Valle de la Luna, you can board these minibuses at Zona Sur's Plaza Humboldt or follow the difficult walking track from near the zoo in Mallasa, which involves a descent to the Río Choqueyapu and then a stiff 600m ascent to the eastern side of the *muela*. To return to La Paz from Pedregal, catch a 'Prado' minibus from the parking area.

Mecapaca

ELEV 2900M (9515FT)

This quaint village is worth visiting for its authenticity and sun-kissed landscapes. Mecapaca is much warmer and greener than the big city of La Paz, and boasts a beautifully restored **church** in its plaza (ask for Erol Castillo for keys; if you buy something from his store and add a donation to the church box, he'll likely oblige). The church is perched on the hillside of the small plaza with wonderful views of the fertile valley beyond. For even better views, head up the snaking path behind the plaza to the hilltop lookout.

🛏 Sleeping & Eating

⭐**DM Hotel Andino** RESORT $$$
(☎ 274-9191; www.dmhoteles.com; Av Manuel Castillo 5; s/d/ste incl breakfast & transport from La Paz US$82/92/106; P 🛜 🏊) La Paz feels a world away at this luxurious country retreat, where your toughest decision will be whether to dip in the regular or hydromassage pool. Adults will appreciate the spa, wine shop and collection of Bolivian art, while kids will enjoy the minigolf and games rooms. The architecture is inspired by the colonial period, but the rooms are decidedly modern.

Trattoria Restaurant ITALIAN $$
(☎ mobile 6513-6708; Av Principal s/n; mains B$30-45; ⊙ 11am-6pm Sat & Sun) Sit under an umbrella in the grass and enjoy a wood-fired pizza or scoop of artisan ice cream (not to mention the mountain views!) at this countryside Italian restaurant. To find it, walk downhill from the plaza toward DM Hotel Andino.

❶ Getting There & Away

Mecapaca lies about 30km south of La Paz and 15km from Mallasa. Take minibus 253 to Macapaca/Valencia from Plaza Belzu in San Pedro (B$5, one hour, departs when full) or from Mallasa. To return to La Paz take the same minibus 253. On weekends, *trufis* (shared car or minibus), minibuses and radio taxis leave constantly from Plaza Humboldt (Zona Sur) for points south.

Valle de las Ánimas

The name Valle de las Ánimas (Valley of Spirits) is used to describe the eerily eroded canyons and fantastic organ-pipe spires to the north and northeast of the barrios of Chasquipampa, Ovejuyo and Apaña (which are rapidly being absorbed into the Zona Sur neighborhoods of La Paz). The scenery resembles that of Valle de la Luna (p81), but on a grander scale. It's worth just getting out here even if you don't hike.

There are two moderately difficult walking routes through the valley, which each take a long day and require some previous backcountry experience: the Río Ovejuyo Route and the Quebrada Negra Route. The **Río Ovejuyo Route** requires a compass

and 1:50,000 topography sheet 5944-II and, for a very short section, topo sheet 5944-I. This option can be challenging, especially because of the altitude. Make sure you carry plenty of water, a hat and snacks.

The **Quebrada Negra Route** heads up Quebrada Negra, over Cerro Pararani and down to Uni village. Although only 7km long, it's a demanding day hike that requires six to seven hours. For this route you'll need a compass and the 1:50,000 topo sheets 5944-I and 6044-III.

It begins at the Quebrada Negra ravine, which crosses the road at the upper (eastern) end of Ovejuyo village. The relatively easy-to-follow 4km route up Quebrada Negra will take you through the most dramatic stretches of the eroded Valle de las Ánimas pinnacles. Near the head of the ravine, you need to traverse southeast around the northern shoulder of Cerro Pararani, until you find the obvious route that descends steeply to Uni. In fine weather, you'll have good views of Illimani along this section. To return to La Paz, follow the road for 2km up over Paso Uni and then for another 1.5km downhill to Apaña, where you'll catch up with regular *micros* and *trufis* returning to the city.

To get to the Valley, take any *micro* with 'V de las Ánimas' in the window. You can catch these from La Paz at the intersection of Calles Lara and Boquerón in San Pedro (one hour, B$4), or Plaza Humboldt in Zona Sur (30 minutes, B$4).

Cañón de Palca

The magnificent Palca Canyon (marked on topo sheets as 'Quebrada Chua Kheri') brings a slice of Grand Canyon country to the dramatic badland peaks and eroded amphitheaters east of La Paz. A walk through this gorge makes an ideal day hike from the city.

For the start of this hike, you need to reach Uni, which is served only by *micros* and *trufis* heading for Ventilla and Palca. These leave at least once daily from near the corner of Calles Boquerón and Lara, two blocks north of Plaza Líbano in the San Pedro district of La Paz. There's no set schedule, but most leave in the morning. You'll have the best luck on Saturday and Sunday, when families make excursions into the countryside. Alternatively, take *micro* 42 or minibus 385, marked 'Ovejuyo/Apaña,' get off at the end of the line, and slog the 1.5km up the road to Paso Uni.

Uni, the small town above the entrance to Cañón de Palca, has a store selling basic supplies, including bottled water and snack foods. You can also find Bolivian *almuerzos* (set lunches) at lunchtime. Meanwhile, Palca is a pleasant, basic town located relatively close to the exit of the canyon. It has a simple *hostal* (hostel), which offers set meals and is popular with Bolivian tourists on weekends. You can also camp around Palca or nearby Ventilla, but beware of the badly polluted surface water, and ask permission before you set your tent up in a field or pasture.

It's best to check on the safety situation before leaving La Paz. Only go to the canyon in groups, as assaults on single hikers have been reported. A good, safe alternative is to head out with La Paz on Foot (p58), which offers excellent guided day hikes through the canyon (US$75 per person, including transportation and lunch). If you arrive in Palca geared up for more hiking, you can also set off from Ventilla along the Takesi Trek (p122).

From Palca back to La Paz, you'll find occasional *camiones* (flatbed trucks), *micros* and minibuses, particularly on Sunday afternoon, but don't count on anything after 3pm or 4pm.

Cerro Chacaltaya

The 5395m-high Cerro Chacaltaya peak atop a former glacier is a popular day trip. The glacier diminished over several decades and, tragically, had melted completely by 2009. Until the 'big melt,' it was the world's highest 'developed' ski area. It's a steep 90-minute ride from central La Paz, and the accessible summit is an easy 200m ascent from there. For visitors and hikers, Chacaltaya offers spectacular views of La Paz, Illimani, Mururata and 6088m Huayna Potosí.

It's a high-altitude, relatively easy (but steep) 100m or so climb from the old ski lodge to the summit of Chacaltaya. Remember to carry warm clothing and water, and take plenty of rests – say, a 30-second stop every 10 steps or so, and longer stops if needed – even if you don't feel tired. If you start to feel light-headed, sit down and rest until the feeling passes. If it doesn't, you may be suffering from mild altitude

sickness; the only remedy is to descend. From Chacaltaya it's possible to walk to Huayna Potosí Refugio (p110), at the base of Huayna Potosí (p110), in half a day. Before you set out, you must obtain instructions and maps from Instituto Geográfico Militar (p77).

You can get your thrills, spills (well, hopefully not) and great views on a 60km-plus mountain-bike trip from Chacaltaya to Zongo and beyond at descents of up to 4100m (vertical drop). La Paz bike outfitters run trips for B$800 to B$1300 per person (depending on group size).

There's no public transportation to Chacaltaya. Most La Paz tour agencies take groups to Chacaltaya for around B$80 per person, and many include it with another attraction for a full-day tour. Bring warm, windproof clothing, sunglasses (100% UV protection) and sunscreen. Those who fly into La Paz from the lowlands will want to wait a few days before visiting Chacaltaya or other high-altitude places.

Tiwanaku

ELEV 3870M (12,696FT)

The ruins of Tiwanaku (sometimes spelled Tiahuanaco or Tihuanaco) make for a good day trip from La Paz for those who want to view a few carved monoliths, archways and arcades, and two decent museums. It's no Machu Picchu or Tikal, but history buffs will love diving into the myths and mysteries of this lost civilization.

Little is actually known about the people who constructed this ceremonial center on the southern shore of Lake Titicaca more than a thousand years ago. However, evidence of their influence, particularly in religion, has been found throughout the vast area that later became the Inca empire.

In the eponymous village nearby, there are a number of hotels, restaurants, a fun little plaza with excellent sculptures inspired by Tiwanaku styles, and a 16th-century church, built, no doubt, with stones from the Tiwanaku site.

History

Although no one is certain whether it was the capital of a nation, Tiwanaku undoubtedly served as a great ceremonial center. At its height the city had a population of 20,000 inhabitants and encompassed approximately 2.6 sq km.

Some say the name roughly translates to 'the dry coast' or 'stone in the center,' and at 3870m (12,696ft) in altitude, the city most likely sat on the edge of Lake Titicaca, serving as the ceremonial center for the regions south of the lake.

While only 30% of the original site has been excavated – and what remains is less than overwhelming – the Tiwanaku culture made great advances in architecture, math and astronomy well before the Inca ascendancy.

Archaeologists divide the development of the Tiwanaku into five distinct periods, numbered Tiwanaku I through V, each of which has its own outstanding attributes.

The Tiwanaku I period falls between the advent of the Tiwanaku civilization and the middle of the 5th century BC. Significant finds from this period include multicolored pottery and human or animal effigies in painted clay. Tiwanaku II, which ended around the beginning of the Christian era, is hallmarked by ceramic vessels with horizontal handles. Tiwanaku III dominated the next 300 years, and was characterized by tricolor pottery of geometric design, often decorated with images of stylized animals.

Tiwanaku IV, also known as the Classic Period, developed between AD 300 and 700. The large stone structures that dominate the site today were constructed during this period. The use of bronze and gold is considered evidence of contact with groups further east in the Cochabamba valley and further west on the Peruvian coast. Tiwanaku IV pottery is largely anthropomorphic. Pieces uncovered by archaeologists include some in the shape of human heads and faces with bulging cheeks, indicating that the coca leaf was already in use at this time.

Tiwanaku V, also called the Expansive Period, is marked by a decline that lasted until Tiwanaku's population completely disappeared around 1200. Were they the victims of war, famine, climate change or alien abductions? Nobody knows, though most archaeologists point to climate change as the most likely cause of the civilization's rapid decline. During this period pottery became less elaborate, construction projects slowed and stopped, and no large-scale monuments were added after a few early examples.

At the request of Unesco, excavations of the site ceased in 2010. Archaeologists are concentrating now on preserving what they've already dug up. About 130,000 visitors come to the site every year.

⊙ Sights

Entrance to the complex is paid at the **ticket office** (Av Puma Punku s/n; B$100; ⊙ tickets 9am-4pm, site 9am-5pm) opposite the museums. If you go on your own, start your visit in the museums to get a basic understanding of the history, then head to the ruins.

Scattered around the Tiwanaku site, you'll find heaps of jumbled basalt and sandstone slabs weighing as much as 25 tons each. Oddly enough, the nearest quarries that could have produced the basalt megaliths are on the Copacabana peninsula, 40km away beyond the lake. Even the sandstone blocks had to be transported from a site more than 5km away. It's no wonder, then, that when the Spanish asked local Aymará how the buildings were constructed, they replied that it was done with the aid of the leader/deity Viracocha.

Museo Lítico Monumental　　　MUSEUM
The star of the show at this Tiwanaku museum is the massive 8m **Monolito Bennett Pachamama**, rescued in 2002 from its former smoggy home at the outdoor Templete Semisubterráneo (p56) in La Paz. You'll also find a basic collection of other monoliths and artifacts dug up on-site here. Labeling is in Spanish.

Much of the collection is currently mothballed, as the roof of the relatively new museum is already collapsing.

Megaphones　　　RUINS
At the entrance to the Tiwanaku site are two stone blocks that can be used as megaphones. Entertain yourself for a minute or two with this interesting pre-Columbian, pre-iPod technology.

Akapana Pyramid　　　RUINS
Climb the hill up to Tiwanaku's most outstanding structure, the partially excavated Akapana pyramid, which was built on an existing geological formation. At its base this roughly square, 16m hill covers a surface area of about 200 sq meters. In the center of its flat summit is an oval-shaped sunken area, which some sources attribute to early, haphazard, Spanish excavation. The presence of a stone drain in the center, however, has led some archaeologists to believe it was used for water storage.

LOST TREASURES

The treasures of Tiwanaku have literally been scattered to the four corners of the earth. Its gold was looted by the Spanish, and early stone and pottery finds were sometimes destroyed by religious zealots who considered them pagan idols. Some of the work found its way to European museums.

Fortunately, a portion of the treasure has been preserved, and some of it remains in Bolivia. A few of the larger anthropomorphic stone statues have been left on the site, and the on-site museums have a decent collection of pottery and other objects. Others are on display at the Museo Nacional de Arqueología Tiwanaku (p55) in La Paz.

Recent findings include craniums, assumed to be war trophies, leading some archaeologists to believe the pyramid may have been a ceremonial temple. Others think it was used for the study of astronomy.

Kalasasaya   RUINS
North of the Akapana Pyramid (p85) is Kalasasaya, a partially reconstructed 130m-by-120m ritual-platform compound with walls constructed of huge blocks of red sandstone and andesite. The blocks are precisely fitted to form a platform base 3m high. Monolithic uprights flank the massive entrance steps up to the restored portico of the enclosure, beyond which is an interior courtyard and the ruins of priests' quarters. Note the size of the top stair – a massive single block.

The **Monolito Ponce** monolith, with his turban (no doubt covering up his deformed cranium), mask, ceremonial vase and walking stick, sits at the center of the first platform. Some say the stick and the vase are symbolic of the dualism of Andean culture (nature versus nurture).

Other stairways lead to secondary platforms, where there are other monoliths including the famous **El Fraile** (priest).

Puerta del Sol   RUINS
(Gateway of the Sun) At the far northwest corner of Kalasasaya is Tiwanaku's best-known structure, the 10-ton Puerta del Sol. This megalithic gateway was carved from a single block of andesite, and archaeologists assume that it was associated with the sun

deity. The surface of this fine-grained, gray volcanic rock is ornamented with low-relief designs on one side and a row of four deep niches on the other.

The gateway was most likely originally located in the center of Kalasasaya Platform and was used as a calendar, with the sun striking specific figures on the solstice and equinox.

There's a smaller, similar gateway carved with zoomorphic designs near the western end of the site that is informally known as the **Puerta de la Luna** (Gateway of the Moon).

Templete Semisubterráneo   RUINS
East of the main entrance to Kalasasaya, a stairway leads down into the Templete Semisubterráneo, an acoustic, red-sandstone pit structure measuring 26m by 28m, with a rectangular sunken courtyard and walls adorned with 175 crudely carved stone faces. In the 1960s archaeologists tried to rebuild these and used cement between the stones.

Putuni   RUINS
(Palacio de los Sarcófagos, Palace of the Sarcophagi) West of Kalasasaya is a 55m-by-60m rectangular area known as Putuni. It is surrounded by double walls and you can see the foundations of several tombs. About 90% of the artifacts collected by amateur enthusiast Fritz Buck in the early 20th century from these tombs are found in La Paz's Museo de Metales Preciosos (p53).

Kantatayita   RUINS
The heap of rubble at the eastern end of the Tiwanaku site is known as Kantatayita. Archaeologists are still trying to deduce some sort of meaningful plan from these well-carved slabs; one elaborately decorated lintel and some larger stone blocks bearing intriguing geometric designs are the only available clues.

Puma Punku   RUINS
(Gateway of the Puma) Across the railway line southwest of the Tiwanaku site, you'll see the excavation site of Puma Punku. In this temple area megaliths weighing more than 130 tons have been discovered. Like Kalasasaya and Akapana (p85), there is evidence that Puma Punku was begun with one type of material and finished with another; part was constructed of enormous sandstone blocks and, during a later phase of construction, notched and jointed basalt blocks were added.

Note also, in the distance of the site's northern boundary, the *sukakollo*, a highly sophisticated system of terraced irrigation.

Museo Cerámico   MUSEUM
Showcases a small collection of the ceramics found at the site, as well as a ceremonially deformed cranium and artifacts from the Chiripa and Wankarani cultures.

☞ Tours

Guided **tours** (🖉 7724-9572; walipini.tiwanacu@gmail.com; Av Ferrocarril s/n; tour for up to 6 people in Spanish/English/French B$150/180/180) are available in English, French and Spanish, and are highly recommended.

The local guides can also arrange onward walking, boating or bus tours from here to Lake Titicaca (just 12km away), which will include camping or stays with local families.

✯ Festivals & Events

Aymará New Year   NEW YEAR
(Willkakuti, Machaq Mara; ⊙ Mar 21, Jun 21, Sep 21) Locals don colorful ceremonial dress and visitors are invited to join the party, drink *singani* (distilled grape liquor), chew coca and dance until dawn at celebrations that take place on fall and spring equinox, when the rays of the rising sun shine through the temple entrance on the eastern side of Kalasasaya. The largest celebration is Aymará New Year on June 21, when as many as 5000 people, including a large contingent of New Agers, arrive from all over the world.

Artisans hold crafts fairs to coincide with the annual celebrations.

Special buses leave La Paz around 4am to arrive in time for sunrise. Dress warmly because the pre-dawn hours are bitterly cold.

🛏 Sleeping & Eating

Hotel Tiahuanacu   HOTEL **$$**
(🖉 289-8548; Bolívar 903; s/d incl breakfast B$100/200) Three blocks east of the Plaza, this is the nicest place to stay, with rooms that are clean, breezy and comfortable. There's a restaurant open daily. We only wish there were better views of the ruins.

Hotel Akapana   HOTEL **$$**
(🖉 289-5104; www.hotelakapana.com; Av Manco Kapac s/n; s/d incl breakfast B$190/330) Just 100m west of the site, this friendly hotel has three levels, simple rooms with good views, hot water 24 hours a day, and a top-floor *mirador* (lookout) with amazing views of the neighboring site.

Restaurante Cabaña del Puma   BOLIVIAN **$**
(Av Puma Punku s/n; almuerzo B$25; ⊙ 9am-6pm) Next to the ruin entrance, this clean eatery offers basic country food, like trout and chicken. A vegetarian meal comes with veggies, potatoes and country cheese. Chef Gloria Aliaga can also offer some more traditional local dishes if you ask.

Inti Wara   BOLIVIAN **$$**
(🖉 289-8543; Av Bolívar s/n; mains B$35; ⊙ 10am-6pm) The only eating option on the north-eastern side of the ruins, with trout, quinoa soup and other local specialties.

ⓘ Getting There & Away

Many La Paz agencies offer reasonably priced, guided, full- and half-day Tiwanaku tours (B$80 to B$150 per person), including transportation and a bilingual (English and Spanish) guide. These tours are well worth it for the convenience; most travelers visit Tiwanaku this way.

Diana Tours (p80) and Vicuña Travel (p80) have round-trip guided trips to Tiwanaku from La Paz, leaving daily at 8:30am and returning around 4pm.

For those who prefer to go it alone, minibuses from La Paz's cemetery leave when full and cost B$15 for the 1½-hour drive. These minibuses are often crowded and pass by the museum near the entrance to the complex. To return to La Paz, you can usually find a waiting minibus at the same point. If not, head to the village's main plaza. Make sure it says Cementerio, otherwise, you'll get dropped off in El Alto's Ceja.

Micros (small buses) to Guaqui and the Peruvian border can be flagged down on the highway 2km away – again, expect crowds.

Taxis to Tiwanaku from La Paz cost from B$210 to B$280 for the round trip.

Empresa Ferroviaria Andina (p80) runs occasional round-trip tourist trains from La Paz's El Alto to Tiwanaku (1½-hour stop) and on to Guaqui on Lake Titicaca (2½-hour stop). The train departs El Alto on the second Sunday of each month at 8am. Check the website or call ahead.

Lake Titicaca

Best Places to Eat

➡ La Cúpula Restaurant (p96)

➡ La Orilla (p97)

➡ Las Velas (p104)

➡ Isla Peñon (p100)

Best Places to Stay

➡ Las Olas (p95)

➡ Hotel Rosario del Lago (p96)

➡ La Estancia Ecolodge (p103)

➡ Palla Khasa (p104)

Why Go?

Everything – and everyone – that sits beside this impressive body of water, from the traditional Aymará villages to the glacier-capped peaks of the Cordillera Real, seems to fall into the background in contrast with the shimmering opal jewel set into the spare altiplano earth. It is not hard to see how Inca legends came to credit Lake Titicaca with the birth of their civilization.

Set between Peru and Bolivia at 3808m, the 8400 sq km lake offers enough activities to keep you busy for at least a week. There are trips to the many islands that speckle the shoreline, hikes to lost coves and floating islands, parties in the tourist hub of Copacabana and encounters with locals that will provide insight into the traditions of one of Bolivia's top attractions.

When to Go
Copacabana

Feb–Nov Sunny days, but bitterly cold nights. Lots of festivals including Semana Santa.

May Fiesta de la Cruz (Feast of the Cross) is popular around the lake.

Aug Fiesta de la Virgin de Copacabana is an annual blessing of cars and other possessions.

Lake Titicaca Highlights

① **Isla del Sol** (p100) Exploring on foot, hiking from shore to hilltop for stunning vistas of distant mountains.

② **Copacabana** (p89) Discovering vestiges of the Inca culture, checking out a baptism (or even a vehicle blessing!) at the cathedral and watching the sunset from the top of Cerro Calvario.

③ **Lakeside villages** (p98) Traveling between Copacabana and Yampupata, taking a spin in a reed boat and eating fresh grilled trout on a (faux) floating island.

④ **Isla Pariti** (p106) Boating out to this tiny island with its lovely museum featuring exquisite Tiwanaku finds from a 2004 excavation.

⑤ **Isla de la Luna** (p105) Skipping the sun and heading straight for the moon, where you'll find ancient ruins and landscapes straight out of the Mediterranean.

History

When you first glimpse Lake Titicaca's crystalline, gemlike waters beneath the looming backdrop of the Cordillera Real in the clear altiplano light, you'll understand why pre-Inca people connected it with mystical events. Those early inhabitants of the altiplano believed that the sun and their god-king, Viracocha, had risen out of its mysterious depths. The Incas, in turn, believed that it was the birthplace of their civilization.

Archaeological discoveries indicate that the areas around the lake have been inhabited since about 1500 BC by civilizations like the Tiwanaku, Aymará and Inca. Discoveries of a subaquatic temple and ancient wall have led some to speculate that the lake area was inhabited as far back as 6000 BC. And while the nearby Tiwanaku ruins are the largest in the area, there are numerous pre-Columbian sites surrounding the lake.

From pre-Columbian times to the present day, the Uru people have lived on artificial floating reed islands on the lake. The islands on the Peruvian side of the lake are still inhabited, while the Bolivian counterparts are made purely as tourist attractions.

Changes to the water level of Lake Titicaca are not uncommon; in the 1980s, a large flood displaced 200,000 people and it took several years for the Río Desaguadero, the lake's only outlet, to drain the floodwaters. Today, with melting glaciers and inconsistent rainfalls, the water is dropping to record-low levels.

Archaeological expeditions continue around – and beneath – the lake. At Isla Koa, north of Isla del Sol, 22 large stone boxes were found, containing a variety of artifacts: a silver llama, some shell figurines and several types of incense burners. And in 2004 the tiny island of Pariti (p106) hit world headlines when a team of Bolivian and Finnish archaeologists discovered elaborate pottery.

❶ Getting There & Away

The road journey between La Paz and Copacabana is impressive in terms of the scenery, so it's a good idea to travel by day. To get to Copacabana by bus, you'll need to cross the Estrecho de Tiquina (Tiquina Straits) on a ferry. The Islas de la Luna and del Sol are accessed by boat from Copacabana or Yampupata.

Copacabana

📌 2 / POP 15,000 / ELEV 3808M

Nestled between two hills on the southern shore of Lake Titicaca, Copacabana is a small, bright and enchanting town. It's long been a religious mecca, and local and international pilgrims still flock to its raucous fiestas, but lakeside strolls and meanderings up El Calvario will get you far from the madding crowd. Copa is the launching pad for visiting Isla del Sol and Isla de la Luna, and makes a pleasant stopover between La Paz and Puno or Cuzco.

History

After the fall and disappearance of the Tiwanaku culture, the Kollas (Aymará) rose to power in the Titicaca region. Their most prominent deities included the sun and moon (who were considered husband and wife), the earth mother Pachamama, and the ambient mountain spirits known as *achachilas* and *apus*. Among the idols erected on the shores of the Manco Capac peninsula was Kota Kahuaña, also known as Copacahuana (Aymará for 'lake view').

Once the Aymará had been subsumed into the Inca empire, Emperor Tupac-Yupanqui founded the settlement of Copacabana as a wayside rest for pilgrims visiting the *huaca* (shrine) known as Titi Khar'ka (Rock of the Puma), a former site of human sacrifice at the northern end of Isla del Sol.

Before the arrival of Spanish priests in the mid-16th century, the Incas had divided local inhabitants into two distinct groups. Those faithful to the empire were known as Haransaya and were assigned positions of power. Those who resisted, the Hurinsaya, were relegated to manual labor. It was a separation that went entirely against the grain of the community-oriented Aymará culture, and the floods and crop failures that befell them in the 1570s were attributed to this social aberration.

This resulted in the rejection of the Inca religion, and the partial adoption of Christianity and establishment of Santuario de Copacabana, which developed into a syncretic mishmash of both traditional and Christian beliefs. The populace elected La Santísima Virgen de Candelaria as its patron saint and established a congregation in her honor. Noting the lack of an image for the altar, Francisco Tito Yupanqui, a direct descendant of the Inca emperor, fashioned a figurine of clay and placed it in the church. However, his rude effort was deemed unsuitable to represent the honored patron of the village and was removed.

The sculptor, who was humiliated but not defeated, journeyed to Potosí to study the arts. In 1582 he began a carving that took eight months to complete. In 1583a sculpture of the Virgen was installed on the adobe altar at Copacabana and shortly thereafter the miracles began. There were reportedly 'innumerable' early healings and Copacabana quickly became a pilgrimage site.

In 1605 the Augustinian priesthood advised the community to construct a cathedral commensurate with the power of the image. The altar was completed in 1614, but work on the building continued for 200 years. In 1805 the *mudéjar* (Moorish-style) cathedral was finally consecrated, but construction wasn't completed until 1820. In 1925, Francisco Tito Yupanqui's image was canonized by the Vatican.

◉ Sights

Copacabana's central attractions can be visited in one long but relaxed day, but there are some great trips further afield. Much of the action in Copa centers on Plaza 2 de Febrero and Av 6 de Agosto, the main commercial drag, which runs from east to west. At its western end is the lake and a walkway (Costañera) that traces the shoreline. The transportation hub is in Plaza Sucre.

★**Cathedral** CHURCH
(Plaza 2 de Febrero) FREE The sparkling white *mudéjar* (Moorish–style) cathedral, with its domes and colorful *azulejos* (blue Portuguese-style ceramic tiles), dominates the town. Check the noticeboard in front of the entrance for the mass schedule.

The cathedral's **Camarín de la Virgen de Candelaria** statue, carved by Incan Emperor Tupac-Yupanqui's grandson, Francisco Yupanqui, is encased above the altar upstairs in the *camarín* (shrine); visiting hours can be unreliable.

The statue is never moved from the cathedral, as superstition suggests that its disturbance would precipitate a devastating flood of Lake Titicaca. **Museo de la Catedral** (Murillo s/n; per person B$10, minimum 8) contains some interesting religious art.

Horca del Inca RUINS
(Inti Watana; B$10) This hillside gate is a fascinating pre-Incan astronomical observatory, surrounded by pierced rocks that permit the sun's rays to pass through onto the lintel during the June solstice, which is the Aymará New Year. Locals use the event to predict everything from the expected rainfall to crop yields, and venture up before sunrise to celebrate the occasion. From near the end of Murillo, a signposted trail leads uphill to the site.

Cerro Kopakati RUINS
Located about 4km down the road from Horca del Inca toward Kasani, this carved stone features pre-Incan ruins and pictographs. The best known, though difficult to distinguish, is **Escudo de la Cultura Chiripa**, a unique icon attributed to the pre-Inca Chiripa culture.

Museo del Poncho MUSEUM
(www.museodelponcho.org; Baptista, near Costañera; B$15; ⊙10am-5:30pm Mon-Sat, to 4pm Sun) A visit to Museo del Poncho will help you unravel the mysteries of the regional textiles. The exhibits, spread over two floors, give a clear insight into the origins and meanings of the poncho – who wears what and why. Labels are in English and Spanish. Hours are irregular and photography is not allowed.

Copacabana Beach BEACH
While Bolivia's only public beach can't hold a candle to its better-known counterpart in Rio de Janeiro, on weekends the festive atmosphere is a magnet for families. You can play foosball against the local talent and rent all manner of watercraft, from paddleboat swans and canoes to small sailboats. Also on offer are horseback rides, bicycles and motorbikes.

Cerro Calvario MOUNTAIN
The summit can be reached in half an hour and is well worth the climb, especially for a view of the sunset. The trail begins near the church at the end of 3 de Mayo and climbs past the 14 Stations of the Cross. You can also enter from a longer winding dirt path that begins at the corner of Calles Jáuregui and Costañera.

You'll need sturdy hiking shoes for the long dirt path.

Museo Pacha Uta MUSEUM
(Av 16 de Julio s/n; ⊙8am-noon & 2-6pm) FREE A small museum by the tourist info center that's dedicated to the natural and human history of the lake.

Intikala RUINS
(Tribunal del Inca; cnr Mejia & Jose Mejia) North of the cemetery on the southeastern outskirts of town is this neglected site of artificially sculpted boulders. Its original purpose is unknown, but there are several carved stones with *asientos* (seats), basins and *hornecinos* (niches), which may have once contained idols.

Museo de Kusijata MUSEUM
(Map p99; ☑mobile 7128-0464; Kusijata; B$10; ⊙8am-noon & 1-5pm) A 3km walk northeast along the shoreline from the end of Calles Junín or Ballivián leads to the community of Kusijata, where there's a former colonial hacienda housing a small, dusty archaeological display. Seek out the long-deceased mummified corpse *(chullpa)* sitting in an upright fetal position, as it was buried. If no one is at the entrance, simply ask around or call.

Copacabana

0   200 m
0   0.1 miles

Tours

Stroll On Walking Tours   WALKING
(☑ mobile 7302-9991; www.strollonwalkingtours.com) Offers a range of English-language walking tours and hikes around Copacabana, as well as Isla del Sol and Isla de la Luna.

Turisbus   TOURS
(☑ 245-1658; www.turisbus.com; Hotel Rosario del Lago, Paredes, near Costañera; ⊙ 8am-noon & 2-6pm) Book your tour with this well-run and professional agency through Hotel Rosario (p96) in Copacabana or La Paz.

Copacabana

Transturin TOURS
(📞 242-2222; www.transturin.com; Achumani Calle 6 No 100, La Paz; ⊙ 9am-7pm Mon-Fri, to noon Sat) This agency runs day and overnight cruises to Isla del Sol in covered liveaboard catamarans or reed boats.

★ Festivals & Events

Copacabana hosts several major annual fiestas. The town also celebrates the **La Paz departmental anniversary** on July 16. Thursdays and Sundays are lively **market days**. Watch your belongings; with lots of partying – and people from out of town – there's an increased chance of petty theft.

Alasitas Festival RELIGIOUS
(⊙ Jan 24) A local tradition is the blessing of miniature objects, such as cars or houses. Supplicants pray that the real thing will be obtained in the coming year.

Fiesta de la Virgen de Candelaria RELIGIOUS
(⊙ Feb 2-5) Honors the patron saint of Copacabana and Bolivia. Copacabana holds an especially big bash, and pilgrims and

dancers come from Peru and around Bolivia. There's much music, traditional Aymará dancing, drinking and feasting. Celebrations culminate with the gathering of 100 bulls in a stone corral along the Yampupata road.

Semana Santa RELIGIOUS
(⊙ Mar or Apr) Easter Week celebrations fill the town with pilgrims on Good Friday – some walk the 158km from La Paz – to do penance at the Stations of the Cross on Cerro Calvario. Beginning at the cathedral (p91) at dusk, pilgrims join a solemn candlelit procession, with a statue of Christ in a glass coffin and a replica of the Virgen in the lead.

At the summit, you may join the locals in lighting incense and purchasing miniatures representing material possessions in the hope of being granted the real things by the Virgin during the year.

Fiesta de la Cruz RELIGIOUS
(Feast of the Cross; ⊙ May) This fiesta is celebrated over the first weekend in May all around the lake, but the biggest festivities are in Copacabana. Expect elaborate costumes and traditional dancing.

WORTH A TRIP

OUTDOOR ADVENTURES FROM COPACABANA

The areas around Copacabana offer plenty of adventure. The trip to Yampupata is a worthwhile excursion by foot, bike, minibus or taxi. Here are a few DIY activities that will take you beyond the standard tourist tracks.

Las Islas Flotantes (Floating Islands) While there aren't any true floating reed islands to visit near Copacabana anymore (for that you'll need to head to Huatajata), there are a few faux islands that locals flock to for fresh *trucha*. You can walk from town to Isla Flotante Kalakota (p100), near Kusijata, or you can hike or take a taxi to the more scenic Isla Peñon (p100) near Chañi.

Lost ruins Ask **Centro de Información Turística** (☑ mobile 7880-4452; cnr Avs 16 de Julio & 6 de Agosto; ⊙ 8am-noon & 2-6pm Mon-Fri) for a list of nearby Inca ruins and strike out on your own. Some, but not all, Inca sites are listed here. Admittedly, many are now neglected or rarely visited.

Hike south of town The stunning peninsula south of town will give you a different perspective of the lake. To start your hike, head out 6km to the village of J'iska Q'ota. Catch a minibus marked 'Kasani' (B$4) and you'll arrive in 10 minutes. Follow the road toward the lake heading in a northeasterly – and then northerly – direction around the peninsula and back to Copa.

Bike from town Hire a bike at Copacabana Beach (p91) and head off into the hills or in the direction of Yampupata – a hilly, but beautiful, journey.

Bolivian
Independence Day   NATIONAL HOLIDAY
(⊙ Aug) Copacabana stages its biggest event during the first week of August. It's characterized by round-the-clock music, parades and brass band performances as well as fireworks displays. This coincides with an annual pilgrimage that brings thousands of Peruvians into the town to visit the Virgin.

🛏 Sleeping

A host of budget options abound, especially along Jáuregui, charging about B$30 to B$40 per person. There are also several midrange options that are well worth the extra bolivianos. During fiestas accommodations fill up quickly and prices increase up to threefold.

Hostal Sonia   HOTEL $
(☑ 862-2019, mobile 7196-8441; hostalsoniacopacabana@gmail.com; Murillo 256; r per person with/without bathroom B$50/40; @ 🛜) This lively spot has bright and cheery rooms, great views from the upstairs rooms and a top-floor terrace, making it one of the top budget bets in town. The proprietors own the swankier (and newer) Hotel Lago Azul (p96), if you want to upgrade.

Suma Samawi   CAMPGROUND $
(Hostel-Camping; ☑ mobile 7525-8093; Costañera s/n; campsite B$20, cabins per person B$30-40)

Just down the beach from town, this colorful youth-oriented campground-cum-hostel has a shared kitchen and a big barbecue pit outside. The laid-back ambience is fostered by owners Martha and Johnny, who'll make you feel a world away from the hubbub of downtown Copa.

Hotel Mirador   HOTEL $
(www.titicacabolivia.com; cnr Av Busch & Costañera; r per person incl breakfast B$50; 🛜) Stunning value for the impressive view of the lake that shines like a beacon from the end of the long rooms. The common areas are dated – and the hotel seems in a perpetual state of being half-open – but its sprawling size gives it the charm of a Los Angeles motel.

Hostal Sucre   HOSTEL $
(☑ 862-2080; Murillo 228; r per person incl breakfast B$50, f B$200) Clearly a smart hotel in former days, this place – now a little tired but perfectly adequate – has local TV, carpeted rooms, reliable hot water, a courtyard and a restaurant. Some rooms are cell-like, but all have external windows.

⭐ **Las Olas**   BOUTIQUE HOTEL $$
(☑ 862-2112, mobile 7250-8668; www.hostallasolas.com; Pérez 1-3; s/d/tr/q US$41/52/68/79; @ 🛜) To say too much about this place is to spoil the surprise, so here's a taste: quirky, creative, stylish, ecofriendly, million-dollar vistas. Plus there are kitchens, private terraces with

hammocks and a solar-powered Jacuzzi. A once-in-a-lifetime experience and well worth the splurge. Reserve one or two weeks ahead.

Hotel La Cúpula   HOTEL $$
(📱mobile 7708-8464; www.hotelcupula.com; Pérez 1-3; s/d/tr from US$17/29/54, s/d/tr ste from US$32/48/60; 📶) International travelers rave about this inviting oasis, marked by two gleaming-white domes on the slopes of Cerro Calvario, with stupendous lake views. The rooms are basic but stylish. The gardens, hammocks, shared kitchen and friendly atmosphere add to the appeal. The helpful staff speak several languages, and you can even buy the artwork in your room.

Ecolodge Copacabana   LODGE $$
(📞862-2500; www.ecocopacabana.com; Av Costañera s/n; per person incl breakfast B$180; 📶) Twenty minutes on foot along the Costañera, this eco-friendly lakefront property offers a tranquil experience. The quirky adobe rooms and apartments (two with kitchens) are self-heated thanks to the mudbricks and have solar-powered water. The bird-filled garden of *kantutas* (a flowering shrub) and roses affords great views of the lake.

Hostal Flores del Lago   HOTEL $$
(📞862-2117; Jáuregui s/n; s/d/tr/q B$100/140/210/300; 📶) This red four-story hotel on the north side of the harbor is a top-tier budget option. The clean rooms are slightly damp, but you'll love the views and the friendly, sunny lobby area, which is the domain of Blanco the cat. Two large 'family-style' rooms for four or more people are available.

Hostel Leyenda   HOSTEL $$
(📱mobile 6707-9158; hostel.leyenda@gmail.com; cnr Av Busch & Constañera; s/d incl breakfast B$100/200, ste B$250; 📶) This is a solid bet for budgeteers, with views of the water, a lush garden and 'Bolivian Boutique' rooms.

The corner rooms have lots of space for the same price while the top-floor suite is a bit pricier and nicer – it even has a *totora*-reed raft and its own terrace.

La Aldea Del Inca   GUESTHOUSE $$
(📞862-2452; www.hostalaldeadelinca.com; San Antonio 2; s/d/tr/q incl breakfast B$170/280/420/525; 📶) Themed like the nearby Incan ruins and with spacious rooms replete with Andean art, this hotel makes for a solid mid-range option. Most rooms have views and all have heat, TVs and access to the hammock-strewn garden.

Hotel Wendy Mar   HOTEL $$
(📞862-2124, mobile 7882-4240; www.hotelwendymar.com.bo; Av 16 de Julio & Potosí; s/d/tr incl breakfast B$120/230/320; 📶) Everything about this excellent budget option is neat and orderly, from the hospital-corner sheets to the spotless floors. Ask for a room with a lake view.

Hotel Utama   HOTEL $$
(📞862-2013; www.utamahotel.com; cnr Pérez & San Antonio; s/d incl breakfast B$140/250; 📶) Set by the hill overlooking the town, this clean, reliable option has firm beds, a central terrace and electric showers. Try to get a room with a view. Free bag storage, a nice garden and a book exchange add to the mix.

Hotel Lago Azul   HOTEL $$
(📞862-2581; cnr Costañera 13 & Jáuregui; s/d B$130/260; @📶) Located right on the lake, this hotel has nicely painted rooms, heaters, small balconies, flat-screen TVs and new mattresses. A bit austere, but you can hardly get a better location.

★Hotel Rosario del Lago   HOTEL $$$
(📞245-1658, La Paz 2-277-6286; www.gruporosario.com; Paredes, near Costañera; s/d incl breakfast US$89/99; @📶) One of the smartest places

---

BENEDICIÓN DE MOVILIDADES

The word *cha'lla* is used for any ritual blessing, toast or offering to the powers that be, whether Inca, Aymará or Christian. On most mornings during the festival season (July to August) from around 10am (and reliably on Saturday and Sunday), cars, trucks and buses decked out in garlands of real or plastic flowers, colored ribbons and flags hover in front of Copacabana's cathedral. The majority are from Peru and they come for a *cha'lla* known as Benedición de Movilidades (Blessing of Automobiles).

Petitions for protection are made to the Virgin and a ritual offering of alcohol is poured over the vehicles – and sometimes consumed by the driver – thereby consecrating them for the journey home. Between Good Friday and Easter Sunday, the *cha'lla* is especially popular among pilgrims and long-distance bus companies with new fleets. Drivers offer the priest donations for their blessings.

LOCAL KNOWLEDGE

EAT LOCAL

The specialty in Copacabana is *trucha criolla* (rainbow trout) and *pejerrey* (kingfish) from Lake Titicaca. The trout were introduced in 1939 to increase protein content in the local diet. The catch of the day is served *ad nauseam* to varying degrees of taste – some resemble electrocuted sardines while others are worthy of a Michelin restaurant rating.

in town, the hacienda-styled sister of Hotel Rosario in La Paz has charming modern rooms with solar-heated showers, double-glazed windows and lake views. The staff also provide excellent service. The altiplano light streams on a pleasant sun terrace.

Eating

Some of the best Titicaca fish is served at **beachfront stalls** (Costanera; trout from B$25; ⊙8am-9pm), though hygiene is questionable. The bargain basement is the market *comedor* (dining hall), where you can eat a generous meal of *trucha* for a pittance, or an 'insulin shock' breakfast of hot *api morado* (hot corn drink; B$4) and syrupy *buñuelos* (doughnuts or fritters; B$3).

Pan America   BAKERY $
(☑ mobile 7881-5278; www.facebook.com/Pan AmericaCopacabana; Plaza 2 de Febrero; mains B$20-40; ⊙10am-6:30pm Fri-Mon) 🥖 The American owners of this bakery, which is next to the cathedral (p91), use the profits to fund development projects in nearby rural communities. Come in the morning for coffee and yummy baked goods, and return for wine and pizza in the afternoon.

El Condor & The Eagle Cafe   CAFE $
(www.facebook.com/elcondorandtheeaglecafe; Av 6 de Agosto s/n; mains B$30; ⊙7am-1pm Mon-Fri; 🛜🥖) Make this cheery traveler's cafe your breakfast spot. It's got great veggie options, French-press coffee and owners who are more than happy to offer advice on Bolivia. There's also a small bookstore and a great collection of journals where fellow travelers offer tips for onward journeys.

Pit Stop   BAKERY $
(☑ mobile 6323-5727; Av 16 de Julio s/n; snacks B$7-15; ⊙8:30am-2pm & 4:30-7pm) Trust the Argentines to bring proper short espressos, and dense cakes to Copacabana. You can find

empanadas and pizza elsewhere in town, but at this hole-in-the-wall where buses stop, Luciano and Maria Jose do it better.

Baguette About It   SANDWICHES $
(Av 16 de Julio s/n; sandwiches B$18-25; ⊙8:30am-2pm & 4:30-7pm) The owners of Pit Stop have opened this (equally tiny) cafe next door. The focus here is on build-your-own sandwiches and craft beers. It's great for a takeaway as it's right by the tourist buses.

La Choza   CAFE $
(Av 16 de Julio, btwn Busch & Av 6 de Agosto; snacks & sandwiches B$10-40; ⊙8am-10pm) This breezy cafe is open all day. It's a nice place to have a sandwich and gaze at the holy trinity of Jimi Hendrix, Bob Marley and Marilyn Monroe posters, while you wait for a bus.

Restaurant Aransaya   BOLIVIAN $
(Av 6 de Agosto 121; almuerzo B$15, mains B$30; ⊙8am-8:30pm Wed-Mon) Super-friendly local favorite for a tall, cold beer and trout heaped with all the trimmings. It's neat, clean, very traditional and popular with the locals.

★La Cúpula Restaurant   INTERNATIONAL $$
(www.hotelcupula.com; Pérez 1-3; mains B$24-59; ⊙7:30am-3pm & 6-10pm, closed lunch Tue; 🖊) An inventive use of local ingredients makes up the extensive international and Bolivian menu here. There's plenty for carnivores and vegetarians alike. Dip your way through the cheese fondue – it's to die for...which leaves the Bolivian chocolate fondue with fruit platter beyond description.

★La Orilla   INTERNATIONAL $$
(☑862-2267; Av 6 de Agosto s/n; mains B$36-60; ⊙9:30am-2pm & 5-9:30pm; 🖊) Some say this cozy maritime-themed restaurant is the best in town, with fresh, crunchy-from-the-vine vegetables and interesting trout creations that incorporate spinach and bacon. They might just be right. Even the high-altitude falafels are pretty good.

Gourmet Ali   INTERNATIONAL $$
(☑7124-6336; Av 6 de Agosto s/n; mains B$40-60; ⊙7am-11pm; 🛜) An unassuming and brightly lit restaurant with seriously good food, including fresh takes on trout, as well as pizzas, pastas and filets of llama.

Terradentro Restaurant   INTERNATIONAL $$
(☑862-2141; Hotel Rosario del Lago, Paredes, near Costañera; mains B$30-60) This hotel restaurant has excellent views of the lake, great

service and well-prepared international dishes. While it is one of the more expensive in town, it also has higher standards than some of its counterparts. Andean soup, grilled llama, Bolivian wines and desserts like tiramisu and mousse ensure a fine-dining experience.

Puerto Viejo INTERNATIONAL **$$**
(www.puertoviejocafecopacabana.blogspot.com; Av 6 de Agosto s/n; mains B$35-50; ☺8:30am-11:30pm; 🐟) You'll find burgers, tacos amid the scarily large menu. Also cocktails and passable espresso coffees. Service is friendly and it's a good place to chat with fellow travelers over the hefty wooden tables.

Huanchaco PERUVIAN **$$**
(Restaurant Peruana; Av 6 de Agosto s/n; mains B$40-110; ☺11am-11pm) Forget Copa's *ad nauseam* pizzas and go for a *Papa a la Huancaino* (potato in spicy yellow sauce) or a *chupe de camarones*, and be transported across the border at this colorful restaurant. The kicker, *suspira a la limeña*, is a heady concoction of pisco, egg whites and condensed milk.

La Posta PIZZA **$$**
(✐ 7252-1244; Av 6 de Agosto s/n; mains B$20-40; ☺9:30am-11pm) Tasty pizzas are served in a cozy, tango-themed setting.

🍷 Drinking & Nightlife

New nightspots come and go as frequently as tour boats. To find out what's happening while you're in town, it's best to ask the touts on Av 6 de Agosto.

KM/0 BAR
(KM Zero; ✐ mobile 7259-0797; Av 6 de Agosto s/n; ☺10am-11pm) This long-running bar has lost a bit of its edge over the years, but it's still got good drink specials and live music nightly at 8pm. It's located just 50m up the road from the big anchor. Friendly service makes all the difference.

Waykys Disco Bar BAR
(www.facebook.com/waykysdiscoteca; cnr Avs 16 de Julio & 6 de Agosto; ☺9pm-late Mon-Sat) Looking for a dark, black-lit bar with loud music, dingy bathrooms and graffiti-covered walls? The kind of place you might make poor decisions at? This is the spot. Be sure to try Evo, a lightning-bolt of a cocktail with *singani* (distilled grape liquor), lemon juice, coca leaves and liquor de coca.

🛍 Shopping

Local specialties include handmade miniatures of *totora*-reed boats and unusual varieties of Andean potatoes. Massive bags of *pasankalla*, which is puffed *choclo* (corn) with caramel, the South American version of popcorn, abound. Dozens of stores sell llama- and alpaca-wool hats and sweaters. Vehicle adornments used in the *cha'lla* and religious paraphernalia are sold at stalls in front of the cathedral.

Spitting Llama
Bookstore & Outfitter BOOKS
(Av 6 de Agosto; ☺9am-noon & 1-6pm) A great collection of secondhand books in English, German and French, as well as plenty of Lonely Planet titles. Also sells trekking maps and camping equipment.

ℹ Information

DANGERS & ANNOYANCES

UV Radiation The thin air, characteristically brilliant sunshine and reflection off the water mean scorching levels of ultraviolet radiation. Wear a hat and sunscreen in this region, and drink lots of water to avoid dehydration.

Crowds Be especially careful during festivals. Stand well back during fireworks displays, when explosive fun seems to take priority over crowd safety, and be wary of light-fingered revelers.

MEDICAL SERVICES

You'll likely get the best care at the tourist-friendly **Medical Health Home** (✐ mobile 7727-8510; www.medicalhome.com.pe; cnr Baptista & Costañera). For serious situations don't think twice – head straight to La Paz.

MONEY

ATMs dot Plaza Sucre. Shops on Av 6 de Agosto will exchange foreign currency (clean dollar bills preferred). Most *artesanías* (crafts stores) sell Peruvian soles.

TELEPHONE

Entel (Murillo s/n; ☺8:30am-12:30pm & 2:30-6:30pm Mon-Fri, 9am-3pm Sat & Sun), Tigo and Viva *puntos* (privately run phone offices) are located along Av 6 de Agosto and around town. Many also offer relatively cheap international calls.

ℹ Getting There & Away

AIR

A new airport opened in 2018. At the time of research it was not yet complete, but was planned to have domestic flight connections to La Paz, Rurrenabaque, Trinidad and Uyuni.

ⓘ ENTERING & LEAVING PERU

Most travelers enter/exit Peru via Copacabana (and the Tiquina Straits) or the scruffy town of Desaguadero (avoiding Copacabana altogether). Note that Peruvian time is one hour behind Bolivian time. Always keep your backpack with you when crossing the border.

Via Copacabana

Micros to the Kasani/Yunguyo border leave Copacabana's Plaza Sucre regularly, usually when full (B$4, 15 minutes). At Kasani you obtain your exit stamp at passport control and head on foot across the border. On the Peruvian side, a taxi or mototaxi can ferry you to Yunguyo (about Peruvian S3, five minutes). From here, you can catch a bus heading to Puno.

An efficient alternative is to catch a tourist bus from La Paz to Puno via Copacabana (from B$60) or vice versa; some allow you a couple of days' stay in Copacabana. Note, though, that even if you've bought a ticket to Cuzco or elsewhere in Peru, you'll change buses in Puno. Buses to Cuzco depart from Puno's international terminal, located about three blocks from the local terminal.

Via Desaguadero

A quicker, if less interesting, route is via Desaguadero on the southern side of the lake. Several bus companies head across this border from/to Peru. The crossing should be hassle-free: you obtain your exit stamp from the **Bolivian passport control** (Desaguadero; ⊙ 8:30am-12:30pm & 2-8:45pm), walk across a bridge and get an entry stamp at *migración* in Peru. Buses head to Puno at hourly intervals (about 3½ hours).

BOAT

Buy your tickets for boat tours to Isla de la Luna and Isla del Sol from agencies on Av 6 de Agosto or from beachfront kiosks. If you're traveling in a big group, consider renting a private boat for B$600 to B$900 per day. Separate return services are available from both islands.

BUS

Most buses leave from near Plazas 2 de Febrero or Sucre. The more comfortable nonstop tour buses from La Paz to Copacabana – including those operated by **Titicaca Tourist Transportation** (☑ 862-2160; www.titicacabolivia.com; cnr Avs 6 de Agosto & 16 de Julio) – cost about B$30 and are well worth the investment. They depart from La Paz at about 8am and leave Copacabana at 1:30pm and 6:30pm (four hours). You will need to exit the bus at Estrecho de Tiquina (Tiquina Straits) to cross via ferry (per person B$2, 15 minutes) between the towns of San Pedro de Tiquina and San Pablo de Tiquina.

Buses to Peru depart and arrive in Copacabana from Av 16 de Julio. You can also get to Puno by catching a public minibus from Plaza Sucre to Kasani (B$4, 15 minutes). Across the border there's frequent, if crowded, onward transportation to Yunguyo (five minutes) and Puno (2½ hours).

A new player in the bus game, Irish-run Bolivia Hop (p80) offers services between Lima, Arequipa, Copa and La Paz, and helps travelers with customs and *hostal* arrangements.

DESTINATION	COST (B$)	TIME (HR)
Arequipa (Peru)	80	10-11
Cuzco (Peru)	80	11-12
La Paz	20-30	4
Puno (Peru)	30	3-4

Copacabana to Yampupata

Hiking, biking or simply busing along the road from Copacabana to Yampupata, a small hamlet about 17km north of town, is a fun little adventure and an interesting alternative to the standard Copa-Isla tour. Along the way, you'll see ruins, stop at (faux) floating islands, get chased by dogs and pass through traditional communities.

◉ Sights

★ **Sampaya**   AREA
This is a beautifully preserved village where the homes are built with flat stones joined in an earthen mortar. There is a stone church on the hilltop overlooking Titicaca and Isla de la Luna in the distance. Take a stroll and get lost in the small alleyways and terraced hills. This will likely be the highlight of any journey north of Copacabana.

Titicachi   VILLAGE
This picturesque village lies on a secluded crescent-shaped bay encased by green hills.

If it's open, there's a basic *tienda* (shop) in town selling soft drinks.

Sicuani   VILLAGE

Ask around town for Hilario Paye Quispe. He can take you on trips around the bay in a *totora*-reed boat or via motorboat to the peninsula opposite (prices negotiable). You can also camp here.

Gruta de Lourdes   CAVE

(Gruta de Fátima; Hinchaca) A cave that, for locals, evokes images of its respective French and Portuguese namesakes. It attracts devotees from across the border in Peru, particularly in August.

Yampupata   VILLAGE

This is a collection of lakefront adobe houses. If you ask around, you'll find rooms for rent for about B$30. Asociación Transport Yampu Tour Lacustre (p105) takes passengers across to the south of Isla del Sol for B$130 (one-way). You can also get to Isla de la Luna for B$250 (round-trip). Prices are per boat.

🏃 Activities

Hiking

The main hiking trek is road-bound, making it a fairly hot and hard slog (allow seven hours one-way if you're stopping along the way). By bike the round trip can be done in a day, while taxi or minibus trips will take under an hour one way. Take your own snacks; there's little, if anything, along the road.

From Copacabana, head northeast on the road that follows the shoreline, past the turnoff to Museo de Kusijata (p92). About 7km into the journey, you arrive at Gruta de Lourdes. To save an hour or so, you can catch a minibus (B$5) or taxi (one-way/return B$50/80) from Copa to the cave, from where the more picturesque hiking begins. At the fork just below the crest of the hill, bear left and descend to the shore and into the village of Titicachi (p99). You pass through Sicuani (p99) and, 17km from Copacabana, you'll reach Yampupata (p99).

An alternative hiking option, especially for those who don't want to head to Isla del Sol, is to catch a taxi (one-way B$80) from Copacabana along the main road and stop at villages along the way.

A highly recommended detour is the unspoiled cobblestone village of Sampaya (p99), 5km from Yampupata, which has basic lodging. You can return on foot, bike or taxi to Copacabana via the higher eastern route.

North of Copacabana

Although this road doesn't pass through main villages, it affords magnificent views and a more nature-bound experience.

 Eating

Isla Peñon SEAFOOD **$**

(Islas Flotantes de Chañi; ☑ mobile 7309-3322; Chañi; mains B$30; ⊗ 8am-7pm) Do as the locals do and make a weekend trip to this faux floating island. It's attached to a rocky outcrop with sweeping views, and the trout comes from right beneath your feet.

Isla Flotante Kalakota SEAFOOD **$$**

(☑ 7623-2516; Kusijata; mains B$30-35; ⊗ 10:30am-6pm) Located just after the Kusijata turnoff, Isla Flotante Kalakota is a good spot to stop for a freshly caught trout lunch.

ⓘ Getting There & Away

Taxis from Copacabana to Yampupata (p99) cost B$80 one-way, or B$200 for a round-trip journey with stops. For those who don't want to walk or catch a taxi, the easiest way to travel between Yampupata and Copacabana is by minibus (B$10, 40 minutes). They leave from Pérez, across from Comedor Central; departures are more regular in the morning, but you can typically catch a ride until 5pm.

Asociación Transport Yampu Tour Lacustre (p105) runs trips from Yampupata to Isla de la Luna (B$250 round-trip) and either Pilko Kaina or Yumani on Isla del Sol (B$130 one-way). Prices are per boat.

Isla del Sol

☑ 2 / POP 3000 / ELEV 3808M

Easily the highlight of any Lake Titicaca excursion, Isla del Sol is a large island with several traditional communities, decent tourist infrastructure such as hotels and restaurants, a few worthwhile pre-Columbian ruins, amazing views, great hikes through terraced hills and, well, lots of sun.

ⓘ VISITING ISLAS DEL SOL & DEL LUNA

To visit Islas del Sol and de la Luna you can either take a ferry or go the luxury route with a La Paz–based tour operator for a guided excursion (adding a night or two in their hotels on Isla del Sol). Recommended operators include:

➡ Crillon Tours (p105)

➡ Transturin (p93)

➡ Magri Turismo (p358)

The island's permanent residents – a mix of indigenous peoples and émigrés – are distributed between the main settlements of Cha'llapampa, near the island's northern end; Cha'lla, which backs onto a lovely sandy beach on the central east coast; and Yumani, which straddles the ridge above Escalera del Inca in the south and is the biggest town on the island. Unfortunately, due to a conflict between island communities, it is only possible to visit Yumani.

Extensive networks of walking tracks make exploration fairly easy, though the altitude and sun may take their toll: carry lunch and ample water. The sun was born here and is still going strong.

History

The Island of the Sun was known to early inhabitants as Titi Khar'ka (Rock of the Puma), from which Lake Titicaca takes its name. This island has been identified as the birthplace of several revered entities, including the sun itself. Legend has it that the bearded white god-king Viracocha and the first Incas, Manco Capac and Mama Ocllo, mystically appeared under direct orders from the sun. Most modern-day Aymará and Quechua peoples of Peru and Bolivia accept these legends as their creation story.

⊙ Sights

Whirlwind half-day tours to Isla del Sol are strictly for the been-there-done-that crowd as the island definitely merits a night or two. That said, the majority of the ruins and associated sights are located on the island's northern half, which is off-limits to tourists. In the limited area you're allowed to roam you'll find a few small ruins, lookouts and walking trails, but most visitors simply kick back and enjoy the view.

Yumani VILLAGE

Yumani is the main village at the south end of the island. Most boats drop you at the village's dock, about 200m downhill from the town proper. The small church, Iglesia de San Antonio, serves the southern half of the island. Nearby you'll find an exploding cluster of guesthouses and fabulous views over the water to Isla de la Luna.

You can climb to the ridge (in about 30 minutes) for a view down to the deep sapphire-colored Bahía Kona on the western shore. From the crest you'll also find routes leading downhill to the tiny pretty village of Japapi.

Isla del Sol

See North of Copacabana Map (p99)

Isla del Sol

◉ Sights

🛏 Sleeping

🍴 Eating

Mirador Palla Khasa   VIEWPOINT

Follow the well-signposted path from Yumani's ridgeline up to this small stone lookout atop Cerro Palla Khasa (4065m) for sweeping sunset views over the lake.

Escalera del Inca   GARDENS

(Yumani; B$10) Just uphill from the ferry dock at Yumani, along the beautifully reconstructed Escalera del Inca (Inca stairway), you'll pass plenty of terraced gardens, small shops and hotels. It's a lung-buster that gains almost 200m in elevation over less than 1km, so take your time – or hire donkeys (B$30) to carry your pack. Pay your admission fee at the dock for access to the stairway and village.

Pilko Kaina   RUINS

(B$10) This prominent ruins complex near the southern tip of the island is about 30 minutes (2km) south by foot from Yumani. It sits well camouflaged against a steep terraced slope. The best-known site is the two-level **Palacio del Inca**, thought to have been constructed by the Incan emperor, Túpac Inca Yupanqui.

Fuente del Inca   SPRING

(Yumani) Early Spaniards believed Yumani's spring was a fountain of youth and for the Incas the three streams represented their national motto: *Ama sua, Ama llulla,* *Ama khella* (Don't steal, don't lie and don't be lazy). Up until 2015, the fountain was a crucial source of water for locals, who came daily to fetch and carry it up the steep trail. Now, most residents have running water.

Lighthouse   LIGHTHOUSE

This lighthouse on the tip of Kakayo-Queña Ridge is technically in an area tourists are allowed to visit, though access by land has been cut off by the blockade.

Ruins   RUINS

Of the more than 80 Inca ruins on the island, most date to the 15th century AD. You could spend a week looking at them all.

🛏 Sleeping

With no cars or roads, and just a wild series of walking paths, it can be difficult to find the hotel you're looking for. To make things worse, many places close or shut down for weeks on end without notice. With a bit of flexibility, you should be able to find a spot to lay your head no matter your budget.

The most scenic place to stay is Yumani – high on the ridge – where guesthouses are growing faster than coca production. Booking ahead, if possible, can save you the grueling uphill hike with your luggage, as many places include a porter service in the price.

THE DARK CLOUD OVER SUN ISLAND

Trekking the length of Isla del Sol from the north to the south was once one of the great joys of visiting Lake Titicaca. Now, that's no longer possible. Tourists have been restricted from traveling north of Yumani (and its satellite village of La Estancia) due to an ongoing conflict between the communities of Cha'lla, in the middle, and Cha'llapampa, to the north.

The conflict began, in earnest, in March 2017 when the people of Cha'lla built a hostel near the ruins of Cha'llapampa in an attempt to cash in on some of the tourism revenue that had long evaded them. This angered the people of Cha'llapampa so much that they blew up the hostel with dynamite. Thing is, the people who now live in Cha'llapampa settled the area from Cha'lla, so the whole ordeal has turned into a family feud writ large.

In retaliation for the hostel incident, the people of Cha'lla instituted a blockade on the north, preventing tourists from traveling there by land or sea. Rather bizarrely (given the cause of the conflict), tourists can't even drop by Cha'lla for a visit, though you should be able to loop around Cerro Palla Khasa.

In theory there should be someone at a guard post stopping you if you walk too far from Yumani. In practice, that's not always the case. Either way, do not be tempted to test your fate. A Korean tourist was stabbed and strangled under mysterious circumstances in early 2018 shortly after a heated exchange between the two communities to the north. No one was charged with the murder, but it was suspected at the time that she had unwittingly crossed into the northern half of the island.

These unfortunate events should by no means stop you from visiting Isla del Sol. Stick to Yumani or La Estancia and your trip will likely be perfectly safe and conflict-free. In fact, you may never even realize that there are troubles brewing in the north. As with any conflict, it's best to check with hotels and tour operators in the region (namely Copacabana) before you depart for Isla del Sol to find out the latest.

Note that prices may double in high season (June to August and during festivals).

If camping, it's best to ask permission from the local authority and then avoid cultivated land (a nominal payment of B$20 should be offered).

Inti Kala Hostal   HOTEL $
(☑ mobile 7151-6293; hotelintikala@gmail.com; Yumani; r per person incl breakfast US$20; ☎) This place has a massive deck and remodeled rooms with solar-heated showers, fluffy bedspreads and Andean motifs.

Hostal Inti Wayra   HOTEL $
(Yumani; r per person B$70) The amicable and rambling Inti Wayra affords great views from most rooms; these vary a great deal – some are larger and more open. A serene, carpeted meditation area dominates the 2nd floor. This family hotel, like a few on the island, isn't always open.

Hostal Templo del Sol   HOTEL $
(☑ mobile 7351-8970; Yumani; r per person with/without bathroom B$60/40; ☎) Expect electric showers and electrifying views from either side of this refurbished hilltop hostel. There are pigs in the yard, and the wi-fi works. What more could you ask for? Oh, breakfast? That would be extra.

Hotel Imperio del Sol   HOTEL $
(☑ 7196-1863, mobile 7373-4303; Yumani; r per person with/without bathroom B$100/50) This peachy and central place on the hillside running into Yumani is a good bet, with clean rooms and friendly, reliable service.

Inti Wasi Lodge   HOSTEL $
(☑ mobile 7196-0223; Yumani; dm per person B$45, cabins per person incl breakfast B$80) This lodge offers seven basic but cozy cabins with smashing views and there's an on-site pizzeria too. To get here, turn right just before Hostal Illampu as you head up the hill.

Inka Pacha   HOTEL $
(☑ mobile 7197-5569; www.inkapachaecolodge.com; Yumani; r per person B$50, with bathroom & breakfast B$100) What this Hostelling International–affiliated place lacks in luxury, it makes up for in friendliness. The communal area is a nice spot to meet fellow travelers.

Utasawa Lodge   CABAÑAS $$
(☑ mobile 7402-4787; s/d US$50/70; ☎) These four little *casitas* are set on a hillside for classic Titicaca views. More comfortable than most Yumani options, they've got big bathrooms with solar-heated showers.

A BOLIVIAN ATLANTIS?

At low tide an innocuous-looking column of rock peeps just a few centimeters above Lake Titicaca's surface, north of Isla del Sol (and thus off-limits to tourists). Most locals dismiss it as a natural stone column, similar to many others along the shoreline. In 1992 stone boxes containing artifacts (including several made of pure gold) were discovered at the underwater site known as **Marka Pampa** (La Ciudad Submergida). In 2000 and 2004 further excavations near the site revealed a massive stone temple, winding pathways and a surrounding wall, all about 8m underwater. Although it remains unclear who was responsible for the structures, it has been postulated that they could be as much as 6000 years old. Some even say they are the lost traces of Atlantis. Investigations – and conspiracy theories – are ongoing.

Hostal Jallalla   HOTEL $$
(☑ mobile 6816-5404; Yumani; r incl breakfast B$300; ☎) Known for having strong wi-fi, Hostal Jallalla is clean and perfectly located near both the restaurants at Yumani and the turnoff to Mirador Palla Khasa. It's banana yellow; you can't miss it.

Hostal Puerta del Sol   HOTEL $$
(☑ mobile 7350-6995; Yumani; s with/without bathroom B$150/40, cabin per person B$150, d B$250) Located on the promontory on top of the hill, this friendly option has good views from most rooms (number 14 is awesome), clean sheets and a nice terrace. The rooms with bathrooms are much better, and the Andean textiles add a nice touch. Passive solar heating in the cabins helps keep you warm at night.

Hostal Las Cabañas   CABIN $$
(☑ mobile 7353-1339; Yumani; s/d incl breakfast B$80/160; ☎) Perched on the hill leading into town from the dock, these simple adobe bungalows afford great views and have 24-hour hot water. However, the beds are a bit bowed and the rooms need some maintenance.

★ La Estancia Ecolodge   LODGE $$$
(☑ 2-244-0989; www.ecolodge-laketiticaca.com; La Estancia; s/d incl breakfast & dinner US$120/154; ☎) ✔ These delightful adobe cottages are set above pre-Incan terraces facing snow-capped Illampu. They are authentically ecological with solar-powered showers, sun-powered

hot-boxes for heaters and Aymará thatched roofs. Staff can arrange hiking, boat trips and mystic ceremonies. La Estancia is a 15-minute walk from Yumani (p100).

★Palla Khasa   CABIN $$$
(☑ mobile 7321-1585; www.pallakhasalodgeand tours.com; Yumani; bungalows incl breakfast B$570-750) About 300m north of Yumani proper, this top choice has beautifully manicured grounds and 14 circular stone bungalows with gas-heated showers, tiled bathrooms and great views. The restaurant is highly recommended for regional cuisine cooked in an earthen oven. Camping is available nearby if you spend money in the restaurant.

La Posada del Inca   HISTORIC HOTEL $$$
(☑ La Paz 2-233-7533; www.crillontours.com; r from B$700) This converted 1700s-era hacienda boasts beautiful wood-carved furnishings, colorful gardens and cloud-like beds. It can only be booked as part of a packaged trip to the island with Crillon Tours (p105).

✗ Eating

There are more pizzerias in Yumani than Titicaca has *trucha*. Many midrange and top-end accommodation options have good restaurants, most of which are blessed with good views – those on the ridge are special for the sunset. Nearly all menus are identical; *almuerzos* (set lunches) and set dinners cost between B$25 and B$30.

Restaurant Pachamama   CAFE $
(☑ mobile 7351-8970; mains B$30; ⊘ 8am-9:30pm; 🖥) Sit back in a rocking chair and enjoy the view while you munch on pizzas, sandwiches or a *tortilla de quinoa*. This is one of the few places in Yumani that opens for breakfast. Wi-fi access costs extra.

★Las Velas   INTERNATIONAL $$
(lasvelassunisland@gmail.com; Yumani; mains B$50-70; ⊘ 4-11pm; 🖉) Want a candle-lit dinner of organic vegetarian pizza at 4000m? Head to this beloved hilltop restaurant with wonderful westerly views. There are also pastas and traditional Bolivian fare like trout and kingfish. Perfect for a beer or wine at sunset, too.

Take the path up to Yumani and turn left into the forest at the sign for Las Velas (bring a flashlight).

You can camp next to Las Velas for free if you frequent the restaurant for food or drinks. There are plenty of board games, cards and musical instruments here to keep you from getting bored.

❶ Getting There & Away

You can reach Isla del Sol by ferry from either Copacabana or Yampupata, or with a guided tour.

Ferry tickets may be purchased at the **Asociación Unión Marines** (Costañera, Copacabana; one-way/round-trip B$20/30; ⊘ departs Copacabana 8:30am & 1:30pm) ticket kiosks on the beach in Copacabana or from town agencies (save yourself the trouble and buy direct). Boats land at either Pilko Kaina or Escalera del Inca near Yumani. Return trips leave Yumani at 10:30am and between 3pm and 4pm (one-way B$25).

CONSTRUCTION OF A TOTORA-REED BOAT

The construction of *totora*-reed boats is an art form. Green reeds are gathered from the lake shallows and left to dry in the sun. Once free of moisture, they are organized into fat bundles and lashed together with strong grass. In former days, a sail of reeds was often added. These bloated little canoes don't last long; after several months of use they become waterlogged and begin to rot and sink. Traditionally, the canoes often would have been stored some distance away from the water to increase their lifespan. Now the boats are made and used mainly for tourism purposes, and are rarely 100% reeds.

Dr Thor Heyerdahl, the Norwegian adventurer and ethnographer, wanted to test his theory that migration and early contact occurred between the ancient peoples of North Africa and the Americas. He planned to show the feasibility of traveling great distances using the boats of the period, in this case, papyrus craft.

Heyerdahl's first and most notable adventure was on the *Kon-Tiki*, which sailed for 101 days and more than 4000 miles (6437km) in 1947 from coastal Peru to Polynesia. In 1970 he solicited the help of the well-known shipbuilders from Lake Titicaca's Isla Suriqui, the Limachi brothers and Paulino Esteban, to design and construct his vessel *Ra II*, which he sailed from Morocco to Barbados (the first *Ra*, made in Lake Chad in Africa, fell apart in the water). Esteban's son, Fermin, showcases reed-building techniques and recounts the stories of his and his father's expeditions with Heyerdahl and others in the Eco Village at Inca Utama Hotel & Spa (p106).

Titicaca Tours (Costañera, Copacabana; round-trip B$30; ⊘ departs Copacabana 8:30am) will take you to both Isla del Sol and Isla de la Luna in half a day – two hours to explore the former and one hour at the latter. However, it's highly recommended to stay overnight or longer on one of the islands.

Asociación Transport Yampu Tour Lacustre runs boats between Yampupata and Isla del Sol for B$130. Prices are per boat.

❶ Getting Around

There are no vehicles on Isla del Sol, so visitors are limited to hiking along rocky trails (some are now paved in Inca style) or traveling by boat.

Isla de la Luna

POP 120 / ELEV 3808M

Legend has it that the small Island of the Moon was where Viracocha commanded the moon to rise in the sky. However, its spiritual significance did not stop the Bolivian government from using this secluded outpost as a political prison for much of the 20th century.

The island is way smaller, way drier and way less touristed than its solar counterpart, and if you only have a day, you are better off heading to Isla del Sol. That said, for slightly more adventurous experiences this is a good alternative, and it's easy enough to tack a half-day here onto your Isla del Sol trip.

Most boats arrive on the eastern side of the island, where you'll find a visitor center, hostel, restaurant and artisan stands.

◉ Sights

Templo de las Vírgenes RUINS
(Map p99; B$10) The ruins of an Inca nunnery and temple dedicated to the Virgins of the Sun occupy an amphitheater-like valley on the northeast shore where most ferries drop you. It's constructed of stone set in adobe mortar and was likely initially built by the Tiwanaku.

🏃 Activities

Bolivia Amphibian Initiative SNORKELING
(www.bolivianamphibianinitiative.org; snorkel trip B$300, with transport from Copacabana B$450) Strap on a snorkel and get out into the lake in search of the Titicaca water frog. Book in advance by email.

Mirador Trail HIKING
A walk up to the eucalyptus grove at the summit where shepherds graze their flocks is rewarded with a spectacular vista of aquamarine waters, Cerro Illampu and the entire snow-covered Cordillera Real.

SANTIAGO DE OKOLA

For a genuine cultural experience, don't miss an overnight stay at **Santiago de Okola** (☑ mobile 7154-3918; www.santiago deokola.com; 3-day program departing from La Paz from US$130) on the road to Apolobamba. With the support of external funding bodies, Okola has formed a community-based agro-tourism company to conserve its rich agricultural heritage and generate income for members. Visitors stay with families and participate in daily life. Great beaches, walks and hikes abound, including a short climb to the crest of a magnificent rocky outcrop known as the Sleeping Dragon. Other activities included in the multi-day programs are weaving classes, a chance to learn about local medicinal plants and Andean cooking classes.

❶ Getting There & Away

Asociación Transport Yampu Tour Lacustre (☑ mobile 7525-4675; Yampupata; ⊘ 8am-6pm) runs round-trip journeys from Yampupata to Isla de la Luna (B$250 per boat).

Asociación Unión Marines (Costañera, Copacabana; one-way/round-trip to Isla del Sol B$20/40, round-trip to Isla de la Luna B$40; ⊘ departs Copacabana 8:30am & 1:30pm) runs trips from Copacabana at 8:30am, returning from the island at 3pm (B$40).

Huatajata

☑2 / POP 3180 / ELEV 3800M

This little lakefront *pueblo* on the road from La Paz to Copacabana is a good kick-off point for trips to Islas Kalahuta, Suriqui and Pariti, as well as a fantastic place to learn about the culture of building reed boats.

The cheapest lodging in town is at **Hostal Inti Karka** (☑ mobile 7197-8959; Ruta Nacional 2, Km 87; r B$80). Maximo, the owner, can take you to the neighboring islands. Inca Utama Hotel & Spa (p106) is run by Crillon Tours and offers moderately upscale resort-style rooms, guided trips to the rest of the lake and four on-site museums.

☞ Tours

Crillon Tours TOURS
(Map p50; ☑ 233-7533; www.titicaca.com; Av Camacho 1223, La Paz; ⊘ 9am-noon & 2:30-7pm Mon-Fri, to noon Sat) An upmarket agency with a hydrofoil service offering various day and multiday

packages on Lake Titicaca kicking off from Huatajata (or La Paz). Inquire at Inca Utama Hotel & Spa in the village.

Valtours TOURS
(Map p54; ☑ mobile 7016-6012; www.valtours.com. bo; Av 16 de Julio 1416, Edificio San Pablo, Office 607, La Paz; ☉ 9am-7pm Mon-Fri, to 12:30pm Sat) Formerly Balsa Tours, this agency offers motor excursions from its resort at Puerto Pérez to Islas Pariti, Kalahuta and Suriqui.

⏢ Sleeping

Inca Utama Hotel & Spa HOTEL $$
(☑La Paz 2-233-7533; www.crillontours.com; Ruta Nacional 2, Km 86; s/d/ste incl breakfast B$340/425/690; ☏) Clean, if a bit dated, this lakefront hotel is worth the extra bolivianos for the on-site museums, which cover reed boats, Kallawaya medicines and altiplano culture. There's also an Andean Observatory for nighttime stargazing and an Eco Pueblo with local weavers. Try to book a room in the newer wing.

ⓘ Getting There & Away

The easiest way to get here is on the Copacabana–La Paz bus line. Buses depart from the cemetery district in La Paz when full (B$20, two hours). When you board, be sure to ask the driver to be dropped off in Huatajata. You can flag down these same buses for onward travel to Copacabana or the return trip to La Paz.

Islas de Wiñaymarka

Lago de Wiñaymarka's most frequented islands, Kalahuta, Suriqui and Pariti, are easily visited in a half-day trip and provide a more authentic look at the region and its people than the islands near Copacabana. Tourism has become an economic mainstay to supplement fishing, but it has not been entirely beneficial to the Kalahuta people who reside on the islands. Please behave sensitively; ask permission before taking photos and refuse requests for money or gifts.

⌕ Tours

Trips to the islands with Crillon Tours (p105) also include a stop at a natural floating island where members of the local Uru community explain how (and why) they used to live atop this lake. Hint: instead of giving up their freedom to the Inca and Tiwanaku they gave up their lands.

Maximo Catari GUIDE
(☑mobile 7197-8959; Hostal Inti Karka, Huatajata) For a local option, try Maximo Catari who is

based in Huatajata. He speaks Spanish and runs informative day visits to Isla Suriqui and Isla Pariti (both islands, B$400), including a stop at a floating island.

ⓘ Getting There & Away

There is no regular public transportation to the islands, though you can easily arrange a boat in Huatajata. Many tour agencies in La Paz, including Valtours and Crillon Tours (p105), offer day trips here.

Isla Kalahuta

When lake levels are low, Kalahuta ('stone houses' in Aymará) becomes a peninsula. Its shallow shores are lined with beds of *totora* reed, the versatile building material for which Titicaca is famous. By day fisherfolk ply the island's main bay in their wooden boats (*totora*-reed boats are no longer used).

During Inca times the island served as a cemetery. The west side of it is still dotted with stone *chullpas* (funerary towers) and abandoned stone houses. Legends abound about the horrible fate that will befall anyone who desecrates the cemetery, and locals have long refused to live beyond the island's only village, **Queguaya**.

Isla Pariti

This tiny island, surrounded by *totora*-reed marshes, made world news in 2004 when a team of Bolivian and Finnish archaeologists discovered ancient Tiwanaku ceramics here in a small circular pit. While the American archaeologist Wendell Bennet was the first to excavate the island in 1934, the more recent finds uncovered some extraordinary shards and ceramics, believed to be ritualistic offerings as they were intentionally destroyed. Many of these stunning pots and *ch'alladores* (vases) are displayed in **Museo de Pariti** (☑mobile 7656-1170; Isla Pariti; B$15), while the remainder are displayed in Museo Nacional de Arqueología in La Paz. These exhibits reflect the high artistic achievements of Tiwanaku potters. Don't miss the *Señor de los patos*.

Isla Suriqui

This island used to be more famous than Isla del Sol as the place where Bolivia's most renowned boat-builders lived. Many of the *totora*-reed crafts used for open-sea expeditions were built by men who honed their skills on Suriqui. Nowadays, the island is better known for its woven handicrafts.

The Cordilleras & Yungas

Best Places to Eat

➡ Toto (p119)

➡ Helados El Oso Goloso (p133)

➡ Carla's Garden Pub (p119)

➡ Villa Bonita (p119)

Best Places to Stay

➡ Hostal Sol y Luna (p117)

➡ Altai Oasis (p133)

➡ Country House (p125)

➡ El Encanto Sorata (p133)

➡ Posada Nirvana Inn (p126)

Why Go?

Caught between the Andes and the Amazon, this rugged region has just about everything you could ask for from your Bolivian adventure.

For the vertically inspired, there are glacier-capped 6000m peaks and adrenaline-charged mountain-bike descents. Nature lovers can seek out the cloud forests and hillside semitropical Yungas towns of Chulumani, Coroico and Sorata, where you can hike to nearby waterfalls, start your river trip into the Amazon, go mountain biking or simply enjoy the breeze from a mountain hideaway.

Far off the tourist trail, the areas around the Quimsa Cruz and Cordillera Apolobamba offer large swaths of wilderness, a few lost ruins and great opportunities for adventure.

Everywhere in between you'll find treks along preserved Inca trails, wildlife-watching opportunities aplenty, warm weather, cool breezes and a pervading air of hard-won tranquility.

When to Go
Coroico

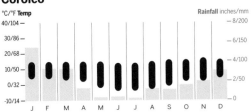

May–Sep Climbing season means dry weather and good visibility.	Oct–Dec Heavy rains make roads challenging and occasionally impassable.	Jan–May Cheaper hotels, fewer people and high rivers. Remote travel can be tough.

The Cordilleras & Yungas Highlights

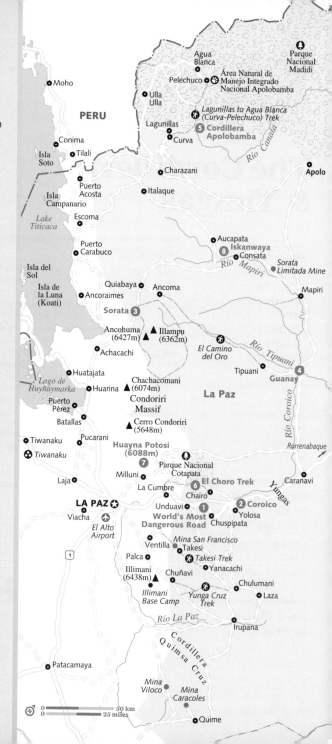

1 World's Most Dangerous Road (p117) Getting dusty as you cheat death on this mountain-bike descent of nearly 3600m.

2 Coroico (p114) Treating yourself to a few days of warm weather, a hammock and a poolside drink.

3 Sorata (p130) Embracing your adventurous spirit while climbing, hiking and mountain biking in the nearby hills.

4 Guanay (p129) Setting off in a boat (or on a raft) along the river road to Rurrenabaque via a series of jungle-clad canyons.

5 Cordillera Apolobamba (p135) Hiking in the footsteps of the mystical Kallawaya healers.

6 El Choro Trek (p120) Traveling on the path of the Inca on an inspiring multi-day journey.

7 Huayna Potosí (p110) Strapping on crampons, swinging an ice axe and bagging a 6000m peak.

8 Iskanwaya (p134) Channeling Indiana Jones as you explore the lost ruins of a little-understood culture.

History

With its steep mountains, plunging valleys and rugged terrain, the Cordillera and Yungas region has been slow to develop economically. Boom-and-bust cycles kept the region a political backwater until the end of the 2000s when new emphasis on coca production brought it to the forefront of national discourse.

The first settlers to the Yungas were indigenous groups from the altiplano, who were inspired by economic opportunity. Gold was discovered in the Tipuani and Mapiri valleys in the days of the Inca empire. When the Spanish arrived they immediately began prospecting. To enrich the royal treasury, they forced locals to labor for them, and the region became one of the continent's most prolific producers of gold. Later, the fertile valleys were used as the agricultural breadbasket to fuel mining operations in the altiplano. Today the rivers of the lower Yungas are ravaged by wildcat prospectors and bigger mining outfits.

Coca and cocaine have also played a central role in the development of the region's modern economy. The Yungas' coca has been cultivated since pre-Columbian times, and much of Bolivia's legal production takes place here. The rise to power of former coca farmer Evo Morales has meant new political weight for the growers of the region. However, they have been unable to find a united voice, with two main factions forming: Las Proteccionistas, the more established highland farmers who want to defend the localized economy, and the more numerous Nacionalistas, from newly colonized lower altitude areas who seek to expand the coca economy. Las Proteccionistas claim that coca is the only viable crop at the altitudes at which they live and that President Morales' policies (which support alternative legalized uses of coca in medicines, foods and drinks) threaten their livelihoods by opening up coca cultivation to farmers beyond the region.

During October 2003 – the dying days of President Sánchez de Lozada's government – the Yungas was the scene of roadblocks and violent clashes between police, the military and *campesinos* (subsistence farmers) protesting at the selling of the nation's natural resources (principally gas) and the mistreatment of the indigenous population. More than 100 tourists found themselves trapped in the town of Sorata for more than a week during the demonstrations, until a military mission was launched to 'rescue' them, sparking violent clashes that left six people dead. The fallout from the violence and mismanagement of the situation led to the resignation of Sánchez de Lozada and ultimately to the election of Morales.

🛈 Getting There & Around

Access is entirely overland and the region's unpaved roads can get mucky and washed out in the rainy season. Scheduled public transportation to many trekking and mountaineering base camps is infrequent, so chartered private transportation from La Paz is used more often here than in other regions of the country.

If you are scared of heights, or don't have much faith in Bolivian bus drivers, ask for an aisle seat. Roads are narrow; drops are steep; and some of the routes, such as to Chulumani or Aucapata, are particularly hairy.

Traveling between towns in the region often necessitates backtracking to La Paz or taking a somewhat costly taxi ride across the valley.

CORDILLERA REAL

Bolivia's Cordillera Real has more than 600 peaks over 5000m, most of which are relatively accessible and many of which are just a few hours' drive from La Paz. They're also still free of the growing bureaucracy attached to climbing and trekking in the Himalaya. There are many peaks to entice the experienced climber, and whether you choose a well-known climb or one of the lesser known, climbing in the Bolivian Andes is always an adventure. The area also has fun treks, bikes and hikes for non-climbers, so you can build your own adventure.

The best season for climbing in the Cordillera Real is May to September. Note that most of the climbs are technical and require climbing experience, a reputable climbing guide and proper technical equipment. You should be fully acclimatized to the altitude before attempting any of the ascents.

Guides & Equipment

By far the easiest way of tackling these mountains is to go on a guided climb. Several La Paz agencies (p58) offer trips that include transportation, *refugio* (mountain hut) accommodations, equipment hire and a guide. Some of the same agencies will rent you equipment if you want to tackle the peaks without taking the tour, but this option should only be considered by those with extensive mountaineering experience at similar altitudes.

Prices start at around B$900 to B$1400 for an ascent of Huayna Potosí, but are significantly higher for more technical climbs – around B$3500-plus for Illimani, for example. A number of agencies and foreign climbing-tour agents (p357) offer packages that bundle ascents of several of the Cordillera Real peaks. The combinations are as endless as, well, your oxygen supply and money. Choose your tour agent carefully; cheaper does not mean better.

You can also independently contract registered mountain guides via The Asociación de Guías de Montaña (www.agmtb.org). If you are in a group, it's worth paying extra to make sure that there are two guides accompanying you, so that if one member of the group succumbs to altitude sickness the ascent isn't compromised.

Huayna Potosí

This is Bolivia's most popular major peak because of its imposing beauty and ease of access, as well as the fact that it's 88m over the magic 6000m figure (but 26ft under the magic 20,000ft figure). While most people come to Huayna Potosí to climb, you can also stay at the mountain lodge, and head out for some fun hikes or mountain biking.

Though some people attempt to climb Huayna Potosí in one day, it is not recommended. You're better off attempting the climb in two or three days (three days is best for newbies to ensure you properly acclimatize and learn the ropes before you hit higher sections). Guided trips cost between B$900 and B$1400.

🏃 Activities

La Paz mountain-bike outfits (p57) take adventurous riders to Huayna Potosí for the descent from the base of the spectacular mountain, past Zongo Dam, and then along a dramatic 40km, 3600m descent into the lush and humid Yungas. This is a dead-end road that lacks a great destination at its finish, but there's little vehicular traffic, so you tend to have the road to yourself and can open up the throttle a little more.

🛏 Sleeping

Huayna Potosí Refugio   REFUGE $
(📞7252-8937; www.huayna-potosi.com; Paso Zongo Km 42; dm incl breakfast B$210, dinner

B$50) Run by a La Paz tour company, this is a comfortable, heated spot and a fine place to acclimatize – there's pretty walking to be done in the area, and plenty of advice and good cheer on hand. Must reserve ahead.

Refugio Casa Blanca   REFUGE $
(Paso Zongo Km 41; dm B$50, incl dinner/full board B$80/120) Right by the La Paz–Zongo road (buses will let you off outside) is this simple but very hospitable spot. You can also camp here.

Huayna Potosí Overnight Hike

A 4WD from La Paz to the trailhead at Paso Zongo costs around B$500 one-way for up to five people. A taxi should cost a bit less with haggling (aim for B$250 one way and make sure your driver knows the way). Daily Trans Zongo minibuses leave when full from Plaza Ballivián in El Alto starting at 6am (B$13, one hour).

Huayna Potosí is popular, so lots of climbers head out that way during the climbing season. If you want a lift, check with specialist climbing agencies; someone will probably have a 4WD going on the day you want, and you can share costs for the trip.

The Route

Start Paso Zongo

End Paso Zongo

Duration Two to three days

Distance 11km (to summit)

Difficulty Medium

There are a number of routes to the top of Huayna Potosí; we describe the North Peak route, which is most popular with visitors and tour companies. It's appealing because it can be climbed by beginners with a competent guide and technical equipment. Fit beginners, that is; it's quite steep toward the end and it's a tough climb.

From the Huayna Potosí Refugio, cross the dam and follow the aqueduct until you reach the third path on your left, signed 'Glacier Huayna Potosí.' Take this path to a glacial stream then through and across the rocks to reach the ridge of a moraine. Near the end of the moraine – where you'll pay B$20 to climb the mountain at a small rock hut – descend slightly to your right and then ascend the steep scree gullies. At the top, bear left and follow the cairns to reach the **Campo Rocas Glacier** (5200m). There are sleeping huts (around B$60 per person) and dry places to camp. Most tours stop here, before commencing the ascent at around 2am.

The glacier is crevassed, especially after July, so rope up while crossing it. Ascend the initial slopes then follow a long, gradually ascending traverse to the right, before turning left and climbing steeply to a flat area between 5500m and 5700m known as **Campo Argentino** (a seldom-used alternate sleeping spot). It will take you about two to three hours to reach this point. Camp to the right of the path if staying here, but note that the area further to the right is heavily crevassed, especially later in the season.

The following morning you should leave from here between 4am and 6am. Follow the path/trench out of Campo Argentino, and head uphill to your right until you join a ridge. Turn left here and cross a flat stretch to reach the steep and exposed **Polish Ridge** (named in honor of the Polish climber who fell and died while soloing in 1994). Here you cross a series of rolling glacial hills and crevasses to arrive below the summit face. Either climb straight up the face to the summit or cross along the base of it to join the ridge that rises to the left. This ridge provides thrilling views down the 1000m-high west face. Either route will bring you to the summit in four to six hours from Campo Argentino.

The descent to Campo Argentino from the summit takes two to three hours; from there, it's another one or two hours back to the *refugios* at Paso Zongo.

Condoriri Massif

Condoriri Massif is actually a cluster of 13 peaks ranging from 5100m to 5648m. The highest of these, Cabeza del Cóndor (Head of the Condor) has twin winglike ridges flowing from either side of the summit. Known as Las Alas (The Wings), these ridges cause the peak to resemble a condor lifting its wings.

Cabeza del Cóndor is a challenging climb following an exposed ridge, and should be attempted only by experienced climbers. However, a number of other peaks in the Condoriri Massif, including the beautiful Pequeño Alpamayo (5370m), can be attempted by beginners with a competent guide. The hike to the glacier is fun for non-climbers.

According to local legend, the massif is the last refuge of the biggest and most ferocious condors in the Andes, which kidnap children and educate them to become

'man-condors', and then return them to the human population to bring terror and death.

Condoriri Massif Overnight Hike

There is no public transportation from La Paz to Condoriri. A 4WD to the start of the walk-in at the dam at Laguna Tuni (or alternatively Riconada, about an hour closer) costs around B$550. You can also trek the 24km from Milluni to the Laguna Tuni dam on the road to Paso Zongo. Take everything you will need with you, as there is nowhere to buy provisions once you begin the trek.

It isn't possible to drive beyond the dam because a locked gate bars the road. Some drivers know a way around it, but if you need to hire pack animals you'll have to do so before you reach the dam. Locals charge B$80 to B$100 per day for mules, and a bit less for llamas, which can carry less. You may have to sign into the Parque Nacional Condoriri.

The Route
Start Laguna Tuni
End Laguna Tuni

Duration Two to three days

Distance 14km (to summit)

Difficulty Hard

Access to the Condoriri Massif begins from Laguna Tuni. Here, a rough road circles south around the lake and continues up a drainage trending north. Once you're in this valley, you'll have a view of the Cabeza del Cóndor and Las Alas.

From the end of the road, follow the obvious paths up along the right side of the valley until you reach a large lake, Chiar Khota. Follow the right shore of the lake to arrive at the base camp, which is an easy three hours from Laguna Tuni. There are toilet facilities here. The community charges B$20 to stay the night, plus a B$30 entrance fee. There are also five basic huts that cost about B$30 per person.

Leave base camp at about 3am and follow the path up the east-trending valley through boulders, passing some lakes on your left. Keep heading up the main trail, on the right-hand side of the valley, until you reach the glacier. You should reach this point in about 1½ hours from base camp.

Here you should rope up and put on crampons. Head left across the glacier before rising to the col (lowest point of the ridge), taking care to avoid the crevasses. Climb to the right up the rock-topped summit Tarija (5240m), which affords impressive views of Pequeño Alpamayo, before dropping 100m down a scree and rock slope to rejoin a glacier on the other side. From there, follow the main ridge to the summit. The ridge has some exposure.

Ancohuma

Ancohuma is the highest peak in the Sorata Massif, towering on the remote northern edge of the Cordillera Real. It was not climbed until 1919 and remains a challenging climb that should only be attempted with a guide for all but the most experienced of mountaineers.

Ancohuma Overnight Hike

The peak is accessed via Sorata, where you can hire a taxi to take you up to La Mina. From here it's just one hour by foot up to the trailhead at Laguna Chillata (4200m). If you have a serious amount of gear, you can rent a mule (B$120) or porter (B$150) to carry it.

The Route

Start Laguna Chillata

End Laguna Chillata

Duration Five days

Distance 15km (to summit)

Difficulty Very Hard

Ancohuma is most often climbed from the more easily accessed western route, using Laguna Glacial as a base camp. Hike from Laguna Chillata (p131) to the base camp at Laguna Glacial. From here the route climbs the obvious moraine and then ascends the glacier, over fields of extremely dangerous crevasses. Most climbers make a high camp at 5400m or 5800m. The route then climbs to the bergschrund (crevasse) and across a relatively level ice plateau to the summit pyramid. This is most easily climbed via the north ridge; the first part is quite steep and icy, but then gets easier toward the summit.

It's essential to seek out advice and information in Sorata (p130), and to hire a guide, as Ancohuma offers some of the most difficult (but rewarding!) climbing in Bolivia.

Illimani

Illimani, the 6438m giant overlooking La Paz, was first climbed in 1898 by a party led by WM Conway, a pioneer 19th-century alpinist. Although it's not a difficult climb technically, the combination of altitude and ice conditions warrants serious consideration and caution.

Technical equipment is essential above the snow line; caution is especially needed on the exposed section immediately above Nido de Cóndores where several climbers have perished.

Illimani Overnight Hike

The easiest way to reach Puente Roto, the first camp, is via Pinaya, a three-hour trip by 4WD from La Paz (about B$850).

Alternatively, a daily 5am bus (B$10) leaves from near La Paz's Mercado Rodríguez to the village of Quilihuaya, from where you'll have a three-hour slog to Pinaya – complete with a 400m elevation gain. Buses return from Quilihuaya to La Paz several days a week at around 8:30am, but if you're relying on public transportation you should carry extra food just in case of delays or changes.

An alternative route to the base camp is via Cohoni. Buses and *camiones* (flatbed trucks) leave La Paz for Cohoni (B$30, five hours) early afternoon Monday to Saturday from the corner of Calles and Boquerón. These return from Cohoni around 8:30am and may take anywhere from five hours to all day depending on which route is followed.

The Route

Start Pinaya

End Pinaya

Duration Four days

Distance 10km (to summit)

Difficulty Hard

The normal route to Pico Sur, the highest of Illimani's five summits, is straightforward but heavily crevassed. If you don't have technical glacier experience, hire a competent professional guide.

At Pinaya you can hire porters (B$150) and mules (B$120) to carry your gear to Puente Roto or to the high camp at Nido de Cóndores. It is a wise investment. From Pinaya, it's two to three hours' walk to the first camp at Puente Roto. An alternative route to the base camp is via Cohoni.

The route to Nido de Cóndores (5400m), a rock platform beside the glacier, is a four- to six-hour slog up a rock ridge from Puente Roto. There's no water at Nido de Cóndores, so you'll have to melt snow – bring sufficient fuel for your stove.

From Nido de Cóndores you need to set off at about 2am. Follow the path in the snow leading uphill from the camp; the path grows narrower and steeper, then flattens out a bit before becoming steeper again. It then crosses a series of crevasses before ascending to the right to reach a level section. From here, aim for the large break in the skyline to the left of the summit, taking care to avoid the two major crevasses, and cross one steep section that is iced over from July onwards. After you pass through the skyline break, turn right and continue up onto the summit ridge. Ascending the final three vertical meters involves walking 400m along the ridge at over 6400m elevation.

Plan on six to 10 hours for the climb from Nido de Cóndores to the summit and three to four hours to descend back to camp.

If possible, continue down from Nido de Cóndores to Puente Roto on the same day. The 1000m descent is not appealing after a long day, but your body will thank you the following day and will recover more quickly at the lower altitude. You'll also avoid having to melt snow for a second night.

On the fourth day you can walk from Puente Roto back out to Pinaya in about two hours.

Chachacomani

This 6074m mountain, named for an Andean medicinal herb, is a relatively new climb that typically takes four days. The first day encompasses a three-hour drive to Alto Cruz Pampa from La Paz, and from there it's a three- to four-hour walk to the base camp at 4600m. It's recommended to hire donkeys or horses to transport your equipment.

On the second day, a three- to four-hour walk takes you to the beautiful high camp, beside the impressive Chachacomani Glacier, at 5200m. For this section, porters charge about B$120 per day to heft 20kg.

Day three is a long hike with crampons and ropes to the summit: a six-hour walk that isn't technically difficult. From up top there are spectacular views of Lake Titicaca and the entire cordillera. Return to base camp that night, and on the fourth day hike back down to vehicles for the journey back to La Paz.

THE YUNGAS

The transition zone between dry highlands and humid lowlands, the Yungas is where the Andes falls away into the Amazon Basin. Above the steaming, forested depths rise the near-vertical slopes of the Cordillera Real and the Cordillera Quimsa Cruz, which halt altiplano-bound clouds, causing them to deposit bounteous rainfall. Vegetation is abundant, and tropical fruit, coffee, coca, cacao and tobacco grow with minimal tending.

The Yungas is composed of two provinces in La Paz department – Nor and Sud Yungas (oddly, most of Sud Yungas lies well to the north of Nor Yungas) – as well as parts of other provinces. Coroico and Chulumani are the main population centers. Most people here claim Aymará descent but there is also a noticeable Afro-Bolivian population. Visitors often find locals to be more friendly here than in the colder altiplano (must be the heat).

Coroico & Yolosa

⬛2 / POP 19,330 / ELEV 1750M (5741FT)

With warm weather, spectacular views, good resort-style hotels for all budgets and an infectious laid-back air, Coroico is the most visited tourist town in the Yungas. It's perched eyrie-like on the shoulder of Cerro Uchumachi and commands a far-ranging view across forested canyons, cloud-wreathed mountain peaks, patchwork agricultural lands, citrus orchards, coffee plantations and dozens of small settlements.

Coroico is derived from the Quechua word *coryguayco*, meaning 'golden hill.' The town's biggest attraction is its slow pace, which allows plenty of time for swimming, sunbathing and hammock-swinging.

The village of Yolosa is located about 7km from Coroico along the World's Most Dangerous Road. It has a few cool hangouts, an animal refuge, and a steady stream of dust-caked Dangerous Road bikers who generally end their rides here.

◉ Sights

★La Senda Verde

Wildlife Sanctuary ANIMAL SANCTUARY

(www.sendaverde.org; Yolosa; B$100, bear visit extra B$20; ☺10am-4pm) At 12-hectare Senda Verde, there's a new concept: humans are 'caged' while most of the 200-plus monkeys run free. This protects people and monkeys alike (adult monkeys can be aggressive, and sick humans can infect their simian cousins). Toucans, caimans, Andean bears, ocelots and margays are among the other wild residents. There's a nice buffet-style restaurant on-site. Located 500m north of Yolosa (B$40 taxi or B$10 minibus from Coroico).

The refuge provides a sanctuary for animals that have been rescued from illegal traffickers. Reservations are required. You can stay overnight (p118), or simply come for an hour-long tour. Volunteering is possible (two-week minimum) for B$1370 per week, including three meals.

☂ Activities

El Encuentro SWIMMING

Book a trip with a Coroico agency for an afternoon swim in this 'secret' spot of emerald pools located at the joining of the Río Santa Bárbara and Río San Cristobal.

Zzip the Flying Fox ADVENTURE

(⬛231-3849; www.facebook.com/ziplinebolivia; Yolosa; single trips B$220; ☺9am-5pm) Three zipline sections take you flying at speeds of up to 85km/h through the forest canopy near Yolosa. The 1500m zipline can be combined with trips down the World's Most Dangerous Road. Book your ticket at agencies in La Paz or Coroico.

Hiking

Hill walking around here is more strolling than trekking, which appeals to stiff-legged hikers straight off the El Choro trek (p120), which ends near Coroico, or those nursing bruised bottoms after the hectic mountain-bike descent from La Paz. Birders might catch a glimpse of the regional symbol, the Andean cock-of-the-rock.

It can get extremely hot while hiking, so carry plenty of water. You should also bring bug spray, and consider wearing long sleeves and pants, as well as bringing a headlamp along. Single travelers – especially women – should check with their hotels about the security situation before heading out.

El Calvario WALKING

For pretty views, El Calvario is an easy 20-minute hike from town. Here, the **Stations of the Cross** lead to a grassy knoll and chapel. You can continue to **Cerro Uchumachi** (a five-hour round-trip), which affords terrific valley views.

El Vagante WALKING, SWIMMING

A good day's walk (7km) will take you to El Vagante, an area of natural stone swimming holes in the **Río Santa Bárbara**.

Follow the road from Coroico toward Arapata for about two hours. Turn left at a fork in the road and head steeply downhill past Comunidad Miraflores; at the second fork, bear right (the left fork goes to Santa Ana). After two hours along this route, which features a stretch with some pre-Columbian terraces, you'll reach a cement bridge. Turn right before the bridge and follow the river downstream for 20 minutes to a series of swimming holes and waterfalls. The water isn't drinkable, so carry water or purification tablets – and bear in mind that the return route is uphill all the way!

Cerro Uchumachi Walk HIKING

For a pretty walk, head uphill toward Hotel Esmeralda (p118) and on up to El Calvario, an easy 20-minute hike. At El Calvario the **Stations of the Cross** lead to a grassy knoll and chapel. From here the trail continues 3km to Cerro Uchumachi, which

Coroico

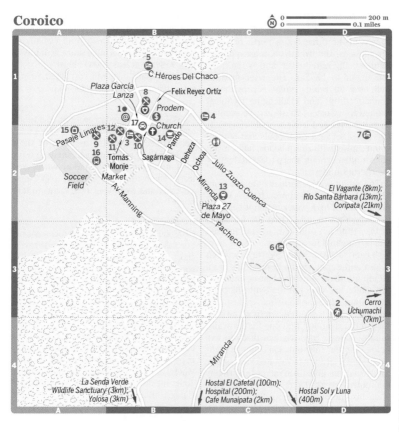

Map labels:

Plaza García Lanza

C Héroes Del Chaco

Felix Reyez Ortíz

Prodem

Church

Pasaje Linares

Tomás Monje

Sagárnaga

Soccer Field

Market

Av Manning

Deheza

Ochoa

Pando

Miranda

Julio Zuazo Cuenca

Plaza 27 de Mayo

Pacheco

El Vagante (8km); Río Santa Bárbara (13km); Coripata (21km)

Cerro Uchumachi (7km)

La Senda Verde Wildlife Sanctuary (3km); Yolosa (3km)

Hostal El Cafetal (100m); Hospital (200m); Cafe Munaipata (2km)

Hostal Sol y Luna (400m)

0 — 200 m / 0 — 0.1 miles

THE CORDILLERAS & YUNGAS COROICO & YOLOSA

Coroico

Activities, Courses & Tours
1 Coroico Travel	B1
2 El Calvario	D3
Tour del Cafe	(see 14)

Sleeping
3 Hostal Kory	B2
4 Hostal Tunqui Eye	C1
5 Hotel Bella Vista	B1
6 Hotel Esmeralda	C3
7 Villa Bonita	D2

Eating
8 Cafe Almendra	B1
9 Carla's Garden Pub	B1

10 Coroico Star	B2
11 Flor de los Andes	B2
12 Toto	B2
Villa Bonita	(see 7)

Drinking & Nightlife
13 Discoteca Búfalo	C2
14 M&M Coffee	B2

Shopping
15 Madres de Clarisa Convent	A2

Transport
16 Bus Terminal	A2
17 Turbus Totaí	B2

towers above the town and affords terrific valley views.

Bring a guide or travel in a group – no incidents have occurred in recent years, but best to play it safe.

Mountain Biking

La Paz agencies take you down the World's Most Dangerous Road (p117) to Yolosa. In Coroico you can rent bikes from Coroico Star (p119) to take you to nearby attractions.

White-Water Rafting

The Río Coroico flows through the Nor Yungas about three hours north of Coroico. This is the country's most popular commercially rafted river, and is the most convenient to La Paz. The river features well over 30 rapids, great surfing holes, dramatic drops and challenging technical maneuvers (most of these can be scouted from the river and from several bridges). It alternates between calm pools and 50m to 900m rapids, with sharp bends, boils, mean holes, undercurrents, sharp rocks and rather treacherous undercuts.

The white water normally ranges from Class II to IV, but may approach Class V during periods of high water (when it becomes too dangerous to raft). There are few spots to take time out and rest, so stay focused and be prepared for surprises.

Access is from the highway between Yolosa and Caranavi; the best put-ins are a 20-minute drive north of Yolosa and near the confluence with the Río Santa Bárbara, a 50-minute drive north of Yolosa. Just look for any track that winds down from the road toward the river and find one that provides suitable access. Trips average three to five hours. For the take-out, look on the right side of the river for a devastated steel bridge (destroyed in a 1998 flood) across a normally diminutive creek. Don't miss it because, after this, climbing to the road up steep jungled slopes is practically impossible, and it's a long, long way to the next possible exit.

The Río Huarinilla flows from Huayna Potosí and Tiquimani down into the Yungas to meet the Río Coroico near Yolosa, and is best accessed from Chairo, at the end of the El Choro trek. Although it's normally Class II and III, high water can swell it into a much more challenging Class IV to V. The full-day trip is best suited to kayaks and narrow paddle rafts. The new Yungas Hwy passes right by the take-out at the confluence of the Ríos Huarinilla and Coroico.

The white water is great, but unfortunately the high tourist season coincides with the dry season. Several agencies in La Paz and around Coroico's plaza offer day-long rafting trips for B$250 to B$350 per person.

🖝 Tours

Cafe Munaipata   TOUR
(☑ 7129-8379; www.cafemunaipata.com; Rincon Munaipata; tours B$120-350) This beautifully manicured coffee plantation 4km from the plaza in Coroico has professional tours that cover everything from picking beans to roasting and taste-testing. It also has on-site lodging (B$200 per person) and a small cafe (the llama filet in a coffee sauce is unmissable). Reserve at least a day ahead.

A taxi from town will cost B$20, or you can catch a passing *micro* for B$5.

Tour del Cafe   TOUR
(☑ 6930-3315; www.facebook.com/tourdelcafe. coroico; Pando s/n, M&M Coffee; 4hr tours B$165) Local coffee expert Mauro, owner of M&M Coffee (p120), runs Spanish-language tours to a nearby coffee plantation where you learn about different strains, pick some 'cherries' and roast your own beans to take home.

Coroico Travel   HIKING
(☑ 7306-3696; www.facebook.com/CoroicoAdmin; Guachalla s/n; ⊙ 8:30am-7pm) Specializes in short day-hikes from Coroico to coca farms, coffee plantations, waterfalls and nearby Afro-Bolivian communities such as Tocaña. Also sells bus tickets to Rurrenabaque. Some guides speak English.

El Vagante Canyoning   OUTDOORS
(☑ 7527-4751; www.elvagante.com; Santa Rosa de Vagante; 6hr tours B$420) Runs canyoning trips from Coroico to Santa Rosa de Vagante, where you'll descend into the Río Vagante. Tours include a picnic lunch. Previous experience is not necessary.

🛏 Sleeping

Coroico has the best lodging options in the Yungas, including everything from sprawling resorts to top-tier budget hotels. On weekends from June to August, hotels are often booked out. It's possible to make advance reservations, but there's no guarantee that all hotels will honor them. On holiday weekends prices may increase by as much as 100%.

Around the tiny village of Yolosa (about 7km from Coroico) there are several ecolodges worth checking out.

Hostal Tunqui Eye   HOTEL $
(☑ 7350-0081; miranda_gui@hotmail.com; Iturralde 4043, Coroico; r per person with/without bathroom B$80/40; ☞) In the ultra-budget spectrum, this solid bet has decent beds with clean(ish) sheets and bizarre panda bedspreads. There are good views from the terrace and some rooms at the end of the halls. An outdoor kitchen is handy for prepping your own grub.

DEADLY TREADLIES & THE WORLD'S MOST DANGEROUS ROAD

Before a new replacement road opened in 2007, the road between La Paz and Coroico was identified as the World's Most Dangerous Road (WMDR) by an Inter-American Development Bank (IDB) report. The moniker was well deserved: an average of 26 vehicles per year disappeared over the edge into the great abyss.

The gravel road is narrow (just over 3.2m wide), with precipitous cliffs, up to 600m drops and few safety barriers. Crosses (aka 'Bolivian caution signs') lining the way testify to the frequency of past vehicular tragedies. The most renowned of these occurred in 1983 when a *camión* (flatbed truck) plunged over the precipice, killing the driver and 100 passengers in the worst accident in the sordid history of Bolivian transportation.

The WMDR is now used almost exclusively by cyclists, support vehicles and the odd tourist bus. Many agencies offering the La Cumbre to Yolosa mountain-bike plunge distribute T-shirts that boast about having survived the road.

Some 27 cyclists have died doing the 64km trip, which has a 3600m vertical descent, and readers have reported close encounters and nasty accidents. Ironically, the now traffic-free road can be more dangerous to cyclists than to vehicles, especially kamikaze freewheeling guides and overconfident cyclists who fail to account for the possibility of oncoming vehicles. Other accidents are due to little or no instruction and preparation, and poor-quality mountain bikes; beware bogus rebranded bikes and recovered brake pads.

Unfortunately, there are no minimum safety standards in place for operators of this trip, and no controls over false advertising, or consequences for unsafe operating practices. In short, many agencies are less than ideal. As such the buyer has to beware, even a bit paranoid; this is one activity where you don't want to be attracted by cheaper deals. Experienced and trained guides, high-quality bikes, well-developed risk-management systems and adequate rescue equipment all cost money, and low-cost companies may stretch the truth about what they provide if it means making another sale. Cost cutting can mean dodgy brakes, poor-quality parts and, literally, a deadly treadly. This, plus inexperienced and untrained guides and little or no rescue and first-aid equipment, is a truly scary combination on the WMDR.

Nuts & Bolts

The trip begins around 7am in La Paz. Your agency will arrange a hotel pickup. From there, you'll bus it up to the *cumbre* (summit), about 45 minutes outside La Paz. Trips cost anywhere from B$325 to B$850, but you get what you pay for. Most operations provide a solid buffet lunch in Yolosa, and some even have arrangements with hotels for showers and swimming pool access. There is a B$50 surcharge to use the old road. Bring sunscreen, a swimsuit and a dust-rag (if they don't provide one), and ask about water allotments. The bus takes you back up in the early evening; expect to arrive back in La Paz around 9pm.

THE CORDILLERAS & YUNGAS COROICO & YOLOSA

Hostal El Cafetal HOTEL **$**
(☑ 7193-3979; Miranda s/n, Coroico; r per person with/without bathroom B$90/55; 🖥🏊) Out of town by the hospital, this French-owned hotel has a lot of potential – tremendous views, a nice pool and large grounds. The rooms with private bathrooms are worth the price, while those without have soft beds and are slightly unkempt. French is spoken.

★ **Hostal Sol y Luna** RESORT **$$**
(☑ 7156-1626; www.solyluna-bolivia.com; Apanto Alto, Coroico; campsites B$50, s B$220-275, d B$380-440, s/d without bathroom B$100/160; 🖥🏊) Set on a jungle-covered hill, this inspiring spot offers appealingly rustic

accommodations in a variety of *cabañas* (cabins), simple rooms and camping spots (dry season only). The rambling grounds over 5 hectares include two pools and a small hot tub. There are yoga classes, secluded bungalows and enchanted forests. A 20-minute uphill walk from town, or a B$20 taxi, provides some reprieve for the non-party set.

Many cabins have kitchens, and there's a top-tier on-site restaurant (p120). Email reservations require a two-night minimum.

Villa Bonita CABAÑAS **$$**
(☑ 7191-8298; Héroes del Chaco s/n, Coroico; cabins per person B$90) Villa Bonita's three charming and colorful cabins lie behind

a beloved cafe of the same name. The English-speaking owners also offer yoga by donation in a small space (Wednesdays at 9:30am and by demand), as well as massages (B$100, one hour).

La Senda Verde Resort   CABAÑAS $$
(www.sendaverde.org; Yolosa; r per person incl breakfast B$200-260) 🐾 This delightful spot is accessed from the Yolosa–La Paz road, 500m south of Yolosa. It has a verdant setting on the banks of two rivers and is a great place to relax. The duplex *cabañas* are excellent, as is the Tarzan-meet-Jane tree house. Note that this is a wildlife refuge (p114) with animals running free. Prices include a tour.

Hotel Esmeralda   HOTEL $$
(📞213-6017; www.hotelesmeralda.com; Julio Suazo s/n, Coroico; s/d B$360/440, dm/s/d without bathroom B$90/160/280; @🛜🏊) A top pick for the party set, this resort-style hotel on the hillside has amazing grounds, tremendous views and a swimming pool. There are rooms for all tastes, from cheap dorms to larger digs with balconies and private bathrooms. The rooms with shared bathrooms can be a bit dark. A book exchange and on-site restaurant mean you may never leave the hotel.

Hotel Bella Vista   HOTEL $$
(📞213-6059; coroicohotelbellavista@hotmail.com; Héroes del Chaco 7, Coroico; s/d without bathroom B$90/180, incl breakfast B$170/250; 🛜) The views truly are something to behold – tropical-bird-filled gardens, coffee and orange plantations in the distance – and while the new management can be a bit inept, you'll love the bright colors, firm mattresses (an oddity in Coroico), cast-iron furniture and...oh yeah, the views!

Hostal Kory   HOTEL $$
(📞7772-1986; Tomás Monje s/n, Coroico; r per person B$120-140, without bathroom B$80; 🏊) Right in the center of town, this rambling six-story complex is one of your best budget bets. There are fabulous views of the valley and Cordillera peaks from the large pool and the rooms. Beds have older sheets, but are clean. The pool is open to nonguests for B$25.

El Jiri Ecolodge   LODGE $$$
(📞7155-8215, 7067-7115; www.jiribolivia.com; Charobamba; 2 days & 1 night per person B$443; 🏊) Near Charobamba, across the valley

---

THE COCA CONTROVERSY

Coca in Bolivia is largely reserved for traditional uses such as chewing the leaf, drinking it in *mate* and using it in religious ceremonies. Its mild alkaloids are said to provide an essential barrier against altitude sickness and fatigue for farm workers and miners in the highlands. However, it is also used to produce the drug cocaine.

Following the expulsion of the US ambassador to Bolivia in September 2008, the US State Department placed Bolivia on its 'drug blacklist' for the country's unwillingness to cooperate on the drug-trafficking problem. In response, President Evo Morales suspended the activities of the US Drug Enforcement Agency in Bolivia. In the 2009 new constitution, he declared coca an intrinsic part of Bolivia's heritage and Andean culture, and at a UN meeting in March 2009 he announced that Bolivia would start the process to remove the coca leaf from the 1961 Single Convention that prohibits the traditional chewing of it.

Morales has been hard at work attempting to establish a new industry of legal coca-based by-products such as tea, medicines and cosmetics, in the hope of growing the market and boosting the income of coca growers. Some see this as opting out of the war on drugs. But, using the motto 'coca yes, cocaine no,' Morales claims to have cracked down on illegal drugs; in April 2009, a new anti-corruption unit was established in Bolivia, mainly to fight drug trafficking and related crime.

In the early days of Morales' presidency, national coca production grew from 24,500 hectares in 2006 to around 31,000 hectares in 2010. By 2017, when Morales bumped up the legal production level from 12,000 hectares to 22,000 hectares, the United Nations Office on Drugs and Crime found that the total figure of coca production in the country had in fact dropped to 23,100 hectares. However, it's estimated that just 14,700 hectares are needed to meet the local demand for chewing and teas. Using new refining processes, Bolivia has been able to increase its cocaine output, and the wealth generated by the drug trade is evident as you travel around the region.

from Coroico, this lodge is a fun spot to stay, with hanging bridges, a pool and meals served under a thatched roof. You're kept busy with walks in Parque Nacional Cotapata and plenty of activities. Ask to see the ruins of an old Jewish settlement nearby. Book ahead.

Río Selva Resort   RESORT $$$
(☑ 241-1818; www.rioselva.com.bo; Pacallo; 3-day all-inclusive packages per 2 people US$335; @ ☒) Five kilometres from the end of the Choro trek in Pacallo you'll find this aging riverside retreat aimed at families and groups. It has seen better days, but amenities include racquetball, a sauna and a swimming pool. Accommodations range from double rooms to cabins sleeping up to six.

🍴 Eating

The plaza in Coroico is ringed by a number of inexpensive local cafes and pizzerias; all have ordinary menus, acceptable fare and a typically tropical sense of urgency and service. Venture further afield for finer options. Saturday and Sunday are market days. On Mondays most stores and restaurants close, and reopen Tuesday morning.

Villa Bonita   INTERNATIONAL $
(☑ 7191-8298; Héroes del Chaco s/n; mains B$12-35; ☺ 8:30am-5:30pm Wed-Sun; ☑) This peaceful garden cafe is just 600m from town but seems like a world away. The personable owners offer delicious homemade ice creams bursting with fresh fruit, tasty sundaes with unusual local liqueurs (try the *yungueña*, an elixir of orange, maracuya and lemon), and an eclectic range of vegetarian dishes.

Cafe Almendra   VEGETARIAN $
(Héroes del Chaco s/n; mains B$10-45; ☺ 10am-5:30pm Sat-Wed; ☑) One block uphill from Hotel Bella Vista, a lovely young couple makes wholesome meals and snacks including delish *sonsos* (pancakes filled with cheese and yucca) and *patacones* (sandwiches made with smashed fried bananas instead of bread). There's a selection of books and local fruit jams for sale. It's a bit hippie but not over the top.

Coroico Star   SOUTH AMERICAN $
(www.facebook.com/coroicostar; Tomás Monje s/n; mains B$25-30; ☺ 10am-10pm; ☎) A few steps down from the main plaza, this popular travelers' meeting point might serve the best *pique a lo macho* (sausages and french fries in sauce) you'll encounter on

your entire trip. The owners also organize a very popular and respected bike ride down the Camino del Muerte. A nice spot to sit on the steps and relax with fellow *mochileros* (backpackers).

Flor de los Andes   INTERNATIONAL $
(☑ 6804-6496; Tomás Monje s/n; mains B$10-50; ☺ 7:30am-6pm) It's a bit sparse, but the views are spectacular and the owners are incredibly welcoming (they lived in Kentucky in the 1970s and can still make a respectable mint julep!). Come for hearty breakfasts (including muffins and bagels with cream cheese), as well as fresh juices, espresso coffees and sandwiches.

★Toto   ITALIAN $$
(☑ 7151-2707; Tomás Monje s/n; mains B$40-60; ☺ 6-11pm Mon, Tue & Thu-Sat) Homemade tagliatelle, gnocchi and ravioli pastas with delicious sauces, not to mention the best pizza in town, make this a must for those wanting a little Italian comfort food. The soft lighting, warm service and soothing music are oh-so inviting.

El Cafetal   INTERNATIONAL $$
(☑ 7193-3979; Miranda s/n; mains B$30-60; ☺ 8am-8:30pm Wed-Mon) This secluded hotel restaurant with unbeatable views has cane chairs and slate-topped tables where you can enjoy a range of dishes prepared with a French touch. The menu includes sweet and savory crepes, soufflés, curries, vegetarian lasagna and specials such as llama goulash. Also runs Bon Apetit Cafe downtown.

La Senda Verde Restaurant   CAFE $$
(Yolosa; lunch buffet B$70, sandwiches B$25; ☺ 1:30-4pm) This restaurant at the wildlife sanctuary (p114) has decent sandwiches and great snacks such as coca-infused *alfajor* cookies and home-produced coffee from a nearby plantation. The main focus, however, is the lunch buffet of all-you-can eat pasta.

Carla's Garden Pub   GERMAN $$
(Back-Stübe Konditorei; ☑ 7207-5620; Pasaje Linares; mains B$20-60; ☺ 1-10pm Wed-Fri, from noon Sat & Sun; ☎) A Dutch pub owner has combined her thatched-roof beer hall with an established German restaurant and moved it to the bottom of the plaza's steep stairs (check for the 'Open' sign). They've maintained the same tasty breakfasts, tempting cakes and pastries, as well as pasta and memorable *sauerbraten* (marinated pot-roast beef) with *spätzle* (German noodles).

Luna Llena

INTERNATIONAL $$

(Apanto Alto, Hostal Sol y Luna; mains B$20-40; ⊙8am-9pm; 🍴) The small outdoor restaurant at the Hostal Sol y Luna has a well-priced, tasty menu of Bolivian and European dishes including vegetarian options. It's a bit of a walk from town, but a worthwhile afternoon excursion.

Drinking & Nightlife

M&M Coffee

COFFEE

(www.facebook.com/cielo.recien.tostado.coroico.bolivia; Pando s/n; ⊙9am-12:30pm & 3-9pm Wed-Sun) Wrap your hands around a mug of some high-quality (and low-priced) local coffee at this small 2nd-story cafe a block east of the plaza. Inquire about tours to a nearby coffee plantation to dig deeper into the local coffee culture.

Discoteca Búfalo

CLUB

(https://bufalocoroico.wordpress.com; Plaza 27 de Mayo; ⊙8pm-3am Fri & Sat) The most happening disco in town when we passed through, with flickering lights, loud music and a good mix of locals and foreigners. It will likely be as fun as the people you bring with you.

🛍 Shopping

Madres de Clarisa Convent

FOOD & DRINKS

(Pasaje Linares; ⊙8am-8pm) The Madres de Clarisa Convent sells homemade cakes, 10 types of creatively flavored biscuits and ridiculously sweet wines. You'll find it down the steps off the southwest corner of the plaza (just across from Carla's Pub); ring the bell to get into the shop area.

ℹ Information

INTERNET ACCESS

Únete (Plaza García Lanza; per hr B$3; ⊙8am-10pm) offers the most reliable internet access in town.

LAUNDRY

Hotels offer laundry services. Prices are typically B$20 per kilo, much higher than La Paz.

MEDICAL SERVICES

There's a basic regional **hospital** (☎213-6002; Miranda s/n; ⊙24hr) near Hostal El Cafetal, but for serious medical treatment you'll be better off in La Paz.

MONEY

There are three ATMs on the main plaza.
Prodem (Plaza García Lanza; ⊙8:30am-4pm Tue-Fri, 8am-3pm Sat & Sun) changes dollars

at a fair rate and does cash advances for 5% commission.

POLICE

The **police station** (Plaza García Lanza) is centrally located.

ℹ Getting There & Away

The La Paz–Coroico road has replaced the World's Most Dangerous Road as the town's access route. It's asphalted along its entirety, but landslides aren't uncommon.

BUS

Buses and *micros* from La Paz arrive either at the **bus terminal** (Av Manning; during peak travel times) or Plaza García Lanza. It's a steep walk uphill to the plaza from the terminal, or you can hop in a taxi (B$5).

From the Villa Fátima area in La Paz, buses and *micros* leave for Coroico (B$25, 3½ hours) at least hourly from 7:30am to 8:30pm, more on weekends and holidays. En route they stop in Yolosita, a dusty crossroads where you can connect with buses heading north to Rurrenabaque (B$100, 12 to 13 hours) and further into the Bolivian Amazon.

For Chulumani, the quickest route is to backtrack to La Paz. Although the junction for the Chulumani road is at Unduavi, few passing *micros* have spare seats at this point.

The road to Caranavi was only open from 4pm to 6am at the time of writing. Buses from Coroico will take you there (and on to other Amazon destinations) for B$30, departing at 2pm, 3pm and 6pm.

TAXI

Turbus Totaí (☎289-5573; Plaza García Lanza) runs comfortable taxi services to La Paz, leaving when full (B$25, two hours).

El Choro Trek

Traversing the Cordillera Real and Parque Nacional Cotopata, the El Choro trek is one of Bolivia's premier hikes. It begins at La Cumbre (4725m), the highest point on the La Paz–Coroico highway, and climbs to 4859m before descending 3250m into the humid Yungas and the village of Chairo (where most hikers end up taking a taxi down to Coroico).

Along the 57km route (which is in the best condition during the April to September dry season), you'll note a rapid change in climate, vegetation and wildlife as you leave the altiplano and plunge into the forest. Energetic hikers can finish the trek in two days, but it's a demanding walk more comfortably done in three.

El Choro Trek

Prepare for a range of climates. It can be pretty cold, even snowy, on the first day, but you'll soon be in sweatier climes. For the lower trail, light cotton trousers will protect your legs from sharp vegetation and biting insects. The Inca paving can be pretty slippery, so make sure you've got shoes with grip and consider using trekking poles. For the best chance of good clear views of the stunning scenery, start as early as possible, before the mist rises out of the Yungas.

Overnight Hike

Once you find the trailhead, the trail is easy to access and follow. From Villa Fátima (p79) in La Paz, catch any Yungas-bound transportation and ask to be dropped at **La Cumbre**, marked by a **statue of Christ**, where the trek begins.

The road climbs steeply out of Villa Fátima toward La Cumbre, less than an hour out of La Paz at the 4725m crest of the La Paz–Yungas road.

You can also taxi to the trail (30 minutes) from La Cumbre, an advantage of this being that you can be taken up the first bit to the pass at **Abra Chucura**, thus avoiding the initial climb – useful if you think it might cause you altitude problems.

The Route

Start La Cumbre

End Chairo

Duration Three days

Distance 57km

Difficulty Medium

El Choro's trekking route begins at the **statue of Christ**, where there is a park registration office. Sign in here. Traditionally this is also the place to perform the ritual *challas*, which asks for blessing from the gods and good luck for your journey. In former times it was an Aymará sanctuary, which was replaced with the Christ monument in the colonial era. In August, *yatiris* (traditional Aymará medicine men) set up tents here to offer benedictions from the *achachillas* (mountain spirits) to people coming from La Paz. From the statue, follow the well-defined track to your left for 1km, then turn off onto the smaller track that turns right and passes between two small **ponds** (one often dry). Follow the track up the hill until it curves to the left and begins to descend.

At this point follow the light track leading up the gravelly hill to your right and toward an obvious notch in the barren hill before you. This is **Abra Chucura** (4859m), and from here the trail runs downhill all the way to its end at Chairo. At the high point is a pile of stones called **Apacheta Chucura**. For centuries travelers have marked their passing by tossing a stone atop it (preferably one that has been carried from a lower elevation) as an offering to the mountain *apus* (sacred places). An hour below Abra Chucura lies the remains of a **tambo** (wayside inn) dating from Inca times.

One hour below the *tambo* is the hamlet of **Estancia Samaña Pampa**, where there's a store that sells water, a grassy campsite, a shelter and another registration hut.

A short way further on is the village of **Chucura** (Achura; 3600m), which has basic supplies. Here you pay a toll of B$10 for maintenance of the trail – you will notice the difference it makes as you head on. An hour's walk from here leads to some **campsites** (B$10 per person), found along the river. The sites are nice, but you may wish to push on down the beautifully paved Inca road to **Cha'llapampa** (2825m), a lovely village with a roofed campsite and simple shelters approximately seven hours from the trail's start point. There are toilets, and water is available from a convenient stream below a bridge close to town.

After two hours following beautiful but slippery stretches of pre-Columbian paving, you'll reach a **suspension bridge** across the Río Chucura at **Choro** (2200m). The track continues descending steadily along the true left (west) side of the Río Chucura, passing through dense vegetation to some small **campsites** (B$10 per person) and a store providing drinks and snacks.

From the ridge above Choro, the trail alternately plunges and climbs from sunny hillsides to vegetation-choked valleys, crossing streams and waterfalls. You'll have to ford the **Río Jucumarini**, which can be rather intimidating in the wet season. Further along, the trail crosses the deep gorge of the **Río Coscapa** via the relatively sturdy Puente Colgante suspension bridge (note that this and the suspension bridge over Río Chucura were both damaged in floods in 2018, but should be restored by the time you read this).

The trail continues through some tiny hamlets, including **San Francisco** and **Buena Vista**, which are separated by the stiff ascent and descent of the **Subida del Diablo**. Some five to six hours from Choro is the remarkable **Casa Sandillani** (2050m), a home surrounded by beautiful gardens where you can camp.

From Casa Sandillani it's an easy 2½ hours downhill to **Chairo**, where camping is also possible in a small, flat, grassed area with no facilities, near the bridge above town.

It's possible to walk the relatively level 12km past the Río Selva Resort (p119) or take transportation from Chairo to **Yolosa** (16km) and then catch an onward service for 7km to **Coroico**. A few private vehicles head to Yolosa and Coroico on most days, but beware of being charged scandalous prices. Don't pay more than B$170 – you could call a cab in Coroico to pick you up for less than that. Infrequent minibuses

also run the route, or you can arrange transport with an agency in La Paz prior to departure.

A growing number of La Paz outfits (p60) offer organized El Choro treks. Most include meals, guides and camping equipment; some include the services of porters.

Takesi Trek

Also known as the Inca Trail, the Takesi trek is one of the most popular and impressive walks in the Andes. The route was used as a highway by the early Aymará, the Inca and the Spanish, and it still serves as a major route to the humid Yungas over a relatively low pass in the Cordillera Real.

The 45km trail conserves expertly engineered pre-Inca paving; it's more like a highway than a walking track. It has been suggested that this paved section was part of a long road that linked the La Paz area with the Alto Beni region. The walk itself is demanding and takes two days, but plan on longer because of unreliable transportation to and from the trailheads. On the first day you will ascend to 4650m, so spend a few days acclimatizing in La Paz before heading off. The trail is hiked by about 5000 people annually, more than half of whom are Bolivians, and suffers from a litter problem due to its growing popularity.

The May to October dry season is best for this trip. In the rainy season the wet and cold, combined with ankle-deep mud, may contribute to a less-than-optimal experience. Since the trail's end is in the Yungas, plan on some rain year-round. The entire route appears on a single 1:50,000 IGM topo sheet: *Chojlla* – 6044-IV.

With a fully serviced lodge two-thirds of the way along the route, the hike is easily done with just a daypack, but agencies can arrange guides and mules if you want them.

Overnight Hike

If you're traveling by public transportation, your first destination will be Ventilla. *Micros* leave from La Paz (B$12, three hours) when full from the market area above Calle Sagárnaga, at the corner of Calles Rodríguez and Lara. Alternatively, groups can charter a taxi (around B$350 for up to four people) to the Choquekhota trailhead. Most La Paz tour agencies can organize this for you, or contact **Fundación**

Pueblo (☎212-4413; www.fundacionpueblo.org; Plaza Libertad, Yanacachi) for advice.

Transportation between Ventilla and the San Francisco mine trailhead is sparse. You will probably have to pay for a taxi, or hike two or three hours uphill to the trailhead.

The Route

Start Ventilla

End Mina Chojlla

Duration Two days

Distance 45km

Difficulty Medium

Begin the hike in Ventilla. About 150m beyond the village, turn left and take the road uphill, following the Río Palca. After climbing for one to 1½ hours, you'll reach the village of **Choquekhota**. After a further hour or two of uphill hiking you'll come to the access road to the **Mina San Francisco**; after crossing a stream, you'll see the signpost indicating the trailhead. The mine route veers left here, but hikers should continue along the signposted track where the original pre-Columbian trail begins.

After an hour of climbing you'll begin switchbacking for 30 minutes for the final ascent, partly on superb precolonial paving, to the 4700m **Apacheta** (Abra Takesi) pass. There you'll find the *apacheta* (shrine of stones) and have a spectacular view of Nevado Mururata (5868m) to the right and the plunging valleys of the Yungas far below. Just beyond the pass you'll see an abandoned **Mina David tunnel**; tungsten and tin are mined around here. Entry is not advisable.

From the pass the trail begins to descend sharply into the valley, passing a series of abandoned mining camps and high glacial lakes. If daylight is on your side, look for another lake, **Laguna Jiskha Huara Huarani**, to the left of the trail midway between the pass and Takesi. The trail from here contains some of Bolivia's finest examples of Inca paving. A little later the trail widens to between 6m and 8m and you will reach **Inka Tambo**. With five rooms, it's a good place to spend the night. If you prefer to push on, you'll next reach the ancient-looking thatched village of **Takesi**, where there's a hut and campsite; you may also find villagers who can prepare simple meals of potatoes and local trout. It is at this point that you will begin to experience the sudden change to Yungas cloud forest vegetation.

Beyond Takesi the increasingly muddy trail winds downhill until it crosses a bridge over the **Río Takesi**, then follows the beautifully churning river before moving upwards and making a long traverse around the **Loma Palli Palli**, where you're protected from steep drop-offs by a pre-Columbian wall. Shortly after passing a particularly impressive *mirador* (lookout), you'll enter the village of **Kacapi**, the heart of the former colonial *estancia* (ranch) that once controlled the entire Takesi valley. Most of the overseers' dwellings have been reclaimed by vegetation, but you can still see the ruins of the chapel, **Capilla de las Nieves**. Kacapi's 10-bed **Albergue Turístico** (dm B$25) and campsite are equipped with solar-powered showers. Basic meals are sometimes available, though the *albergue* is occasionally closed without warning.

After Kacapi the track drops sharply to a bridge over the **Río Quimsa Chata** (which suffers varying degrees of damage each rainy season), then climbs past a soccer field on the left to reach a pass at the hamlet of **Chojlla**. From there the route descends to the final crossing of the Río Takesi via a concrete bridge, marking the end of the pre-Columbian trail. It's then a 1½ hour trudge along an **aqueduct** to the ramshackle mining settlement of **Mina Chojlla** (2280m), where there is a cheap *alojamiento* (basic accommodation) and food stalls.

From Mina Chojlla, crowded buses leave for Yanacachi (B$3, 30 minutes) and La Paz (B$12, three hours) at roughly 5:30am and 1pm daily – buy your ticket on arrival. If you can't endure a night in Mina Chojlla (and few people can), keep walking about one hour down the road past the headquarters of the hydroelectric power project to the more pleasant village of **Yanacachi**.

Yunga Cruz Trek

This is a relatively little-trodden trek between the village of Chuñavi and the Sud Yungas' provincial capital, Chulumani. Declared a national monument in 1992, it preserves good stretches of pre-Columbian footpaths and archaeological remains dating from the Tiwanaku and Inca periods.

This is one of your better bets for wildlife watching, as it has less traffic than other treks (though mining is on the rise). Keep your eyes peeled for Andean foxes, condors, and plenty of birds and butterflies.

Takesi Trek

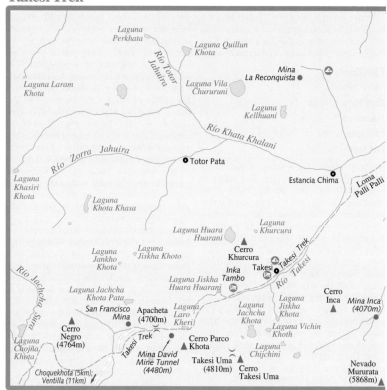

Laguna Perkhata

Laguna Quillun Khota

Río Totor Jahuira

Mina
La Reconquista

Laguna Laram Khota

Laguna Vila Chururuni

Laguna Kellhuani

Río Khata Khalani

Río Zorra Jahuira

Totor Pata

Laguna Khasiri Khota

Estancia Chima

Loma Palli Palli

Laguna Khota Khasa

Laguna Khurcura

Laguna Huara Huarani

Takesi Trek

Laguna Jankho Khota

Laguna Jiskha Khoto

Cerro Khurcura

Inka Tambo

Takesi

Río Takesi

Río Jachcha Sura

Laguna Jachcha Khota Pata

Laguna Jiskha Huara Huarani

Cerro Inca

Mina Inca (4070m)

San Francisco Mina

Apacheta (4700m)

Laguna Laro Kheri

Laguna Jachcha Khota

Laguna Jiskha Khota

Laguna Chojña Khota

Cerro Negro (4764m)

Takesi Trek

Mina David Mine Tunnel (4480m)

Cerro Parco Khota

Takesi Uma

Laguna Vichin Khoth

Laguna Chijchini

Cerro Takesi Uma

Nevado Mururata (5868m)

Choquekhota (5km); Ventilla (11km)

Takesi Uma (4810m)

There are a couple of variations to the standard trek, including a pass over the northern shoulder of **Illimani** to get you started, as well as an alternative – and considerably more spectacular – route over **Cerro Khala Ciudad**, which begins beyond **Lambate**. Some guides even offer the trek backwards, starting at **Chulumani**, but that's a fairly punishing alternative. Crossing several passes at over 5000m, it's easily the most demanding of the Inca trails and usually takes three or four days.

There are no official campsites along the route, although there are plenty of easy-to-find spots along the way to set up camp. If you are going to attempt this trek you'll need to carry the 1:50,000 topo sheets *Palca – 6044-I, Lambate – 6044-II* and *Chulumani – 6044-III* or, even better, arrange a guide (highly recommended). Many agencies in La Paz offer this trek, with guides, a cook and pack animals. Note that there is no

water available on the last day, so stock up ahead of time.

There's a good case for hiring a 4WD to take you to the trailhead at Lambate. Otherwise you can go straight to Chuñavi (four hours) or Lambate (five hours) by *micro* from La Paz, with departures from Calle Venancio Burgoa, near Plaza Líbano, leaving daily from 5am.

The return to La Paz from Chulumani and Irupana is straightforward: catch one of the many daily buses or *camiones* (flatbed trucks) from the *tranca* (police post) in Chulumani.

Chulumani

♪ 2 / POP 2000 / ELEV 1700M (5577FT)

Perched scenically on a hillside, this peaceful little burg has a friendly town square, a bustling market and tropical attitude. And with far fewer international visitors

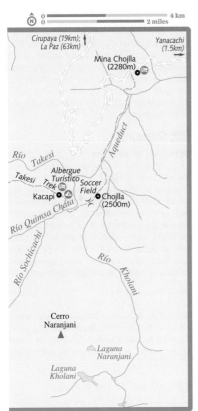

than tourist-center Coroico, it's way more tranquil.

Chulumani is a paradise if you're into birds and butterflies – there are clouds of the latter, and several endemic species of the former. At a tropically warm and often wet altitude, the town makes a great trekking base camp and a relaxing weekend retreat with great views. The only time its pervasive tranquility is interrupted is during the week following August 24, when Chulumani stages the riotous **Fiesta de San Bartolomé**.

History

Chulumani was founded because of the supposed healing qualities of the area's mineral streams. However, when its fertile soils provided bumper crops of coca (the country's best leaf for chewing), citrus, bananas, coffee and cacao, Chulumani soon became important as a trade center for nearby farming communities (300 of them now flock to the weekend market here).

Chulumani does have its ghosts. Nazi war criminal and local narco-trafficker Klaus Barbie lived in the sawmill above town after World War II. A recent documentary, *The Road to Chulumani,* documents the presidency of Jose Luis Tejada Sorzano, local resident and president of Bolivia during the Chaco War. Tejada Sorzano died in exile and it's said his ghost, as well as that of his mistress, haunts the nearby Castillo del Loro built by Paraguayan prisoners of war.

🛏 Sleeping

Hostal Dion   HOTEL **$**
(☑289-6034; Bolívar s/n; r per person with/without bathroom incl breakfast B$80/60) Half a block south of Plaza Libertad, this is the best of the central options. The homey setting includes extremely clean rooms, cable TV, electric showers and sparkling tile floors. Enjoy the courtyard garden, but be sure to ask about the curfew.

★Country House   HOTEL **$$**
(☑7528-2212; Tolopata 13; r per person incl breakfast B$150; 🐾) Easily your best bet in town, this welcoming home is 10 minutes west of the plaza, by the basketball court. Lovingly decorated rooms have hot water showers and plant-packed patios. Great breakfasts, abundant birdlife and delicious home-cooked dinners (killer quinoa pie!). Owner Javier is a gregarious host who can organize many local excursions.

**Tarapari Guesthouse
& Biodiversity Garden**   GUESTHOUSE **$$**
(☑7154-3918; www.lapazonfoot.com; Camino al Cementerio; r per person without bathroom US$18) 🌿 This ecofriendly adobe guesthouse from the team at La Paz on Foot (p58) sleeps up to six people and has shared bathrooms. All proceeds support Tarapari's environmental education and biodiversity conservation initiatives, and you'll find a butterfly garden, coffee plantation and small farm on the property. Find it on the road to the cemetery.

🍴 Eating

Country House Restaurant   INTERNATIONAL **$$**
(☑7528-2212; Tolopata 13; mains B$50; ⊙9am-10pm) Peruse the hand-drawn menu for yummy comfort foods such as fish and chips, pizza and pasta, as well as local favorites such as quinoa pie. Upstairs tables

offer great views over the valley. If you're not staying at the on-site hotel, be sure to reserve in advance.

ℹ️ Information

INTERNET ACCESS

The Entel office on Plaza Libertad is one of several central phone offices. Internet connections are sporadic but try **Rayito Internet** (Sucre s/n; ⊙11am-9:30pm).

MONEY

There's no ATM in Chulumani. Prodem (two blocks west of the plaza on Pando) changes US dollars and gives cash advances on credit cards (5% commission).

TOURIST INFORMATION

Chulumani's tourist office is in a kiosk on the main plaza, but it's rarely open. If you are thinking of exploring the region it is worth seeking out hotel owners such as English-speaking Javier Sarabia at the Country House (p125).

ℹ️ Getting There & Away

Since the closure of the original La Paz–Coroico road, the nail-biting route from La Paz to Chulumani, which extends on to Irupana, has claimed the title of the World's Most Dangerous Road (p117). If you can keep your nerves in check, it is actually an exceptionally beautiful route, though it's hard to appreciate when your bus is reversing round a blind, muddy bend in search of a section wide enough to let oncoming traffic past.

The town is also readily accessed from Yanacachi at the end of the Takesi trek (p122). From Yanacachi, walk down to the main road and wait for transportation headed downhill; it's about 1½ hours to Chulumani.

From Villa Fátima in La Paz (Minasa Terminal), various bus companies depart when full for Chulumani (B$30, four hours) from 8am to 4pm. From Chulumani, La Paz–bound buses wait around the *tranca* (police post). Theoretically, there are several departures before 10am and after 4pm.

Coming from Coroico, get off at Unduavi and wait for another vehicle. It will likely be standing-room only; if a seat is a priority, you'll have to go all the way back to La Paz and start from there.

It's also possible to go to Coroico via Coripata; take a La Paz–bound bus and get off at the crossroads just after Puente Villa at Km 93. Here, wait for a bus or *camión* to Coripata and then change again for a lift to Coroico. It's a long and dusty but worthwhile trip. An easier option is to hire a taxi; expect to pay B$400 for the trip to Coroico for up to four people.

Around Chulumani

The area around Chulumani is a beautiful, fertile zone with patches of intact cloud forest and plenty of farms producing coca, coffee, bananas and citrus fruits. Walking, biking or busing your way between the small colonial-era towns of the region is a worthwhile experience.

🛏️ Sleeping

⭐**Posada Nirvana Inn**   LODGE **$$**
(☑213-6154; Sector Chiriaca; cabañas per person incl breakfast B$180; ☀) In the *barrio* of Chiriaca at the top of Irupana (past the soccer field, turn right), Nirvana houses five sublime *cabañas* in an immaculate hillside garden full of citrus trees. Considerate hosts tend rooms that are comfortable and romantic with log fires – and there are optional kitchen facilities, a swimming pool and sauna. Staff can arrange forest walks.

Hotel Bougainvillea   HOTEL **$$**
(☑213-6155; Sucre 246; s/d incl breakfast B$150/200; ☀) An attractive, modernized, whitewashed building built around a pool. Rooms are clean and appealing, although we've found management is not overly welcoming.

ℹ️ Getting There & Away

Regular *micros* drive the 31km from Chulumani to Irupana (B$15, one hour) and there are also some direct connections to Irupana from La Paz. *Micros* run to the smaller villages from Chulumani and Irupana, though schedules are erratic and many only operate on weekends.

One of the most comfortable ways to see the places in this region (except in the rainy season, December to February) is to hire a taxi from Chulumani. For the whole circuit, expect to pay around B$200 to B$300 for a day's hire. It's worth getting hold of a driver who can also act as a guide; ask Javier Sarabia at the Country House (p125) in Chulumani for a recommendation.

Irupana to Ocabaya Day Hike

A beautiful hike is the four-hour walk from Chulumani to Chirca, where there's a church of a revered local virgin (a guide is suggested to see this site). For something longer and more demanding, try the hike back from Irupana.

The Route

Start Irupana

End Ocabaya

Duration Six hours

Distance 21km

Difficulty Moderate

This moderately difficult hike dips into – and rises out of – two lush mountain valleys for classic Yungas views. Along the way, you'll get a taste of rural life and a glimpse of some remote Afro-Bolivian communities.

To begin the hike, take a *micro* from Chulumani to **Irupana** (B\$15, one hour), an attractive, sleepy colonial town founded in the 18th century on one of the few bits of flat ground in the area. Irupana is the birthplace of noted astronomer and poet Agustín Aspiazu, and has plenty of shops where you can stock up on supplies or grab a hearty breakfast.

Descend from Irupana along the little-used dirt road to the principal Afro-Bolivian town, dusty **Chicaloma** – known for its annual town festival on May 27, which features lots of traditional *saya* music (a hybrid of African, Aymará and Spanish styles). About 4km into the journey you'll cross over the **Río Puri**, and it's another 4km uphill until you reach Chicaloma.

From here, it's a long and sun-baked 7km down to the **Río Solacama**, whose banks are populated by numerous butterflies. This a lovely spot to bathe on a hot day.

Cross the bridge, as the final 6km leg is on the far side of the river. On your way up look out for coca leaves being harvested and dried (and remember that while much coca production in the region is legal, farmers may be sensitive about pictures or lots of questions).

Tiny, postcard-pretty **Ocabaya** lies at the top of the hill. It has one of the oldest churches in Bolivia, fronted by a liberty bell and a memorial to two local martyrs of the struggle for *campesino* rights. From here, it's another 10km back to Chulumani; most hikers hail one of the frequent *micros* (B\$5, 20 minutes).

Note that the route has vast changes in elevation and long shade-less stretches, so you'll need to be in good shape and well equipped with plenty of water and sunscreen. You may be able to purchase snacks in Chicaloma, but don't count on it.

If you do the hike in reverse, Irupana makes a pleasant place to lay your head before returning to Chulumani, where there are several hotels and basic eateries.

AFRO-BOLIVIANS: UNDERSTANDING BOLIVIA'S INVISIBLE MINORITY

The hill villages of the Chulumani region are home to a high proportion of the country's Afro-Bolivian population. An estimated 35,000 Bolivians are descended from African slaves who were brought to Bolivia by Spanish colonialists to work in the Potosí silver mines. An astronomical percentage died living underground for up to four months continuously. Because of the high death rate, enslaved Afro-Bolivians were deemed to be three times more expensive than local labor, and as a result the Spanish transferred them to domestic labor and farm work.

Simón Bolívar's original Bolivian constitution technically ended the practice of slavery, but slaves were still indebted to their owners, and it wasn't until 1851 that slavery ended. After slavery was abolished, many Afro-Bolivians were forcibly settled in the Yungas, where they were virtually enslaved under a sharecropper-style system for another 100 years. While Afro-Bolivians never fully assimilated into local culture – and remain one of Bolivia's most marginalized communities both economically and politically today – they adopted the Aymará language and, for women, the Aymará traditional dress. Afro-Bolivians are recognized by Bolivia's new constitution, but still lack a voice on the national stage.

In Afro-Bolivian *saya* music (a haunting hybrid of African, Aymará and Spanish styles) and funerary rites, you will see distinct African overtones. See www.solidarity insaya.com for a documentary on how Afro-Bolivians are using *saya* music as a form of social protest.

Traditional Bolivian dance the *morenada* has its roots in a portrayal of an African slave train arriving at the mines. More information about Afro-Bolivian history and culture can be found on the Fundación Activos Culturales Afro website (www.programa acua.org).

Guanay

📍 2 / POP 11,530 / ELEV 670M (2200FT)

The only reason to visit isolated Guanay is to hop on a boat for the scenic ride up to Rurrenabaque. Chatting with the down-to-earth miners and *barranquilleros* (panners) while you're here can make for a particularly interesting experience, as can joining them for some karaoke. This area and other spots upriver are frontier territory reminiscent of the USA's legendary Old West (albeit with a tropical twist).

🛏 Sleeping

La Piscina   HOTEL $

(r B$140; ❄) This decent new five-room hotel doesn't have a name but everyone calls it *'la piscina'* because it's the only place in town with a pool. Find it just west of the *fútbol* (football) field.

❶ Getting There & Away

BOAT

Charter boats take travelers from Guanay to Rurrenabaque, but these are pricey to arrange on your own (B$4000 for a 10-person boat, 12 hours). Several agencies in La Paz offer a multiday version of this trip with camping and jungle excursions from about B$1990 per person. These include Deep Rainforest (p60), Gravity (p354) and Banjo Tours (p60).

BUS

The bus offices are all located around the plaza, but buses actually depart a block away toward the river. Four companies offer daily runs to and from La Paz via Caranavi and Yolosa (B$45, 10 hours). Departures in La Paz are from along Av Las Americas daily at 1pm or 1:30pm (10:30am on Sunday). For Coroico, get off at Yolosa and catch a lift up the hill.

El Camino del Oro

For nearly 1000 years this Inca road has been used as a commerce and trade link between the altiplano and the lowland goldfields. The Tipuani and Mapiri valleys were major sources of the gold that once adorned the Inca capital, Cuzco. While the upper route remains magnificent, the fields today are worked primarily by bulldozers and dredgers owned by mining cooperatives.

Overnight Hike

It's possible to start the hike right from Sorata, but many people cut some time off

the lengthy journey by zipping ahead to Ancoma. You'll have to bargain for a 4WD from Sorata to Ancoma, but expect to pay at least B$400. It's likely just as economical to hire a local guide in Sorata to make the arrangements.

The Route

Start Sorata

End Llipi

Duration Six to seven days

Distance 100km

Difficulty Hard

Almost all hikers follow El Camino del Oro from Sorata down the valley to Tipuani and Guanay, simply because it's generally downhill. If you don't mind a climb, however, you might prefer to do it in reverse, thus leaving the prettiest bits to last. Either way, it is best with a guide.

There are three options for the route between Sorata and Ancoma. First, you can rent a 4WD in Sorata and cut two days off the trek. Second, a challenging alternative is the steep route that begins near the cemetery in Sorata. The route roughly follows the **Río Challasuyo**, passing through the village of **Chillkani** and winding up on the road just below the **Abra Chuchu** (4658m). The third, shorter and more scenic option is to follow the route through the village of **Lakathiya** and over the **Abra de Illampu** (4741m) to meet up with the road about 1½ hours above Ancoma. Foreigners are charged B$10 per person to camp anywhere in the vicinity of Ancoma or you can ask about lodging in the school room. There is also a B$3 charge for crossing the bridge. Alternatively, continue a few kilometers on to **Tushuaia** where there is a flat terrace that makes for excellent camping (recommended).

Once you're in **Ancoma**, the route is fairly straightforward. Leave the 4WD track and follow the southern bank of the **Río Quillapituni** (which eventually becomes the **Río Tipuani**). At a wide spot called **Llallajta**, 4½ hours from Ancoma, the route crosses a bridge and briefly follows the north bank before recrossing the river and heading toward Sumata. An Inca-engineered diversion to the north bank has been destroyed by bridge washouts, forcing a spontaneously constructed, but thankfully brief, detour above the southern bank.

Just past the detour is the village of **Sumata**. A short distance further along

THE SLOW BOAT TO RURRENABAQUE

River travel was once the only lifeline connecting remote Amazonian communities to the rest of Bolivia. However, with the advent of a new network of roads over the last decade, many rivers have been all but abandoned (or taken over by gold-mining operations). While it's harder than ever to find regular boats navigating these magnificent waterways, the journey between Guanay and Rurrenabaque is one shining exception.

Though rarely used by local commuters these days, this route is frequented by several La Paz–based tour operators who market it as a more picturesque alternative to the 15-hour bus ride or 45-minute plane trip to Rurrenabaque. And picturesque it most certainly is.

Most companies offer journeys of between two and five days, departing Guanay along the Río Kaka en route to **Paso Retamas** and its natural swimming pools. At **Mayaya**, the last town before the long slog to Rurrenabaque, you stop for any last-minute supplies and then turn north past a row of gold mines to the junction with Río Alto Beni. The two rivers merge to become the Río Beni just before the magnificent **Cañon del Beu**.

From here you'll have the remote wilds of **Parque Nacional Madidi** to your left and **La Reserva de Biósfera Pilón Lajas** to your right. After passing through the towering cliffs of **Cañon del Chepete**, the river widens and the landscape flattens out for a while. This is a particularly good spot for bird-watching and jungle walks. The waterway becomes slightly more populated with indigenous communities as you continue downriver, and you'll begin to see small fishing boats, and children splashing in the sandy banks.

Soon after the turn-off for Río Tuichi, home to most of Madidi's community-based tourism projects, the Río Beni squeezes through **Cañon del Bala** and deposits sun-baked travelers into the tourist hamlet of Rurrenabaque.

Most tours involve wild camping on riverside beaches, fishing for basic camp meals and treks into some of the more remote stretches of Parque Nacional Madidi in search of wildlife. Bring sunscreen, insect repellent, a flashlight and a good sense of adventure, as you won't see toilets, showers or cell (mobile) signal for the entire journey. What you will see in spades are hungry, opportunistic mosquitoes. Be sure to check the latest news before setting out. The Bolivian government has big plans for a mega-dam project along the Río Beni (at Cañon del Chepete and Cañon del Bala) that could make this route impassable in the coming years.

from the trail junction is **Ocara**. From here, the path goes up the slope – don't follow the river. After 1½ hours you'll reach **Lambromani**, where a local may ask you to pay B$3 per person to pass. You can camp here in the schoolyard.

An hour past Lambromani you'll reach **Wainapata**, where the vegetation grows thicker and more lush. Here, the route splits (to rejoin at Pampa Quillapituni); the upper route is very steep and dangerous, so the lower one is preferable. A short distance along, the lower route passes through an interesting tunnel drilled through the rock. There's a popular myth that it dates from Inca times, but it was actually made with dynamite and likely blasted out early in the 20th century by the Aramayo mining company to improve access to the Tipuani goldfields. At **Pampa Quillapituni**, 30 minutes beyond, you'll find a favorable campsite.

Four hours after crossing the swinging bridge at the **Río Coocó**, you'll reach the little settlement of **Mina Yuna**, where you can

pick up basic supplies. It's possible to camp on the soccer field.

An hour further down is **Chusi**, which is four hours before your first encounter with the road. There's no place to camp here, but you can stay in the school. **Puente Nairapi**, over the Río Grande de Yavia, is a good place for a swim to take the edge off the increasing heat.

The scene on this former Inca trail grows increasingly depressing once you reach the road due to modern-day mining activity. For a final look at relatively unaffected landscape, follow the shortcut trail, which begins with a steep **Inca staircase** and winds up at **Baja Llipi** and the **Puente de Tora** toll bridge (B$2) over the **Río Santa Ana**.

After crossing the bridge, climb up the hill and hope for a *camioneta* (flatbed truck) or 4WD to take you to **Tipuani** and **Guanay**. *Camionetas* from the Río Santa Ana bridge to **Unutuluni** cost B$5 per person; it's an additional B$15 to continue on to Tipuani or Guanay.

You can pick up basic supplies at Ancoma, Wainapata, Mina Yuna, Chusi and Llipi, as well as at all the lower settlements along the road. Spartan accommodations may be found in Unutuluni, Chima (rough-and-ready and not recommended), Tipuani and Guanay, all of which are along the road.

Sorata

📞 2 / POP 23,020 / ELEV 2670M (8759FT)

Knocked back a peg in the early 2000s by social unrest, Sorata is making a slow recovery, and in fact is a bit of a Yungas gem. While it doesn't have the shiny digs of its arch nemesis Coroico, this semi-tropical village sitting high above a verdant agricultural valley does offer great weather, access to some of Bolivia's best treks, kick-ass downhill mountain biking and an atavistic air that may just become intoxicating.

In colonial days Sorata (from the Aymará *shuru-ata* or 'shining peak') provided a link to the Alto Beni's goldfields and rubber plantations, and a gateway to the Amazon Basin. These days, mining is the main source of employment in the region. But it really is worth your while to pick up a guide in La Paz – or better yet, hire a local one in Sorata (p132) – and explore this under-appreciated mountain playground.

History

In 1791 Sorata was the site of a distinctly unorthodox siege by indigenous leader Andrés Tupac Amaru and his 16,000 soldiers. They constructed dykes above the town, and when these had filled with runoff from the slopes of Illampu, they opened the floodgates and the town was washed away.

◉ Sights

There isn't much of specific interest in Sorata itself – its main attractions are its historic ambience and a maze of steep stairways and narrow cobbled lanes. Step outside city limits, however, and the opportunities for adventure are endless.

★ **Gruta de San Pedro**   CAVE
(B$20; ⊙ 9am-5pm) A popular excursion, San Pedro Cave, known in the Aymará language as Chussek Uta (House of Owls), is approximately 500m deep, with an enclosed lagoon that can be crossed in pedal boats (B$5 per person, and recommended). Guides with

the necessary lamps will help you find your way around. PCMB, the Bolivian program to conserve bats, has identified three nectar- and insect-eating bats in the pitch-black surroundings.

It's a scenic 15km hike to the cave along a dirt road (two hours each way). Taxis will do the return trip for around B$80, including waiting time. The local community has also set up two simple *albergues* (basic accommodations) to overnight in. There are a total of four rooms with a single bed in each and prices are B$30 per person.

Mirador Wila Kollu   VIEWPOINT
(Camino a Laripata) This vertigo-inducing lookout 3035m above Sorata is, quite literally, breathtaking. To reach it, walk (or hire a taxi, B$80) up the road to Laripata. Just before Laripata you'll see a small trail off to the left leading to a railed-in platform.

Las Cuevas del Rio San Cristobal   CAVE
A short 3km round-trip hike down the road past Altai Oasis takes you to these small caves by the river where rural farmers used to sleep before market days in Sorata. The caves themselves aren't super impressive but if you continue 100m past them you'll reach a viewpoint over a beautiful canyon. Come in the morning to see squawking parrots flying through the valley.

The path isn't terribly well marked, but just keep left to follow the river and you should be able to find your way.

Puente Colgante   BRIDGE
(Camino del Río) A nice walk below town on Camino del Río leads to a hanging bridge over Río San Cristobal with gorgeous views down the valley.

Plaza General Enrique Peñaranda   PLAZA
The main square, Plaza General Enrique Peñaranda, is Sorata's showcase. With the town's best view of the *nevados* (snow-capped mountain peaks), it's graced by towering date palms and immaculate gardens.

Casa Günther   HISTORIC BUILDING
(Plaza) It's worth taking a look at Casa Günther, a rambling, historic mansion in the northeast corner of the plaza that now houses the Residencial Sorata. It was built in 1895 as the home of the Richters, a quinine-trading family, and was later taken over by the Günthers, who were involved in rubber extraction until 1955. Python skins on the walls; bullet holes in the doors!

🏃 Activities

Hiking

Sorata is best known as a convenient base for hikers and climbers pursuing some of Bolivia's finest high-mountain landscapes. Peak hiking season is from May to September.

Ambitious adventurers can do the seven-day El Camino del Oro trek (p128), an ancient trading route between the altiplano and the Río Tipuani goldfields. Otherwise there's the challenging seven-day **Illampu circuit**, though there have been reports of robberies on this route in recent years and it's recommended to go with a guide who can make monetary offerings to ensure a safe journey.

The ultimate hardcore challenge is the 20-day **Trans Cordillera route**: eight days gets you from Sorata to Lago Sistaña, with possible four-day (to Huayna Potosí) and eight-day (to Illimani) extensions. Hikers should carry the *Alpenvereinskarte Cordillera Real Nord* (Illampu) 1:50,000 map, available online.

While it's possible to hike independently, it is best to hook up with a guide (p109), mainly because of the need to be aware of local sensibilities and the difficulty of finding passable routes. The most economical, authorized option is to hire an independent Spanish-speaking guide from the Asociación de Guías de Sorata (p132).

Laguna Chillata   HIKING

Laguna Chillata is a popular hike from Sorata. It's a pretty spot with great views of the surrounding sierra and Lake Titicaca. The former trail is now mostly a road, so you can take a taxi to La Mina and hike one hour up to the lagoon. On the right-hand side of the lagoon are ruins of a small Incan stone village. It's worthwhile taking a guide, as it's easy to get lost.

A steep ascent the following day can take you up to **Laguna Glacial**, a top spot where you can watch big chunks of ice cracking off into the water. It's at 5100m, so take it easy; the altitude can make it a tough climb.

It's possible to overnight, and leave the tent and your gear at Laguna Chillata. However, it'll get nicked if you haven't brought a guide, who can detail someone to watch over it.

Mountain Biking

With its thrillingly steep descents and spectacular mountain scenery, the Sorata area

makes a top two-wheel destination. The **Jach'a Avalancha (Grand Avalanche) Mountain Bike race** takes place in Sorata each year, typically in October. This is the biggest downhill race course in South America based on the Mega Avalanche format. It is a 2000m descent using a mass start, and draws riders from across the world.

One of the best trips around is the descent into town from the mountains astride Lake Titicaca. From La Paz, take a Sorata-bound bus to the pass north of Achacachi and then choose either the main road or any of the downhill routes along unpaved roads. Most routes eventually lead to Sorata – or come at least within view of it (but it's wise to have a map). Throughout the ride you're presented with superb views of towering snow-capped peaks, plunging valleys and tiny rural villages. La Paz–based Gravity (p132) and local company Sorata Xtreme offer guided rides here.

Sorata Xtreme Bike   MOUNTAIN BIKING

(☑ 7157-2302; sorataxtremebike@gmail.com; Plaza; ☺ 9am-noon & 2-6pm) Runs single-day bike trips to Gruta de San Pedro and from the altiplano to Sorata along the Loma-Loma track. Also does hiking and biking trips to Iskanwaya. Stop by the office for great area maps.

🧭 Tours

Sorata Travel   TOURS

(☑ 7121-0044; cnr Calles 14 de Sepiembre & Samuel Tejerina; ☺ 2-7:30pm) A new agency offering half- and full-day tours to Laguna Chillata, Mirador Wila Kollu, Gruta de San

Sorata

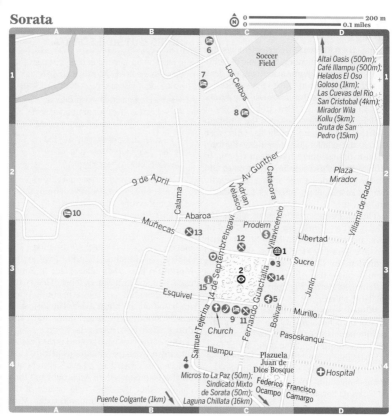

Soccer Field

Altai Oasis (500m);
Café Illampu (500m);
Helados El Oso
Goloso (1km);
Las Cuevas del Río
San Cristobal (4km);
Mirador Wila
Kollu (5km);
Gruta de San
Pedro (15km)

Plaza
Mirador

Prodem

Libertad

Sucre

Murillo

Pasoskanqui

Plazuela
Juan de
Dios Bosque

Hospital

Micros to La Paz (50m);
Sindicato Mixto
de Sorata (50m);
Laguna Chillata (16km)

Puente Colgante (1km)

Church

Illampu

Esquivel

Pedro and other nearby attractions. It also offers overnight trips to Aucapata and the ruins of Iskanwaya, as well as hikes along the Camino del Oro.

Gravity Assisted
Mountain Biking   MOUNTAIN BIKING
(7670-3000; www.gravitybolivia.com; Linares 940, La Paz; 9am-7pm Mon-Fri, 10am-3pm Sat, 2-6pm Sun) This La Paz–based operator is your best bet for single-track rides near Sorata. A remarkable six-day trip can take you from La Paz to Rurrenabaque, including a night in Sorata.

Asociación de Guías
y Portaedores de Sorata   TOURS
(Sorata Guides & Porters Association; 213-6672; http://guiasorata.com; Plaza) Offers Spanish-speaking guides, rents out equipment of varying quality and arranges many different treks. Cooking equipment is included in the price, but food is extra.

Clients are expected to pay for the guide's food. The cooperative benefits workers and community-based projects. Unfortunately, hours are extremely erratic and the office opens whenever someone feels like being there. Email ahead of time.

Sleeping

Hostal Las Piedras   HOTEL $
(7191-6341; soratalaspiedras@yahoo.com; Villa Elisa Calle 2 s/n; s/d/tr B$120/160/195, s/d without bathroom B$70/110) This joint has amazing views from most rooms, clean sheets, a shared kitchen and a fun common area. Breakfast (B$30 to B$46) is optional.

Residencial Sorata   HOTEL $
(Casa Günther; 213-6672; Plaza; r per person with/without bathroom B$60/35) This ultra-characterful colonial-style mansion makes a romantic place to stay. Do your eyes a favor and ask to see the old-style rooms; do your back a favor and stay in one of the

Sorata

new ones (with private bathroom). There's a laundry service, a wild garden and a warm welcome. This is a good spot to gather info on local hikes.

Hostal Santa Lucia HOTEL $
(☑ 7151-3812; Los Ceibos s/n; r per person with/without bathroom B$65/55) Located near the soccer field, this is one of the cleanest and neatest budget options in town. The bright-yellow hotel does have a slightly institutional feel, but in return you get nice mattresses (by Sorata standards), crisp linens and tidy shared facilities. The elderly owner, Serafín, is as friendly as they come.

Hotel Panchita HOTEL $
(☑ 7120-5651; Plaza; r per person with/without bathroom B$80/35) Built around a clean and sunny courtyard on the south side of the plaza, the Panchita has cell-like rooms (some a bit dark). The management is friendly; there's hot water and good mattresses; and you are right on the plaza (no walk uphill!). It's above La Casa del Turista.

Reggae House HOTEL $
(☑ 7323-8327; Muñecas s/n; r per person B$25-30) There's a distinctly relaxed vibe at the aptly named Reggae House. Sorata-farians will love the wonderful terrace for guitar jams and drum circles, but the tiny moldy rooms

with single beds and personalized graffiti/art leave something to be desired. The whole place is rather dirty, but, hey, that's part of the deal, right?

★**El Encanto Sorata** HOTEL $$
(☑ 7709-2511; Villa Elisa Calle 2 s/n; r per person B$112) This new brick building down past the soccer field has the cleanest, smartest and sunniest rooms in town, all with private bathrooms and valley views. The flowery garden below makes it a super-tranquil oasis.

★**Altai Oasis** LODGE $$
(☑ 7151-9856; www.altaioasis.com; Camino a la Gruta, Zona Quincirka; campsites B$30, cabins B$750-900, s/d B$300/500, dm/s/d without bathroom B$100/125/290; 🛜🏊) This really does feel like an oasis, with a lush garden, hammocks and a pretty balcony cafe. The riverside retreat offers grassy campsites, comfortable rooms, and romantically rustic *cabañas* (cabins), intricately and fancifully painted. The English-speaking owner can offer great local tips.

To get here, follow the track past the soccer field to the river, climb back up to the road and turn left before reaching Cafe Illampu.

🍴 Eating

★**Helados El Oso Goloso** ICE CREAM $
(☑ 7208-1805; Camino a la Gruta; 1 scoop B$5; ☉7am-7pm) Dig in to some seriously good artisanal ice cream under the watchful eye of rescued rheas at this eccentric outdoor *heladería* (ice cream shop) on the road to Gruta de San Pedro (p130). Try local flavors such as *chirimoya* (custard apple), *chilto* (Peruvian groundcherry) or *karicari* (wild blackberry). Also serves traditional Bolivian food and fresh fruit juices.

Cafe Illampu CAFE $
(Camino a la Gruta, Zona Quincirka; sandwiches B$28; ☉9am-6pm Wed-Mon, closed Jan & Feb) This small open-air cafe with a wild and rickety lookout tower serves sandwiches (using homemade bread), cakes and espresso coffees. It has a great lending library of books and board games, as well as a grassy field for camping (B$18 per person).

La Casona BOLIVIAN $
(Plaza; almuerzo B$10-15; ☉7:30am-8:30pm) For a good *almuerzo* (set lunch) at a great price and with fantastic service, do as the locals do and head to this old-school eatery on the plaza.

THE CORDILLERAS & YUNGAS SORATA

Mercado
MARKET **$**

(Muñecas s/n; mains B$5-20; ⊙8am-10pm) Head to the market to grab goods for a picnic lunch. There are some food stands here, too (mostly fried chicken).

Restaurant Jalisco
MEXICAN **$**

(Plaza; mains B$25-30; ⊙8am-10pm; 🖉) On the east side of the plaza, Jalisco delivers an ambitious menu of pizza, pasta, Bolivian fare, and creditable attempts at Mexican food such as tacos and burritos. There are quite a few vegetarian options.

La Casa del Turista
INTERNATIONAL **$$**

(Plaza; mains B$25-35; ⊙8am-10pm) This friendly eatery offers the best pizza on the plaza, traditional international favorites such as pasta and tacos, and a few tried-and-true Bolivian treats like *pique a lo macho* (heaping plate of rice, beef, sausage, french fries, boiled eggs, tomato and onion). It's cleaner than most restaurants in town.

Altai Oasis
INTERNATIONAL **$$$**

(www.altaioasis.com; Camino a la Gruta, Zona Quincirka; mains B$50-150; ⊙8am-7:30pm Tue-Sat, to 2pm Sun; 🖉) The peaceful balcony restaurant at this lovely retreat 20 minutes' walk from town serves coffee, drinks and a range of vegetarian dishes. There are T-bone steaks and, for an Eastern European touch, Polish borscht and tasty goulash. It's a great place to just sit with a drink, too, absorbing views over the valley and the tinkle of wind chimes.

ⓘ Information

MEDICAL SERVICES

Sorata has a **hospital** (🖉7352-5447; Villamil de Rada s/n; ⊙24hr) for basic ailments.

MONEY

Prodem (Villaricencio s/n; ⊙12:30-4pm Mon, 8:30am-4pm Tue-Fri, 8am-3pm Sat) changes US dollars, does credit-card cash advances for a 5% commission and has Western Union facilities, but there are no ATMs. Be sure to bring all the cash you'll need.

POLICE

The police are located on the central plaza.

TELEPHONE

Top up your phone at **Entel** (Plaza).

TOURIST INFORMATION

There's a small **tourist information** (🖉7910-0320; Plaza; ⊙8am-noon & 2-6pm Tue-Fri, to noon Sat) center on the plaza.

ⓘ Getting There & Away

Sorata is a long way from other Yungas towns, and there's no road connecting it directly with Coroico, so you must go through La Paz via a paved road.

Buses leave for Sorata from near La Paz's cemetery regularly between 4am and 5:30pm (B$20, 3½ hours). From Sorata, **La Paz–bound** *micros* depart when full and *flotas* (long-distance buses) leave on the hour between 4am and 5pm. **Sindicato Mixto de Sorata** (🖉7321-9976; Samuel Tejerina s/n) offers services to Copacabana (B$45) and Coroico (B$50) when there is demand. It also runs regular trips to Achacachi (B$15) and Haurina (B$20).

For Copacabana you can also get off at the junction town of Huarina and wait for a connecting bus. Similarly, for Charazani you should change at Achacachi, but to do so you'll need to start out from Sorata very early.

Sindicato Mixto de Sorata also services the towns on the rough 4WD track to the gold-mining settlement of Mapiri, including Quiabaya (B$20), Tacacoma (B$40) and Constata (B$40), with no continuing service to Mapiri. The departure is typically 11am. The biggest drawbacks are the horrendous mud, the road construction and some river crossings that are passable only with a 4WD.

Vagonetas (4WD vehicles) leave Sorata sporadically for the grueling journey to Consata (five hours) and on to the Sorata Limitada mine (seven hours) and Mapiri (eight hours). Ask around in town for prices and times.

Aucapata & Iskanwaya

🖉2 / POP 200 / ELEV 2640M (9290FT)

The tiny, remote village of Aucapata – a charming mountain town with stone-built homes and a serene plaza – is about as far off the beaten track as most people will get in Bolivia. Perched on a ledge, on the shoulder of a dramatic peak, it's a great place to hole up for a couple of days' reading, hiking and relaxing.

While most of Aucapata's very few visitors want to see Iskanwaya – somewhat optimistically dubbed 'Bolivia's Machu Picchu' – they may well take one look at the 1500m descent to the ruins (and the corresponding climb back up) and seek out the small Iskanwaya museum in the village itself. That would be a shame. The spectacular setting, marred ever so slightly by a new gold mine, is worth the journey alone. And the chance to explore a sight like this in absolute solitude is a rare treat indeed.

⊙ Sights

Iskanwaya
RUINS

The major but near-forgotten ruins of Iskanwaya, on the western slopes of the Cordillera Real, sit in a cactus-filled canyon, perched 250m above the Río Llica. Thought to date from between 1145 and 1425, the site is attributed to the Mollo culture. This large citadel was built on two platforms and flanked by agricultural terraces and networks of irrigation canals. It contains more than 70 buildings, plus delicate walls, narrow streets, small plazas, storerooms, burial sites and niches.

While Iskanwaya isn't exactly comparable to Peru's Machu Picchu, the 13-hectare site is outwardly more impressive than Tiwanaku near La Paz. The government finally allocated money for restoration efforts in 2018; however, discussions over who would manage these funds was ongoing at the time of research.

Unfortunately, many of the passionate guides who once took tourists to the ruins have now either moved into mining jobs or passed on, but you could try your luck with Spanish-speaking **Manuel Huaqui** (☑ 7191-8141). For background reading, *Iskanwaya: La Ciudadela que Sólo Vivía de Noche,* by Hugo Boero Roja (1992), contains photos, maps and diagrams of the site, plus information on nearby villages.

Pukara
RUINS

A set of Mollo ruins so little explored that locals say you can still find ceramic pieces and other artifacts. It lies like a fortress on the peak above Aucapata and can be reached on a 1½-hour hike from Aucapata's plaza (look for the cross and you'll see the ruins just above). When clouds rise out of the valleys, this site offers a privileged view of the entire region.

Museum
MUSEUM

(Plaza) FREE This small, poorly maintained museum contains artifacts from the Iskanwaya site, including ceramics, copper utensils and bone flutes. Admission is free but you'll need to ask at Residencial Iskanwaya for the keys.

🛏 Sleeping

Residencial Iskanwaya
HOTEL $

(☑ 6316-9913; r per person B$35) Aucapata's smart-looking (if basic) hotel has clean rooms, hot showers and a nice internal patio.

ℹ Getting There & Away

Aucapata lies about 145km northwest of Sorata, but is most easily reached from La Paz. A **Trans Muñecas** (☑ 298-5960) bus departs at 3am from Reyes Cardona in the cemetery district of La Paz every Tuesday and Friday (B$40, nine to 10 hours). You might have better luck getting a Charazani-bound bus to the *cruce* (turnoff) for Aucapata, but don't bank on it. Buses return to La Paz at 2am on Wednesdays and Sundays.

Access from Sorata is difficult and involves a four-day hike via Payayunga. Guides are available in Sorata. Note that there's no accurate map of the area, and in the rainy season hiking is dangerous on the region's exposed routes and not recommended. Alternatively, both Sorata Xtreme (p131) and Sorata Travel (p131) offer regular tours here if you're willing to endure the grueling eight-hour drive, mostly along the Mapiri road.

To avoid the 14km round-trip hike from Aucapata to Iskanwaya, you can hire a taxi to drive you down, wait and bring you back up for B$160.

CORDILLERA APOLOBAMBA

The remote Cordillera Apolobamba, flush against the Peruvian border north of Lake Titicaca, is a burgeoning hiking, trekking and climbing destination. Mountaineers in particular will find a wonderland of tempting peaks, first ascents and new routes to discover, and the trek from Lagunillas to Agua Blanca – through magnificent Andean landscapes – is one of the most memorable in the country.

While access is improving, it must be emphasized that this is an extremely isolated region, and far from being set up for tourism. There are few services; transportation isn't reliable; and the people here maintain a fragile traditional lifestyle. Comparatively few locals speak more than rudimentary Spanish (mostly men). Being sensitive to the local sentiments of this highly traditional Aymará- and Quechua-speaking area will help keep its distinctive character intact.

Charazani

☑ 2 / POP 13,020 / ELEV 3250M (10,662FT)

Charazani is the administrative and commercial center and transportation axis of Bautista Saavedra province, and by far the largest town in the area. You can hike through the moss-green hills from here

Cordillera Apolobamba

Chupi Orco Norte (6000m)

Paso Pura Pura

Nevada de Salluyo (5808m)

Chupiorco (6044m)

PERU

Flor de Roca (5808m)

Lago Chocnacota

Chucuyo Grande (5430m)

Sorel Oeste (5641m)

Paso Rite

Queara

Lago Cacanicoche

Palomani Cunca (5769m)

Manresa (5655m)

Sorel Este (5471m)

Lago Saihuanlcocha

Lago Chucuyo Grande

Presidente (5700m)

Azucarani (5580m)

Lago Churococha

Trapiche

Machu Suchi Coochi (5679m)

Katantica (5592m)

Paso de Queara (4770m)

Calliapata

Pelechuco Huaracha (5650m)

Lloco Lloco (5605m)

Agua Blanca

Pelechuco

Lago Suches

Huanchuchiri (5400m)

Suches

Paso de Pelechuco

Albergue Agua Blanca

BOLIVIA

Huanacuni (5796m)

Cerro Cerebro (5550m)

Nevado Nube (5710m)

Huanacuni Este (5500m)

Río Suches

Antaquilla

Lago Cololo

Lago Nube

Lago Dadacorane

Cololo (5916m)

Quello

Río Cololo

Hichacollo (Sorapata)

Sunchuli (5306m)

Posnansky (5430m)

Cochauau

Paso Osipal

Área Natural de Manejo Integrado Nacional (Anmin) Apolobamba

Lago Quello

Lago Pullo Pullo

Iscacuchu (5650m)

Mita (5500m)

Pullo Pullo

Bofedales

Ulla Ulla

Lago Kanahuma

Lago Alueta

Lago Chojna Khota

Kotapampa

Lago Cacho Khota

PERU

Phujro Utano

to the trailhead for the Lagunillas–Agua Blanca trek.

Services in Charazani have increased slightly in recent years, but the NGOs who were once involved in promoting sustainable tourism seem to have packed up and left. That said, weary hikers will certainly enjoy the hot springs.

Two **fiestas** are held in Charazani; the biggest takes place around July 16 and the smaller one around August 6. There's also a wonderful **children's dance festival** (around November 16) in honor of the Virgen del Carmen, an invocation of the Virgin Mary. Market day is Sunday.

⊙ Sights

Chari   VILLAGE
The traditional Kallawaya village of Chari, a 6km walk from Charazani (90 minutes), is a blend of terraces, flowers and vegetable gardens. The town is home to a **Kallawaya cultural museum**, a stone and thatch structure with exhibits pertaining to medicinal plants and textile arts.

Pre-Incan Ruins   RUINS
(Chari) About an hour's walk outside Chari are some pre-Incan ruins, reached by walking through town and turning left at the enormous boulder that creates a small cave. Follow this path to the cemetery, keep left until you gain the ridge, then continue 200m up to the ruins. To avoid suspicion it's best to advise locals where you're headed before setting off.

🏃 Activities

Termas de Charazani Phutina   HOT SPRINGS
(B$5; ⊙7am-9pm) Along the river, about 10 minutes' walk upstream from town, you'll pass the Termas de Charazani Phutina, a hot-springs complex where you can bathe and enjoy a hot shower. Other natural thermal baths, complete with a steaming-hot waterfall, can be found a two-hour hike away. Head down the valley from Charazani along the Apolo road alongside the Río Kamata.

🛏 Sleeping & Eating

Accommodations are basic no matter where you look. Don't expect heat, and use the thermal springs if you want a hot shower.

Hotel Akhamani   HOTEL **$**
(☏7201-0646; Lionel Alvarez s/n; r per person B$25, apt B$140) A block below the plaza,

Hotel Akhamani has the highest standards and the widest variety of options, including a four-bed mini-apartment with private bathroom and small kitchen.

Pension Doña Sofia BOLIVIAN **$**
(📱7490-2589; Peru s/n; mains B$10; ⏱7:30am-9pm) Just off the plaza on the road to **Residencial Inti Wasi** (📱249-5185; Peru s/n; r per person B$25), Doña Sofia is your best bet for a decent meal. Try the *mate de la basura,* a 'trash tea' of local herbs.

ℹ Information

Technically there's a tourist information kiosk in the plaza but it's rarely open. Similarly, if you happen to find it open, the public Nawiriywasi Library has books on medicinal plants and Kallawaya culture, as well as maps and information for hikers, trekkers and climbers.

There's no ATM, so be sure to bring cash with you.

ℹ Getting There & Away

From La Paz, **Trans Altiplano** (📱7320-7113) buses depart daily at 6am from Reyes Cardona in the cemetery district (B$30, six to seven hours), returning from Charazani daily at 8pm. Book tickets in advance, as the schedule for the return trip often changes. An onward bus to Lagunillas will cost B$6 and typically leaves between noon and 1pm.

A 4WD route winds down from Charazani to the Yungas village of Apolo at the edge of the Amazon Basin, where you can stay overnight at a basic hotel. The route is frequently negotiated by buses during the dry season, but several serious stream crossings and risks of landslide mean it's often closed to traffic during the rains (November to April).

THE KALLAWAYA

Originating in 10 villages around Charazani in the Apolobamba region, the Kallawaya people are healers who pass ancient traditions down the generations, usually from father to son. Around a quarter of the inhabitants of these villages become involved in the healing tradition, although there are many more people throughout the Andes that pass themselves off as authentic Kallawaya when they are not.

The origins and age of the Kallawaya tradition are unknown, although some Kallawaya claim to be descended from the vanished people of Tiwanaku. The Kallawaya language, Machaj Juyai, used exclusively for healing, is derived from Quechua, the language of the Incas. With only 100 to 200 Kallawaya speakers left in the world, the language is at risk of extinction – around half of the 7000 languages spoken globally may disappear in the next 100 years. Check out www.livingtongues.org to hear recordings of Kallawaya and learn more about language preservation initiatives.

For the Kallawaya people, language, knowledge and skills are passed down through generations, although it's sometimes possible for aspiring healers to study under acknowledged masters. Women don't become healers, but play an important part in the gathering of herbs. A hallmark of Kallawaya dress is the *alforja* (medicine pouch) carried by the men.

Early Kallawaya were known for their wanderings and traveled all over the continent in search of medicinal herbs. The most capable of today's practitioners will have memorized the properties and uses of 600 to 1000 different healing herbs. Their practices also involve magic and charms. They believe that sickness and disease are the result of a displaced or imbalanced *ajallu* (life force). Incantations and amulets are intended to encourage *ajallu* back into a state of equilibrium within the body.

The Kallawaya legacy has been recorded by several anthropologists and medical professionals; German university psychiatrist Ina Rössing has produced an immense four-volume work titled *El Mundo de los Kallahuaya* about her ongoing research, and Frenchman Louis Girault has compiled an encyclopedia of herbal remedies employed by the Kallawaya, entitled *Kallahuaya, curanderos itinerantes de los Andes.*

There's a small exhibition about the Kallawaya people in the **Museo Interpretativo Center** in Lagunillas, and a larger exhibit at the Inca Utama Hotel (p106) in Hautajata. For a guided journey through Kallawaya lands, consider a tour with **Pacha Trek** (📱6317-7688; www.facebook.com/pachatrek.bolivia; 3-day tours per 2/4/8 people B$1950/1176/793).

Área Natural de Manejo Integrado Nacional Apolobamba

In the late 1990s the Reserva Nacional de Fauna Ulla Ulla was renamed the Área Natural de Manejo Integrado Nacional (Anmin) Apolobamba and was expanded by nearly 300,000 hectares to 484,000 hectares. It now includes the entire Cordillera Apolobamba and most of the renowned Lagunillas–Agua Blanca trek along the range's eastern slopes. At its northern end, it abuts Parque Nacional Madidi to form one of the western hemisphere's most extensive protected areas.

The park is home to several thousand alpacas and vicuñas, and also has one of Bolivia's densest condor populations. In addition to popular hiking routes, you'll find excellent wild trekking around Lagos Cololo, Nube, Quello, Kanahuma and Pullo Pullo, all of which enjoy snow-covered backdrops and rich waterbird populations, including flamingos and several species of Andean geese.

🛏 Sleeping

There are ranger stations at Antaquilla, Charazani, Lagunillas, Kotapampa, Pelechuco, Pullo Pullo, Suches and Hichacollo; the latter three were designed by a La Paz architect, and blend adobe construction, domed thatched roofs and passive solar walls to reflect both modern and traditional styles. Hikers can camp at any of these sites or stay in the stations – sufficient space and Spanish skills permitting.

Noncampers may find accommodations in local homes for B$20 per person.

Lagunillas Albergue   GUESTHOUSE $
(📷 7250-3217; Lagunillas; per person B$25, incl meals B$65) This large modern building by the football field has dorm beds, kitchen facilities and a fireplace. Hot water is not always guaranteed, and the place might not be clean if you haven't reserved ahead. Ask around town for Marco and Anna, who have the keys.

Agua Blanca Albergue   GUESTHOUSE $
(📷 7321-2250; Agua Blanca; per person B$25, incl meals B$65) Dorm beds, hot showers, kitchen facilities and a fireplace in a modern building. Reserve ahead, if possible, or you'll have to search the town for the keys.

ℹ Information

A team of park rangers roams between several far-flung Casas de Guardaparques, which are all linked by phone but infrequently staffed during the day. For pre-departure information contact Servicio Nacional de Áreas Protegidas (p79) in La Paz.

ℹ Getting There & Away

Trans Altiplano (📷 La Paz 2-238-3010; cnr Reyes Cardona & Av Kollasuyo, La Paz) buses run to Lagunillas from La Paz (B$30, daily at 6am, six to seven hours) from Reyes Cardona in the cemetery district. Trans Norte (📷 La Paz 2-6807-4905; Terminal Interprovincial El Alto, La Paz) runs to Agua Blanca and Pelechuco from the Terminal Interprovincial in El Alto (B$45, daily at 7am, 12 hours). Double-check departure times and book one day in advance.

A more expensive but considerably easier and more comfortable option is 4WD. A vehicle and driver from La Paz to Lagunillas (B$2100, six hours) or Agua Blanca (B$2500, 10 hours) may be worthwhile because it allows for daylight travel through some incomparable scenery. However, for that kind of money you're probably better off trekking with an agency and leaving the logistics to them.

Lagunillas to Agua Blanca Trek

This fantastic five-day hike (93km) passes through splendid and largely uninhabited wilderness. There is an extreme lack of support services along the way, so unless you are a highly experienced backcountry hiker, it's recommended to go with a guide.

The Route

Start Lagunillas

End Agua Blanca

Duration Five days

Distance 93km

Difficulty Hard

Most people do the trek from south to north – Lagunillas (also known as Tilinhuaya) to Agua Blanca.

From the albergue in Lagunillas it's a short walk to the village of **Curva**, center of the Kallawaya community. From Curva, head toward the **cross** on the hill north of the village and skirt the right side of the hill. About an hour out of Curva, you'll cross a stream. Continue uphill along its right bank. At a cultivated patch about 200m before the valley descending from the right flank of the snowy peak, cross the stream to join a well-defined path on your left. If you continue along this path, you'll reach an excellent flat, streamside campsite. Alternatively, keep following the path for another 1½ hours to an ideal campsite at **Jatunpampa** (4200m).

From Jatunpampa, head up the valley and across a small plain to the *col* (saddle between two peaks) with a cairn, about two hours along. Known as the **Cumbre Tambillo**, this 4700m pass offers fabulous views of Akamani off to the northwest. One to two hours further along you'll arrive at a good campsite (4100m) near the **Incacancha Waterfall** (aka Incachani).

The following morning's zig-zag ascent of the **Akamani Sacred Hill** looks a bit daunting, but it isn't that bad. Cross the bridge below the waterfall and follow the switchbacks up the scree gully. As you ascend, enjoy distant views of Ancohuma and Illampu. After two hours or so you'll reach **Mil Curvas** (4800m), another high pass.

From the pass, traverse gently uphill to the left until you gain the ridge, which affords great views of the Cordillera Real to the south and Cuchillo II to the north. At this point the obvious trail descends past a small lake before arriving at a larger **lake** with a good view of Akamani.

Climb up to the next ridge before descending an hour to the small mining settlement of **Viscachani**, where you'll strike the 4WD track toward Hilo Hilo (aka Illo Illo). In another hour this road ascends to the **Cumbre Viscachani** pass (4900m), which also provides superb views of the Cordillera Real to the south and the Sunchulli Valley to the north and west.

At the pass the road drops into the valley; at the point where it bears right, look for a path turning off to the left. This will take you to a point above the **Sunchulli gold mine**. From Sunchulli, follow a contour line above the aqueduct for about an hour, until you see an idyllic **campsite** (4600m) below Cuchillo I.

The fourth day of the hike is probably the finest, as it includes sections that have been used for centuries by miners and *campesinos* (subsistence farmers). From the campsite, the road ascends for about two hours via a series of switchbacks to the **Cumbre Sunchulli** (5100m) pass. From the pass, you can scramble up to a cairn above the road for excellent views dominated by **Cololo**

(5916m), the southern Cordillera Apolobamba's highest peak.

Descend along the road for a few minutes, then jog right down a steep but obvious path that crosses a stream opposite the **glacier lake** below Cuchillo II before descending to the valley floor. If you follow the valley floor, you'll rejoin the road a couple of minutes above the picturesque stone-and-thatch village of **Piedra Grande**, three hours from the pass. Camping is possible here.

Follow the road for about an hour, then join the precolonial road turning off downhill to your right. After you cross a bridge, you should follow the obvious path to the right, leading you up into the village of **Hilo Hilo** in about an hour. Here you'll find small stores selling basic supplies and it may even be possible to rent a room for the night.

When leaving Hilo Hilo don't be tempted onto the path to the left, which leads west to Ulla Ulla (although this is also a viable trek). The correct route is to the right, leaving the village above the school between the public facilities and the cemetery. From there, cross the llama pastures until the path becomes clear again. After crossing a bridge (about an hour out of town) and beginning up the **Palca Valley** with a sharp rock peak at its head (if it's too overcast to see the rock, look for several small houses on your left and turn there), you'll stumble onto an ideal campsite set in a bend in the valley, where there are a number of large fallen rocks.

From the campsite, head up the valley for about 1½ hours until you reach a bridge over the stream. At this point the route begins to ascend to the **Cumbre Kiayansani** pass (4900m), which you should reach in another 1½ hours. From the pass, descend past a **lake**, crossing pastures full of llamas, and follow some pre-Columbian paving as well as stone steps cut into the rock that date from the same period. In less than two hours you'll arrive in **Pelechuco**, a quaint colonial village founded by Jesuits in 1560.

There are a couple of simple *alojamientos* (basic accommodations) in Pelechuco, but a 30-minute walk further, passing two intriguing pre-Columbian settlements, takes you to the mining village of **Agua Blanca**, where there's an albergue (p139), for a well-deserved rest.

Note that there is an extreme lack of support services along the way, so unless you are a highly experienced backcountry hiker, it's recommended to do this trek with a guide.

Cordillera Quimsa Cruz

Although close to La Paz, the Cordillera Quimsa Cruz is a largely undiscovered wilderness of 5000m-plus peaks, some of which have only been climbed for the first time in recent years. Basque climbing magazine *Pyrenaica* once labeled it a 'South American Karakoram.' In 1999, near the summit of Santa Veracruz, Spaniard Javier Sánchez discovered the remains of an 800-year-old ceremonial burial site with ancient artifacts and weavings.

The Quimsa Cruz is separated from the Cordillera Real by Río La Paz. Geologically speaking, it's actually a southern outlier of that range that's just 50km from end to end, with lower peaks than in other Bolivian ranges. The highest peak, **Jacha Cuno Collo**, rises to 5800m, and other glaciated peaks range from 4500m to 5300m. Granite peaks, glaciers and lakeside camping make Quimsa Cruz an unforgettable, untouristed Andean experience.

🏃 Activities

Climbing

The Quimsa Cruz lies at the northern end of Bolivia's tin belt, and tin reserves have been exploited here since the late 1800s. For climbers, this means that mining roads in every valley provide access to the impressively glaciated peaks. The area offers some of the finest adventure climbing in Bolivia, and although all of the *nevados* (snowy peaks) of the Quimsa Cruz have now been claimed, there are still plenty of unclimbed routes, and climbers are likely to have the mountains to themselves. If you have no previous climbing experience, find a guide who really knows the area at a La Paz agency (p60).

Hiking

Trekking is possible throughout the range, which is covered by IGM mapping. The main route is the two- to three-day Mina Viloco to Mina Caracoles trek, which crosses the range from west to east. Of interest along this route is the renowned site of a 1971 airplane crash, which had already been stripped by local miners before rescue teams arrived at the scene two days later. Mina Viloco is 70km southeast of La Paz, and is centered on a major tin mine. Mina Caracoles is still worked by cooperatives, and is 13km northwest of Quime.

ℹ️ Getting There & Away

Road access is relatively easy because of the number of mines in the area, and it's possible to drive to within 30 minutes' walk of some glaciers. Others, however, are up to a four-hour hike from the nearest road.

The easiest access is provided by **Flota Trans-Inquisivi** (Map p50; ☎ 228-4050; Main Bus Terminal, La Paz), which leaves daily in the early morning from La Paz for the eastern side of the range (to Quime, Inquisivi, Cajuata, Circuato, Suri, Mina Caracoles and, less often, Yacopampa and Frutillani).

Trans Araca (☎ 228-4050; cnr Av Francisco Carvajal & Calle 8, Barrio Villa Dolores, El Alto) serves communities and mines on the western side of the range from its office in El Alto. A bus to Mina Viloco, Araca or Cairoma departs daily at 7am (seven to 10 hours).

Those with a bit more ready cash can rent a 4WD and driver for the five- to seven-hour journey from La Paz (expect to pay at least B$2000); any of the services used by mountaineers and trekkers can organize the trip.

Southern Altiplano

Best Places
to Eat

➡ Las Delicias (p150)

➡ Tika (p164)

➡ Salteñas Especiales
Marianita (p175)

➡ Minuteman Revolutionary
Pizza (p164)

➡ Milan Center (p175)

Best Places
to Stay

➡ La Petite Porte (p163)

➡ Albergue Ecoturístico
Tomarapi (p156)

➡ Luna Salada Hotel (p169)

➡ Hotel Mitru (p175)

➡ Piedra Blanca Hostel
(p161)

Why Go?

The harsh and sometimes almost primeval geography of the Southern Altiplano will tug at the heartstrings of visitors with a deep love of bleak and solitary places. Stretching southwards from La Paz, this high-plains wilderness is framed by majestic volcanic peaks, endless kilometers of treeless stubble and the white emptiness of the eerie *salares* (salt deserts), which are almost devoid of life. At night the stargazing is spectacular, but it's as cold as you could ever imagine.

The area around Parque Nacional Sajama offers some breathtaking scenery and climbing, while revelers may wish to hit up Carnaval (p151) celebrations in the gritty, straight-talking mining city of Oruro (p153). Further south Salar de Uyuni (p156) is the star attraction, and a three-day jeep tour of the region is at the top of most travelers' itineraries. From here, you can head to the warmer cactus-studded valleys around Tupiza (p177) for horseback riding and mountain biking.

When to Go
Uyuni

| **May–Sep** The best time for salt-flat and wilderness trips. | **Oct–Nov** Good deals on *salar* tours and the chance to see the salt flat flooded. | **Jan–Mar** Eye-catching Carnaval costumes, dance troupes and a huge water-balloon fight. |

History

The prehistoric lakes Minchín and Tauca once covered most of this highland plateau. They evaporated around 10,000 years ago, leaving behind a parched landscape of brackish puddles and salt deserts. Pre-Columbian civilizations didn't leave much of a mark on the region; some time in the mid-15th century an Inca ruler sent his son Tupac-Yupanqui southward to conquer all the lands he encountered. Tupac-Yupanqui and his troops marched on across the wastelands to the northern bank of Chile's Río Maule, where a fierce band of Araucanian people inspired them to stake out the southern boundary of the Inca empire and turn back toward Cuzco.

These days, outside the major towns and cities, most people cluster around mining camps. During the late 1980s a mining crisis sent miners fleeing to lower elevations. But with commodity prices up and the world's largest stash of lithium in the early stages of exploitation, mining is back and, with it, controversy. In fact, much of Bolivia's social conflict now revolves around contamination from mines, and the nationalization and management of the industry. Climate change and desertification are affecting the region's natural and social landscape in a major way as well, making it easier to sow lucrative quinoa crops at higher elevations and triggering a tenfold spike in land prices.

National Parks

Parque Nacional Sajama (p154), Bolivia's first national park, is a region of magnificent peaks, plains and wildlife habitat. It is also home to the world's highest and some of South America's loftiest hot springs. Even if you're not into hardcore mountaineering, an evening dip in the clear springs at the base of Volcán Sajama (p154) in the company of a few camelids is worth the trek. Reserva Nacional de Fauna Andina Eduardo Avaroa (p170) is a highlight of Southwest Circuit tours and the gateway to Chile for those headed to San Pedro de Atacama.

ℹ Getting There & Away

From La Paz the Southern Altiplano is easily accessed by bus, and as the once-bumpy, unpaved intercity roads of the region are now almost all tarmacked, it's easier than ever. The central highland cities of Potosí and Sucre are now linked by paved roads to Tupiza (p171), Oruro and Uyuni (p159). The overland route from Chile is a scenic mountain traverse on a good road from Arica, and Villazón has an easy border crossing with Argentina.

ORURO & THE NORTH

Oruro

📱 2 / POP 265,000 / ELEV 3706M (12,158FT)

Oruro's Carnaval (p151) celebrations are famous throughout South America for their riotous parties, lavish costumes and elaborate parades. The culmination of the city's rich dance and musical heritage, the festivities attract revelers from across Bolivia and beyond. Outside Carnaval season, there are some worthwhile museums to visit in the city and plenty to see in the area.

At first glance Oruro is a sprawl of sun-baked buildings in shades of terracotta and dusty tan, but there's something about this gritty miners' city that endears it to visitors. In many ways Oruro (which means 'where the sun is born') is an intriguing place, where 90% of the inhabitants are of indigenous heritage. *Orureños* (Oruro locals) refer to themselves as *quirquinchos* (armadillos), after the carapaces of their *charangos* (traditional Bolivian ukulele-like instruments). The city makes for an oddly atavistic experience that some may find intoxicating.

◉ Sights

Monumento Escultérico
Virgen del Socavón   MONUMENT
(Cerro Santa Bárbara; B$10; ⊗9am-5pm) Oruro's **teleférico** (one-way/return B$10/15, during Carnaval B$20/30; ⊗11am-7pm Wed, Sat & Sun) zips passengers on a three-minute journey from Plaza del Folklore up to the towering statue of Virgen del Socavón, perched atop Cerro Santa Bárbara (3883m), from where there are impressive views of the city and beyond. Inside the monument, stairs lead to viewing platforms and a small exhibition of carnival posters and photographs, some dating back to 1910. At 45.4m, the statue is the tallest of its kind in South America.

Santuario de la
Virgen del Socavón   CHURCH
(Plaza del Folklore; ⊗7:30am-7pm) **FREE** Dedicated to the Virgen de Candelaria (the patron of Oruro miners), this small church is a colorful 19th-century reconstruction of the 1771 original and figures prominently in Oruro's Carnaval (p151).

The ceiling features a star-studded night sky with painted depictions of the four creatures that, according to local legend, were sent by the spirit of the sky, Huari, to destroy the Uru people: a serpent, a lizard, a giant frog and ants.

Southern Altiplano Highlights

1 Salar de Uyuni (p167) Strapping on some sunglasses and posing for photos with a plastic dinosaur on the salty expanse.

2 Los Lípez (p169) Traversing Dalí-esque landscapes and gazing out at colorful lakes populated with flamingos in the country's far southwest.

3 Tupiza (p171) Whistling the theme from your favorite Western as you guide your horse up the narrow gullies.

4 Parque Nacional Sajama (p154) Hiking out to geysers, relaxing in hot springs and climbing the snow-topped volcano, Bolivia's loftiest peak.

5 **Carnaval** (p151)
Donning a mask and joining the revelers at Oruro's boisterous party.

6 **Curahuara de Carangas** (p153)
Ogling at Bolivia's version of the Sistine Chapel in this remote village.

7 **Oruro** (p143)
Exploring the city's museums and taking a ride in a cable car.

Oruro

Museo Sacro, Folklórico, Arqueológico y Minero   MUSEUM

(Plaza del Folklore; B$12; ⏱ 9-11:45am & 3:15-6pm) An excellent double museum attached to Santuario de la Virgen del Socavón. Access is by guided tour only, beginning with a descent down from the church to a mining tunnel lined with tools and representations of El Tío, spirit of the underground. Upstairs are a variety of archaeological and folklore exhibits, from Wankarani-period stone llama heads to Carnaval costumes.

Tours leave every 45 minutes. The guides for the mining museum are miners who are happy to talk about the industry and life in the mines, though most don't speak English. Some exhibits have bilingual explanations.

Casa de la Cultura Simón Patiño   MUSEUM

(Soria Galvarro 5755; B$10; ⏱ 8:30-11:30am & 3-6:30pm Mon-Fri, 9am-3pm Sat) The grand former residence of tin baron Simón Patiño is now a museum, displaying his furniture, personal bric-a-brac, musical instruments and fine toys (you're not allowed to play with them though). Entry is by guided tour only.

The museum is reached via an ornate art-nouveau staircase. Temporary art exhibitions are displayed in the downstairs lobby; admission is free.

respect to Pachamama, which you are welcome to join; call ahead.

Museo Antropológico
Eduardo López Rivas   MUSEUM
(España cnr Urquidi; B$5; ⊙10am-6pm) Located south of the city center, this anthropological and archaeological museum is worth the hike. The fascinating hodgepodge of exhibits includes mastodons, Carnaval costumes, stone-carved llama heads, mummies from nearby *chullpares* (funerary towers) and skulls exhibiting the horrific cranial deformations once practiced on children.

Take any *micro* (small bus) marked 'Sud' from the northwest corner of Plaza 10 de Febrero or opposite the train station (p152).

Faro de Conchupata   MONUMENT
(Montecinos s/n) **FREE** On November 17, 1851, Bolivia's flag was first raised at Faro de Conchupata: red for the courage of the Bolivian army, gold for the country's mineral wealth and green for its agricultural wealth. The spot is now marked by a platform and column topped by a glass globe, and is illuminated at night. It provides a fine view over the town.

Plaza del Folklore Stairway   VIEWPOINT
(Plaza del Folklore) **FREE** Starting from the western side of Plaza del Folklore, a stairway takes you huffing and puffing to a handful of interesting murals depicting Carnaval images and religious themes.

Portada del Beaterio   CONVENT
(Soria Galvarro 1764) It's worth checking out this facade of a convent, which is carved with ornate plant and bird motifs. It's located a couple of blocks southeast of Plaza 10 de Febrero.

🎓 Courses

Centro de Aprendizaje
de Lenguas Modernas   LANGUAGE
(📞528-7676; Pagador 5635; ⊙8:30am-noon & 4-8pm) Drop by for Quechua or Spanish classes, which cost B$1664 for a 20-hour course. Students can choose how many hours of classes they wish to take per day.

👉 Tours

Charlie Tours   TOURS
(📞524-0666; charlietours@yahoo.com) Run by the knowledgeable Juan Carlos Vargas, Charlie Tours is a real specialist in the region. In addition to city tours, mine visits and excursions to nearby attractions such as Cala Cala (p153) and Termas de Obrajes (p153), it offers

Museo Casa Arte
Taller Cardozo Velasquez   MUSEUM
(📞527-5245; juegueoruro@hotmail.com; Junín 738; B$8; ⊙hours vary; call ahead) A family of seven artists – Gonzalo (sculptor), his wife María (potter) and their five daughters – open their whimsical house and art studio to visitors. Take a peek at their collection of Bolivian art and into the nooks and crannies of their workshop, overflowing with artsy bric-a-brac. A leafy patio is the site of Gonzalo's fascinating sculptures – the one in the middle is devoted to Pachamama (Mother Earth).

On the first Friday of the month, they hold a *k'oa* ceremony, an Andean ritual that pays

SOUTHERN ALTIPLANO ORURO

Oruro

trips to places further afield, including the Chipaya (p158), Salar de Coipasa and Sajama. The offices are outside town, so call or email.

Mina San José TOURS
There are several mines in the Oruro area, many operated by *cooperativos* (small groups of miners who purchase temporary rights). One of the most important is Mina San José, which has been in operation for over 450 years. For a half-day tour of the mine, contact Charlie Tours (p147) or Hostal Graciela. The mine is located 2km west of the city center.

🛏 Sleeping

Oruro has some decent midrange business-style hotels, but little in the way of luxury accommodations. Budget lodgings can be bitterly cold at night.

Accommodations are often booked solid during Carnaval (p151), when there's also a three-night minimum stay. It's wise to reserve well ahead of time or ask the tour-ist office (p152) about rooms in local homes.

Expect to pay up to five or six times the usual price for a room.

Hostal Graciela HOSTEL $
(☑525-2082; www.facebook.com/OruroHostalGraciela; Herrera 47; dm/s/d/tr incl breakfast B$56/85/140/180; 🛜) Colorful murals and friendly, English-speaking staff make for a warm welcome at Graciela, though the unheated rooms are pretty cold at night. Dorms are small and rather dank; the street-facing private rooms are brighter. The top-floor common area with a small kitchen and bar is a good place to hook up with other travelers.

The hostel runs a free city walking tour at 10am daily, and offers a number of cycling and hiking tours in the surrounding area.

Residencial Gran Boston HOSTEL $
(☑527-4708; Pagador 1159; s/d B$100/150, with shared bathroom B$50/100; 🛜) A class above most Oruro *residenciales* (simple accommodations), this place makes an effort with its airy yellow courtyard that nicely sets off

the sun. You'll have to decide whether this makes up for the windowless rooms and lack of heating.

★ Flores Plaza Hotel   HOTEL $$
(☏525-2561; www.floresplazahotel.com; Adolfo Mier 735; s/d/tr incl breakfast B$300/450/550; 🅿@🤖) A top midrange choice right on the main plaza, this eight-story, three-star hotel offers nicely renovated rooms, good city views, an ample breakfast buffet and friendly management. Request a room on a higher floor for better views.

Hotel Virgen del Socavón   HOTEL $$
(☏528-2184; Junín 1179; s/d/ste incl breakfast B$300/400/480; 🅿🤖) This modern option has rooms looking right onto Plaza del Folklore, making it the most sought-after hotel in town come Carnaval (p151) time when prices spike. Outside Carnaval season, it's still a worthwhile option, with fresh bedspreads, contemporary decor and excellent balconies overlooking the action on the plaza.

Hotel Repostero   HOTEL $$
(☏525-8001; hzavaleta1947@yahoo.com; Sucre 370; s/d/tr incl breakfast B$180/250/300; 🅿🤖) You'll love the sign at this faded but likable old place, which conjures up a sense of old-school travel and adventure. It has a variety of rooms in two wings, all with cable TV and hot showers.

Hotel Edén   BUSINESS HOTEL $$$
(☏521-0671; www.hoteledenbolivia.com; Bolívar 777; s/d/ste incl breakfast B$623/1106/1386; 🅿@🤖🛗) If you're looking for a comfortable, well-equipped business hotel, then this is it. Rooms are huge, with big beds and flat-screen TVs, and there's an on-site gym and indoor pool. Guests are zipped up to their rooms in a glass elevator overlooking the plaza. Rates are often cheaper online.

✕ Eating
Oruro's culinary offerings are not exceptional, but with some decent grill restaurants and comforting pizzerias you won't go hungry. Local specialties include *thimpu de cordero* (a mutton-and-vegetable concoction smothered in *llajua*, a hot tomato-based sauce) and *charquekan* (sun-dried llama meat with corn, potatoes or beans, eggs and cheese).

Restaurant Ardentia   INTERNATIONAL $
(Soria Galvarro 5865; almuerzo B$15, mains B$13-26; ⊙11am-2:30pm & 7-11pm Mon-Sat) It's not known how Halle Berry would feel about the

restaurant using her likeness for its publicity, but copyright infringement issues aside, you can get a good meal here. The menu features lasagna, simple but savory chicken and beef dishes, and other familiar standards.

Govinda   VEGETARIAN $
(Junín, btwn Soria Galvarro & Calle 6 de Octubre; mains B$6-19; ⊙noon-2pm & 4-10pm Mon-Sat; ✍) Forget you're in Bolivia at this Hare Krishna–devoted restaurant behind a modern glass front, where vegetarian meals are fresh, cheap and creative, the decor light, and the music ambient. Good juices and milkshakes too, some with soya milk, of course.

Mercado Campero   MARKET $
(Adolfo Mier, btwn Pagador & Soria Galvarro; dishes B$5-15; ⊙6am-7:30pm) There are rows of lunch spots at this market, as well as stalls serving *mate* (a herbal infusion of coca, chamomile or similar), *api* (a local drink made of maize) and coffee. Tuck into filling soups and other typical fare at long tiled tables.

Mercado Fermín López   MARKET $
(Cochabamba, btwn Av Presidente Montes & Washington; dishes B$12-25; ⊙6am-8pm) Fresh juices and *licuados* (smoothies) as well as local plates such as *picante de pollo* (chicken with a spicy tomato sauce) are served in this vibrant market.

Irupana   SUPERMARKET $
(Soria Galvarro 5891; ⊙9am-9pm Mon-Sat) This health-food chain has a great selection of nutritious snacks.

La Casona   ITALIAN $$
(Av Presidente Montes 5969; mains B$21-40; ⊙9am-1pm & 4-11pm) Straight-out-of-the-oven *salteñas* (meat and vegetable pasties) for lunch and Oruro's best pizzas for dinner keep this little place buzzing, especially at night when it gets really busy and warm.

Pagador   BOLIVIAN $$
(Pagador 1440; almuerzo B$22, mains B$45-75; ⊙11am-9:30pm Mon-Sat) This no-frills restaurant is deservedly popular with locals. The *almuerzo* (set lunch) is especially good on the covered patio outside. Pay at the counter and collect a token before taking your seat.

Bravo's Pizza   PIZZA $$
(☏525-5551; cnr Camacho & Bolívar; mains B$28-45; ⊙9am-11pm) This well-established Oruro favorite serves 20 varieties of pizza, including a spicy one with dried llama meat, plus pasta, sandwiches, burritos and breakfasts

(B$32 to B$34). Call for a delivery if it's too cold to go outside.

★ Las Delicias BARBECUE $$$
(☑ 527-7256; Rodríguez, btwn Calle 6 de Octubre & Av La Paz; almuerzo B$20, mains B$45-90; ☺ 9am-10:30pm) This is arguably the best *churras-quería* (grilled-meat restaurant) in town, with attentive service, sizzling tableside *parrilladas* (plates of mixed grilled meats), great *almuerzos* (set lunches) and top-notch Argentine-imported beef.

Nayjama BOLIVIAN $$$
(☑ 527-7699; cnr Aldana & Pagador; mains B$55-150; ☺ 11:30am-9:30pm Mon-Sat, to 3pm Sun; 🛜) This appealing choice serves high-quality traditional *orureño* (local) food with a dash of innovation in a bright dining room warmed by an open fire. The servings are huge, so ask for half a portion. Lamb is the specialty, served with salad and dehydrated potatoes.

Bravo's Grill BOLIVIAN $$$
(☑ 528-0980; Montecinos, btwn Pagador & Velasco Galvarro; almuerzo B$22, mains B$45-86; ☺ noon-3pm Sun-Tue, noon-3pm & 4:30-11pm Wed-Sat) An upscale grill (by Oruro standards) offering meat and fish dishes. If you can't make up your mind what to choose, go for the house special Triple Delicia Combo (B$80), which includes chicken, pork and prawns slathered in barbecue sauce.

Las Retamas INTERNATIONAL $$$
(☑ 525-2375; Murguía 930; almuerzo B$30, mains B$58-90; ☺ noon-3pm & 7-10pm Mon-Sat, noon-3pm Sun) This fancy restaurant occupies a series of cozy rooms with leafy views and offers an ambitious menu of international mains, including steaks, trout and chicken dishes. The selection of cakes is stellar.

🍷 Drinking & Nightlife

As an urban hub where young people come to work and study, Oruro has a few fairly good bars, cafes and juice stalls, and even a thumping nightclub.

★ Dali BAR
(cnr Calle 6 de Octubre & Cochabamba, 2nd fl; ☺ 3pm-1am Mon-Sat, 4pm-midnight Sun) The closest place you'll find to a hip hangout in Oruro is this chilled cafe-bar that caters to the city's young set. Come for the drinks, not the food. It's a perfect launch pad for a night out on the town.

El Gato Negro CAFE
(www.facebook.com/ElGatoNegroOruro; Adolfo Mier, btwn Soria Galvarro & Calle 6 de Octubre;

☺ 8:30am-noon & 3:30-8:30pm Mon-Sat) Java junkies can get their fix at the black cat cafe, one of the few places in Oruro to serve lattes made with freshly ground beans, as well as pies, cakes and pastries (B$4 to B$9).

Sounder CLUB
(www.complejosounder.com; Petot 1140; ☺ Tue-Sun) This is three discos in one. Pick your music to dance to, from pop and electronic to Bolivian traditional.

Fruit Juice Stalls JUICE BAR
(cnr Velasco Galvarro & Bolívar; ☺ 8am-midnight) On sunny days, locals flock to the row of excellent fruit juice stalls around Mercado Campero (p149).

☆ Entertainment

Cine Gran Rex CINEMA
(☑ 525-8720; www.facebook.com/CinemaGranRex; Adolfo Mier 551; ☺ 3-9pm Mon & Tue, 10:30am-1pm & 3-9:30pm Wed, Thu, Sat & Sun, 3-9:30pm Fri) Shows international films daily. It's located a block away from Plaza 10 de Febrero.

Bravo Bravo KARAOKE
(Montecinos, btwn Pagador & Velasco Galvarro; ☺ 9pm-3am Wed-Sun) The owners of Bravo's Grill offer drinking, dancing and the best karaoke in town.

🛍 Shopping

The design, creation and production of artistic Diablada (dance of the devil) masks and costumes is the main focus of retail in Oruro. Av La Paz, between León and Villarroel, is lined with small workshops offering devil masks, headdresses, costumes and other devilish things. For herbal remedies and witchcraft items, head to the shops on Junín between Galvarro and Av 6 de Agosto.

The Super Feria street market takes over the streets surrounding Mercado Fermín López on Wednesday and Saturday. Near the train station, you'll find hawkers selling indigenous musical instruments such as cheap *zampoñas* (pan flutes made of hollow reeds) and *charangos* (traditional Bolivian ukulele-like instruments).

Mercado Fermín López MARKET
(Cochabamba, btwn Washington & Av Presidente Montes; ☺ 10am-7pm) The impressive Mercado Tradicional in the middle row of Mercado Fermín López has more dried llama fetuses and amulets than a voodoo master has pins. The affable vendors are more than happy to explain the usage of their wares, but make sure to ask if you want to take a photo.

A DEVIL OF A GOOD TIME

Oruro's **Carnaval** (⊙ Feb or Mar) has become Bolivia's largest and most renowned annual celebration. There are two sides to this party of all parties. For the angels in all of us, there are processions, dances and religious pageantry; for our inner devils, there's plenty of drinking, debauchery and water-fights.

In a broad sense, these festivities can be described as reenactments of the triumph of good over evil, but the festival is interlaced with threads of both Christian and indigenous myths, fables, deities and traditions.

Orureños (Oruro locals) maintain that the festival commemorates an event that occurred during the early days of their own fair city. Legend has it that one night a thief called Chiruchiru was seriously wounded by a traveler he'd attempted to rob. Taking pity on the wrongdoer, the Virgen de Candelaria gently helped him reach his home near the mine at the base of Cerro Pié del Gallo and succored him until he died. When the miners found him there, an image of the Virgin hung over his head. Today, the mine is known as **Socavón de la Virgen** (Grotto of the Virgin), and a church, Santuario de la Virgen del Socavón (p143), has been built over it to house the Virgin, the patron saint of the city.

This legend is combined with the ancient Uru tale of Huari, the spirit of the hills who sent four plagues – a lizard, a giant frog, a serpent and a horde of ants – to destroy the Urus (they were saved by a princess who turned the monsters to sand or stone), and the biblical story of archangel Michael (San Miguel), who leads the angels in a war against Satan and the seven deadly sins.

Ceremonies begin several weeks before Carnaval itself, with various processions as dance groups practice boisterously in the city's streets. On the morning of the Saturday before Carnaval (10 days before Ash Wednesday, in February or March), thousands of bands gather to play together in the **Festival de Bandas** on Plaza del Folklore. The next day, the dance troupes meet for a final rehearsal along the entire 3.5km Carnaval parade route. On Thursday, locals from the surrounding villages arrive in Oruro to perform their traditional dances in the **Anata Andina** procession. The following day, miners perform *cha'lla* libations, in which alcohol is sprinkled over worldly goods to invoke a blessing.

The main event kicks off on the Saturday before Ash Wednesday with the spectacular *entrada* (entrance procession). For 24 hours, some 50 carnival troupes make their way down the parade route to Santuaro de la Virgen, which they enter on their knees to receive a blessing. At dawn on Sunday a mass is held in honor of the Virgin.

There's another, less spectacular *entrada* on Sunday afternoon, when anyone can put on a mask and join the dancing. Yet more dance displays take place on Monday, including a series of dances in which San Miguel fights off the dancing devils. The next day, Shrove Tuesday, is marked by family reunions and *cha'lla* libations, and the following day people make their way into the surrounding countryside where four rock formations – the Toad, Viper, Condor and Lizard – are also subjected to *cha'lla* as an offering to Pachamama.

Tickets typically cost between B$200 and B$350 for the seats along Av 6 de Agosto. On the main plaza, prime seats cost between B$800 and B$1200.

ARAO Artesanías Oruro ARTS & CRAFTS
(Adolfo Mier, btwn Soria Galvarro & Calle 6 de Octubre; ⊙ 9:30am-12:30pm & 3-7:30pm Mon-Fri, 10:30am-5:30pm Sat) Offers a small selection of high-quality, cooperatively produced handicrafts from four communities in Oruro.

ℹ Information

DANGERS & ANNOYANCES

The region has been mined since pre-Columbian times and there is an estimated two million tons of mining waste sitting on the hillsides outside town. This waste contaminates the water, the air and the general environment, and clashes between mining and agricultural interests are on the rise. Be sure to drink only bottled water and ask at your hotel or the tourist office (p152) to find out if protests or roadblocks are likely.

IMMIGRATION

Migraciónes (☏ 527-0239; www.migracion. gob.bo; cnr Cochabamba & La Plata; ⊙ 8:30am-12:30pm & 2:30-6:30pm Mon-Fri)

INTERNET ACCESS

There are plenty of places to get online in Oruro (for about B$2 per hour), with a concentration of options on Calle 6 de Octubre on the blocks between Mier and Ayacucho. Most also offer cheap international calls.

LAUNDRY

Limpieza Virgen del Socavón (Ayacucho 5801; per kilo B$16; ⊙ 8:30am-12:30pm & 2-7:30pm Mon-Sat) Offers a same-day laundry service.

MEDICAL SERVICES

Policlínica Oruro (☑ 527-5082; Rodríguez 579)

MONEY

There are several banks with ATMs in town, particularly around Plaza 10 de Febrero.

→ **Banco Bisa** (Plaza 10 de Febrero)

→ **Banco de Crédito** (Plaza 10 de Febrero)

TOURIST INFORMATION

Caseta de Información Turística (Tourist Information Office; cnr Velasco Galvarro & Aldana; ⊙ 8:30am-noon & 2:30-7pm Mon-Fri)

❶ Getting There & Away

AIR

Domestic flights leave from Oruro's **Aeropuerto Juan Mendoza** (☑ 527-8333), 5km east of the city center. **Boliviana de Aviación** (BoA; ☑ 511-2473; www.boa.bo; Potosí, btwn Sucre & Bolívar; ⊙ 8:30am-12:30pm & 2:30-6:30pm Mon-Fri, 9am-1pm Sat) flies at least once daily to Cochabamba (30 minutes, from B$296) continuing on to Santa Cruz (2½ hours, from B$458). A taxi from the airport to Oruro city center costs B$30.

BUS

Long-distance buses use the **new bus terminal** (Gregorio Reynolds), 5km east of the city center. To get here, take any minibus marked 'nueva terminal' traveling north along Av 6 de Agosto. There's a luggage storage office (B$5) on the ground floor of the terminal.

Buses to La Paz depart every half-hour, and there are departures throughout the day for Cochabamba, Potosí, Sucre and Uyuni. Trans Copacabana and Chino Bus offer services to Santa Cruz via Cochabamba, departing in the late afternoon (B$100). There are daily services to Arica, Calama and Iquique in Chile, which depart in the evening.

DESTINATION	COST (B$)	TIME (HR)
Arica (Chile)	140	8
Calama (Chile)	150	14
Cochabamba	30	5
Iquique (Chile)	70-100	8
La Paz	35	3
Potosí	30	5
Sucre	50-80	8
Tarija	60-80	12
Tupiza	50-60	10-12
Uyuni	25-35	4½
Villazón	70-120	12

TRAIN

Trains run south from Oruro to Villazón on the border with Argentina, passing through Uyuni, Atocha and Tupiza along the way. At the time of research, no trains were running south of Uyuni due to damage to the track caused by flooding in the Tupiza area. Repairs were underway to the section north of Tupiza, which suffered less damage. The section from Tupiza to Villazón is expected to take longer to repair.

Expreso del Sur is slightly more luxurious with heating, departing Oruro at 2:30pm on Tuesdays and Fridays. Cheaper service is available on the Wara Wara line, which leaves Oruro on Wednesdays and Sundays at 7pm. There is a return service on Expreso del Sur arriving at 7:10am on Thursdays and Sundays, and on the Wara Wara line arriving at 9:10am on Tuesdays and Fridays.

Buy tickets at least a day ahead from the **train station** (☑ 527-4605; www.fca.com.bo; Velasco Galvarro; ⊙ ticket office 9am-noon & 2:30-5:30pm Mon, Wed, Thu & Sun, 8am-5pm Tue & Fri). Don't forget to bring your passport. On train days, there's a left-luggage kiosk here.

Expreso del Sur

ROUTE	COST (B$ COACH/1ST CLASS)	ARRIVAL TIME
Oruro to Uyuni	60/120	9:20pm
Oruro to Tupiza	107/239	3am
Oruro to Villazón	126/279	6:05am

Wara Wara

ROUTE	COST (B$ NORMAL/ COACH/1ST CLASS)	ARRIVAL TIME
Oruro to Uyuni	32/47/102	2:20am
Oruro to Tupiza	56/80/181	8:35am
Oruro to Villazón	67/100/220	12:05pm

❶ Getting Around

Micros (half-sized buses; B$1.50 to B$2.50) and minibuses (B$1) connect the city center with outlying areas. Their routes are designated by their letters, colors and signs (and in the case of minibuses, numbers). It's a fairly confusing system, so check with the driver before boarding. Note that *micros* and minibuses are small and crowded so, if possible, avoid carrying luggage aboard.

Taxis around the center cost B$5, slightly more if you wander further afield. **Radio taxis** (☑ 527-7775) cost around B$10.

Around Oruro

There's plenty to see around Oruro, particularly along the road south toward Uyuni, where bleak and epic scenery surrounds old mines and the remnants of ancient lakeside cultures.

◉ Sights & Activities

Cala Cala   HISTORIC SITE
(B$20; ⊙9am-5pm Mon-Fri) A worthwhile trip, this site consists of a series of rock paintings of llamas and humans in red and orange tones, dating to the 1st millennium BC. It's located under an overhang 3.5km beyond the village of Cala Cala, 26km east of Oruro.

Stop in the village to locate the current guardian of the key; this can be tricky, as residents take turns in the role. Try asking in the small store on the left as you enter the village.

The site itself is a 30-minute walk beyond the village, near the old brewery. It was a place of rest for ancient llama trains heading for the Potosí and Cochabamba valleys, where Wankarani traders would shelter in the caves while their llamas grazed. Even if you can't locate the key, it's possible to see the clearest of the paintings from beyond the locked gate. The views from the site of the exceptionally beautiful valley, which provides some of Oruro's water, are spectacular.

There's no public transport; expect to pay at least B$100 for a taxi. Charlie Tours (p147) offers a half-day tour to the site (B$300).

Termas de Obrajes   HOT SPRINGS
(B$15; ⊙7am-4pm) These hot springs, located 25km northeast of town, are a popular weekend destination. It's a well-run complex, with a pool and private bathrooms with tubs, which you can reserve for half an hour and gradually fill up with the magnesium-rich water. Make sure you have a swimming costume to enter the public pool.

Obrajes *micros* (B$10, 45 minutes) leave when full from the corner of Caro and Av 6 de Agosto in Oruro; buses are more frequent at weekends, when the pools are more crowded. Last return around 3pm.

Curahuara de Carangas

📝2 / POP 4,200 / ELEV 3898M (12,789FT)
This scenic village halfway between Oruro and Sajama is home to a lovely adobe-and-thatch church called La Capilla Sixtina del Altiplano. The village also has a simple

hostel and plenty of hiking opportunities nearby. It's tricky to reach, but the church is worth the trip.

◉ Sights & Activities

Curahuara de Carangas is the site of a major military base and was once the place where political prisoners were subjected to torture and hard labor in freezing fields.

★**La Capilla Sixtina del Altiplano**   CHURCH
(Sistine Chapel of the Altiplano; Plaza Principal; B$50; ⊙hours vary) Like its famous counterpart in Vatican City, the interior of this lovely adobe-and-thatch church is covered with frescoes. But unlike the other Sistine Chapel, these gorgeous 17th-century paintings have a strong local influence and depict themes such as the three kings visiting Jesus on a llama train. There are plenty of biblical scenes plus some interesting artifacts in a small room behind the altar.

If the church is closed, look for a note pasted on the garage to the left of the church with the phone number of a key holder.

Museo Militar   MUSEUM
(Plaza Principal; B$5; ⊙8:30am-6pm Mon-Fri) This chilling museum details the horrifying treatment of political prisoners, and is adorned with distorted mannequins illustrating painful consequences of refusing to toe the government line during the military

---

LAGO POOPÓ: THE DISAPPEARING LAKE

It was once Bolivia's second largest body of water, but over recent years Lago Poopó has been shrinking at an alarming rate. The size of the lake has always fluctuated, filling with water in the rainy months and shrinking as water evaporates during the dry winter period. But in 2015 the lake dried up almost completely for the first time, forcing local communities who made their living fishing to seek work elsewhere. The Bolivian government blames climate change for the evaporating waters, but environmental experts point to a problem with the flow of water from Lake Titicaca via the Río Desaguadero: water from the river is diverted to supply mines, which in turn are a source of contamination. Although a small body of shallow water is still visible just south of Oruro, sadly, the lake has all but disappeared.

dictatorship. Ask at the military base for the museum curator.

Pukara de Monterani ARCHAEOLOGICAL SITE
Ask around town for directions to this nearby mountain fortress with terracing, stone walls and *chullpares* (burial towers). Cloaked in legend and a site of great cultural importance, the flat-topped mountain has been revered by local indigenous communities for centuries. Ancestral rituals are performed here on January 1 each year.

Palestras de Qala Chua CLIMBING
Located just 2km from town, this climbing spot has interesting natural formations and makes for a good afternoon jaunt. The chain of rocks resembles a precariously balanced row of dominoes.

🛏 Sleeping & Eating

With advance warning, Hostal Kory Wara can prepare meals, and there are a couple of small stores and simple local cafes located near the main square.

Hostal Kory Wara HOSTEL **$**
(📞 7197-5356; hkorywara@hotmail.com; Av Principal; r per person incl breakfast B$50) This simple hostel has small rooms with Andean textiles. There are heaters in the rooms, but it's still

CHULLPA TOMBS

A *chullpa* is a funerary tower or mausoleum that various Aymará groups built to house the mummified remains of some members of their society, presumably people of high rank or esteem within the community. Oruro is particularly rich in *chullpas*, especially along the shores of Lago Poopó and around the Sajama area. The biggest concentration is found along the road from Patacamaya to Tambo Quemado at the border with Chile.

A *chullpa* was constructed of stone or adobe, and typically had a beehive-shaped opening, which nearly always faced east toward the rising sun. The body was placed in the fetal position along with various possessions. Some communities would ritually open the *chullpas* on feast days and make offerings to the mummified ancestors. Most of the tombs, however, have been looted, apart from some bones here and there, and the mummies can now be found in museums, such as Museo Antropológico Eduardo López Rivas (p147) in Oruro.

good to bring a sleeping bag if you've got one. The family that runs the establishment can provide plenty of tips for trips to the nearby countryside. The hostel is located near the entrance to town.

❶ Getting There & Away

To get here, take the hourly Trans Sajama service from Patacamaya (B$10, 2½ hours). Buses leave every half-hour on Sundays. The last minibus back to Patacamaya leaves Curahuara de Carangas at 4pm and continues on to Oruro.

You can also take an Arica-bound bus from La Paz and ask to be dropped at the highway turnoff, but it's a long 5km walk into town, or take a taxi (B$25). From the highway you can pick up westbound buses toward Parque Nacional Sajama and the border at Tambo Quemado.

Parque Nacional Sajama

Bolivia's first national park, Sajama (B$100) was created on November 5, 1945, to protect 1000 sq km of wondrous scenery, home to rare wildlife that inhabits this northern extension of the Atacama Desert. With increased protection, vicuña populations are on the rise and you may spot flamingos, puna rheas and giant coots. The park offers expansive high-plains views, geyser fields, hot springs, and climbing and hiking opportunities aplenty.

According to legend, Mururata, the most gigantic of all Andean mountains, lost much of its grandeur when it annoyed Pachamama, who angrily decapitated it. The rolling head formed the Sierra Nevada from the gushing blood as it bounced along, before coming to a standstill and turning into Volcán Sajama, the majestic centerpiece of this breathtakingly beautiful national park. At 6542m, Sajama is Bolivia's highest peak.

◎ Sights & Activities

Most climbers come to summit Volcán Sajama (6542m; a three-day climb). Other options include one-day climbs up Acotango (6052m; it's possible to drive up to 5500m, from where it's a three-hour climb to the top) and Parinacota (6348m). Hostels can help organize climbing expeditions and equipment.

Volcán Sajama CLIMBING
(Nevado Sajama) The star of Parque Nacional Sajama, this extinct volcano (6542m) is a popular mountain to climb, but the altitude and icy conditions make the peak more challenging than it initially appears. Some La Paz

Parque Nacional Sajama

agencies offer organized climbs or you can contract a local guide in Sajama – expect to pay around B$3500 for a three-day climb with all equipment included.

Hostal Sajama (p156) offers guided climbs and rents equipment. Only consider going without a guide if you have experience with high-altitude climbing, but prepare for extremely cold and icy conditions and carry lots of water close to your body (otherwise it will freeze). Do not try to climb the volcano between November and February; wet weather and electrical storms make this a dangerous time to ascend.

Hot Springs   HOT SPRINGS
(B$30; ☺ 7am-6pm) For a relaxing warm soak, there are four lovely 35°C hot springs 8km northwest of Sajama village, an easy one-hour walk; look for the bright-orange house to the left of the road. Ask at your hotel about other undeveloped hot springs in the area – there are several.

Geysers   GEYSER
About 7km (1½ hours on foot) due west of Sajama is an interesting spouting geyser field. It makes for a great hike from Sajama. Take the road downhill from the plaza and continue straight; the route is signposted. The geysers steam and sporadically spout water throughout the day.

Lagunas de Altura   HIKING
Tour operators offer one-/two-day (B$160/500 per person) treks from Sajama, beginning with a vehicle trip to the geysers, before setting off hiking to a series of high-altitude lagoons including Khasiri (4820m), Sorapata (4900m) and Chiar Kota (4960m). It takes you right up to the Chilean border.

Laguna Huañakota   LAKE
Flamingos can often be spotted on Laguna Huañakota, about 12km north of Sajama village. It's a pleasant hike here along the road from Sajama, though the lake is sometimes dry or frozen in winter.

Queñua Forest
FOREST

The foothills flanking Volcán Sajama are covered with the world's highest forest, consisting of dwarf *queñua* trees, an endemic and ancient altiplano species. While technically a forest, it's a little underwhelming – the 'trees' look more like little bushes.

🍽 Sleeping & Eating

Most people stay in the village of Sajama (4250m), where there are several guesthouses. Camping is fine just about anywhere in this sparsely populated region; bring a good, cold-weather sleeping bag.

All guesthouses in Sajama village serve meals. There are also a few small stores in the village selling snacks and basic supplies.

Hostal Oasis
HOSTEL $

(📞 7372-2394; hostaloasissajama@gmail.com; r per person B$60-100; 🅿 @ 🛜) At the entrance to Sajama village is the well-run Hostal Oasis, offering private rooms, meals, transport to sights around the park and hiking guides. The upstairs rooms have windows, private bathrooms and chunky wooden furniture, while the cheaper 1st-floor rooms are smaller and darker. The lounge area is a relaxing place to compare hiking notes with other travelers.

Hostal Sajama
HOSTEL $$

(📞 7150-9185; r per person B$70-100; 🅿 🛜) With traditional-style thatched-roof adobe *lakauta* huts, firm beds, clean sheets and electric heaters, this is an atmospheric option at the southern entrance to Sajama village. The arched ceilings give a feeling of openness to the otherwise tight rooms, with Andean textiles adding to the overall charm. There's even wi-fi access in the restaurant.

Owner Eliseo is an experienced climbing guide who can arrange guides and rent equipment for climbs up Volcán Sajama (p154), Volcán Parinacota and Volcán Acotango. It's also possible to rent bikes (B$35 per day).

★ Albergue Ecoturístico Tomarapi
LODGE $$$

(📞 7247-2785; www.ecotomarapi.com; s/d/tr incl meals B$400/550/650) 🍃 On the northern edge of the park in the tiny, charming hamlet of Tomarapi, 12km beyond Sajama, is this enticing community-run 35-bed ecolodge, which offers the area's most comfortable accommodations. Occupying lovely thatched buildings, styled along traditional local architectural lines, it has simple rooms with heating, private bathrooms and hot water, and a very welcoming log fire.

It also offers excellent food, featuring lots of llama meat. Twenty-five families from the nearby village of Caripe work the lodge on a rotating basis. With advanced notice transport can be arranged from Tambo Quemado (B$250).

🛈 Information

Park admission (B$100, for which you are also provided with a small map) is payable at the Servicio Nacional de Areas Protegidas (SERNAP) office at the entrance to the park, immediately after the highway turnoff and 12km south of sleepy Sajama village. The fee applies to all foreigners, including those who are only visiting the village.

🛈 Getting There & Away

There is a daily Trans Sajama bus from the town of Patacamaya to Sajama village (B$30, noon, three hours). Look for the minibus outside the Capitol restaurant on Avenida Principal in Patacamaya; the bus leaves when full, usually between noon and 1pm. A return bus departs Sajama village at 6am Monday to Saturday and 4am on Sunday.

Patacamaya is easily reached on most buses from La Paz to Cochabamba, Oruro and Arica. There are frequent returns from Patacamaya to La Paz (B$12, one hour) and Oruro (B$15, 1½ hours).

Minibuses take the paved road between Oruro and Tambo Quemado at the border with Chile (B$30, 3 hours), leaving Tambo Quemado at around 6am, noon and 6pm. From Oruro, minibuses leave when full starting at around 6am, from the roundabout at the southern end of Avenida Dehene, just north of the university and about 4km southeast of the city center. With advance notice, hostels in Sajama village and Tomarapi can pick you from Tambo Quemado (B$100 to Sajama Village or B$250 to Tomarapi).

La Paz–Arica buses pass the entrance to Parque Nacional Sajama (p154; 12km from Sajama village). The turnoff for Tomarapi is 24km east of the main park entrance at Cruce Tomarapi (signed); Tomarapi village is about 15km from the turnoff.

The border crossing between Tambo Quemado (Bolivia) and Chungará (Chile) 12km away is straightforward and open from 8am to 8pm.

UYUNI & THE SOUTHWEST CIRCUIT

Bolivia's southwestern corner is an awe-inspiring collection of diverse landscapes ranging from the blinding white Salar de Uyuni (which can only be visited on a guided tour, either from Uyuni, Tupiza or

ANDEAN CAMELIDS

There's nothing like them on earth – playful, elegant, independent, ecological and cute as hell – the camelids of the Andes are the species that define a continent.

The western hemisphere had few grazing mammals after the Pleistocene era, when mammoths, horses and other large herbivores disappeared from North and South America. For millennia, the Andean people relied on the New World camelids – the wild guanaco and vicuña, and the domesticated llama and alpaca – for food, fiber and companionship.

Both of the domesticated varieties are highly ecological, friendly animals. Cross the altiplano and you are likely to see perfect circles of llama poop. Yes, in order to fulfill their Darwinian obligations, llamas and alpacas all poop in the same place, protecting the delicate Andean high plains from turning into a veritable desert. They also emit less noxious gas than other livestock – not insignificant considering that 18% of the world's CO_2 emissions come from livestock according to the Food and Agricultural Organization, and most of that comes from the 1.5 billion cows now living on our little blue planet. Don't want to become a vegan just yet? No worries, the low CO_2-emitting llamas also have low-fat, zero-cholesterol meat. And it tastes great – somewhere between steak and lamb – whether in a stew, steak or jerky.

Until around 2008, many Bolivian pastoralists had fairly large llama herds, but they kept them more as pets and pack animals, only sacrificing animals on occasion for big feasts. This asset-rich, cash-poor scenario – llamas are worth about US$100 each, and most high-plains ranchers have herds of around 80 head – prompted the Bolivian government to invest heavily in camelids through projects like Pro-Camélidos, a five-year program that aims to protect the environment, reduce desertification and provide new uses for camelids throughout the high plains. Now, with demand rising on international markets for llama meat and alpaca and vicuña wool, many Bolivian ranchers are also turning back to their Inca roots and getting rid of their sheep and cattle herds in favor of alpacas and llamas.

Species at a Glance

Alpaca *(Vicugna pacos)* These domesticated animals are prized for their fine wool, which is used to make shawls, sweaters and scarves. Smaller and more delicate than their llama brethren, alpacas require well-watered grasslands and are more common in lower elevations.

Guanaco *(Lama guanicoe)* These wily brownish animals are rarely seen in Bolivia, even though they will inhabit a much wider range than their vicuña cousins: from sea level up to 4000m or higher. They are sometimes seen in the highland plains of Reserva Nacional de Fauna Andina Eduardo Avaroa (p170).

Llama *(Lama glama)* The taller, rangier and hardier llama has relatively coarse wool that is used for blankets, ropes and other household goods. It also works as a pack animal, but thanks to the introduction of the *camión* (flatbed truck), llama trains are increasingly rare in Bolivia. Llamas can survive in dry, poor pastures, making them ideal animals for the harsh altiplano.

Vicuña *(Vicugna vicugna)* Nearly hunted to extinction for their fine wool – once reserved exclusively for Inca emperors – the delicate rusty-orange vicuñas are rebounding throughout the Andes. Innovative catch-and-shear programs and increased patrols have cut down on poaching, and there are now around 350,000 vicuñas across Argentina, Bolivia, Chile, Ecuador and Peru. Bolivia has around 60,000, and the populations are on the rise. You are likely to see them in Parque Nacional Sajama (p154), Reserva Nacional de Fauna Andina Eduardo Avaroa, Área Natural de Manejo Integrado Nacional Apolobamba and in other wild areas above 4000m. Ongoing threats to the vicuñas include a lack of continuous protected areas, degraded land and poaching. Vicuña blood is believed to cure all kinds of ailments, and the wool is worth US$400 in local markets and up to US$2000 in international markets per pound.

VISITING THE CHIPAYA

Immediately north of Salar de Coipasa, on the Río Sabaya delta, live the Chipaya people. Some researchers believe the Chipaya were the altiplano's first inhabitants and that they may in fact be a remnant of the lost Tiwanaku civilization. Much of this speculation is based on the fact that their language is vastly different from both Quechua and Aymará, and is probably a surviving form of Uru. They occupy two main desert villages, Santa Ana de Chipaya and Ayparavi.

Though it is rare to see these days, the Chipayas are best recognized by their earth-colored clothing and the women's unique hairstyle, which is plaited into 60 small braids. These are, in turn, joined into two large braids and decorated with a *laurake* (barrette) at each temple. Traditionally they lived in mud huts in a unique circular (*huayllichas*) or conical (*putucus*) shape, with doors made from cactus wood and which always face east, though few of these now remain. Museo Antropológico Eduardo López Rivas (p147) in Oruro has a replica of a Chipaya home and photographs of the community.

Chipaya tradition maintained that their people came into the world when it was still dark, and that they are descended from the 'Men of Water' – perhaps the Uru. Their nature-based religion was complex and symbolic, deifying phallic images, stones, rivers, mountains, animal carcasses and ancestors. The village church tower was worshipped as a demon – one of 40 named demons that represent hate, ire, vengeance, gluttony and other evils. These were believed to inhabit the whitewashed mud cones that exist within a 15km radius of the village, where they were appeased with libations, sacrifices and rituals to prevent their evil from invading the village.

The commemoration of dead ancestors culminated on November 2, **Día de los Muertos** (Day of the Dead), when bodies were disinterred from *chullpas* (funerary towers). They were feted with a feast and informed about recent village events and the needs of the living. Those who were chiefs, healers and other luminaries were carried to the church, where they were honored with animal sacrifices. Due to Christian evangelism such practices have died out, but ancestors who died during the previous year are still celebrated with a feast of their favorite foods in their honor on November 1.

Río Lauca, on which the Chipaya have depended for thousands of years, has been drying up during winter in recent years. Many Chipaya thus emigrate to Chile during this period, returning to plant their quinoa with the rains. The traditional way of life of the region's most ancient people has now all but disappeared.

In the past tourists haven't been especially welcome, but there is now a community-run **albergue** (☑7373-1515, 7155-4206; www.chipaya.org; Santa Ana de Chipaya; d incl breakfast B$120, dinner B$60) (hostel) in Chipaya village. Accommodation is in round adobe huts, with tiled floors, hot water and electricity. Expect to be charged for taking photographs of people (and ask permission first!).

The distinctive, conical houses are found in the Ayparavi community, 30km outside Chipaya. Here you might also see women with their hair plaited in the traditional style. Ask around in Chipaya for a guide to take you to Ayparavi and negotiate a price; the area may be inaccessible in wet weather.

There is now an asphalt road from Oruro to Santa Ana de Chipaya. Minivans leave when there is sufficient demand, from Oruro's Mercado Avaróa on Velasco Galvarro, 1.5km south of the train station (B$40, 4½ hours). There are most likely to be people making the trip on Wednesday and Saturday afternoon, after the market.

In addition, a few tour companies organize visits to Chipaya; check with Charlie Tours (p147) in Oruro.

San Pedro de Atacama across the border in Chile) salt flat to the geothermal hotbed of Los Lípez (p169), one of the world's harshest landscapes and a refuge for Andean wildlife. The ground here literally boils with minerals, and the spectrum of colors is extraordinary. A circuit from Uyuni takes you through unforgettable landscapes and is the highlight of a visit to Bolivia.

Although it gets plenty of visitors, Bolivia's southwest is still oddly remote, with rough dirt roads, scattered mining settlements, quinoa-producing villages and little public transportation. The main town, Uyuni, is a military outpost with a frontier feel. It's the launching point for expeditions into the region, from the desolate expanses of the *salares* to the craggy hills of Los Lípez, which rise into the high Andean peaks along the Chilean frontier.

Uyuni

🖉 2 / POP 10,300 / ELEV 3669M (12,037FT)

Standing in defiance of the desert-like landscape that surrounds it, Uyuni occupies a desolate corner of southwestern Bolivia. Mention Uyuni to a Bolivian and they will whistle and emphasize *harto frío* (extreme cold). Yet despite the icy conditions, the town has a cheerful buzz about it, with hundreds of travelers passing through every week to kick off their tour of Salar de Uyuni or the Southwest Circuit.

Founded in 1889 by Bolivian president Aniceto Arce, Uyuni remains an important military base. Tourism and mining are the other major sources of employment in the town. The world's largest lithium reserve – about 100 million tons – lies beneath the neighboring salt flat, and could potentially fuel all the smart phones and electric cars the world could build over the next century. While work on building extraction and processing facilities has been proceeding slowly, expect more and more mining activity near Uyuni in the coming years.

◉ Sights

Cementerio de Trenes HISTORIC SITE
(Train Cemetery) FREE The only real attraction in Uyuni, Cementerio de Trenes is a rusty collection of historic steam locomotives and rail cars dating back to the 19th century, when there was a rail-car factory here. Today they sit decaying in the yards about 3km southwest of the modern-day station along Av Ferroviaria.

They're fun to climb on, and it's a nice walk from town to keep you warm. Most tours visit the train cemetery as a first or last stop on the three-day *salar* (salt desert) circuit.

Museo Arqueología y Antropológico de los Andes Meridionales MUSEUM
(Av Arce, near Colón; B$5; ◔8:30am-12:30pm & 2:30-6:30pm Mon-Fri) A small museum featuring mummies, long skulls, fossils, ceramics and textiles. There are Spanish descriptions of the practices of cranial deformation. At research time the museum was closed for renovations.

Museo Ferrocarril MUSEUM
(Train Museum; Tomás Frias; B$20; ◔8:30am-12:30pm & 2:30-6:30pm Mon-Fri) Serious train-spotters might want to take a look inside this huge hangar of a museum, which houses several salt-crusted train engines and carriages. It's not possible to board the trains and there is little signage, making the exhibits rather dull.

☞ Tours

Salty Desert Aventours TOURS
(🖉7237-0444; www.saltydesert-uyuni.com; Av Ferroviaria, btwn Av Arce & Bolívar; ◔10am-12:30pm & 2:30-7:30pm) This operator gets good reviews. Tours with an English-speaking guide are available for an extra cost.

Quechua Connection TOURS
(🖉693-3923; www.quechuaconnection4wd.com; cnr Bolívar & Cabrera; ◔7:30am-noon & 3-8pm) This company offers salt flat tours with English-speaking guides. Its best-sellers are tours that include the chance to cycle 3km across the salt flats.

Hidalgo Tours TOURS
(🖉693-2989; www.salardeuyuni.net; Av Potosí 113, Hotel Jardines de Uyuni; ◔7am-7:30pm) This upscale agency offers high-end, private tours with accommodations at luxury salt hotels.

Red Planet TOURS
(🖉7240-3896; www.redplanetexpedition.com; Av Ferroviaria, btwn Sucre & Camacho) This agency is slightly pricier than other tour companies, but it offers English-speaking guides as well as one-, two- and three-day tours. It accepts payment by credit card with a 7% surcharge.

Cordillera Tours TOURS
(🖉693-3304; www.cordilleratraveller.com; Av Ferroviaria 314; ◔7:30-11am & 1:30-7pm) Offers the usual salt flat tours as well as transfers to Chile (from B$350 per person).

Andes Salt Expeditions TOURS
(🖉622-5175; www.andes-salt-uyuni.com.bo; Av Ferroviaria 56) This agency offers a range of tours at various price points. Its founder, ex-miner Raul Braulio Mamani, worked as the guide for *The Devil's Miner* documentary, a 2005 film about two brothers working in mines near Potosí.

★ Festivals & Events

Annual Festival FESTIVAL
(◔July) On July 11 Uyuni celebrates the anniversary of the founding of the town with parades, speeches, dancing, music and, naturally, lots of drinking.

SOUTHERN ALTIPLANO UYUNI

Uyuni

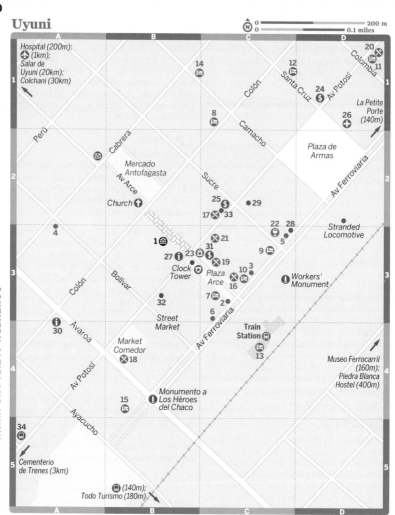

SOUTHERN ALTIPLANO UYUNI

🛏 Sleeping

Reserve ahead in high season, especially if you're chugging in on a late-night train. Only better hotels offer heating – bring a sleeping bag if you have one. In the rainy season, prices are slightly lower and it's not as cold at night. Note that there are water rations in Uyuni year-round. Do not sleep with a propane heater in your room.

Hotel Avenida HOTEL $
(☑ 693-2078; Av Ferroviaria 11; per person B$70, with shared bathroom B$50; @ 🛜) Located near the train station, this place is popular for its

neat rooms, friendly staff and laundry sinks. It's good value for the price, but it doesn't have heating. Newer rooms in the covered area are nicer and warmer.

El Cactu Urkupiña Hostal HOSTEL $
(☑ 693-2032; Av Arce 46; s/d incl breakfast B$75/150, with shared bathroom B$60/120) A bit disorganized in the common areas, this budget spot earns points for the clean rooms, central location and buffet breakfast. The mattresses are a bit lumpy but the owners have plans to install heaters, which should make for a more comfortable night's sleep.

Uyuni

◎ Sights
1 Museo Arqueología y
   Antropológico de los
   Andes Meridionales............................ B3

⊕ Activities, Courses & Tours
2 Andes Salt Expeditions........................ C3
3 Cordillera Tours C3
   Hidalgo Tours.................................(see 11)
4 Quechua Connection............................ A3
5 Red Planet... C3
6 Salty Desert Aventours........................ C3

⊜ Sleeping
7 El Cactu Urkupiña Hostal...................... C3
8 Hostal La Magia de Uyuni.....................C1
9 Hotel Avenida....................................... C3
10 Hotel Julia C3
11 Jardines de Uyuni D1
12 Los Girasoles Hotel...............................C1
13 Onkel Inn Wagon Sleepbox.................. C4
14 Tambo Aymará B1
15 Toñito Hotel.. B4

⊗ Eating
16 Arco Iris.. C3
17 Lithium Club C2
18 Mercado Campesino............................ B4

Minuteman Revolutionary
   Pizza..(see 15)
19 Restaurant 16 de Julio C3
20 Tika.. D1
21 Wiphala Pub C3

⊕ Drinking & Nightlife
22 Extreme Fun Pub................................... C3

⊕ Shopping
23 Market...B3

⊕ Information
24 Banco Mercantil Santa Cruz................. D1
25 Banco Nacional de Bolivia.................... C2
   Banco Unión...................................(see 25)
26 Clínica las Carmelitas D1
27 Infotur...B3
28 Lavarap.. C3
29 Migración.. C2
30 Office of Reserva Nacional de
   Fauna Andina Eduardo Avaroa..........A4
31 Prodem.. C3

⊕ Transport
32 Amazonas..B3
33 Boliviana de Aviación............................ C2
34 Buses to San Cristóbal..........................A5

★ **Piedra Blanca Hostel**   HOSTEL **$$**
(☑ 7643-7643; www.piedrablancabackpackers.hos tel.com; cnr Loa & Tomás Frías; dm B$77, d with/ without bathroom B$290/220) This appealing hostel is in a modern building featuring plenty of concrete and wood, a bright central courtyard and common areas. The private rooms are simple but cozy and dorms have large pine bunks, comfy mattresses, lockers and thick comforters; all rooms are heated. There's a bar and a well-equipped kitchen, and breakfast is included in the room rates. Waiting for a train? Stop by for a hot shower (B$20) before heading on your way.

Toñito Hotel   HOTEL **$$**
(☑ 693-3186; www.tonitouyuni.com; Av Ferroviaria 60; s/d incl breakfast B$400/500; P☎) An appealing choice built around a covered central courtyard that warms up nicely during the day, Toñito has a set of pleasant rooms with spacious beds and solar showers. It remains a consistent top pick among tour groups, so book ahead.

Onkel Inn Wagon Sleepbox   HOTEL **$$**
(☑ 7722-4522; www.onkelinn.com/wagon-sleep box; Av Ferroviaria s/n, Train Station, 2nd fl; s/tw with shared bathroom B$111/208, d/wagon with private bathroom B$452/515; ☎) Located on the 2nd floor of the train station's ticket office building, this railway-themed hotel is gimmicky but fun. The wood-paneled rooms mimic sleeping compartments in railway carriages, and are cozy and warm (most share bathrooms). Outside, in front of the station, are three (heated) railway wagons that have been turned into double rooms, with private bathrooms. Breakfast is included.

Tambo Aymará   HOTEL **$$**
(☑ 693-2227; www.hoteltamboaymara.com; Cama-cho, near Cabrera; s/d incl breakfast B$390/500; ☎) This homely option has terrific common areas and rooms decorated with Bolivian textiles, huge beds and handmade wooden furniture. There are also flannel sheets and electric heaters to keep you warm. Some rooms are a bit dark but there's reliable hot water and service is friendly. Touch the ring to get in.

Los Girasoles Hotel   HOTEL **$$**
(☑ 693-3323; www.girasoleshotel.hostel. com; Santa Cruz 155; s/d/tr incl breakfast B$330/520/680; ☎) This spacious and handsome hotel has attractive, heated

❶ SALAR DE UYUNI & SOUTHWEST CIRCUIT TOURS

Theoretically you can visit the Salar de Uyuni (p167) and the attractions of the Southwest Circuit independently, but it's extremely challenging due to unreliable transport and the remoteness of the area. The vast majority of people take an organized tour from either Uyuni or Tupiza, which probably works out cheaper than doing it alone anyway.

From the end of December to the end of March, the salt flat floods and many agencies shut down, and you can only visit the edges of the salt flat at this time.

Costs

Tours cost B$800 to B$1200 for three days at a standard agency, and B$1200 to B$1500 at a high-end agency. The cheapest tours do not include English-speaking guides. It's cheaper to book in Uyuni; you'll pay more if you book elsewhere. Tours include a driver (who also serves as your guide, mechanic and cook), two nights' accommodation (quality varies depending on the agency), three meals a day and transport. You'll also pay a B$30 entrance fee to **Isla Incahuasi** (p167) and a B$150 fee to enter **Reserva Nacional de Fauna Andina Eduardo Avaroa** (p170). Those traveling on to Chile will need B$20 to B$50 for the border crossing. Most agencies don't accept credit cards.

What to Bring

You'll want to bring several liters of water, snacks, a headlamp, sunscreen, sunglasses, a sunhat, warm clothes, a camera and chargers, and a plastic dinosaur (for photos, of course). Bring cash for entry to the national parks, and small change for bathroom fees (usually B$5). A sleeping bag is also highly recommended. Some agencies provide sleeping bags for no extra fee; check when booking if a sleeping bag is included.

Choosing an Agency

Generally, it doesn't matter which agency you book with (other than the high-end ones), as most agencies run the same routes, share drivers and sort travelers into groups of five or six people (don't accept more!). This means that while you may book with Agency A, you may end up traveling with Agency Z.

This said, you do have some power here. Talk to returning travelers and multiple agencies, and use your judgment to pick a good operator. If you are custom-building an itinerary, have the agency put it in writing. If you can make your own group (try the pub), you'll be better off. The high-end agencies have better hotels, can customize tours and have more reliable cars.

Though things are improving, a number of travelers have died on this trip, mostly in drunk-driving accidents. Ask to see the car you will be traveling in and to meet the driver ahead of time. If the agency tries to switch drivers or cars on you, call them on it. Along the way, make sure your driver is not drinking alcohol (and demand to switch cars if he is).

Day Tours

You can book a day trip (B$200) to Isla Incahuasi, but really, you've come all this way, so you might as well go on with the rest of the pilgrims.

rooms with big comfortable beds, a TV and cactus-wood paneling. Rooms face an internal courtyard (the lack of external windows helps to keep out the cold), but are bright nonetheless.

Hostal La Magia de Uyuni   HOTEL **$$**
(☑ 693-2541; www.hostalmagiauyuni.com; Colón 432; s/d in old section B$210/350, in new section B$280/490; @ 🛜) One of the pioneers of Uyuni tourism, this choice hacienda-inspired hotel is a solid midrange choice. The rooms

in the older wing have less creature comforts and are smaller and darker, while the newer rooms have nice antique furniture, new beds, thick comforters and heaters. Breakfast is included.

Hotel Julia   HOTEL **$$**
(☑ 693-2134; www.hoteljuliauyuni.com; cnr Avs Ferroviaria & Arce; s/d/tr B$220/330/450, s/d with shared bathroom B$120/220; @ 🛜) This neat and tidy option right in the center of town has heated rooms and hot showers. It's worth

If you do decide to make a quick trip, you'll typically depart around 10am in high season, stopping first at Cementerio de Trenes (p159) and the Colchani (p168) salt extraction areas (where you can buy souvenirs), before heading on to Playa Blanca Salt Hotel (p168) and Isla Incahuasi (p167).

At this point the day-trippers turn back, and the hard-core travelers continue on to enjoy the dramatic rainbow-colored sunset before heading on to their hotel.

Standard Tours

The most popular tour is the three-day circuit taking in the **Salar de Uyuni**, **Laguna Colorada**, **Sol de Mañana**, **Laguna Verde** and points in between.

The quality of food varies, though many agencies use the same caterers. Vegetarians should make arrangements with the operator ahead of time (and bring plenty of snacks just in case). Higher-end operators offer nicer hotels – with heaters and down comforters – and better food.

Many tours do the Isla Incahuasi trip on the first day and spend the night in the handful of salt hotels around the village of **Chuvica** that sits on the eastern edge of the salt flat.

After entering the remote and beautiful region of **Los Lípez** (p169) on the second day, many tour groups spend the second night in the dormitory accommodation at Laguna Colorada, or a little further on in the village of Huayajara, for the coldest night on the trip. On day three of the standard tour, you wake at dawn to visit the large geyser field dubbed **Sol de Mañana** (p170).

If you're not heading to Chile, the final afternoon drive back to Uyuni has a few potential worthwhile stops in **Valles de Rocas** (p171) and **San Cristóbal** (p171).

Custom Tours

Ask your agency about the possibility of reversing the standard circuit. That way you will arrive at the *salar* early in the morning on the third day, when the lighting is at its best.

If you have the time and cash to customize a trip, consider creating a custom tour that includes a volcano climb (p165), a visit to local communities and a possible drop-off in Tupiza. These customized trips are usually pricier than typical three-day jaunts but involve a real sense of discovery. This region is a land of bizarre lava formations, active volcanoes, abandoned villages, badlands, salt flats, pre-Incan cave cemeteries, lone quinoa fields, multicolored lagoons and sulfur lakes.

You can visit **Coquesa** (p169) and some less-visited attractions such as **Isla Cáscara de Huevo**, **Aquaquiza**, **Salar de Coipasa** and the **Sud Lípez Lakes area** (p171). These are places where you won't be surrounded by packs of jeeps and other travelers, where the feel of the last frontier is true and real.

If you are heading to Chile, the three-day circuit can end on the morning of the final day with a border drop-off after Laguna Verde, just in time for an onward connection to the pretty town of San Pedro de Atacama. When booking, check that the price of the transfer to San Pedro is included.

paying more for a room with bathroom as these have more light. Breakfast is included.

★ La Petite Porte　　BOUTIQUE HOTEL **$$$**
(☑7388-5960;　　www.hotel-lapetiteporte-uyuni. com; Av Ferroviaria 742; s/d B$620/725; @🛜) This gorgeous boutique hotel oozes with understated class and pizzazz. Rooms have a unique ceiling heating system that ensures they are toasty and warm even when it's freezing outside, and little touches like free tea and coffee make you feel at home.

Jardines de Uyuni　　HOTEL **$$$**
(☑693-2989; www.hotelesrusticosjardines.com; Av Potosí 113; s/d/tr incl breakfast B$610/800/1068; @🛜🛇) Built around a courtyard in a delightful rustic style, this adobe hotel has the best common areas and overall panache in town. The rooms are on the small side but all are well appointed with tasteful decorations and comfy beds. Needless to say, it's a popular choice for high-end tour groups, so book ahead.

ℹ WARNING: SALAR TOURS

Operators are piled high in Uyuni: there are currently more than 100 legal agencies offering trips to the *salar*. While the competition may mean more choice, remember that cost-cutting leads to operators corner-cutting – at the expense of your safety and the environment.

The results of this have included deadly accidents. At least 26 people have been killed in jeep accidents on the Salar de Uyuni salt plains since May 2008, including an accident in 2016 in which five tourists died. There have been alarming reports of ill-equipped vehicles without seat belts, speeding tour operators, a lack of emergency equipment, breakdowns, drunk drivers and disregard for the once-pristine environment of the *salar*.

Eating

Uyuni's tourist footfall and remote location push up prices, but it's easy to get a decent meal in town. There are plenty of places serving satisfying pizza and pasta dishes, as well as a few high-end restaurants offering more sophisticated local and international dishes.

Mercado Campesino MARKET **$**
(Avaroa, cnr Av Potosí; meals B$5-10; ⊙ 6am-noon) For quick eats, cheap meals are on offer at the market's *comedor* (dining hall) and nearby street food stalls.

★Tika BOLIVIAN **$$**
(☑ 693-2989; www.tikarestaurante.com.bo; Av Potosí 113; mains B$40-92; ⊙ 4-10pm; 🛜) Tika's chic, modern dining room is an appealing setting to sample contemporary takes on traditional Bolivian dishes, such as *charque lipeño* (sun-dried llama meat with potatoes, cheese and corn) and *k'alaphurka*, a gurgling corn soup served with a hot volcanic stone. There's also a well-stocked bar and a lengthy wine list.

★Minuteman Revolutionary Pizza PIZZA **$$**
(☑ 693-3186; Av Ferroviaria 60; mains B$55-65; ⊙ 8-10am & 5-9pm) This convivial spot inside Toñito Hotel (p161) is run by Chris from Boston and his Bolivian wife Sussy, and is a travelers' favorite. Sample the best pizzas in town as well as tasty gourmet salads. It's also

a cozy spot for a beer, glass of Tarija wine or a hearty breakfast (B$20 to B$50).

Wiphala Pub PUB FOOD **$$**
(☑ 693-3545; Av Potosí 325; mains B$35-50; ⊙ 2-11pm) Named after the multicolored indigenous flag, this place has a traditional atmosphere and welcoming feel with its wooden tables, earthy vibe and board games. It serves pizza and tasty Bolivian dishes, specializing in llama meat and quinoa, and has quinoa beer (B$35). Service can be slow.

Arco Iris PIZZA **$$**
(Av Arce 27; mains B$35-50; ⊙ 8am-10pm) Something of an Uyuni classic for its menu of pizza, pasta, soups and drinks, this place with wooden benches and local Bolivian decor is friendly and popular.

Restaurant 16 de Julio INTERNATIONAL **$$**
(Av Arce; mains B$45-80; ⊙ 8am-midnight) Located along the main strip, this place offers a full spectrum of international and Bolivian dishes, including the obligatory llama steak, and plenty of choices for vegetarians. Not hungry? Try a coca beer instead.

Lithium Club BOLIVIAN **$$$**
(☑ 693-3399; Av Potosí 24; mains B$70-120; ⊙ 10:30am-10pm Mon-Sat, 4-10pm Sun) This upper-end choice has international takes on traditional Bolivian dishes like *charque de llama* (llama jerky) and *pailita de llama* (llama stew), bringing together authentic flavor combinations with a smidgen of European styling.

🍷 Drinking & Nightlife

There are a few welcoming options in town for a night of pre- or post-salt tour drinking. Many of Uyuni's restaurants double as bars and offer a good selection of beer, wine and cocktails.

Extreme Fun Pub PUB
(La Llamita; Sucre 23; ⊙ 2:30pm-1am) For a night of extreme fun head to Uyuni's top drinking spot. The extensive cocktail list features concoctions such as Sexy Llama Bitch and Sensual Llama's Navel, as well as hot cocktails to warm you up on cold nights. There are salt floors, drinking games, friendly service and beautiful *salar* photos. Guitars are on hand for impromptu music sessions.

🛍 Shopping

Market MARKET
(Av Potosí; ⊙ Sun & Thu) The big market day in Uyuni is Thursday when Av Potosí gets taken

over by stalls selling anything from arts and crafts to television sets; Sunday is a smaller market day.

❶ Information

DANGERS & ANNOYANCES
Watch your cash, especially around the train and bus stations. There have been reports of groups of young men pretending to help buy tickets or transfer luggage to a bus, and then taking off with backpacks. If you are robbed, you can get a police report from the **Tourist Police** (cnr Avs Potosí & Arce) at their office in the clock tower.

IMMIGRATION
Migración (📋7307-9328; www.migracion.gob.bo; Av Potosi, near Sucre; ⊗8:30am-12:30pm & 2:30-6:30pm Mon-Fri, 8:30am-12:30pm Sat) Visa extensions only. Get your visas and exit/entry stamps at the border.

INTERNET ACCESS
There are several internet places in town, especially around Plaza Arce. An hour costs between B$4 and B$5. Wi-fi is available in nearly all hostels and hotels, many restaurants and most tour operator offices.

LAUNDRY
Most hotels offer some sort of laundry service, but it can be pricey.
Lavarap (Av Ferroviaria, btwn Sucre & Camacho; per kilo B$20; ⊗8am-8pm) Handy and efficient.

MEDICAL SERVICES
Hospital Obrero (Caja Nacional de Salud; 📋693-2025; Av Arce, btwn Fernando Alonzo & Calvimontes)
Clínica las Carmelitas (📋693-3539; Santa Cruz, btwn Avs Potosí & Ferroviaria)

MONEY
There are several cash machines in town. Several places on Av Potosí between Arce and Bolívar buy Chilean and Argentine pesos.
Banco Mercantil Santa Cruz (cnr Av Potosí & Santa Cruz)
Banco Nacional de Bolivia (cnr Av Potosí & Sucre)
Banco Unión (cnr Sucre & Av Potosí)

SOUTHERN ALTIPLANO UYUNI

CLIMBING VOLCANOES

Though not included on the standard tours, there is plenty of scope for hiring your own driver and climbing some volcanoes. Guides are easy to find in the region's settlements or can be organised through a tour company in Uyuni. The challenging aspect of most of the climbs is the altitude rather than technical difficulty.

The most frequently climbed is **Volcán Licancabur** (5960m); it takes about eight hours to climb to the summit and two to get down. Several Uyuni and Tupiza agencies can include a guided climb of the volcano in a Southwest Circuit route, adding an extra day to the trip. You can normally find a guide near the campsite in Laguna Blanca – they tend to charge about B$500 for an ascent of the mountain, which has a beautiful lagoon at the top. The climb can be done comfortably (if you handle the altitude) in one day. As the volcano is sacred to the locals, the guides usually perform a ritual for Pachamama, asking the earth goddess for her permission to climb.

Nevado Candelaria (5995m), southwest of Salar de Coipasa, is also an exhilarating climb. The active **Volcán Ollagüe** (5865m) on the Chilean border southwest of San Pedro de Quemez is another interesting option, with spectacular views.

A rounded promontory juts into Salar de Uyuni diagonally opposite Colchani, and on it rises **Volcán Tunupa** (5432m), which you can approach from the village of Coquesa (10 hours there and back, including a visit to the caves that house pre-Incan mummies). Local guides charge around B$500. Altitude aside, this hulking yellow mountain is a relatively easy climb. One legend linking it to the origins of the salt flat states that 16th-century Inca ruler Atahualpa slashed the breast of a woman called Tunupa on the mountain's slopes, and the milk that spilled out formed the *salar*. Another story tells that in ancient days, mountains were men and women. Right after giving birth to their baby, Tunupa learned her man was living with another woman. Devastated, she wept and wept, spilling her salty tears over her breast milk and creating this vast area of sadness and beauty that is now the *salar*.

It's also possible to climb **Uturuncu** (6020m), which is an active volcano; jeeps can drive up to 4800m, from where you can hike to the top – an easy way to say you've climbed a 6000m-high volcano!

SOUTHERN ALTIPLANO UYUNI

PULACAYO

At the virtual ghost town of **Pulacayo** (B$10), brilliantly colored rocks rise beside the road and a mineral-rich stream reveals streaks of blue, yellow, red and green. The silver mines north of the village closed in 1959, and today only a few hundred hardy souls remain. Take any bus to Potosí and ask to be dropped off at Pulacayo (B$5, 30 minutes) or book a tour. There is a fee of B$10 to enter the village.

Also worth seeing here is the mansion of the 22nd president of Bolivia, Aniceto Arce Ruíz. Nearby is a collection of decaying steam locomotives that were originally imported to transport ore. They include Bolivia's first steam engine, *El Chiripa*, and the train that was robbed by legendary bandits Butch Cassidy and the Sundance Kid, including a wooden rail car that bears the bullet holes from the attack.

Prodem (Plaza Arce; ⊙8am-4pm Mon-Fri, 9am-noon Sat)

POST
Post Office (☑693-2405; cnr Av Arce & Cabrera)

TOURIST INFORMATION
Infotur (☑693-3666; cnr Avs Potosí & Arce; ⊙8am-noon & 2:30-6:30pm Mon-Fri) Well stocked with leaflets on Uyuni and the rest of Bolivia. At research time the office was located in the bus terminal while the office on Avenida Arce was being renovated.

Office of Reserva Nacional de Fauna Andina Eduardo Avaroa (REA; ☑693-2225; www. boliviarea.com; cnr Colón & Avaroa; ⊙9am-6pm Mon-Fri) Administrative office for the park in Uyuni. You can buy your park entry (B$150) here if going under your own steam.

① Getting There & Away

AIR
The quickest way to get to Uyuni is by flying direct from La Paz to Aeropuerto Joya Andina, 1km north of town.

Amaszonas (☑693-3333; www.amaszonas. com; Av Potosí s/n; ⊙8:30am-7pm Mon-Fri) and **Boliviana de Aviación** (BoA; ☑693-3674; www.boa.bo; Av Potosí, near Sucre; ⊙8:30am-12:30pm & 2:30-6:30pm Mon-Fri, 8:30am-12:30pm Sat) both operate two flights a day to La Paz (from B$700, one hour).

BUS
At the time of research, Uyuni's gleaming new **bus terminal** (Avaroa) was complete and awaiting the official sign-off for bus companies to begin operating here. All long-distance buses will no doubt depart from the new terminal. There's a choice of companies to most destinations, so ask around to get the best price, time and service.

Potosí buses leave hourly; for Sucre it's easiest to head to Potosí and change there.

The highway between Uyuni and Oruro is now fully paved, making for quicker and more comfortable journeys as well as a more frequent bus service to Oruro and further north to La Paz.

The safest and most comfortable terrestrial transport to La Paz is with **Todo Turismo** (☑693-3337; www.todoturismo.bo; Avaroa; one-way B$250), which runs a heated bus service, departing daily at 8pm.

At research time, the road south to Tupiza and Villazón was nearly completely paved, cutting journey times. Buses leave at 6am and 8pm daily.

For Calama, Chile, Cruz del Norte buses depart at 5am (B$130, nine hours).

DESTINATION	COST (B$)	TIME (HR)
Cochabamba	130	10
La Paz	100-250	8-9
Oruro	30	4½
Potosí	30	4
Sucre	60	7
Tupiza	40	5
Villazón	50	6

TRAIN
Uyuni has a modern, well-organized **train station** (☑693-2153; www.fca.com.bo; Av Ferroviaria s/n). Trains take you north to Oruro and south to Villazón. Seats often sell out, so buy your ticket several days in advance or get an agency to do it for you. There are numerous reports of slow trains, cancelled trains and large gaps in service – but that's all part of the adventure.

At research time, no trains were running south of Uyuni due to damage to the track caused by flooding in the Tupiza area. Repairs were underway to the section north of Tupiza, which suffered less damage. The section from Tupiza to Villazón is expected to take longer to repair.

Depending on size, you may have to check your backpack/suitcase into the luggage compartment. Look out for snatch thieves on the train just before it pulls out.

Expreso del Sur
Expreso del Sur is the slightly more luxurious line, departing Uyuni for Oruro on Thursdays and Sundays at 12:05am and heading south for Atocha, Tupiza and Villazón on Tuesdays and Fridays at 9:40pm.

ℹ CROSSING THE BORDER TO CHILE

Most tour agencies now offer cross-border connections to **San Pedro de Atacama** as part of Southwest Circuit tours, by arrangement with Chilean operators. You'll make the connection around 9am not long after visiting Laguna Verde (p171), giving you limited time to enjoy the hot springs. Arrange this ahead of time with your operator. The Hito Cajón border post charges an exit tax of B$15 to B$30 here (B$21 is the standard).

Some of the tour companies, including Cordillera Tours (p159), offer direct jeep transfers to San Pedro for B$350 per person, via the border crossing at Hito Cajón. The jeeps typically leave at 4pm, there's a sleepover in Mallcu Villamar, and you arrive in San Pedro at noon the next day.

In winter the road to Hito Cajón is occasionally impassable because of heavy snow. It may be possible to cross the border at Ollagüe instead; a transfer via Ollagüe with Cordillera Tours costs B$500 per person, with a night in Villa Alota or Culpina.

ROUTE	COST (B$ COACH/1ST CLASS, ONE-WAY)	ARRIVAL TIME
Uyuni to Oruro	60/120	7:10am
Uyuni to Tupiza	47/120	3am
Uyuni to Villazón	72/180	6:05am

Wara Wara

Wara Wara offers a cheaper service that leaves Uyuni on Tuesdays and Fridays at 1:45am for Oruro. On Thursdays and Mondays at 2:50am, it heads south to Atocha, Tupiza and Villazón.

ROUTE	COST (B$ COACH/1ST CLASS/ EXECUTIVE, ONE-WAY)	ARRIVAL TIME
Uyuni to Oruro	32/47/102	9:10am
Uyuni to Tupiza	25/38/76	8:35am
Uyuni to Villazón	38/56/118	12:05pm

Salar de Uyuni

An evocative and eerie sight, the world's largest salt flat (12,106 sq km) sits at 3653m (11,984ft). When the surface is dry, the *salar* is a pure white expanse of the greatest nothing imaginable – just blue sky, white ground and you. When there's a little water, the surface perfectly reflects the clouds and the blue altiplano sky, and the horizon disappears. If you're driving across the surface at such times, the effect is surreal; it's hard to believe that you're not flying through the clouds.

Salar de Uyuni is now a center of salt extraction and processing, particularly around the settlement of Colchani. The estimated annual output of the Colchani operation is nearly 20,000 tons, 18,000 tons of which is for human consumption while the rest is for livestock. And beneath the surface, massive lithium deposits should fuel Bolivia's economy for the next 100 years.

Formation

Between 40,000 and 25,000 years ago, Lago Minchín, whose highest level reached 3760m, occupied much of southwestern Bolivia. When it evaporated, the area lay dry for 14,000 years before the appearance of short-lived Lago Tauca, which lasted for only about 1000 years and rose to 3720m. When it dried up, it left two large puddles, Lagos Poopó and Uru Uru, and two major salt concentrations, Salares de Uyuni and Coipasa.

This part of the altiplano is drained internally, with no outlet to the sea; the salt deposits are the result of the minerals leached from the mountains and deposited at the lowest available point.

◉ Sights

★ **Isla Incahuasi**   ISLAND

(B$30) One of the highlights of a Salar de Uyuni tour is a hike around the spectacular Isla Incahuasi, otherwise known as Inkawasi. It's located in the heart of the *salar*, 80km west of Colchani. This hilly outpost is covered in *Trichocereus* cactus and surrounded by a flat white sea of hexagonal salt tiles.

It was once a remarkably lonely, otherworldly place but since the advent of *salar* tours it receives large numbers of visitors every day. Nonetheless, it's still a beautiful sight if you forget the crowds.

You have to pay an entry fee to climb the hill (B$30), and tour groups clamber over the hiking trails chasing the perfect photo

SOUTHERN ALTIPLANO SALAR DE UYUNI

Salares de Uyuni & Coipasa

N 0 — 50 km
0 — 25 miles

Oruro (82km)
Oruro (56km)

1

Huachacalla
Payrumani
Esmeralda
Escara
Romero Pampa
Ayparavi
Sabaya
Santa Ana de Chipaya
Check Post
Peruguanu
601
Villa Vitalina
Laguna Coipasa
Pisiga
Villakollo
Coipasa
Oruro
Pampa Aullagas
Condo
Quillacas
Tambo Tambillo
Sevaruyo
Iquique (105km)
Irpa
Tonavi
603
CHILE
Salar de Coipasa
Potosí
Hizo
Tres Cruces
Salinas de Garci-Mendoza
Chacoma
Lavaxa
Río Mulatos
Bella Vista
Cha'llacollo
Caquena
Volcán Tunupa (5432m)
Nevado Candelaria (5995m)
Llica
Tahua
Coquesa
BOLIVIA
Salar de Uyuni
602
Canquella
Isla Pescador
Ojos del Salar
Hotel Palacio de Sal
Salar de Empexa
Isla Incahuasi
Playa Blanca
Bloques de Sal
Colchani
Toja
Potosí (210km)
Empexa Hot Springs
Chuvica
Uyuni
El Desierto
Petrified Forest
Atulcha
Isla Cáscara de Huevo
Tupiza (225km);
Villazón (320km)
701
San Pedro de Quemez
Colcha K (Villa Martín)
San Juan (20km);
Chiguana (40km);
Laguna Colorada (175km)
Avaroa (120km);
Calama (245km)

Lago Poopó

SOUTHERN ALTIPLANO SALAR DE UYUNI

of cacti and salt. It's a 15-minute walk to the top of the island, with a trail that loops back, but it's worth it. Note that during the wet season when the *salar* is flooded, the island is inaccessible.

Playa Blanca Salt Hotel   NOTABLE BUILDING
Although it is now closed to overnight visitors, you can still check out the salt sculptures inside and the **Dakar Rally** and **Flag Monuments** outside (add your flag if you've brought one). Find your own isolated piece of salt desert to enjoy and take out your props – it's here that plastic dinosaurs come out, as photographers play with the bizarre

perspective caused by the bright blue skies and super-flat landscape. Many tour groups stop for lunch here.

Colchani   VILLAGE
Located right on the edge of Salar de Uyuni, Colchani is the easiest place to access the great salt flat and the place to go if you just want a glimpse of the *salar*. Most salt flat tours stop here to visit the souvenir stalls and small **salt museum**, which is built from salt and contains salt sculptures (admission is free). Colchani is 22km north of Uyuni; buses to Oruro pass the village (B$5, 40 minutes).

The families here make their living from salt extraction as part of a cooperative; you can see small pyramids of salt draining on the *salar*, close to the village.

🛏 Sleeping

When you're on a salt flat, what better place to spend the night than in a salt hotel? The simple salt hotels in Coquesa, Chuvica and San Juan are nearly identical, with salt floors, furniture and walls, and common dining rooms where you can eat dinner (and shiver). The hotels have no heating, but an extra B$10 gets you a hot shower. There are also more luxurious salt hotels.

Luna Salada Hotel   BOUTIQUE HOTEL **$$$**
(☑ 7121-2007; www.lunasaladahotel.com.bo; r incl breakfast from B$1250; 🅿 🛜) This luxurious salt hotel is located 7km from Colchani on the edge of the *salar*. Its cozy rooms have colorful local fabrics, and its restaurant offers panoramic views. Facilities include a spa with a steam room, and bicycle rental.

Hotel Palacio de Sal   BOUTIQUE HOTEL **$$$**
(☑ 6842-2088; www.palaciodesal.com.bo; r incl breakfast from B$1050; 🛜) Right on the edge of the *salar,* near Colchani, is this luxurious salt complex, the first such hotel to open in the region. There is a games room with a pool table and magnificent salt flat views, and a good on-site restaurant. The hotel is booked through Hidalgo Tours (p159); it comes cheaper as part of a package.

Hotel Tayka de Piedra   HOTEL **$$$**
(☑ 693-2987; www.taykahoteles.com; San Pedro de Quemes; s/d/tr B$560/665/810) At the southwestern tip of the *salar*, off the beaten track, is Hotel Tayka de Piedra. Built of rugged local stone, it lies near the village of San Pedro de Quemes, by the burned-down ruins of a pre-Columbian settlement.

Coquesa

☑ 2 / POP 60 / ELEV 3689M (12.103FT)
At the village of Coquesa on the northern edge of the *salar*, take time to explore the **ruined ancient villages** and **burial grounds** nearby. Ceramic, gold and copper artifacts, and articles of clothing have been discovered at some of the sites, indicating the presence of an advanced but little-known culture. Unfortunately, the sites' remoteness has left them vulnerable to amateur treasure hunters who have plundered several items of archaeological value. Coquesa is also the starting point for climbs

up **Volcán Tunupa**. Local guides charge B$500 to take you up.

🛏 Sleeping

Maya Hostal de Sal   HOTEL **$**
(r per person B$50) Run by a local Aymará family in Coquesa, this is a nice, traditional choice. The beds are built on salt blocks, the doors and windows of cactus wood, and the dining room has salt tables with a splendid view over the *salar*. At night, a campfire and candlelight illuminate the place.

Hotel Tayka de Sal   HOTEL **$$$**
(☑ 7202-0069; www.taykahoteles.com; Tahua; s/d incl breakfast US$560/830) This hotel is located in the village of Tahua, just west of Coquesa. It's built entirely of locally extracted salt, apart from the thatched roof and the black stone bathrooms. This is a luxury, heated option. Reservations are required.

ℹ Getting There & Away

Most people visit Coquesa as part of a tour from Uyuni (p159). It's also accessible by road, coming from the north. There is no public transport.

Los Lípez

Wild and otherworldly, Los Lípez is the kind of place where you can feel like you and your companions are the only people on earth. Though tours leave Uyuni in convoys, by the time you reach the military checkpoint of Colcha K (*col-*cha-*kah*) the other groups are well dispersed across this vast region, allowing you to enjoy the scenery and ponder your own insignificance.

◉ Sights

There is a pleasant adobe church at **Colcha K** and a series of fairly rudimentary dormitory accommodations, but the indescribably beautiful landscapes, displaying an artist's palette of colored rocks in remarkable formations, are the real attraction of this area.

About 15km past Colcha K is the quinoa-growing village of **San Juan** (elevation 3660m), which has a small store. It also has a lovely adobe church, a population of 1000, and several volcanic-rock tombs and burial *chullpas* (funerary towers) in its vicinity.

At this point, the route that most tour groups follow turns west and starts across the borax-producing **Salar de Chiguana**,

BOLIVIA: SET TO BECOME THE SAUDI ARABIA OF LITHIUM?

Bolivia could hold the key to an environmentally sustainable future – the government claims that 70% of the world's lithium deposits, a mineral essential for hybrid and electric vehicles, is found in the salt flats of Uyuni.

Several major players in the global auto industry have their eyes set on this untapped potential. But progress has been slow, in part due to Evo Morales' reluctance to court foreign investment. Instead, with an investment of US$6 million, Comibol, the state agency that oversees mining projects, was charged with constructing a pilot plant in the salt flats. The agency lacked expertise and the project suffered numerous setbacks, but in 2016 the plant made its first shipment of 10 tons of lithium to China.

Spurred on by skyrocketing lithium prices, which had more than doubled in two years, in late 2017 Morales began talks with overseas companies, while stipulating that Bolivia must remain a majority stakeholder in any deal. In 2018 a US$1.3 billion deal to produce lithium batteries with a German company was announced. Work is scheduled to begin in late 2019 and Morales hopes the country will produce 15,000 metric tons per year after 2020.

Meanwhile, with the electric car market booming, demand for lithium continues to grow and is projected to outstrip supply by 2023.

SOUTHERN ALTIPLANO LOS LÍPEZ

where the landscape opens up and snow-capped **Ollagüe** (5865m), an active volcano straddling the Chilean border, appears in the distance.

The route then turns south and climbs into high and increasingly wild terrain, past several mineral-rich lakes filled with flamingos and backed by hills, including **Lagunas Cañapa**, **Hedionda** and **Honda**.

The road south through **Desierto de Siloli** takes you past **Árbol de Piedra**, from where it's another 18km or so to Laguna Colorada, at the entrance to Reserva Nacional de Fauna Andina Eduardo Avaroa.

★ **Reserva Nacional de Fauna Andina Eduardo Avaroa**   NATIONAL PARK
(REA; www.bolivia-rea.com; B$150) Tucked away in the southwestern corner of Los Lípez near the Chilean border is the remote Reserva Nacional de Fauna Andina Eduardo Avaroa. It's a rough bumpy road through marvelous Martian landscapes to get there, but worth every bang of the head along the way.

The park headquarters is located opposite Laguna Colorada, where you can pick up informative materials, pay your fee, and learn more about local flora and fauna.

The reserve was created in 1973 to cover an area of 7150 sq km. It receives in excess of 50,000 visitors annually and emphasizes the conservation of the vicuña, James's flamingo and the yareta plant, all of which are globally threatened species.

Laguna Colorada   LAKE
Laguna Colorada is a rusty-burnt-orange-hued lake (4278m) that covers approximately 60 sq km and reaches a depth of just 80cm. The rich red coloration on the lake is derived from algae and plankton that thrive in the mineral-rich water, and the shoreline is fringed with brilliant white deposits of sodium, magnesium, borax and gypsum. More apparent are the flamingos that breed here; all three South American species are present.

The lake sediments are rich in diatoms (tiny microfossils used in the production of fertilizer, paint, toothpaste and plastics, and as a filtering agent for oil, pharmaceuticals, aviation fuel, beer and wine). The clear air is bitterly cold and winter nighttime temperatures can drop below -20°C.

Sol de Mañana   GEYSER
Most tour groups wake at dawn to visit the large geyser field dubbed Sol de Mañana. This 4850m-high geyser basin has bubbling mud pots, hellish fumaroles and a thick and nauseating aroma of sulfur fumes. Approach the site cautiously; any damp or cracked earth is potentially dangerous and cave-ins do occur, sometimes causing serious burns.

Termas de Polques   HOT SPRINGS
(B$6) At the foot of **Cerro Polques** lies Termas de Polques, a small 29.4°C hot-spring pool, and an absolute paradise after the chilly *salar* nights. Although they're not boiling by any means, they're suitable for bathing, and the mineral-rich waters are thought to relieve the symptoms of arthritis and rheumatism. There's a restaurant here, and changing sheds with toilet facilities.

Laguna Verde   LAKE
The stunning blue-green Laguna Verde (4400m) is tucked into the southwestern corner of Bolivian territory, 52km south of Sol de Mañana (p170). The incredible green color comes from high concentrations of lead, sulfur, arsenic and calcium carbonates. Most tours visit this in the morning, but it's at its most dramatic during the afternoon when incessant icy winds have whipped the water into a brilliant green-and-white froth.

This surface agitation, combined with the high mineral content, means that it can remain liquid at temperatures as low as -21.2°C. Behind the lake rises the cone of **Volcán Licancabur** (5960m), whose summit is said to have once sheltered an ancient Inca crypt.

Desierto de Dalí   NATURAL FEATURE
Where the route splits about 20km south of Sol de Mañana, the more scenic left fork climbs up and over a 5000m pass, then up a stark hillside dotted with enormous rocks, which appear to have been meticulously placed by the surrealist master Salvador Dalí.

ⓘ Getting There & Away

The best way to explore this area is on a tour from Uyuni or Tupiza. In winter (June to August) the roads in this area may become impassable due to snow, and the Reserva Nacional de Fauna Andina Eduardo Avaroa (p170) and Hito Cajón border crossing may be closed.

Valles de Rocas

In the midst of high, lonesome country stretch several valleys of bizarre eroded rock formations known as **Valles de Rocas**. These strangely shaped badlands are great for a wander and snapping some photos. From the dusty village of **Alota** nearby, it's a three-hour jostle to Uyuni through a string of 'authentic villages', the most picturesque of which is **Culpina K**, which has colorful little houses and a cafe.

San Cristóbal

🎵 2 / POP 750 / ELEV 3800M (12,467FT)
The mining village of San Cristóbal is worth a stop for the lovely 350-year-old Jesuit **church** (Sucre s/n; B\$15; ⊘10am-5pm). In 1999 the entire village, including the church and the cemetery, was moved 20km from its original location next to the mine by the American–Japanese mining project that took over the area digging for lead, zinc and silver.

If you don't come on a tour, you can take a bus to San Cristóbal from near the **military base** (cnr Av Potosí & Ayacucho) in Uyuni at 8am, 2pm and 6:30pm. Return buses depart San Cristóbal at 8am, 4:30pm and 6pm (B\$15, two hours).

Sud Lípez Lakes & Around

The blue lake of **Laguna Celeste** or, more romantically, 'heaven lake', is still very much a peripheral trip for most Uyuni agencies, but it's gaining popularity with adventurous travelers as a one-day detour. A local legend suggests the presence of a submerged ruin, possibly a *chullpa*, in the lake. Behind the lake, a road winds its way up **Volcán Uturuncu** (6020m) to the **Uturuncu sulfur mine**, in a 5900m pass between the mountain's twin cones. That means it's more than 200m higher than the road over Khardung La in Ladakh, India, making it quite possibly the highest motorable pass in the world.

In the vast eastern reaches of Sud Lípez are numerous other fascinating mineral-rich lakes that are informally named for their odd coloration and have so far escaped much attention. Various milky-looking lakes are known as **Laguna Blanca** (white lake), sulfur-colored lakes are **Laguna Amarilla** (yellow lake) and wine-colored ones are known as **Laguna Guinda** (cherry lake). These are more often included in trips from Tupiza than Uyuni.

About 120km northeast of Laguna Verde and 30km southwest of Laguna Celeste is the small mining settlement of **Quetena Chico**, which has a few basic services and supplies, a military post and a couple of simple *albergues* (hostels). It also has **Centro de Ecología Ch'aska**, where you can see an exhibition about the geology and biology of the Los Lípez region, and the lives of the local llama herders. Just 6km southeast from here is the picturesque abandoned village of **Barrancas**, which nestles against a craggy cliff.

TUPIZA & AROUND

Tupiza

🎵 2 / POP 22,233 / ELEV 2950M (9678FT)
The pace of life in tranquil Tupiza seems a few beats slower than in other Bolivian towns, making this a great place to relax for a few days, head out for a rip-romping

Tupiza

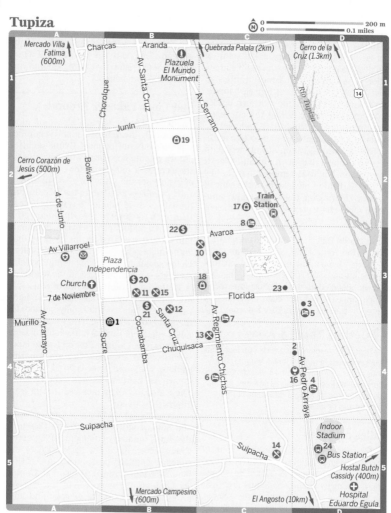

cowboy adventure like Butch Cassidy and Sundance did more than 100 years ago, or trundle off on the back road to Salar de Uyuni.

Set in a spectacular 'Wild West' countryside, the capital of the southern Chichas region is in a corner of Río Tupiza Valley, surrounded by rugged scenery – cactus-studded slopes and eroded rainbow-colored rocks cut by gravelly *quebradas* (ravines, usually dry).

The climate is mild year-round, with most of the rain falling between November and March. From June to August, days are hot,

dry and clear, but nighttime temperatures can drop to below freezing.

History

The tribe that originally inhabited the region called themselves Chichas and left some archaeological evidence of their existence. Despite this, little is known about their culture or language, and it's assumed these were distinct from those of the tribes in neighboring areas of southern Bolivia and northern Argentina.

Officially, Tupiza was founded on June 4, 1574, by Captain Luis de Fuentes (who was

Tupiza

◎ Sights
  1 Municipal Museum B4

✪ Activities, Courses & Tours
  2 Alexandro Adventure Travel D4
    La Torre Tours .... (see 6)
    Tupiza Tours .... (see 7)
  3 Valle Hermoso Tours D3

🛏 Sleeping
  4 Anexo Valle Hermoso D4
  5 Hostal Valle Hermoso D3
  6 Hotel La Torre C4
  7 Hotel Mitru C3
  8 Hotel Mitru Anexo C2

✖ Eating
  9 Alamo C3
  10 Churrasqueria Moises C3
  11 Cremalin... B3
  12 Italiana... B3
  13 Milan Center C4

  14 Rinconcito Quilmes C5
  15 Salteñas Especiales
    Marianita B3

🍷 Drinking & Nightlife
  16 Vinoteca El Origen................................ D4

🛍 Shopping
  17 Feria Serrano C2
  18 Mercado de Ferias C3
  19 Mercado Negro B2

ℹ Information
  20 Banco Fie B3
  21 Banco Union B3
  22 Latin America
    Cambio B3
  23 Super Clean Laundry C3

ℹ Transport
  24 Rapiditos.. D5

also the founder of Tarija). From Tupiza's inception through the War of Independence, its Spanish population grew steadily, lured by the favorable climate and suitable agricultural lands. Later, the discovery of minerals attracted even more settlers. More recently, *campesinos* (subsistence farmers) have drifted in from the countryside and many unemployed miners have settled here.

◎ Sights

Cerro de la Cruz   VIEWPOINT
A steep, rocky path leads to the top of Cerro de la Cruz, affording breathtaking views of Tupiza and the surrounding hills. The hike takes about two hours; bring plenty of water.

The hill is 2km north of the train station, on the other side of the river; the trail begins behind a small white church. It's best to get a moto-taxi (B$4) to the start of the path, as it can be tricky to find.

Cerro Corazón de Jesús   MONUMENT
The short hike up this hill leads to a monument of Jesus flanked by the Stations of the Cross. It's a pleasant morning or evening outing when the low sun brings out the fiery reds of the surrounding countryside.

Municipal Museum   MUSEUM
(Sucre; ⊙8am-noon & 2-6pm Mon-Fri) **FREE** Tupiza's municipal museum houses a jumble of historical and cultural artifacts in two rooms. The artifacts include an antique

cart, old photographs, archaeological relics, donated household items and historic farming implements.

⤳ Tours

All agencies offer **horseback riding** (B$210/300/420 for three/five/seven hours). They also offer the **triathlon** (B$300 to B$380 per person, including lunch, based on four people), which is an active full-day tour of the surrounding area by jeep, horseback and mountain bike. You can also arrange a **jeep tour** (B$480 to B$600 per day) or a **guided hike** (B$150 to B$275 per half-day).

Tupiza Tours   TOURS
(✑694-3003; www.tupizatours.com; Av Regimiento Chichas 187, Hotel Mitru; ⊙8am-8pm) This outfit pioneered many of the Tupiza-area routes now also offered by competitors. As well as tours to Uyuni via the *salar,* it runs a useful daily bus service to nearby sights, including La Poronga, Puerta del Diablo, El Cañón del Duende (p178) and el Sillar (p177).

La Torre Tours   TOURS
(✑694-2633; www.latorretours-tupiza.com; Av Regimiento Chichas 220, Hotel La Torre; ⊙7am-8pm) Run by a friendly couple, this agency offers personalized tours of Tupiza's surroundings and the *salar.* It rents bikes at B$80 for three hours.

SOUTHERN ALTIPLANO TUPIZA

❶ TOURING THE SOUTHWEST CIRCUIT FROM TUPIZA

An increasing number of operators in Tupiza offer trips through the Southwest Circuit (p156) ending in Uyuni or back in Tupiza. Tupiza is a great place to start this trip, as you get to explore the lesser-known wild lands of Sud Lípez (p171) as well as seeing the well-established highlights at different times to the large convoys of 4WDs that visit them out of Uyuni. Tours out of Tupiza often kick off with a visit to El Sillar (p177) or Quebrada Palala (p177), before heading on to the Sud Lípez lakes, including several that aren't visited on standard circuits that start from Uyuni. The *salar* itself is visited on the final day, with the option to see the sunrise over the salt well worth getting out of bed for.

The downside is that you may have to wait a while in Tupiza to get a group together (although the larger outfits have departures almost daily). While the standard *salar* tour starting in Uyuni is three days, Tupiza to Uyuni tours require four days, and therefore cost a little more. Expect to pay between B$1200 and B$1600 per person for the standard four-day trip, based on four people in a jeep, during the high season. This price typically includes all meals, transport and basic accommodations, but does not include the B$150 entrance to Reserva Nacional de Fauna Andina Eduardo Avaroa (p170), snacks, sleeping-bag rental or bottled water. Customized trips, many including climbing options, will cost a bit more but they're worth the extra.

While most tour operators display enthusiastic comments from satisfied customers, the truth is that standards vary widely. Try to avoid buying through your hotel and chat to a few operators. Professionalism, honesty and flexibility are the things to look for, not willingness to haggle on the price. The same safety precautions (p164) apply as in Uyuni when looking for the right tour operator for you.

Alexandro Adventure Travel   TOURS
(☑ 6791-8495; aleadventure4x4@hotmail.com; cnr Av Pedro Arraya & Chuquisaca; ⊙ 6:30am-8pm) This friendly and experienced agency offers English-speaking guides who are excited to show travelers spots that are off the beaten path. It offers tours to the *salar* as well as activities in and around Tupiza.

Valle Hermoso Tours   TOURS
(☑ 694-2592; www.vallehermosotours.com; Av Pedro Arraya 478, Hostal Valle Hermoso; ⊙ 7am-midnight) This agency inside Hostal Valle Hermoso offers tours to the *salar* and a range of tours in the surrounding area, including Butch Cassidy tours to San Vicente (B$1200 for up to four people).

🛏 Sleeping

The accommodations here won't win any prizes for cutting-edge design, but nonetheless there are some comfortable and welcoming budget and midrange options. It can be cold at night during the winter months, so consider looking for a room with heating.

★ Hostal Butch Cassidy   HOSTEL $
(☑ 7944-8880, 7183-3271; hostalbutch@hotmail. com; Av Jose Luis San Juan Garcia s/n; s/d/tr incl breakfast B$120/160/240; 🛜) Located across the river from town and a 10-minute walk

from the bus station (p176), this hostel has 13 spacious rooms with gleaming tiled floors, bright and comfortable common areas and a well-equipped kitchen. It's run by Franklin, who can also arrange tours of the surrounding area and to Uyuni via the *salar*.

Ask for a room at the back, with mountain views. There is a small supermarket next door.

Hotel La Torre   HOTEL $
(☑ 694-2633; www.latorretours-tupiza.com; Av Regimiento Chichas 220; s/d incl breakfast B$80/150, r per person with shared bathroom B$60; @ 🛜) Run by a retired nurse and doctor, this hotel offers clean rooms with good beds and smart bathrooms with gleaming tiles. Rooms at the front of the rambling colonial-era home receive more daylight but are chillier, and the beds can be a bit lumpy. Guests have use of a kitchen, roof terrace and TV lounge – the latter is a good place to meet other travelers.

Hostal Valle Hermoso   HOSTEL $
(☑ 694-2592; www.vallehermosotours.com; Av Pedro Arraya 478; dm B$55, s/d with private bathroom B$100/150, r with shared bathroom B$125; 🛜) This old-school hostel has a book exchange, roof terrace, kitchen and plenty of social space. It's HI-affiliated (members get a 10% discount). Breakfast is included.

Anexo Valle Hermoso HOSTEL **$**
(☑ 694-3441; www.vallehermosotours.com; Av
Pedro Arraya 505; dm B$60, s/d B$80/140, d with
shared bathroom B$120; 🛜) Close to the bus
station with passable rooms and cable TV.
The price includes breakfast.

★**Hotel Mitru** HOTEL **$$**
(☑ 694-3001; www.hotelmitru.com; Av Regimiento
Chichas 187; s B$280-380, d B$380-480, s/d with
shared bathroom B$90/160; @ 🛜 ⊠) The best
and most reliable hotel in town, Mitru has
been run by the same family for generations
and is a relaxing choice built around a swim-
ming pool that's just the ticket after a dusty
day on horseback. It has a variety of rooms
in two sections: the older 'garden' part and
the newer 'cactus' area. Breakfast is included.

The suites with a fridge and minibar
are particularly appealing, and the rooms
with shared bathrooms are top value in the
budget range.

Hotel Mitru Anexo HOTEL **$$**
(☑ 694-3002; www.hotelmitru.com; cnr Avs Ava-
roa & Serrano; s/d incl breakfast B$150/250, with
shared bathroom B$80/130; 🛜) A marginally
cheaper offshoot of Hotel Mitru with a similar vibe but no pool (you can use the Mitru's
for free), this place is good value. The rooms
have cable TVs, phones and hot water.

✖ Eating

Pizza and pasta dominate the restaurant
scene, but you'll also find places serving
quality beef (some imported from nearby
Argentina) and decent ice cream as well as
good local food. For a morning treat, head to
Mercado de Ferias (p176) after 9am for *charque*-filled *tamales* (cornmeal dough filled
with llama meat; B$3).

★**Salteñas Especiales**
Marianita BOLIVIAN **$**
(☑ 7917-8578; Florída; per salteña B$4; ⊙ 8am-
5pm) Get these hot-from-the-oven chicken
and beef *salteñas* (savory pies) to eat in or
take away. They're some of Bolivia's best!

Cremalin ICE CREAM **$**
(Plaza Independencia; cones B$2.50-9, sundaes
B$10-22; ⊙ 10am-2pm & 2:30-6pm) Choose
from 14 flavors of homemade ice cream as
well as a lengthy menu of indulgent sundaes,
including papaya splits and *selva negra*
(four scoops of chocolate ice cream, Oreo
cookies, chocolate cake, nuts, cream and
cherries). If it's available, try the *chirimoya*
(custard apple) ice cream, a local specialty.

★**Milan Center** PIZZA **$$**
(cnr Av Regimiento Chichas & Chuquisaca; mains
B$25-55, pizza B$33-35; ⊙ 9am-10pm Mon-Sat,
4-10pm Sun; 🛜) For the best pizza in town,
head over to Milan Center, which serves
crispy thin-crust pizzas with a variety of
topping options. The covered back patio is
a nice break from the streets of Tupiza. It's
also a good place to come for a coffee.

Alamo MEXICAN **$$**
(cnr Av Regimiento Chichas & Avaroa; snacks B$10-
30, mains B$30-60; ⊙ noon-2pm & 6-10pm Mon-
Sat) A saloon-style spot where locals and
tourists mingle in the fun two-story space
with a Hollywood vibe and lots of knick-
knacks. The menu features mainly meat
dishes, like *pique a lo macho* (beef chunks
and sausages over french fries with lettuce,
tomatoes, onions and spicy *locote* peppers),
and comes in huge tasty portions.

Churrasqueria Moises BARBECUE **$$**
(cnr Av Regimiento Chichas & Avaroa; almuerzo
B$20, churrasco B$60; ⊙ noon-10pm) A reason-
able carnivore hangout for chunks of *chur-
rasco* accompanied by rice, salad and sweet
potato. It fills up with locals around 8pm, so
get in early to find a table.

Rinconcito Quilmes ARGENTINE **$$**
(Suipacha 14; almuerzo B$15, mains B$40-100;
⊙ 10:30am-10:30pm) You'll see few other tourists in this little spot known for cheap, filling
lunches served in a spacious dining room
with patio tables. It's popular on weekends
for its *asados* (barbecues) with quality meat
from Argentina.

Italiana INTERNATIONAL **$$**
(Florida, nr Santa Cruz; mains B$30-48; ⊙ 10am-
10:30pm) A decent selection of pizzas, pastas,
burgers, sandwiches, soups and salads, as
well as fresh fruit smoothies, cocktails and
local wine is on offer here. All of the very
similar restaurants around this block are
run by different members of the same fam-
ily, as you can probably tell from the decor
and menus.

🍷 Drinking & Nightlife

Most of Tupiza's restaurants are also bars,
serving coffee and tea, fresh juices and
smoothies, cold beers and local wines.

★**Vinoteca El Origen** WINE BAR
(☑ 7252-6746; Av Pedro Arraya 80; ⊙ 9am-
12:30pm & 3-11:30pm Mon-Sat) More than 10
different wines from small, mostly organic

ON THE TRAIL OF BUTCH CASSIDY & THE SUNDANCE KID

San Vicente is a remote mining town that wouldn't even rate a mention were it not the legendary spot where the outlaws **Butch Cassidy and the Sundance Kid** met their untimely demise. Located 100km west of Tupiza, it's a long drive out here over rough roads through a barren, mountainous landscape. Even hardcore Butch and Sundance fans are sometimes a little disappointed by San Vicente, a dusty spot with little tourist infrastructure. Bring your imagination: you can still see adobe houses similar to those where the bandits holed up and eventually died, and visit the cemetery where they were buried.

The pair are honored in a tiny but charming adobe **museum** (B$10; ⊙ 8am-noon & 2-6pm). Enlarged photographs of the real-life duo and their celluloid counterparts adorn the walls, and there's information (in Spanish) about their life and death as well as an assortment of items like saddles and old typewriters. The museum is kept locked. To look inside, ask the key holder to open up; she works in the small store next door.

The only public transport between San Vicente and Tupiza is set up to allow residents of San Vicente to make day trips to Tupiza, and the timing is inconvenient for travelers wishing to do the reverse; there is no tourist accommodation in San Vicente. The easiest way to go is with an agency from Tupiza; Valle Hermoso Tours (p174) offers the trip. One-day trips to San Vicente and back are a long, expensive slog (B$1200 for a carload) but at least you'll see plenty of llamas and rugged mountainous scenery on the way.

Bolivian vineyards can be sampled by the glass at this artists' hangout, which also serves local craft beer and coffee from the Yungas. It's run by Goyo, who plays Bolivian records from behind the bar. The furniture is made from recycled TVs, suitcases and heaters, and there's regular live music.

🔒 Shopping

Tupiza is a market town, and there is no shortage of opportunities to find yourself a bargain, with some kind of market taking place somewhere every day.

Mercado de Ferias   MARKET
(Florida, btwn Avs Regimiento Chichas & Santa Cruz; ⊙ 6:30am-10pm) The central Mercado de Ferias has lots of produce stalls and *come-dores* (dining halls) upstairs.

Mercado Negro   MARKET
(Junín, btwn Avs Santa Cruz & Regimiento Chichas; ⊙ 9am-7pm Mon-Sat) The *mercado negro* (black market) has a mishmash of consumer goods, and occupies an entire block between Avs Santa Cruz and Regimiento Chichas.

Mercado Villa Fatima   MARKET
(Tumusla; ⊙ 9am-6pm Sun) This popular local Sunday market in the north of the city deals in imported Argentinian products.

Feria Serrano   MARKET
(Av Serrano; ⊙ Thu & Sat) Starting at the train station (p177), this street market extends north along Av Serrano, swallowing whole blocks on Thursdays and Saturdays.

ℹ Information

INTERNET ACCESS
There are several internet places along Calle Florida that charge B$3 per hour, and most of them also offer phone calls.

LAUNDRY
Super Clean Laundry (Florída, cnr Av Serrano; ⊙ 8am-8pm) Same-day washes for B$10 per kilo.

MONEY
Banco Union (cnr Florída & Santa Cruz)
Banco Fie (Plaza Independencia)
Latin America Cambio (Avaroa 160; ⊙ 8am-9pm Mon-Sat) Changes many currencies but not always at the best rates.

TOURIST INFORMATION
With no official tourist office, the hotels and tour agencies are your main source of information, but be sure to distinguish the sales pitch from helpful advice.

ℹ Getting There & Away

BUS
The **bus station** (Av Pedro Arraya) has buses to most major destinations or hubs in the region. There are services throughout the day, though the majority of buses leave in the evening.

For Villazón and the border crossing to Argentina, take a *rapidito* (minibus or van), which leave when full (B$20, one hour). The **boarding point** (Av Pedro Arraya) is next to the bus terminal.

Rapiditos also run to Potosí (B$80, 3½ hours) and Uyuni (B$80, three hours), and get there much faster than the bus.

DESTINATION	COST (B$)	TIME (HR)
Cochabamba	80	15
La Paz	50-100	14
Oruro	50-80	10
Potosí	30-70	5
Tarija	50	7
Uyuni	40	4½
Villazón	15-22	2

TRAIN

The ticket window at the **train station** (🖋 694-2529; www.fca.com.bo; Av Serrano) opens irregularly on days when there's a train, so it can be easier to have a tour agency buy your tickets for a small surcharge.

At the time of research, no trains were running to or from Tupiza due to damage to the track caused by flooding. Repairs were underway to the section north of Tupiza, which suffered less damage. The section from Tupiza to Villazón is expected to take longer to repair.

Expreso del Sur is the most comfortable service. Southbound trains to Villazón leave on Wednesday and Saturday at 3:10am. Northbound services to Uyuni and Oruro leave on the same days at 6:25pm. The cheaper Wara Wara heads south to Villazón on Monday and Thursday at 9:05am, with the northbound service departing Tupiza at 7:05pm.

Expreso del Sur

ROUTE	COST (B$ COACH/1ST CLASS, ONE WAY)	ARRIVAL TIME
Tupiza to Villazón	25/60	6:15am
Tupiza to Uyuni	47/120	11:50pm
Tupiza to Oruro	107/239	7:10am

Wara Wara

ROUTE	COST (B$ COACH/1ST CLASS, ONE WAY	ARRIVAL TIME
Tupiza to Villazón	14/20/45	12:05pm
Tupiza to Uyuni	25/38/76	1:15am
Tupiza to Oruro	56/80/181	10:05am

Around Tupiza

Much of Tupiza's appeal lies in the surrounding landscape, a visually stunning wilderness of *quebradas* (ravines), thirsty riverbeds and thriving cacti that'll have you whistling a Western theme tune in no time. It's great hiking country and also perfect for exploration on horseback or 4WD – most Tupiza operators offer these excursions.

If you're hiking without a guide, it's not easy to get lost, but take a map anyway – you can get them from various tour agencies. Carry at least 3L of water per day in this dry desert climate. It's wise to wear shoes that can withstand assault by prickly desert vegetation, and to carry a compass or GPS if you're venturing away from the tracks. Flash flooding is also a danger, particularly in the summer months; avoid camping in the *quebradas* or entering the canyons, especially if it looks like rain.

⊙ Sights & Activities

El Sillar   VIEWPOINT

El Sillar (the Saddle), located 17km northwest of Tupiza, is where a road straddles a narrow ridge between two peaks and two valleys. Throughout this area, rugged amphitheaters have been gouged out of the mountainsides and eroded into spires that resemble a stone forest. The easiest way to get here is on the 3:30pm Tupiza Tours (p173) bus (B$70); it's possible to hire a bike and cycle back to Tupiza for an extra B$80.

The road continues on to San Vicente, of Butch Cassidy and Sundance fame. This entire route is part of a centuries-old trade route. From May to early July you may see a trickle of llama, alpaca and donkey trains (or nowadays more likely *camiones*, pickup trucks) humping salt blocks 300km from the Salar de Uyuni to trade in Tarija.

Quebrada Palala   NATURAL FEATURE

About 3km northwest of Tupiza is Quebrada Palala, a broad *quebrada* (wash) lined with some very impressive red formations known as fins. During the rainy season it becomes a tributary of Río Tupiza. Beyond the dramatic red rocks, the wash rises very gently into hills colored greenish-blue and violet by lead and other mineral deposits.

To get here, head north on Tupiza's Av La Paz from Plazuela El Mundo; 2km ahead, along the railroad line, you'll see the mouth of the *quebrada*. Alternatively, take minibus 2 from Tupiza town center to Palala village (10 minutes, B$1.50); it drops you right at the start of the *quebrada*. About 5km further along, the route passes fin formations and continues up the broad *quebrada* into increasingly lonely country, past scrub brush and cacti stands.

SOUTHERN ALTIPLANO AROUND TUPIZA

ℹ CROSSING THE BORDER TO ARGENTINA

The Bolivian side of the main border crossing to Argentina is the town of **Villazón**, a sprawling, dusty, chaotic sort of place. The frontier and bus station are always busy, as numerous Bolivians work in Argentina. Watch out for the usual scammers who tend to congregate at borders; dodgy banknotes and petty theft are not unknown.

The **Argentine consulate** (☑ 597-2011; http://villazon.consulado.gob.ar; cnr Tarija & Calle 20 de Mayo, Villazón; ◷ 8am-1pm Mon-Fri) is on the main square. Numerous *casas de cambio* (money changers) near the bridge along Av República Argentina offer reasonable rates of exchange for US dollars and Argentine pesos, less for Bolivianos, and there is an ATM on the plaza.

All northbound buses depart from the **Villazón bus terminal** (Av Tumusla), 3km north of the border. All except those bound for Tarija pass through Tupiza (B$15 to B$20, two hours). It's slightly quicker and no more expensive to take a *rapidito* (minibus or van). It's a beautiful trip, so try to go in the day and grab a window seat. Regular bus services also head to Potosí (B$30, seven hours), La Paz (B$50, 15 hours), Uyuni (B$40, 6½ hours) and Oruro (B$50, 12 hours). Daily evening buses run the rough but amazing route to Tarija (B$50, seven hours).

Argentine bus companies have ticket offices at Villazón's terminal, but all Argentine buses leave from the La Quiaca bus terminal, across the border. You'll be hassled by ticket sellers for both Argentine and Bolivian bus services; don't be rushed into buying a ticket as there may be a service leaving sooner. The first bus south to Salta from La Quiaca is at 8:30am Argentinian time (7:30am Bolivian time).

The **Villazón train station** (☑ 597-2565; www.fca.com.bo; Calle 20 de Mayo) is 1.5km north of the border crossing – a taxi costs B$5. Trains run north to Tupiza (B$14 to B$60, three hours), Uyuni (B$38 to B$180, eight to nine hours) and Oruro (B$67 to B$279, 16 to 18 hours) at 3:30pm on Monday, Wednesday, Thursday and Saturday. Expreso del Sur is more comfortable than the basic Wara Wara service.

On the north side of the international bridge, **Bolivian customs and immigration** (Av JM Deheza, btwn Junín & Tupiza; ◷ 6am-11pm) issues exit and entry stamps (valid for 30 days). There is no official charge for these services, but a 'service fee' is sometimes leveraged. Argentine immigration and Argentine customs are open from 7am to 11pm. Formalities are minimal but the wait and exhaustive custom searches can be very long. In addition, those entering Argentina may be held up at several control points further south of the border by more customs searches.

Quebrada Palmira
NATURAL FEATURE

Cañon del Inca, 8km west of Tupiza, makes a great destination for a half-day hike via Quebrada Palmira, a normally dry wash flanked by tall and precarious fin formations. The route leads past the **Puerta del Diablo** rock formation, 5km outside Tupiza. The right fork of the wash is rather comically known as **Valle de los Machos** (Valley of Males); the name stems from the clusters of exceptionally phallic pedestal formations.

It's also possible to reach the canyon on a three-hour round trip on horseback.

Cañón del Duende
CANYON

This canyon, located 9km outside Tupiza, can be reached from the town on a great half-day hike through towering red rock formations of the nearby Quebrada de Santa Elena; ask any of the tour agencies in Tupiza for a map and directions.

El Angosto
TUNNEL

(Entre Ríos) This scenic spot 10km south of Tupiza is the site of a narrow tunnel carved into the mountain, known as the *angosto* (narrow). Until 2011, the tunnel was the only thoroughfare for traffic coming to and from Villazón at the border with Argentina. The tunnel is near the juncture of the rivers Tupiza and San Juan. Where the two meet there are some striking rock formations, including *la torre* (the tower). The area makes for a pleasant hike.

Central Highlands

Best Places to Eat

➜ El Huerto (p210)

➜ Casa de Campo (p189)

➜ Café Gourmet Mirador (p209)

➜ Clementina (p189)

Best Places to Stay

➜ Casa Verde (p208)

➜ Samary Boutique Hotel (p208)

➜ Hacienda Cayara (p231)

➜ Samary Wasi (p219)

➜ Running Chaski Hostal (p186)

Why Go?

Geographically – and some would say metaphorically – the heart and soul of the country, the Central Highlands are a mix of lively urban centers and vast pastoral and mountainous regions dotted with remote villages. Gorgeous whitewashed Sucre, where independence was declared in 1825, is the gateway to trekking the Cordillera de los Frailes. Potosí is a powerful symbol of the natural wealth of the country, built on the silver deposits extracted from nearby Cerro Rico. Much-lower-altitude Cochabamba is one of Bolivia's most pleasant cities, with a perfect climate and modern vibe.

Throughout, there are lovely, little-known colonial towns; it's well worth eschewing the city-to-city mode of travel to explore them. A more distant past is evoked by the Inca ruins in the Cochabamba Valley, but Parque Nacional Torotoro has the last laugh on the age front: it's bristling with dinosaur footprints and fossils, some of which date back 300 million years.

When to Go
Potosi

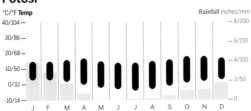

Mar Indigenous festival Pujllay bursts into life on the third Sunday in March.

Aug Catch merrymaking at the Fiesta de la Virgen de Urkupiña.

Oct–Mar Target the summer months to avoid the worst of Potosí's chills.

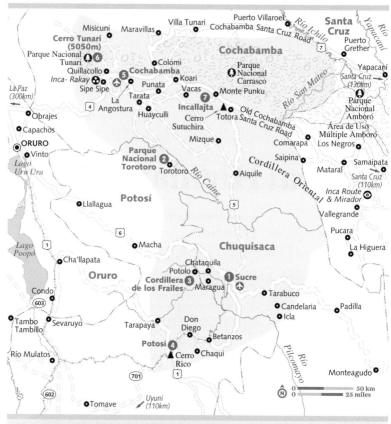

Central Highlands Highlights

1 Sucre (p201) Viewing the whitewashed, red-roofed colonial panorama from high above in La Recoleta.

2 Parque Nacional Torotoro (p197) Spelunking and climbing where the dinosaurs once were.

3 Cordillera de los Frailes (p214) Trekking this mountainous region with

its one-of-a-kind geology and intriguing Jal'qa communities.

4 Casa Nacional de la Moneda (p221) Learning about the origin of money at this country's most fascinating museum, located in Potosí.

5 Cochabamba (p181) Packing on the pounds and

partying them away while visiting this city's lively food and nightlife scene.

6 Cerro Tunari (p194) Summiting this high peak with Andean condors overhead and views below.

7 Incallajta (p195) Visiting these mystical ruins, Bolivia's version of Machu Picchu.

History

Prior to Spanish domination, the town of Charcas, where Sucre now stands, was the indigenous capital of the valley of Choque-Chaca. It served as the residence of local religious, military and political leaders, and its jurisdiction extended to several thousand inhabitants. When the Spanish

arrived, the entire area from Southern Peru to the Río de la Plata in present-day Argentina came to be known as Charcas.

In the early 1530s Francisco Pizarro, the conquistador who felled the Inca empire, sent his brother Gonzalo to the Charcas region to oversee indigenous mining activities that might prove to be valuable to the

Spanish realm. He was not interested in the altiplano and concentrated on the highlands east of the main Andean cordilleras. As a direct result, in 1538 a new Spanish capital of the Charcas was founded. Following in the conquered population's footsteps, he chose the warm, fertile valley of Choque-Chaca for its site. The city, later to become Sucre, was named La Plata – silver was God in those days.

Whereas previously all territories in the region had been governed from Lima, in 1559 King Felipe II created the Audiencia (Royal Court) of Charcas, with its headquarters in the young city, to help administer the eastern territories. Governmental subdivisions within the district came under the jurisdiction of royal officers known as *corregidores*.

In 1776, a new Viceroyalty was established in what is now Buenos Aires and the Charcas came under its control. 'La Plata' was renamed Chuquisaca (a Spanish corruption of Choque-Chaca), as there were too many La Platas around for comfort.

The city had received an Archbishopric in 1609, according it theological autonomy. That, along with the establishment of the University of San Xavier in 1622 and the 1681 opening of the Academía Carolina law school, fostered continued development of liberal and revolutionary ideas and set the stage for 'the first cry of Independence in the Americas' on May 25, 1809. The mini-revolution set off the alarm throughout Spanish America and, like ninepins, the northwestern South American republics were liberated by the armies of the military genius Simón Bolívar.

After the definitive liberation of Peru at the battles of Junín and Ayacucho, on August 6 and December 9, 1824, Alto Peru – historically tied to the Lima government – was technically free of Spanish rule. In practice, however, it had been administered from Buenos Aires and disputes arose about what to do with the territory.

On February 9, 1825, Bolívar's second-in-command, General Antonio José de Sucre, drafted and delivered a declaration that rejected the authority of Buenos Aires and suggested the political future of the region should be determined by the provinces themselves.

Bolívar, unhappy with this unauthorized act of sovereignty, rejected the idea, but de Sucre stood his ground, convinced that there was sufficient separatist sentiment in Alto Peru to back him up. As he expected, the people of the region staunchly refused to wait for a decision from the new congress, which was to be installed in Lima the following year, and also rejected subsequent invitations to join the Buenos Aires government.

On August 6, the first anniversary of the Battle of Junín, independence was declared in the Casa de la Libertad at Chuquisaca and the new republic was christened Bolivia, after its liberator. On August 11 the city's name was changed for the final time to Sucre, in honor of the general who'd promoted the independence movement.

National Parks

The region's protected areas include the remote Parque Nacional Torotoro (p197), peppered with thousands of dinosaur footprints, and Parque Nacional Tunari (p194), easily accessible from the city of Cochabamba.

➊ Getting There & Away

The Central Highlands' major population centers are well served by intercity buses. Getting between towns in the region is a bit more of a challenge – that is, slow and sometimes uncomfortable – if venturing beyond the Potosí–Sucre paved highway; the route between Cochabamba and Sucre is a particularly slow one. Coming from La Paz, the majority of travelers choose to reach Potosí and Sucre from the south via Oruro.

There are frequent flights to Cochabamba and Sucre from La Paz and Santa Cruz; Cochabamba has one of the busiest airports in the country with connections to various regions. It's a quick and cheap flight between Cochabamba and Sucre. There's no functioning airport in Potosí.

COCHABAMBA

🖊 4 / POP 1.24 MILLION / ELEV 2553M

Busy, buzzy Cochabamba is one of Bolivia's boom cities and has a distinct, almost Mediterranean, vitality that perhaps owes something to its clement climate. While much of the city's population is typically poor, parts of town have a notably prosperous feel. The spacious, ever-expanding new-town avenues have a wide choice of restaurants, eagerly grazed by the food-crazy *cochabambinos,* and the bar scene is lively, driven by students and young professionals. It's also the base for outdoor adventures further

Cochabamba

N 0 ____ 400 m
0 ____ 0.2 miles

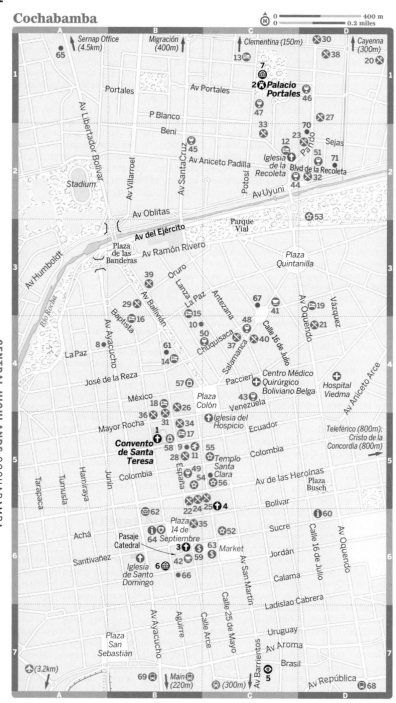

Cochabamba

afield, including trips to Parque Torotoro. You could easily find yourself staying a lot longer than planned.

The city's name is derived from the Quechua *khocha pampa,* meaning 'swampy plain.' Cochabamba lies in a fertile green bowl, 25km long by 10km wide, set in a landscape of fields and low hills. To the northwest rises Cerro Tunari (5050m), the highest peak in central Bolivia.

History

Founded in January 1574 by Sebastián Barba de Padilla, Cochabamba was originally named Villa de Oropeza in honor of the Count and Countess of Oropeza, parents of Viceroy Francisco de Toledo, who promoted its settlement.

During the height of Potosí's silver boom, the Cochabamba Valley developed into the primary source of food for the miners in agriculturally unproductive Potosí. Thanks to its maize and wheat production, Cochabamba became known as the 'breadbasket of Bolivia.' As Potosí's importance declined during the early 18th century, so did Cochabamba's and grain production in the Chuquisaca (Sucre) area, much closer to Potosí, became sufficient to supply the decreasing demand.

By the mid-19th century, however, the city had reassumed its position as the nation's granary. Elite landowners in the valley grew wealthy and began investing in highland mining ventures. Before long, the altiplano mines were attracting international capital, and the focus of Bolivian mining shifted from Potosí to southwestern Bolivia. Cochabamba again thrived and its European–mestizo population gained a reputation for affluence and prosperity.

In 2000 the eyes of the world turned to Cochabamba when its citizens took to the barricades to protest against increases in water rates. The World Bank had forced the Bolivian government to sell off its water company to US giant Bechtel in order to provide financing for a tunnel that would bring water from the other side of the mountains. The resultant rate hikes brought hundreds of thousands of citizens out in protest, sparking uprisings elsewhere in the country and eventually driving Bechtel out. Dubbed 'the Water War,' it helped usher Evo Morales and his party Movement Towards Socialism (MAS) to power. However, as of 2017 a large percentage of Cochabamba residents were still without regular piped water services, many in newer parts of the rapidly expanding city. Hundreds of community wells have been dug as a better solution than accessing water from mobile trucks.

Politically, Cochabamba is suspended somewhere between the pro-Morales altiplano and the pro-autonomy lowlands.

◎ Sights

Cochabamba is Bolivia's largest market town and shopping and gastronomy are what draw in the locals. The town is also blessed with a couple of interesting museums and a number of attractive churches, though the latter are usually open only during Mass.

★ **Palacio Portales** PALACE
(c.pedagogicocultral@fundacionpatino.org; Potosí 1450; incl guide B$25; ⊙ gardens 3-6:30pm Tue-Fri, 9:30-11:30am Sat & Sun, palace guided tours in English 2pm, 5pm & 6pm Tue-Fri, 10:30am & 11:30am Sat, 11:30am Sun) Nothing symbolizes Bolivia's

gilded mineral age like tin baron Simón Patiño's European-style Palacio Portales. Though he never actually inhabited this opulent mansion completed in 1927, it was stocked with some of the finest imported materials available at the time – Carrara marble, French wood, Italian tapestries and delicate silks. The gardens and exterior were inspired by the palace at Versailles, the games room is an imitation of Granada's Alhambra and the main hall takes its design inspiration from Vatican City.

The property also houses an arts and cultural complex as well as a teaching center, and the gardens are a wonderful place to pass the time with a book while waiting for your tour to begin. The house is located in the upscale neighborhood of Queru Queru; take *micro E* north from east of Av San Martín. Tours in Spanish are more frequent and at different times than the English options.

★ **Cristo de la Concordia** LANDMARK
(Innominada, Zona la Chimba; ⊙ 10am-6pm Tue-Sat, 9am-6pm Sun) This immense Christ statue standing atop Cerro de San Pedro (2800m) behind Cochabamba is the second largest of its kind in the world. It's 44cm higher than the famous *Cristo Redentor* in Rio de Janeiro, which stands 33m high, or 1m for each year of Christ's life. *Cochabambinos* justify the one-upmanship by claiming that Christ actually lived *'33 años y un poquito'* (33 years and a bit). Fantastic 360-degree panoramic views of the city and valley are worth the trip.

There's a footpath from the base of the mountain (1250 steps), near the eastern end of Av de las Heroínas, but robberies have been reported and signs along the route not so subtly suggest that you should take the **teleférico** (return B$12; ⊙ closed Mon). In addition, the steps up are extremely steep and only worth considering if you're in the mood and shape for an intense cardio workout. On Sunday you can climb right to the top of the statue (B$2) for a Christ's-eye view of the city. The closest public-transport access is on *micro E* from the corner of San Martín and Sucre. Taxis charge B$40 for the round trip to the top, including a half-hour wait.

★ **Convento de Santa Teresa** CONVENT
(☑ 452-5765; cnr Baptista & Ecuador; guided tour B$50; ⊙ tours hourly 9-11am & 2:30-4:30pm Mon-Sat) The noble, timeworn Convento de Santa Teresa is straight out of a Gabriel García Márquez novel. Guided tours (around 45

minutes) of this gracefully decaying complex allow you to see the peaceful cloister, fine altarpieces and sculptures (from Spanish and Potosí schools) and the convent church. However, it's not so much the quality of the architecture or art that's noteworthy, but rather the challenge to your imagination in picturing and conceiving what life was like for the cloistered nuns (p187) here.

After the original building, built in 1760, was destroyed in an earthquake, a new church was built in 1790 with an excess of ambition, but was too big to be domed. Beginning in 2014, much of the building was slowly and painstakingly restored; several boarded up passageways and unused pulpits have been revealed. There's still a Carmelite community here, but its handful of nuns are now housed in more comfortable modern quarters next door.

La Cancha   MARKET
(Av Aroma; ⊙9am-8pm) Sprawling, chaotic and claustrophobic, Cochabamba's main market, while lacking an attractive mise-en-scène, is nevertheless a colorful place to wander. The largest and most accessible area is **Mercado Cancha Calatayud**, which spreads across a wide area along Av Aroma and south toward the former railway station. It's your best opportunity to see local dress, which differs strikingly from that of the altiplano.

The **Mercado de Ferias** spills out around the old railway station. *Artesanías* (stores selling locally handcrafted items) are concentrated along the alleys near the junction of Tarata and Arce, at the southern end of the market area. The fruit and vegetable section is on the shore of Laguna Alalay in the southeast of town.

Catedral Metropolitana   CHURCH
(Plaza 14 de Septiembre; ⊙8am-noon & 5-7pm Mon-Fri, 8am-noon Sat & Sun) On the arcaded Plaza 14 de Septiembre, Cochabamba's cathedral is the valley's oldest religious building, begun in 1542 as a tiny stone-and-adobe structure. Later additions and renovations have removed some character, but a fine eastern portal has been preserved. Inside it is light and airy, with various mediocre ceiling paintings. There are statues of several saints, a gilded altarpiece and a grotto for the ever-popular Inmaculada (Virgin of the Immaculate Conception).

Museo Arqueológico de la UMSS   MUSEUM
(⎘425-0010; www.museo.umss.edu.bo; cnr Jordán E-199 & Aguirre; B$25; ⊙8am-6pm Mon-Fri,

8:30am-12:30pm Sat) The Museo Arqueológico provides an excellent overview of Bolivia's various indigenous cultures. The collection is split into three sections: the archaeological collection, the ethnographic collection and the paleontological collection. There's good information in Spanish and an English-speaking guide is available for 1:30pm and 4pm tours Monday to Friday.

**Museo de Historia
Natural Alcide d'Orbigny**   MUSEUM
(⎘448-6969; www.museodorbigny.org; Potosí 1458; B$5; ⊙9am-noon & 3-6pm Mon-Fri) `FREE`
Adjacent to the Palacio Portales (p184) is the city's old-fashioned, neglected and low-key natural history museum. With its creaky wooden floors and array of stuffed birds and mammals, this is a good way to kill half an hour while waiting for your Palacio Portales tour to begin. You can also take a look at the small geological collection.

**Iglesia y Convento
de San Francisco**   CHURCH
(cnr Calle 25 de Mayo & Bolívar) Constructed in 1581, the Iglesia y Convento de San Francisco is Cochabamba's second-oldest church. However, major revisions and renovations occurred in 1782 and 1926, and little of the original structure remains. The attached convent and cloister were added in the 1600s. The cloister was constructed of wood rather than the stone that was customary at the time. The pulpit displays good examples of mestizo design and there's a fine gold-framed altarpiece.

La Angostura   LAKE
This artificial lake on the ever-expanding southern outskirts of Cochabamba is a popular spot for *cochabambinos*. However, the lake itself is not an especially pretty sight (though the mountain views are) and there's not much to do other than fill up on enormous plates of *trucha* (trout) or *pejerrey* (king fish) with rice, salad and potato served from one of the shoreline places in the village of the same name.

You can also hire paddleboats, rowboats and kayaks on weekends. A taxi from Cochabamba should run around B$40 each way, or you can head to the corner of Av Barrientos and Manuripi in Cochabamba, take any *micro* toward Tarata or Cliza and get off at the Angostura bridge; if you see the dam on your right, you've gone too far (just). Nearby is the famous **Las Carmelitas** (RN 7, Km 15,

Angostura; empanadas B$4), where you can get delicious and hefty-sized empanadas.

Courses

Instituto Cultural Boliviano Alemán   LANGUAGE
(ICBA; 412-2323; www.icbacbba.org; Lanza 727) Offers group Spanish lessons.

Juntacha   LANGUAGE
(768-5180; http://juntucha.org; cnr Junquillos & Flor de Lino) Classes (B$50 to B$65) are offered daily in the morning, afternoon and evening at this school far from the center of town.

Tours

Because tourism in Cochabamba is relatively low key, it's challenging for solo travelers to book excursions to outlying destinations; unless in a group, prices are prohibitively high. It's best to try arranging in advance, otherwise you'll likely have to stick around for several days at least before there's a departure. Many companies, including some of those we recommend, only have Spanish-speaking guides.

★**El Mundo Verde Travel**   OUTDOORS
(534-4272; www.elmundoverdetravel.com) An extremely knowledgeable and passionate Dutch-Bolivian couple runs this full-service tour company operating throughout Bolivia. Their base is in Cochabamba and they specialize in trekking Cerro Tunari; two- and three-day trips to Torotoro; and visits to Incallajta (p195), other ruins and small villages in the area. Also arrange treks further afield to Huayna Potosí and Illimani, and customized Uyuni journeys.

Andes Xtremo   ADVENTURE
(036-5816; www.andesxtremo.com; La Paz 138) Day trips to Cerro Tunari and multiday treks, as well as paragliding and rock climbing. Best for outdoor adventures in the area.

Bolivia Cultura   ADVENTURE
(452-7272; www.boliviacultura.com; Ecuador E-0342) Professionally guided trips to Parque Nacional Torotoro and other regional attractions. Friendly and accustomed to dealing with foreign travelers; some English is spoken.

Festivals & Events

Santa Veracruz Tatala   RELIGIOUS
(May 2) At the fiesta of Santa Veracruz Tatala, farmers gather at a chapel 7km down the Sucre road to pray for fertile soil during the coming season. Their petitions are accompanied by folk music, dancing and lots of merrymaking.

Heroínas de la Coronilla   CULTURAL
(May 27) This major annual event is a solemn commemoration to honor the women and children who defended the city in the battle of 1812.

Fiesta de la Virgen de Urkupiña   RELIGIOUS
(mid-Aug) For four or so days in Quillacollo, basically a district of Cochabamba 13km to the east, the *chicha* flows liberally (as does *garapiña*, a strong blend of *chicha*, cinnamon, coconut and *ayrampo*, a local mystery ingredient from a cactus that colors the drink red). Folkloric musicians and dancers from around the country perform amid large cheering and intoxicated crowds.

Sleeping

Two good hostels draw the majority of backpackers. Hotels are abundant, but they're generally lacking in character compared to other well-traveled cities in the region. Don't be tempted by the rock-bottom prices in the market areas and around the bus station. They're cheap for a reason: the area is dodgy after dark.

Staying in nearby Quillacollo or Tiquipaya is also an option.

★**Running Chaski Hostal**   HOSTEL $
(425-0559; www.runningchaski.com.bo; España 449; dm B$75-89, s/d/tr B$130/250/300; @) Easily the best choice for budget-minded travelers, Running Chaski is justifiably busy – reserve in advance, especially for weekends. The handsome colonial-style entryway leads to a small grassy back garden. Wood-floored rooms have modern furnishings and the extremely helpful staff can provide travel advice.

★**Las Lilas Hostel**   HOSTEL $
(7740-1222; www.hostellaslilas.com; Zona Linde, Tiquipaya; dm from B$57, r with shared/private bath B$70/85;) With relatively quick access to Cochabamba (it depends on traffic), but in a lovely rural setting, Las Lilas is a stately looking adobe home in front with an arts-and-craft-style patio out the back. There are several dorm rooms of varying configurations, and basic private rooms as well. Hammocks and lounge chairs are provided in the large back garden.

Bicycles are free for guests, and the hostel can arrange trips to Tunari and Torotoro. Bus J runs down Av Ayacucho in Cochabamba and drops you two blocks from the hostel.

Jaguar House   HOSTEL **$**
(☑ 459-1813; jaguarhousehostel.godaddysites.com; Baptista 746; dm B$65-70, s B$110-140, d B$190-220; ☎) The whitewashed paint job and sunny courtyard gives Jaguar House a cool Mediterranean-style vibe. Its rooms are comfortable, if basic. Service is hit-or-miss, as front-desk staff are often newly arrived guests just learning the job. Loungey common areas; best for those looking to socialize and party. No towels provided in dorms.

Monserrat Hotel   HOTEL **$$**
(☑ 452-1011; www.hotelmonserrat.com; España N-342; s/d incl breakfast B$230/350; @ ☎) This centrally located solid midrange choice is housed in a renovated historic building with a handful of happening bars nearby. The carpeted rooms are comfortable, though they're dated and could use more light. Breakfast is above average, and it's worth noting the nice views of the Cristo de la Concordia (p184) from the end of the hallway on the 2nd floor.

THE NUNS OF SANTA TERESA

The Santa Teresa convent (p184) in Cochabamba houses what remains of an order of cloistered Carmelite nuns. A strict Catholic order with a strong devotion to the Virgin Mary, the Carmelites are thought to have been founded in the 12th century on Mt Carmel (hence the name). The order believes strongly in the power of contemplative prayer and shuns the excesses of society.

Local families believed that a daughter in the convent guaranteed the entire family a place in heaven, so there was strong pressure on the first daughter of every *cochabambino* family to enter into the convent. Such was the demand to get some real estate in heaven that there was even a waiting list set up when no vacancies were available. An elderly nun had to pass on before a new young nun was allowed in.

Life inside was tough, and a rigid class system operated. Those who paid a considerable dowry (equivalent to more than US$150,000 in modern money) earned themselves a *velo negro* (black veil) and a place on the council under the control of the Mother Superior. The council was responsible for all the decisions in the convent. As the elite members of the order, *velos negros* were blessed with a private stone room with a single window, where they spent most of their day in prayer, religious study and other acceptable activities such as sewing tapestries.

Each *velo negro* was attended by members of the *velo blanco* (white veil), second-class nuns whose family paid a dowry, but could not afford the full cost of a *velo negro*. *Velo blancos* spent part of their day in prayer and the rest in the personal service of the *velo negros*. Daughters of poor families who could not afford any kind of dowry became *sin velos* (without veils). They slept in communal quarters and took care of the cooking, cleaning and attending to the needs of the *velo blancos*.

The rules inside the convent were strict. Personal effects weren't permitted and communication with other nuns was allowed for only one hour a day – the rest was spent in total silence. Meals were eaten without speaking and contact with the outside world was almost completely prohibited. Once a month each nun was allowed a brief supervised visit from their family, but this took place behind bars and with a black curtain preventing them from seeing and touching each other. The only other contact with the city was through the sale of candles and foodstuffs, which was performed via a revolving door so that the vendor and the client were kept apart. Such transactions were the sole source of income for the nuns who were otherwise completely self-sufficient.

In the 1960s the Vatican declared that such conditions were inhuman and offered all cloistered nuns the world over the opportunity to change to a more modern way of life. Many of the nuns in Santa Teresa rejected the offer, having spent the better part of their life in the convent and knowing no different. Today most of the few remaining nuns are of advancing years and while the rules are no longer as strict as they once were, the practices have changed little. These days the cloistered lifestyle is understandably less attractive to young girls in an age where their families permit them to exercise their own free will.

CENTRAL HIGHLANDS COCHABAMBA

Hotel Luxor   HOTEL $$
(☑ 452-4048; luxoraparthotel@hotmail.es; La Paz 439; s/d incl breakfast B$270/380; ❄ 🛜) On a leafy and quiet residential street only a block from Av Ballivián, this multistory tower has no-frills, spick-and-span rooms with faux-wood floors, excellent light and old TVs.

★Hotel Aranjuez   HOTEL $$$
(☑ 428-0076; www.aranjuezhotel.com; Av Buenos Aires E-563; r from B$630; ❄ @ 🛜) As you walk around the wonderfully decorated salons in this elegantly furnished hotel on a quiet street in the wealthy Recoleta district, you could be forgiven for thinking you were staying in one of Patiño's palaces. In fact, the Palacio Portales (p184) is just a half block away. This is old-world luxury, so not the place for those seeking contemporary style.

Gran Hotel Cochabamba   HOTEL $$$
(☑ 448-9520; www.granhotelcochabamba.com.bo; Plazuela Ubaldo Anze E-415; s/d from B$570/650; ❄ @ 🛜) Officially Cochabamba's top hotel, this five-star beauty is essentially attached to the Iglesia de la Recoleta and is in the same historic building that once housed the city's first hotel. It's classy and elegant and yet manages to provide friendly, informal

---

PATIÑO'S PAIRUMANI VILLA

If you haven't already had your fill of Simón Patiño's legacy in Oruro and Cochabamba, you can visit **Villa Albina** (☑ 401-0470; Pairumani; B$10; ⏲ 8am-4pm Mon-Fri, 9am-1pm Sat) 🍴 in the village of Pairumani and tour the home the tin baron occupied. This enormous white mansion, with its long palm-tree-lined entrance roadway, was named after Simón's wife, Albina. She was presumably as fussy as her husband when it came to the finer things in life, and the elegant French decor of the main house seems fit for royalty.

As well as the house, there's a formal garden, complete with topiary, and the family mausoleum, made from Carrara marble, in which the don and his wife were finally laid to rest.

The villa is only 18km from Cochabamba, but traffic can be bad. Best to take a taxi and try to avoid rush hours. Alternatively, from Quillacollo, take a Pairumani *trufi* from the Plaza Bolívar and get off at Villa Albina.

---

service that most hotels in this category lack. There's also a wonderful patio.

El Poncho Eco Center   CABAÑAS $$$
(☑ 439-2283; www.elponcho.org; Calle Innominada, Zona Marquina, Quillacollo; s/d incl breakfast B$330/520; @ 🛜) You might think you've stumbled onto a film set for *The Lord of the Rings*. This psychedelic-looking place, with a stunning mountain backdrop the equal of any CGI-rendered fantasy land, has uniquely designed, mostly stone and thatch-roof bungalows scattered around a well-manicured garden. Massage, tai chi and a sauna are only a few of the offerings.

Hotel Diplomat   HOTEL $$$
(☑ 425-0687; www.hdiplomat.com; Av Ballivián 611; s/d B$550/690; ❄ @ 🛜) An upmarket business hotel clinically efficient in its service with great views from some of the well-appointed rooms. Centrally located on Av Ballivián, known as 'El Prado' – a center for shopping or barhopping. Free airport transfer.

Toloma Gran Hotel   BUSINESS HOTEL $$$
(☑ 466-4627; www.tolomahotel.com; Av Oquendo 690; s/d B$480/550; ❄ @ 🛜) Conveniently located with concentrations of restaurants in several directions (Recoleta is within walking distance), this towering hotel has a rather grand entrance with several flags marking its international ambitions. Service is friendly and some staff speak English.

🍴 Eating

Cochabambinos pride themselves on being the most food-loving of Bolivians and their city's reputation as the culinary capital of the country is deserved. The highest concentration of good restaurants is in La Recoleta, an upscale neighborhood north of the center; there are several recommended Argentinian-style *churrasquerías* in a pedestrian plaza here.

★Vainilla   INTERNATIONAL $
(cnr Salamanca & Antezana; mains B$25-36; ⏲ 8am-10:30pm Mon-Sat, to 9:30pm Sun; 🛜) This contemporary, bright and airy restaurant has the look, feel and healthy menu choices of a southern California cafe. The umbrella-shaded outdoor patio is an ideal place for a breakfast of eggs, a fruit smoothie and a cappuccino.

María Bonita   MEXICAN $
(Beni 0539; mains B$15-25; ⏲ 6-11pm Mon-Sat, 11am-9pm Sun) This charming and friendly

spot decorated with bright colors and Mexican signifiers such as Frida Kahlo posters and football jerseys is run by the son of a Mexico City–Bolivian couple. Tasty burritos, enchiladas and chimichangas are nicely presented, and the Sunday brunch of ceviche and *sopa de frijol* (black bean soup) is a good deal.

Mikuy Cafe Cultural
CAFE **$**
(cnr Bolivar & España; mains B$17-45; ⊘ 8am-10pm Mon-Sat; 🛜) The light-filled atrium with faux-stone flooring at this restored colonial-era building is a pleasant place to break up a walk around downtown. Sandwiches, crepes and pasta make up the bulk of its basic menu, but it's equally good for a pastry and cappuccino.

Palacio Silpancho
BOLIVIAN **$**
(cnr Baptista & Mayor Rocha; mains B$18; ⊘ 24hr) No-frills joint that only serves several versions of *silpancho* (schnitzel-style meat topped with a fried egg on a bed of rice and boiled potatoes), one of the city's specialty dishes.

Empanadas Otah
EMPANADAS **$**
(empanadas B$9; ⊘ 8:30am-8:30pm Mon-Sat) Hole-in-the-wall spot with a couple of tables where you can quickly tackle large, juicy empanadas washed down with a juice or even a surprisingly good espresso.

★Clementina
INTERNATIONAL **$$**
(📱 425-2151; www.clementina.com.bo; mains B$38-48; ⊘ 7-11pm Tue-Sat) A corrugated shipping container facade conceals this intimate and sophisticated scene. Dishes include creative salads, like quinoa with tandoori chicken, burgers and a dozen pasta dishes (gluten free upon request). Lamps hanging in mason jars and a dimly lit back patio give it a romantic vibe.

★Casa de Campo
LATIN AMERICAN **$$**
(Pasaje del Blvd 618; mains B$43-70; ⊘ 11:30am-midnight; 🛜) A Cochabamba classic, this loud and cheerful partly open-air restaurant is a traditional spot to meet and play *cacho* (dice). There's a big range of Bolivian dishes and grilled meats; the food is fine (and piled high on the plates), but the lively, unpretentious atmosphere is better.

★Menta
VEGETARIAN **$$**
(España; mains B$29-45; ⊘ noon-3pm & 6:30-10pm Mon-Sat) A sparsely designed white-brick space with several long picnic-style tables and a menu of Bolivian-style vegetarian dishes and good fruit juices.

Cayenna
INTERNATIONAL **$$**
(www.cayenna.com.bo; Alvestegui; mains B$30-65; ⊘ 8:30am-12:30am; 🛜) On the ground floor of an upscale apartment building lining a narrow suburban park, Cayenna has a large, eclectic menu ranging from *pita silpancho* (sliced beef, potatoes, onions, tomatoes and fried egg) to vegetarian pizzas, steak chimichurri and trout in a vinaigrette sauce; photos are a help. Also an extensive wine list.

Beef & Buns
BURGERS **$$**
(cnr Av América & Aguirre; burgers B$32; ⊘ noon-3pm & 6:30-11pm) Classic Americana decor and a variety of juicy 200g beef burgers; equally above-average chicken sandwiches.

De K'ffe
INTERNATIONAL **$$**
(Pando 1143; mains B$30-120; ⊘ 8am-midnight; 🛜) Homey and a little old-fashioned, at least as far as decor goes, this is nevertheless a convivial place, where regulars have been congregating for years. The menu, imitating an American deli, is wide-ranging – if anything there are too many choices – making it a good place for everything from early morning breakfasts to late-night drinks.

Gopal
VEGETARIAN **$$**
(España 250; buffet B$18, mains B$20-40; ⊘ 11am-2pm Mon-Sat; 🍴) Stop by for the buffet lunch at this long-running chain with a few locations in the city serving half-decent vegetarian dishes, including soy-based versions of Bolivian dishes and a few curries. It's in the rear of the courtyard for the Ñaupa House Hostel.

La Estancia
ARGENTINE **$$$**
(Av Uyuni 0786; mains B$50-95; ⊘ 11:30am-midnight) One of a knot of spacious restaurants just across the river in Recoleta, this Argentine-style grill is a fine place. There are thick, juicy steaks (it's worth upgrading to the Argentine meat), ribs and kidneys, as well as fish and chicken, all sizzled on the blazing grill in the middle. There's also a decent salad bar and very good service.

Sole Mio
PIZZA **$$$**
(📱 428-3379; Av América E-826; pizzas B$55-80; ⊘ 6-11pm Tue-Sun) The best pizza in Cochabamba. The owners, encouragingly, are from Napoli and import the ingredients for their robust brick-oven, wood-fired pizzas – thin crust, light on the sauce. Soft opera music, rich Italian wines and excellent

LOCAL SPECIALTIES

There's a dazzling array of local specialties, including *pico a lo mancho* (a gut-busting portion of various meats and sausages, onions, spicy peppers and tomatoes on a bed of thick french fries); *silpancho* (schnitzel-style meat on rice and potatoes); *lomo borracho* (beef with egg in a beer soup); and *picante de pollo* (chicken in a spicy sauce).

Street Eats

There's tasty street food and snacks all over Cochabamba; the *papas rellenas* (potatoes filled with meat or cheese) at the corner of Achá and Av Villazón are particularly delicious. Great *salteñas* (meat and vegetable pasties) and empanadas are ubiquitous, and locals swear by the sizzling *anticuchos* (beef-heart shish kebabs).

Sweet Treats

At the corner of Av de las Heroínas and España – crowding one another in a jumble of fluorescent lights, neon signs of child-friendly mascots, and kaleidoscopic displays of gelato flavors – are a jumbo-sized **Dumbo** (Av de las Heroínas E-345; mains B$10-79; ⊙ 8am-11pm; 🛦), **Cristal** (Av de las Heroínas E-352; mains B$18-47; ⊙ 8am-11pm) and **Donal** (Av de las Heroínas; mains B$20-55; ⊙ 7:30am-midnight; 🛦). All serve a range of foods throughout the day, from pancakes to bland-but-decent burgers, but crowds flock here in the evening for *helados* (ice creams), shakes and gut-busting servings of cake. Competing for *cochabambinos'* ice-cream and dessert bolivianos is Globo's, with four locations across the city; the multistory outlet on **Av Pando** (Pando 1236; mains B$27-79; ⊙ 24hr) in La Recoleta is an impressive mix of child-friendly elements with a sophisticated nightclub feel for adults.

service make this a comfortable place to linger a while. It also serves a range of meat and pasta dishes.

Páprika INTERNATIONAL $$$
(www.paprika.com.bo; Chuquisaca; mains B$30-110; ⊙ 11:30am-midnight; 🕾) Classy and fashionable, this popular restaurant-bar has an eclectic menu, both Bolivian and international, including tasty baked potatoes and fondues, and more unusual plates such as ostrich and llama. After dark it becomes a trendy spot for a late drink and is also a good place to meet up with young bolivianos.

Bufalo's Rodizio BRAZILIAN $$$
(☑ 425-1597; Av Oquendo N-654, Torres Sofer, 2nd fl; buffet B$91; ⊙ 6-11pm Mon, noon-11pm Tue-Sat, to 2:30pm Sun) This all-you-can-eat Brazilian-style grill has smart waiters bringing huge hunks of delicious meat to your table faster than you can pick up your fork. There's a large salad bar but, let's face it, it's designed for the carnivore.

Suiza INTERNATIONAL $$$
(Av Ballivián; mains B$50-120; ⊙ 11:30am-2:30pm & 6-11pm Mon-Sat) Formally attired waitstaff and an overall air of old-school traditional aloofness permeates Suiza. However, the *almuerzo ejecutivo* is a good deal at B$50, and the pasta is above average. The restaurant's specialty is fish, either pejerrey, surubí, trout or corvina, prepared in a number of ways, including our favorite, *sudado* (stew).

La Cantonata ITALIAN $$$
(☑ 425-9222; cnr España & Mayor Rocha; mains B$50-110; ⊙ 11am-2:30pm & 6:30-11:30pm Tue-Sat, noon-2:30pm Sun; 🕾) A little stuffy in an old-school way with menus the weight of a hardcover book and formal, waistcoated waiters, this long-running Italian place remains the most reputable restaurant in this part of town. Choose from a long list of pizza, pasta and meat dishes; better value at lunch.

Self-catering

IC Norte SUPERMARKET $
(cnr Av América & Pando; ⊙ 8:30am-9pm Mon-Fri) Well-stocked US-style supermarket with imported and unique, export-quality Bolivian products.

Hipermaxi SUPERMARKET $
(Ballivián 1185; ⊙ 7:30am-10:30pm) Large centrally located supermarket. On weekends there's a grill set up out front serving up burgers and *silpancho* (schnitzel-style meat topped with a fried egg on a bed of rice and boiled potatoes). Five banks have separate ATMs right out the front.

🍷 Drinking & Nightlife

There's a flourishing bohemian-style bar scene popular with mostly university-aged students along España, between Mayor Rocha and Colombia. In La Recoleta, a slightly older crowd heads to spots along Paseo del Blvd, and El Pasaje Portales has several nightclubs playing Latin and electronic music. The nightlife along El Prado (Av Ballivián) mostly involves drinking at street-front restaurants.

★ Muela del Diablo   BEER GARDEN
(Potosí 1392; ◷5:30pm-2am; 🕾) The central patio of this exceptionally charming place, wonderfully lit up at night by candles and glowing heat lamps, is surrounded by archways and columns. The feel is of a cool hideaway in an abandoned villa in a European city. Indoors, the bar is more downtown trendy and has live music some weekend nights. The menu is also worthy, with artisanal wood-fired pizza (B$43 to B$60).

★ Suassuna por
Cafe Fragmentos   BEER GARDEN
(Chuquisaca, btwn Lanza & Valdiviezo; ◷5-11:30pm Mon-Sat) Lively on weekend nights when the outdoor garden tables lit with candles are filled with young couples and small groups of friends enjoying cheap drinks (B$20 for two Cuba Libres), snacks and small dishes.

Tambo Cafe   BAR
(España 449; ◷3-11pm) One of the nicer places for a drink, or an afternoon snack and dinner for that matter, is the vine-covered cobblestone courtyard of the Running Chaski Hostal (p186). Live jazz some Friday nights.

Capresso Cafe   CAFE
(Salamanca 860; ◷7am-11pm Mon-Fri, from 8am Sat, 9am-10pm Sun; 🕾) Contemporary-style cafe with pleasant front porch seating, especially good for a long Sunday afternoon stay when other places are closed. Upstairs has more loungey seating options, popular with laptop-toting locals and foreigners alike.

Mandarina Lounge   LOUNGE
(www.facebook.com/MandarinaLOUNGE; Pasaje Portales; ◷5pm-late) Uber-urban, contemporary and fashionable, this place could be dropped in Soho in NYC or Miami Beach. The soundtrack is a mix of hip-hop, latin pop and house. Leave your sneakers and T-shirts and come dressed to impress.

Vinoppolis   WINE BAR
(www.facebook.com/Vinoppolis-14945409174 68075; Paseo del Blvd (Blvd de la Recoleta); ◷6pm-2am Tue-Sun) Classy wine bar with tapas.

Novecento   BAR
(Chuquisaca 711; ◷noon-late Mon-Fri, 6pm-late Sat, noon-5pm Sun; 🕾) Live performance space, cultural center, bar and restaurant all in one; but true to its name, film is the inspiration and movies are shown in a small screening room most nights at 8:30pm. There's also live jazz Wednesdays at 9pm. But it's always a good spot to hang out, and the menu is large and eclectic.

Dishes span the gamut, from tacos to beef stroganoff to pizzas and risotto (mains B$35 to B$65).

La Tirana y Olé   WINE BAR
(Venezuela 635; ◷7-11:30pm Wed & Thu, to midnight Fri & Sat, noon-3pm Sun) This multistory maze of a place is all Spanish style, from its chef and tapas menu to its sangria (B$100 for 1.5L) and cozy brick-walled ground floor, which resembles an Andalucían bodega. Live music doesn't get started upstairs until after 11pm on weekend nights.

Simón Boliche   BAR
(España E-250; ◷6:30pm-1am Mon-Sat; 🕾) Girls in glasses reading Pablo Neruda while sipping artisanal beer. Young guys barbecuing meat on a portable grill just outside the entrance. Live performances by 'new reggae' bands. Warhol-style paintings of Evo Morales. This snapshot of a single night should give you an idea of the vibe of this hip, casual spot above the entrance to the Ñaupa House Hostel.

Espresso Café Bar   CAFE
(Arce 340; ◷8:30am-10:30pm Mon-Sat; 🕾) Just behind the cathedral, this traditional-looking place is filled with regulars, mostly men chatting with old buddies or perusing the papers while sipping large cups of espresso. Good juices and pastries are also served up by professional, quick-to-please waitstaff.

Lujo's Discoteca y Karaoke   CLUB
(Beni E-330; ◷8pm-late Wed-Sun) A popular dancing spot is Lujo's Discoteca y Karaoke, which, when the clientele don't take the music into their own hands, plays salsa and pop.

Levoa   CLUB
(Paseo del Blvd (Blvd de la Recoleta); ◷9pm-late Fri & Sat) This loud and trendy dancing place gets crowded on weekends.

CENTRAL HIGHLANDS COCHABAMBA

☆ Entertainment

The new Hupermall in La Recoleta has a cinema, as does the multiplex **Cine Center** (www.cinecenter.com.bo; Ramón Rivero 789; tickets B$45) with several screens showing the latest Hollywood flicks (plus there's a food court and ATMs). More atmospheric, if also dingy, are the **Cine Heroínas** (Av de las Heroínas s/n; tickets B$25-35), **Cine Teatro Capital** (cnr Calle 25 de Mayo & Colombia; tickets B$30) and the smaller **Cine Astor** (cnr Sucre & Calle 25 de Mayo; tickets B$25-35). For information about what's on, see the newspaper entertainment listings.

Teatro Adela Zumudio THEATER
(cnr Av de las Heroínas & Calle 25 de Mayo) Built in the 1940s and refurbished in the last decade, this theater in the center of the city hosts everything from jazz to folkloric dances to contemporary bands.

🛍 Shopping

Spitting Llama BOOKS, OUTDOOR EQUIPMENT
(☑ 452-2147; www.spllama.com; España 301; ⊙ 9am-7pm Mon-Fri, to 1pm Sat) International brands of camping equipment and trekking clothing and gear for sale or rent, and foreign-language books, including Lonely Planet guidebooks.

Asarti CLOTHING
(www.asarti.com; cnr Calle México & Av Ballivián, edificio Colon; ⊙ 10am-1pm & 3-8pm Mon-Fri, 10am-4pm Sat) Expensive but reliable Asarti, on the ground floor of an office building, makes export-quality alpaca clothing.

ℹ Information

DANGERS & ANNOYANCES

➡ According to locals, the streets south of Av Aroma are dangerous at night and are best avoided. The bus station is around here, so don't be surprised if, when arriving in the early hours of the morning, you're strongly discouraged from leaving until sunrise.

➡ Pickpocketing and petty theft aren't uncommon in the markets.

➡ The parkland areas Colina San Sebastián and Coronilla Hill near the bus station are both considered dangerous throughout the day – avoid them.

➡ As in any large city, it's best to travel with others late at night and keep your wits about you.

Police

Tourist Police (☑ 450-3880, emergency 120; Plaza 14 de Septiembre; ⊙ 24hr)

INTERNET ACCESS

Wi-fi is common in cafes, restaurants and even some public parks (but signals in the latter are iffy). Internet cafes are thick on the ground in the blocks surrounding the university; most charge B$4 per hour.

LAUNDRY

Most hotels offer laundry services, but they tend to be pricey and charge per piece. The two hostels are more affordable and charge per kilo. For commercial *lavanderías* try **Limpieza Superior** (España 616; ⊙ 8:30am-1pm & 2-7pm Mon-Fri, 8am-1pm & 2-5pm Sat), which charges B$18 per kilo.

MEDICAL SERVICES

Centro Médico Quirúrgico Boliviano Belga (☑ 422-9407; Antezana N-455; ⊙ 24hr) Private clinic.

Hospital Viedma (☑ 453-3240; Venezuela; ⊙ 24hr) Full-service public hospital.

MONEY

Moneychangers gather along Av de las Heroínas and near the market at **Calle 25 de Mayo** (Calle 25 de Mayo); some only accept US cash. **Amanda Casa de Cambio** (Pasaje de la Catedral 340; ⊙ 8:30am-5:30pm) is quick and professional. You're never far from an ATM, with clusters on Av Ballivián, including five separate ones in front of the Hipermaxi (p190) supermarket and at the corner of Avs Heroínas and Ayacucho.

POST

The main **post office and Entel** (cnr Avs Ayacucho & de las Heroínas; ⊙ 6:30am-10pm) are together in a large complex. Downstairs from the main lobby is an express post office.

TOURIST INFORMATION

The **tourist office** (☑ 425-8030; www.cocha bambaturistica.com.bo; Plaza 14 de Septiembre; ⊙ 8am-noon & 2:30-6:30pm Mon-Fri) hands out good city material. There are several information kiosks, which also open Saturday mornings, including at the bus station and airport.

Cochabamba has a superb website for visitors (www.brujulaturistica.com/cochabamba), with details and information about places of interest, links to flight information, hotel listings, photos and local events.

Visit the **Instituto Geográfico Militar** (IGM; ☑ 425-5563; Calle 16 de Julio S-237; ⊙ 8am-noon & 2-6pm Mon-Fri) for topographic maps (useful for hikers) of Cochabamba department. The **Sernap office** (Servicio Nacional de Areas Protegidas; www.sernap.gob.bo) has limited information about national parks. Private tour companies are usually better equipped to answer questions.

Head to the **Migración** (☑ 452-4625; Av Rodríguez Morales, btwn Santa Cruz & Potosí;

⊗ 8.30am-12:30pm & 2:30-6:30pm Mon-Fri) office for visa and length-of-stay extensions.

ℹ Getting There & Away

AIR

The flight between La Paz and Cochabamba's Jorge Wilstermann International Airport (p352) – only 4km southwest of the center – must be one of the world's most incredible (sit on the left coming from La Paz, the right from Cochabamba), with fabulous views of the dramatic Cordillera Quimsa Cruz and a (disconcertingly) close-up view of the peak of Illimani. Most flights between Santa Cruz and La Paz touch down briefly at Cochabamba and the city also connects them with flights to Sucre.

BoA (☑ 414-0873; www.boa.bo; cnr Jordán & Aguirre; ⊗ 8:30am-7pm Mon-Sat), **Ecojet** (www.ecojet.bo; Plazuela Constitución 0879, cnr 16 de Julio; ⊗ 8:30am-7:30pm), **Amazonas** (☑ 479-4200; www.amaszonas.com; Av Bolívar 0-1509; ⊗ 8:30am-12:30pm & 2:30-6pm Mon-Fri, 8:30am-12:30pm Sat) and **TAM** (☑ 458-0547; www.tam.bo; Av Aniceto Padilla 755; ⊗ 8:30am-1pm & 2:30-7pm Mon-Fri, 8:30am-1pm Sat) combined, run a bunch of daily flights between Santa Cruz and La Paz via Cochabamba and a couple of daily flights to Sucre. There are also daily flights to Oruro, Trinidad and Tarija, the latter continuing on to Yacuiba a couple of days a week (the schedule changes). Flights to Uyuni generally connect via La Paz.

Micro B (B$2) shuttles between the airport and the main plaza. Taxis to or from the center cost B$25 to B$30. To Quillacollo or Tiquipaya it's B$50.

BUS

Cochabamba's **main bus terminal** (☑ 422-0550; Ayacucho; terminal fee B$4), just south of the center, has an information kiosk, a branch of the tourist police, ATMs, luggage storage and a *casa de cambio* (money exchange bureau). The traffic around the terminal is a mess; if bags are small and light and it's daytime, it might be worth walking a few blocks to hail a taxi.

Trufis (collective taxis) and *micros* to eastern Cochabamba Valley villages leave from a variety of spots south of the center, along Av República at the corners of Barrientos, Av 6 de Agosto and Mairana.

Torotoro *micros* (B$35) with **Sindicato de Transporte Mixto Toro Toro Turistico** (☑ 7144-2073; Mairana, near Av República) depart daily, when full, from around 7am until late in the afternoon, but waits can vary; 1½ hours isn't unusual. Arrive around 7am or go with a group and it should be quick. Services to the western part of the valley leave from the corner of Avs Ayacucho and Aroma. For Villa Tunari, *micros* to **Chapare**

(Av Oquendo, near Av República) leave from the corner of Avs República and Oquendo.

Expreso Campero (p197) runs minivans to Aquile and Peña Colorada leaving Cochabamba at noon, 4pm and 6pm.

Departures to La Paz and Santa Cruz leave frequently throughout the day. Oruro and Potosí are mostly nighttime trips.

Bolívar and Trans Copacabana generally have the most qualified drivers and so are the most recommended bus lines.

Best to buy your tickets in the morning the day of your trip. If you turn up in the evening, shortly before departure, we've heard stories of people being scammed.

DESTINATION	COST (B$)	TIME (HR)
Buenos Aires	900	54
La Paz	40-100	9
Oruro	20-50	5
Potosí	80-120	12
Santa Cruz	95-130	12
Sucre	65-95	8-9
Villa Tunari	bus 15, trufi 35	bus 4, trufi 3

ℹ Getting Around

BUS

Convenient lettered *micros* and *trufis* display their destinations and run to all corners of the city (B$2). *Micros* to **Quillacollo, Pahirumani & Sipe Sipe** (cnr Avs Aroma & Ayacucho) leave from the intersection of Avs Ayacucho and Aroma near the bus terminal.

CAR & MOTORCYCLE

Rental cars are available at **Europcar** (☑ 7889-7884; cochabamba@europcar.com.bo; Jorge Wilstermann International Airport; ⊗ 8:30am-11pm) and **Sudamericana Rent-a-Car** (☑ 428-3132; www.sudamericanarentacar.com; Pando 1187), but there's no reason to rent just to get around the city and the immediate environs. If you want to explore further afield, you'll need a 4WD. Traffic around downtown, especially at rush hour, is bumper to bumper.

TAXI

The taxi fare around the center of Cochabamba is B$6 per person. An extra boliviano is charged if you cross the river or go far to the south. At night, a taxi to La Recoleta runs around B$10. Drivers will ask for B$15 from the center to various *micro* stops south of Av 6 de Agosto. To accommodations around Quillacollo it's B$35 to B$40. For a radio taxi, ring **Radio Taxi SJ** (☑ 428-0002).

AROUND COCHABAMBA

Parque Nacional Tunari

This easily accessible 3090 sq km park was created in 1962 to protect the forested slopes above Cochabamba and the wild summit of Cerro Tunari. It encompasses a wide diversity of habitats, from dry inter-Andean valleys to the more humid and highly endangered *Polylepis* forests of the Cordillera Tunari; because of habitat destruction the endemic Cochabamba mountain finch is also endangered.

Cochabamba Area

A good dirt road zigzags its way from the park gate (open until 4pm) up the steep mountain face. About 3km after the gate, you'll reach a **picnic site** with barbecues and a playground. Beyond here is a *sendero ecológico* (nature trail). Don't expect too much in the way of *ecología,* but it's a well-made path that gains altitude rapidly, winding into thickening mature woodland. The views are tremendous, with Cochabamba spread out below, and in the opposite direction, Cerro Tunari and the Cordillera. With an early start and plenty of water you should be able to make it up to some of the nearer peaks on a long day hike.

The Sernap office (p192) in Cochabamba may have simple walking maps of the park.

Coming from town take *trufi* 109 (B\$2) along Av Ayacucho to the last stop, which will drop you a three-minute walk from the park entrance, at a big wooden archway with a fire-risk indicator. You may have to show ID and sign in to access the park. From the gate turn right, then left after 100m; the road winds up past the playground to some mountain lakes.

Cerro Tunari Area

Snow-dusted Cerro Tunari (5050m) is the highest peak in central Bolivia (it's the second peak from the left on the Taquiña beer label). Its flanks are 25km northwest of Cochabamba along the road to Morochata and Independencia. This spectacular area offers excellent hiking and camping and the chance to spot Andean condors, but access is less than straightforward on your own. For climbs, pick up the 1:50,000 map *Cordillera de Tunari* (sheet 6342III) from the Instituto Geográfico Militar (p192).

From the beautiful forested Parque Pairumani near Quillacollo (the south face

route) it's a complicated four- to five-hour ascent to the summit, with some sections requiring technical equipment. Experienced climbers can manage the round-trip in a long day, but the high-altitude ascent will be more pleasant if you allow two days and camp overnight. You'll need a guide.

An easier route along the north face ascends from Estancia Chaqueri or Tawa Cruz, 12km beyond Cruce Liriuni at 4200m. *Micros* and *camiones* (flatbed trucks) toward Morochata leave on Monday, Thursday and Saturday at 7am from three blocks off the main plaza in Quillacollo; they return to Cochabamba in the afternoon on Tuesday, Friday and Sunday. The relatively easy path, which takes around five hours, ascends the north face of the peak.

Of course, it's easier and much more recommended to simply go with a tour company out of Cochabamba. Rates for one- or two-day trips with Andes Xtremo (p186) and the highly recommended El Mundo Verde Travel (p186) depend on the number in the group. Trips involve a very early morning departure time and cold weather gear.

🛏 Sleeping

Berghotel Carolina   LODGE **$$$**
(📞 7213-0003; www.berghotelcarolina.com; Combuyo, Vinto; s/d/tr/q incl breakfast B$558/732/976/1150) German-owned Berghotel Carolina is a mountain refuge with trillion-boliviano views located at the foot of Cerro Tunari, northwest of Quillacollo. Simple and spacious suites, a sauna and outdoor deck create a sense of rustic luxury, and staff arrange all manner of trekking in the park.

ℹ Getting There & Away

Coming from Cochabamba take *trufi* 109 (B$2) along Av Ayacucho to the last stop, which will drop you close to the park entrance. You may have to show ID and sign in to the park. From the gate turn right, then left after 100m; the road winds up past the playground to some mountain lakes.

EASTERN COCHABAMBA VALLEY

Tarata & Huayculli

📋 4 / POP 3500

Tarata, 35km southeast of Cochabamba, is one of the region's loveliest towns, a picturesque but decaying beauty that's worth a visit for its noble buildings, cobbled streets and gorgeous plaza filled with palm trees and jacarandas. The town's name is derived from the abundant *tara* trees, the fruit of which is used in curing leather. Tarata is famous as the birthplace of president General Mariano Melgarejo, who held office from 1866 to 1871 and whose remains lie in the town church. While citizens aren't proud of his achievements, they're proud of producing presidents (populist military leader René Barrientos, who ruled from 1964 to 1969, was also born here).

Huayculli, 7km from Tarata, is a village of potters and glaziers. The air is thick with the scent of eucalyptus being burned in cylindrical firing kilns. The local style and technique has been passed down from generation to generation and remains unique.

◉ Sights

Tarata's enormous neoclassical **Iglesia de San Pedro** was constructed in 1788 and restored between 1983 and 1985; several of the interior panels include mestizo-style details carved in cedar. The 1772 **Franciscan Convent of San José**, which contains lovely colonial furniture and an 8000-volume library, was founded as a missionary training school. It now operates as a museum and contains the ashes of San Severino, Tarata's patron saint, whose feast day is celebrated on the last Sunday in November.

The village also has several other historic buildings: the **Palacio Consistorial** (government palace) of President Melgarejo (built in 1872) and the homes of President Melgarejo, General don Esteban Arce and General René Barrientos.

❶ Getting There & Away

From Cochabamba, taxis (B$7, 30 minutes) leave for Tarata when full and *micros* (B$5, 45 minutes) leave every 15 minutes between 5am and 8pm from the corner of Av Barrientos and Magdalena – the stop is clearly marked with a sign. There are no *micros* to Huayculli, but minibuses running between Tarata and Anzaldo can drop you there.

Incallajta

The nearest thing Bolivia has to Peru's Machu Picchu is this remote, rarely visited site (meaning 'Land of the Inca'), 132km east of Cochabamba on a flat mountain spur above the Río Machajmarka. This was the easternmost outpost of the Inca

---

WORTH A TRIP

CHICHA IN PUNATA

This small market town 50km east of Cochabamba is said to produce Bolivia's finest *chicha* (fermented corn drink). Tuesday is **market day** and May 18 is the riotous **town festival**. Access from Cochabamba is via *micros* (B$8, one hour) and taxis (B$10) that depart when full from Plaza Villa Bella at the corner of Av República and Av 6 de Agosto between 5am and 8pm.

---

empire; after Tiwanaku it's Bolivia's most significant archaeological site. The most prominent feature is the immense stone fortification that sprawls across alluvial terraces above the river, but at least 50 other structures are also scattered around the 30-hectare site.

Incallajta was probably founded by Inca Emperor Tupac-Yupanqui, the commander who had previously marched into present-day Chile to demarcate the southern limits of the Inca empire. It's estimated that Incallajta was constructed in the 1460s as a measure of protection against attack by the Chiriguanos to the southeast. In 1525, the last year of Emperor Huayna Capac's rule, the outpost was abandoned. This may have been due to a Chiriguano attack, but was more likely the result of increasing Spanish pressure and the unraveling of the empire, which fell seven years later.

The site is on a monumental scale; some researchers believe that, as well as serving a defensive purpose, it was designed as a sort of ceremonial replica of Cuzco, the Inca capital. The site's most significant building, the **kallanka**, measures a colossal 78m by 26m. The roof was supported by immense columns. Outside it is a large boulder, probably a speakers' platform. At the western end of the site is a curious six-sided tower, perhaps used for astronomical observation. On the hilltop, a huge zigzag defensive wall has a baffled defensive entrance.

The ruins were made known to the world in 1913 by Swedish zoologist and ethnologist Erland Nordenskiöld, who spent a week at the ruins measuring and mapping them. However, they were largely ignored – except by ruthless treasure hunters – for the next 50 years, until the University of San Simón in Cochabamba launched its investigations.

TIQUIPAYA

The town of Tiquipaya, whose name means 'Place of Flowers,' is located 11km northwest of Cochabamba. It is known for its **Sunday market**, and for its array of unusual festivals: in late April or early May there's an annual **Chicha Festival**; in July there's a **Potato Festival**; the second week in September sees the **Trout Festival**; around September 24 is the **Flower Festival**; and in the first week of November there's the **Festival de la Wallunk'a**, which attracts colorful, traditionally dressed women from around the Cochabamba department.

Micros leave half-hourly from the corner of Ladislao Cabrera and Av Oquendo in Cochabamba. A taxi costs about B$50.

At Pocona, 17km from the ruins, there's an information center and a small exhibition of archaeological finds from the site.

Without your own transportation or a guided tour, visiting Incallajta will prove inconvenient at best. If you can't arrange lodging in private homes or prefer the outdoors, you can camp at the site next to the ruins; be sure to take plenty of water, food and warm clothing, and have the proper gear.

Cochabamba agencies run day trips to Incallajta; most recommended is El Mundo Verde Travel (p186), which adds a visit to the colonial village of **Chimboata** and will do the trip for one or two, and, of course, larger groups. Bolivia Cultura (p186) is another option. Beware of tours that seem suspiciously cheap or that involve 'trekking.' That usually means getting a cab part way and walking a good distance to the site.

Totora

⏰ 4 / POP 2000 / ELEV 2300M

Totora, 142km east of Cochabamba, huddles in a valley at the foot of Cerro Sutuchira. It is on the main route between Cochabamba and Sucre, but few travelers ever see it because most buses pass through at night. Nevertheless it is a lovely village, built around a postcard-pretty plaza with colorful buildings and arcades. In May 1998 the town was struck by an earthquake measuring 6.7

on the Richter scale. While the damage was extensive and rebuilding was slow, most things have since been lovingly restored.

⭐ Festivals & Events

The annual **town festival** is on February 2, though be warned that it features bullfights, an event known for its animal welfare issues. There's a **piano festival** at the end of September, but Totora's most charming and famous festival is that of **San Andrés**. On November 2, giant swings are erected on the streets and throughout the month young women who are hoping for marriage are swung high on them. The women on the swings are also believed to be helping the wandering souls, who descended to earth on All Souls' Day, to return to heaven.

🛏 Sleeping

Villa Eva Casa de Huespedes   B&B $
(☎ 434-1254; villaevatotora@gmail.com; Rodolfo Soriano; r B$170) Several homey rooms in an impressive-looking colonial-style home with Spanish tile rooftop.

ℹ Getting There & Away

Expreso Campero (☎ in Aiquile 695-1569, in Cochabamba 453-7046; Mairana) *micros* (B$35, three hours) destined for Aiquile leave daily for Totora when full from the corner of Calle Mairana and Av República in Cochabamba.

Mizque

⏰ 4 / POP 27,000 / ELEV 2000M

This pretty colonial village enjoys a lovely pastoral setting on the Río Mizque. Founded as the Villa de Salinas del Río Pisuerga in 1549, it soon came to be known as the Ciudad de las 500 Quitasoles (City of 500 Parasols), after the sun shields used by the locals. It makes a nice escape from the cities and main tourist sights, and the few visitors who pass through on trips between Sucre and Cochabamba are impressed by the beauty of the Mizque and Tucuna Valleys, where flocks of macaws squawk in the early morning. There's a small archaeological and historical **museum**, and the **Iglesia Matríz**, lovingly restored after a 1998 earthquake, which once served as the seat of the Santa Cruz Bishopric (until the seat was shifted to Araní in 1767).

There's an indigenous Rankay Pampa community in the surrounding hills; Monday is the day many come to town for supplies.

☞ Tours

Mizque Tours y Aventuras OUTDOORS
(☑ 758-9773) This place has experience showing foreign travelers the outdoor adventures on the town's doorstep. Great for guided tours to area waterfalls (B$140 per day), mountain biking day tours (B$320 per person) and even rappelling the Kuri bridge (B$220 per person) or a nearby canyon (B$80 per person). Can also provide transportation from Cochabamba.

★☆ Festivals & Events

Besides its cheese and honey, Mizque is best known for its **Feria de la Fruta** (April 19), which coincides with the *chirimoya* (custard apple) harvest and **Semana Santa**. From September 8 to 14, Mizque holds the lively **Fiesta del Señor de Burgos**, which features much revelry and bull- and cockfighting. Monday is **market day**.

🛏 Sleeping

Residencial Hotel Mizque PENSION **$**
(☑ 420-0224; Morales; per person B$45) Set amid gardens, this clean place is the easiest to find if you arrive at night.

Hostal Graciela PENSION **$**
(☑ 434-2124; Bolívar 968; per person B$55) A good option with rooms that have decks; it's affiliated with the also-recommended Restaurant Plaza.

❶ Getting There & Away

Three daily Expreso Campero (p196) Aiquile-bound *micros* leave Cochabamba for Mizque (B$20, four hours) from the corner of Mairana and República at noon, 4pm and 6pm; from Mizque they depart for Cochabamba at 8am, 10am and noon from the east side of Plaza Héroes de la Independencia. Occasional *micros* travel between here and Totora – 31km on a rough road.

Parque Nacional Torotoro

One of Bolivia's most memorable national parks surrounds the remote and tranquil colonial village of Torotoro. The area's geography can seem like a practical demonstration of geology on an awe-inspiring scale. Beds of sedimentary mudstone, sandstone and limestone, bristling with marine fossils and – from drier periods – dinosaur footprints, have been muscled and twisted into the sharp, inhospitable hillscapes of the Serranías de Huayllas and de Cóndor Khaka. In places, the immensity of geological time is showcased, with exposed layers revealing fossils below a hundred meters or more of sedimentary strata.

◉ Sights

★Dinosaur Tracks ARCHAEOLOGICAL SITE
As you might have guessed from the dinosaur figure in the plaza or the dinosaur head sticking out of city hall, Torotoro has become synonymous with paleontology. The village, which sits in a wide section of a 20km-long valley at an elevation of 2600m, is flanked by enormous, inclined mudstone rock formations bearing bipedal and quadrupedal dinosaur tracks from the Cretaceous period (spanning 145 million to 65 million years ago).

There are numerous tracks *(huellas)* all over the place and much work remains to be done on their interpretation. Many different dinosaur species are represented, both herbivorous and carnivorous.

The closest tracks are at **Cerro Huayllas**, at the entrance to the village, on the other side of the river. It's behind a locked fence so you'll need an official guide to enter (most people visit as part of the hike to Cañon de Torotoro & El Vergel; p198). Above the water but below the road are the area's largest tracks, made by an enormous quadruped dinosaur (diplodocus or similar) and measuring 35cm wide, 50cm long and 20cm deep. Near here, just above the road, the angled plane of rock reveals a multitude of different tracks, including a long set from a heavy quadrupedal dinosaur that some have posited are those of the armadillo-like ankylosaurus.

Along the route to Umajalanta cave (p198), the flat area known as the Carreras Pampa site has several excellent sets of footprints (on both sides of the path). These were made by three-toed bipedal dinosaurs, both herbivores (with rounded toes) and carnivores (pointed toes, sometimes with the claw visible).

All the tracks in the Torotoro area were made in soft mud, which then solidified into mudstone. They were later lifted and tilted by tectonic forces. For that reason, many of the tracks appear to lead uphill. Many local guides, however, incorrectly believe that the footprints were made in lava as the dinosaurs fled a volcanic eruption.

CENTRAL HIGHLANDS PARQUE NACIONAL TOROTORO

AIQUILE

Aiquile is known as Bolivia's capital of the *charango* (a traditional ukulele-type instrument); it produces more than 400 a year, many exported to communities in Ecuador and Peru (prices range from B$500 to B$7000). The small **Museo del Charango** (Campero, Aiquile; B$10; ☺8:30am-5pm Mon-Fri) has some archaeological pieces and holds a collection of the instruments, including ones that have won prizes at the Feria del Charango, held in late November.

The town lies on the main route between Cochabamba and Sucre, but most intercity buses pass in the wee hours of the night. Expreso Campero (p197) minivans to Aiquile (B$20, six hours) depart daily at noon, 4pm and 6pm from Calle Mairana and Av República in Cochabamba. It's about two hours between Aiquile and Mizque, from where there are a couple of *micros* a day.

★**Caverna de Umajalanta**　　　CAVE
(guide B$150, transportation B$150, equipment rental B$12) The Río Umajalanta, which disappears beneath a layer of limestone approximately 22m thick, has formed the impressive Umajalanta Cavern, of which 4.5km of passages have been explored. Inside are some spectacular stalagmite and stalactite formations and waterfalls, as well as a resident population of vampire bats that have produced an impressively large pile of steaming guano over the years. A guide is mandatory, as it's easy to get lost, and helmets with headlamps are provided.

The exciting descent is moderately physical and you must expect to get both wet and dirty (wear long pants since you'll do some sliding on your bum); there are several parts where you need to crawl and wriggle to get through and a couple of short roped descents. Make sure you have good nonslip shoes on. You eventually descend to a small underground lake and river, which is populated by small, white, completely blind catfish. The ascent from here is fairly easy, as it takes a more direct route.

There are numerous other caverns in the area, most of which are virtually unexplored.

The 8km one-way walk to the cavern entrance takes two hours from the village; it's a completely exposed uphill slog. Most people arrive via transportation with a guide from Torotoro.

Ciudad de Itas　　　NATURAL FEATURE
(guide B$150, transportation B$300, entrance fee B$5) Though the weirdly shaped set of caverns, once the refuge of isolated communities, are striking, they aren't the main reason to make the 21km, often white-knuckle drive here from Torotoro. It's the breathtaking views you should come for, which, at 3770m, provide an expansive perspective on the unique geology of the region. Visible cross sections of sloping mountains appear in isolation like massive spaceships that have been abandoned for millennia.

There are a couple of tricky spots, including one that involves climbing up a nearly vertical rock wall on a ladder.

Cañon de Torotoro & El Vergel　　　CANYON
(guide B$180, optional transportation B$70) Three kilometers from Torotoro, the ground drops away into an immense and spectacularly beautiful canyon, more than 250m deep. From the *mirador* (lookout) at the top you can gaze along it, watching vultures wheeling. From here, following the diminishing canyon to the left, you come to a flight of 800 stairs that lead down to El Vergel (also called Huacasenq'a, meaning 'cow's nostrils' in Quechua), which always has water and is filled with incongruous mosses, vines and other tropical vegetation.

In addition to the *mirador*, there's a semicircle viewpoint pitched vertiginously out and over the canyon. The cliffsides here are home to the rare *paraba frente roja* (red-fronted macaw), which you have a good chance of seeing, or at least hearing. At the bottom, a crystal-clear river tumbles down through cascades and waterfalls, forming idyllic swimming pools. Ask your guide to return via the longer alternative path, so as to avoid climbing the same 800 steps back to the top.

If walking and not going all the way to the falls, guides cost only around B$100.

Sea Fossils　　　ARCHAEOLOGICAL SITE
In a side gully, an hour's walk southwest of Torotoro on the Cerro de las Siete Vueltas (Mountain of Seven Turns; so called because the trail twists seven times before reaching the peak), there is a major sea-fossil deposit.

At the ravine's base you may see petrified shark teeth, while higher up, the limestone and sedimentary layers are set with fossils of ancient trilobites, echinoderms, gastropods, arthropods, cephalopods and brachiopods. The site is thought to date back about 350 million years.

Llamachaki   RUINS
(guide B$250, transportation B$350) A challenging 19km hike around the Cerro Huayllas Orkho, or more commonly a drive in a 4WD vehicle from Torotoro, will take you to the ruins known as the Llamachaki (Llama's Foot). The multilevel complex, which dates from Inca times, rambles over distinctive terraces and includes a maze of rectangular and semicircular walls, plus a fairly well-preserved watchtower. Given its strategic vantage point, it probably served as a military fortification and may have been somehow related to Incallajta (p195), further north.

Batea Q'ocha
Rock Paintings   ARCHAEOLOGICAL SITE
Above the third bend of the Río Torotoro, 1.5km downstream from the village, are several panels of ancient rock paintings collectively called Batea Q'ocha because the pools below them resemble troughs for pounding laundry. The paintings were executed in red pigments and depict anthropomorphic and geometric designs as well as fanciful representations of serpents, turtles and other creatures.

Pachamama Wasi   MUSEUM
(Guadalupe; B$10; ⊙ 2:30-6pm Mon-Fri, 9am-noon & 2:30-5pm Sat) This amazing house-museum is the quirky home of a man who has spent years of his life pacing the *cerros* (mountains) with a rockhound's eye. The house is like a botanic garden, but made of stones: fossils, geological quirks and unusually shaped rocks form a unique, soothing ensemble. It's only open when the owner or his family are at home, so the opening hours listed here are just a guide.

🎊 Festivals & Events

Fiesta del Señor Santiago   RELIGIOUS
(⊙ Jul) From July 24 to 27, the village stages the Fiesta del Señor Santiago, which features sheep sacrifices, dynamite explosions, colorful costumes, lots of *chicha* and some light *tinku* (traditional Bolivian fighting). An interesting time to visit with more public transportation than usual, but the natural attractions are crowded.

🛏 Sleeping & Eating

Palacio Asteria   HOSTAL $
(☎ 7272-0973; www.comoencasa.com.bo; cnr Olvido & Guadalupe; r B$140) Large, grand-looking building – nay, palatial from the outside – with spacious simple rooms (beds are a little lumpy) and an inner patio for lounging. The water pressure in the showers is hit-or-miss, as is the breakfast selection. However, the friendly owner does her best to please.

★ Villa Etelvina   HOSTAL $$
(☎ 7073-7807; www.villaetelvina.com; Sucre s/n; camping B$550, s/d B$180/240, 5-person bungalow B$780; 🛜) A welcoming oasis with simple, comfortable accommodations, nice bathrooms with good hot water pressure and delicious home cooking, including tasty vegetarian fare, available on request. Books, board games and DVDs are available for guests to pass the time. The owners can organize transfers from Cochabamba and professional tours of nearby attractions. It's a five-minute walk south of the plaza.

Wi-fi is very slow so don't count on doing any downloading. It's best to book ahead in the high season.

Hotel El Molino   B&B $$
(☎ 424-3633; www.elmolinotorotoro.com; s/d/ tr B$100/180/250) The nicest place to stay in this renovated country home with spacious rooms, nice common areas and outdoor space to relax after a day of hiking. It's family run, with excellent, gracious service, and can help arrange transport from Cochabamba. However, it's located nearly 2km south of the central plaza. Two-day tours (B$600 per person) are offered every Saturday.

Cabañas Umajalanta   CABAÑAS $$
(☎ 7274-6253; s/d/tr B$130/240/330) If Torotoro feels too big city, try these attractive stone and red-tile-roofed cabins 8km away, high above town on an exposed slope past Caverna de Umajalanta (p198). Beds are comfortable and the views are fantastic, but it can feel lonely with no one else around. Lunch (B$25), which changes daily, is available to nonguests. Transfer from the village costs B$55.

Cafe Dinosaur   INTERNATIONAL $$
(Saenz; mains B$25-55; ⊙ 8:30am-12:30pm & 3-9:30pm Mon-Sat) One of the village's more reliable options (in terms of opening hours and having food that's on the menu), this is a good spot to share stories with fellow travelers over large portions of spaghetti and

ℹ️ PARQUE NACIONAL TOROTORO REGISTRATION & GUIDES

In order to protect the park's geological wonders, it is compulsory to take a guide on any excursion outside the village. Entry tickets (B$100 for four days) are purchased at the **park office** (📞 7149-4473; Olvido; ⏰ 7am-noon & 1:30-5pm) next door to the office where you arrange **guides** (📞 7435-9152; Olvido; ⏰ 7am-noon & 1:30-4:30pm). Hang on to your ticket at all times as it will be inspected by park rangers. Guides are unlikely to speak English, but their knowledge of the surroundings greatly enhances your visit and contributes positively to the local community.

The going rate for a guide is about B$80 to B$100 per person for a full day of excursions for groups of no more than six (ie for a full day to Ciudad de Itas and Caverna Umajallta it's B$106 in a group of five). Most people go to Caverna de Umajalanta (p198), Ciudad de Itas (p198) and Cañon de Torotoro & El Vergel (p198), combining Ciudad de Itas with one of the other two sights on one day and doing the remaining one in the afternoon of their arrival or morning of departure.

If on your own, the easiest and most affordable sight to visit is Cañon de Torotoro and El Vergel.

Turn up at the guides office around 7:30am to book morning and full-day trips; if you're just looking to join with others for the afternoon, it's best to hang out there starting at around 1:30pm.

acceptable pizzas. Also does espresso and has happy hour with two-for-one drinks in the restaurant or attached bar decorated to resemble Caverna de Umajalanta (p198).

ℹ️ Information

INTERNET ACCESS

Only Villa Etelvina (p199) has wi-fi and it's spotty, so desperate travelers congregate around a unique little machine called **TUINFO** (cnr Montes & Saenz; 30min for B$3; 📶) stationed in the entrance to a little shop across from the main market. Place your phone directly, without a cover, where it says 'coloca aqui,' insert B$3 and grab a seat on the curb for 30 minutes of weak wi-fi.

MONEY

Bring all the cash you'll need. There are no ATMs and no money changers, but you might be able to change dollars or euros in a pinch at a restaurant or hotel. Villa Etelvina (p199) and Hotel El Molino (p199) accept credit cards.

SHOWERS

There are public showers (B$5) next to the police station, just behind the small central market.

ℹ️ Getting There & Away

Parque Nacional Torotoro is 135km southeast of Cochabamba in Potosí department. The road is very slowly being improved, but much of the way is along a rough rocky and sandy road, muddy in the rainy season (November to February), when access can be problematic. Once it's completely paved, the driving time should be only around 2½ hours (or so we're told optimistically).

BUS & MINIVAN

It's now quite easy to reach Torotoro via public transportation. Trans Mixto, **Sindicato Mixto Torotoro** (📞 7147-7601) or Trans del Norte minivans (B$35, four to six hours in the dry season from May to September) depart Cochabamba throughout the day, when full, from the corner of Avs República and Mairana. They generally seat 11, so if you have a group you can rent the entire vehicle for around B$400. The front seat is most comfortable and has unobstructed views of the passing countryside. You might be in for a long wait, depending on the time of day and month of the year (show up at the office in Cochabamba around 7am to guarantee a quick departure). It can be a much longer trip or even impassable in the rainy season.

Minivans return to Cochabamba from near the plaza in Torotoro. Best to get a group together to shorten wait times.

The much slower bus (B$25) traveling between Cochabamba and Torotoro is much less recommended. There's one departure daily, but times vary depending on the day of the week.

CAR & MOTORCYCLE

The most comfortable, if pricey, terrestrial way to get to Torotoro is by 4WD, and El Mundo Verde Travel (p186), Andes Xtremo (p186) and Bolivia Cultura (p186), tour companies in Cochabamba, can arrange this. Villa Etelvina (p199) and Hotel El Molino (p199) in Torotoro can also provide transportation as part of a package for guests at their *hostales*.

You can also rent 4WDs in Cochabamba, but keep in mind there's no place to buy petrol in Torotoro itself. The route there can be confusing; be sure to have a GPS device or good app (www.maps.me is recommended), as well as a good physical road map. Check on weather and road conditions in advance.

The only option to reach Sucre directly is with a new private 4WD service offered by the Oficina de Guiaventura (p200), for a maximum of six people (B$1450). You have to reserve in advance.

SUCRE

📞 4 / POP 278,000 / ELEV 2750M

Proud, genteel Sucre is Bolivia's most beautiful city and the symbolic heart of the nation. It was here that independence was proclaimed, and while La Paz is the seat of government and treasury, Sucre is recognized in the constitution as the nation's capital. Set in a valley surrounded by mountains with a glorious ensemble of whitewashed buildings sheltering pretty patios, it's a spruce place that preserves a wealth of colonial architecture. Sensibly, there are strict controls on development and it was declared a Unesco World Heritage Site in 1991. Both the city and its university enjoy reputations as focal points of progressive thought within the country.

With a selection of excellent accommodations, a mild and comfortable climate, a wealth of churches and museums, and plenty to see and do in the surrounding area, it's no surprise that visitors end up spending much longer in Sucre than they bargained on.

🔘 Sights

Sucre is positively overflowing with impressive museums and architecture. For the best view in town, inquire about climbing the cupola at the national police office inside the **Prefectura de Chuquisaca** (State Government Building; cnr Estudiantes & Arce), next to the cathedral. Note the murals depicting the struggle for Bolivian independence as you go upstairs.

★**Museo de Arte Indígena**   MUSEUM
(📞 645-6651; www.asur.org.bo; Pasaje Iturricha 314; B$22; ⊙ 9am-12:30pm & 2:30-6pm Mon-Fri, 9am-noon & 2:30-6pm Sat) This superb museum of indigenous arts is a must for anyone interested in the indigenous groups of the Sucre area, focusing particularly on the woven textiles of the Jal'qa and Candelaria (Tarabuco) cultures. It's a fascinating display and has an interesting subtext: the rediscovery of forgotten ancestral weaving practices has contributed to increased community pride and revitalization. Information in English is

available and you can observe the weavers patiently at work.

★**Casa de la Libertad**   MUSEUM
(www.casadelalibertad.org.bo; Plaza 25 de Mayo 11; admission incl optional guided tour B$15; ⊙ 9am-noon & 2:30-6:30pm Tue-Sat, 9am-noon Sun) For a dose of Bolivian history, it's hard to beat this museum where the Bolivian declaration of independence was signed on August 6, 1825. It has been designated a national memorial and is considered the birthplace of the nation. Spanish-speaking guides are top flight – you'll likely applaud at the end of your guided tour.

The first score of Bolivian congresses were held in the Salón de la Independencia, originally a Jesuit chapel. Doctoral candidates were also examined here. Behind the pulpit hang portraits of Simón Bolívar, Hugo Ballivián and Antonio José de Sucre. Bolívar claimed that this portrait, by Peruvian artist José Gil de Castro, was the most lifelike representation ever done of him. The charter of independence takes pride of place, mounted on a granite plinth. A fine inlaid wooden ceiling and elaborate choir stalls are also noteworthy.

English- and French-speaking guides are available for groups of three or four minimum; you can, though, ask for free use of a tablet computer with text in English.

★**Museo Nacional de Etnografía y Folklore**   MUSEUM
(www.musef.org.bo; Ortiz; ⊙ 9:30am-12:30pm & 2:30-6:30pm Mon-Fri, 9:30am-12:30pm Sat) **FREE** Known locally as MUSEF and housed in the impressive former Banco Nacional building, this museum brings together a series of fascinating temporary exhibitions that vividly illustrate the great diversity of Bolivia's ethnic cultures. In the past, these have included native Bolivian fiesta masks, costumes and apparel; reconstructions of Uru-Chipaya village life; Catholic religious iconography; and *topos*, an ornament used to fasten women's clothing, once used as a weapon and in rituals.

Museo del Tesoro   MUSEUM
(www.museodeltesoro.com; Plaza 25 de Mayo; B$25; ⊙ 9am-12:30pm & 3-6:30pm Mon-Fri, 9am-12:30pm Sat) Wondering why millions labored for centuries under terrible conditions, and still do, including in mines around nearby Potosí? Check out the highly polished collection of precious metals and stones on display here in one of the city's newest museums (opened in

Sucre

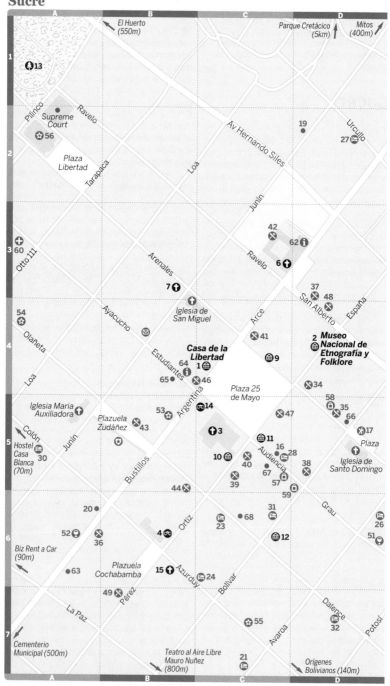

El Huerto (550m)

Parque Cretácico (5km)

Mitos (400m)

13

Pilinco

Supreme Court

Ravelo

56

Plaza Libertad

Tarapaca

Av Hernando Siles

Loa

19

Urcullo

27

Junín

42

62

60

Otto III

Arenales

Ravelo

6

37

48

San Alberto

España

7

Iglesia de San Miguel

Ayacucho

Arce

54

Olañeta

Loa

Casa de la Libertad

1

64

65

Estudiantes

46

41

9

Museo Nacional de Etnografía y Folklore

2

34

Plaza 25 de Mayo

58

35

66

Iglesia Maria Auxiliadora

Colón

Junín

Plazuela Zudáñez

53

43

Argentina

14

47

17

Plaza

Hostel Casa Blanca (70m)

30

3

11

Iglesia de Santo Domingo

Bustillos

10

40

16

28

Audiencia

67

38

39

57

59

44

20

Ortiz

31

Grau

26

52

36

4

23

68

12

51

63

Plazuela Cochabamba

15

Azurduy

24

Bolívar

Biz Rent a Car (90m)

49

Perez

Dalence

Potosi

La Paz

55

Avaroa

32

Cementerio Municipal (500m)

Teatro al Aire Libre Mauro Nuñez (800m)

21

Orígenes Bolivianos (140m)

CENTRAL HIGHLANDS SUCRE

2015) housed in one of the oldest buildings, circa 1560s. Guides, some English-speaking, add insight and provide excellent historical context.

Catedral   CHURCH
(Plaza 25 de Mayo; ⊘Mass 9am Thu & Sun) Sucre's cathedral dates from the middle of the 16th century and is a harmonious blend of Renaissance architecture with later baroque additions. It's a noble structure, with a bell tower that is a local landmark. Inside, the white single-naved space has a series of oil paintings of the apostles, as well as an ornate altarpiece and pulpit. If you are not attending Mass, you can enter as part of a visit to the Museo Eclesiástico de Sucre next door.

Museo Eclesiástico de Sucre   MUSEUM
(Ortiz 31; B$30; ⊘9am-noon & 2:30-6:30pm Mon-Fri, 2:30-6:30pm Sat) Next door to Sucre's cathedral, this museum holds one of Bolivia's best collections of religious relics. There are four sections, ritually unlocked as your guided tour progresses.

In the entry room is a series of fine religious paintings from the colonial era. Next, a chapel has relics of saints, and fine gold and silver chalices. The highlight, however, comes in the **Capilla de la Virgen de Guadalupe**, which was completed in 1625. Encased in the altar is a painting of the Virgin, the city's patron. She was originally painted by Fray Diego de Ocaña in 1601, but the work was subsequently coated with highlights of gold and silver and adorned in robes encrusted with diamonds, amethysts, pearls, rubies and emeralds donated by wealthy colonial parishioners. The jewels alone are worth millions of dollars, making it the richest Virgin in the Americas.

Convento de San Felipe Neri   VIEWPOINT
(Ortíz 165, enter via school; B$15; ⊘ 2:30-6pm Mon-Fri, 9am-6pm Sat) The view from the bell tower and tiled rooftop of the San Felipe Neri convent more than explains Sucre's nickname – the 'White City of the Americas.' In the days when the building served as a monastery (it is now a parochial school), asceticism didn't prevent the monks from appreciating the view while meditating; you can still see the stone benches on the roof terraces.

Museo de la Recoleta   MUSEUM
(Plaza Anzures; B$15; ⊘9-11:30am & 2:30-4:30pm Mon-Fri, 3-5pm Sat) Overlooking the city of Sucre from the top of Calle Polanco, La Recoleta was established by the Franciscan Order

Sucre

in 1601. It has served not only as a convent and museum, but also as a barracks and prison. The highlight is the church choir and its magnificent wooden carvings dating back to the 1870s, each one intricate and unique, representing the martyrs who were crucified in 1595 in Nagasaki.

The museum is also worthwhile for its anonymous sculptures and paintings from the 16th to 20th centuries, including numerous interpretations of St Francis of Assisi.

Outside are courtyard gardens brimming with color, and the renowned *Cedro Milenario* (Ancient Cedar), a huge tree that is one of the few survivors of the cedars that were once abundant around Sucre.

Parque Cretácico
(Cal Orck'o)   ARCHAEOLOGICAL SITE
(Cretaceous Park; www.parquecretacicosucre.com; B$30; ⊙9am-5pm Mon-Fri, 10am-8pm Sat, to 5pm Sun; ⊕) It seems that 65 million years ago the

site of Sucre's Fabrica Nacional de Cemento SA (Fancesa) cement quarry, 5km north of the center, was the place to be for large, scaly types. When the grounds were being cleared in 1994, plant employees uncovered a nearly vertical mudstone face bearing about 5000 tracks of at least eight different species of dinosaur – the largest collection of dinosaur footprints in the world.

You can see some of the prints from outside the park's chain-link fence, but of course you get a better panorama inside; the best light for photographs is during the afternoon. From the terrace, you can examine the tracks on the rock face opposite with binoculars, though the exposed prints are increasingly eroded with every passing winter. There are a number of kitschy life-size models of dinosaurs (good for kids) and a room with unimpressive fossil displays. Recommended are the optional guided tours that take you down into the quarry for close-up views. There's a basic restaurant on site.

Micro 4 (B$1.50) runs from the center past the site; tell the driver where you want to get off. Taxis are B$30 each way and the park runs a double-decker bus (B$10 each way) that leaves from in front of the cathedral on Plaza 25 de Mayo; it's worth taking for the views of the city and surrounding countryside from the top.

Templo Nuestra Señora de la Merced   CHURCH
(Pérez 1; B$10; ⊘9am-noon & 3-5pm Mon-Fri) After several years of restoration work (the completion date was still unknown at the time of research), this church's interior is still mostly bare, but the views from the bell tower are splendid. Because the order of La Merced left Sucre for Cuzco in 1826, taking its records with it, the church's founding date is uncertain, but it's believed to be sometime in the 1540s.

Museos Universitarios   MUSEUM
(☑645-3285; www.usfx.bo/museos-universitarios; Bolívar 698; B$20; ⊘9am-noon & 2:30-6:30pm Mon-Fri, 9am-12:30pm Sat) Housed in a beautifully restored 17th-century building with a picture-perfect colonial courtyard, the Museos Universitarios consist of three separate halls housing colonial relics, anthropological artifacts and modern art. Most interesting are the cases filled with dolls dressed in traditional ethnic fiesta clothing and, for the more macabre, a collection of skulls and mummified remains. The permanent gallery of paintings are mostly dark and

dour portraits of generals and politicians; the quality of the contemporary exhibitions varies. Spanish and English text.

Cementerio Municipal   CEMETERY
(entrance on Calle José Manuel Linares; ⊘8-11:30am & 2-5:30pm Mon-Fri, 8am-5:30pm Sat) Sucre's immaculately maintained cemetery is evidence that inequality doesn't die when we do. Mausoleums of wealthy colonial families and their descendants, interspersed with arches carved from poplar trees, as well as picturesque palms, are larger and certainly more elaborate than most living residents' homes. At weekends it's jam-packed with families. You can walk the eight blocks from Plaza 25 de Mayo south along Junín, or take a taxi or *micro A*.

Museo Gutiérrez Valenzuela   MUSEUM
(Plaza 25 de Mayo; B$10; ⊘9am-12:30pm & 2:30-6:30pm Mon-Fri, 9:30am-noon Sat) Run by the university, this museum is an old aristocrat's house stocked with a hodgepodge collection of gaudy 19th-century decor. Think gilded gold mirrors, red-velvet-upholstered chairs, marble candle holders and dinner plates etched with pastoral scenes. To justify a visit you need the help of the excellent guides (Spanish-speaking only).

Parque Bolívar   PARK
A short walk north of Plaza Libertad, the elongated Parque Bolívar is sandwiched between two avenues flanked with trees and overlooked by the imposing Supreme Court building. It's a pleasant place for a stroll and its European style is highlighted by the presence of a miniature replica of the Eiffel Tower; remarkably, it was built by the same hand as the original in 1906. Kids will like the large playground, and there's a tennis club and small outdoor food court.

Museo de Santa Clara   MUSEUM
(Calvo 212; B$15; ⊘2-6pm Mon-Fri, to 5:30pm Sat) Located in the Santa Clara Convent, this museum of religious art, founded in 1639, contains several works by Bolivian master Melchor Pérez de Holguín and his Italian instructor, Bernardo de Bitti. In 1985 it was robbed, and several paintings and gold ornaments were taken. One of the canvases, however, was apparently deemed too large to carry away, so the thieves sliced a big chunk out of the middle and left the rest hanging.

Convento de Santa Teresa   CHURCH
(San Alberto; ⊘3-6pm Tue-Sat) The brilliant-white Convento de Santa Teresa belongs to

an order of cloistered nuns. They sell home-made candied oranges, apples, figs and limes daily by way of a miniature revolving door.

Iglesia de Santa Mónica   CHURCH
(cnr Junín & Arenales) The Iglesia de Santa Mónica was begun in 1574 and was originally intended to serve as a monastery for the Ermitañas de San Agustín. However, the order ran into financial difficulties in the early 1590s, resulting in its conversion into a Jesuit school. The interior is adorned with mestizo carvings, and the courtyard is one of the city's finest. The church now serves as a civic auditorium and is only open to the public during special events.

Iglesia de San Francisco   CHURCH
(Arce 106; B$15; ⊘ 9am-noon & 3-5:30pm Mon-Fri, 9am-noon Sat) The Iglesia de San Francisco was established in 1538 soon after the founding of the city, but was turned over to the military in 1809. The soldiers weren't big on maintenance and it fell into disrepair before eventually being reconsecrated in 1925. Its most interesting features are its *mudéjar* (Moorish-style) paneled ceiling and the **Campana de la Libertad**, Bolivia's Liberty Bell, which called patriots to revolution in 1825.

 Courses

Sucre is a very popular place to learn Spanish, and a number of group and individual programs are available for all levels.

Instituto Cultural Boliviano Alemán   LANGUAGE
(ICBA; ☑ 645-2091; www.icba-sucre.edu.bo; Calvo 217; ⊘ 9:30am-12:30pm & 3-9pm Mon-Fri, 10am-noon Sat) Offers recommended Spanish lessons with homestay options and also runs Quechua classes. ICBA has a German-language library and listings of rooms for rent.

Me Gusta Spanish   LANGUAGE
(☑ 645-8689; www.megustaspanish.com; Junín 333, 2nd fl) Can tailor lessons to subjects of interest such as sports, cooking or walking tours of the city; can also help arrange homestays.

South American Spanish School   LANGUAGE
(☑ 7033-5141; www.sas-school.com; Plazuela San Francisco 107) Group or private conversational Spanish classes, plus salsa and folkloric dancing and cooking classes. Can help organize homestays and volunteer opportunities.

 Tours

While Sucre is traditionally visited for its colonial architecture and wealth of museums, there are also plenty of worthy destinations in the surrounding area, most notably hiking in the Cordillera de los Frailes. Most tour companies can organize trips, with a few, like Condor Trekkers, more recommended than others. Some agencies now cater to adrenaline-fueled travelers with offerings such as off-road mountain, motorbiking and quad biking, paragliding and rock climbing.

Agencies are a dime a dozen in town and nearly all offer trips to Tarabuco (B$40 per person) for the Sunday market; many hotels and *hostales* can also arrange this trip. Make a point of comparing prices before you sign on the dotted line.

★**Condor Trekkers**   HIKING
(☑ 7289-1740; www.condortrekkers.org; cnr Calvo & Bolívar; ⊘ 8:30am-6:30pm Mon-Sat) Popular and recommended tour agency, housed in the cafe of the same name, which organizes a variety of multiday hikes in the surrounding region. You can put your name on the whiteboard and hope to find other takers to share the cost. The agency has very high-quality guides and can customize any trip. A portion of earnings go toward social development projects.

★**Off Road Bolivia**   OUTDOORS
(☑ 7033-8123; www.offroadbolivia.com; Audiencia 44) These are the safest and best-quality quad-biking, motorcycle and mountain-biking tours in Sucre. For newbies, they even offer lessons on riding off-road motorbikes.

Bolivia Specialist   TOURS
(☑ 643-7389; www.boliviaspecialist.com; Audiencia 80; ⊘ 8:30am-noon & 2:30-7pm Mon-Fri, 8:30am-noon Sat) All-purpose travel agency that can book flights, buses and organized tours all over Bolivia as well as in the region around Sucre, including Cordillera de los Frailes hikes.

Climbing Sucre   CLIMBING
(☑ 7713-0781; www.climbingsucre.com) Half- and full-day trips for all levels led by experienced locals.

Festivals & Events

Sucre celebrates its birthday on May 24 to 25 and this usually involves a visit by the president and no shortage of marching bands.

CANDELARIA & ICLA
. . . .

To experience Central Highlands culture in an environment unmediated by tourism, head to the more off-the-beaten-path villages of Candelaria or Icla, both to the south of Tarabuco.

The former, around 88km southeast of Sucre, produces some of the highest quality hand weavings – blankets, rugs, ponchos and bags – in the local style. The community has established a weaving association, which owns a museum and textile store that explain the meaning and significance of their intricate designs. The store has a large selection of the same high-quality weaving found in Sucre, but at lower prices, with 100% of the profits going back into the small fair-trade association.

Some Sucre operators run tours leaving for Candelaria on Saturday, staying the night and proceeding to Tarabuco's market on Sunday morning. The weaving association can also arrange stays in private homes, but this is best arranged in advance through an agency in Sucre. Do not arrive in town without an arrangement for accommodations, as there are no formal hotels.

Icla, another 13km south, is set in an imposing canyon dripping with waterfalls and riddled with caves, some with interesting geological formations and cave paintings. It's remote and extremely beautiful, with scores of dinosaur footprints in the surrounding area. The local government is trying to promote trekking in the region. Homestays are available; try asking for doña Nora or doña Rosa.

Bus company 12 de Marzo has a daily departure at 4pm from Sucre to Candelaria (B$15) and Icla (B$20, four hours); buses leave from Bustillos near the bus terminal. Return trips to Sucre leave from Icla at around 1pm.

**Fiesta de la Virgen
de Guadalupe** RELIGIOUS
(☉Sep) On the weekend closest to September 8, people from all over the country flock to join local *campesinos* in a celebration of the Fiesta de la Virgen de Guadalupe with songs, traditional dances and poetry recitations. The following day, they dress in colorful costumes and parade around Plaza 25 de Mayo carrying religious images and silver arches.

Todos Santos RELIGIOUS
(☉Nov) On November 2 Todos Santos (All Saints' Day) is celebrated with much fervor.

🛏 Sleeping

Accommodations in Sucre are on the whole good value, with no shortage of hostels; most of the choices are in attractive whitewashed colonial buildings built around pretty central courtyards. Some midrange to upmarket places have boutique features in historic buildings. For an authentic Bolivian experience ask at the various language schools or travel agencies about homestay options. The cheapest places cluster near Mercado Central (p209) and along Ravelo and San Alberto.

★**Kultur Berlin** HOSTEL $
(📞646-6854; www.kulturberlin.com; Avaroa 326; 4-/8-bed dm B$75/55, s/d incl breakfast B$85/200; @🛜) Sprawling and social, this is easily the best hostel for those looking to meet up with

other gringo travelers. It's a big operation housed in a colonial-era building, but couples or those just interested in quiet aren't excluded – ask for one of the uniquely configured and furnished upper-floor rooms in the back building.

Colors House Hostel HOSTEL $
(📞644-3841; www.colorshousesucre.com; Dalence 109; dm B$48, d $145-180; @🛜) Colorfully painted colonial building with a pretty inner patio and basic dorm rooms. The private rooms are irregularly shaped and have old furniture. Salsa, cooking and Spanish language lessons offered on site.

Beehive HOSTEL $
(📞763-3346; www.thebeehivesucre.com; Avaroa 607; dm B$55, d B$172; 🛜) This messy, even grungy, place is nevertheless popular with low-maintenance backpackers looking for a laid-back vibe and longer-term stays while working on their Spanish or volunteering in a nearby community. Bare-bones concrete-floored dorm rooms are large and the garden area has hammocks for lounging.

La Dolce Vita GUESTHOUSE $
(📞691-2014; www.dolcevitasucre.com; Urcullo 342; s/d/tr B$90/140/195, s/d without bathroom B$55/100; @🛜) A newly whitewashed facade makes this traveler-friendly guesthouse on a quiet street more appealing. Offers basic rooms for a variety of budgets. The kitchen

is somewhat ratty, but the terrace is a good spot to catch some sun. Discounts offered for long-term stays.

Hostel Casa Blanca   HOSTEL $
(📞 7142-4313; Loa 909; dm B$48, r B$150; 🛜) Small and intimate, with a warm and welcoming vibe and two outdoor patio areas with hammocks for lazing about and swapping travel tales. Private rooms are small and have low ceilings.

Papa Imilla Hostel   HOSTEL $
(📞 646-4754; papaimillahostel@gmail.com; Colón 220; s/d B$70/100; 🛜) This backpacker-geared hostel housed in a yellow-walled colonial home with Spanish tile roof has a charming and leafy central patio. Some rooms have odd design features. It's best to choose wooden-floored rooms over the more bedraggled carpeted ones. Kitchen available for guests.

★ Casa Verde   B&B $$
(📞 645-8291; www.casaverdesucre.com; Potosí 374; s/d/ste B$145/260/340; @🛜🏊) Immaculate Casa Verde is a real home away from home. It's deservedly popular and frankly under-priced given the quality of service: Belgian owner Rene almost bends over backwards to help his guests. Rooms, arranged around a small courtyard with a pool, are named after Rene's children and grandchildren. If you visit in winter you'll be thankful for the thick duvets.

Casa Al Tronco   GUESTHOUSE $$
(📞 642-3195; www.casaaltronco.com; Topater 57; s/d without bathroom B$180/360, d B$440; 🛜) This homey guesthouse in the Recoleta district has just three rooms, so book in advance. Glorious views of the city from two terraces and use of the kitchen might make you stay longer than planned. Stay more than five nights and there is a price reduction.

Casa Kolping   HOTEL $$
(📞 642-3812; www.casakolpingsucre.com; Pasaje Iturricha 265; s/d B$300/360; @🛜) High on a hill by Plaza Anzures, with great views over Sucre, this excellent hotel caters mostly for conferences, but is an appealing place to stay. It boasts clean, comfortable, well-equipped (if somewhat generic) rooms, plus efficient service and a good restaurant. It's also a good place for kids, with family apartments, plenty of space and a ping-pong table.

La Selenita   B&B $$
(📞 643-4239; www.sucrelife.com/places/la-sele nita-bb; Mostajo 145; s/d B$180/310; 🛜) This

French-owned place has a beautifully maintained garden with several simply furnished self-contained cottages. There's a kitchen and bright common room, but you'll want to spend your leisure time outside looking out over the city. Best to call in advance lest no one is home on arrival.

★ Samary Boutique Hotel BOUTIQUE HOTEL $$$
(📞 642-5088; www.samaryhotel.com; Dalence 349; s/d from B$380/500; ❄@🛜🏊) Samary has an ambitious concept – reproducing a traditional Chuquisaca village in hotel form – and it pulls it off surprisingly well. There's a plaza, a chapel and even a *chichería* selling authentic home-brew liquor. Rooms are of the highest standard, adorned with Yamparaez textiles and replica rock carvings.

Attention to detail is king here. Even the bread is baked fresh every morning in a traditional oven on the breakfast terrace.

★ La Posada   BOUTIQUE HOTEL $$$
(📞 646-0101; www.hotellaposada.com.bo; Audiencia 92; s/d B$345/552; @🛜) This comfortable and classy property has charming, tastefully furnished and comfortable rooms with an appealing colonial ambience and wooden trimmings. There are views over town, a stylish and intimate feel, and a good family suite. The courtyard restaurant is recommended and a great spot for your breakfast. Service is professional.

Hostal de Su Merced   BOUTIQUE HOTEL $$$
(📞 645-1355; www.desumerced.com; Azurduy 16; s/d/tr B$370/550/660; 🛜) In true Sucre style, this lovely hotel in a restored 18th-century home is decorated with antiques, old-fashioned furnishings and paintings, with rooms set around an intimate, tiled courtyard. Room No 7 is particularly nice, and the view from the rooftop terrace is stunning. The helpful staff speak English and there's also a restaurant.

**Parador Santa
María la Real**   HISTORIC HOTEL $$$
(📞 643-9592; www.parador.com.bo; Bolívar 625; r from B$836, ste B$1300; @🛜) Elegant and refined, this five-star hotel is a time capsule to 18th century luxury. It boasts an arcaded courtyard, antique furniture, a communal spa bath with a view, and a curious historic underground section with an atmospheric restaurant.

Hotel Villa Antigua   BOUTIQUE HOTEL $$$
(📞 664-3437; www.villaantiguahotel.com; Calvo 237; s/d B$365/587; 🛜) From the colonnaded

walkways to the polished wood floors, nary a nail is out of place in this restored classic colonial-era mansion. The rooms themselves, generally spacious if simply furnished, aren't as lovely.

Eating

Sucre has a good variety of quality restaurants and it's a great place to spend time lolling around in cafes. You can find good *salteñas* (meat-and-vegetable pasties) and the Sucre specialty *mondongo chuquisaqueño* (spicy pork stew on top of a large corn kernel). Thanks to the city's status as Bolivia's chocolate capital, shops cater to those with a sweet tooth.

Mercado Central   MARKET
(cnr Ravelo & Junín; ⊙ 7am-7.30pm Mon-Sat, to 11am Sun) Don't miss the fresh juices (B$7) – the vendors and their blenders always come up with something indescribably delicious; try *jugo de tumbo* (unripe passion-fruit juice). Upstairs, above the clothing vendors, tasty, cheap meals are fried up and served at picnic tables from morning to night. Sensitive stomachs might want to pass.

Bienmesabe   VENEZUELAN $
(Grau 289; mains B$20; ⊙ 11am-2pm & 4-8pm Mon-Sat) Venezuelan/Bolivian-owned casual place selling a variety of *arepas* (pancakes made with fresh corn) and *cachapas* (pancakes made with fresh corn, cornmeal and sugar). Everything is gluten-free and made to order, so it can take 15 minutes or so for your meal to arrive. The *arepa de chocolate* dessert, made with fruit, caramel, chocolate syrup and coconut shavings, is excellent.

Prem   VEGAN $
(San Alberto 54; set lunch B$25; ⊙ 11am-3pm & 7-9pm Mon-Sat; 🍴) Tiny, crowded spot when locals crowd the few tables for a tasty vegan set lunch. Good juices, smoothies and cupcakes as well.

Monky's Churros   DESSERTS $
(Dalence; churros B$5; ⊙ 9am-9pm) *Churros* (fried dough) and nothing but at this newly opened postage-stamp-sized place. *Dulce de leche* or chocolate filling.

El Patio   FAST FOOD $
(San Alberto 18; salteñas B$8; ⊙ 8am-12:30pm) This bakery, with seating under umbrellas in the courtyard of a lovely whitewashed building, specializes in *salteñas* (meat and vegetable pasties); get there early as they sell quickly.

Negro Café   CAFE $
(Dalence 95; mains B$5-15; ⊙ 4-7:30pm Mon-Fri; 🛜) Mostly older women, friends of the owner, gather at this cozy cafe housed in the historic Casa Rodriguez building for a regular coffee catch-up. Join them to enjoy a selection of quick bites, such as empanadas, plus sandwiches, paninis and Chuquisaca specialty cakes, at one of the few tables inside or in the large, covered courtyard patio.

El Paso de los Abuelos   FAST FOOD $
(Bustillos 216; salteñas B$8; ⊙ 8am-1pm) Come early to get your *salteñas* (meat and vegetable pasties) from this *salteñería* bakery – the tasty treats sell out fast.

★Om   INTERNATIONAL $$
(cnr Potosí & Grau; mains B$30-70; ⊙ 8:30am-10pm) The tapas-style plates are equal to the beautifully sophisticated Mediterranean-like courtyard patio here, which, since it's one of the most pleasant places to eat in the city, is no small compliment. The menu ranges from blue-cheese-and-walnut-stuffed dates wrapped in bacon to Cajun shrimp and mains like mesquite-smoked trout with rosemary foam. Heaters on hand for cool nights; hours may vary.

★Café Gourmet Mirador   CAFE $$
(Pasaje Iturricha 297, Mirador de la Recoleta; mains B$25-45; ⊙ 9am-8pm; 🛜) Settled in a lounge chair looking out over the city's rooftops and surrounding mountains you'll likely be inspired to scour the classifieds for Sucre real estate. No matter the time (though bring a hat and sunscreen during the day) it feels quite Edenic – catching up on your reading, sipping an espresso or smoothie and snacking on a sandwich or tortilla.

After climbing the steep steps up Grau, turn right and it's just below the colonnaded walkway of Plaza Anzures.

★Florín   INTERNATIONAL $$
(Bolívar 567; mains B$35-45; ⊙ 10am-2am Mon-Fri, 8:30am-late Sat & Sun; 🛜) This atmospheric bar-restaurant serves a mixture of typical Bolivian food and international dishes (the latter, such as chicken tandoori, pad thai or moussaka, are generally pale imitations), including a 'full English' breakfast. Popular with locals and gringos alike, who line up along the enormous 13m-long bar at night to swill down the beers.

The drinks menu includes the owner's own Belgian-style brewed beers and Bolivian specialties like *chufflay* and *aguardiente de coca*, as well as absinthe.

CENTRAL HIGHLANDS SUCRE

Imaynalla Restaurant   BOLIVIAN $$
(Ortiz 46; mains B$20-80; ☺ 7am-midnight Mon-Sat; 🛜) In the hostel of the same name, Imaynalla's three-story inner courtyard is a great spot for a meal or a drink. Cool music and candlelit tables add to the scene. Skip the burgers and pastas and try a traditional dish like the gut-bustingly large *pique a lo macho* (beef, onions, potatoes, peppers and boiled eggs), which can easily satisfy three.

La Posada   INTERNATIONAL $$
(www.hotellaposada.com.bo; Audiencia 92; mains B$30-60; ☺ noon-8pm Mon-Sat, to 3pm Sun; 🛜) Situated in the handsome hotel (p208) of the same name, this is one of Sucre's most appealing spots for a meal or drink, offering elegant indoor and outdoor seating around its stone-flagged courtyard. There are tasty fish and meat dishes, pastas and salads, and good-natured service and reasonably priced *almuerzos* (set lunches).

Papavero   ITALIAN $$
(☑ 204-6380; Estudiantes 1, 2nd fl; mains B$28-55; ☺ 12:15-2pm & 6-10pm) The elegant light-filled dining room on the 2nd floor of a regal colonial-era building on the corner of Sucre's central plaza is reason enough for a meal here. But the *almuerzo* (set lunch; B$28) is a good deal and the pizzas are excellent.

Café Metro   INTERNATIONAL $$
(cnr Calvo & España; mains B$25-60; ☺ 8am-midnight; ✳🛜) Deservedly popular with gringos on laptops and smartphones – as much for its prime location on the eastern corner of Plaza 25 de Mayo as for its strong wi-fi signal. Snag a table fronting the large street-front windows for prime people-watching, order a frappuccino and cake, and you won't want to leave. It's expanded to add another level of seating.

The menu of salads, soups, pastas, sandwiches and even sushi (four/eight pieces B$22/45) is almost an afterthought, though enough to tide you over.

Pizzeria Napolitana Restaurante   PIZZA $$
(España 30; mains B$35-55; ☺ 8:30am-11:30pm Mon-Sat, 9am-6pm Sun) Casual and friendly, bustling with families on weekend nights, this long-running pizzeria on Plaza 25 de Mayo turns out more than adequate pies, plus pasta and burgers.

Joy Ride Café   INTERNATIONAL $$
(www.joyridebol.com; Ortiz 14; mains B$35-85; ☺ 7:30am-2am Mon-Fri, 9am-2am Sat & Sun; 🛜) This wildly popular gringo-tastic cafe, restaurant and bar has everything from dawn espressos to midnight vodkas and nightly movies to weekend table-dancing. It's spacious, friendly and you'll need an hour just to read through the menu. Service can be slow on busy nights.

Chifa y Thai   ASIAN $$
(Calvo; mains B$38-48; ☺ 11:30am-10:30pm Mon-Sat; 🍴) What better value than three menus and three cuisines in one? Thai, Chinese and vegetarian dishes, including standards like pad thai, but also specialties like fried Amazon fish and lizard tail, as well as stir-fried vegetables with quinoa. Good service and spacious dining room.

★**El Huerto**   INTERNATIONAL $$$
(☑ 7612-3300, 645-3587; www.elhuertorestaurante.net; Av Cabrera 86; mains B$65-95; ☺ noon-4pm Mon, Tue & Sun, noon-4pm & 7-10pm Wed-Sat) Set in a lovely secluded garden, El Huerto has the atmosphere of a classy lawn party, with sunshades and grass underfoot. There's great service and stylishly presented traditional plates (especially the chorizo) that don't come much better anywhere in the country. Other specialties are the prawns, Peruvian- and Bolivian-caught fish and chateaubriand, plus an excellent wine selection.

La Taverne   FRENCH $$$
(☑ 645-5719; www.lataverne.com.bo; Arce 35; mains B$70-140; ☺ 9am-10:30pm Mon-Sat, 4-10pm Sun) With a quiet and cozy atmosphere, the restaurant of the **Alliance Française** (☑ 645-3599; www.afbolivia.org; Arce 35; ☺ 8:30am-noon & 2:30-7pm Mon-Fri) makes for a nice night out. The short, select menu has a French touch and there are excellent daily specials, including hefty Argentinian-style steaks and filet mignon, as well as a good wine selection.

Self-Catering

Supermercado SAS   SUPERMARKET $
(Pérez 331; ☺ 8am-10pm) A large grocery store in a minimall (where the movie theatre (p211) is located); carries Bolivian and foreign brands.

🍸 Drinking & Nightlife

Many restaurants, especially Joy Ride Café, Florín (p209), Imaynalla and Kultur Berlin (p207) are popular drinking spots, and get lively – especially during their respective happy hours. Om (p209) is easily the most stylish. Sureña is the locally brewed beer and comes in five varieties; Chanchito is the darkest. For *discotecas* (weekends only), head north of the center; it's easiest by taxi.

La Quimba BAR
(Grau 238; ⏱7:30pm-late Tue-Sat) Somehow, in this postage-stamp-sized spot, there's space made for musicians to perform most Friday nights. There are drinks, of course, a laid-back bohemian vibe, and a menu of vegetarian dishes such as lentil and quinoa burgers (B$20).

Goblin Brew Pub BAR
(Grau 246; ⏱8pm-late Thu-Sat) This high-ceilinged family-run place resembles a Spanish taverna and offers a good selection of its very own craft beers.

Kulturcafé Berlin BAR
(www.kulturberlin.com; Avaroa 326; ⏱8am-12:30am; ☎) Most gringo backpackers end up at this spacious and happening bar for a night or two. There's outdoor patio seating, sports on the TV, regular game nights and even folkloric dancing and live music. There's also a menu of the usual Bolivian fare, plus Mexican and German specialties and good desserts.

Salfari PUB
(Bustillos 237; ⏱8:30pm-1am) This cozy little pub has a loyal local crowd and lively games of poker and *cacho* (dice) usually going on. Try the tasty but potent homemade fruit shots.

Mitos CLUB
(Cerro 60; women/men B$5/10; ⏱8pm-late Thu-Sat) Mitos is a spacious basement spot a 15-minute walk north of the center. It really fills up after midnight and plays well-loved Latin and international hits.

☆ Entertainment

Orígenes Bolivianos LIVE PERFORMANCE
(☑645-7091; www.origenes.com.bo; Azurduy 473; dinner & show B$170, show only B$120; ⏱8:30pm Tue-Fri, 8pm Sat) A dinner theater that features a Bolivian folkloric show, including dances, music and costumes from across the country. The talented performers certainly give it their all, but the venue is dated (the video that's screened appears to be from the 1970s), the food mediocre and the service overly punctilious (best to eat beforehand and get drinks at the show).

Cine SAS CINEMA
(www.facebook.com/cinesassucre; Pérez 331; tickets B$25-35) Inside the Supermercado (p210)

minimall, Cine SAS has three screens showing the latest Hollywood releases.

Teatro Gran Mariscal de Ayacucho THEATER
(Plaza Libertad) This opulent old opera house today hosts a wide range of live performances – the tourist office (p212) and the **Casa de la Cultura** (☑643-9621; sucrecultural@hotmail.com; Argentina 65) both distribute a monthly calendar of events.

Teatro al Aire Libre Mauro Nuñez LIVE MUSIC
(La Paz) Southeast of the center, this large outdoor amphitheater hosts regular live musical and other performances.

Cultural Centers
There's a monthly brochure detailing Sucre's cultural events; look for it at tourist offices or in bars and restaurants. Art centers **La Guarida Espacio Cultural** (☑7756-7432; www.facebook.com/laguaridaespaciocultural; Azurduy 118) and **El Mercado** (☑644-3154; Olañeta 277; ⏱hours vary Thu-Sat) draw a local bohemian crowd. Other establishments provide language courses and host cultural events.

🛍 Shopping

The best place to learn about traditional local weavings is the Museo de Arte Indígena (p201), but to buy them you are best off going direct to the villages. Prices are steep by Bolivian standards, but the items are high quality. Several shops near the central plaza sell locally made clothing, from high-quality alpaca sweaters to cheap ponchos.

Inca Pallay TEXTILES
(☑646-1936; www.incapallay.org; Audiencia 97; ⏱8:30am-12:45pm & 2:30-7pm Mon-Sat) This weavers' and artisans' cooperative has an impressive array of high-quality handmade crafts, not all from the Sucre area. Prices are high, but this is the store that returns the highest percentage to the weavers themselves. You can sometimes see weavers at work on the patio.

Arte y Cultura Sucre ART
(www.arteculturasucre.com; Audiencia 89; ⏱9am-12:30pm & 2:30-7:30pm Mon-Sat, 2:30-7:30pm Sun) Gallery shop selling local artists' works, from paintings to ceramics and jewelry.

Awaj Warmi CLOTHING
(☑645-1502; www.awajwarmi.com.bo; Calvo 74; ⏱9am-12:30pm & 3:30-7:30pm Mon-Fri, 9:30am-12:30pm Sat) Some of the highest quality alpaca designs you'll find, with prices to match.

SUCRE'S MARKETS

A trip to the **Mercado Americano** (☺8am-7pm), around the junction of Mujía and Reyes, will keep clothes lovers busy for hours, while the enormous and maze-like **Mercado Campesino** (☺6am-7pm) is a fascinating mix of stalls selling traditional and authentic food and everyday housewares and junk. Take *micro* 7 or G northbound from the center.

ℹ Information

DANGERS & ANNOYANCES

Sucre has long enjoyed a reputation as one of Bolivia's safest towns, but if you have a problem, report it to the **tourist police** (📞648-4811; Dalence 1, Plazuela Zudáñez).

INTERNET ACCESS

Most accommodations have wi-fi, as do a large number of restaurants and cafes.

LAUNDRY

There are a handful of *lavanderías*, including **Laverap** (Ortiz; per kg B$9; ☺8am-8pm Mon-Sat, to noon Sun) and **Superlimp** (Estudiantes 26; per kg B$12; ☺8:30am-8pm Mon-Sat) that charge per kilo around town; most need a half day or more. All but one or two are closed Sundays.

MEDICAL SERVICES

For medical emergencies try **Hospital Santa Bárbara** (📞643-5240; cnr Ayacucho & René Moreno, Plazuela Libertad; ☺24hr).

MONEY

ATMs

ATMs are located all around the city center, but not at the bus station.

Changing Money

Businesses that display 'compro dólares' signs only change cash. Street moneychangers, who operate outside the market along Av Hernando Siles, are handy on weekends when banks are closed, but check rates beforehand.

Credit Cards

Credit cards are widely accepted at hotels and many restaurants.

POST

The tranquil **main post office** (cnr Estudiantes & Junín; ☺8am-8pm Mon-Fri) has an *aduana* (customs) office downstairs for collecting *encomiendas* (parcels).

TOURIST INFORMATION

Infotur (📞645-5983; San Alberto 413; ☺8am-noon & 4-6pm Mon-Sat, 9am-noon & 2:30-6pm Sun) has a moderately helpful office in town and has booths at the airport, bus terminal and Plaza Libertad. The **Oficina Universitaria de Turismo** (📞644-7644; Estudiantes 49; ☺4-7pm Mon-Sat, 2-7pm Sun), run by university students, sometimes offers guides for city tours.

The **Migración** (📞645-3647; www.migracion.gob.bo; Bustillos 284; ☺8:30am-12:30pm & 2:30-6:30pm Mon-Fri) office is a no-fuss place to extend visas and lengths of stay.

Stop by the **Instituto Geográfico Militar** (📞645-5514; Arce 110; ☺8:30am-noon & 2:30-6pm Mon-Fri) for topographic maps of the Chuquisaca department.

ℹ Getting There & Away

AIR

You can fly internationally between Sucre and Buenos Aires, Madrid, Salta and São Paulo on **BoA** (📞691-2360; www.boa.bo; Audiencia 21; ☺8:30am-12:30pm & 2:30-6:30pm Mon-Fri, 8:30am-12:30pm Sat).

BoA, **Ecojet** (📞691-4711; www.ecojet.bo; Dalence 138; ☺8:30am-12:30pm & 2:30-6:30pm Mon-Fri) and **Amaszonas** (📞643-7000; www.amaszonas.com; Calvo 90; ☺8:30am-12:30pm & 2:30-6:30pm Mon-Fri) offer several flights a day to Cochabamba, La Paz and Santa Cruz; Amaszonas also flies to Uyuni (around B$374 one way) daily Monday, Wednesday and Friday. There are direct flights on BoA to Tarija several days a week. TAM also serves Sucre, La Paz and Santa Cruz; however, the location of its local office was in flux when we last visited.

The city's new airport named **Alcantarí International Airport**, located in Yamparáez, 30km south of the city, is still a work in progress. The space feels mostly vacant, with few shops or eateries open, especially for night flights. There is an ATM, but no money exchange. Unlike the old airport, however, it's less vulnerable to bad weather and certainly isn't in danger of being overrun by housing developments. Departure tax is B$11.

The airport is a 40-minute taxi ride (B$50) from the city at night (longer during the day when there's more traffic). Or you can grab a shared one, minimum two people (B$60), from **Plaza Tréveris** or a *micro* that leaves when full from a **spot** near Plaza Camargo (B$8).

BUS & SHARED TAXI

The **bus terminal** (📞644-1292; Av Ostria Gutiérrez) is a 3km uphill walk from the center along Av Gutierrez and most easily accessed by *micros* A or 3 (B$1.50) from along Ravelo, or by taxi (as the *micros* are too crowded for lots of luggage). You can also walk and get there quicker in midday gridlock. Unless you're headed for Potosí, it's wise to book long-distance buses a day in advance in order to reserve a seat. There's a terminal tax of B$2.50; services include an information kiosk, but no ATM. To save the trip to the bus station, many centrally located travel agents also sell tickets on selected services for a small commission.

There are plans to build a new bus station in the next couple of years.

Take an early evening bus to La Paz, as opposed to an afternoon one, so you don't arrive at an ungodly hour. A new company called El Mexicano (leaves 6pm) is the best for the Santa Cruz route, and Andes Bus to Oruro or Tarija is like flying 1st class on a plane.

If you are headed to Tarija or Villazón, you'll have more luck going to Potosí; the quickest and comfiest (if not the cheapest) way to get there is in a shared taxi (B$50, two hours), which can be arranged through your hotel or by calling direct. Try **Super Movil** (📷 645-2222).

For Uyuni, we recommend 6 de Octubre buses (either *cama,* ie fully reclining, or *semi-cama*), which leave at 9am and 8pm daily.

DESTINATION	COST (B$)	TIME (HR)
Camiri	120	18
Cochabamba	80-90	10
La Paz	150-260	12
Oruro	40-70	7-8
Potosí	30-50	3
Santa Cruz	94-105	12
Uyuni	80-90	8½

❶ Getting Around

BUS & MICRO

Lots of buses and *micros* (B$1.50) ply slow and circuitous routes around the city's one-way streets, and all seem to congregate in a logjam at or near the market between runs. They're usually crowded, but fortunately Sucre is a town of short distances. The most useful routes are *micros* 7, C and G, which climb the steep Av Grau hill to La Recoleta, and *micro* A, which serves the main bus terminal.

CAR & MOTORCYCLE

If you want to brave the rough roads outside Sucre you can try **Biz Rent a Car** (📷 643-8725; www.biz.com.bo; La Paz 703; ⊗ 8:30am-12:30pm & 2:30-6:30pm Mon-Fri, 9am-noon Sat) for high-quality 4WD rentals starting at US$65 per day.

TAXI

The city center is small enough to walk to most places, but taxis are readily available, including

Sur (📷 645-1351) and **Chasqui** (📷 645-3535) if you want to go further afield or can't face hills.

AROUND SUCRE

Tarabuco

📷 4 / POP 19,500 / ELEV 3284M

This small, predominantly indigenous village 65km southeast of Sucre is famous for its textiles, which are among the most renowned in all of Bolivia. To travelers though, Tarabuco is best known for its annual Pujllay celebrations in March and its colorful, sprawling Sunday market, a popular day trip from Sucre.

◉ Sights

★**Sunday Market** MARKET
(⊗ 7am-4pm) Despite the presence of other camera-wielding gringos and the ubiquity of travel agencies in Sucre selling 'tours,' Tarabuco's Sunday market is well worth experiencing. Look out for high-quality *artesanías* such as pullovers, *charangos,* coca pouches, ponchos and weavings that feature geometric and zoomorphic designs. Items (and prices) more geared towards tourists, and some produced far from the area, are sold on and close to the plaza. The further in you wade, the less likely this is the case.

✸ Festivals & Events

Pujllay CULTURAL
(⊗ Mar) On March 12, 1816, Tarabuco was the site of the Battle of Jumbati, in which villagers, led by doña Juana Azurduy de Padilla, ambushed a battalion of Spanish soldiers, liberating the town in the process. In commemoration of the event, Tarabuco stages this celebration on the third Sunday in March; more than 60 surrounding communities attend in local costume.

The celebration begins with a Quechua mass and procession followed by the Pukara ceremony, a Bolivian version of Thanksgiving. Folk dancers and musicians perform throughout the two-day weekend fiesta. It's one of Bolivia's largest festivals and is great fun – just don't think too long on the fate of those Spaniards. Only the Spanish drummer boy survived and the hearts of the others were eaten in an act of ritual revenge.

🛏 Sleeping & Eating

Centro Ecológico Juvenil HOSTEL **$**
(cnr Azurduy & Murillo; dm B$45) Only a block from the northeast corner of the plaza, this

ⓘ TARABUCO TOURS

Condor Trekkers (p206) in Sucre has recently inaugurated a Sunday trip to Tarabuco (B$180 per person) that involves a 7km hike in the surrounding foothills.

and 3:30pm from just outside the tourist office in Tarabuco.

Many tourists these days arrive by 'chartered' minivans (B$40 round-trip, two hours each way) from Sucre. Tickets must be bought in advance from bigger hotels or any travel agent. From Tarabuco, the minivans return to Sucre any time between 1pm and 3pm.

Hostelling International property, concealed behind imposing walls and a grand wooden doorway, is a classic colonial-era mansion with a Spanish tile roof and a sunny central courtyard. With only three rooms in total and no wi-fi, it's a peaceful refuge.

Water supply is an issue, especially in October and November, so showers might not always be possible.

★ **Pukari Wasi** BOLIVIAN $
(Olañeta 31; mains B$25; ⊙ 11:30am-3pm Sun) An absolutely charming family-run spot only a block from the southeast corner of the town plaza with a central patio lined with potted plants and flowering trees. *Almuerzos* (B$35) come with *cazuela da maní* (peanut soup, cooked with onions, potatoes and vegetables), seasonal fruit and a chicken or meat dish.

Tables are reserved in advance by groups, so get there early for lunch on market (p213) days.

Samay Wasi BOLIVIAN $$
(☑ 644-3425; tarabucosamaywasi@gmail.com; Mendieta 147; set lunch B$40; ⊙ 11am-2pm Sun) Every Sunday when tourists descend on the market (p213), Samay Wasi puts on a dance show performed by children. A set lunch of traditional dishes is served. Often booked out by large groups with travel agencies in Sucre, especially during the high season.

ⓘ Information

Bring all the cash in bolivianos you'll need. Some of the high-quality textiles aren't cheap. There are no ATMs and credit cards aren't accepted.

Tourist Office (cnr Calle 1° de Mayo & Potosí)

ⓘ Getting There & Away

It's quite easy to use public transportation to travel to Tarabuco. *Micros* (B$10, 1½ hours) leave when full from the intersection of Avs de las Américas and Mendoza in Sucre on Sunday between 6:30am and 9:30am; large buses for the same fare, though slightly slower, are less regular. Returns to Sucre leave between 11am

Cordillera de los Frailes

The imposing serrated ridge forming Sucre's backdrop creates a formidable barrier between the departments of Chuquisaca and Potosí. Only a short drive heading northwest out of Sucre, roads turn rough, carving their way around forested mountains leaving modern Bolivian urban life far behind. Home to the Jal'qa people, this region of bizarrely shaped and multi-hued rocks and deceptively tall and remote peaks is a trekker's dream.

◉ Sights

Museo Apus MUSEUM
(Maragua; B$10) This amateur anthropology museum is dedicated to the preservation of indigenous culture and the passion of Crispin Ventura whose home houses the collection of fossils, ceramics, rocks, ritual weavings and musical instruments. It's in Irupampa, a short walk from Maragua. Opening hours aren't set – if Crispin's around, he'll open up for visitors.

🏃 Activities

Hiking

The best way to see this region is on foot. Keep in mind you'll be hiking at high altitude and it can be strenuous.

A recommended three- or four-day circuit taking in several Cordillera highlights and the villages at the heart of the community tourism project begins at Chataquila, on the ridge above Punilla, 35km northwest of Sucre. From here (with an optional side trip to the abstract red, white and black man-animal rock paintings at Incamachay and Pumamachay) you descend to Chaunaca, then head to the Cráter de Maragua, before ending with the spectacular six- to seven-hour walk – via *chullpa* (funerary towers) and with a short diversion to see the dinosaur footprints at Niñu Mayu – to Potolo. From Potolo there is daily transportation back to Sucre.

There are numerous walking routes through the Cordillera de los Frailes, some of which are marked on the 1:50,000 topo sheets *Sucre,* sheet 6536IV, and *Estancia Chaunaca,* sheet 6537III. Maps are essential if hiking independently; you can get them at the Instituto Geográfico Militar (p212) in Sucre.

Guided Trips
We strongly recommend taking a guided hiking tour to increase your enjoyment of the region and to communicate with the Quechua-speaking *campesinos* (subsistence farmers). A responsible guide will help you avoid local hostility, minimize your impact and get a better feel for the local culture.

Almost every Sucre travel agency advertises quick jaunts into the Cordillera, including one-day trips to see the rock paintings of Incamachay and Pumamachay or a two-day circuit from Chataquila to Incamachay and Chaunaca. It's important to go with a responsible operator committed to contributing to the communities you visit. Exploitative day trips have created an atmosphere of hostility toward visitors in some villages, and it is up to you to ensure that your visit does't exacerbate the problem.

Prices per day vary depending on the number in your group, as well as whether private transportation is provided. If it's not, count on long, likely uncomfortable bus rides, which might diminish your enjoyment, especially at the end of a long, tiring day of trekking. In general, guided trips run around B$650 for three days and B$800 for four days per person.

Condor Trekkers (p206) in Sucre is highly recommended; if short on time, its two-day, one-night trip (B$500, minimum four) along the Inca Trail from Chataquila to Maragua (p217) is a memorable experience. It, along with most other agencies, can customize trips to your hiking abilities and available time.

Chataquila to Chaunaca
On the rocky ridge top at Chataquila (3560m) is a lovely stone **chapel** dedicated to the Virgen de Chataquila, a Virgin-shaped stone dressed in a gown and placed on the altar (it's concealed behind a wall). The chapel was built from the local rock, and, like the next door amphitheater (used for fiestas), it blends in with its surroundings. The spot is also the site where Tomás Katari (p218), the leader of an indigenous revolt against the Spanish, was executed in 1781.

From Chataquila look around on the south side of the road for an obvious notch in the rock, which leads into a lovely pre-Hispanic route that descends around 2300ft, sometimes steeply, for 6km to the Río Ravelo canyon and the village of Chaunaca, 41km from Sucre. Lots of good paved sections remain and it's easy to follow.

Chaunaca is home to a school, a tiny church and an interpretation and information center on the Jal'qa region. Beds are available in the information center, but you'll have to find your own food. There's also a campsite and the renovated colonial hacienda, Samay Huasi (p219), which offers high-quality accommodation with hot showers.

For a head start, *camiones* (flatbed trucks) run the route from Sucre to Chaunaca and Chataquila, departing from Av Juana Azurduy de Padilla. From Chaunaca you have the option of continuing west 15km direct to Potolo, or taking the very rewarding detour south via Maragua and Humaca. The latter will add an extra day to your hike, but takes in some sites of real geological and paleontological interest.

Incamachay & Pumamachay
A worthwhile side trip from Chataquila or Chaunaca leads to two fascinating sets of ancient rock paintings estimated to be up to 2000 years old. At the first major curve on the road west of Chataquila, a rugged track heads north along the ridge. For much of its length the route is flanked by craggy rock formations, but it's relatively easy going until you've almost reached the paintings, where you face a bit of a scramble. The first set, Pumamachay, lies well ensconced inside a rock cleft between two stone slabs. The pictographs here depict humans and geometric shapes in monochrome black. A more impressive panel, Incamachay, is 15 minutes further along beneath a rock overhang that contains anthropomorphic, zoomorphic and geometric motifs painted in red and white. Guides at the entrance charge B$10 – you will need one to find the paintings.

From Incamachay, you can continue downhill for a couple of hours until you hit the road at the **Toma de Agua** aqueduct, where there's drinking water and a campsite. From there take the road 6km to the Chataquila–Chaunaca road, where you can either ascend to Chataquila or descend to Chaunaca from where you can find transportation back to Sucre.

Cordillera de los Frailes

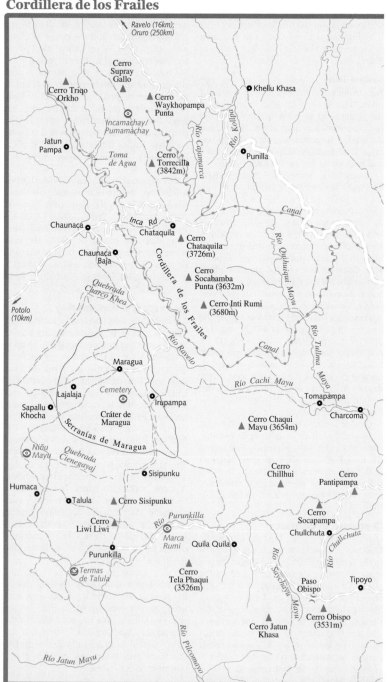

Ravelo (16km);
Oruro (250km)

Cerro
Supray
Gallo

Cerro Triqo
Orkho

Khellu Khasa

Cerro
Waykhopampa
Punta

Incamachay/
Pumamachay

Río Cajamarca

Río Kollpa

Jatun
Pampa

Toma
de Agua

Cerro
Torrecilla
(3842m)

Punilla

Canal

Chaunaca

Inca Rd

Chataquila

Cerro
Chataquila
(3726m)

Río Quikuqui Mayu

Chaunaca
Baja

Cerro
Socabamba
Punta (3632m)

Quebrada
Charco Khea

Cerro Inti Rumi
(3680m)

Río Tullma Moya

Potolo
(10km)

Cordillera de los Frailes

Río Ravelo

Canal

Maragua

Río Cachi Mayu

Lajalaja

Cemetery

Irupampa

Tomapampa

Sapallu
Khocha

Cráter de
Maragua

Cerro Chaqui
Mayu (3654m)

Charcoma

Serranías de Maragua

Niñu
Mayu

Quebrada
Cienegayaj

Sisipunku

Cerro
Chillhui

Cerro
Pantipampa

Humaca

Talula

Cerro Sisipunku

Cerro
Socapampa

Cerro
Liwi Liwi

Río Purunkilla

Chullchuta

Río Chullchuta

Purunkilla

Marca
Rumi

Quila Quila

Termas
de Talula

Cerro
Tela Phaqui
(3526m)

Río Sayçhuru Mayu

Paso
Obispo

Tipoyo

Cerro Obispo
(3531m)

Cerro Jatun
Khasa

Río Pilcomayo

Río Jatun Mayu

Cráter de Maragua

This unearthly natural formation, sometimes called the Ombligo de Chuquisaca (Chuquisaca's Belly Button), features surreal settlements scattered across an 8km-wide red-and-violet crater floor, and bizarre slopes that culminate in the gracefully symmetrical pale green arches of the Serranías de Maragua. These scallop-shaped cliff faces make it one of the most visually striking places in Bolivia. There's plenty to see, including waterfalls, caves and a picturesque **cemetery** in the middle of the crater that dates from pre-Hispanic times.

The village of Maragua (3100m) is an active weaving center. The weavers have set up a store and will take visitors into their homes where you can watch them creating the textiles. Maragua has three *cabañas* and a campsite. A kilometer from the village, in Irupampa, is the lovely stone and red-tile-roofed Samary Wasi (p219), with cozy and comfortable beds and often after-dinner visits from a trio of village musicians. You can also camp here.

Maragua is a sometimes challenging three-plus-hour hike, involving some steep stretches. If you'd prefer a lift, ask about shared 4WD taxis at one of the Sucre tourist agencies.

Maragua to Potolo

From Maragua, it's a spectacular walk to Potolo. You can get there in five hours, but there's plenty to see on the way to slow you down. In the area around **Humaca** you will find *chullpa* (funerary towers) and a pale-ontological deposit where embedded fossils are clearly visible in the rocks. Additionally, dinosaur footprints (around 100) at **Niñu Mayu** can be visited if you are prepared to add an extra hour or so to your hike. These places can be found most easily with a local guide. Ask around in the villages and negotiate a price that is fair to the community.

Another side trip from Humaca could take you to the **Termas de Talula**, 5km away. You'll need to ford the Río Pilcomayo twice. The Talula hot springs issue into rock pools that have temperatures of up to 46°C. Camping is possible anywhere in the vicinity.

From Talula it's 500m to the constricted passage that conducts the Río Pilcomayo between the steep walls of the Punkurani gorge. When the river is low, you can cross over to the Potosí shore and see the many **rock-painting sites** above the opposite bank.

Potolo

The village of Potolo, one of the region's larger towns, has some typically stunning weaving going on in the workshops. It also has a little museum of traditional medicine, which demonstrates vernacular healing practices and other aspects of the culture. There are three *cabañas* here, a store and a campsite.

Camiones run infrequently to Potolo from Av Juana Azurduy de Padilla in Sucre via Chaunaca and Chataquila. They return to Sucre from Potolo when full.

Quila Quila

The beautiful village of Quila Quila, three hours southeast of Maragua by foot, is another worthwhile destination. It's a formerly deserted village of largely mud buildings that is being slowly repopulated. The tower of the colonial church dominates the skyline and adjacent to it are the buried remains of the revered 18th-century indigenous leader Tomás Katari, who was murdered at the chapel in Chataquila in 1781. In 1777 Katari walked to Buenos Aires to confront colonial leaders and claim rights for the Aymará and returned triumphantly with a document signed by the viceroy ceding to his demands and recognizing him as *cacique* (chieftain). Upon his return to Bolivia he was imprisoned, sparking a widespread uprising that eventually led to his death. A few kilometers away are the Marca Rumi monoliths with pictographs. The area is rich in pre-Columbian archaeological artifacts.

It's a challenging but doable hike from here to the summit of Cerro Obispo, at 3531m, one of the highest peaks in the area.

Daily *camiones* to Talula via Quila Quila (B$12, three to four hours) depart at 6:30am from Osvaldo Molina in Sucre, returning the afternoon of the same day. Alternatively negotiate with a taxi driver. Some visitors have reported a less than welcoming reception by villagers, so your best bet is to go with a guide.

🛏 Sleeping

If you're on your own, most homestays or tourist *cabañas* run around B$30 to B$60 per person. Samary Wasi (p219) and Samay Huasi (p219), community-run projects in

THE JAL'QA COMMUNITIES

The Cordillera de los Frailes is home to the Quechua-speaking Jal'qa people, of whom there are some 10,000 in the area around Potolo and Maragua. They have traditionally made a living from farming potatoes, wheat and barley, and herding sheep and goats. The weaving of elaborately patterned *axsus* (an apron-like skirt) is an important craft tradition, and these Escher-like red-and-black garments are instantly recognizable, being patterned with inventive depictions of *khurus* – strange, demon-like figures – inspired by weavers' visions of a mythic underworld called Ukhu Pacha. It was only in the 1990s that *axsus* began to be designed and sold as tapestries, as a means of preserving the dying tradition and to provide income for Jal'qa women.

The Jal'qa have embraced low-key, sustainable tourism, in a way meant to benefit the community without destroying its traditions. They have developed a series of accommodations, cultural centers and guiding services, all involving maximum community participation, with the villages receiving 100% of profits.

Accommodations and restaurant services have been set up in the villages of Maragua and Potolo. Sets of attractive thatched *cabañas* have been constructed using traditional methods and materials; they boast comfortable beds, hot water and attractive wooden furniture, and are decorated with local textiles. The cost is B$60 per person per night; for B$100 per person, meals and cultural displays are included. The villages are also well placed for hiking and have good camping areas. In Chaunaca, there's a camping area and some beds set up in the information center, but no restaurant service.

If you go with a tour group you will eat traditional Bolivian *campesino* meals – such as *kala purca,* a maize soup cooked by immersing hot stones in it. Cultural activities that can be organized include demonstrations of *pujllay* dancing, folkloric music or a visit to a *curandera,* a traditional healer. Weaving workshops can be found in all the villages mentioned, as well as some others, while Chaunaca has an interpretation center and Potolo a museum of indigenous healing. Note that the Jal'qa aren't fond of being photographed.

To book the Maragua or Potolo *cabañas* on your own, it's easiest to ask at the Museo de Arte Indígena (p201) in Sucre.

Maragua and Chaunaca respectively, are very comfortable and pricier. Camping is possible, but always ask for permission.

★**Samary Wasi** HOSTAL **$$**
(☑ 693-8088; Maragua; s/d/tr B$152/207/276)
A kilometer from the village of Maragua, in Irupampa, is this lovely stone and red-tile-roofed *hostal* with three bedrooms, heaps of heavy blankets for cool nights, a toilet and shower, and a little sitting area for meals. There are electrical outlets for charging devices.

Often, a trio of local musicians stops by to play traditional folkloric music for visitors at nighttime.

Samay Huasi HOSTAL **$$$**
(☑ 645-4129; Chaunaca; per person B$480)
This renovated colonial hacienda offers high-quality accommodations. The price includes three meals a day, and transportation can be arranged for a small fee. Sitting on the outdoor patio with a drink at the end of the day with mountains in the near distance is quite idyllic.

❶ Getting There & Away

Most travelers arrive via private transportation arranged by trekking companies in Sucre. If taking public transportation, the easiest way is probably to take a Potolo-bound *trufi* (shared car or minibus) from the Parada a Ravelo in Sucre to Chataquila.

POTOSÍ

☑ 2 / POP 190,000 / ELEV 4070M

The conquistadors never found El Dorado, the legendary city of gold, but they did get their hands on Potosí and its Cerro Rico, a 'Rich Hill' full of silver. Indeed, the city was founded in 1545 as soon as the ore was discovered and pretty soon the silver extracted here was bankrolling the Spanish empire. Even today, something very lucrative is said to *vale un Potosí* (be worth a Potosí).

During the boom years, when the metal must have seemed inexhaustible, Potosí became the Americas' largest and wealthiest city. Once the silver dried up, however, the city went into decline and its citizens slipped into poverty. The ore, plus tin, lead and other minerals, is still being extracted by miners in some of the most abysmal conditions imaginable. But the rest of Potosí – its grand churches and ornate colonial architecture – is also worth getting to know.

History

No one is certain how much silver has been extracted from Cerro Rico over its four centuries of productivity, but a popular boast was that the Spanish could have constructed a silver bridge to Spain and still had silver left to carry across it. The Spanish monarchy, mortgaged to the hilt by foreign bankers, came to rely completely on the yearly treasure fleets that brought the Potosí silver. On the rare occasions when they were intercepted by storms or pirates, it was a national disaster.

Although the tale of Potosí's origins probably takes a few liberties with the facts, it's a good story. It begins in 1544 when a local Inca, Diego Huallpa, searching for an escaped llama, stopped to build a fire at the foot of the mountain known in Quechua as 'Potojsi' (meaning 'thunder' or 'explosion,' although it might also have stemmed from *potoj,* 'the springs'). The fire grew so hot that the very earth beneath it started to melt and shiny liquid oozed from the ground.

Diego immediately realized he had run across a commodity for which the Spanish conquerors had an insatiable appetite. Perhaps he also remembered the Inca legend associated with the mountain, in which Inca Huayna Capac had been instructed by a booming voice not to dig in the hill of Potojsi, but to leave the metal alone, because it was intended for others.

Whatever the truth of this, the Spanish eventually learned of the enormous wealth buried in the mountain of Potojsi and determined that it warranted immediate attention. On April 1, 1545, the Villa Imperial de Carlos V was founded at the foot of Cerro Rico, thousands of indigenous slaves were forced into service, and large-scale excavation began.

The work was dangerous, however, and so many workers died of accidents and silicosis pneumonia that the Spanish imported millions of African slaves to augment the labor force. The descendants of the very few to survive mainly live in the Yungas.

In order to increase productivity, in 1572 the Viceroy of Toledo instituted the *Ley de la Mita,* which required all indigenous and African slaves over the age of 18 to work shifts of 12 hours. They would remain underground without seeing daylight for four months at a time, eating, sleeping and working in the mines. When they emerged from a 'shift,' their eyes were covered to prevent damage from the bright sunlight.

Potosí

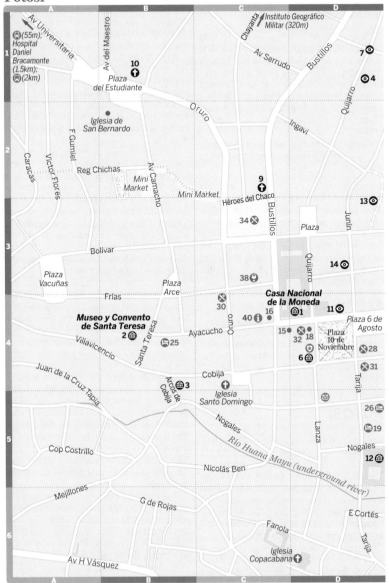

Naturally these miners, who came to be known as *mitayos,* didn't last long. Heavy losses were also incurred among those who worked in the *ingenios* (smelting mills), as the silver-smelting process involved contact with deadly mercury. In all, it's estimated that over the three centuries of colonial rule (1545–1825) as many as eight million Africans and indigenous Bolivians died in these appalling conditions.

In 1572 a mint was established to coin the silver, reservoirs were constructed to provide

As with most boom towns, Potosí's glory was not to last. The mines' output began to decline in the early 19th century and the city was looted during the independence struggles in Alto Perú. The population dropped to less than 10,000 and the mid-19th-century drop in silver prices dealt a blow from which Potosí has never completely recovered.

In the present century only the demand for tin has rescued Potosí from obscurity and brought a slow but steady recovery. Zinc and lead have now taken over from tin as Bolivia's major metallic exports, but silver extraction continues on a small scale.

Most of the operations in Cerro Rico today are in the control of miner-owned cooperatives, which operate under conditions that have changed little from the colonial period. The dream of the lucky strike (there are still a few) keeps them going, although the number of miners is steadily dwindling.

◉ Sights

In 1987 Unesco named Potosí a World Heritage Site in recognition of its rich and tragic history and its wealth of colonial architecture. Stroll around the narrow streets to take in the ornate doorways and facades, as well as the covered wooden balconies that overhang the streets. Architecturally notable homes and monuments include the mustard-colored **El Cabildo** (City Hall; Plaza 10 de Noviembre), the pretty Casa de las Tres Portadas (p224) and the **Arcos de Cobija** (Arches of Cobija; Arcos de Cobija) on the street of the same name.

On Calle Junín, between Matos and Bolívar, you'll find the especially lovely and elaborate **Portón Mestizo** (doorway), flanked by twisted columns. It once graced the home of the Marqués de Otavi, but now ushers patrons into the Banco Nacional.

★**Casa Nacional de la Moneda** MUSEUM
(☑ 622-2777; www.casanacionaldemoneda.bo; Ayacucho, near Bustillos; admission by guided tour B$40, photo permit B$20; ⊙ tours 9am, 10:30am, 2:30pm & 4:30pm Tue-Sat, 9am & 10:30am Sun) The National Mint is Potosí's star attraction and one of South America's finest museums. Potosí's first mint was constructed on the present site of the Casa de Justicia in 1572 under orders from the Viceroy of Toledo. This, its replacement, is a vast and strikingly beautiful building that takes up a whole city block. You don't have to be a numismatist to find the history of the first global currency fascinating.

water for the growing population and European consumer goods found their way up the llama trails from Arica and Callao. Amid the mania, more than 80 churches were constructed and Potosí's population grew to nearly 200,000, making it one of the largest cities in the world.

Potosí

The building was built between 1753 and 1773 to control the minting of colonial coins; legend has it that when the king of Spain saw the bill for its construction, he exclaimed 'that building must be made of silver' (expletive presumably deleted). These coins, which bore the mint mark 'P', were known as *potosís*.

The walls are more than a meter thick and, not surprisingly, it has not only functioned as a mint, but also done spells as a prison, a fortress and, during the Chaco War, the headquarters of the Bolivian army. As visitors are ushered into a courtyard from the entrance, they're greeted by the sight of a stone fountain and a freaky mask of Bacchus, hung there in 1865 by Frenchman Eugenio Martin Moulon for reasons known only to him. In fact, this aberration looks more like an escapee from a children's funfair, but it has become a town icon (known as the *mascarón*).

Apart from the beauty of the building itself, there's a host of historical treasures. They include a fascinating selection of religious paintings from the Potosí school (especially remarkable are those by Melchor Pérez de Holguín), culminating in *La Virgen del Cerro,* a famous anonymous work from the 18th century, as well as the immense assemblies of mule-driven wooden cogs that served to beat the silver to the width required for the coining. These were replaced by steam-powered machines in the 19th century. The last coins were minted here in 1953; the Bolivian coins you may have used to pay to enter the museum are made in Canada and Chile from cheaper materials like zinc and copper.

The guided tour is long (two hours) and the temperatures inside chilly, so be sure to have a jacket on hand. Although there are English and French tours available on request, the quality of the Spanish one is higher and the visit more comprehensive, so it's worth doing, even if your language skills aren't quite up to scratch.

★ Museo y Convento de Santa Teresa   MUSEUM
(www.museosantateresa.blogspot.com; cnr Santa Teresa & Ayacucho; admission by guided tour B$21, photo permit B$10; ⊙9am-12:30pm & 2:30-6pm

Mon & Wed-Sat, 2:30-6pm Tue, 3-6pm Sun) The fascinating Santa Teresa Convent was founded in 1685 and is still home to a small community of Carmelite nuns who have restored the sizable building and converted part of it into a museum. The excellent guided tour (1¾ hours; in Spanish and English) explains how girls from wealthy families entered the convent at the age of 15, getting their last glimpse of parents and loved ones at the door.

There are numerous fine pieces, including a superb Madonna by Castilian sculptor Alonso Cano, several canvases by Melchor Pérez de Holguín, Bolivia's most famous painter, and a room of painted wooden Christs. Some of the artworks verge on the macabre, as does the skull sitting in a bowl of dust in the middle of the dining room and a display of wire whisks that some of the nuns used for self-flagellation.

The building itself is as impressive as the works of art on show (a good portion of which were paid for by the sizable dowries given for the privilege of entering the convent), with two pretty courtyards housing numerous cacti and a venerable apple tree. It provides a glimpse into a cloistered world that only really changed character in the 1960s, with the reforms of the Second Vatican Council. Note that some of the rooms are particularly chilly.

Museo y Convento
de San Francisco   MUSEUM
(☑ 622-2539; cnr Tarija & Nogales; admission by guided tour B$15; ☺tours 9:30am, 11am, 3pm & 4pm Mon-Fri, 9am & noon Sat) This convent, founded in 1547 by Fray Gaspar de Valverde, is the oldest monastery in Bolivia. Owing to its inadequate size, it was demolished in 1707 and reconstructed over the following 19 years. The museum has a fine collection of religious art, including paintings from the Potosí school, such as *The Erection of the Cross* by Melchor Pérez de Holguín, various mid-19th-century works by Juan de la Cruz Tapia and 25 scenes from the life of St Francis of Assisi.

The highlight of the excellent tour (1½ hours; English-speaking guides are unlikely) comes at the end, when you're ushered up the tower and onto the roof for grand views of Potosí. You also visit the catacombs, which have a smattering of human bones and a subterranean river running nearby.

A gold-covered altar from this building is now housed in the Casa Nacional de la Moneda (p221). The statue of Christ that graces the present altar features hair that is said to grow miraculously.

La Catedral   ARCHITECTURE
(Cathedral; Plaza 10 de Noviembre; ☺3-6:30pm Mon-Fri, hours subject to change) Construction of La Catedral was initiated in 1564 and finally completed around 1600. The original building lasted until the early 19th century, when it mostly collapsed. Most of what is now visible is the neoclassical construction, and the building's elegant lines represent one of Bolivia's best exemplars of that style. The interior decor represents some of the finest in Potosí. You can visit the **bell tower** (Junín; B$15; ☺9am-noon & 3-6pm Mon-Fri) for nice views of the city.

Iglesia y Museo de
San Lorenzo de Carangas   CHURCH
(cnr Héroes del Chaco & Bustillos; museum B$100; ☺9am-12:30pm & 2:30-6:30pm) The ornate mestizo baroque portal of this church, probably one of the most photographed in Bolivia, is an explicit expression of the *mezcla* (mixture) between Aymará and Spanish Catholic beliefs. Check out the bas-reliefs of a guitar-playing indigenous mermaid and a sword-carrying Archangel San Miguel. It was carved in stone by master indigenous artisans in the 16th century, but the main structure wasn't completed until the bell towers were added in 1744.

La Capilla de Nuestra
Señora de Jerusalén   CHURCH
(Plaza del Estudiante; ☺9am-7pm Sun) This church is a little-known Potosí gem. Originally built as a humble chapel in honor of the Virgen de Candelaria, it was rebuilt more lavishly in the 18th century. There's a fine gilt baroque *retablo* (portable box with depictions of religious and historical events) – the Virgin has pride of place – and a magnificent series of paintings of Biblical scenes by anonymous Potosí school artists. The impressive pulpit has small paintings by Melchor Pérez de Holguín.

Torre de la Compañía de Jesús   CHURCH
(Ayacucho, near Bustillos; mirador B$10; ☺8-11:30am & 2-5:30pm Mon-Fri, 8am-noon Sat) The ornate and beautiful bell tower, on what remains of the former Jesuit church, was completed in 1707 after the collapse of the original church. Both the tower and the doorway are adorned with examples of mestizo baroque ornamentation. Also the location of the Potosí tourist office (p231).

THE JOB FROM HELL

In the cooperative mines on Cerro Rico, all work is done with mostly primitive tools and underground temperatures vary from below freezing – the altitude is more than 4200m – to a stifling 115°F (46°C) on the 4th and 5th levels. Miners, exposed to all sorts of noxious chemicals and gases, normally die of silicosis pneumonia within 10 to 15 years of entering the mines.

Women are admitted to many cooperative mines, but only five are allowed to be in the mine's interior at any one time. This is because quite a few miners still hang on to the superstition that women underground invite bad luck although, in many cases, the taboo applies only to miners' wives, whose presence in the mines would invite jealousy from Pachamama (Mother Earth). At any rate, lots of Quechua women are consigned to stay right outside the mines, picking through the tailings to glean small amounts of minerals that may have been missed.

Since cooperative mines are owned by the miners themselves, they must produce the goods in order to scrape a living. The majority of the work is done by hand with explosives and tools they must purchase themselves, including the acetylene lamps used to detect pockets of deadly carbon monoxide gas.

Miners prepare for their workday by socializing and chewing coca for several hours, beginning work at about 10am. They work until lunch at 2pm, when they rest and chew more coca. For those who don't spend the night working, the day usually ends at 7pm. On the weekend, each miner (or a group of miners) sells their week's production to the buyer for as high a price as they can negotiate.

When miners first enter the mine, they offer propitiation at the shrine of the miners' god Tata Kaj'chu, who they hope will afford them protection in the harsh underground world. Deeper in the mine, visitors will undoubtedly see a devilish figure occupying a small niche somewhere along the passageways. As most of the miners believe in a god in heaven, they deduce that there must also be a devil beneath the earth in a place where it's hot and uncomfortable. Since hell (according to the traditional description of the place) must not be far from the environment in which they work, they reason that the devil himself must own the minerals they're dynamiting and digging out of the earth. In order to appease this character, whom they call Tío (Uncle) or Supay – never Diablo – they set up a little ceramic figurine in a place of honor.

On Friday nights a *cha'lla* (offering) is made to invoke Supay's goodwill and protection. A little alcohol is poured on the ground before the statue, lit cigarettes are placed in his mouth and coca leaves are laid out within easy reach. Once formalities have been dispensed with, the miners smoke, chew coca and proceed to drink themselves unconscious. While this is all taken very seriously, it also provides a bit of diversion from an extremely harsh existence. It's interesting that offerings to Jesus Christ are only made at the point where the miners can first see the outside daylight.

In most cooperative operations there is a minimal medical plan in case of accidents or silicosis (which is inevitable after seven to 10 years working underground) and a pension of about US$15 a month for those so incapacitated. Once a miner has lost 50% of his lung capacity to silicosis, he may retire, if he so wishes. In case of death, a miner's widow and children collect this pension.

Casa de las Tres Portadas HISTORIC BUILDING
(Bolívar 1052) An architecturally notable home that once housed lay sisters of the Franciscan order. It has three separate and widely spaced doorways with finely filigreed designs on brick, and is covered in lime to resemble stone or marble.

Iglesia de la Merced CHURCH
(cnr Hoyos & Millares; ⊙9am-7pm Sun) Constructed between 1555 and 1687, the restored Iglesia de la Merced has a carved pulpit, a gorgeous wooden ceiling and a beautiful 18th-century silver arch over the altarpiece.

Calle Quijarro ARCHITECTURE
North of the Iglesia de San Agustín, Calle Quijarro narrows as it winds between a wealth of colonial buildings, many with doorways graced by old family crests. It's thought that the bends in this street were an intentional attempt to inhibit the cold winds

that would otherwise whistle through and chill everything in their path.

During colonial times Quijarro was the street of potters, but it's now known for its hatmakers. The intersection of Quijarro and Modesto Omiste, further north, has been dubbed the **Esquina de las Cuatro Portadas** because of its four colonial doorways.

Los Ingenios HISTORIC BUILDING
On the banks of the Río Huana Mayu, in the upper Potosí barrios of Cantumarca and San Antonio, are some fine ruined examples of the *ingenios* (smelters) formerly used to extract silver from the ore hauled out of Cerro Rico. Some remaining ones – there were originally 82 along a 15km stretch – date back to the 1570s and were in use until the mid-1800s. Most Cerro Rico mine tours include a stop at a working *ingenio*.

Pasaje de Siete Vueltas ARCHITECTURE
(Passage of Seven Turns) This passageway, an extension of Calle Ingavi, east of Junín, wends around a series of angular turns, displaying some interesting architectural quirks along the way.

☞ Tours

In addition to mine tours, there are a variety of guided offerings by over two dozen local agencies, including a three-hour city tour (B$70 to B$100, not including entry fees) of the museums and monuments. Other popular options include the Tarapaya (p226) hot springs (B$50 to B$100); guided trekking trips around the Lagunas de Kari Kari (p226) (B$160 to B$280); and tours of colonial haciendas around Potosí (B$150). Many outfits also book Salar de Uyuni tours for those heading in that direction. You can generally book tours at your hotel, too, as most properties either run their own tours or work with the agencies.

Koala Tours TOURS
(☑622-2092; www.koalabolivia.com.bo; Ayacucho 5) Ground floor of the similarly named **cafe** (Ayacucho 5; mains B$15-45; ☺7am-10pm) and popular with backpackers, partly because it also operates two Potosí hostels. It runs twice-daily mine tours Monday to Friday (B$130; 8:45am and 1:30pm), and a small portion of the profits goes to the mining community. Also runs trips to Tarapaya (p226; B$150) and trekking trips to Kari Kari, and can help book onward bus tickets.

For the truly adventurous, there are tinku (p230; ritual fighting) excursions (four-day trip B$800) and a nine-day trek along the ancient llama caravan route to Cochabamba.

Big Deal Tours TOURS
(☑623-0478; www.bigdealtours.blogspot.com; Bustillos 1092; mine tours B$150; ☺8am-8pm Mon-Sat) The specialty of this outfit run by current and former miners is, of course, mine tours. Guides are informative, passionate and have a good sense of humor, plus clearly have a good relationship with the mine workers encountered along the way.

Altiplano Tours TOURS
(☑622-5353; Ayacucho 19; mine tours B$140) At the end of Altiplano's mine tours, you can try some of the work yourself. This company also offers tinku excursions.

Hidalgo Tours TOURS
(☑622-9512; www.salardeuyuni.net; cnr La Paz & Matos; ☺9am-12:30pm & 2:30-7:30pm) One of the better upmarket options running 4WD trips to Uyuni and customized journeys in the altiplano around Potosí.

★ Festivals & Events

Fiesta del Espíritu SPIRITUAL
(☺Jun & Aug) Potosí's most unusual event happens on the last three Saturdays of June and the first Saturday of August. It's dedicated to Pachamama (Mother Earth), whom the miners regard as the mother of all bolivianos. *Campesinos* bring their finest llamas to the base of Cerro Rico to sell to the miners for sacrifice. The ritual is conducted to a meticulous schedule.

At 10am, one miner from each mine purchases a llama, and their families gather for the celebrations. At 11am, everyone moves to the entrance of their respective mine. The miners chew coca and drink alcohol from 11am until precisely 11:45am, when they prepare the llama for Pachamama by tying its feet and offering it coca and alcohol. At noon, the llama meets its maker. As its throat is slit, the miners petition Pachamama for luck, protection and an abundance of minerals. The blood of the llama is splashed around the mouth of the mine to ensure Pachamama's attention, cooperation and blessing.

For the next three hours, the men chew coca and drink while the women prepare a plate of grilled llama. The meat is served traditionally with potatoes baked along with *habas* (fava beans) in a small adobe oven. When the oven reaches the right temperature, it is smashed in on the food, which is baked beneath the hot shards. The stomach,

WORTH A TRIP

DAY TRIPS FROM POTOSÍ

Lagunas de Kari Kari

The Lagunas de Kari Kari are artificial lakes (ranging from an elevation of 4500m to 5025m) constructed in the late 16th and early 17th centuries by 20,000 indigenous slaves to provide water for Potosí and for hydropower to run the city's 82 *ingenios* (smelters). Of the 32 original lakes only 25 remain and all have been abandoned – except by waterfowl, which appreciate the incongruous surface water in this otherwise stark region.

The easiest way to visit Lagunas de Kari Kari is with a Potosí tour agency, which charge about B$180 per person per day based on a group of three. If you prefer to strike out on your own, carry food, water and warm clothing. In a long day, you can have a good look around the *lagunas* and the fringes of the Cordillera de Kari Kari, but it may also be rewarding to camp overnight in the mountains (if you're fully kitted out with cold-weather gear).

Access is fairly easy, with public transportation from Potosí. Or negotiate with a taxi driver for the day; you can ask them to follow the road to Tupiza before making a left onto a rough, dirt road that leads up to the shore of Laguna San Sebastián. It's still best to inquire with one of the agencies in town and make sure you get a good map of the area. The Cordillera de Kari Kari is included on the IGM topo sheet *Potosí (East)*, sheet 6435; nearby Cerro Kari Kari Central tops out at 5010m.

Tarapaya

Belief in the curative powers of Tarapaya (3600m), the most frequently visited hot-springs area around Potosí (21km northwest of the city), dates back to Inca times. It even served as the holiday destination for Inca Huayna Capac, who would come all the way from Cuzco (now in Peru) to bathe. The most interesting sight is the 30°C **Ojo del Inca**, a perfectly round, green lake in a low volcanic crater, 100m in diameter.

Along the river below the crater are several very developed *balnearios* (resorts) with medicinal thermal pools (B$10) utilizing water from the lake, but best to stay close to the edge since *remolinos* (whirlpools) make bathing here a hazardous affair.

Camiones leave for Tarapaya (B$4, 30 minutes) from Mercado Chuquimia near the **old bus terminal** (Av Universitaria) in Potosí on Av Antofagasta roughly every half hour from 6am to 7pm. Taxis cost about B$70 one way. The last *micro* from Tarapaya back to Potosí leaves between 5pm and 6pm.

feet and head of the llama are buried in a 3m hole as a further offering to Pachamama, then the music and dancing begin. In the evening, celebrants are taken home in transportation provided by the miner who bought his mine's llama.

Fiesta de San Bartolomé
(Chu'tillos)
CULTURAL

(⊙ Aug or Sep) This rollicking celebration takes place on the final weekend of August or the first weekend of September and is marked by processions, student exhibitions, traditional costumes and folk dancing from all over the continent. Given all the practicing during the week leading up to the festival, you'd be forgiven for assuming it actually started a week earlier. Booking accommodations essential.

Exaltación de la Santa Vera Cruz
RELIGIOUS

(⊙ Sep) This festival, which falls on September 14, honors Santo Cristo de la Vera Cruz. Activities occur around the Iglesia de San Lorenzo de Carangas and the railway station. Silver cutlery features prominently, as do parades, dueling brass bands, dancing, costumed children and, of course, lots of alcohol.

🛏 Sleeping

Accommodations in Potosí aren't of the kind to tempt you to prolong a visit. Only central options (other than Hacienda Cayara) should be considered. Usually only the mid-range to top-end hotels have heating, and they sometimes need to be persuaded to use it. There may be blanket shortages in the cheapies, so you'll want a sleeping bag.

⭐**La Casona Hostal**
HOSTEL **$**

(🖉 623-0523; www.hotelpotosi.com; Chuquisaca 460; dm B$40, s/d/tr/q B$100/140/200/240, without bathroom B$70/90/135/180; @ 🗟) Housed in an attractively crumbling

18th-century colonial house in the center of town with an equally handsome yellow and stone slab inner atrium. The private rooms have nice wood floors, heavy blankets and clean, hot-water showers. Backpackers give the dorms mixed reviews, in part because of the state of the shared bathrooms.

Casa Blanca HOSTEL $
(✆ 7142-4313; luiszilvetiali@gmail.com; Tarija 35; dm B$40, d B$100) The graffiti-painted walls of the inner courtyard give this otherwise whitewashed place a splash of color. Rooms are otherwise ordinary and the bathrooms could use a bit of work. Staff are friendly and helpful.

★Hostal Colonial HOTEL $$
(✆ 622-4265; www.hostalcolonialpotosi.com.bo; Hoyos 8; s/d/tr B$320/420/505; @ 🛜) In a well-kept colonial building near the main plaza, this warm whitewashed retreat has smallish rooms with windows onto a central courtyard; all rooms have minibars and cable TV, and some have bathtubs. It's a longstanding favorite with midrange travelers and boasts very helpful English-speaking staff and a great location.

Hostal Carlos V Imperial HOTEL $$
(✆ 623-1010; frontdesk@hostalcarlosv.com; Linares 42; s/d B$180/B$240, without bathroom B$80/160, ste B$300; 🛜) Not bad value for Potosí, especially for the views from the rooftop terrace; however, the rooms with shared bathroom can feel cramped and dark. The en-suite rooms are worth the extra bolivianos and the spacious and light-filled suite is a bargain, the equal of any room in a higher-priced hotel.

Hostal Patrimonio HOTEL $$
(✆ 622-2659; Matos 62; s/d B$275/440; 🛜) Comfortable, if generic hotel rooms opening onto a shiny, light-filled central atrium. Friendly and helpful front-desk staff and reliable hot water make up for the lack of character, and it is better than most options in this price range in Potosí. The windowless breakfast room is a bit dreary.

Hostal Tukos la Casa Real HOTEL $$
(✆ 623-0689; www.hostaltukoslacasareal.com; Hoyos 29; s/d/tr B$175/262/303; 🛜) An attractive covered inner courtyard and a rooftop terrace with city views justify a stay here. The rooms are barely furnished and vary in terms of sunlight and bathroom quality; check out a few before committing.

Hotel Santa Teresa HOTEL $$
(✆ 622-5270; www.hotelsantateresa.com.bo; Ayacucho 43; s/d B$280/440; @ 🛜) This hotel by the convent of the same name on a quiet block in central Potosí has seen better days. But with less than fierce competition, its small, overly green rooms aren't a bad choice; the upstairs units have more light. The courtyard restaurant is a somewhat overly priced formal affair.

Hotel Coloso Potosí HOTEL $$$
(✆ 622-2627; www.potosihotel.com; Bolívar 965; s/d/tr B$530/670/920, ste B$707-884; @ 🛜 🏊) Luxurious for Potosí, the city's only five-star option wouldn't beat out your average Holiday Inn, at least as far as room features and design go. But there's a pool, restaurant, sauna and room service, if slightly stuffy formality. Some rooms have great city views.

🍴 Eating

Culinary diversity is as thin as the air (as are open restaurants on Sundays), though there are a few spots to ward off the night-time chill with a hearty meal. The city is especially known for its quality *salteñas* (meat-and-vegetable pasties), sugary pastries filled with a variety of nuts and dried

> **ℹ POTOSÍ MINES WARNING**
>
> The cooperatives are not museums, but working mines that are fairly nightmarish places. Anyone planning to take a tour needs to realize that there are risks involved. People with medical problems – especially claustrophobia, asthma and other respiratory conditions – should avoid them. While medical experts including the NHS note that limited exposure from a tour lasting a few hours is extremely unlikely to cause any lasting health impacts, if you have any concerns whatsoever about exposure to asbestos or silica dust, you should not enter the mines. Accidents can also happen – explosions, falling rocks, runaway trolleys etc. For these reasons, all tour companies make visitors sign a disclaimer absolving them completely from any responsibility for injury, illness or death. If your tour operator does not, choose another. Visiting the mines is a serious decision. If you're undeterred, you'll have an eye-opening and memorable experience.

ℹ️ VISITING THE COOPERATIVE MINES

A visit to the cooperative mines will almost certainly be one of the most memorable experiences you'll have in Bolivia, providing an opportunity to witness working conditions that are among the most grueling imaginable. We urge you not to underestimate the dangers involved in going into the mines and to consider the voyeuristic factor involved in seeing other people's suffering. You may be left stunned and/or ill.

Dozens of Potosí operators offer guided tours through the mines. The best guides tend to be ex-miners, who know the conditions and are friendly with the men at work. The safety standards are hit-and-miss; you really are going down at your own risk.

Mine visits aren't easy and the low ceilings and steep, muddy passageways are best visited in your worst clothes. You'll feel both cold and hot at times, there will likely be a bit of crawling and shimmying through narrow shafts, and the altitude can be extremely taxing – cases of acute mountain sickness (AMS) following a tour have been reported. On some tours, you'll end up walking 3km or 4km inside the mountain. You'll be exposed to noxious chemicals and gases, including silica dust (the cause of silicosis), arsenic gas and acetylene vapors, as well as asbestos deposits. Anyone with doubts or medical problems should avoid going. The plus side is that you can speak with the friendly miners, who will share their insights and opinions about their difficult lot. The miners are proud of their work in such tough conditions and generally happy for visitors to observe their toil.

Tours begin with a visit to the miners' market at Plaza el Calvario, where miners stock up on acetylene rocks, dynamite, cigarettes and other essentials. You'd be very unpopular if you didn't supply a handful of coca leaves, cigarettes, juice, soda, or pens and notebooks (for their children) – luxuries for which the miners' meager earnings are scarcely sufficient. Photography is permitted. Avoid taking plastic bags into the mine; accumulation of garbage is a problem.

The tours then generally visit an *ingenio* (smelter), before heading up to Cerro Rico itself (Candelaria, Santa Rita, Rosario and Santa Rosita are the most commonly visited sections). Note that it's illegal for tour companies to give demonstrations of dynamite explosions, which destabilize the mountain and potentially threaten lives. Ask your tour company vendor if a dynamite explosion is included. If they say yes, choose another operator. It is unlikely to be the only corner they are cutting.

Tours run in the morning or afternoon and last from four to five hours. The standard charge is between B$100 and B$150 per person; slightly lower rates may be available during the low season. This price includes a guide, transportation from town and equipment (pants, jacket, helmet, boots and lamp). Note the claim that '15% of profits donated to miners' is a well-known marketing scam; all companies pay the same fee for entry into the mines and it is considerably less than 15%. If you want to help the miners, choose a company run by miners. Wear sturdy clothing, carry plenty of water and have a handkerchief/headscarf handy to filter some of the noxious substances you'll encounter. There is less activity in the mines on Sundays.

fruits, and *quesitos de leche* (pastries filled with cheese).

★ Café la Plata
CAFE $

(Plaza 10 de Noviembre; mains B$14-45; ⊙1:30-11pm Mon, 10am-11pm Tue-Sat) The city's most sophisticated cafe by far, this handsome, high-ceilinged place is comfortable and chic in a restored sort of way, and a good place to hang out, especially at one of the window seats with plaza views. There are rich espressos, magazines to read and wine served by the glass. Pastas, cakes, salads, sandwiches – it's all done well.

La Salteña
LATIN AMERICAN $

(Padilla 6; salteña B$3.50; ⊙10am-1:30pm) Most Bolivians acknowledge, when pushed, that Potosí does the best *salteñas* (meat and vegetable pasties) – juicy, spicy and oh-so-tasty. Go no further than La Salteña, where one of these delicious items goes for B$3.50.

Mercado Central
MARKET $

(Oruro; snacks B$6; ⊙6am-7pm) Stalls in the *comedor* (dining hall) serve inexpensive breakfasts of bread, pastries and coffee. Downstairs there are some excellent juice stands. Cheese or meat empanadas are sold around the market until early afternoon, and in the evening, street vendors sell *humitas* (cornmeal filled with cheese, onion, egg and spices, baked in the oven or boiled).

Potocchi   CAFE $
(🕿 622-2759; Millares 13; mains B$18-30; ⊘ 8am-11pm; 🛜🍴) This pleasant family-run place serves llama steak and quinoa soup as the specialties, and has plenty of vegetarian choices. It hosts an acoustic *peña* (folk-music performance; cover B$15) nightly during the high season (otherwise on Wednesday and Friday).

Phishqa Warmis   INTERNATIONAL $
(Sucre 55; meals B$20-40, almuerzo B$25; ⊘ 8am-midnight Mon-Fri, 8am-4pm & 7pm-midnight Sat) A pleasingly cozy little restaurant lounge with colored walls and a vaulted ceiling. The pub-style à-la-carte food gets mixed reviews, but the buffet *almuerzo* (set lunch) is better. Attentive service and a refined but friendly atmosphere make it worth a try.

Cheery's   INTERNATIONAL $
(Padilla 8-10; mains B$12-35; ⊘ 8am-10pm; 🛜) Simply furnished place with bad coffee, but worth noting for being open on Sunday. It has a wide-ranging menu, including basic sandwiches and Bolivian dishes.

El Fogón   INTERNATIONAL $$
(cnr Oruro & Frías; almuerzo B$30, mains B$30-70; ⊘ 10am-10pm) This spacious, colorful and brightly lit central restaurant is popular for its range of international and Bolivian food, including llama steaks. In truth though, portions aren't huge and the service is slow and less than attentive.

Pizzeria Lobo's Cafe-Pub   INTERNATIONAL $$
(Padilla; mains B$35-70; ⊘ 10am-11pm) This dim and chilly place overlooks a narrow cobblestone street. It has a large menu of the usual beef and chicken standards, plus burgers and sandwiches, though the two dozen varieties of pizzas are, of course, the specialty. The decor is a hodgepodge of football posters and hanging musical instruments, and there's a billiards table.

★**4.060**   INTERNATIONAL $$$
(🕿 622-2623; www.cafepub4060.com; Hoyos 1; mains B$45-90; ⊘ 4-11:30pm Mon-Sat) Potosí's most au courant restaurant, 4.060 is popular with groups of travelers looking for a comfortable and familiar night out. This spacious contemporary cafe-bar has earned plenty of plaudits for its pizzas, burgers and Mexican food (and paella, if you order it in advance) as well as being a sociable spot for a drink. There's a good beer selection.

While it doesn't roll off the tongue, the restaurant's name refers to the city's altitude.

El Tenedor de Plata   INTERNATIONAL $$$
(cnr Tarija & Linares; mains B$30-100; ⊘ noon-3pm & 6-10pm Mon-Sat, noon-3pm Sun) This fine-dining restaurant has an upscale, white-tablecloth mentality. It's an appealing and warm brick-walled place and the pricier chops and steak dishes are above average. Try the *tawas-tawas* (sweet fritters dusted with sugar) for dessert. Popular with business and government groups.

🍷 Drinking & Nightlife

La Casona Pub   PUB
(Frías 41; ⊘ 6pm-12:30am Mon-Sat) This atmospheric pub is tucked away in the historic 1775 home of the royal envoy sent to administer the mint. It's a friendly watering hole with pub grub. On Friday it stages live music performances.

☆ Entertainment

Ask around at the bars, cafes and restaurants for live music; several occasionally host acoustic *peñas* (gatherings where traditional folkloric music is played). Potosí has two cinemas; the **Multicine Universal** (🕿 622-6133; Padilla 31; tickets B$40) screens relatively recent releases. Real Potosí, the local soccer team, is one of Bolivia's most successful; it plays at the town stadium on the hilariously named Av Highland Players.

🛍 Shopping

Favored Potosí souvenirs include silver and tin articles (earrings, spoons and platters) available from stands near the market entrance on Calle Oruro. Many of these were produced in the village of Caiza, 80km south of Potosí, which now has its own co-op store featuring naturally dyed wool items. Several souvenir and handicraft shops cluster on Calle Sucre, north of Bolívar.

ℹ Information

INTERNET ACCESS
There are numerous places to get online, mostly charging between B$3 and B$4 per hour. Some cafes and restaurants have wi-fi, as do most accommodations.

TINKU: THE ART OF RITUAL MAYHEM

Native to the northern part of Potosí department, *tinku* fighting, which takes place on May 3, ranks as one of the few Bolivian traditions that has yet to be commercialized. This practice lies deeply rooted in indigenous tradition and is thus often misunderstood by outsiders, who can make little sense of the violent and often grisly spectacle.

Tinku may be best interpreted as a type of ritualized means of discharging tensions between different indigenous communities. Festivities begin with singing and dancing, but celebrations soon erupt into mayhem and frequently violence, as emotions are unleashed in hostile encounters.

A *tinku* usually lasts two or three days, when men and women in brightly colored traditional dress hike in from surrounding communities. The hats worn by the men strongly resemble those originally worn by the Spanish conquistadors, but are topped, Robin Hood–style, with one long iridescent feather.

On the first evening, the communities parade through town to the accompaniment of *charangos* and *zampoñas* (a type of pan pipe). Periodically, the revelers halt and form two concentric circles, with women on the inside and the men in the outer circle. The women begin singing a typically repetitious and cacophonous chant, while the men run in a circle around them. Suddenly, everyone stops and launches into a powerful stomping dance. Each group is led by at least one person – usually a man – who uses a whip to ensure slackers keep up with the rhythm and the pace.

This routine may seem harmless enough, except that alcohol plays a significant and controlling role. Most people carry bottles filled with *puro* (rubbing alcohol), which is the drink of choice; by nightfall, each participating community retreats to a designated house to drink *chicha*.

This excessive imbibing inevitably results in social disorder. Roaming the streets, individuals encounter people from other communities with whom they may have some quarrel, either real or imagined, and may challenge them to fight.

The situation rapidly progresses past yelling and cursing to pushing and shoving, before it turns into an almost choreographed form of warfare. Seemingly rhythmically, men strike each other's heads and upper bodies with extended arms. This has been immortalized in the *tinku* dance, which is frequently performed during Carnaval in highly traditional Oruro. To augment the hand-to-hand combat, the fighters may also throw rocks at their opponents, occasionally causing serious injury or death. Any fatalities, however, are considered a blood offering to Pachamama in lieu of a llama sacrifice for the same purpose.

The best known and arguably most violent *tinku* takes place in the village of Macha during the first couple of weeks of May, while the villages of Ocurí and Toracarí, among others, also host *tinkus*.

As you'd imagine, few foreigners aspire to witness this private and often violent tradition, which categorically cannot be thought of as a tourist attraction; many people who have attended insist they'd never do it again. For the terminally curious, however, Altiplano Tours (p225) in Potosí conducts culturally sensitive – and patently less-than-comfortable – visits to several of the main *tinku* festivities. Note, however, that if you do go it will be at your own risk. Keep a safe distance from the participants and always remain on the side of the street to avoid being trapped in the crowd. When walking around the village, maintain a low profile, speak in soft tones and ignore any taunting cries of 'gringo.' Also, bear in mind that these traditional people most definitely do not want hordes of foreign tourists gawking at them and snapping photos; avoid photographing individuals without their express permission and do not participate.

LAUNDRY

Most hotels can organize laundry services for their guests. Not surprisingly, hostels will do it cheapest by the kilo. You should have no problems taking your laundry to a hotel or hostel even if you're not a guest.

MAPS

The **Instituto Geográfico Militar** (1° de Abril 28 028; ☉8am-noon & 2-6pm Mon-Fri) sells topographic sheets of all areas of Potosí department.

MEDICAL SERVICES

If experiencing severe symptoms of altitude sickness, your best bet is to get to a lower altitude as quickly as possible.

The **Hospital Daniel Bracamonte** (☑ 624-4960; Italia s/n; ⊙24hr) has some English-speaking doctors.

MONEY

ATMs are common in the center of town. Lots of businesses along Bolívar, Sucre and in the market change US dollars at reasonable rates; stalls along Héroes del Chaco also change euros and Chilean and Argentine pesos. Many hotels now accept credit cards, primarily Visa and Mastercard.

POST

Post Office (cnr Lanza & Chuquisaca; ⊙8am-8pm Mon-Fri, to 5:30pm Sat, 9am-11:30pm Sun)

TOURIST INFORMATION

InfoTur de Potosí (☑ 622-7404; http:// infoturpotosi.blogspot.com; Ayacucho; ⊙8am-noon & 2-6:30pm) has quite helpful Spanish-speaking staff, good city maps and loads of brochures on city sights; it's located at the entrance to the Torre de la Compañía de Jesús (p223). Another useful site is www.brujulaturistica.com/potosi.

The **tourist police** (Plaza 10 de Noviembre; ⊙8am-noon & 2-6pm) on the ground floor of the Gobernación building can be helpful; there's also a branch at the new bus terminal.

Head to the **Migración** (☑ 622-2745; Linares 136; ⊙8:30am-12:30pm & 2:30-6:30pm Mon-Fri) office for visa extensions.

🛈 Getting There & Away

AIR

Potosí boasts one of the world's highest airports, Aeropuerto Capitán Rojas. However, unless you're the president, you won't be flying here. There are no operating commercial flights. Sucre's Alcantarí International Airport (p212) is 121km away.

BUS & SHARED TAXI

All road routes into Potosí are quite scenic and arriving by day will always provide a dramatic introduction to the city. The **new bus terminal** (Av Circumvalación) is about 2km north of the center on Av Las Banderas and nearly all *flotas* (long-distance buses; except for Uyuni) depart from here. *Micros I* or *A* run between the bus terminal and the cathedral.

There are direct *flotas* to La Paz, but in many cases it can be quicker to look for a connection in Oruro. Similarly for Sucre shared taxis (B$50, 2¼ hours) are pricier than the *flotas,* but are faster and more comfortable and can pick you

HACIENDA CAYARA

This **hotel** (☑ 740-9024; www.hotelmuseocayara.com/en; r per person B$180), 25km down the valley northwest of Potosí, is perfect for a peaceful retreat or some comfortable hill walking. Set amid lovely scenery at 3550m, this beautiful working farm produces vegetables and milk for the city, and as a place to stay is light years ahead of anywhere in town.

The building dates back to colonial times, but these days it's owned by the English Aitken family, who converted it into a hostel in 1992. The hacienda is part hotel and part museum: an opulent colonial mansion furnished with original paintings and period furniture. Guests have use of the fireplace and extensive library, which includes works dating from the 17th century. Lunch and dinner can be organised for B$50.

up at your hotel. Try **Cielito Express** (☑ 624-6040) or **Correcaminos** (☑ 624-3383); if solo, it's quicker to go to their offices behind the old bus terminal (p226) as they won't depart without a full car.

For Uyuni (B$40, five hours) buses depart from the old terminal 15 minutes downhill on foot from the center on Av Universitaria roughly every half hour from 7am to noon and then several more in the early evening. The rugged 210km route is quite breathtaking. *Micros* to Tarija also depart from this location.

Autobuses Quirquincho (www.autobuses quirquincho.com) and two other companies service Buenos Aires, Argentina.

DESTINATION	COST (B$)	TIME (HR)
Cochabamba	52-120	10
La Paz	52-135	9-10
Oruro	25-40	4
Sucre	20	3
Tarija	100	5-6
Tupiza	40-100	6
Villazón	50-90	8-9

🛈 Getting Around

Micros and minibuses (B$1.50) shuttle between the center and the Cerro Rico mines, as well as to the old (p226) and new bus terminal. Taxis charge B$4 per person around the center, slightly more at night, and B$10 or so to the new bus terminal.

South Central Bolivia & the Chaco

Best Places to Eat

➡ El Fogón de Gringo (p243)

➡ Bodega Casa Vieja (p248)

➡ Macondo de Pizza Pazza (p243)

➡ Pappillon (p243)

Best Places to Stay

➡ Casona Señorial Gloria (p241)

➡ Valle de los Condores Farmhouse (p250)

➡ Resort Hotel Los Parrales (p241)

➡ Kiwi Casita Apart-Hotel (p247)

➡ Hotel El Rancho Olivo (p252)

Why Go?

Generally seen by travelers as a way station to several international borders, this region of southern Bolivia sees relatively few tourists. The culture gravitates toward neighboring Argentina and dreams of being closer to faraway Andalucía. Famed for its dances, wines and Mediterranean feel, Tarija especially is worth a visit in its own right. Only a short distance from its charming, tightly packed, colonial center are vineyards, waterfalls and hiking trails in high alpine country.

Further to the east in the isolated Gran Chaco, the greenery fades to flat, petroleum-rich, scrubby red-earth expanses backed by stark highlands. This is where you'll find Bolivia's hottest town, Villamontes, and a series of remote, difficult-to-access reserves where wildlife abounds and few people tread. If you're well-outfitted and self-sufficient or plan far enough in advance with a tour company, a trip here could be one of your most memorable experiences in Bolivia.

When to Go
Tarija

Late Mar Rosillas goes cow crazy during the Fiesta de Leche y Queso.

Aug The coolest time of year to visit blistering Villamontes is during the fishing festival.

Sep Tarija's colorful Fiesta de San Roque starts the first Sunday in September.

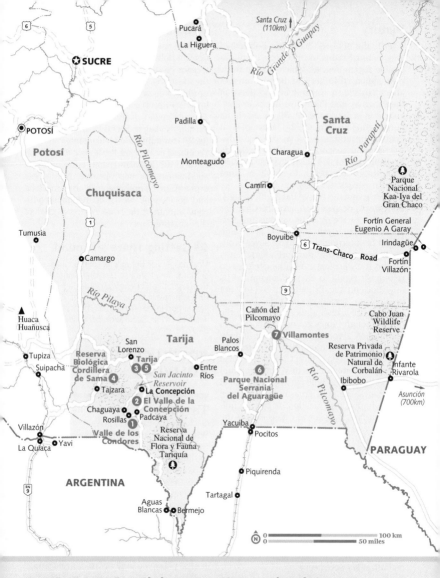

South Central Bolivia & the Chaco Highlights

1 Valle de los Condores
(p250) Sleeping under the stars and waking to condors soaring overhead.

2 El Valle de la Concepción
(p246) Sampling some of the world's highest-grown wines in this bucolic valley.

3 Tarija (p234) Strolling the city's tranquil colonial streets

and people-watching at a plaza cafe.

4 Reserva Biológica Cordillera de Sama (p248) Marveling at the thousands of lagoon-stepping flamingos.

5 Chapaco Carnaval
(p244) Celebrating, dancing and partying in Tarija's streets for weeks.

6 Parque Nacional Serranía del Aguaragüe
(p252) Discovering spectacular Chaco wildlife in the region's remote parks and reserves.

7 Villamontes (p251) Snacking on some fresh fish in this scorching town.

History

Prior to the 1932–35 Chaco War, Bolivia had long claimed rights to the Chaco, an inhospitable region beneath which rich oil fields were supposed to lie. The disputed area of about 240,680 sq km stretched northeast of the Paraguay and Pilcomayo Rivers in Paraguay, and included the 168,765 sq km chunk of Argentina north of the Río Bermejo. With political turmoil in Paraguay causing a distraction and economic hardship in Bolivia providing a stimulus, the Bolivians saw their opportunity and began to slowly advance into Paraguayan territory.

After losing the War of the Pacific in 1884, Bolivia was desperate to have the Chaco as an outlet to the Atlantic via the Río Paraguay. Hoping that physical possession would be interpreted as official sovereignty, the Bolivian army set up a fort at Piquirenda on the Río Pilcomayo and then refused to relinquish rights to Fuerte Vanguardia, its only port on the Paraguay river (and not in Bolivian territory). In 1928 Paraguay responded by sending its army to seize the fort. Although things got heated, both sides maintained a conciliatory attitude, hoping that a peaceful solution might be possible.

Things, however, didn't go as planned. During settlement talks in Washington and under orders from Bolivian President Daniel Salamanca, the Bolivian army tried to seize land without authorization, triggering full-scale warfare. Bolivia was widely seen as the aggressor in diplomatic circles and its case generated little support.

As the war progressed the Bolivians were driven back beyond their existing borders, though they continued to fight, with their most successful battle in the town of Villamontes in 1934. The hot, dry climate made access to fresh water a decisive factor in the war, and capturing and keeping access to wells became a key strategy. Conditions were miserable, soldiers were ill equipped and disease was rife. As a result, casualties on both sides were heavy.

Though no decisive victory was reached in the war, both nations had grown weary of fighting and peace negotiations four years later awarded most of the disputed territory to Paraguay. To date, no oil has ever been found in the Chaco, though prospectors are still searching. Ironically the smaller area of Chaco awarded to the Bolivians harbors enormous natural gas reserves that have boosted the Bolivian economy and are the envy of the Paraguayans on the other side of the border.

National Parks & Reserves

Remote, wild and off the beaten track, South Central Bolivia's parks and reserves are perfect for hard-core adventure seekers. Easily, the most accessible is the Reserva Biológica Cordillera de Sama (p248) outside Tarija, followed by Reserva Nacional de Flora y Fauna Tariquía (p250) southeast of Padcaya and Parque Nacional Serranía del Aguaragüe (p252) extending from Villamontes south to Yacuiba. The Reserva Privada de Patrimonio Natural de Corbalán (p252) is little visited and involves the most planning. Natural gas exploration, simultaneously controversial and coveted by local and regional politicians, threatens the conservation of parts of these nature reserves.

⚫ Getting There & Around

Most people visit Bolivia's far south on the way to or from somewhere else. Overland connections from Argentina, Paraguay and other regions within Bolivia involve long bus rides. Tarija has the biggest airport in the area and daily flights to Cochabamba, La Paz, Sucre and other major towns.

SOUTH CENTRAL BOLIVIA

Tarija

📱 4 / POP 205,300 / ELEV 1905M

With its pleasantly mild climate and easily walkable colonial center, you may find yourself lingering in Tarija longer than expected on your way to or from Argentina or Paraguay. Despite the fact that many Bolivians from bigger cities regard South Central Bolivia as a backwater, Tarija's palm-lined squares, tight streets, laid-back feel and lively restaurants feel just the right amount of cosmopolitan and sophisticated. After an afternoon with a glass of local vino on the central plaza you might consider relocating.

Tarija is also the base for excursions further afield, especially to the vineyards on its doorstep in El Valle de la Concepción and to surrounding villages and nature reserves.

Chapacos – as *tarijeños* (Tarija locals) are otherwise known – are culturally distinct from other parts of the country.

History

Tarija was founded as La Villa de San Bernardo de Tarixa by don Luis de Fuentes y Vargas on July 4, 1574, under the orders of

WORTH A TRIP

EL PICACHO

The riverfront **hacienda** (near Lajas Merced) of former Bolivian president Jaime Paz Zamora was designed by Zamora himself as his own version of Gabriel García Márquez' Macondo. Zamora, equally passionate about the arts and nature, will likely be around to point things out, from the bay-leaf tree given to him by Papa Juan Pablo II (Pope John Paul II) to a small bottle with a bit of the first petroleum discovered in Bolivia in it. Contact Macondo de Pizza Pazza Hotel (p241) in Tarija for tour information.

Originally the property of 'Moto' Méndez in the 1800s, it was turned into a refuge for artists escaping dictatorial regimes in neighboring countries like Argentina in the 1970s. The name of the estate Zamora purchased from a friend in the late 1980s comes from the large and unique rock formation just in front on the Río Guadalquivir. Other features worth checking out are portraits of Zamora painted by Ecuadorean artist Oswaldo Guayasamín; a piece of the wing from the plane crash in 1980 that Zamora was the only one of eight passengers to survive – the result of a bomb placed on board meant to kill Zamora (he celebrates his 'second birthday' every year on June 2, the day of the crash); and a Gastón Ugalde painting made entirely from coca leaves.

Visitors are allowed to wander along a nature path past a variety of trees, selected and planted by Zamora, an amateur horticulturalist. (Ironically, one of Tarija's most traffic-congested major roadways is named after him.) Also, check out the big-bellied toborochi tree on the house's grounds.

The two-hour tour ends with a tasting of locally produced cheeses, ham and *singani*, all served outside on a massive stone table built from millennia-old slabs of rock (with embedded fossils) Zamora found in the countryside.

Viceroy don Francisco de Toledo. He named the river flowing past the city the Guadalquivir (after Andalucía's biggest river), and left the *chapacos* with a lilting dialect of European Spanish. In 1810 the region declared independence from Spanish rule. Although the breakaways weren't taken seriously by the Spanish, the situation erupted into armed warfare on April 15, 1817 at the Batalla de la Tablada when the *chapacos* won a major victory over the Spanish forces.

In the early 19th century, Tarija actively supported Bolivia's struggle for independence. Although Argentina wanted to annex the agriculturally favorable area, Tarija opted to join the Bolivian Republic when it was established in 1825.

◉ Sights

In and of themselves, the sights within the center of Tarija aren't especially noteworthy. However, the city's narrow streets, colonial architecture and laid-back feel make it an extremely pleasant place to stroll. It's also the base for trips to nearby small towns, a natural reserve, mountain trekking and a winery region.

Basílica de San Francisco   CHURCH
(cnr Campos & La Madrid; ⊙ museum 8am-6pm Mon-Fri) FREE This basilica was founded in 1606 as the Jesuit 'base camp' in Bolivia and is now a national monument. The 16th-century convent library and archives, which may conjure up images reminiscent of *The Name of the Rose,* can be used only by researchers who have been granted permission by the Franciscan order; it holds an important archive of baroque music compositions. Inside the basilica, the free **Museo Franciscano Fray Francisco Miguel Mari** displays ecumenical paintings, sculptures and artifacts.

Santa Ana Astronomical Observatory   OBSERVATORY
(☑ 613-9810; B$15; ⊙ 6-8pm Mon-Fri) The country's first observatory, built in collaboration with the then USSR, is around 14km southeast of Tarija. Best to call in advance.

El Mercado de los Campesinos   MARKET
This sprawling maze-like scene covers several city blocks with row upon row of vendors selling everything from lemons to electronics. The vegetable and fruit sections are an especially kaleidoscopic display of colors. Watch your head as the canvases covering outdoor sellers sit low.

Mirador Loma de San Juan   VIEWPOINT
This park area above the tree-covered slopes of the Loma de San Juan provides a grand city view and makes it a favorite with smooching students. Climb uphill to the end of Bolívar, then turn right behind the hill

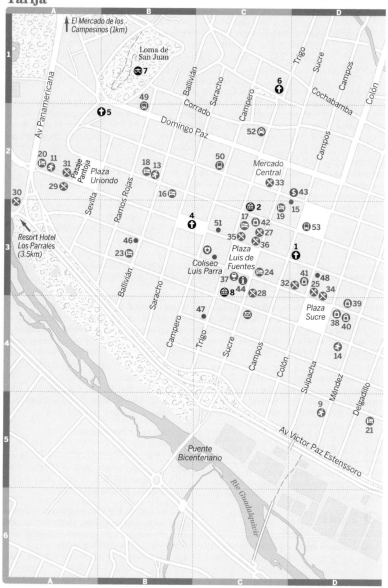

and follow the footpath up the slope that faces away from the city.

San Jacinto Reservoir
LAKE

This 17-sq-km reservoir, 7km southwest of town, makes for a pleasant afternoon trip, especially on hot days. It gets very busy on weekends with families and university students feasting on crabs and dorado (a delicious local fish) served from a handful of little *cabañas* (open 10am to 5pm) perched over the edge of the water just past the dam

Trufis to San Jacinto (p246; B$3, 10 minutes) run every 20 minutes from the corner of Ingavi and Campos (outside the Palacio de la Justicia) in Tarija. Taxis cost B$15 to B$20 each way and it's a common stop with tour companies in Tarija.

Museo de Arqueología y Paleontología   MUSEUM

(☑663-6680; freddypar67@hotmail.com; cnr Lema & Trigo; ⊙8am-noon & 3-6pm Mon-Fri, 9am-noon & 3-6pm Sat) FREE The university-run Archaeology & Paleontology Museum provides a glimpse of the prehistoric creatures and lives of the early peoples that once inhabited the Tarija area. Downstairs you'll see well-preserved animal remains and upstairs the focus is on history, geology and anthropology, with displays of old household implements, weapons, ceramics and various prehistoric hunting tools, including a formidable cudgel known as a *rompecabezas* (head-breaker).

Casa Dorada   MUSEUM

(Ingavi O-370; guided tour B$5; ⊙by guided tour hourly 9-11am & 3-5pm Mon-Fri, 9-11am Sat) With heavy coats of gold and silver paint, the appropriately named Gilded House whose roof is topped with a row of liberating angels looks impressive from afar but less so upon closer inspection. Entry is by guided visits only, which leave on the hour.

Cathedral   CHURCH

(cnr Campero & La Madrid) This rather dull-looking cathedral contains the remains of prominent *chapacos*, including Tarija's founder, don Luis de Fuentes y Vargas. It was constructed in 1611 and has some interesting stained glass depicting harvest scenes.

Iglesia de San Roque   CHURCH

(Trigo) Architecturally, Tarija's most unusual church and major landmark is the bright, white 1887 Iglesia de San Roque. Dedicated to the city's patron saint, the church sits on the hill at the end of Trigo, lording it over the town. Its balcony once served as a lookout post.

Iglesia de San Juan   CHURCH

(Bolívar) The Iglesia de San Juan was constructed in 1632 and it was here that the Spanish signed their surrender to the liberation army after the Batalla de la Tablada. The garden serves as a *mirador* (lookout) over Tarija and its dramatic backdrop of brown mountains.

(an almost vertical stairway leads to the base of the dam).

There's a place to rent canoes or, if you feel the need for speed, jet skis. Those who prefer tranquility can take short walks along the shore and surrounding ridges.

Tarija

Castillo de Moisés Navajas NOTABLE BUILDING
(Castillo Azul; Bolívar E-644; ◷9-11:30am Mon-Sat) The exterior of this oddly prominent and deteriorating private mansion is worth a look for its garish blue-and-white-striped extravagance. It's still inhabited and is occasionally open for informal tours – check with the Infotur (p245) office.

🏃 Activities

★ **Valle de los Condores** WILDLIFE WATCHING
(⌨7023-2025; www.valledeloscondores.com; Virginio Lema 284; ◷by appointment) This pioneering company runs two- to four-day treks (p250) in what it describes as the 'Yungas of Tarija' in order to spot majestic condors gliding over and around high-altitude cliffs.

Most of the hiking is done between 2000m and 3000m and nights are spent in traditional adobe homes.

Sur Bike CYCLING
(⌨761-9420; cnr Ingavi & Ballivián; ◷9am-12:30pm & 3-6:30pm Mon-Fri) Ernesto, the friendly and in-the-know owner at Sur Bike rents out bicycles by the hour and day. Also rents pick-up trucks for around US$70 per day.

Nivel Fitness Club GYM
(La Madrid 1030; ◷6am-10:30pm Mon-Fri, 8am-noon & 3-7pm Sat, 9am-1pm Sun) This gym, easily the best in the city with spin and yoga classes, an indoor pool, steam room and sauna, is attached to Hotel Los Ceibos

(p241). Guests of the hotel have complimentary access to all the facilities.

Tours

Half a dozen or so companies offer standard packages to area sights, including tours to the wineries (p246) from B\$130 for a half-day trip (four hours). Most of the full-day options, for around B\$230, involve adding on either a city tour or, more recommended, spots like San Lorenzo (p242), Coimata (p240) and Tomatitas (p240) not far to the north. They're pleasant trips in a minibus with generally well-informed guides (some are English speaking) and can often be arranged at the last minute with hotel pickups. Most have morning (8:30am or 9:30am) and afternoon (2:30pm) departures.

Explora Tarija   TOURS
(☑ 666-5500; Ingavi 649) This company seems to run its tours, the standard Ruta del Vino and Campiña Chapaca routes, more frequently than others. Oftentimes you can just turn up at its pick-up point at the southeastern corner of the central plaza a few minutes before departures (either 8:30am or 9:30am and 2:30pm) and join up with a trip.

VTB Tours   TOURS
(☑ 664-4341; www.vtbtourtarija.com; Ingavi O-784) One of the city's longest established agencies, with a reliable reputation and English-speaking guides, is located inside Hostal Carmen (p241; ask for Javier). With advance notice and a minimum of three people, this is a good bet for the Inca Trail or Tajzara Lagoons (p248) in the Reserva Biológica Cordillera de Sama (B\$1600 per person for two days).

Bolivian Wine Tours   OUTDOORS
(☑ 7187-1626; viviugarte@gmail.com; Méndez 175, btwn Avaroa & La Américas) Does all the standard wine tours and also runs highly recommended two-day tours to Reserva Biológica Cordillera de Sama (B\$390 per person). It also has one-day tours (B\$295 per person), but it's a lot of driving and you miss out on the experience of spending the night and stargazing. Costs per person go up for groups smaller than five.

Prometa   TOURS
(☑ 663-3873; www.prometa.org.bo; Alejandro del Carpio E-659; albergue r per person B\$100-150) Prometa operates seven camps in Tariquía and has information on visiting Tajzara (p248) in the Reserva Biológica Cordillera de Sama.

CHAPACOS
....

Chapacos, people from Tarija, have close cultural connections to Argentina. This isn't surprising, considering the region was part of Argentina until 1825.

➡ Most follow River Plate and Boca Juniors, Argentinian football teams.

➡ Many have family in Salta or elsewhere in northern Argentina or Buenos Aires.

➡ People drink *mate* like Argentinians.

➡ 'Che,' an Argentinian colloquialism meaning 'hey' or 'buddy,' is commonly heard.

➡ Siestas are religiously followed.

➡ Music and dance resemble Argentinian folkloric traditions.

➡ And, of course, wine is a popular drink.

Viva Tours   TOURS
(☑ 663-8325; vivatours.turismo@gmail.com; Bolívar 251, 2nd fl; ☺ 8am-12:30pm & 3-7pm Mon-Fri, 8am-12:30pm Sat) For wine tours and adventurous ecotrips to Tarija's hinterlands – including nearby national reserves – it's tough to beat Viva Tours.

🎉 Festivals & Events

Tarija is one of Bolivia's most festive towns and its Carnaval (p244) one of the most animated in Bolivia when all *chapacos* (Tarija locals) come out to dance, sing and party the days away. Ask around about the **arts fair** in October and the **Wine and Jam Festival** at the Hotel los Parrales (p241) in November.

Every April, in the middle of the month, a **baroque music festival** is held at the Basílica de San Francisco (p235; part of a larger fiesta in Santa Cruz). Pedro Ximénez Abril y Tirado's *Sinfonía 16* was performed for the first time in 200 years at the 2018 event.

If you find yourself in the region during a fiesta, you can expect unique music and dance traditions. The folk music of Tarija features unusual woodwind instruments, such as the *erque* and *quenilla*, the *caña* and the *camacheña*. The song that accompanies the music is called a *copla* – a direct import from Spain – with comic verses, sung in a duet. The dance that tops it all off is the traditional Chuncho; dancers wear colorful outfits, feathered headgear and masks,

SOUTH CENTRAL BOLIVIA & THE CHACO TARIJA

INTER-ANDEAN VALLEYS

During the summertime, there are several places in the valley to go swimming in the rivers, including Tomatitas, Coimata and Chorros de Jurina. The tour companies operating out of Tarija generally include Coimata and sometimes Tomatitas on their 'Campiña Chapaca' half-day tours.

Tomatitas, with its natural swimming holes, three lovely rivers (the Sella, Guadalquivir and Erquis) and happy little eateries serving *cangrejitos* (soft-shelled freshwater crabs), is popular with day-trippers from Tarija 5km to the south. The best swimming is immediately below the footbridge, where there's also a park with a campground and barbecue sites.

From here you can walk the 9km to **Coimata**. If coming from Tarija, turn left off the main San Lorenzo road (*micros* from the city to Coimata leave from Calle Comercio at the Mercado de los Campesinos; p235). After less than 1km, you'll pass a **cemetery** on the left, which is full of flowers and brightly colored crosses. Just beyond it, bear right towards Coimata. Once there, turn left at the soccer field and continue to the end of the road. Here you'll find a small cascade of water and a **swimming hole** that makes a great escape, as lots of *tarijeño* families can attest. There's also a choice of small restaurants serving *misquinchitos* and *doraditos* (fried local fish with white corn), as well as *cangrejitos* (small freshwater crabs). From this point, you can follow a walking track 40 minutes upstream to the base of the two-tiered **Coimata Falls**, which has a total drop of about 60m.

Another swimming hole and waterfall are found at **Rincón de la Victoria**, 6km southwest of Tomatitas in a green plantation-like setting. Instead of bearing right beyond the colorful cemetery, as you would for Coimata, follow the route to the left. From the fork, it's 5km to Rincón de la Victoria.

The twin 40m waterfalls at **Chorros de Jurina**, 26km northwest of Tarija, also make an agreeable destination for a day trip. Set in a beautiful but unusual landscape, one waterfall cascades over white stone while the other pours over black stone. In late winter, however, they may diminish to a mere trickle or dry up completely.

The route from Tarija to Jurina passes through some impressive rural landscapes. From near the flowery plaza in San Lorenzo (p242), follow the Jurina road, which turns off beside the Casa de Moto Méndez. After 6km, you'll pass a school on the left. Turn left 200m beyond the school and follow that road another 2.5km to the waterfalls. From the end of the road, it's a five-minute walk to the base of either waterfall. The one on the left is reached by following the river upstream; for the other, follow the track that leads from behind a small house.

Micros A and *B* to Tomatitas leave every 20 minutes from the corner of Domingo Paz and Saracho in Tarija (B$2), some continuing on to Jurina (B$7) via San Lorenzo. Get off near the school and then walk the rest of the way. For Coimata, similarly frequent departures leave from the corner of Campesino and Comercio (B$3) in Tarija.

symbolizing the Chiriguano tribes and their long-term resistance against the conquerors.

Rodeo Chapaco   RODEO
(Parque Héroes de la Tablada; ⊙ Apr 15-21) In keeping with its gaucho heritage, Tarija stages an annual rodeo, beginning on the departmental holiday. Rodeo Chapaco includes all the standard cowboy events. To get there, take *micro C* from the center.

Fiesta de San Roque   RELIGIOUS
(⊙ Sep) This well-known festival, which officially begins in mid-August, gives thanks to the saint whose appearance supposedly marked the end of the plague and leprosy in the area. The main celebration begins the first Sunday of September, continuing for eight days. It features traditional musical performances and a colorful Chuncho (an indigenous tribe) procession where participants wear 'coveralls' traditionally worn by lepers.

Fiesta de las Flores   RELIGIOUS
(⊙ 2nd Sun Oct) This annual festival is a religious celebration dedicated to the Virgin of Rosario. It begins with a procession, which sets off from the Iglesia de San Juan (p237). Along the route, spectators shower participants with petals. The highlight of the day is a colorful fair and bazaar in which the faithful spend lavishly for the benefit of the Church.

🛏 Sleeping

Budget accommodations are found mainly north of Bolívar, though most places in this price tier do not have heating and you may need it in winter. Many good midrange options are within several blocks of the central plaza; the city's only real high-end place is a few kilometers north of the center.

Casa Blanca — HOSTEL $

(☑ 664-2909; www.hostelcasablancatarija.com; Ingavi 645; dm B$60; @ 🛜) The whitewashed colonial-era facade and shady courtyard make Casa Blanca easily the most attractive of the city's budget accommodations. Three dorm rooms have two bunk beds each and the bathrooms are kept clean and have reliably hot showers. It's on a quiet block a short walk to the central plaza; but the soundness of your sleep depends on other guests.

Kultur Berlin Guesthouse — HOSTEL $

(☑ 186-2725; Ballivián 367; dm B$75, s/d/tr B$110/160/230; 🛜) Good-value place with a friendly owner, comfortable beds, a pleasant courtyard and sort of a roof patio; the basic bathrooms could use an upgrade. An especially good breakfast for this price bracket of homemade yogurt and granola, fruit, eggs and freshly made bread is served at a large communal table. Knock loudly even if it looks closed from the outside.

★Casona Señorial Gloria — BOUTIQUE HOTEL $$

(☑ 7824-5070; www.sites.google.com/view/casona gloria; Trigo 0680; B$280-385; 🏵🛜) Worthy of an upscale design magazine, five-room family-run Casona Gloria is a mix of historic colonial-era architecture and contemporary boutique stylings. The cherry on top, as it were, is its location: above and behind the owner's ice-cream shop. Rooms have high ceilings, brick walls, paintings by Bolivian artists and luxurious bedding, not to mention spa-quality bathrooms.

Macondo de Pizza Pazza Hotel — HOTEL $$

(☑ 666-3566; cnr Sucre & Calle 15 de Abril; s/d B$245/290; 🏵🛜) You'll find eight modestly furnished rooms with wood flooring ideally situated on the top floor of the Club Social Tarija building on the corner of the plaza principal. Part of the highly recommended restaurant (p243) of the same name.

Hostal del Sol — HOTEL $$

(☑ 666-5259; www.hoteldelsol.com.bo; Sucre 782; s/d incl breakfast B$230/350; 🏵@) Good value and conveniently located only two blocks from the central plaza, Hostal del Sol is a

reliable choice for its sunny street-facing rooms with minibalconies and breakfasts served in a similarly light-filled 2nd-floor dining room. Interior rooms are darker and less preferred but all have flat-screen TVs and sparkling-clean marble floors.

Hotel Mitru — HOTEL $$

(☑ 664-3930; www.hotelmitrutarija.com; Avaroa 450; s/d/tr B$270/380/460; 🏵@🛜) Don't expect any bells and whistles, just clean and modern efficiently designed rooms in a low-slung orange building a few minutes' walk from the central plaza. There are a few benches and sitting areas in a little inner courtyard garden.

Hostal Carmen — HOTEL $$

(☑ 664-3372; www.hostalcarmentarija.com; Ingavi 0-0784; s/d from B$190/280; @🛜) On a quiet block, this professionally run place offers standard rooms in a large three-story building. However, it can feel dark and abandoned if you're the solo guest. Less expensive, top-floor rooms are more basic, though you have quick access to the rooftop's city views. On-site tour company VTB (p239) is recommended and staff are accustomed to helping foreign tourists.

★Hotel Los Ceibos — HOTEL $$$

(☑ 663-4430; www.hotellosceibos.com; Av Pan-americana 612; r B$550; 🏵@🛜) The downtown area's largest hotel is only a little more than a half-dozen blocks from the central plaza and delivers the most bang for your bolivianos. Several towering palm trees give the pool area a tropical resort vibe. Guests have complimentary access to Nivel Fitness Club (p238), a fabulous gym attached to the hotel.

★Resort Hotel
Los Parrales — LUXURY HOTEL $$$

(☑ 664-8444; www.losparraleshotel.com; Urbanización Carmén de Aranjuez; s/d from B$575/830; 🏵@🏊) In a relaxed setting 3.5km from the center, Tarija's only five-star option delivers a complimentary cocktail on arrival and has a spa, a giant Jacuzzi and a lovely open-air dining area overlooking the countryside. The rooms are colonial-style luxury, with very comfy beds. Significant discounts (up to 45%) are available for one-night-plus stays during the low season.

Hotel Terravina — BOUTIQUE HOTEL $$$

(☑ 666-8673; www.terravinahoteldelvino.net; Bolívar E52; s/d/tr B$475/630/770; 🏵🛜) Calling itself a 'hotel del vino' is a bit of a marketing

WORTH A TRIP

SAN LORENZO

San Lorenzo (population 21,400), 14km north of Tarija along the Tupiza road, is a quaint village with freshly whitewashed adobe facades, cobblestone streets, carved balconies, a church built in 1709 and a charming plaza shaded by towering palm trees. Next to the plaza is a tiny market with vendors selling a variety of pastry specialties including *rosquetes* (basically a crunchy, dry doughnut with white frosting).

The town is best known as the home of José Eustaquio 'Moto' Méndez, the hero of the Batalla de la Tablada (p234), whose former house is now the **Museo Moto Méndez** (⊗9am-noon & 3-6pm Tue-Sun) FREE, aka 'Casa de los Libertadores de America.' The popular **Fiesta de San Lorenzo** takes place here on August 10 and features *chapaco* musical instruments and dancing. During Easter, yellow flowers are hung along the streets and buildings, providing a dash of color to the town's white stucco palette. After seeing the museum, head 2km north to the former Méndez family chapel, **Capilla de Lajas**, which is delicate, exquisitely proportioned and a fine example of colonial architecture.

Just to the north is the former home of erstwhile Bolivian president Jaime Paz Zamora, with an adjacent billboard paying homage to him. Only a few kilometers north of here, you can arrange in advance for a guided tour of El Picacho (p235), Zamora's beautiful estate – he'll likely be on hand to regale visitors with stories.

Micros and *trufis* (B$3, 30 minutes) to San Lorenzo leave from the corner of Av Domingo Paz and Calle Rojas in Tarija approximately every 20 minutes during the day. All of the tour companies in Tarija include a stop in San Lorenzo on at least one of their designated itineraries.

ploy, but it does offer tastings of wines sold here and most of the rooms have super-enlarged wine-themed photos as wallpaper. The furnishings are otherwise fairly basic.

🍴 Eating

Chapaco cuisine is unique and Tarija's restaurants pay it due homage. Get a copy of the *Guía Gastronomica* from the tourist office (p245) for mouthwatering ideas. It's worth noting that the majority of restaurants and cafes, except those around the central plaza, shut down for siesta between 12:30pm and 2:30pm or 3pm. Most are also closed Sundays.

★**Mercado Central**   BOLIVIAN $
(cnr Sucre & Bolívar; mains B$7-15; ⊗6am-10pm Mon-Sat) Despite its sterile suburban mall-like interior, the newly built central market is a great place to sample local specialties. The ground floor is divided into zones for bread, meat, cheese, vegetables etc, while the 2nd floor's food stalls serve dishes like *piqué macho* (beef, potatoes, onions and peppers), *saice* (spicy diced beef and vegetables) and *sopa de maní* (peanut soup).

★**Entre Frutas**   HEALTH FOOD $
(Calle 15 de Abril 142; mains B$15-40; ⊗8am-noon & 4-9pm Mon-Fri) Açaí bowls and fruit smoothies are the specialties here, with salads and ceviches rounding out the healthy menu. A

few front seats are good for watching passersby and the enclosed cobblestone back patio is nice for a longer stay.

El Puente Night Market   BOLIVIAN $
(Av Estenssoro; dishes B$5-12; ⊗4-11pm) More than a dozen stalls with apron-clad women serving up local specialties like *falso conejo* (ground meat with vegetables, onions and rice), *saice* (spicy diced beef and vegetables), *sonso* (grilled mashed yucca with cheese) and more basic meat and rice dishes. Miniature plastic tables and chairs line the street.

Belén   BOLIVIAN $
(Colón; mains B$17-36; ⊗7am-10pm Mon-Sat, to 3pm Sun; 🛜🖉) A US- and Australian-trained chef/owner created this homey, eclectically decorated restaurant serving artisan sandwiches, excellent burgers and a lightly seasoned trout dish for lunch. Equally good for breakfast of poached eggs and the yogurt and granola bowl.

Paleta de Yucatan   DESSERTS $
(Trigo; ice pops B$8-16; ⊗11am-9pm) Shopfront selling a variety of ice pop flavors, some quite unique like *mousse de maracuyá* (passion fruit mousse) and cheesecake *frutilla* (strawberry).

Don Vico   CEVICHE $
(ceviche B$25; ⊗8am-1:30pm Mon-Sat) A change of pace from your standard *almuerzo*, basic

bare-bones Don Vico has a few plastic tables and serves tasty Brazilian-style ceviche and seafood soup dishes.

Chocolate Cafe
CAFE $
(Sucre, btwn Madrid & Ingavi; ⊗8:30am-12:30pm & 3-8pm Mon-Fri, 9am-1pm Sat) Strong Italian espresso drinks and gourmet, locally crafted chocolates (cake as well) with a window on a busy downtown street.

★Pappillon
SEAFOOD $$
(☑7189-8676; E-1005 Arce; mains B$50; ⊗12:30-4pm Sat) Popular with locals, especially older men who come here for *cacho* (a dice game), guitar strumming and fish like *pacu* (from the Amazon around Beni), *sabalu* (from Villamontes) and *surubí*. It's located on a road commonly referred to as Av Pescado for the number of fish restaurants. Pappillon (also the owner's nickname) is tough to find without some help.

Look for the light-brown stucco wall with a brown gate covering the driveway. If you call a day ahead you can ask for *dorado relleno*, a big fish split open, filled with tomatoes, onions and other vegetables, then closed up and cooked. It's only for groups of six or more and best eaten slowly because it's filled with bones. There's no sign and you have to ring the bell and make your way through a patio and garage.

Tío Lucho
SEAFOOD $$
(☑7189-8676; Av Echazú 2171; mains B$35-80; ⊗6-11pm Tue-Fri, 12:30-3pm & 6-11pm Sat) Argentinian-owned traditional fish place with basic furnishings, but outstanding trout, shrimp and squid dishes.

Cabaña de Don Pedro
BOLIVIAN $$
(☑664-2681; Av Padilla; mains B$40, adult/child buffet B$75/35; ⊗noon-3pm Sun) This Tarija culinary institution serves local, regional and Bolivian specialties to families who have been gathering in its large, light-filled dining room for generations. Originally opened in 1974 in a different location, the founder's children have carried on their parent's tradition, offering an ever-popular Sunday buffet that includes their own version of *sopa de maní* (quinoa and peanut soup).

Mokka Cafe
INTERNATIONAL $$
(Calle 15 de Abril; mains B$40; ⊗8am-10pm Mon-Sat) Fronting Plaza Sucre, this long, narrow space with attentive service is good for basics like lasagna and enchiladas, large frappés and cakes, as well as strong espresso drinks. *Almuerzos* (set lunches; B$49 to

LOCAL SPECIALTIES

You'll need to be brave to try *sopa la poderosa* (soup with vegetables, rice and bull's penis), *ranga ranga* (tripe with onion, tomato and chili) and *chan faina* (diced lamb guts with potatoes and greens), but even delicate stomachs will enjoy *guiso de karas* (stew of pork skin, potatoes and mote, a corn-like grain), *chancao de pollo* (spicy chicken), *sopa de maní* (peanut soup) or *saice* (spicy ground beef and vegetables with rice or noodles), which is just as commonly eaten for breakfast as dinner. Don't forget to sample the desserts too – *dulce de lacayote* (caramelized squash), *pepitas de leche* (cinnamon fudge) and *tojori* (pancakes with cloves and aniseed) are all favorites.

The best places to try these are the Mercado Central (p242), El Mercado de los Campesinos (p235) and El Puente Night Market (p242).

B$59), with soup, main, drink and dessert, are good value.

Taberna Gattopardo
INTERNATIONAL $$
(cnr La Madrid & Sucre, Plaza Principal; mains B$20-55; ⊗8am-midnight; 🛜) Worthy of repeat visits if only for people-watching while sipping an espresso, this European-run tavern and cafe occupies one of the central plaza's choicest corners. The menu is large and eclectic, the food merely mediocre – salads, burgers, pizzas, a few Bolivian specialties, steaks and fondue bourguignonne. Inside, the high-ceilinged dining room is cavernous.

★El Fogón de Gringo
STEAK $$$
(La Madrid 1051; mains B$70-100; ⊗7-11pm Mon-Fri, noon-3pm & 7-11pm Sat, noon-3pm Sun; 🛜) The quality and value of El Fogón's choice steaks equal the appeal of its warm ambience, which echoes the casual sophistication of a southern Spanish bodega's restaurant. All mains come with a tasty buffet of salad, rice, potatoes and pasta and there's an excellent wine selection.

★Macondo de Pizza Pazza Restaurant
PIZZA $$$
(☑664-2107; macondopizzapazza@gmail.com; Sucre 508; mains B$55-110, pizza B$60-110; ⊗3:30pm-midnight Mon-Thu, to 3am Fri, 9am-midnight Sat, 9am-2:30pm & 6-11pm Sun; 🛜) Exuberant host Edith Paz Zamora and her

son Hector have put together a really unique blend of art and, you guessed it, pizza, on the ground floor of the Club Social Tarija. But the homemade pastas are equally good (the all-you-can-eat Sunday pasta buffet for B$70 is excellent) and the menu also includes steak and fish dishes.

La Parilla del Gordo Aviles STEAK **$$$**

(☑ 7299-8765; Calle 6 de Junio, Juan 23; mains B$60-100; ⊘ 7-11pm Tue-Fri, noon-3pm & 7-11pm Sat, noon-3pm Sun) The owner of La Parilla took the leap from hosting *asados* at home to opening and running one of the city's best steakhouses. It's busy with locals downing bottles of wine who all seem to know one another.

El Quincho de Quiliu STEAK **$$$**

(☑ 7021-1133; La Madrid 1022; mains B$70; ⊘ 7-11:30pm Tue-Sat, noon-3pm Sun) While the decor is simpler and more casual at El Quincho, the quality of the meat is equally high. It's located directly across the street from the well-known steakhouse El Fogón de Gringo (p243).

Drinking & Nightlife

⭐ **Macondo de Pizza Pazza Bar** BAR

(☑ 7022-2022; https://macondopizzapazza.neg ocio.site; cnr Sucre & Calle 15 de Abril; ⊘ 6:30pm-midnight, to 3am Fri; ☎) For a Bolivia highlight, head here on Friday 'bohemian nights' (B$40; free for hotel guests), an intoxicating scene with live folkloric music, dancing and bottles of local vino and *sin-gani*. The action starts at 10pm (call for reservations or else you'll be stuck peering through doorways); like clockwork, Hector and his mum Edith start dancing on tables around midnight.

Xoxo BAR

(Calle 15 de Abril; ⊘ 8am-midnight) Adorned with pop art and drink cans from across the globe, this bar-cafe with outdoor seating on the main plaza generally attracts a young crowd at night. Worth considering for a meal (burgers, pastas, pizza, salads from B$30 to B$68) on Sunday, when it's one of the few places in the center open all day.

THE CHAPACO CARNAVAL

Tarija is Bolivia's music and dance region, famous for its unique traditions and loud, colorful festivals, especially during Carnaval, when all *chapacos* (Tarija locals) come out to dance, sing and party the days away. If you find yourself in the region during a fiesta, here's what to expect.

The folk music of Tarija features unusual woodwind instruments, such as the *erque* and *quenilla,* the *caña* and the *camacheña.* The song that accompanies the music is called a *copla* – a direct import from Spain – with comic verses, sung in a duet. The dance that tops it all off is the traditional *Chuncho*; dancers wear colorful outfits, feathered headgear and masks, symbolizing the Chiriguano tribes and their long-term resistance against the conquerors.

Tarija's Carnaval is one of the most animated in Bolivia and brilliant fun. To launch the festivities, two Thursdays before Carnaval Tarija celebrates the **Fiesta de Compadres** (⊘ 3rd week Feb). This unique fiesta is Tarija's largest pre-Carnaval festival. It's assumed that the celebration, originating in the village of Pola de Siero in the northern Spanish region of Asturias, was inspired by the wives of Spanish colonial authorities and soldiers, who saw to it that social customs and morals were strictly followed. It was eventually adopted by the local indigenous population and is now celebrated by the entire community with music, dancing and special basket tableaux constructed of bread known as *bollus preñaus*. Flowers, fruits, tubers, small cakes and other gifts are passed between female friends and relatives.

Throughout the Carnaval season, the streets fill with dancing, original *chapaco* music and colorfully costumed country folk who turn up in town for the event. There's a Grand Ball in the main plaza after the celebration and the entire town comes out for the dancing and performances by folk groups, bands and orchestras. Beware: water balloons figure prominently in the festivities.

On the Sunday after Carnaval, the neighborhood near the cemetery enacts a 'funeral' in which the devil is burned and buried in preparation for Lent. Paid mourners (actors pretending to mourn the death of the devil) lend the ritual a morose air – although we suspect they're actually lamenting that they must now remain vice-free for the 40 days until Easter.

🛍 Shopping

Bodegas **Aranjuez** (☑664-5651; www.vinos aranjuez.com; Calle 15 de Abril 254; ☺8am-noon & 2:30-6:30pm Mon-Fri, 8am-12:30pm Sat), **Kohlberg** (☑663-6366; www.kohlberg.com.bo; 15 de Abril E-275; ☺8am-noon & 2:30-6:30pm Mon-Fri, 8am-12:30pm Sat), **La Concepción** (☑663-2250; www.bodeglaconcepcion.com; Colón 585; ☺8am-noon & 2:30-6:30pm Mon-Fri, 8am-12:30pm Sat) and **Campos de Solana** (☑664-5498; www.camposdesolana.com; Calle 15 de Abril E-259; ☺8am-noon & 2:30-6:30pm Mon-Fri, 8am-12:30pm Sat) all have shops near one another just off Plaza Sucre. For cloyingly sweet artisan wines, hit one of the shops lining Calle Sucre between Domingo Paz and Cochabamba.

★**La Vinoteca**   WINE
(☑7299-6486; lavinoteca@hotmail.com; Ingavi 371; ☺9am-12:30pm & 3-7pm Mon-Fri, to 1pm Sat) The best shop to pick up a bottle of the local vino, *singani* or other specialty food products. Carlos, the owner, is happy to open bottles to try by the glass.

ℹ Information

DANGERS & ANNOYANCES

Police (☑664-2222; cnr Campero & Calle 15 de Abril)

LAUNDRY

Telo Lavo (cnr Calle 15 de Abril & Ballivián; ☺8am-8pm Mon-Fri) is convenient for washing and drying laundry. Otherwise ask at your hotel and expect to pay B$2 to B$3 per item.

MEDICAL SERVICES

Hospital San Juan de Dios (☑664-5555; Santa Cruz s/n) For medical emergencies.

MONEY

There are numerous banks with ATMs around the plaza and at the airport.

Several **casas de cambio** (Bolívar; ☺8am-1pm & 3-8pm Mon-Fri, 8am-1pm Sat), which change US dollars, euros and Argentine pesos, are conveniently located on Bolívar between Sucre and Daniel Campos. Most are open from 8am to 1pm and 3pm to 8pm Monday to Friday and only in the morning on Saturday.

POST

Post Office (cnr Sucre & Virginio Lema)

TOURIST INFORMATION

Infotur (☑666-7701; www.tarijaturismo.com; cnr Calles 15 de Abril & Sucre; ☺8am-noon & 2:30-6:30pm Mon-Fri, 9am-noon & 4-7pm Sat & Sun) distributes basic town maps and is reasonably helpful with queries regarding sights in and around town – Spanish-speaking only. Also, check out the excellent www.brujulaturistica.com/tarija for transportation, food and other helpful tourist information.

Head to the **migración** (☑664-3450; cnr La Paz & Oruro; ☺8:30am-12:30pm & 2:30-6:30pm Mon-Fri) office in front of Parque Bolívar for entry/exit stamps or to extend your stay.

Conduct all your business in the morning or you'll have to wait until after the siesta because Tarija becomes a virtual ghost town between 1pm and 4pm.

The **Protección del Medioambiente del Tarija** (Prometa; www.prometa.org.bo; Tarija) works in the Gran Chaco region on a series of social and conservation initiatives.

ℹ Getting There & Away

AIR

The **Capitán Oriel Lea Plaza Airport** (☑664-2195; Av Victor Paz Estenssoro) is 3km east of town off Av Jaime Paz Zamora. **TAM** (☑664-5899; www.tam.bo; La Madrid O-470; ☺8:30am-1pm & 3-7pm Mon-Fri, 8:30am-1pm Sat), **BOA** (☑611-2787; www.boa.bo; Trigo, btwn Alejandro del Carpio & Lema; ☺8:30am-12:30pm & 2:30-6:30pm Mon-Fri, 9am-noon Sat), **Ecojet** (☑611-3427; www.ecojet.bo; cnr Colón & Madrid; ☺8:30am-1pm & 3-7pm Mon-Fri, 8:30am-1pm Sat) and Amazonas (www.amazonas.com) service La Paz, Santa Cruz, Sucre and Cochabamba (tickets range from B$220 to B$450; for La Paz and Sucre it can sometimes involve a stop in Cochabamba). TAM and Amazonas also make the short hop to Yacuiba (B$300 to B$500) one to two days a week.

Syndicate taxis from the airport to the center cost B$20 to B$25, but if you walk 100m past the airport gate (visible from outside the terminal), you'll pay as little as B$12 per person for a normal taxi. Otherwise, cross the main road and take a passing *micro A* or *trufi*, which run by the old bus terminal and the Mercado Central.

BUS

The new, modern and very large **bus terminal** is 7km south of town. There's a wine shop, charging station for electronics, luggage storage, money exchange, shops selling snacks and light eats, and an information desk with usually one English-speaking staff on hand.

Most long-haul services leave in the afternoon between 4:30pm and 8:30pm. Lince and Platinum's daily 7pm buses (B$195 to B$265) offer the most luxurious service to La Paz; expect 180-degree reclining seats, wi-fi, USB outlets, private video screens with headphones, clean bathrooms, plus snacks and water.

Services to Santa Cruz pass through Villamontes from where there are connections to Yacuiba and Asunción in Paraguay, though frustratingly the latter pass through in the early hours of the morning, meaning you'll have to wait a long time for your onward ride.

The bus company Trans Tours Juarez C has Tuesday, Thursday and Sunday departures direct all the way to Salta in Argentina (B$320 to B$400, 10 hours, 7pm) via the Bermejo crossing (p248); it's highly recommended for fairly luxurious buses (every *cama* seat has its own TV) and expediting the border-crossing process.

Micros for northern destinations like Camargo and Potosí leave from **Parada del Norte**. While waiting for the minivans to fill, you can grab a snack or coffee from a handful of basic stalls.

Micros to Padcaya (Hwy 1, btwn Avs Sossa & Moreno, Parada del Chaco) leave from the Parada del Chaco.

Trufis to San Jacinto (Ingavi, btwn Campos & Colón; B$3) (B$3, 10 minutes) run every 20 minutes from the corner of Ingavi and Campos (outside the Palacio de la Justicia) in Tarija.

Many of the roads in the area, most notably the ones to Potosí, Tupiza and Villamontes (work remains to be done on a scary, narrow stretch near Villamontes), have been upgraded, improving safety and shortening driving times.

DESTINATION	COST (B$)	TIME (HR)
Bermejo	50	3½
Camiri	60	11
Cochabamba	130-256	15
La Paz	120-260	18
Oruro	60-103	12
Potosí	60-70	5-6
Sucre	80-180	12
Santa Cruz	90-254	12-13
Tupiza	50-80	7
Villamontes	60-100	8
Villazon	45	6
Yacuiba	60	6

TAXI

Colectivos in all shapes and sizes, though primarily Subaru station wagons and minivans, service every regional destination (for either Villamontes or Yacuiba it's B$100 and six hours) and some further afield. They are in general a little more expensive, though arguably more comfortable than buses (depending on your seat). However, they leave when full so waits vary. *Colectivos* to Bermejo (B$45, three hours) on the Argentinian border leave frequently.

❶ Getting Around

BUS

City *micros* and *trufis* cost B$2.50 per ride. Routes are clearly marked on the front windows of vehicles.

Take **minivans** (Corrado) marked 'V' to El Valle de la Concepción.

CAR & MOTORCYCLE

If you want to get to spots outside the city on your own schedule, check out **Rocas Rent a Car** (☑ 7023-3246; www.rocasrentacar.com; Av Zamora, btwn Ruiz & España; ◷ 8am-noon & 1-6pm Mon-Fri, 8am-noon Sat), which rents 4WD Toyotas and Nissans (US$90 to US$120 per day).

TAXI

Although you can walk just about anywhere in Tarija, taxis cost B$4/8 per person for day/night trips around the center. It's B$12 for one person to or from the bus terminal, B$20 for two or more. It costs slightly more at night for all trips. **Movil Andaluz** (☑ 663-3010) is one of more than a dozen radio taxi companies operating in the city.

El Valle de la Concepción

☑ 4 / ELEV 1900-2100M

The region south of Tarija, the Concepción Valley or simply 'El Valle,' is the heart of Bolivian wine production. It may be able to claim the title as the 'world's highest wines,' outside of Manischewitz, but the wines produced here are also some of the sweetest. No doubt, they're maturing, evolving and improving, and several of the larger wineries are producing sophisticated and textured wines the equal of their South American neighbors.

Most people breeze on through on organized day trips from Tarija (advertisements for 'Ruta del Vino' trips are everywhere), but the village of La Concepción, with picturesque colonial architecture, a plaza sporting lovely flowering ceibo trees and a sleepily prosperous feel, is worth lingering over.

🏃 Activities

Winery visits usually involve a quick tour of the production facilities, which vary from the basement of a suburban-style home to larger operations with industrial-size equipment. The main wineries are Campos de Solana (☑ 466-4549; www.camposdesolana.com; ◷ 9-11am & 1-4pm Mon-Fri, 9-11am Sat), Bodega Kuhlmann (☑ 664-4346; www.bodegakuhlmann.com), Kohlberg (☑ 663-6366; www.kohlberg.com.bo; Av Jorge Paz; ◷ 8am-noon & 2:30-6:30pm Mon-Fri), Casa Real (a distillery), Bodega La Concepción (☑ 664-5040; www.bodegaslaconcepcion.com; ◷ 8am-5pm Mon-Fri, to noon Sat) and Aranjuez (at the time of research this one was due to open to visitors in September 2018). Most tours include visits to two of these, plus a smaller artisan bodega.

If you go on your own, you'll pay around B$5, plus the cost of whatever bottle you like for a 'tasting.' Keep in mind, most places are open from 9am to 11am and 2pm to 4pm Monday to Friday and only in the mornings Saturday.

When in a group at one of the artisan bodegas, the traditional way of tasting is to line up glasses full of different varieties all in a row or to form a circle and pass around each glass – either way, everyone sips from the same source. Cheese, ham and olives are typically part of the tastings.

🎉 Festivals & Events

Fiesta de la Uva   CULTURAL
(Vendimia Chapaca; ☉ Mar) The Fiesta de la Uva (Grape Festival) is held in La Concepción for three days in March, coinciding with the grape harvest.

🛏 Sleeping & Eating

Hostería Valle D'Vino   HOSTAL **$**
(☑ 665-1515; https://valledivinotarija.com; 6 de Julio, Uriondo; camping B$25, dm B$50, s/d/tr/q B$100/140/210/280; 🛜) As eccentric as its owner, this shabby-looking vineyard is one of the only wineries to offer accommodations, including camping in an equally messily maintained grassy area, large dorm rooms and a few basic private ones with varying bed layouts. While there, take a gander at its one-of-a-kind 'museum,' a hodgepodge collection of animal skins, fossils, beehives, luggage etc.

Kiwi Casita Apart-Hotel   APARTMENT **$$**
(☑ 599-6674; www.kiwicasita.com; Rojas, Uriondo; r B$276; 🛜) A couple of apartments in a 19th-century adobe home just a few blocks from Uriondo's central plaza with vineyard views. The DIY decor is charming, with repurposed grape crates as shelves, bedside tables made from vine-post wood and old newspapers as wallpaper.

Tarija's Wine Country

★ **Bodega Casa Vieja** BOLIVIAN $
(☑666-2605; www.lacasavieja.info; mains B$20-60; ⊗10am-6pm) Home to the best *patero* (foot-trodden) wine, this atmospheric winery has a lovely restaurant with a trellis-covered courtyard and covered outdoor patio with beautiful mountain views. Serves classic Chaco dishes like *saice* (spicy ground beef over potatoes and rice) and *chancho de la cruz* (whole hog). It's in the village of La Concepción, about 30km from Tarija.

ⓘ Getting There & Away

For a half-day or day-long guided visit to the valley's wineries, contact any of the recommended tour agencies in Tarija (p239). If you prefer to visit under your own steam, El Valle lies off the route toward Bermejo; take the right fork at the *tranca* (police post) east of Tarija. Using public transportation really isn't a convenient option if you want to visit more than one winery; taxis (around B$35 one way) and *micro V* leave when full (B$6, 30 minutes) from the corner of Corrado and Trigo.

Reserva Biológica Cordillera de Sama

The Sama Biological Reserve protects sandy Sahara-like dunes, tens of thousands of flamingos and startling clear night skies, all within several hours of Tarija. On the cold and windy *puna* (high open grasslands) portion of the reserve (3400m above sea level, nearly the same altitude as La Paz), you can visit the Tajzara Lagoons, a Ramsar site of international importance for aquatic birds. Here, several shallow flamingo-filled lagoons appear like jewels in the harsh altiplano, vegetated only by *thola* (a small desert bush) and *paja brava* (spiky grass of the high altiplano).

Tarija's New Agers consider Tajzara to be a natural power site while the locals claim that the lakes are haunted by nocturnal spirit voices and woe betide anybody who stays out after dark. The night air does produce some eerie voice-like cries, but unimaginative people ascribe the phenomenon to winds rushing through the *thola*.

◉ Sights

Entry to the reserve costs B$100 and the fee is not usually included in prices quoted by tour companies.

Sama has experienced several bad fires in the last couple of years, including one in 2017 that destroyed nearly 15,000 hectares of forested park.

Tajzara Lagoons NATURAL FEATURE
Along the eastern shores of the lagoons, the wind has heaped up large *arenales* (sand dunes). An interesting climb takes you to the symmetrical peak of **Muyuloma**, which rises about 1000m above the plain. The summit affords views across the lagoons and beyond to the endless expanses of the southern altiplano – thousands of Andean and James' flamingos can often be seen in the waters here. The return climb takes the better part of a day.

Observatorio de Aves VIEWPOINT
A favorite with bird-watchers in search of three of the world's six flamingo species, and the rare horned and giant coots.

🏃 Activities

Hikers can spend an enjoyable six to eight hours on the wonderful **Inca Trail** as it descends from the starting point at Abra Calderilla 2000m to the valley below. We've also heard of mountain bikers tackling

---

ⓘ CROSSING THE BORDER TO ARGENTINA

These days, Bermejo/Aguas Blancas is the most convenient crossing to Argentina for those coming directly from Tarija or Salta in Argentina; the border is open from 8am to 5pm. The bus company Trans Tours Juarez C (www.facebook.com/juarezcinfo) has highly recommended Tuesday, Thursday and Sunday departures (B$320 to B$400, 10 hours, 7pm) via this crossing; it helps expedite the process and you don't have to change buses.

Otherwise, it's a more complicated ordeal. Bermejo's bus terminal is eight blocks southeast of the main plaza. Buses leave every couple of hours from Tarija to Bermejo (B$20, three hours) between 7:30am and 9pm, but you'll need to get a morning service (last departure 10:30am) if you want to cross the border the same day; *colectivos* (B$45) are more frequent and leave when full. It's a quick B$3 *chalana* (ferry) ride across the river frontier to Aguas Blancas in Argentina (be sure to pick up an exit stamp before crossing). From here, buses to Orán (US$2, one hour) depart hourly from the terminal opposite the immigration office. From Orán, you can connect to Argentina's Salta, Jujuy and Tucumán.

WINE & SINGANI

The grapevines, first brought to the region by 17th-century missionaries, grow at a staggering 1600m and 2150m and are only 22° south of the equator. They ripen quicker than their sea-level cousins and the wine is given a head start in the maturing process, making rich reserves easier to produce. The grapes grown here, all hand-harvested, are mainly a mix of muscat of Alexandria (also, the primary grape for *singani*) and Californian (like cabernet sauvignon and sauvignon blanc), but with a taste all their own. Most wineries have recently been experimenting with other grapes like malbec, petit verdot and tannat grapes, including Aranjuez, which has produced some award-winning vintages (Juan Cruz Aranjuez Grand won a gold prize in 2012, the country's first gold in an international competition).

Some bottles to look out for are Esther Ortiz 2015 and Unico from Campos de Solana (p246), Tannat Origen from Aranjuez, and Kohlberg 200 from Kohlberg (p246). They run from around B$85 to B$320 for a bottle in a restaurant (whereas bottles of Argentinian wines usually start at around B$320).

Santa Cruz, as a city, is the largest consumer of Bolivian wine. A few bodegas now export to the US, Japan and Europe. Dozens of small artisan wineries, some only producing enough bottles to supply their own extended families, are south of El Valle, closer to Chaguaya. It's also worth noting El Valle de los Cintis, the area around Camargo, 162km north of Tarija (three hours) on the way to Potosí, as another especially beautiful region with vineyards and artisan producers; at around 2400m, most are even higher than Tarija.

Most bodegas also produce *singani,* a distilled muscat grape spirit (40%) considered Bolivia's national drink, along with, of course, *chicha* (fermented maize liquor). It's a booming industry with a certificate of origin akin to Champagne. The cheapest are harsh, the more expensive tend to be smoother (unlike somewhat similar brandy, no aging is involved). Don Lucho Oro from Casa Real, which is distilled four times, is one of the best and goes for B$295. Bodegas and offices in Tarija sell bottles at factory prices (B$15 to B$300).

Surprisingly, the American film director Steven Soderbergh has done more than anyone to raise the drink's profile abroad, or at least in cocktail bars in large cities in the US. Enraptured by *singani* after his first taste, he's partnered with Casa Real to export his own brand, *Singani* 63 and even produced a documentary titled *La Storia de Singani.*

Chuflay (two fingers *singani* with ginger ale and lemon or lime) is the most common way to drink it. Other cocktails made from *singani* are *leche de tigre* (*singani,* warm milk and cinnamon); *mokachinchi* (*singani,* sun-dried peaches, ginger ale, lime and a stick of cinnamon); *mojito chapaco* (*singani,* lemon, soda, bitters and mint); and, of course, simply 'on the rocks,' best only for higher-end brands. All are around B$25 in a restaurant.

For *singani*-produced hangovers, do as the locals do and slurp down a bag of Karpil (branded as Pilfruit in Sucre), a fruit-flavored milky-cheese byproduct (the liquid that remains after making cheese); it's available at any grocery.

sections. With luck, you may see vicuñas, condors or mysterious petroglyphs of unknown origin.

🛏 Sleeping

Albergue de Pujzara HOSTAL $
(per person B$50) This large stone and adobe building on a rocky slope run by the local community is the only accommodations in Sama. Basic and simple meals are offered and it's great for stargazing. Most people arrive as part of a tour; to organize a stay independently, contact **Servicio Nacional de Áreas Protegidas** (Sernap; 663-3873; www.sernap.gob.bo; Av Paz Estenssoro, Tarija) in Tarija.

ℹ Information

Temperatures in the highlands stay quite chilly year-round but are slightly more comfortable in the drier winter months (May to August). The best time to visit the lower elevations is in the summer, when it's warm enough to swim.

ℹ Getting There & Away

The best way to visit Sama is with a tour company (p239) in Tarija. They organize overnight trips to the most accessible areas of the reserve, but require a minimum of three people and an advance booking. The extremely self-sufficient can consider taking a Tupiza- or Villazón-bound bus or *micro* from Tarija to Iscayachi (B$40) and a taxi from there to the dunes (it's around a

WORTH A TRIP

VALLE DE LOS CONDORES TOUR

In the mountains around 11km south of Padcaya, west of the road cutting through the valley, a large population of Andean condors (some say 200 pairs) can be seen gliding high above the highest peaks. Locals actually call them *cuervos* (crows), but they're majestic birds, one of the world's largest, with wingspans that can measure over 3m. The casual slight is largely because *campesinos* say condors kill their grazing cows, when in fact they're scavenging off the dead animals after they've lost their footing on the steep slopes and fallen to their deaths. For baby condors' inaugural flights, when they turn six or seven months, cliffs measuring at least 400m are required and there's no shortage here. To differentiate between male and female, look for the beard-like plumage of the former. Vultures, urubi and eagles can also be spotted.

It's a steep hike up from the valley road to a plateau where you camp and begin to see the birds soaring on warm updrafts. Most people opt to climb higher to a rocky outcropping with even more majestic 180-degree panoramic views. Dinner is cooked over a fire, with wine, an amazingly civilized meal amid such stunning and remote scenery.

The hike back to the road follows another steep path, with a few challenging and slippery switchbacks through a dense jungle-like stretch (we spotted a tarantula!) that ends at a waterfall – you can take a dip in the pool at the base if you don't mind the chilly water.

Contact Valle de los Condores (p238) in Tarija to arrange a trip. On its standard three-day/two-night journey, guests are transported from Tarija to the company's idyllic country **farmhouse** (www.valledeloscondores.com; Cruce de Rocillas; r B$103-173), just south of the village of Cruce de Rocillas. Here guests can wander around the property and try their hand at milking a cow. When you arrive, bread will likely already be cooking in the outdoor oven. Dinner with hosts Julia and Vincent is a feast, with various meats, including llama, and cheeses cooked on a Swiss-style raclette. Six rooms, all with extremely comfortable bedding and modern bathrooms, are scattered around the compound. Hikes leave early the following morning.

After returning in the early afternoon from the mountains, there's an equally fantastic *asado* (also heavy on the llama) waiting for you in a flower-filled garden setting. Most people won't want to leave and imagine immigrating to this slice of Eden.

three-hour journey). Private taxi hire from Tarija all the way to Tajzara will run B$500. Try Omar Jurado (☏ 7511-8145).

Padcaya & Chaguaya

Visiting Padcaya, south of Tarija, brings full meaning to the old saying that 'it's better to travel than to arrive,' with the route twisting its way through 45km of lovely mountainous desert and green river valleys. The town itself has a few old colonial buildings and is located in an area rich in fossils, meaning you are more likely to bump into a paleontologist than another tourist.

Chaguaya, 68km south of Tarija, is home to the pilgrimage shrine **Santuario de la Virgen de Chaguaya**. The **Fiesta de la Virgen de Chaguaya** begins on August 15; celebrations follow on the subsequent Sunday. Alcohol is forbidden at this time. Pilgrims from all over Bolivia arrive during the following month, some making the trip on foot via a large, approximately 10-hour procession from Tarija.

◉ Sights

A few kilometers north of Chaguaya in Juntas del Rosario is the 500-year-old San Vicente Juntas church, one of the oldest still-functioning churches in the country.

Reserva Nacional de Flora y Fauna Tariquía　　　WILDLIFE RESERVE

The lovely and little-known 2470 sq km Tariquía Flora & Fauna Reserve (created in 1989) protects a large portion of cloud forest and a smaller area of polylepis woodland on the eastern slopes of the department of Tarija's mountains. Ranging in altitude from 400m to 1500m, it houses rare animals such as the spectacled bear, as well as hundreds of bird species including the threatened rufous-throated dipper and the spectacular military macaw.

The largely wild reserve's pristine future has been in doubt for many years now after the discovery of large deposits of natural gas. Access is complicated and there are no formal tours. Hiking is possible but extremely challenging in this remote area and should not be attempted without a guide. Contact the Prometa (p239) office in Tarija for details on how to visit or Eiber Sibila (☑7513-1714), a guide based in Tarija who can organize trips. They operate a few camps in Tariquía, including a simple *albergue* with camping and cooking facilities in the heart of the reserve, but it's a two-day hike in from the road. The best time to visit is during the dry winter months (May to September) when the climate is mild and river crossings are possible.

The way from Padcaya to Pampa Grande-Motoví, the access point to Tariquía, is along a rough dirt road and takes around three hours. Shared taxis (B$70) from Padcaya need six people to leave – it will be a long wait if you're not in a group.

❶ Getting There & Away

Micros (B$8, 90 minutes) from Tarija to Padcaya depart every 20 minutes from the Parada del Chaco at Plaza Sucre. Less frequent services run to Chaguaya from the same place, leaving midafternoon. From Padcaya, it's only two hours by taxi to the town of Bermejo on the Argentine border (p248).

Sindicato de Taxis 8 de Noviembre Padcaya (☑654-5025) has comfortable vehicles servicing Tarija, Padcaya, Chaguaya and Bermejo.

THE CHACO

Flat and sparsely populated, the Chaco is a vast expanse of thorn scrub covering most of southeastern Bolivia and western Paraguay and stretching into neighboring Argentina. Dispersed throughout this wilderness are pockets of ranchers, isolated indigenous villages and Mennonite farming communities, as well as outposts of police and military troops. Wildlife abounds in the undisturbed and protected parts of the Chaco. With humans a relatively rare species, animals are bolder and more visible here than in the Amazon and this is one of the best places in South America (if also one of the more logistically difficult) to see large mammals like the tapir, jaguar and puma.

Plant life amazes with a series of bizarre (and often spiny) adaptations to the xeric environment. Apart from being prickled by various species of cacti, you'll be surprised by brilliant flowering bushes and trees, such as the yellow carnival bush; the white-and-yellow *huevo* (egg) tree; the pink or white thorny bottle tree, locally known as the *toboroche* or *palo borracho* (drunken tree), associated with various mythical legends; and the red-flowering, hard *quebracho* (axe-breaker) tree whose wood, too heavy to float, is one of the Chaco's main exports.

Villamontes

☑4 / POP 39,800 / ELEVATION 383M

Despite the heat and hot dry winds that coat everything with a thick layer of dust, Villamontes, officially Bolivia's hottest town, is a welcoming place. The majority-indigenous Guaraní population means that lovely woven baskets and furniture made from natural Chaco materials can be found in the market. Villamontes' biggest employer is the local gas plant, which is responsible for an influx of migrant workers from across the

---

❶ CROSSING THE BORDER TO PARAGUAY

Crossing the border into Paraguay is fairly easy. The infamous Ruta Trans-Chaco is paved along its entire length on the Paraguay side, though it takes a slight detour away from the original Trans-Chaco at La Patria; the detour crosses into Bolivia at the military checkpoint of Infante Rivarola. Several bus services from Santa Cruz via Villamontes now run this route to Asunción on a daily basis.

Bolivian customs formalities take place at Ibibobo. You will need to present your passport and visa to both customs and military representatives. Buses typically pass here around 4am or 5am, so don't expect a tranquil night's sleep. From here the Paraguayan border point, Infante Rivarola, is another hour or so away but Paraguayan customs formalities are not carried out until you are well beyond here, at the *aduana* (customs office) in Mariscal Estigarribia. Buses typically arrive here around 7am or 8am.

This is a notorious smuggling route so expect to be lined up with your bags as customs officials and sniffer dogs rifle through your private possessions. Once you are given the OK to proceed, you get your entry stamp from the small immigration office just outside the main compound. There is a service station here that sells food if you're peckish and, provided you are not carrying anything you shouldn't be, it is as simple as that!

SOUTH CENTRAL BOLIVIA & THE CHACO VILLAMONTES

RESERVA PRIVADA DE PATRIMONIO NATURAL DE CORBALÁN

This private 18 sq km **reserve** on the Paraguayan border was established in 1996 to protect a choice piece of Gran Chaco – its northern section is contiguous with the Paraguayan Reserva Privada Cañada del Carmen with which it shares a transnational conservation plan. Jaguars, pumas, tapirs, giant anteaters and giant armadillos are found here, though you'll more likely see Azara's fox, the three-banded armadillo and birds such as the blue-fronted Amazon parrot and Chaco chachalaca.

The only access route is a poor road from Villamontes, which takes at least four hours with a good vehicle. If you plan to visit, accommodations are limited to a simple park rangers' camp, and you'll need to bring your own food, water and other supplies. Ask at Prometa (p239) in Tarija for further information.

border in Paraguay. The 6pm whistle that rings out across town signals the end of the working day.

◉ Sights

Parque Nacional Serranía del Aguaragüe
NATIONAL PARK

The long and narrow 1080 sq km Aguaragüe National Park takes in much of the mountains of Serranía del Aguaragüe, which divide the vast Gran Chaco and the highlands of Tarija department. The park's name comes from Guaraní, meaning 'the lair of the jaguar,' because the range is famous for being home to this lovely spotty (and scary) cat. Foxes, tapirs, anteaters, assorted parrots, numerous plant species and 70% of the region's potable water sources can also be found here.

Right in the center of the region known for being the hottest in Bolivia, it is best visited in the cooler winter months (May to October). In the beautiful **Pilcomayo Canyon** at **El Chorro Grande** waterfall, fish are prevented from swimming further upstream. Abundant surubí, sábalo and dorado are easily caught, making the area a favorite with anglers from all over the country. The predatory dorado is prized by game fishers because of its legendary fight; it's particularly interesting because it has an odd hinge at the front of its jawbone that allows its mouth to open wide horizontally.

There are great views from the restaurants 7km to 10km west of Villamontes where you can sample local fish dishes.

Although it lacks visitor facilities, the Cañón del Pilcomayo is easily accessible from Villamontes. Take any Tarija-bound transportation, or taxi to the *tranca* (highway police post) and walk from there. Where the road forks, bear right and continue another 2km to the mouth of the gorge. Or, more conveniently, you can negotiate with a taxi driver in Villamontes. One of the tour companies in Tarija might be able to arrange a trip with sufficient notice and a minimum of three people.

🛏 Sleeping

Hotel El Rancho Olivo
HOTEL **$$$**

(📞 672-2059; www.elranchoolivo.com; Av Méndez Arcos; s/d/tr B$420/520/570; ❄ 🏧 @ 🛜 🌊) Only a few blocks from the bus station, this is the place of choice in Villamontes for those with a bit of money to spend. Stained wooden furniture and decorative lamps add a touch of luxury to the tile-floored rooms. A pleasant but pricey restaurant sits by the side; also a popular event space.

ⓘ Getting There & Away

Buses, *micros* and *trufis* run to Tarija (B$100, eight hours) and Santa Cruz (B$120, eight to 11 hours) after 6pm from the terminal two blocks west of the El Pescadito statue. *Trufis* for Camiri (B$30, two hours) leave when full from the main road a block north of El Pescadito, and for Yacuiba (B$20, 1½ hours) from three blocks south.

The main reason for stopping in Villamontes, however, is to catch a bus connection for Asunción in Paraguay (B$300, 15 hours) via the border crossing (p251) at Infante Rivarola before continuing on to the Trans-Chaco Road. All companies have their offices on the main road close to El Pescadito and buses pass through in the early hours of the morning. You should buy your ticket in advance, but you will be allocated to a bus irrespective of which company sold you the ticket. Unfortunately, the quality of service varies considerably between companies and which one you get is pot luck.

The *Ferroviaria Oriental* (www.fo.com.bo) to Yacuiba (B$11, 2¾ hours) passes through on Friday morning at 5am and returns to Santa Cruz (B$38, 14 hours) on Friday evening at 7:45pm, but the route is painfully slow. The train station is two blocks north of the bus terminal.

Santa Cruz & Gran Chiquitania

Best Places to Eat

➡ Sach'a Rest (p261)
➡ Café Jardín (p273)
➡ Jardín de Asia (p261)
➡ El Arriero (p261)
➡ Latina Café (p273)

Best Places to Stay

➡ Refugio los Volcánes (p269)
➡ CasaPatio Hotel Boutique (p260)
➡ Cosmopolitano (p260)
➡ Jodanga Backpackers Hostel (p259)
➡ Nómada (p272)

Why Go?

The Bolivian Oriente is not what you generally see in Bolivian tourist brochures. This tropical region, the country's most prosperous, has a palpable desire to differentiate itself from Bolivia's traditional highland image. The region's agriculture boom has brought about a rise in income and a standard of living unequaled by any other Bolivian province.

Santa Cruz is Bolivia's most populous city with a cosmopolitan population, yet it retains a small-town atmosphere. From here you can visit charming Jesuit mission towns with the country's loveliest examples of Jesuit architecture, tour pre-Inca ruins near the village of Samaipata or embark on a revolutionary pilgrimage to where Che Guevara met his maker around Vallegrande. Prefer nature? There are miles of hikes and tons of wildlife at Parque Nacional & Área de Uso Múltiple Amboró, the so-called 'elbow of the Andes' where the ecosystems of the Chaco, the Amazon Basin and the Andes meet.

When to Go
Santa Cruz

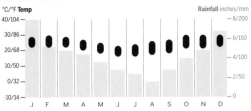

Apr Catch Santa Cruz's Theater Festival or Baroque Music Festival.

May–Aug Visit lowland Chiquitania now to avoid the worst of the heat.

Oct Join the faithful at Vallegrande's Che Festival, in memory of the revolutionary.

Santa Cruz & Gran Chiquitania Highlights

1 Jesuit Mission Circuit (p278) Traversing dusty roads and exploring beautifully restored churches.

2 Vallegrande (p274) Following in the footsteps of a legendary revolutionary on the Che Trail.

3 Santa Cruz (p255) Savoring the international cuisine in a modern city with a small-town feel.

4 Parque Nacional Amboró (p267) Hiking among giant ferns and spotting wildlife.

5 El Fuerte (p270) Exploring pre-Inca ruins and taking in the views.

6 Chochis (p283) Visiting a breathtaking sanctuary and snapping photographs of street art.

7 Samaipata (p269) Sipping coffee in artsy cafes

and eating vegetarian lunches at organic farms.

8 La Paraba Frente Roja Lodge (p277) Spotting the endangered macaw and other birds at this community lodge.

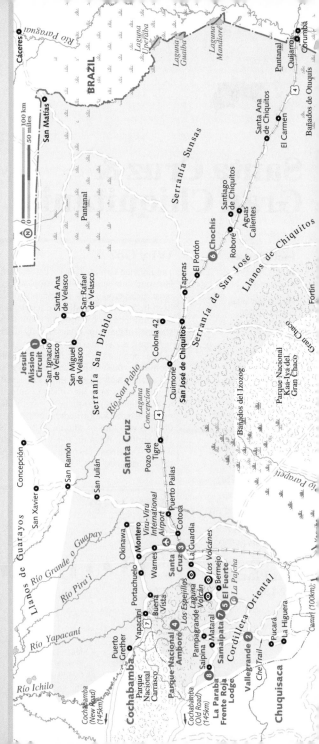

National Parks

Parque Nacional Amboró is an unquestion-able highlight of the region. In the south of the region the remote Parque Nacional Kaa-Iya del Gran Chaco is Latin America's largest park, but is largely inaccessible. Parque Nacional Noel Kempff Mercado is virtually closed to tourists these days, and most of the camps once used by visitors are in a state of disrepair or totally abandoned. Adventure-tour companies in Santa Cruz may be able to put together a package for you to visit these remote parks – expect it to be rough and expensive, though probably pretty exciting!

❶ Getting There & Away

Santa Cruz is the country's most connected city. Many flights from Europe and neighboring coun-tries fly directly to Santa Cruz and are worth considering if you're arriving from sea level and don't want to spend days acclimatizing in La Paz. International flights depart daily for Asunción, Buenos Aires, Miami, São Paulo and Rio de Ja-neiro, and there is a comprehensive network of domestic routes, though some destinations are reached only via Cochabamba.

Trains trundle south to Argentina and east to the Brazilian Pantanal, and long-distance bus routes crisscross the country to all major destinations.

SANTA CRUZ

🗩 3 / POP 1.4 MILLION / ELEV 417M (1368FT)

Santa Cruz may surprise you with its small-town feeling, colonial buildings and relaxed tropical atmosphere. Bolivia's largest city oozes modernity yet clings stubbornly to tradition. The city center is vibrant and thriving, its narrow streets crowded with suited businesspeople sipping *chicha* (a fermented-corn drink) at street stalls. Locals still lounge on benches in the main square listening to *camba* (eastern lowlands) music, restaurants close for siesta and little stores line the porch-fronted houses selling cheap, local products.

This is not the Bolivia that you see on postcards, but it is the place with the greatest population diversity in the country – from the overall-wearing Mennonites strolling past Goth kids, to the Japanese community, altiplano immigrants, Cuban doctors, Brazil-ian settlers and fashionable *cruceños* (Santa Cruz locals) cruising the tight streets in their SUVs. It's worth spending a few days here, eating at the international restaurants and checking out the nightlife.

⦿ Sights

Though the city has no standout sights there is plenty to see and do around town. If the heat saps your energy though you may prefer to just stroll around, sip a fruit juice in one of the city's many cafes or do some people-watching in the shade of the buzzing **Plaza 24 de Septiembre**.

Basílica Menor de San Lorenzo   CATHEDRAL
(Plaza 24 de Septiembre; ⦿7:30am-noon & 3-8pm Mon-Sat, 6:30am-1pm & 5-9pm Sun) **FREE**
Although the original cathedral on Plaza 24 de Septiembre was founded in 1605, the present structure dates from 1845 and wasn't consecrated until 1915. Inside, the decorative woodwork on the ceiling and silver plating around the altar are worth a look. There are good views of the city from the **bell tower** (Plaza 24 de Septiembre; B\$3; ⦿8am-noon & 3-6pm Tue, Thu, Sat & Sun).

Inside the church is a small **museum** (🖸332-4683; B\$10; ⦿9am-noon & 3-6pm Mon-Fri) displaying a collection of religious icons, vestments and medallions.

Casa Melchor Pinto   CULTURAL CENTER
(Sucre 50; ⦿9am-10pm Mon-Fri, 3-10pm Sat, 11am-7pm Sun) **FREE** This cultural center is in the impeccably restored family home of Dr Melchor Pinto Parada, a wealthy and influ-ential *cruceño* who died in 1982. There are several gallery spaces hosting temporary exhibitions, regular concerts and events as well as activities such as tango classes. Call in to see what's happening while you're in town.

Museo de Arte Contemporáneo   GALLERY
(MAC; Sucre; ⦿9am-noon & 3-8pm Mon-Fri) **FREE** In an appealing 1920s building with a breezy central patio, this small gallery displaying temporary exhibitions is worth a look for its thought-provoking contempo-rary pieces by Bolivian artists.

Museo de Historia Regional   MUSEUM
(🖸336-5533; Junín 151; ⦿8am-noon & 3-6:30pm Mon-Fri) **FREE** In the former home of the Gutiérrez Jiménez family, completed in 1920, this museum has four rooms with displays covering regional history. The first is dedicated to former president and *cru-ceño* Gabriel René Moreno, and there are further rooms containing displays on pre-Columbian history in Chiquitano, the Jesuit missions and the masks used in local festi-vals. All displays are in Spanish.

Santa Cruz

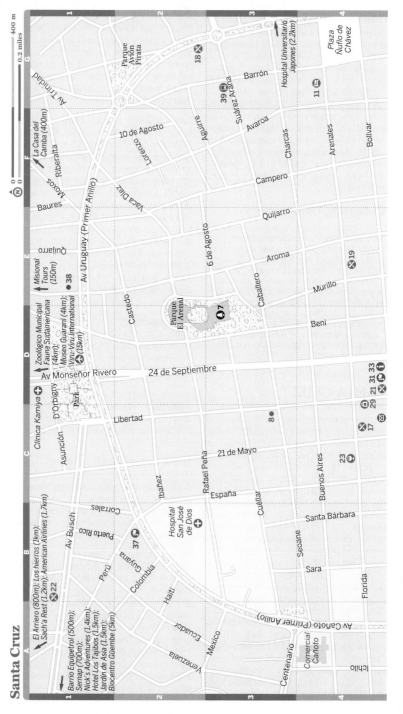

0.2 miles
400 m

El Arriero (800m); Los Iheríos (1km);
Sach'a Rest (1.2km); American Airlines (1.7km)

Barrio Equipetrol (500m);
Sernap (700m);
Nick's Adventures (1.4km);
Hotel Los Tajibos (1.5km);
Jardín de Asia (1.5km);
Biocentro Güembé (5km)

Clínica Kamiya

Zoológico Municipal
Fauna Sudamericana
(4km);
Museo Guaraní (4km);
Viru-Viru International
(15km)

Misional
Tours
(150m)

La Casa del
Camba (400m)

Parque
Avión
Pirata

Hospital Universitario
Japones (2.2km)

Plaza
Nuflo de
Chávez

Av Trinidad

Riberalta

Noxos

Baures

10 de Agosto

Lorenzo

Vaca Diez

Av Uruguay (Primer Anillo)

Castedo

Parque
El Arenal

Quijarro

Aguirre

6 de Agosto

Caballero

Suárez Arana

Barrón

Avaroa

Charcas

Campero

Quijarro

Aroma

Murillo

Beni

Arenales

Bolívar

Av Monseñor Rivero

24 de Septiembre

D'Orbigny

Park

Asunción

Libertad

21 de Mayo

Rafael Peña

España

Ibáñez

Cuéllar

Buenos Aires

Santa Bárbara

Seoane

Sara

Florida

Corrales

Av Busch

Puerto Rico

Guyana

Perú

Colombia

Haití

Hospital San José
de Dios

Ecuador

Venezuela

México

Centenario

Av Cañoto (Primer Anillo)

Comercial
Cañoto

Ichilo

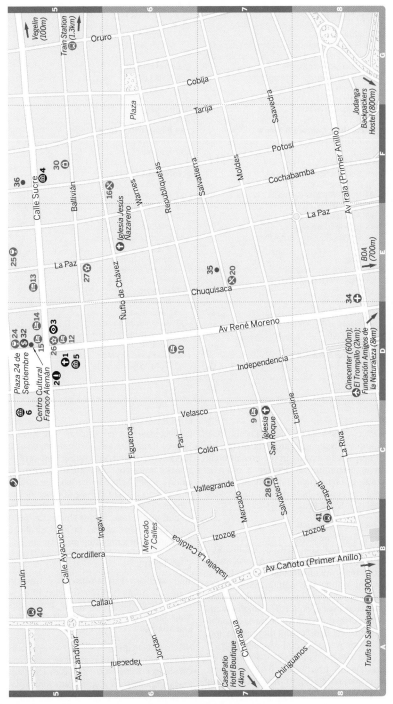

Santa Cruz

Parque El Arenal
PARK

(Murillo; ⊘8am-9pm) **FREE** Locals relax around the lagoon at Parque El Arenal, but it's best not to dawdle in the area at night. On an island in the lagoon, a bas-relief mural by renowned Bolivian artist Lorgio Vaca depicts historic and modern-day aspects of Santa Cruz.

Zoológico Municipal
Fauna Sudamericana
ZOO

(Radial 27; adult/child B$10/5; ⊘9am-5:30pm Tue-Sun) Santa Cruz zoo has a collection of native birds, mammals and reptiles kept in pleasingly humane conditions, although the llamas are a bit overdressed for the climate. Keep your eyes open for free-ranging sloths and squirrel monkeys in the trees. It's popular with local families and there can be long queues on weekends and school holidays.

Take *micro* (minibus) 55 from Vallegrande, 76 from Santa Bárbara or anything marked 'Zoológico.' Taxis for up to four people cost around B$20 from the center.

Museo Guaraní
MUSEUM

(www.facebook.com/museoguarani; Av Marcelo Terceros Bánzer, 3er anillo; ⊘9am-6pm Mon-Fri) **FREE** A small but interesting and professionally presented exhibition of Guaraní culture, located close to the zoo. The curator is happy to explain the significance of the exhibits, if you speak Spanish. Look for the animal masks and *tinajas* (huge clay pots) used for making *chicha* (a local alcoholic drink made by fermenting maize).

👉 Tours

Tour agencies can arrange day trips to Lomas de Arena (p261) and longer tours to Parque Nacional Amboró, the Jesuit missions and the jaguar conservation area of San Miguelito.

Nick's Adventures
TOURS

(📱334-1820; www.nicksadventuresbolivia.com; Celia Salmón, Edificio Isuto, office 208) Excellent tour company with a strong ethos of social responsibility and promoting conservation through tourism. Especially good for wildlife tours, including tours to the San Miguelito Jaguar Reserve and the Pantanal.

Misional Tours   TOURS
(🖰332-7709; www.misionaltours.com; Av Beni, 9th fl, Edificio Top Center, office 9-E; ⊘9am-12:30pm & 2-7pm Mon-Fri, 9am-1pm Sat) One of the most well-organized and reliable tour operators. Specializes in the Mission Circuit, but just as good for other attractions across Bolivia.

Bird Bolivia   BIRD-WATCHING
(🖰356-3636; www.birdbolivia.com) Professional birding and wildlife tours with expert guides for those with a special interest in nature. Based in Santa Cruz but without a public office; arrange tours by phone or email.

Amboró Tours   TOURS
(🖰339-0600, cell 7261-2515; www.amborotours. com; Libertad 417, 2nd fl; ⊘9am-noon & 2:30-6pm Mon-Wed, 9am-5pm Thu & Fri) Offers trips to Parque Nacional Amboró and the Pantanal. Ask about visiting Kaa-Iya and Noel Kempff Mercado national parks.

🎊 Festivals & Events

Carnaval   CULTURAL
(⊘Feb or Mar) If you're in Santa Cruz during Carnaval, you should most certainly head for the paintball-plagued streets and join in the collective chaos. Carnaval occurs annually in February or March, one week before Lent begins.

International Theater Festival   THEATER
(www.festivalesapac.com/teatro.htm; ⊘mid-Apr) Theater groups from all over the world perform in venues around the city. Held in odd-numbered years only, it's a great time to be in Santa Cruz.

Festival de Música
Misiones de Chiquitos   MUSIC
(www.festivalesapac.com/musica.htm; ⊘late Apr–early May) A 10-day biennial festival held in even-numbered years, celebrating the area's baroque musical tradition. Concerts are held in Santa Cruz and the Jesuit mission towns.

🛏 Sleeping

Santa Cruz's accommodations are more expensive than elsewhere in Bolivia, and those on a tight budget might find the quality of lodgings poor. Nonetheless, there are some good hostels and a growing number of midrange hotels, as well as some sleek boutique hotels. Luxury options are generally

away from the center and are more like resorts than hotels.

Nomad Hostel   HOSTEL $
(🖰7530-8001; www.facebook.com/nomad316; René Moreno 44; dm/d B$50/180) Still a work in progress at research time, Nomad opened in 2018 and is sure to become one of the city's best budget options. It's right on the edge of Plaza 24 de Septiembre; the hostel's roof terrace overlooks the cathedral. Dating from 1895, the building has been carefully restored to create a homey feel. Beds have thick mattresses.

★ Jodanga Backpackers Hostel   HOSTEL $$
(🖰339-6542; www.jodanga.com; El Fuerte 1380, Zona Parque Urbano; dm B$85-100, d/tr B$300/340, d without bathroom B$210; ❄@≋) This superbly equipped hostel has a pool, pool table and seriously groovy, air-conditioned rooms, as well as a party atmosphere inspired by its own bar. A quieter complex across the road houses three well-appointed rooms (with private bathroom) in converted shipping containers. Jodanga is near Parque Urbano in a leafy neighborhood, a 25-minute walk from the city center.

The hostel also organizes great-value Spanish classes from B$80 per hour.

Backpacker Bar & Suites   HOSTEL $$
(🖰339-8027; www.facebook.com/bedbarback packers; cnr Monseñor Salvatierra & Velasco; dm B$55-65, r B$190-250, r without bathroom B$150; ❄🛜) Occupying a prime corner plot near the city center, Backpacker is a solid option. Rooms are spacious and equipped with cable TV; some have a balcony. Facilities include a kitchen, book exchange, lockers, a bar (of course) and a terrace that's perfectly positioned for sunset views. Breakfast is included.

Hostal Río Magdalena   HOTEL $$
(🖰339-3011; www.facebook.com/Hostal-río-Mag dalena-1538060872938774; Arenales 653; s/d/ tr B$140/200/270; ❄🛜≋) This is an atmospheric midrange option with comfortable rooms, an inviting pool and a roof terrace with glorious views of the city.

Residencial Ikandire   HOTEL $$
(🖰339-3975; www.residencialikandire.com; Sucre 51; s/d from B$170/250, without bathroom from B$110/190; ❄) A converted 18th-century colonial house that retains a number of original features. Rooms are spacious, with high ceilings, fridge and cable TV. All in all this place isn't bad value compared to other

central options, and it's just half a block from the main plaza. Prices include breakfast.

Residencial Bolívar HOSTEL **$$**
(📞 334-2500; Sucre 131; dm B$100, r with shared bathroom B$220, s/d with private bathroom B$220/270; 🐦) It's been in business since 1905 and is reputedly the city's oldest hotel. There are leafy tropical patios, a toucan snoozing on a branch and clean, if small, rooms. You can laze in the hammocks or read in the courtyard and there is a kitchen for guests to use. Prices include breakfast.

★Cosmopolitano BOUTIQUE HOTEL **$$$**
(📞 332-3118; www.cosmopolitano.com.bo; Pari 70; r incl breakfast B$450-600; ❄@🐦) An oasis of contemporary design in the city center, the Cosmopolitano has just eight spacious rooms arranged on two levels around a central courtyard with a small pool. The aesthetic here is sleek lines, wood and concrete, with splashes of color and carefully chosen furniture, including modern and antique pieces. Staff are beyond helpful.

★CasaPatio Hotel Boutique BOUTIQUE HOTEL **$$$**
(📞 333-1728; www.casapatio-hotelboutique.com; Av Ibérica Calle 5, Las Palmas; s/d incl breakfast B$450/580, restaurant almuerzo B$30, mains B$39-46; ❄🐦🖥) Out by the fourth *anillo*, this boutique hotel is worth every boliviano. The rooms have a delicate, understated appeal, as well as quirky names such as the '*No se lo digas a nadie habitación matrimonial*' ('Don't tell anybody matrimonial suite'). The owners are warm, welcoming hosts and the patio is exquisite. You'll need to take taxis into town.

Hotel Los Tajibos HOTEL **$$$**
(📞 342-1000; www.lostajiboshotel.com; Av San Martín 455, Equipetrol; d/ste incl breakfast from B$1400/2400; ❄@🖥) From the impressive lobby with its grand, carved wooden doors and oversized chandelier to the huge pool and on-site art gallery, Los Tajibos has top-rate facilities and a luxurious feel. The 208 rooms are set in lush tropical gardens, patrolled by resident peacocks, and there are three on-site restaurants including the excellent Jardín de Asia (p261). A good choice for families.

Senses Boutique Hotel Plaza BOUTIQUE HOTEL **$$$**
(📞 339-6666; www.sensescorporacion.com; cnr Plaza 24 de Septiembre & Sucre; r incl breakfast from B$550; ❄@🖥) Prepare yourself for sensory overload at this modern hotel. From the reception area with its half-ball chairs and flat-screen TVs, down to the luxurious rooms with king-size beds and walk-in closets, the owners have gone all-out in the name of contemporary design. Look out for frequent special offers.

🍴 Eating

The international population has rolled up its sleeves and opened some fine restaurants, so what the city lacks in attractions it makes up for in gastronomic offerings. Av Monseñor Rivero is lined with snazzy restaurants that get posher, or more expensive, the further you walk from the center. At the other end of the scale, cheap fast-food joints line Ayacucho.

Vegelin VEGAN **$**
(www.facebook.com/vegelinhouse; Fray del Pilar 143; per kilo B$65; ⏰11:30am-2:30pm) Pile your plate high at this vegan buffet, which charges by weight (about B$20 to B$35 per plate). The dishes have a range of international influences and include vegan sushi, Italian pastas and Chinese-style stir-fries.

Hipermaxi SUPERMARKET **$**
(Flórida, near 21 de Mayo; ⏰7am-11pm) For a good variety of (relatively expensive) ingredients to prepare meals yourself, try this central supermarket.

El Aljibe BOLIVIAN **$$**
(Ñuflo de Chávez; mains B$35-65; ⏰noon-3am & 7-11:30pm Mon-Sat) A cute little restaurant in a charming old colonial house. It specializes in *comida típica* (typical food) which is increasingly difficult to find in cosmopolitan Santa Cruz.

Ken JAPANESE **$$**
(📞 333-3728; Uruguay 730; mains B$35-72; ⏰11:30am-3pm & 6-10:40pm Tue-Sun) Low-key Japanese restaurant dishing out reliable noodles and sushi. The *yaki soba* (stir-fried noodles) is massive, laden with chicken and cashews. Just check out all the folk from the Japanese community licking their lips in satisfaction.

La Casa del Camba BOLIVIAN **$$**
(www.casadelcamba.com; Av Cristóbal de Mendoza 539; mains B$35-95; ⏰11:30am-11:30pm) You are likely to end up at this lively, sprawling landmark if you ask Bolivian friends where to find the 'most typical' *cruceño/camba*

(local) experience. Juicy meat comes sizzling off the grill while live singers holler traditional tunes and straw-hatted waiters attend to your every need.

Aviator Wings & Beer AMERICAN $$
(3er anillo, Av San Martín, Equipetrol; mains B$35-80; ⊙noon-3pm Mon, noon-3pm & 6pm-1am Tue-Fri, 6pm-1am Sat & Sun) Cozy little resto-bar with a lively atmosphere. Great beer and burger selection, and delicious chicken wings.

Pizzería Marguerita PIZZA $$
(📞337-0285; Libertad 116, Plaza 24 de Septiembre; mains B$32-95; ⊙9am-midnight Mon-Fri, from 4pm Sat & Sun) Long known for its high-quality pizza, pasta and salads, and always popular with visitors for its central location, this convenient hangout on the north side of the plaza is good for a casual meal.

★**Sach'a Rest** PERUVIAN $$$
(www.facebook.com/sacharest; Av Profesor Noel Kempff 761, 3er anillo; mains B$75-150; ⊙6:30pm-midnight Mon-Fri, noon-4pm & 6:30pm-midnight Sat, noon-4pm Sun; 🐾) Lip-smackingly good Peruvian food served in a bright and modern dining room,

decorated with fab wall murals. The ceviches are made with fresh paiche, a local river fish, and come with a range of sauces including a killer *leche de tigre* (citrus marinade). The Pisco sours might be the best you'll find this side of Lima.

★**Jardín de Asia** FUSION $$$
(📞342-1000; www.jardindeasia.com; Av San Martín 455, Hotel Los Tajibos; mains B$110-179; ⊙noon-3pm & 7:30pm-1am Mon-Sat; 🐾) The chefs at Jardín de Asia fuse Bolivian ingredients with Asian flavors and culinary techniques to create original dishes with plenty of local flair, served in a candlelit setting. This stylish and atmospheric restaurant is the hottest ticket in town, so book ahead. Kick things off with a perfectly prepared cocktail.

★**El Arriero** STEAK $$$
(📞333-1694; www.facebook.com/elarrierobolivia; cnr Av San Martín & 4 Este, Equipetrol; mains B$70-184; ⊙noon-3pm & 7-11:30pm Mon-Sat, noon-3:30pm Sun; 🐾) Locals say this is the place to go for the country's best steaks and we agree. There's a buzz about El Arriero, with its multicolored cow statues, high-pitched roof and eye-catching central light sculpture. The

DAY TRIPS FROM SANTA CRUZ

Jardín Botánico (📞362-3101; Carretera a Cotoca KM 8½; adult/child B$10/5; ⊙8am-6pm) Santa Cruz's lush botanical gardens, 12km east of the city center, make for a tranquil escape from the urban scene. Covering more than 200 hectares, the gardens feature woodland trails, a lake, a cactarium (cactus garden) and plenty of exotic plants. Climb the wooden viewing platform for vistas across the treetop canopy to the city skyline. The gardens are teeming with wildlife, too; look out for tortoises and sloths.

To get here, take the green minibus marked Cotoca from the corner of Suárez Arana and Barrón and ask the driver to drop you at the entrance to the Jardín Botánico (B$2.50, 25 minutes).

Biocentro Güembé (📞370-0700; www.biocentroguembe.com; Km 5, Camino Porongo, Zona Urubó; adult/child B$150/50; ⊙8:30am-6pm) A great day trip from Santa Cruz, Biocentro Güembé (12km west of the city) has a butterfly farm, orchid exhibitions, 15 natural pools and sports facilities. You can go fishing and hiking in the surrounding forest. There's a restaurant with international cuisine, so you won't go hungry, and there are cabins and a campsite if you wish to stay the night.

It's best to travel by taxi from Santa Cruz. If it's a hot day get here early: the place fills up fast!

Lomas de Arena (📞327-0963; B$10; ⊙8:30am-5pm) This protected area, 12km south of Santa Cruz, is a strange and striking sandy desert that seems out of place in Santa Cruz's humid environs. It's a good spot for bird-watching and you may also see sloths. The best way to visit the dunes is on a half-day trip with a Santa Cruz tour company such as Nick's Adventures (p258), which include sandboarding. Bring sunscreen and water.

From Santa Cruz city center, bus 21 (B$2, 45 minutes) can drop you at the park entrance, from where it's a long, hot 7km walk to the dunes. It's also possible to come by taxi (about B$200), but unless you have a 4WD you will need to walk about 4km to reach the sand.

various beef cuts are imported from Argentina; portions are huge. Service is excellent.

La Casona
INTERNATIONAL $$$

(📋 337-8495; www.bistrolacasona.com; Arenales 222; mains B$52-140; ☺ 11:30am-midnight Mon-Sat) This German-run bistro has seating in a shady courtyard or inside, where colorful indigenous art adorns the walls. The food is diverse, with a variety of salads, German dishes or pasta in a spicy, palate-tingling *arrabbiata* (spicy tomato sauce). There's a good selection of beer and other drinks too.

Chalet La Suisse
SWISS $$$

(📋 343-6070; www.chaletlasuisse.com/santacruz; Los Gomeros 98; mains B$88-198; ☺ noon-2:30pm & 7pm-midnight Mon-Fri, 7pm-midnight Sat) Popular Swiss restaurant with a refined yet relaxed atmosphere. Consistently figures among the best restaurants in the city. Book ahead if you want to guarantee a table.

Yorimichi
JAPANESE $$$

(📋 334-7717; www.facebook.com/restaurantyorimichisrl; Av Busch 548; mains B$60-110; ☺ 6:30-11:30pm Mon-Sat, 11am-2:30pm Sun) This swish Japanese restaurant with bamboo screens separating eating spaces and traditional music tinkling from the speakers, this is the place to come for brilliant sushi, sashimi, tempura and heart-warming sips of sake. It's a favorite of upmarket *cruceños* (Santa Cruz locals).

Los Hierros
ARGENTINE $$$

(📋 337-1309; www.facebook.com/loshierrosbolivia; cnr Av San Martín & Calle 9; mains B$85-180; ☺ noon-3pm & 7pm-midnight) Argentinian-style *churrasquería* (grilled-meat restaurant) serving excellent steaks. Hanging on the wall is a rifle that supposedly once belonged to Butch Cassidy.

Michelangelo
ITALIAN $$$

(📋 334-8403; Chuquisaca 502; mains B$85-138; ☺ 7-11:30pm Mon, noon-2:30pm & 7-11:30pm Tue-Sat, noon-2:30pm Sun) Located in an elegant house, complete with fireplaces and marble floors, this is a good choice for a romantic evening or a little Italian self-indulgence, though sometimes the food doesn't match the classy surroundings. On the plus side, the pastas are homemade and there's a good wine list.

🍷 Drinking & Nightlife

The hippest nightspots are along Av San Martín, between the second and third *anillos* (rings) in **Barrio Equipetrol** (B$15 to $B20 taxi from the center). Hot spots change frequently so it's best to dress to impress, cruise the *piranhar* (strip) and see what catches your fancy. Cover charges cost B$20 to B$70. Most places don't warm up until 11pm.

★Patrimonio Cafetería SCZ
CAFE

(www.facebook.com/patrimoniocafescz; Sucre 50; ☺ 8am-11:30pm) The best lattes in town can be found at Patrimonio, a third-wave coffee shop serving brews made with beans from the Yungas, as well as sandwiches and cakes (B$27 to B$32). It's inside Casa Melchor Pinto (p255), a beautifully renovated former home which is now a cultural center and gallery. Drink your flat white in the breezy central patio.

★Duda Bar
BAR

(www.facebook.com/dudapub; Florída 228, 2nd fl; ☺ 9:30pm-2am Tue & Wed, to 3am Thu-Sat) There's a cool vibe to this colorful bar occupying the 1st floor of an elegant old building in the city center. Under plaster arches and between pillars you'll find retro furniture, badminton rackets and the odd garden gnome. Come for cocktails or beers.

Kiwi's
BAR

(Bolívar 208; ☺ 3-11pm Mon-Fri, 4pm-1am Sat) A laid-back place where you can sip on *bebidas extremas* (extreme drinks) served in two-liter receptacles. Great snacks and sandwiches too, all served with their trademark *papas kiwi* (kiwi potatoes; sandwiches B$16 to B$20).

A *milonga* (Argentine tango night) is held here on Saturday nights (B$20, including tango class).

Irish Pub
IRISH PUB

(Plaza 24 de Septiembre, Shopping Bolívar, 2nd fl; ☺ 9am-1am Mon-Sat, from 4pm Sun) On the east side of the plaza, this place is something of a second home to travelers in Santa Cruz. It serves comfort food such as Irish stew and chicken curry (mains B$70 to B$100), though most people while the hours away drinking beer and watching the goings-on in the plaza below.

☆ Entertainment

Cafe Lorca
LIVE MUSIC

(www.facebook.com/cafelorcasc; Sucre 8; ☺ 9am-midnight Mon-Thu, to 3am Fri & Sat, 6pm-midnight Sun) A meeting point for the city's arty and diversity-loving crowd, Lorca is perfect for a chilled caipirinha or mojito while you enjoy the live music (B$40 cover).

Tapekuá LIVE MUSIC
(☑ 334-5905; cnr La Paz & Ballivián; ⊙ 7:30pm-2:30am Wed-Sat) This casual yet upscale Swiss- and Bolivian-owned place serves good, earthy food (mains B$69 to B$85) and has live music most nights from 10:30pm (B$40 cover).

Cinecenter CINEMA
(https://cinecenter.com.bo/theater/cine-center-santa-cruz/; Av El Trompillo; tickets B$38-53) Twelve-screen cinema that shows all the latest Hollywood releases, located in a modern mall with a food court.

 Shopping

Av René Moreno is a good place for general souvenirs. Wood carvings from the tropical hardwoods *morado* and the more expensive *guayacán* are unique to Santa Cruz. Relief carvings on *tari* nuts make good, portable souvenirs. Locals also make beautiful macramé *llicas* (root-fiber bags). Note that prices are much higher here than in La Paz for llama- and alpaca-wool goods.

Artecampo ARTS & CRAFTS
(Salvatierra 407; ⊙ 9am-12:30pm & 3:30-7pm Mon-Fri, 9am-12.30pm Sat) The best place to find fine *artesanías* (locally handcrafted items), this store provides an outlet for the work of 1000 rural *cruceña* women and their families. The truly inspired and innovative pieces include leatherwork, hammocks, weavings, handmade paper, greeting cards and lovely natural-material lampshades.

Ventura Mall MALL
(☑ 343-2121; www.venturamall.bo; cnr Av San Martín & 4to anillo; ⊙ 10am-10pm Mon-Sat, from 11am Sun) Sleek, modern mall out by the fourth *anillo*, with a huge choice of international chain stores, bars, restaurants, banks and a cinema.

Paseo Artesanal La Recova ARTS & CRAFTS
(Libertad; ⊙ 9:30am-7:30pm Mon-Sat) An alleyway packed with little stores selling both authentic and fabricated handicrafts at reasonable prices.

🛈 **Orientation**

Roughly oval in shape, Santa Cruz is laid out in *anillos* (rings), which form concentric circles

around the city center, and *radiales* (spokes) that connect the rings. Radial 1, the road to Viru-Viru airport, runs roughly north–south; the *radiales* progress clockwise up to Radial 27.

Within the *primer anillo* (the first, innermost ring) Junín is the street with most banks, ATMs and internet cafes, and Av René Moreno is lined with souvenir stores and bars. To the northwest of the center, Av San Martín, otherwise known as Barrio Equipetrol, is the main area for the party crowd, being full of bars and clubs.

🛈 **Information**

DANGERS & ANNOYANCES
Beware of bogus immigration officials and carefully check the credentials of anyone who demands to see your passport or other ID. No real police officer will ever ask to see your documents in the street; be especially wary of 'civilian' police who will most certainly turn out to be fraudsters.

Police
Tourist Police (☑ 800-14-0099; Plaza 24 de Septiembre)

IMMIGRATION
Migración (☑ 351-9579; cnr Sucre & Quijarro, Edificio Guapay; ⊙ 7:30am-3pm Mon-Fri) Visa extensions are available here.

INTERNET ACCESS
There are numerous internet places along Junín and wi-fi in all but the very cheapest *residencial-es* (simple accommodations), so you will have no problem getting online.

LAUNDRY
Lavandería Fichalav (Salvatierra 142; per kilo B$17; ⊙ 8am-noon & 3-7pm Mon-Fri)

MEDICAL SERVICES
Clínica Foianini (☑ 336-2211; www.clinicafoianini.com; Av Irala 468) Hospital used by embassies, but be aware that some travelers have reported unnecessary tests and being required to stay longer than necessary to push up their bill.
Clínica Kamiya (☑ 336-3400; Av Monseñor Rivero 265)
Hospital San José de Dios (☑ 335-2866; Cuellar)
Hospital Universitario Japonés (☑ 346-2038; 3er anillo interno) On the third *anillo*, east side; recommended for inexpensive and professional medical treatment.

MONEY
ATMs line Junín and most major intersections. Street money changers shout '¡Dólares!' on the main plaza, but make sure you know the value

of what you are changing or use an official office (there are plenty nearby).

Casa de Cambio Alemán (Plaza 24 de Septiembre; ◷8:45am-12:30pm & 2:45-6:30pm Mon-Fri, 9am-12:30pm Sat) The easiest place to change cash. On the east side of the plaza.

POST

Main Post Office (Junín; ◷8am-8pm Mon-Sat, 9-11:30am Sun)

TELEPHONE

Tonytel (Junín 322) Local cell-phone rates are cheap. Chips with precharged credit can be bought here.

TOURIST INFORMATION

Online information about the city of Santa Cruz and the main attractions of the Oriente region can be found at www.visitbolivia.org.

Armonía Office (☑356-8808; www.armoniabolivia.org; Lomas de Arenas 400; ◷8:30am-12:30pm & 2:30-6pm Mon-Fri) Visit the Armonía office in Santa Cruz for more information about conservation programs and details on visiting the lodges.

Casa de Gobierno (Plaza 24 de Septiembre, Palacio Prefectural; ◷9am-5pm Mon-Fri) A small information kiosk on the north side of the plaza is good for quick inquiries, but has little or no printed information.

Fundación Amigos de la Naturaleza (FAN; ☑355-6800; www.fan-bo.org; Carr a Samaipata, Km 7.5; ◷8am-4:30pm Mon-Thu, to 2pm Fri) A good source of national parks information. It's west of town off the old Cochabamba road.

Infotur (☑336-9581; www.gmsantacruz.gob.bo; Sucre; ◷9am-noon & 3-7pm) Within the Museo de Arte Contemporáneo, this office provides information for the whole region and the rest of the country.

Servicio Nacional de Áreas Protegidas (Sernap; ☑339-4311; www.sernap.gob.bo; Calle Efesios 4, near Av Nueva Jerusalen; ◷8:30am-6:30pm Mon-Fri) Theoretically provides information on national parks, especially Amboró.

❶ Getting There & Away

AIR

Viru-Viru International Airport (p352), 15km north of the center, handles some domestic and most international flights. International destinations served by direct flights include Asunción, Buenos Aires, Lima, Madrid, Miami, Panama City, São Paulo and Santiago de Chile.

The smaller **Aeropuerto El Trompillo** (☑352-6600), in the southeast of the city receives some domestic flights.

Flights to national destinations leave frequently and it's easy enough to find a seat to anywhere, or at least a suitable connection via Cochabamba.

Aerolíneas Argentinas (☑333-9776; Junín 22; ◷8am-noon & 2:30-6:30pm Mon-Fri)

Amazonas (☑311-5393; Av Las Ramblas, Edificio ALAS 2, 4th fl, btwn Los Cedros & Av San Martín; ◷8:30am-12:30pm & 2:30-6:30pm Mon-Fri)

American Airlines (Map p61; ☑800-100-541; www.aa.com; Calle 15 No 8054, San Miguel; ◷9am-6pm Mon-Fri, to 1pm Sat); **Av San Martín office** (☑800-100-541; Av San Martín, Comercial Fidalga; ◷9am-6pm Mon-Fri, to 1pm Sat)

Boliviano de Aviación (BOA; ☑312-1343; www.boa.bo; Aroma, Edificio Casanova, 1st fl, office 7; ◷8:30am-12:30pm & 2:30-6:30pm Mon-Fri, 9am-1pm Sun)

TAM (☑353-2639; Aeropuerto el Trompillo; ◷8am-6:30pm Mon-Fri, to 1pm Sat)

BUS, MICRO & SHARED TAXI

The full-service **bimodal terminal** (☑348-8482; terminal fee B$3), the combined long-distance bus and train station, is 1.5km east of the center, just before the third *anillo* at the end of Av Brasil. For departmental destinations turn right on entering, for national and international destinations turn left.

The main part of the terminal is for *flotas* (long-distance buses) and the train; on the other side of the tunnel is the *micro* (minibus) terminal for regional services. Most *flotas* leave in the morning before 10am and in the evening after 6pm. Taking a series of connecting *micros* or taxis can be a faster, if more complicated way, of reaching regional destinations, rather than waiting all day for an evening *flota*.

To the Jesuit missions and Chiquitania, *flotas* leave in the morning and early evening (after 8pm). *Micros* run throughout the day, every two hours or so, but only go as far as Concepción. Buses to San Rafael, San Miguel and San Ignacio (B$60 to B$70, eight hours) run via San José de Chiquitos and depart between 6:30pm and 8pm.

Smaller *micros* and *trufis* (shared car or minibus) to regional destinations in Santa Cruz department leave regularly from outside the old bus terminal and less regularly from the *micro* platforms at the bimodal terminal. **Trufis to Buena Vista** (Izozog; B$23, two hours), wait on Izozog (Isoso), near the old bus terminal. **Trufis to Samaipata** (☑333-5067; cnr Av Grigota & Aruma, 2do anillo; B$30, three hours), leave from Calle Aruma near Av Grigota, one block past the 2do *anillo*. **Trufis to Vallegrande** (Doble Vía La Guardia, Km 6, behind the Shopping del Automóvil; B$60, five hours) depart from behind the shopping center 'Shopping del Auto-movil' at Km 6 on Doble Vía La Guardia, beyond the sixth *anillo*. *Flotas* to Vallegrande (B\$35) leave from the same place at 9am, 1pm, 3pm, 6:30pm and 7:30pm.

DESTINATION	COST (B\$)	TIME (HR)
Camiri	30-40	5
Cochabamba	80-131	10
Concepción	35	5
La Paz	100-220	17-18
Quijarro	70-150	9
San Xavier	35	4
San José de Chiquitos	50	4
San Matías	120-150	15
Sucre	70-120	13
Tarija	80-100	11-14
Trinidad	49-140	10-11
Yacuiba	70-100	8

TRAIN

Trains (☑ 338-7000; www.fo.com.bo; Av Internacional, Terminal Bimodel; ☺ ticket office 8am-12:30pm & 2:30-6pm Mon-Thu, to 4pm Fri, 8am-noon Sat, 4-6pm Sun) depart from the bimodal terminal bound for Yacuiba on the Argentine border and Quijarro on the Brazil border. For access to the platform you need to buy a platform ticket and show your passport to the platform guard.

The Yacuiba train departs at 3:30pm on Thursday (B\$47, 18 hours) and returns on Friday at 5pm arriving back in Santa Cruz at 9:55am. It runs via Villamontes (B\$38, 14 hours) – the connection point for buses to Paraguay – arriving inconveniently at 5:13am.

With the recent completion of the road paving all the way from Santa Cruz to Quijarro, the relevance of the Trans-Chiquitano train has declined sharply. No longer the harrowing journey that once earned this line the nickname 'Death Train,' these days its a nice lazy route, and is more comfortable than the bus if you have time on your hands.

Two types of train run this line via San José de Chiquitos and Roboré (for Santiago de Chiquitos). The slowest and cheapest service is the Expreso Oriental, departing Santa Cruz at 1:20pm on Monday, Wednesday and Friday, which operates a single comfortable Super Pullman class. The fastest, comfiest and priciest is the Ferrobus, departing Santa Cruz at 6pm on Tuesday, Thursday and Sunday. There is rarely a problem getting a seat from Santa Cruz or Quijarro, but if joining the service midway along the line then tickets are best bought in advance – only a limited number of seats are allotted for

these stations. Hot and cold food and drinks are available during daylight hours.

Expreso Oriental

ROUTE	COST (B\$)	ARRIVAL
Santa Cruz to San José	35	7:30pm
Santa Cruz to Roboré	50	11:42am
Santa Cruz to Quijarro	70	6:02am

Ferrobus

ROUTE	COST (B\$)	ARRIVAL
Santa Cruz to San José	70	11:08pm
Santa Cruz to Roboré	80	2:12am
Santa Cruz to Quijarro	120	7am

❶ Getting Around

TO/FROM THE AIRPORT

Handy **minibuses** (cnr Junín & 1er anillo; B\$6; ☺ every 20min 6:30am-10pm) leave Viru-Viru for the center (30 minutes). Taxis for up to four people cost B\$70 from Viru-Viru or B\$30 from the more central El Trompillo.

BUS

Santa Cruz's system of city *micros* connects the transportation terminals and all the *anillos* with the center. *Micros* 17 and 18 circulate around the first *anillo*. To reach Av San Martín in Barrio Equipetrol, take *micro* 23 from anywhere on Vallegrande. **Buses to the Jardín Botánico** (cnr Suárez Arana & Barrón) leave from the corner of Suárez Arana and Barrón. A *Guía de Micros* documenting all the city routes is available from bookstores and kiosks (B\$25 to B\$50).

CAR

Driving around the tight, one-way city streets can be a harrowing and confusing experience, but now that roads around the department have been paved, renting a car and getting out to explore is a more realistic possibility. Most rent-a-car companies have their offices at the airport.

TAXI

Taxis are cheap but there is no rigid price structure. Typically the price is higher if you are in a group, are carrying lots of luggage or wish to travel after 10pm, and drivers will quote a fee that they consider fair for the journey. If you think it is too much, refuse, and try the next one: there are plenty to choose from. Typically a trip for one person within the first *anillo* during the day is about B\$15, rising to B\$20 if you stray to the second *anillo*. Agree on your price in advance to avoid arguments.

AROUND SANTA CRUZ

Buena Vista

📞 3 / POP 14,400

Buena Vista is a nice little town two hours (103km) northwest of Santa Cruz, serving as an ideal staging point for trips into Parque Nacional Amboró's forested lowland section. Though most foreigners prefer Samaipata for national-park exploration, Buena Vista has some of the best places to view wildlife, observe birds and see local traditions. The downside is a sweatier, more humid climate and significantly less choice on where to stay and eat. The town website (www.buenavista.com.bo) is a good resource.

◉ Sights & Activities

**Iglesia de los
Santos Desposorios**   CHURCH
(Plaza Principal; ⊙ hours vary) FREE Buena Vista's Jesuit mission was founded in 1694 as the fifth mission in the Viceroyalty of Peru, but its current form dates from 1767. When the Jesuits were expelled from Bolivia later that year, the administration of the church passed to the bishop of Santa Cruz. The church is only open when the priest is around; he is often out of town from Monday to Thursday.

El Cairo   SWIMMING
This lovely swimming hole is an hour's walk from town. To get there, head downhill from the plaza past the *alcaldía* (town hall) and follow the road as it curves to the right. About 2km from town, take the unpaved left fork and cross over a bridge. El Cairo is further down, on the right.

Río Surutú   RIVER
Río Surutú is a popular excursion for locals, and there's a pleasant sandy beach ideal for picnics, swimming and camping during the dry season. From Buena Vista it's an easy 3km walk to the river bend's nearest town. The opposite bank is the boundary of Parque Nacional Amboró.

🛏 Sleeping

La Casona   PENSION $
(📞 932-2083; Plaza Principal; s/d B$100/150, per person without bathroom B$50; ☀) This is a colorful place on the western corner of the plaza, with a friendly owner and a nice patio with hammocks. The rooms are simple with good beds. Food is available on request.

Residencial Nadia   PENSION $
(📞 932-2049; Sevilla 186; s/d B$100/150, without bathroom B$40/80; ☀) Just off the northwest corner of the plaza, this is a budget option with spacious rooms in a friendly family home with a central patio.

Hotel Carmen   HOTEL $$
(📞 932-2135; Plaza Principal; r B$200, pool B$50; ☀) The simple rooms here are a bit pokey but comfortable enough; all have air-con, private bathroom and cable TV. The Carmen's big draw, though, is the fabulous pool surrounded by lawns – perfect for a posthike dip. It's on the south side of the plaza.

Hacienda El Cafetal   HOTEL $$$
(📞 935-2067, cell 7372-8911; incl breakfast d B$400, 4-person cabin B$500; P ☀ 🛜 ☀) Set up to support Bolivian coffee growers and their families, this hacienda is 5km southwest of town. The accommodations are good, with stylish, self-catering *cabañas* and suites, all with good views. You can go around the plantations and see how coffee is produced (tours B$35), taste different types of the strong black stuff, and then, caffeine-pumped, go bird-watching.

🍴 Eating

Cafe Rogelia   CAFE $
(Plaza Principal; snacks B$8-15; ⊙ 7am-9pm) A low-key snack bar on the south side of the plaza with a cheap and simple menu of sandwiches, empanadas, juices and other bits to pick at.

La Cunumisita   INTERNATIONAL $$
(Plaza Principal; mains B$30-110; ⊙ 9am-noon Tue-Sun) A surprisingly varied international menu with Chinese, Italian, Peruvian and French dishes among others, and some pleasant outdoor tables on the west side of the plaza to enjoy them at (if you can phase out the noise of passing motorbikes!). Breakfast is available until midday (B$15 to B$30).

❶ Information

Banco Fassil (Plaza) Has an ATM.
Tourist office (Plaza Principal; ⊙ 8am-noon & 2:30-6pm Mon-Fri) In the Casa Municipal de Turismo y Cultura on the southwest corner of the plaza; it can be helpful supplying names and contact numbers for guides.
Servicio Nacional de Áreas Protegidas (Sernap; 📞 932-2055; www.sernap.gov.bo; ⊙ 9am-noon & 2:30-6pm) Has information on Parque Nacional Amboró. Pick up an entry permit and ask about park regulations and accommodations options. It's a block south of the plaza.

ⓘ Getting There & Away

From Santa Cruz, *trufis* leave for Yapacaní (B$23, two hours) from Izozog (Isoso). Make it clear that you want to get off at Buena Vista. Returning *trufis* cruise around the plaza with horns blaring in search of passengers. Most go only as far as Montero (B$10, one hour), but you can catch a quick and easy onward connection to Santa Cruz there.

Moto-taxis loiter at the southwestern corner of the plaza and are a convenient way to get out into the countryside.

Parque Nacional & Área de Uso Múltiple Amboró

This 430,000-hectare park lies in a unique geographical position at the confluence of three distinct ecosystems: the Amazon Basin, the Chaco and the Andes.

The park was originally created in 1973 as the Reserva de Vida Silvestre Germán Busch, with an area of 180,000 hectares. In 1984, due to the efforts of British zoologist Robin Clarke and Bolivian biologist Noel Kempff Mercado, it was given national park status; in 1990 it was expanded to 630,000 hectares. In late 1995 however, amid controversy surrounding *campesino* (subsistence farmer) colonization inside park boundaries, it was pared down to its current size.

The park's range of habitats means that both highland and lowland species are found here. Mammals include elusive spectacled bears, jaguars, tapirs, peccaries and various monkeys, while more than 800 species of birds have been documented. The park is the stronghold of the endangered horned curassow, known as the unicorn bird.

Buena Vista Section

Access to the eastern part of the reserve requires crossing over the Río Surutú, either in a vehicle or on foot. Depending on the rainfall and weather, the river may be anywhere from knee- to waist-deep.

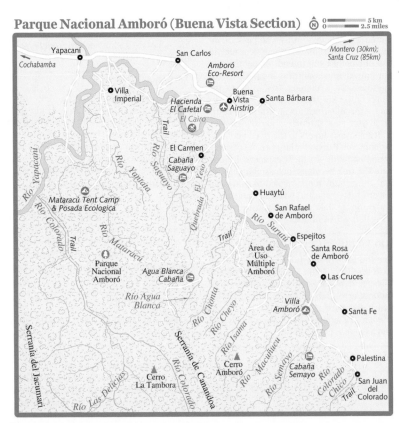

Parque Nacional Amboró (Buena Vista Section)

Inexperienced hikers should not attempt any of the treks in the park without a guide.

Note that at research time, Sernap had introduced a B$100 fee to enter the park. Supposedly, all visitors to the park must first pass by the Buena Vista office (p266) to pay the entrance fee and collect a ticket. However, the fee is disputed by communities living within the park, who continue to impose their own informal community fees on visitors. There is some question over whether the Sernap fee will be maintained and how it will be enforced going forward. At press time, it was not necessary to pay the Sernap fee to enter the park from the southern side.

Río Macuñucu

The Río Macuñucu route is the most popular into the Área de Uso Múltiple Amboró and begins at **Las Cruces**, 35km southeast of Buena Vista. From there it's 7km to the Río Surutú, which you must drive or wade across; just beyond the opposite bank you'll reach Villa Amboró where there is a **campsite** (☑ Adrian Rodríguez 7368-6784, Hugo Rojas 7368-6784; camping B$150). Villagers may charge an entrance fee to any tourist who passes their community en route to Macuñucu, regardless of whether you intend to stay there or not – avoid unpleasantness and pay.

From here a popular trek runs to the banks of the **Río Macuñucu** and follows its course through thick forest. After four hours or so you pass through a narrow canyon, which confines hikers to the river, and a little later you'll reach a large rock overhang accommodating up to 10 campers. Beyond here the trek becomes increasingly difficult and the terrain more rugged as you head toward some beautiful waterfalls and a second campsite. Take a guide if you are considering doing the full hike.

Río Isama & Cerro Amboró

The Río Isama route turns off at the village of **Espejitos**, 28km southeast of Buena Vista, and provides access to the base of 1300m Cerro Amboró, the bulbous peak for which the park is named. It's possible to climb to the summit, but it is a difficult trek and a guide is essential.

Mataracú

From near Yapacaní, on the main Cochabamba road, a 4WD track heads south across the Río Yapacaní into the northern reaches of the Área de Uso Múltiple Amboró and, after a rough 18km, rolls up to Amboró Eco-Resort's Mataracú Tent Camp (p269).

Samaipata Area

Samaipata sits just outside the southern boundary of the Área de Uso Múltiple Amboró and provides the best access point for the Andean section of the park. There's no real infrastructure, or any public facilities, in this area. The best guides to the region are available in Samaipata. A popular day hike is through a nearby cloud forest known for its giant ferns.

Mairana Area

From Mairana, it's 7km uphill along a walking track (or take a taxi) to **La Yunga**. It's in a particularly lush region of the Área de Uso Múltiple Amboró, surrounded by tree ferns and other cloud-forest vegetation. From La Yunga, a 16km forest traverse connects with the main road near Samaipata.

To enter the park here, visit the guard post at the south end of the soccer field in La Yunga. Access to Mairana is by *micro* (three-quarter-size bus) or taxi from Samaipata (B$7 per person).

Los Volcánes

The beautiful region known as **Los Volcánes** features an otherworldly landscape of tropical sugarloaf hills, right on the edge of the park boundary. The access point is the village of Bermejo, 85km southwest of Santa Cruz. It's marked by a hulking slab of red rock known as **El Portón del Diablo**, which is flaking and chipping into nascent natural arches.

Near here are several excellent accommodations and some good hikes. **Laguna Volcán** is an intriguing crater lake 6km up the hill north of Bermejo. A walking track climbs from the lake to the crater rim; it begins at the point directly across the lake from the end of the road.

Comarapa Area

Northwest of Comarapa, 4km toward Cochabamba, is a little-used entrance to the Área de Uso Múltiple Amboró. After the road crosses a pass between a hill and a ridge with a telephone tower, look for the minor road turning off to the northeast at the settlement of **Khara Huasi**. This road leads uphill to verdant stands of cloud forest, which blanket the peaks. The main attraction here is the Laguna Verde, a striking green lake with interpretive trails.

🛏 Sleeping

Ginger's Paradise   AGRITURISMO **$$**
(☑6777-4772, 7310-1864; www.gingersparadise.com; Barmejo; per person incl meals r/camping B$150/110, volunteer r/camping B$90/70) 🍃 A great place to stay in Barmejo is the pleasant eco/agrotouristic organic farm Ginger's Paradise, surrounded by virgin forest and run by an ex-rockstar. It's a hit with birdwatchers, offers reductions for working volunteers and is famed for its homegrown organic meals, included in the price.

★Refugio los Volcánes   LODGE **$$$**
(☑7316-6677; www.refugiolosvolcanes.com; Bermejo; s/d incl meals B$700/1200; P☎) 🍃 Folks rave about this place in the breathtaking Los Volcánes region, 5km up a dirt track off the Santa Cruz–Samaipata road, near Bermejo. Accommodations are in eco-friendly, solar-powered *cabañas* (cabins) with hot showers. Activities on offer include bird-watching and guided hikes through wonderfully wild landscapes, with pools for swimming. It's popular, so book well ahead.

Prices include meals such as pizza baked in a clay oven, and the coffee is made with beans grown at the Refugio. There is a **booking office** (Bolívar; ☑8:30am-noon & 2:30-7pm) in Samaipata.

Mataracú Tent Camp   CABAÑAS **$$$**
(☑932-2020, Santa Cruz 3-342-2372; www.mataracu.com; Mataracú; per person incl meals B$1000-1400; ☎) This jungle camp has a range of accommodations, from beds in tents to more comfortable cabins. It's surrounded by woodland, with a natural pool for dips on-site, plus waterfalls and hiking trails nearby. Meals at the on-site restaurant are included; book ahead through the Santa Cruz office. Access is by 4WD; transfers from **Amboró Eco-Resort** (☑932-2020; www.amboroecoresort.com; Ruta Nacional 4; s/d/ste incl breakfast B$418/523/594; P☎) cost US$100 per car.

ℹ Getting There & Away

By far the easiest and safest way to visit the park is by guided tour with one of the recommended tour agencies in Santa Cruz or Samaipata – not all the roads and paths are regularly maintained and an experienced guide will know the way around. To do it yourself, a *micro* heads south

HIKES IN PARQUE NACIONAL AMBORÓ

Bosque de Helechos Gigantes (Giant Fern Forest; trail B$15) Starting 17km north of Samaipata, just past Chorolque community, is a 11km trail through an ancient cloud forest famous for its giant ferns, some of them more than 4m high. To access the trail you need to be with a guide, so it's easiest to book a tour from Samaipata with transport included (from B$175 per person).

Codo de los Andes A turnoff to the community of Bella Vista, 100km from Santa Cruz on the Samaipata road, leads to a trail known as the Codo de los Andes, but check if it is passable before heading out. This dramatically beautiful area is a great place for spotting condors. Agencies in Samaipata and Santa Cruz offer guided hikes.

from Buena Vista through Huaytú, San Rafael de Amboró, Espejitos, Santa Rosa de Amboró, Las Cruces and Santa Fe. This boundary provides access to several rough routes and tracks that lead southwest into the interior, following tributaries of the Río Surutú. To really probe into the park though, you will need a 4WD and a good deal of previous experience in jungle trekking. Note that all access to the park along this road will require a crossing of the Río Surutú.

Samaipata
☑3 / POP 4400 / ELEV 1650M (5413FT)

Samaipata has developed into one of the top gringo-trail spots in eastern Bolivia, but don't let that put you off. This sleepy village in the foothills of the Cordillera Oriental has held on to its tranquil vibe, and since it's now brimming with well-run hostels and restaurants, you can enjoy a decent coffee as well as stunning views of the verdant landscape.

Visitors come to see the pre-Inca site of El Fuerte; some come searching for a dose of the ancient site's supposed mystical energy. Increasingly Samaipata is the main jumping-off point for forays to Parque Nacional Amboró. It's also a popular weekend destination for *cruceños* (Santa Cruz locals) seeking to escape the city. The Quechua name, meaning 'Rest in the Highlands,' could hardly be more appropriate.

Samaipata

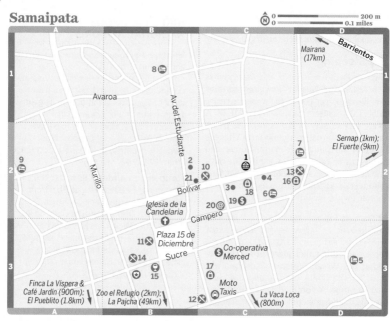

Samaipata

⊙ Sights

★ El Fuerte
RUINS

(B$50; ☺9am-4:30pm) The mystical site of El Fuerte exudes such pulling power that visitors from all over the world come to Samaipata just to climb the hill and see the remains of this pre-Inca site. A designated Unesco World Heritage Site since 1998, El Fuerte occupies a hilltop about 10km from Samaipata and offers breathtaking views across the valleys.

Allow at least two hours to fully explore the complex, and take sunscreen and a hat with you.

First occupied by diverse ethnic groups as early as 2000 BC, it wasn't until AD 1470 that the Incas, the most famous tenants, first arrived. By the time the Spanish came and looted the site in the 1600s it was already deserted. The purpose of El Fuerte has long been debated, and there are several theories. The conquistadors, in a distinctly combative frame of mind, assumed the site had been used for defense, hence its Spanish name, 'the fort.' In 1832 French naturalist Alcide d'Orbigny proclaimed that the pools and parallel canals had been used for washing gold. In 1936 German anthropologist Leo Pucher described it as an ancient temple to the serpent and the jaguar; his theory, incorporating worship of the sun and moon, is now the most accepted. Recently the place has gained a New Age following; some have claimed that it was a take-off and landing ramp for ancient spacecraft.

There are no standing buildings, but the remains of 500 dwellings have been discovered in the immediate vicinity and ongoing excavation reveals more every day. The **main site**, which is almost certainly of religious significance, is a 100m-long stone slab with a variety of sculpted features: seats, tables, a conference circle, troughs, tanks, conduits and *hornecinos* (niches), which are believed to have held idols. A total of seven steps leading up to the main temple represent the seven phases of the moon. Zoomorphic designs on the slab include raised reliefs of pumas and jaguars (representing power) and numerous serpents (representing fertility). *Chicha* (fermented corn) and blood were poured into the snake designs as an offering to Pachamama (Mother Earth). Sadly, these designs are unprotected from the elements and erosion is making them harder to discern with every passing year.

About 300m down an obscure track behind the main ruin is **Chincana**, a sinister hole in the ground that appears all the more menacing by the concealing vegetation and sloping ground around it. It's almost certainly natural, but three theories have emerged about how it might have been used: that it served as a water-storage cistern; that it functioned as an escape-proof prison; and that it was part of a subterranean communication system between the main ruin and its immediate surroundings.

On the approach to the site look out for **La Cabeza del Inca**, apparently a natural rock formation that bears a startling resemblance to the head of an Inca warrior, so much so that many insist it is a human-made project that was abandoned halfway

through. Watch too for condors soaring on thermals overhead.

There are two **observation towers** that allow visitors to view the ruins from above, and a kiosk with food and water next to the ticket office.

Taxis for the round-trip, including a two-hour wait at the ruins, charge B$100 for up to four people from Samaipata. Gluttons for punishment who prefer to walk up should follow the main highway back toward Santa Cruz for 3.5km and turn right at the sign pointing uphill. From here it's 5km to the summit.

Museo Arqueológico   MUSEUM
(Bolívar; B$5, museum & El Fuerte B$50; ⊙8am-noon & 2-6pm Mon-Fri, 8am-4pm Sat & Sun) Samaipata's small archaeological museum displays pieces excavated from El Fuerte and provides information about the site. It's worth coming here before visiting the ruins. There are five, well-arranged rooms with artifacts from different peoples and periods, with good explanations.

Zoo El Refugio   ZOO
(☑944-6169; adult/child B$20/10; ⊙8:30am-6pm) This charming and responsible little zoo is a refuge for rescued animals. The zoo accepts volunteers (one month minimum) who can lodge for free in exchange for their labor, and there is an attractive wooded campsite if you fancy spending a night among the animals. Horses are available for hire for B$40 per hour.

It's a pleasant 3km walk here, heading south from Samaipata.

🕝 Tours
Several agencies organize trips to nearby attractions and almost every hotel runs its own tours. Local taxi syndicates also run transportation to many of the local attractions and rates are very reasonable, though not up for negotiation.

Jukumari Tours   TOURS
(☑7576-0013; www.facebook.com/jukumaritours; Av del Estudiante) An excellent locally run agency; in addition to the local attractions it offers packages to the Che Trail and the Jesuit Mission Circuit.

Roadrunners   TOURS
(☑944-6294; Bolívar) Visit Olaf and Frank at German- and English-speaking Roadrunners for guided hikes to Amboró's waterfalls, cloud forests and El Fuerte (p270).

WATERFALLS NEAR SAMAIPATA

La Pajcha (B$10) This series of three beautiful waterfalls on a turbid mountain river plunge 45m into a dreamy tropical lagoon. La Pajcha has a sandy beach for swimming and some inviting campsites. It's 42km south of Samaipata, toward San Juan, where there is a turnoff that leads 7km to the falls. The site is privately owned and visitors are charged B$10 to swim here.

The easiest way to get here is in a taxi from the plaza in Samaipata (B$250, one hour), or on a tour.

Las Cuevas (B$15; ⊙ 8:30am-6pm) These three lovely waterfalls are 20km east of Samaipata on the road to Santa Cruz. Walk upstream on a clear path away from the road to reach two of the waterfalls, spilling into swimmable lagoons bordered by sandy beaches. About 100m beyond is the third waterfall, the biggest of the set. It gets busy at weekends. Taxis from Samaipata charge B$100 with a two-hour wait. Alternatively, jump on a bus or *trufi* (shared car or minibus) heading toward Santa Cruz.

Michael Blendinger Tours TOURS
(☑ 944-6227; www.discoveringbolivia.com; Bolívar; ⊙ 9am-7:30pm Mon-Sat, 10am-2pm & 5-8pm Sun) Biologist-run orchid, birding and full-moon tours, in English and German.

🛏 Sleeping

El Jardín HOSTEL $
(☑ 7311-9461; www.eljardinsamaipata.blogspot.com; Arenales; camping per person B$25, s/d B$35/80, cupola r B$130) Hippy-style hangout squirreled away in a wild garden in the southeast corner of town. Chilled music, basic digs and a relaxed scene for those who like to take it easy. There is a kitchen for guest use and a pair of unique cupola rooms if you can't abide the idea of a room with corners.

Hostal Siles PENSION $
(☑ 944-6408; Campero; s/d B$60/100, without bathroom B$40/80; 🛜) A neat and tidy little hostel. Rooms are simple but well kept and there is even a communal kitchen for those who prefer to cook for themselves. The roof terrace with hill views is a plus.

Hotel Colibri PENSION $
(☑ 944-6086; jcesarvalenzuelarocha@gmail.com; Bolívar 20; s/d incl breakfast B$140/180, r without bathroom B$120; 🛜) Minimalist whitewashed rooms, some with private bathroom and TV, are set around the standard shady courtyard, which is liberally scattered with hanging plants.

★ Nómada HOSTEL $$
(☑ 944-6446, cell 7782-8132; www.facebook.com/nomadahostelresto; Avaroa, Plaza del Estudiante; incl breakfast, camping per person B$45, dm/s/d

B$77/195/305, s/d without bathroom B$130/191; ⊙ cafe 8am-4pm Thu, to 9pm Fri & Sat) Care has been taken to make this hostel a welcoming and relaxing place. Rooms are cozy and decorated with local fabrics and original artwork, and there are gorgeous gardens with fruit trees. The on-site cafe has a changing menu of local dishes and pizzas (B$40 to B$90); on public holidays, the Argentinian owners fire up the barbecue.

Finca La Víspera CABIN $$
(☑ 944-6362; www.lavispera.org; campsite per person B$40, d B$350, cabins for 2/3/7 people B$480/520/1100) 🍃 This relaxing organic farm and retreat is a lovely place on the outskirts of Samaipata. The attractive rooms with shared kitchen, and five self-contained guesthouses (for two to seven people), enjoy commanding views across the valley. The campsite includes hot showers and kitchen facilities. It's an easy 15-minute walk southwest of the plaza.

Guests can eat breakfast and lunch at Café Jardín (p273) and help themselves to vegetables from the garden for dinner.

La Posada del Sol HOTEL $$
(☑ 944-6366; www.laposadadelsol.info; Avarao; s/d incl breakfast B$140/220; ❄🛜) A pleasant, midrange choice with spacious rooms set around an attractive garden with spectacular views. It's three blocks north of the plaza, heading uphill.

★ El Pueblito RESORT $$$
(☑ 944-6383; www.elpueblitoresort.com; Carr Valle Abajo 1000; s/d incl breakfast B$400/550, house d/tr/q B$700/850/1000; 🅿🛜❄) This four-star resort is arranged like a little

village complete with its own church and plaza. Each room is uniquely styled after a village shop and positively dripping with creativity. There's a swimming pool (B$40 for nonguests), *artesanía* shops and an excellent **restaurant-bar** (El Pueblito; mains B$20-70; ☺noon-2:30pm & 6:30-8:30pm).The resort is set on a hillside with marvelous views of Samaipata in the valley below.

✕ Eating

La Pizzeria   PIZZA **$**
(Arenales; small pizzas B$7-12; ☺5:30-9:30pm) Great-value, thin-crust pizzas are served hot from the oven at this cozy little joint opposite the market.

Caffé Art   CAFE **$**
(www.facebook.com/atteliersandraserrate; Bolívar 111; snacks B$6-25; ☺3-7:30pm Mon-Thu, 8:30am-12:30pm & 2:30-7.30pm Fri-Sun; 🐾) As well as serving coffee, juices, cakes, pies and snacks, this cafe doubles as a gallery for the work of artist Sandra Serrate, whose studio occupies part of the space. Almost every surface in the cafe is painted with beautiful flower motifs, from the wooden tables and chairs to the lampshades and napkin holders. Her pieces are also for sale.

★Café Jardín   HEALTH FOOD **$$**
(Finca La Víspera; mains B$40-60; ☺8am-3pm; 🖊) 🍃 Gaze at Finca La Víspera's (p272) organic garden from its sunny, alfresco cafe and see kitchen staff running up and down to pick your salad fresh from the ground. Famed for its slow food, this vegetarian cafe serves all-day breakfasts and lunches, and special dietary needs are catered for on request. Finish your meal with a tea infusion made with homegrown herbs.

From Samaipata it's a pleasant 20-minute walk here, heading south from the village.

★Latina Café   INTERNATIONAL **$$**
(📞944-6153; www.facebook.com/latinacafe samaipata; Bolívar 3; mains B$35-70; ☺6-10pm Mon & Wed-Fri, noon-2:30pm & 6-10:30pm Sat, noon-3pm & 6-10pm Sun) This bar-restaurant serves some of the best food in town: juicy steak, saucy pasta, vegetarian delights and gorgeous brownies. The lighting is intimate and the sunsets beautiful. Happy hour is from 6pm to 7pm.

Tierra Libre   INTERNATIONAL **$$**
(Sucre 70; mains B$30-65, sandwiches B$25-45; ☺11am-10pm Wed-Mon; 🐾) This place is loved by backpackers for its ample and affordable eats and pleasant garden to enjoy them in. Top-notch dishes from around the globe are served in a bohemian setting. Veggie meals are among those on offer as well as hearty soups and meaty treats including succulent *lomo* (steak).

Luna Verde   INTERNATIONAL **$$**
(Posada del Sol; mains B$50-60; 🐾) Tasty Tex-Mex dishes with a choice of salads and sides. Pick your main course, your accompaniments, grab yourself a refreshing cocktail and enjoy your evening. Great breakfasts too.

La Chakana   INTERNATIONAL **$$**
(Rubén Terrazas, Plaza 15 de Diciembre; mains B$26-60; ☺8am-10:45pm; 🐾) The long-established Chakana, on the west side of the plaza, serves reasonably priced breakfasts, sandwiches, vegetarian meals, excellent pizzas, homemade sweets, cocktails and European specialties.

La Vaca Loca   ICE CREAM **$$**
(www.facebook.com/restaurantelavacaloca; Camino a San Juan; mains B$45-72, pools adult/child B$20/30; ☺10:30am-6:30pm Thu-Sun) This is where Samaipatans go for ice cream. It's 1km south of town in an alpine-style chalet, overlooking gardens with a children's play area and three pools. The menu features beef, *milanesas* (breaded cutlets), pasta and pizza, as well as pancakes and coffee.

🍷 Drinking & Nightlife

Stroll around the main square and take your pick from a number of cafes and bars.

★La Boheme   BAR
(Plaza 15 de Diciembre, cnr Sucre & Rubén Terrazas; ☺5-11pm Tue-Thu & Sun, to 2am Fri & Sat; 🐾) This bumping little bar on the south corner of the plaza has a wide selection of intoxicating cocktails and, if you get the munchies, a chalkboard snack menu of burgers and sandwiches (B$22 to B$28). With 15 different beers to try on the starry roof terrace you have good reason to keep going back. Happy hour is 5pm to 7pm.

🛍 Shopping

Mucho Mundo   ARTS & CRAFTS
(Bolívar; ☺9am-7pm Tue-Sun) Sells all kinds of bric-a-brac designed by a group of resident

artists. One of several similar places along this street.

Asopec ARTS & CRAFTS
(Asociación de Productoras Ecológicas; Campero; ☺9am-2pm Sat & Sun) Asopec offers *artesanías* (artisan goods) produced and sold by Bolivian women from local communities, with all proceeds going to the makers. Wool, ceramics, soap, candles, liquor and honey are on offer. During the week opening hours are irregular.

Information

INTERNET ACCESS
Internet Sebastián (Campero; per hour B$4; ☺8am-9pm)

MONEY
Banco Union (Campero) Samaipata's only ATM. Accepts Visa, but not all foreign cards.

Co-operativa Merced (🖉944-6171; Sucre; ☺8am-noon & 2:30-6pm Mon-Fri, 8:30am-12:30pm Sat) If the ATM on Campero is down you can draw cash on a credit card with your passport here.

TOURIST INFORMATION
There is no official tourist office, though many of the tour companies and hostels can help you with information about the local sites.

Check out Samaipata's excellent tourist website www.samaipata.info.

Servicio Nacional de Áreas Protegidas The park's office is 1km outside of town on the road to Santa Cruz.

Getting There & Away

Trufis (p264; shared car or minibus) run throughout the day when full between Santa Cruz and Samaipata (B$30, three hours). From Samaipata, services depart from the main plaza.

The quickest and easiest way to get to Vallegrande is to organize a group and take a *trufi* (around B$300 for a carload to Vallegrande).

For Cochabamba buses leave from nearby Mairana (15km west of Samaipata) at 8am and 3pm (seven hours, B$80). A taxi to Mairana costs B$7 per person.

Buses to Sucre leave at 8pm from opposite the gas station on the main road. Buy tickets in advance from Nueva Turista cafe (10 hours, B$100).

Getting Around

There are a few hills and dirt roads in Samaipata. A quick and easy way to navigate is by **moto taxi**

(Arenales), some of which hang around near the market. Expect to pay around B$4 one way.

Vallegrande

🖉3 / POP 17,200 / ELEV 2100M (6890FT)

Vallegrande's claim to fame is that it was the spot where Che Guevara's corpse was exhibited before its burial, and it is the main base for the **Che Trail**, a community-based tourism project. The trail follows Che's final movements through the hills near La Higuera, the school where he was held as a prisoner after he was captured and where he was killed, and sites in Vallegrande where his body was brought and later buried.

Most visitors to the town are passing through on a Che pilgrimage, but Vallegrande is also a nice spot to relax and walk in the hills. It's a quiet little town set in the Andean foothills and that enjoys a lovely temperate climate.

◉ Sights

Museo del Che MUSEUM
(Av Ernesto Che Guevara; B$15; ☺8am-noon & 2-6pm Mon-Sat, 8am-noon Sun) This museum is inside the impressive **Centro Cultural Ernesto Che Guevara**, which was completed in 2016 in time for the 50th anniversary of Che's death the following year. It contains a photo-documentary of events leading to the capture of Che and of the days immediately afterward, featuring objects and artifacts that belonged to the guerrilla group. There is also a copy of Che's diary detailing his time in Bolivia.

El Mausoleo del Che MAUSOLEUM
(Che's Mausoleum; Av Ernesto Che Guevara) In 1995, 28 years after Che's death, a soldier who carried out the burial revealed that Che's body lay beneath Vallegrande's airstrip. After two years of searching, Che's body was discovered in 1997. The spot is marked by a mausoleum adorned with the smiling image of Che beaming out across the valley.

The Bolivian and Cuban governments had him exhumed and officially reburied in Santa Clara, Cuba on October 17, 1997. The interior can only be visited by guided tour (p276).

Hospital Señor de Malta HISTORIC SITE
(Señor de Malta) After Che's execution in La Higuera, south of Vallegrande, his body was brought to the hospital laundry and put

on display for the world's press. The hospital still functions, but the laundry itself has been cordoned off as a pilgrimage site, where graffiti pays homage to this controversial figure. The laundry can only be visited as part of a guided tour (p276).

✦ Festivals & Events

Che Guevara Festival   CULTURAL
(☉ Oct) Since the bodies of Che and several of his comrades were recovered from the airport in 1997, the town has celebrated an annual Che Guevara festival in October, featuring folk art and cultural activities.

🛏 Sleeping

Hostal El Marques   HOTEL $
(☎ 942-2336; Pedro Montaño; s/d incl breakfast B$120/170) Hidden away a block south of the Mercado Campesino, this nice hotel has rooms with lovely wooden furniture, attractive decor and cable TV; the best rooms have balconies overlooking the valley.

SANTA CRUZ & GRAN CHIQUITANIA VALLEGRANDE

HASTA SIEMPRE, COMANDANTE

As you travel around Bolivia, the iconic image of Che – the revolutionary with a popularity status reached only by rock stars, and remembered in Cuban songs such as 'Hasta siempre, Comandante' (Forever with You, Commander) – will be staring at you from various walls, paintings, posters and carvings. Bolivia is where Che met his death and where his image has been fervently resurrected.

Fresh from revolutionary success in Cuba (and frustrating failure in the Congo), Ernesto 'Che' Guevara de la Serna was in search of a new project when he heard about the oppression of the working classes by dictator René Barrientos Ortuño's military government in Bolivia. Strategically located in the heart of South America, Bolivia seemed like the perfect place from which to launch the socialist revolution on the continent.

Che's Bolivian base was established in 1966 at the farm Ñancahuazú, 250km southwest of Santa Cruz. Initially his co-revolutionaries had no idea who he was, and only when his trademark beard began to grow back (he had shaved it off to arrive incognito in Bolivia) did they realize that they were in the presence of a living legend. Che hoped to convince the campesinos (subsistence farmers) that they were oppressed and to inspire them to social rebellion, but was surprised to be met only with suspicion. In fact a cunning move by Ortuño to grant campesinos rights to their land had guaranteed their support and all but doomed Che's revolution to failure before it had even begun.

Bolivian Diary was written by Che during the final months of his life. Despite occasional minor setbacks Che considered things to be moving along nicely and in his last entry on October 7, 1967, 11 months after his arrival in Bolivia, he wrote that the plan was proceeding 'without complications.'

The following day he was captured near La Higuera by CIA-trained Bolivian troops under the command of Capitán Gary Prado Salmón, receiving bullet wounds to the legs, neck and shoulder. He was taken to a schoolroom in La Higuera and, just after noon on October 9, he was executed in a flurry of bullets fired by Sergeant Mario Terán, who had asked for the job following the deaths of several of his close friends in gun fights with the guerrillas.

The body was flown to Vallegrande, where it was displayed in the hospital laundry room to prove to the whole world that 'El Che' was finally dead. Local women noted an uncanny resemblance to the Catholic Christ and took locks of his hair as mementos, while the untimely deaths of many of those involved in his capture and assassination has led to widespread belief in the 'Curse of Che,' a sort of Tutankhamen-style beyond-the-grave retribution.

In October 2017, thousands of visitors from around the world descended on Vallegrande to commemorate the 50th anniversary of Che's death. Evo Morales and Che's four children also attended the events, many of them held in Vallegrande's impressive Centro Cultural Ernesto Che Guevara, completed the year before in preparation for the anniversary. Every year new murals appear at the hospital laundry where Che's body was displayed, and flags and personal letters to Che are left in the schoolhouse at La Higuera by travelers wishing to pay tribute to the revolutionary. Their message is scrawled across the museum walls: Che vive! (Che lives on!).

ⓘ TOURING THE RUTA DEL CHE

The tourist office on the east side of the plaza runs the **Ruta del Che City Tour** (B$40; ☺ tours depart 8:30am, 11:30am, 2:30pm & 5pm Mon-Sat, 8:30am & 11:30am Sun) with a fixed timetable. These excellent two-hour guided walking tours cover the Che Guevara sights in Vallegrande. Starting at the tourist office, the tour visits the laundry at the Hospital Señor de Malta (p274), La Fosa de los Guerrilleros, where 12 guerrillas are buried, and the Che Guevara Cultural Center, containing Che's mausoleum (p274) and the Museo de Che (p274). Only one of the four guides speaks English, so if you don't speak Spanish ask if she's available to be your guide. Entrance fees are included in the tour price.

Longer tours including La Higuera and sites outside town start from B$250 per car. It's possible to go to La Higuera in the morning and return to Vallegrande in time to do the city tour in the afternoon. This way you see the sites in chronological order.

Hostal Juanita
HOSTEL **$**

(☎ 942-2231; Manuel María Caballero 123; s/d B$80/160, with shared bathroom B$60/120) This is a family-run hostel just two blocks southwest of the plaza, where you get decent value for money and a flowery courtyard with a fountain. It's a long-term favorite of budget tour groups.

Plaza Pueblo Hotel
HOTEL **$$**

(☎ 942-2630, cell 7503-1880; Virrey Mendoza 132; s/d incl breakfast B$120/200; P �rm) Two and a half blocks uphill from the Mercado Campesino, Plaza Pueblo has plain, motel-style rooms and friendly, helpful staff. Though it's hardly luxurious, it is one of Vallegrande's more high-end sleeping options and is a comfortable enough place to rest your head after a day out exploring the Che trail.

✗ Eating & Drinking

Mercado Samuel Villazón
MARKET **$**

(Virrey Mendoza; snacks B$1-10; ☺ 6am-4pm) One of four markets in Vallegrande, Mercado Samuel Villazón is great for a breakfast smoothie and excellent baked goods, such as *pan de maíz con queso* (corn bread with cheese).

El Mirador
BOLIVIAN **$$**

(☎ 942-2341; El Pichacu; mains B$35-80; ☺ 9am-10pm Tue-Sun; �rm) Literally the top spot in town, with excellent views, and good fish and meat dishes served in a cozy dining room. Portions are generous.

★ Los Paraus
CAFE

(Escalante y Mendoza 103, cnr Señor de Malta; snacks B$8-35; ☺ 3-11pm; �rm) Tourist guide Leo and his wife Paola run this cozy pub-cafe, a block southeast of Plaza 26 de Enero. There are books to leaf through and Che paraphernalia to peruse while sipping coffee, wine or beer and snacking on sandwiches, burgers, pizzas or *chorizo chuquisaqueño* (a type of sausage).

Leo is a fount of local knowledge, and this is a great place to hook up with other travelers looking to share transport to La Higuera.

ⓘ Information

There are several banks with ATMs in town, including **Banco Fassil** (Santa Cruz 108).

Tourist Office (Bolívar, Plaza 26 de Enero; ☺ 8am-noon & 2-5pm Mon-Sat, 8am-2pm Sun)

ⓘ Getting There & Away

In Santa Cruz *trufis* (shared car or minibus) for Vallegrande depart from behind the shopping center Shopping del Automóvil at Km 6 on Doble Vía La Guardia, beyond the sixth *anillo* (B$60, five hours). They leave when full; it can sometimes be a long wait. Buses to Vallegrande leave from the same place at 9am, 3pm and 6:30pm (B$35, six hours). From Samaipata, you can haggle for a shared taxi; expect to pay around B$300 for a carload.

Vallegrande's bus terminal is 1km north of the center. *Trufi* services run every couple of hours to Santa Cruz (B$35 to B$60, 8am to 6pm), passing Samaipata. There are buses to Santa Cruz at 8:30am, 1pm and 9:30pm. There is also a 6pm bus to Cochabamba (B$50, 11 hours). For Sucre, take a Cochabamba- or Santa Cruz-bound bus or a *trufi* as far as Mataral on the main highway (B$10, one hour), where you can pick up a westbound bus to Sucre; they pass from about 7pm onward.

La Higuera

☎ 3 / POP 120

The isolated village of La Higuera is where Che Guevara was held prisoner following his capture. An oversized bust of the revolutionary lords over the dusty **Plaza del Che**, while a full-body cement statue of Che, at twice life-size, stands nearby. The schoolroom where Che was kept before being executed is just off the plaza with a star monument in front. It is now a museum, though the building has been altered from its original design.

◎ Sights

Quebrada del Churo   HISTORIC SITE
(B$10) A steep path leads down a hillside to the sheltered clearing where Che and 16 fellow guerrilla fighters evaded capture for 10 days until, on October 8, 1967, they were surrounded by troops and a gun battle ensued. A badly wounded Che surrendered and was taken to La Higuera.

The Quebrada del Churo is 5km north of La Higuera on the road to Vallegrande; the starting point for the trail is signed. The hike takes around two hours. Bring water.

The spot is marked with a pebble-filled star and concrete benches. It's an atmospheric place to hear stories from your guide about Che's final days. The trail crosses private land so there is a B$10 entrance fee; it can be slippery in wet weather.

Museo Comunal La Higuera   MUSEUM
(B$10; ⊗8am-noon & 2-6pm) This museum is a re-creation of the school room where Che was held prisoner and executed on October 9, 1967. It's covered with photographs, letters and flags left in tribute to Che by visitors from around the world.

If you find the museum locked, ask around the village for the person with the key.

⌷ Sleeping & Eating

Los Amigos   PENSION $
(⏿7108-8433; www.lahigueradelche.blogspot.com; per person B$90) This French-run pension has simple rooms with furniture made by the eccentric owners and a lively bar full of Che paraphernalia. It also serves delicious meals prepared using vegetables grown in the garden (three courses B$60), but you need to book ahead. Rooms have shared bathrooms. There are plans to put in a pool.

Casa del Telegrafista   PENSION $$
(⏿7160-7893; www.facebook.com/hotelposada camping; per person B$100) ⌀ This charming place has a gorgeous cobbled patio and tastefully decorated but rustic rooms in a historic house, with all electricity provided by solar panels. You can also camp here. Meals are available for B$65 per person, and there's a small bar. The dining room houses an exhibition of Che photographs; visitors are welcome to take a look.

❶ Getting There & Away

Getting to La Higuera independently is difficult and doing it as part of a tour from Vallegrande is about the cheapest way; ask at the tourist office (p276) for help finding a taxi or guide. From Vallegrande an *expreso (trufi)* to Pucará costs about B$250 for up to four people. From there it's possible to walk 15km through the hills to La Higuera. Alternatively negotiate with a taxi driver. Taxis to La Higuera (at least B$250, two hours) depart from the market, two blocks east of the main plaza along Sucre.

GRAN CHIQUITANIA

The Gran Chiquitania is the area to the east of Santa Cruz where the hostile, thorny Chaco and the low, tropical savannas of the Amazon Basin are at a standoff. Watched by the foothills of the Cordillera Oriental

SANTA CRUZ & GRAN CHIQUITANIA LA HIGUERA

LA PARABA FRENTE ROJA

The endangered red-fronted macaw (*Ara rubrogenys*), known locally as *paraba frente roja*, reflects its Bolivian specialty status in its red, green and yellow plumage – the colors of the national flag. Found only in dry inter-Andean valleys in the Vallegrande area, this handsome bird has a world population of just 1000. Thanks to an extensive public-awareness campaign, local conservation NGO Armonía was able to raise the funds to purchase a small reserve close to the town of Saipina that is dedicated to the conservation of the bird.

Contact the Armonía office (p264) in Santa Cruz for more information about its conservation programs and how to visit **La Paraba Frente Roja Lodge** (⏿in Santa Cruz 3-356-8808; www.armoniabolivia.org; near Peña Colorada Sur; r incl meals B$1000; ℗) ⌀. The macaw isn't the only threatened bird that calls the lodge home; look out for the raucous cliff parakeet and somber Bolivian blackbird in the area too. For a guided birding tour contact Bird Bolivia (p259).

to the west, the Llanos de Guarayos to the north and the international boundaries of Paraguay and Brazil to the south and east, these two vastly different landscapes stand together, never making peace.

The flat landscapes of the Chiquitania are broken and divided by long, low ridges and odd monolithic mountains. Much of the territory lies soaking under vast marshes, part of the magnificent Pantanal region. It's also the area of Jesuit mission towns with their wide-roofed churches and fascinating history.

The region takes its name from the indigenous Chiquitanos. The name Chiquitanos (meaning 'little people') was coined by the Spanish who were surprised by the low doorways to their dwellings.

History

In the days before eastern Bolivia was surveyed, the Jesuits established an autonomous religious state in Paraguay in 1609. From there they fanned outwards, founding missions in neighboring Argentina, Brazil and Bolivia and venturing into territories previously unexplored by other Europeans.

Keen to coexist with the numerous indigenous peoples of the region, the Jesuits established what they considered an ideal community hierarchy: each settlement, known as a *reducción*, was headed by two or three Jesuit priests, and a self-directed military unit was attached to each one, forming an autonomous theocracy. For a time the Jesuit armies were the strongest and best trained on the continent. This makeshift military force served as a shield for the area from both the Portuguese in Brazil and the Spanish to the west.

Politically, the Bolivian *reducciones* were under the nominal control of the *audiencia* (judicial district) of Chacras, and ecclesiastically under the bishop of Santa Cruz, though their relative isolation meant that the *reducciones* basically ran themselves. Internally, the settlements were jointly administered by a few priests and a council of eight indigenous representatives of the specific tribes who met daily to monitor community progress. Though the indigenous population was supposedly free to choose whether it lived within the missionary communities, the reality was that those who chose not to were forced to live under the harsh *encomienda* (Spanish feudal system) or, worse still, in outright slavery.

The Jesuit settlements reached their peak under the untiring Swiss priest Father Martin Schmidt, who not only built the missions at San Xavier, Concepción and San Rafael de Velasco, but also designed many of the altars, created the musical instruments, acted as the chief composer for the *reducciones* and published a Spanish-Chiquitano dictionary. He was later expelled from the region and died in Europe in 1772.

By the mid-1700s, political strife in Europe had escalated into a power struggle between the Catholic Church and the governments of France, Spain and Portugal. When the Spanish realized the extent of Jesuit wealth and influence they decided to act. In 1767, swept up in a whirlwind of political babble and religious dogma, the missions were disbanded and King Carlos III signed the order of expulsion, which evicted the Jesuits from the continent. In the wake of the Jesuit departure the settlements fell into decline, their amazing churches standing as mute testimony to their achievements.

Jesuit Mission Circuit

The seven-town region of *Las Misiones Jesuíticas* has some of Bolivia's richest cultural and historic sites. Forgotten by the world for more than two centuries, the region and its history captivated the world's imagination when the 1986 Palme d'Or winner *The Mission* spectacularly replayed the last days of the Jesuit priests in the region (with Robert de Niro at the helm). The growing interest in the unique synthesis of Jesuit and native Chiquitano culture in the South American interior resulted in Unesco declaring the region a World Heritage Site in 1991. Thanks to 25 years of painstaking restoration work, directed by the late architect Hans Roth, the centuries-old mission churches have been restored to their original splendor.

❶ Getting There & Away

If you wish to travel the mission circuit on public transportation, the bus schedules synchronize better going counterclockwise: that is starting the circuit at San José de Chiquitos. A much less time-consuming way is by taking a guided tour from Santa Cruz (around US$500 per person for a four-day package), taking in all the major towns. Misional Tours (p259) is a recommended operator.

SANTIAGO DE CHIQUITOS

Set in the hills, the Jesuit mission at Santiago de Chiquitos, 20km east of Roboré, provides a welcome break from the tropical heat of the lowlands. Its church is well worth a look, and there are some great hikes from the village, including to **El Mirador,** a rocky hilltop with dizzying views of the Tucavaca valley. The three-hour round-trip, if walking from town, is particularly lovely in the late afternoon when the light hits the rocks. You can also hike to **La Colina,** a refreshing waterfall 3km from the village, or to **Las Pozas** natural pools, 3.5km outside town. Another walk takes you to **Las Cuevas de Miserendino** (Miserendino Caves) which contain a number of wall paintings; it's best to visit with a guide (guide fees B$180 to B$200; ask at hostal **Churapa** (☑7262-2193; Jorge Tomas Haight, Santiago de Chiquitos; s/d incl breakfast B$150/200, mains B$30-70; ⊙restaurant 6-8pm)). There are a few places to stay in town, including Churapa, one block east of the square. Churapa also has a good restaurant. A taxi to Santiago from Roboré costs B$70; there is no public transportation.

San Xavier

☑3 / POP 15,400

The first (or last, depending on which way you travel) settlement on the circuit, San Xavier, founded in 1691, is the oldest mission town in the region. It's also a favorite holiday destination for wealthy *cruceño* (people from Santa Cruz) families. Swiss priest Martin Schmidt arrived in 1730 and founded the region's first music school and a workshop to produce violins, harps and harpsichords. The village sits on a lovely forested ridge with a great view over the surrounding low hills and countryside.

◎ Sights

Iglesia de San Xavier   CHURCH
(Plaza Principal; museum & church B$20; ⊙8:30am-noon & 2-6pm) Swiss priest Martin Schmidt designed the present church, which was constructed between 1749 and 1752. Restoration work was completed in 1992 to beautiful effect, and the newly restored building manages to appear pleasantly old and authentic. The beguiling whitewashed interior is distinct from other missions on the circuit. Outside mass times, access to the church is via the Museo Misional next door.

Museo Misional   MUSEUM
(Plaza Principal; museum & church B$20; ⊙8:30am-noon & 2-6pm) Adjacent to the church is this interesting little museum outlining the history of the Chiquitos people and the missions. There is also a small gift shop selling wooden carvings and souvenirs.

Museo Casa Natal German Busch   MUSEUM
(Plaza Principal; ⊙8am-noon & 2:30-6pm) FREE
This is the one-time home of the former president and Chaco War hero German Busch, who died in mysterious circumstances aged 35. There is a bit of clutter here and some old photos, as well as a small exhibition of work by local artists. The tourist office (p280) is at the northeast corner of the plaza.

🛏 Sleeping

There are a number of hotels in San Xavier, but none of them are particularly appealing. Consider continuing to Concepción or Santa Cruz (depending on your direction of travel) to spend the night.

Residencial de Chiquitano   PENSION $
(☑7739-2077, 963-5072; Av Padre José de Arce; s B$70-150, d B$90-200, tr B$150-250; P 🞲) This bright two-story hostel decorated with toucan and macaw motifs is on the main road opposite the entrance to town. There's a terrace with killer views of the surrounding hills, but don't even think of getting a room without a fan unless it's cold outside.

Gran Hotel Reposo del Guerrero   HOTEL $$
(☑963-5022; Nicolás Suárez 56; per person incl breakfast B$100; 🞲) Although slightly faded, this is the closest thing to a good hotel in the town center. Despite a grand entrance the rooms are a little boxlike and don't live up to the attractiveness of the garden. It's two blocks east of the plaza.

🍴 Eating

It's mostly fast-food joints in this town. Try the market, two blocks east of the square, for fresh fruit and vegetables.

Dolce Capricho   DESSERTS $
(Av Principal; snacks B$4-10; ⊙3:30-11pm Tue-Sun) Head here for homemade cakes and ice

cream. It's on the main road, one block west of the entrance to town.

Pascana
BOLIVIAN $

(Plaza Principal; mains B$20-25; ⊙7am-8pm) The food here is home cooked and good value, and the family atmosphere and smiling waiters make all the difference. It serves breakfast, lunch and coffee and empanadas (stuffed, savory pastries) in the evening.

ⓘ Information

There are several ATMs on the main road.
Banco Union (Av Principal)

ⓘ Getting There & Away

All Santa Cruz–Concepción buses pass through San Xavier (B$30, six hours), stopping on the main road a short walk from the main plaza. Connections to Concepción pass through every three hours or so from midday to midnight. Along the way look out for the **Piedras de Paquio** rock formation on your right side at Km 322. *Trufis* (shared car or minibus) for San Ignacio de Velasco (via Concepción) leave at 12pm and 3pm.

For the return to Santa Cruz you can avoid the often overcrowded buses by taking a *trufi* (B$35, four hours); these leave when full. Listen for them honking for passengers along the main road. Otherwise, buses for Santa Cruz leave at 11:30am, 2:30pm, 5:30pm, 6:30pm, 7:30pm, 9pm and 11pm.

You can check transport times at the **Tourist Office** (Plaza Principal; ⊙8am-noon & 2:30-6pm).

Concepción

🚍 3 / POP 20,380

'Conce' *(Conchay),* as Concepción is known, is a dusty village with a friendly, quiet atmosphere in the midst of an agricultural and cattle-ranching area. It stands 182km west of San Ignacio de Velasco and is the center for all the mission restoration projects. The town is the most visited of the missions, partly because of its accessibility, but also because its picture-perfect church is one of the most elaborate on the circuit.

⊙ Sights

Catedral de Concepción
CHURCH

(Plaza Centrál; museum pass B$25; ⊙8am-noon & 2-6pm Mon-Sat, 10am-noon Sun) Built in 1709, the elaborately restored cathedral on the east of the plaza has an overhanging roof supported by 121 huge tree-trunk columns

and a similar bell tower. It is decorated with golden baroque designs depicting flowers, angels and the Holy Virgin. Outside mass times, access to the church is via a small museum, which displays interesting historical photos of the church before and after it was restored in the 1970s.

If the church museum is closed, ask at the Museo Misional across the square; the same person is responsible for both.

Museo Misional
MUSEUM

(Plaza Centrál; museum pass B$25; ⊙8am-noon & 2-6pm Mon-Sat, 10am-noon Sun) Intricate art-restoration work is performed in the Museo Misional on the south side of the plaza which, apart from being the birthplace of the former Bolivian president Hugo Banzer Suárez, also has scale models of all the churches on the mission circuit and some fine examples of Jesuit carving.

Restoration Workshops
ART STUDIO

(Baviera; museum pass B$25; ⊙7:30am-noon & 1:30-5:45pm Mon-Fri) Architecture aficionados should visit the restoration workshops behind the church, where many of the fine replicas and restored artworks are crafted.

🛏 Sleeping & Eating

Gran Hotel Concepción
HOTEL $$

(📞964-3031; www.granhotelconcepcion.com.bo; Plaza Centrál; s/d/tr incl breakfast B$250/450/650; 🅿❄🛜🏊) A charming, unapologetically Jesuit-styled hotel with a pool, a quiet patio with a lush, pretty garden and intricately carved wooden pillars. The laundry comes in handy if you are finishing the dusty mission circuit. It's on the west side of the plaza.

La Casona
HOTEL $$

(📞964-3064; Av Killian; s/d with fan B$100/180, air-con B$140/220; ❄) Though not exactly going out on a limb in terms of decor and layout (courtyard, wall paintings, you know the type!), rooms are good value. There are hammocks and a generally relaxed atmosphere, though the place is tidy and well maintained. Breakfast is included.

Hotel Oasis Chiquitano
HOTEL $$

(📞964-3223; German Busch; r per person with/without air-con B$150/100; ❄🛜🏊) This well-maintained hotel with simple rooms and an orchid garden is one block north of the plaza. The price includes access to the

LA RUTA DEL JAGUAR

Bolivia's once thriving jaguar population is increasingly under threat. The forests they inhabit have become smaller as land is lost to soy farming and ranchland, and the soaring demand for illegally traded teeth and skulls, most of which are smuggled to China, makes them more vulnerable to poachers.

The **San Miguelito Jaguar Conservation Ranch** (www.wildlifeconservationtour.com), near the mission town of San Antonio de Lomerío, hopes tourism may counter this trend. Most of the forest surrounding the ranch has been cleared by local farmers for agriculture, leaving a pocket of protected wetland that is densely populated with jaguars. This means it's often possible to see the cats. Camera traps put in place as part of a World Conservation Society study have shown that the reserve is home to six different cat species; jaguar, puma, ocelots, margay, Geoffrey's cat and the jaguarundi. **La Ruta del Jaguar** is a new ecotourism project which works with the local community (who see the cats as a threat to their cattle) and provides an incentive for jaguar conservation.

The ranch is 190km east of Santa Cruz. Tours to San Miguelito (minimum two-night stay), include accommodations in a lodge. Tour companies also offer hikes on which you can check camera traps, canoe on the Río San Julian, and go horseback riding and bird-watching. Contact Nick's Adventures (p258) in Santa Cruz.

Oasis Chiquitano pool complex (nonguests B$15) next door. Breakfast is included.

El Buen Gusto   BOLIVIAN $$
(Plaza Centrál; almuerzo B$30, mains B$45-65; ☺8am-10pm) Portions are generous and the salad bar makes a welcome change from the greasy fare that's often the only option on the mission circuit. Take a seat in the leafy, quiet patio out back. Locals insist this is the best place to eat in town. It's on the north side of the plaza.

ℹ️ Information

Banco Union (Plaza Centrál) This bank on the southwest corner of the plaza has an ATM.

Infotur Office (Padre Lucas Caballero; ☺8am-noon & 2-6pm Mon-Fri) Half a block north of the plaza with information on the entire mission circuit.

ℹ️ Getting There & Away

Buses (B$35, seven hours) from Santa Cruz to Concepción run every two or three hours from 7:30am to 11:15pm via San Xavier (B$20, two hours). They drop off on the main road (a 15-minute walk from the plaza or a B$3 mo-to-taxi ride away) or at the respective company offices. *Trufis* (shared car or minibus, B$50, five hours) to Santa Cruz leave when full from near the market.

If you are thinking of visiting Concepción and continuing on to San Ignacio de Velasco on the same day, you need to leave Santa Cruz very early. The San Ignacio buses from Santa Cruz (B$60, eight hours) pass through Concepción

around 5pm, stopping on the main road 1km from the plaza. *Trufis* to San Ignacio (three hours, B$50) leave from the market when full.

San Ignacio de Velasco
📞 3 / POP 52,400

San Ignacio de Velasco is a thriving commercial center and the largest town on the mission circuit. There's a real buzz about the place, and it's worth planning your route to include an overnight stop here. The church here is a modern reconstruction. Attached to it is an incongruous 1950s tower, which is all that remains of a second church, an ugly building that was later knocked down and replaced with the replica that occupies the site today.

Several attractive, large wooden crosses (a trademark of Jesuit mission towns and villages) stand at intersections just off the plaza.

👁️ Sights

Iglesia de San Ignacio   CHURCH
(Plaza 31 de Julio; ☺8am-noon & 2-8:30pm) **FREE** The first mission church at San Ignacio de Velasco, founded in 1748, was once the largest and most elaborate of all the mission churches. It was demolished in the 1950s and replaced by a modern abomination. Realizing they'd made a hash of it, the architects razed the replacement and designed a reasonable facsimile of the original structure. The new version retains a beautiful altar and wooden pillars from the

original church and overlooks an extensive and well-pruned plaza.

**Museo Misional
de Ignacio de Velasco**   MUSEUM
(cnr Comercio & La Paz, Plaza 31 de Julio; ⊗8am-noon & 2:30-6:30pm Mon-Fri) `FREE` Inside the Casa de Cultura is a small museum with photographs of all the churches on the circuit and background information on the missions. The tourist office is here.

★ Festivals & Events

San Ignacio holds a fete for its patron saint every July 31. The festivities begin on the night of July 30, with music in the main square, followed by a morning parade and dance displays on July 31.

🛏 Sleeping

Hotel Palace   HOTEL $
(☑962-2063; Comercio, Plaza 31 de Julio; s/d incl breakfast B$100/160) 'Palace' is overdoing, but for budget travelers this simple hotel, in the shadow of the church on the west side of the plaza, couldn't be better placed. Rooms have fans but no air-con; those at the front have balconies overlooking the square.

Hotel La Misión   HOTEL $$
(☑962-2333; www.hotel-lamision.com; Libertad, Plaza 31 de Julio; s B$400-550, d B$470-610, ste B$710; 🐕🖥) For a bit of luxury, neocolonial style, try this place on the east side of the plaza. It has chic rooms, a little pool and opulent suites. Breakfast is included.

Hotel San Ignacio   HOTEL $$
(☑962-2283; hotelsanignacio@hotmail.com; Libertad, Plaza 31 de Julio; s/d incl breakfast B$200/300; 🖥🐕) Rooms with high ceilings and wooden furniture, and a pretty central courtyard garden make Hotel San Ignacio an appealing choice. It's on the east side of the square.

🍴 Eating

Pizzeria Napolitano   PIZZA $$
(☑7538-0724; cnr Calle 24 de Septiembre & Av Santa Cruz; mains B$35-60; ⊗6pm-midnight Tue-Sun) At weekends it seems every family in town is at Pizzeria Napolitano, vying for an outdoor table. As well as deep-pan pizzas, the menu spans pasta, meat dishes and excellent salads. It's one block northwest of San Ignacio church.

Club Social   INTERNATIONAL $$
(Plaza 31 de Julio; almuerzo B$25; ⊗11:30am-2:30pm Mon-Sat) Has good-value *almuerzos* (set lunches), which include soup and a main course. The menu changes daily but often features *majadito de charque,* a typical local dish made with rice and dried meat. The restaurant is on the west side of the plaza.

ℹ Information

Banco Union (Plaza 31 de Julio)

Tourist Office (☑962-2211; cnr Comercio & La Paz, Plaza 31 de Julio; ⊗8am-noon & 2:30-6:30pm Mon-Sat) The Casa de la Cultura on the southwest corner of the plaza houses a small tourist office.

ℹ Getting There & Away

The bus terminal is 2.5km south of the main square; a moto-taxi costs B$3.

Trufis (shared car, minibus) to San Rafael via Santa Ana leave at 10:30am and 3:30pm (2½ hours, B$20). *Trufis* to San Miguel leave when full (1½ hours, B$15). *Trufis* to Santa Cruz (seven hours, B$70) via Concepción (three hours, B$50) leave at 8:30am, 10:30am, 1pm and 3:30pm, and at 6pm to Concepción only.

Buses to San Matías and the border with Brazil leave at 12:30am and 3am (six hours, B$180).

San Miguel de Velasco

☑3 / POP 11,400

Sleepy San Miguel hides in the scrub, 37km south of San Ignacio. Its **church** was founded in 1721 and is, according to the late Jesuit priest and Swiss architect Hans Roth, the most accurately restored of all the Bolivian Jesuit missions.

◎ Sights

Jesuit Mission Church   CHURCH
(Plaza Principal; ⊗8am-noon & 12:30-6pm) `FREE` The church of San Miguel's spiral pillars, carved wooden altar with a flying San Miguel, extravagant golden pulpit, religious artwork, toy-like bell tower and elaborately painted facade are simply superb. Although not designed by Martin Schmidt, the church does reflect his influence and is often considered the most beautiful of Bolivia's Jesuit missions.

ℹ Information

Banco Fassil (Plaza Principal) On the south side of the main square.

CHOCHÍS

Tiny Chochís, 360km east of Santa Cruz, sits at the base of the imposing red rock known as la Torre. The main reason for visiting is to see the remarkable **Santuario Mariano de la Torre** (⊙9am-6pm) FREE, a religious sanctuary and memorial built to commemorate the victims of a flood. Though relatively modern (the disaster occurred in 1979), the wood carvings that adorn the sanctuary are the rival of anything seen in the Jesuit missions. The site has a palpable sense of mourning that allows you to share in the grief of the townsfolk.

The surrounding countryside is great for walking and local guides can take you to waterfalls, stunning viewpoints and hidden natural pools. In 2018, 12 street artists from around the world visited Chochís and spent a week painting as part of a festival. Their evocative murals can be seen on buildings around the main square.

Trufis (shared car or minibus) to Chochís leave when full from the main square in Roboré (B$30, 45 minutes). From San José, *trufis* to Roboré can drop you in Chochís (B$40, 1½ hours).

From Chochís a *trufi* leaves for Roboré at around noon and for San José at about 8pm. There are buses to San José at 2:30pm, 3:30pm and 10pm (B$30, 1½ hours), and to Roboré at 5am, 5pm and 10pm (B$20, 1 hour).

Tourist Office (☑962-4222; Calle 29 de Septiembre; ⊙8am-noon & 2-6pm Mon-Fri, to noon Sat)

❶ Getting There & Away

Trufis (shared car, minibus) leave for San Ignacio (1½ hours, B$12) to the north at about 2pm and 6:30pm, but ask around for the latest timetables as departures vary. The road is unpaved and rain can cause delays, a change in route or no service at all. *Trufis* to San Rafael are irregular, but usually leave in the late morning and midafternoon (one hour, B$12). They leave from near the ATM on the main square.

Santa Ana de Velasco
☑3 / POP 680

Of all the villages on the mission circuit, tiny Santa Ana de Velasco is the most peaceful and perhaps the most charming. Reached by a dusty, bumpy road from San Ignacio, it feels barely connected to the modern world. The tranquility of the large grassy square is interrupted only by free-roaming chickens and the occasional sounds of children's music practice.

❍ Sights

Iglesia de Santa Ana   CHURCH
(Plaza Principal; ⊙8am-noon & 2-5pm) FREE
Santa Ana church, with its wooden altar and reed roof, is more rustic than others on the mission circuit and recalls the first churches constructed by the Jesuit missionaries upon their arrival. The interior contains exquisite religious carvings and paintings.

Of particular interest is the church organ, which dates from 1754; the pipes have been replaced but the wooden exterior is original.

🛏 Sleeping & Eating

If you find yourself in Santa Ana for the night, contact Tito Irving Rocha who rents rooms in his informal **pensión** (☑7467-5400; Nanauma; per person B$50).

Restaurante El Tacu   BOLIVIAN $
(☑6781-4229; Plaza Principal; breakfast B$10, 2-course meal B$20; ⊙hours vary, call ahead) Tucked away behind the main square to the east of the church is this lovely restaurant serving hearty home-cooked meals. Seating is at outdoor tables shaded by fruit trees; the grapefruits and limes they bear are used by owner Emma Silva to make juices. Call ahead if you plan to eat here.

❶ Getting There & Away

There is a *trufi* (shared car or minibus) to San Rafael at around 11:30am and 4:30pm (one hour, B$12). Going the other direction to San Ignacio, *trufis* leave Santa Ana at around 11am and 5pm (45 minutes, B$10). It's a bumpy, dusty road out here from San Ignacio; the road may become impassable and transportation canceled in heavy rain.

San Rafael de Velasco
☑3 / POP 7500

San Rafael de Velasco, a dusty little village 132km north of San José de Chiquitos, was founded in 1696. Its church was constructed between 1743 and 1747. In the 1970s and 1980s the building was restored, along with the churches in Concepción and San José de Chiquitos. Aside from checking out the magnificent mission there's not much to see in this tiny town.

⊙ Sights

Jesuit Mission Church CHURCH
(Plaza Principal; ⊙ hours vary) **FREE** The restored interior of this 1747 mission is particularly beautiful, and the original paintings and woodwork remain intact. The pulpit is covered with a layer of lustrous mica, the ceiling is made of reeds and the spiral pillars were carved from *cuchi* (ironwood) logs. If you find the church locked, look on the main door for the phone number of the key holder.

🛏 Sleeping & Eating

Pascana Rafaeleña PENSION $
(☎ 962-4018, 7639-2747; Chiquitos, Plaza Principal; s/d incl breakfast B$70/120; ✳) Just a few meters from the church on the main square is this neat pension, with a high-pitched roof, cool floor tiles, air-conditioning and cable TV. Rooms lead off a long, narrow patio and are decorated with paintings of the missions.

Las Palmeras BOLIVIAN $
(Plaza Principal, cnr Av Velasco & Barba; mains B$15; ⊙ 7:30am-9pm) Simple local restaurant on the square serving soups and mains such as *milanesas* (breaded cutlets).

❶ Getting There & Away

Trufis (shared car or minibus) to San José de Chiquitos in the south leave at 2pm daily (four hours, B$50). From San José, *trufis* leave at 9am.

Going north, *trufis* to San Ignacio (2½ hours, B$20) via San Miguel (one hour, B$12) leave at 1pm and 5pm. There are *trufis* to Santa Ana at 10am, 1pm and 4pm (45 minutes, B$10).

San José de Chiquitos

📝 3 / POP 16,600

An atmospheric place, San José de Chiquitos has the appeal of an old Western film set. The frontier town, complete with dusty streets straight out of *High Noon* and footpaths shaded by pillar-supported roofs, is flanked on the south by a low escarpment and on the north by flat, soggy forest. With an enormous and handsome plaza shaded by *toboroche* (thorny bottle) trees, the most accessible Jesuit mission town is also arguably the most appealing. It's particularly beautiful at sunset, when the stone glows pink.

⊙ Sights

Jesuit Mission Church CHURCH
(Plaza Principal; museum & church B$20; ⊙ 9am-noon & 3-6pm Tue-Sun) San José has the only stone Jesuit mission church and merits a visit even if you miss all the others. Although the main altar is nearly identical to those in other nearby missions and has vague similarities to churches in Poland and Belgium, the reason behind its unusual exterior design remains unclear.

---

❶ CROSSING THE BORDER TO BRAZIL

The main border crossing to Brazil is at **Quijarro** at the end of the train line, with a second, minor crossing at **San Matías**, the access point to the northern Brazilian Pantanal. The route through San Matías is an adventurous border crossing; the road east of San Ignacio is still unpaved. Buses run between San Matías and Santa Cruz (the route may be impassable in heavy rain). If you are crossing the border in your own vehicle, Brazilian entry or exit stamps should be picked up from the Polícia Federal office at Rua Antônio João 160 in Cáceres; get your exit and entry stamps for Bolivia in Santa Cruz.

You'll more than likely arrive in **Puerto Quijarro** by bus or by train between 6am and 7am to be greeted by a line of taxi drivers offering to take you the 3km to the border (B$20). **Immigration offices** (Ruta Nacional 4; ⊙ 8am-6pm) are on opposing sides of the bridge. Bolivian officials have been known to charge an unofficial fee for the entry stamp (usually around B$18). Crossing this border you are generally asked to show a yellow-fever vaccination certificate. On the Brazilian side of the border buses or taxis will take you into Corumbá. Brazilian entry stamps are given at the border.

Museum
MUSEUM

(Plaza Principal; museum & church B$20; ☺ 9am-noon & 3-6pm Tue-Sun) Next to the church is a small museum with information about all 10 Jesuit missions in the area. The admission fee includes entrance to the church.

Parque Histórico
Santa Cruz la Vieja
RUINS

(Av El Sutó; B$10; ☺ 8am-4pm Mon-Fri) A few kilometers outside town, this is the site of the original city of Santa Cruz de la Sierra. The only thing left behind of the old city is an abandoned guardhouse. It's 2.5km south of the main plaza.

Just beyond here is a statue of town founder Ñuflo de Chávez next to a reconstructed *choza* – a typical Chiquitano dwelling with the characteristic low doorway used for defensive purposes. Uphill from there you can hike to the **Cataratas del Suton waterfall** and a stunning **viewpoint**. It's easy to get lost though and a guide is recommended. Ask at the tourist office.

🛌 Sleeping

Hotel Turubó
HOTEL $

(☎ cell 7264-5153; Bolívar, Plaza Principal; s B$100-120, d B$140-160; P ❋ 🛜) A good-value option with friendly helpful staff and neat rooms with TV and private bathroom. On the west side of the plaza.

★ Hotel Villa Chiquitana
BOUTIQUE HOTEL $$

(☎ 7315-5803; www.villachiquitana.com; 9 de Abril; incl breakfast s B$295-395, d B$380-495; ☺ restaurant noon-2pm & 7-9:30pm; P ❋ 🛜 🏊) The spacious rooms here are tastefully decked out with their own theme and have large modern bathrooms. It's a little outside the center, and the pool garden full of palm trees, orchids and tropical birds is a tranquil oasis where you can escape the dusty streets in style. There is an excellent on-site restaurant and bar.

Hotel Misiones de Chiquitos
BOUTIQUE HOTEL $$

(☎ 7800-8062; www.misioneshotels.com; Mons Carlos Gericke, Plaza Principal; r incl breakfast B$350; 🛜 🏊) It comes as a surprise to discover this slick, contemporary hotel on the missions circuit. Rooms have gleaming white floor tiles, flat-screen TV and luxury bathroom, and are arranged around a pool. There's a terrace bar and even a gym.

🍴 Eating

Head to the plaza for good-value, typical local fare. For something more refined, try the restaurant at the Hotel Misiones de Chiquitos.

Sabor Chiquitano
BOLIVIAN $

(Santa Cruz, Plaza Principal; mains B$18-25; ☺ 8:30am-3pm & 5:30-10pm) Delicious juices and a good choice of mains as well as snacks such as tasty empanadas make this a solid choice. Service is friendly and there's an outdoor terrace right on the square.

Churrasquería El Rafa
BARBECUE $$

(cnr Bolívar & Santa Cruz; mains B$25-50; ☺ 11am-2pm & 6-11pm) Locals give this place on the southwest corner of the plaza the thumbs up, but your arteries might not. The lunchtime buffet includes more salads and pasta in addition to meat.

ℹ️ Information

Infotur (☎ 972-2084; cnr Bolívar & Mon Carlos Gericke; ☺ 7:30am-noon & 2:30-6:30pm Mon-Sat) A useful tourist information office in the *alcaldía* (mayor's office) just off the northwest corner of the plaza, with information about all the missions.

There are several ATMs in town.

Banco Prodem (cnr Av Gallardo & 9 de Abril)

Banco Union (cnr Av Gallardo & 9 de Abril)

ℹ️ Getting There & Away

Buses and *trufis* (shared car, minibus) leave from the bus station, 1.5km north of the town center. A moto-taxi into town costs B$3.

The road between San Rafael and San José is unpaved and public transportation is infrequent. A *trufi* to San Rafael leaves at 9am daily (four hours, B$50) and makes the return journey from San Rafael at 2pm.

Buses from Santa Cruz depart daily from the bimodal terminal between 4pm and 6pm (B$50, four hours). Five services return from San José to Santa Cruz, all leaving between 3pm and 11:30pm. To Quijarro on the Brazilian border buses leave at 2pm and 3:30pm (B$50 to B$80, six hours).

A more leisurely way to travel between San José and Santa Cruz or Quijarro is by Ferrobus train or the slower Expreso Oriental train. You'll need to show your passport on purchasing your ticket and again to access the platform.

SANTA CRUZ & GRAN CHIQUITANIA JESUIT MISSION CIRCUIT

Amazon Basin

Why Go?

The Amazon Basin is one of Bolivia's largest and most mesmerizing regions. The rainforest is raucous with wildlife and spending a few days roaming the sweaty jungle is an experience you're unlikely to forget. But it's not only the forests that are enchanting: it's also the richness of the indigenous cultures, traditions and languages that exist throughout the region.

Mossy hills peak around the town of Rurrenabaque, most people's first point of entry into the region and the main base camp for visits to the fascinating Parque Nacional Madidi. This is home to a growing ethno-ecotourism industry established to help local communities. The village of San Ignacio de Moxos is famous for its wild July fiesta; Trinidad, the region's cosmopolitan hub, is encased by buzzing wetlands and is the transit point toward Santa Cruz. North of here the frontier towns of Riberalta and Guayaramerín are in remote regions few travelers dare to tread.

Best Places to Eat

➡ Churrasquería La Estancia (p310)

➡ El Secreto de Mama (p317)

➡ El Nomádico (p298)

➡ Juliano's (p299)

Best Places to Stay

➡ Sadiri (p302)

➡ Chalalán Ecolodge (p301)

➡ Hostal El Lobo (p295)

➡ Serere Ecolodge (p300)

➡ Hostal Mirador (p291)

When to Go
Rurrenabaque

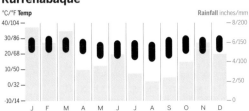

May–Oct Make travel a whole lot easier by avoiding the rain.

Mid-Jun Bull running and mayhem at the Fiesta de la Santísima Trinidad.

Jul The village goes wild during the San Ignacio de Moxos fiesta.

History

The Bolivian Amazon has always oozed mystery. The Incas believed that a powerful civilization lived in the great rainforest and tried to conquer the area in the 15th century. Legend has it that the indigenous peoples of the western Bolivian Amazon, mainly the Moxos tribe, offered mighty resistance to the invading army. Once the Inca realized they were unable to beat the Moxos, they sought an alliance and settled among them.

The tale of the Incas' experience fired the imagination of the Spanish conquerors a century later – they were chasing their own legend: the kingdom of El Dorado (the Golden One) which they thought lay somewhere east of the Andean Cordillera, near the source of the Río Paraguay. The Spanish spent the entire 16th century trying to find the elusive kingdom, but found nothing but death and disease. By the 17th century they moved their search elsewhere.

Though the Spanish were disappointed with their search in the Moxos region, the Jesuits saw their opportunity to 'spread the word' to the highly spiritual *moxeños*. The missionaries were the first Europeans to significantly venture into the lowlands. They founded their first mission at Loreto in 1675. While they imposed Christianity and European ways, the Jesuits also recognized the indigenous peoples' expertise in woodwork, which eventually produced the brilliant carvings now characteristic of the missions. The region is now under increasing pressure from the expansion of the agricultural frontier, as vast tracts of forest are converted into ranch land.

Following the expulsion of the Jesuits in 1767, the Franciscan and Dominican missionaries, as well as the opportunistic settlers who followed, brought mainly slavery and disease. Otherwise, the vast, steamy forests and plains of northern Bolivia saw little activity for decades.

More recently, finding a way to sustainably exploit the natural resources of the region has become an increasingly hot potato. A proposed 300km road that would link Villa Tunari with San Ignacio de Moxos was canceled following demonstrations by indigenous groups and environmentalists who complained that the route would bisect the Tipnis Reserve (Territorio Indígena y Parque Nacional Isiboro Sécure).

Representatives of the 50-plus indigenous communities marched to La Paz in opposition and were met with some violence (four deaths) in 2011. This inspired a countermarch in 2012 by indigenous groups from the Moxos and Tunari areas who insisted that the road was vital for the economic development of their isolated homeland.

In 2014, the project was put on hold as the government promised to address regional poverty, but Supreme Decree 2366 in May 2015 opened the national parks to oil and gas exploration, and the road was on again. Construction remained ongoing in late 2018, though the road is far from complete. Its future remains unwritten.

National Parks & Reserves

The Bolivian Amazon is part of the most biodiverse biome on earth, and the country's best-known national parks and reserves are located here: a paradise for bird-watchers, monkey lovers and jaguar seekers. You can choose between the jungles and wild rivers of lush Parque Nacional Madidi (p301), the less-frequented, *cerrado* savannas of Reserva Biosférica del Beni (p303), the Reserva Barba Azul (p314) – home to one of the world's rarest parrots – and the virtually unexplored 'lost world' of Parque Nacional Noel Kempff Mercado (p293). Several smaller municipal reserves lie near the region's main population centers, helping raise awareness among Bolivians of their natural treasures and providing easy access to nature.

① Getting There & Away

Rurrenabaque in the west and Trinidad in the east are the main access towns to the region. Though it's easy enough to get to Trinidad from Santa Cruz, delving deeper into the region either involves flying (if you're smart and cashed up) or uncomfortably long bus rides (get ready to push if it rains!).

Many roads, including the one linking Rurrenabaque with Trinidad, are in the process of being entirely asphalted. However, this is very much a work in progress: if there is even a hint of a shower, bank on your bus taking at least twice as long as the ticket salesman tells you. Particularly tedious is the route from La Paz to Rurrenabaque. Many people decide to wing it (or take a faster 4WD) after surviving the initial bus ride.

The main airlines all fly to the region, with **BOA** (Boliviana de Aviación; ☑ 901-105-010; www.boa.bo; cnr Sucre & Cipriano Barace; ☉ 8:30am-12:30pm & 2:30-6:30pm Mon-Fri, 9am-1pm Sat) and **EcoJet** (☑ 465-2617, 901-105-055; www.ecojet.bo; cnr Avs 6 de Agosto & Santa Cruz; ☉ 8:30am-12:30pm & 2:30-6:30pm Mon-Fri,

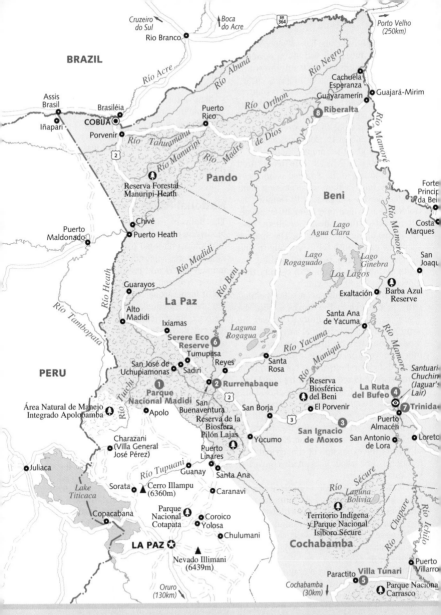

Amazon Basin Highlights

1 **Parque Nacional Madidi** (p301) Boating into the world's most biodiverse park.

2 **Rurrenabaque** (p294) Probing the nearby pampas for caiman, capybara and frighteningly large anaconda.

3 **San Ignacio de Moxos** (p305) Partying with locals at the Amazon's best village fiesta.

4 **La Ruta del Bufeo** (p309) Floating down the serene Río Ibare in search of the elusive pink river dolphins.

5 **Villa Tunari** (p290) Rafting, canyoning and

BR 364

Ji-Paraná

BRAZIL

0 — 200 km
0 — 100 miles

Río Guaporé (Iténez)

Itonamas

Bella Vista

Río San Martín

agdalena

aguna n Luis

Piso Firme

Porvenir

Parque Nacional Noel Kempff Mercado

Reserva de Vida Silvestre Ríos Blanco y Negro

Perseverancia

Reserva Biológica Laguna Bahía

La Florida

Río Negro

Río Blanco

Santa Cruz

Tarvo

Río San Pablo

Asunción de Guarayos

Santa Rosa de la Roca

Río Grande o Guapay

Concepción

San Javier

San Ignacio de Velasco

Santa Ana de Velasco

San Matías

Río Piray

ío Yapacaní

San Ramón

San Miguel de Velasco

San Rafael de Velasco

Santa Cruz (125km)

trekking through the rainforest at this adventure-tourism hub.

6 **Serere Eco Reserve** (p300) Learning about Bolivia's most prominent

conservation warrior at her private wildlife refuge.

7 **Trinidad** (p307) Enjoying the nightlife of the most cosmopolitan city in the Bolivian Amazon.

8 **Riberalta** (p315) Forgoing the beaten path to explore little-visited wildlife reserves and remote açaí-producing communities.

8:30am-12:30pm Sat) specializing in the more remote destinations. Though handy, flights are frequently canceled during inclement weather (or because of 'maintenance').

Boat travel is big here, especially in the rainy season, when it can be a more viable option. Riverboat travel isn't for everyone: it's relaxing but slow-going, and there are no real schedules. While the scenery can be mesmerizing, it changes little, so you'll want to bring a couple of books along. Passenger comfort is the last thing cargo-boat builders have in mind, but Bolivian accommodation standards are still superior to those on the Brazilian 'cattle boats' that ply the Amazon proper.

CHAPARE REGION

The Chapare stretches out beyond the last peaks of the Andes into the dramatically different landscape of the upper Amazon Basin, where lush, moist rainforest replaces the dry, barren mountains. The contrast is breathtaking on the spectacular road between Cochabamba and Villa Tunari, where twists around the high peaks and mountain lakes drop steeply into deep, steaming tropical valleys.

The Chapare region is heavily populated with highland *campesinos* (subsistence farmers) who emigrated here in the 1970s and turned the region into Bolivia's main source of coca grown for the manufacture of cocaine. (Yungas coca, on the other hand, makes up the bulk of what Bolivians themselves chew, make into tea etc.) Subsequent eradication attempts by the US Drug Enforcement Administration (DEA) made the region unstable, and Morales' government expelled the DEA in 2008.

❶ Getting There & Away

Access to the Chapare is relatively easy, as it lies on the main highway between Cochabamba and Santa Cruz. You can catch one of the regular buses from either hub, though vans and shared taxis are often the fastest mode of transport.

Villa Tunari

⬛4 / POP 77,380 / ELEV 300M (984FT)

Strung out along the Cochabamba–Santa Cruz highway, Villa Tunari is an odd combination of truck stop and tourist town that offers a tame introduction to the wilder Amazon. It's a pleasant spot to hike or swing in a hammock, and the hot, steamy jungle air will make you grateful for the proximity of *las pozas*, a series of natural swimming holes.

As visitor numbers increase – mostly weekenders from Cochabamba – the town has developed into something of a tourist trap and your bolivianos won't go as far here as they do further north in the Amazon. That said, it's a great base for probing into the wonderful Parque Nacional Carrasco (p292).

◉ Sights

There is a preponderance of parks with caged wildlife, canopy walks, zip lines and thematic flourishes (including Jurassic Park–inspired dinosaurs). Most are tourist traps and are not worth your time.

Parque Machía   WILDLIFE RESERVE
(Inti Wara Yassi; ☑ mobile 7178-5619; www.intiwara yassi.org; Av Integración; B$6; ⊙9:30am-4pm Tue-Sun) This 37-hectare wildlife refuge houses more than 200 free-range poached or injured critters, and another 300 or so in enclosures. Those who run free (mostly monkeys) make cameos on the 1km hike up to a scenic overlook. An international crew of volunteers tends to the animals' every need, but no attempts are made to reintroduce them into the wild (the animals, not the volunteers!).

⚡ Activities

Pozas (swimming holes) are the main source of fun in Villa Tunari. In addition to those at Hotel de Selva El Puente (p292), there are several free (or very cheap) *pozas* around town along the Río San Mateo and Río Espíritu Santo. Two of the most popular are **Padresama** and **Tres Arroyos**. Great opportunities for fishing and white-water rafting abound in the surrounding rivers, but ask around to see what's safe before heading out on your own.

⌖ Tours

Villa Tunari is a focus area for La Paz–based Fremen Tours (p358), which arranges all-inclusive tours, accommodations, river trips and other activities at out-of-the-way sites.

Local operators specialize in rafting, canyoning and jungle trekking.

★Ranabol   OUTDOORS
(☑ mobile 7350-8590; www.facebook.com/ranabol rafting; cnr Av Integración & Pando; ⊙8am-8pm) Villa Tunari's most-established tour operator specializes in 10km to 19km rafting trips, and seven- to 10-day rafting and trekking

expeditions that connect Cochabamba with Coroico. Also offers multiday community-based trekking adventures in **Territorio Indígena y Parque Nacional Isiboro Sécure**, and a recommended day-long trekking, rappelling and (mild) canyoning circuit. The owners can speak basic English.

Bolivia Rafting   RAFTING
(☑ mobile 7642-2990; bolivia.rafting@gmail.com; Av Integración & La Paz; ☺ 8am-4pm) Runs rafting trips down Río Espíritu Santo that can be combined with hiking, rappelling and ziplining.

★☆ Festivals & Events

Festival de San Antonio   RELIGIOUS
(☺ Jun) The Festival of San Antonio, the town's patron saint, is celebrated in the first week of June.

Feria Regional del Pescado   FOOD & DRINK
(☺ Aug) For delicious and unique Amazonian fish dishes, be in town the first week of August for the Feria Regional del Pescado.

🛏 Sleeping

Villa Tunari has a huge selection of hotels, most of which are expensive by Bolivian standards and provide poor value for money.

★ **Hostal Mirador**   HOSTAL $
(☑ mobile 7547-5435; www.facebook.com/hostal mirador.villatunari; Calle Tarija; dm with/without breakfast B$62/47, s/d/tr/q incl breakfast B$160/190/285/380, camping per person B$35; 🛜 🎿) The most happening spot in town (and the only place you'll encounter other gringos) is this hostel with colorful wall murals, fast wi-fi, a small pool, an outdoor gym, a shared kitchen, pool and ping-pong tables, inviting

AMAZON BASIN VILLA TUNARI

SACRED COCA?

Erythroxylum coca is the scientific name for coca, a plant native to northwestern South America. A small tree growing to a height of 2m to 3m, the species is identified by its long, opaque leaves and clusters of yellowish-white flowers, which mature into red berries. In Bolivia the plant grows primarily in the Yungas, north of La Paz, and in the Chapare region.

But, unless you are a botanist, you are likely to have heard of coca for other reasons – prince among them being its role in the production of the narcotic cocaine. To make the drug, leaves are dried, soaked in kerosene and mashed into a paste. Then they are treated with hydrochloric and sulfuric acids to form a foul-smelling brown base. Further treatment creates cocaine.

For most Bolivians, the white powder snorted by party-goers worldwide has nothing to do with their sacred plant, and they resent the suggestion that they should be held responsible for anyone else's misuse of it. President Evo Morales, a former *cocalero* (coca grower) himself, has vowed to continue the war against drug-trafficking, but not at the expense of the country's coca industry.

Critics argue that his policies have enabled a huge black market for illegal cocaine production in Bolivia. Visitors will no doubt notice that drug money is pouring into the Chapare region, Morales' former home. In 2015, a US$40-million international airport with Bolivia's largest runway opened at the site of an old US Drug Enforcement Agency base in Chimoré, population 21,000, renewing cries of a narco-state.

Coca has formed a part of the religious rituals of the inhabitants of the altiplano since the pre-Inca period, as an offering to the Gods Apus (mountains), Inti (sun) and Pachamama (Mother Earth). It is drunk as a tea *(mate de coca)* or chewed to combat altitude sickness, fatigue and hunger. *Picchar* (to chew coca, from the Aymará) involves masticating a pile of leaves stored as a bolus in the cheek, which has a mild stimulant and anaesthetic effect; it also serves as a powerful symbol of cultural identity.

Outside Bolivia, most people know that cocaine was the original active ingredient in Coca-Cola. Medical company Stepan imports 100 tonnes of dried leaf annually, some of it for the manufacture of medicines, some of it for the production of the Coca-Cola flavoring agent.

Regardless of its status in Bolivia, coca is illegal in most of the world and travelers should not attempt to take any coca leaves home. Most countries consider the leaf and the narcotic as one and same, and you could be charged with possession of a Class A drug for having even a single petiole in your pocket.

hammocks and, most importantly, sweeping river views. Dorms are a better deal than the rooms, some of which have zero furniture beyond the bed.

Hotel Los Cocos HOTEL **$**
(✉ mobile 7177-1796; cnr Benigno Paz & Santa Cruz; s/d B$100/180, without bathroom s/d B$70/140; 🛜🏊) One of Villa Tunari's best budget options, with well-tended rooms, modern bathrooms and a glorious pool to cool off in. Owner Ray Charles Paz is helpful, friendly and, fortunately or unfortunately, doesn't own a piano!

Hotel de Selva El Puente RESORT **$$**
(✉ mobile 7174-2596; http://hotelchapare.com/es; s/d/tr B$270/365/460; ❄🏊) This gorgeous place is set in 22 hectares of rainforest 4km outside Villa Tunari. Handsome (though basic) stone cabins center on a courtyard, and there's a hammock salon on the top floor of reception. The big attractions here are 'Las Pozas,' 14 idyllic natural swimming holes (B$15 for nonguests) deep in the forest.

The hotel is run by Fremen Tours (p358). It's near the Ríos San Mateo and Espíritu Santo confluence. From the center it's B$10 by moto-taxi or B$20 by taxi.

Hotel Las Palmas HOTEL **$$**
(✉ mobile 7570-6100; Av Integración; s/d/tr B$260/400/480; 🅿❄🛜🏊) This aptly named hotel with plenty of perky palms has a refreshing swimming pool and enormous tiled rooms. On the south side of the main road, there are superb views of the river and surrounding hills.

Los Tucanes CABIN **$$**
(✉ 413-6506; www.lostucaneshotel.com; 4-person cabins B$840, s/d B$285/478; ❄🏊) Comfortable cabins (six with river views) boast good beds, homey decor and a nearby pool to lounge around. Each room is individually decorated with its own unique art and it's a great spot for total vacation surrender. It's at the Santa Cruz entrance to town opposite the turnoff for Hotel El Puente (B$3 by moto-taxi).

✗ Eating

Restaurant San Silvestre INTERNATIONAL **$$**
(www.facebook.com/ressansilvestre; Av Integración; mains B$25-70; ⏱ 9:30am-10pm; 🛜) It's a bit expensive and over the top, but San Silvestre, on the main road next to Las Palmas, remains unchallenged as the best restaurant in town. The *surubí al coco* (a local catfish

in coconut sauce) is a real standout, though the gargantuan *pique macho* (beef, sausage and chips) is great if you want to pig out.

Leños Ardientes INTERNATIONAL **$$**
(Av Integración; mains B$20-60; ⏱ 6-10pm Tue-Sun; 🛜) Need your international fix? In addition to grilled fish and meat, this generic-looking restaurant does everything from pizza to pasta, chicken wings and Swiss fondue. There's also a nice wine menu, espresso coffees and fresh juices.

❶ Information

There's an ATM at Banco Unión, located on the far side of Av Integración from Restaurant San Silvestre.

❶ Getting There & Away

Buses taking the newer road between Cochabamba and Santa Cruz pass through Villa Tunari. Buses (B$20, four hours) and *micros* (small buses; B$30, three hours) from Cochabamba leave from the corner of Avs Oquendo and 9 de Abril throughout the day.

Getting a shared taxi from Santa Cruz is much faster than the bus, but means several changes – this typically involves hopping out of one taxi and straight into the next. From the old bus terminal take a taxi to Yapacani (B$25, two hours), from there go to Bulo-Bulo (B$15, one hour), then on to Ivirgazama (B$15, 1½ hours), then another to Shinahota (B$12, 45 minutes) and finally one to Villa Tunari (B$6, 30 minutes). It sounds more complicated than it really is and is a good way of avoiding waiting around for a bus, though you can expect more people to be piled into each cab than actually fit!

Parque Nacional Carrasco

Created in 1988, this 622,600ha **park** (B$100; ⏱ Kawsay Wasi guides 8:30am-3:30pm) has some of Bolivia's most easily explored cloud forest. It skirts a large portion of the road between Cochabamba and Villa Tunari, and also includes a big lowland area of the Chapare region. The rainforest hides a vast variety of mammal species, together with a rainbow of birds, crawling reptiles, amphibians, fish and insects.

The most popular way to visit is to do the hike to the **Cavernas del Repechón** (Caves of the Night Birds), where you'll see the weird, nocturnal *guáchero* (oilbird) and six bat species. Access is from the village of Paractito, 8km west of Villa Tunari. This half-day excursion involves a short slog through

PARQUE NACIONAL NOEL KEMPFF MERCADO

The wonderfully remote and globally important **Noel Kempff Mercado National Park** is home to a broad spectrum of Amazonian flora and fauna and has a wide range of dwindling habitats, from open cerrado (savanna) to dense rainforest. The park lies in the northernmost reaches of Santa Cruz department, between the banks of the Ríos Verde, Guaporé (Río Iténez on Bolivian maps) and Paraguay.

It encompasses more than 1.5 million hectares of the most dramatic scenery in northern Bolivia, including rivers, rainforests, waterfalls, plateaus and rugged 500m escarpments. An attempt to generate a tourist trail to the park appears to have failed, and camps at Flor de Oro and Los Fierros have not been maintained. Loggers, ranchers and energy companies have recently shown interest in the region, but the park remains an exciting off-the-beaten-track option for adventurous travelers. Due to the lack of infrastructure, visits are best done with a Santa Cruz–based tour agency. Nick's Adventures (p358) and Amboró Tours (p259) both run tours.

The park is administered by Sernap and every prospective visitor to the park must first visit a park-information office in La Paz (p79) or Santa Cruz (p264) to register their trip.

the rainforest and a zippy crossing of the **Río San Mateo** in a cable-car contraption.

For more details on this contact **Kawsay Wasi** (www.facebook.com/EcoturismoKawsayWasi), the organization of indigenous guides who work in the park. You'll find them waiting at the park entrance, or you can book a multiday trip with them in advance through Tusoco Travel (p358), a La Paz–based organization that brings together indigenous Bolivians around the country and helps them develop responsible tourism in their regions.

Access to the rest of the park is much more difficult and potentially dangerous as it's become a haven for hidden coca farms. The Conservation International–backed **Camino en las Nubes** (Walk in the Clouds), a trek descending from 4000m to 300m along the old Cochabamba–Chapare road, is now largely used by drug traffickers and unsafe for tourists.

Puerto Villarroel

🚤 4 / POP 2,500 / ELEV 167M (548FT)

This muddy, tropical port on the Río Ichilo is a small settlement with tin-roofed houses raised off the ground to defend them from the mud and wet-season floods. The population here is composed almost entirely of indigenous Yuki and Yuracaré, as well as Quechua groups. The town is a friendly place that has tried hard to promote tourism, but there isn't much to actually see – unless you're excited by a military installation, a petroleum plant and a loosely defined port

area. However, if you fancy gliding down the Río Ichilo to view pink river dolphins, go bird-watching or fish for *surubí* (local catfish), this is your best bet in the Chapare.

🏃 Activities

Ask around at the port or in El Cliper for owners of *lanchas* (small boats). For a negotiable fee they can organize day-long fishing or camping trips to nearby river beaches, as well as visits to indigenous settlements. In the spirit of responsible tourism offer to pay what you consider a fair price; a gift of diesel is always welcome. Short one-hour sightseeing trips cost just B$10 per person with a six-person minimum.

🍴 Eating

El Cliper SEAFOOD $
(📱 mobile 7175-7891; Av Beni; mains B$20; ⊙10am-6pm Tue-Sun) This three-story open-air lookout tower by the port is your one-stop shop for food, local crafts and tourist information. Dine on fish like *surubí* while you arrange a boat trip down the Río Ichilo.

ℹ Getting There & Away

Micros (small buses) from Cochabamba to Puerto Villarroel, often marked 'Chimore' (B$25, five to seven hours), leave from the corner of Avs 9 de Abril and Oquendo, near Laguna Alalay. The first one sets off around 6am, and subsequent vehicles depart every couple of hours.

Alternatively, from the old bus terminal in Santa Cruz take a shared taxi to Yapacani (B$25, two hours); from there go to Bulo-Bulo (B$15, one hour); and finally take a third taxi to Puerto Villaroel (B\$10, one hour).

Note that transportation between Cochabamba and Santa Cruz doesn't stop at Puerto Villarroel, but you can get off at Ivirgarzama and take a taxi the remaining 30-minute stretch (B\$6).

WESTERN BOLIVIAN AMAZON

This is the Amazon as it's meant to be. Rich with wildlife, flora and indigenous culture, you may never want to leave. In the midst of the tropical lushness is the lovely town of Rurrenabaque, a major gringo-trail hangout. Pampas, jungle and ethno-ecotourism options are innumerable here, but vary significantly in quality and price. Parque Nacional Madidi, one of South America's and the world's most precious wilderness gems, sits on Rurrenabaque's doorstep.

Rurrenabaque

🖉 3 / POP 10,000 / ELEV 229M (751FT)

The gentle whisking of brooms on the plaza serves as a wake-up call in sleepy Rurre, a gringo crossroads sliced by the deep Río Beni and surrounded by mossy green hills. Mesmerizing sunsets turn the sky a burnt orange, and a dense fog sneaks down the river among the lush, moist trees. Once darkness falls, the surrounding rainforest comes alive with croaks, barks, buzzes and roars. This is civilization's last stand.

Backpackers fill the streets, and restaurants, cafes and hotels cater mainly to Western tastes. Some travelers spend their days relaxing in the ubiquitous hammocks, but at some stage the majority go off on riverboat adventures into the rainforest or pampas.

The area's original people, the Tacana, are responsible for the curious name of 'Rurrenabaque,' which is derived from 'Arroyo Inambaque,' the Hispanicized version of the Tacana name 'Suse-Inambaque,' the 'Ravine of Ducks.'

⊙ Sights

Though there isn't really that much to do in town, Rurrenabaque's appeal is in its surrounding natural beauty. It's easy to pass a day or three here while waiting to join a tour. Scramble up a 295-step staircase two blocks from the plaza, and then up a dirt-and-stone pathway to a *mirador*, and finally to a big cross (La Cruz) overlooking town and the Beni. Bring your hiking boots!

San Buenaventura   VILLAGE

Sleepy San Buenaventura sits across the Río Beni from Rurrenabaque, watching all the busy goings-on, but content with its own slower pace. The Centro Cultural Tacana (p299) has a handicrafts store on the southwest side of the plaza and celebrates the Tacana people's cosmovision. The official **Sernap office** (🖉 892-2540, mobile 6822-6337; Libertad, San Buenaventura; ⊙ 7am-3pm) for Parque Nacional Madidi is also here, near the market.

🏃 Activities

Canopy Zip Line
Villa Alcira   ADVENTURE SPORTS
(🖉 mobile 7284-3874; http://ziplinevillalcira.com; Comercio, near Santa Cruz; trip B\$350) A series of *tranquilo* (quiet/low-key) community-run tourism projects operate in Parque Nacional Madidi – but if you need more adrenaline, try the company formerly known as Biggest Canopy in Bolivia. It's a forest-canopy zip line for those with a head for heights, a strong stomach and a need for speed. Book at the Rurrenabaque office.

El Chorro   SWIMMING
El Chorro is an idyllic waterfall with a series of pools apt for swimming. You'll find it at the end of Calle Santa Cruz, following a well-worn trail 500m upstream into the jungle. It's popular with local families, but you should still be sure to watch your belongings.

Piscina El Mirador   SWIMMING
(Barrio El Camuy; entry B\$30; ⊙ 9am-6pm) On a *mirador* above town, this is a fabulous spot where you can swim and swoon over stunning views of the Beni lowlands. Food and cocktails are available at the bar. It's a B\$10 moto-taxi ride from the center of town, or a 3km walk (turn uphill by the gas station on the road to the bus terminal). BYO towel.

☞ Tours

Most agencies have offices on Avaroa. Tours can usually be paid for with credit cards.

Bala Tours   TOURS
(🖉 mobile 7112-2053; www.balatours.com; cnr Santa Cruz & Comercio; ⊙ 7:30am-7pm Mon-Sat, 7:30am-noon & 4-6pm Sun) Has its own jungle camp, Caracoles, a comfortable pampas

ℹ CHOOSING A JUNGLE OR PAMPAS TOUR

Jungle and pampas tours are Rurrenabaque's bread and butter, but quality of service provided by the numerous tour agencies varies considerably; in the name of competition, some operators are much less responsible than they ought to be. This is largely a result of overdemanding budget travelers expecting low prices with big results, bartering prices down and compromising their own safety and levels of service in the process. In the interests of responsible travel, consider the following carefully before you hand over your cash:

➡ Cheaper most definitely does not mean better. Local authorities have set minimum prices at B$1,200 for a three-day, two-night excursion; be suspicious of any company that undercuts those rates and do not barter for a lower price.

➡ Every company uses the word 'ecofriendly' as a throwaway sales gimmick. Catch out the conmen by asking the vendor to explain how their company is ecofriendly.

➡ There are no guarantees of spotting wildlife. Any company that offers them is likely to be breaking the rules. Guides are forbidden from feeding, handling or disturbing animals. If your guide offers to capture anacondas, caiman or other animals, object and explain why.

➡ Use only Sernap-authorized operators, as these are the only ones allowed to legally enter Parque Nacional Madidi (p301).

➡ Foreigners must be accompanied by a local guide, but not all speak good English. If this is likely to be a problem, ask to meet your guide.

➡ Talk to other travelers about their experiences and boycott companies that break the rules. Be responsible in your own expectations.

➡ Better still, opt for one of the community-run ecotourism ventures, which, although more expensive, are definitely more worthwhile and aim to help sustain communities and preserve the richness of the rainforests for the generations to come.

Jungle Tours

The Bolivian rainforest is full of more interesting and unusual things than you could ever imagine. Local guides can explain animals' habits and habitats and demonstrate the uses of some of the thousands of plant species, including the forest's natural remedies for colds, fever, cuts, insect bites (which come in handy!) and other ailments. Note that you are likely to see a lot more plants than animals.

Most trips are by canoe upstream along the Río Beni, and some continue up the Río Tuichi, taking shore and jungle walks along the way, with plenty of swimming opportunities and hammock time. Accommodations are generally in agencies' private camps.

Rain, mud and *mariguí* (sandflies) make the wet season (especially January to March) unpleasant for jungle tours, but some agencies have camps set up for wildlife watching at this time.

Pampas Tours

It's easier to see wildlife in the wetland savannas northeast of town, but the sun is more oppressive, and the bugs can be worse, especially in the rainy season. Bring binoculars, a good flashlight, extra batteries and plenty of strong antibug juice. Highlights include playful pink river dolphins, horseback riding and night-time canoe trips to spot caiman.

lodge on Río Yacumo and a forest lodge in Tacuaral.

Fluvial Tours   TOURS
(☑ mobile 7126-9357; http://fluvialtoursbolivia.com; Avaroa, near Santa Cruz; ⊙ 10am-6pm) This is Rurrenabaque's longest-running agency with cheap three-day pampas and jungle tours. Some readers have complained of poor quality.

🛏 Sleeping

★ **Hostal El Lobo**   HOSTEL **$**
(☑ mobile 6770-7582; hostalellobo@gmail.com; Comercio; dm per person B$60, r B$140; ☏ ▨)

Rurrenabaque

Río Beni

San Buenaventura (250m);
Sernap Parque Nacional
Madidi Office (500m);
Centro Cultural Tacana (600m)

Ferry

Internet Cyber
Ronaldo @   ●29

●19

25   ●23   Prodem

15

Moto-Taxi
Parada   ●1   18   ●16
14   28

Ferries to/from San   31●   ●32
Buenaventura   10   20   24
                         2
Banco   San Miguel   22   13
Unión   del Bala Office   Santa Cruz
30   7   17

Madidi Jungle   Chalalán   ●3
Booking Office   Ecolodge   21
            Booking Office   8

5
9   Avaroa

4   Plaza 2
      de Febrero   Campero

6   Templo de la   Sadiri
      Virgen de la   Booking
      Candelaria   Office
      Camacho   Busch

Hostal El
Lobo (50m)

      Sucre
27

26

11   La Cruz;
            Mirador

18 de Noviembre
Comercio
Avaroa
Junín
12
Aniceto Arce
Bolívar
Pando
Costanera
Comercio
Vaca Diez
Bolívar

Two hundred meters from the main plaza, this former mutt is now a buzzing playground for backpackers. A complete makeover includes crafty *tacuara* (bamboo) doors, a kidney-shaped swimming pool overlooking the Beni and a sweet hammock-filled terrace with pool tables and a bar. Dorms have screened windows and catch a cool breeze. Private rooms have river-facing balconies.

invariably be raving about what an excellent place it is – and it really is. Comfy rooms, great showers, garden hammocks for snoozing and big breakfasts are included in the price.

Hostal Turístico Santa Ana HOTEL **$**
(mobile 7128-2751; Avaroa, near Campero; s/d B$120/130, without bathroom B$50/100;) A good, clean value hotel with beautifully tiled pathways leading through a lush garden. As with most places there is the obligatory hammock zone. Unlike most places, there is a shared kitchen.

Hotel Pahuichi HOTEL **$**
(892-2558; cnr Comercio & Vaca Diez; d/tr incl breakfast B$130/170, with air-con B$200-250;) It's amazing what a good face-lift can do to an ageing hotel. The newly renovated suites here are tasteful, colorful and dare we say it stylish (almost!), with sleek wooden furniture and sparkling tiled private bathrooms.

Hotel Takana HOTEL **$$**
(892-2118, mobile 7205-1565; Plaza 2 de Febrero; s/d with air-con B$230/250, s with fan B$180;) This newer joint on the main plaza is a cut above the rest with hefty wooden furnishings and Jacuzzi tubs in some rooms. It's worth paying a bit extra for air-con although you can get away with the ceiling fans. Nice view from the back pool to the Río Beni.

La Isla de los Tucanes CABIN **$$**
(892-2127; www.islatucanes.com; Bolívar; s/d B$280/380;) An ecological cabin complex 1km north of town with thatched bungalows designed to make you feel even further away. With pool tables, an international restaurant and two clean swimming pools there is no real reason to leave – unless, of course, you are going into the jungle proper.

Centro de Recreación del Ejército PENSION **$$**
(892-2377; Plaza 2 de Febrero; r per person B$100, without bathroom B$80) If only all army barracks were like this they might not have so much trouble getting people to sign up! It's a strange concept, almost an officers' club, but it's essentially a good, modern, budget hotel with a river terrace. Just remember to salute if somebody calls your name and expect disciplined reception staff!

Hotel Oriental HOTEL **$**
(892-2401; www.facebook.com/hoteloriental rurre; Plaza 2 de Febrero; s/d/tr B$100/150/210;) If you meet people who are staying at the Oriental, right on the plaza, they'll

AMAZON BASIN RURRENABAQUE

Rurrenabaque

Hotel Rurrenabaque   HOTEL $$

(☑ mobile 7771-9363; Vaca Diez, near Bolívar; s/d B$150/210, without bathroom B$100/170; P ☎) A mustard-colored, porticoed edifice, with muted wood-floored rooms. There are no frills here except for on the curtains, but the new beds (circa 2015) give it an edge over the competition. All rooms include a nice buffet breakfast.

🍴 Eating

Eating options are varied, from quick chicken to fresh fish along the riverfront and fantastic international cooking. In addition to the Beni standard, *masaco* (mashed yuca or plantains, served with dried meat, rice, noodles, thin soup and bananas), try the excellent *pescado en dunucuabi* (fish wrapped in a rainforest leaf and baked over a wood fire).

The Sunday **feria** along the riverfront attracts local farmers with all their wild and wonderful produce.

Pizza al Paso   PIZZA $

(La Bella Italia; ☑ mobile 6728-5349; Avaroa near Pando; pizzas B$25-80; ☺ 5-10pm Wed-Mon; ☎) This popular (and incredibly friendly) street-side pizzeria offers four thin-crust pie sizes and an unlimited choose-your-own toppings menu at fixed prices. Toss in cheap

juices and beers and it adds up to a great value for groups.

Luz de Mar   BAKERY $

(Avaroa, near Pando; mains B$12-45; ☺ 7:30am-10:30pm Tue-Sun; ☎☑) With the biggest selection of sweets in town, this cute little bakery (full of spinning dream catchers) is the spot to go for banana bread, brownies and apple or mango pie. There's also an ambitious menu of mains, including ample vegetarian and vegan options.

Panadería París   BAKERY $

(Avaroa near Vaca Diez; items B$5-15; ☺ 6:30am-12:30pm & 3:30-6:30pm Mon-Fri, to 12:30pm Sat) Across from Fluvial Tours (p295; look for the mini Eiffel Tower!), this might be your only pretour breakfast option. The bread and pastries are almost worthy of its lofty name.

Market   MARKET $

(cnr Avaroa & Pando; snacks B$5-10; ☺ 6am-8pm) Rurrenabaque's market is a good place to stock up on nuts, chocolates and other jungle snacks. Also has cheap juices, empanadas and baked goods.

★ El Nomádico   INTERNATIONAL $$

(☑ mobile 7284-3850; Avaroa, near Aniceto Arce; mains B$50-65; ☺ 10am-10pm Fri-Wed) Set down a long brick alleyway in a candlelit courtyard, this 'hidden' upscale eatery has a hearty menu of delicious steaks, veggie pastas, chicken wings and curries. The fish curry, in particular, is legendary!

★ **Juliano's**   EUROPEAN **$$**
(Santa Cruz, btwn Avaroa & Bolívar; mains B$45-90; ⊙5-11pm; 🐾) Fusion in the jungle! This Tunisian emigre to Bolivia, via Paris, makes some awesome fish dishes (*pescado Juliano* is tasty) and has the only imported Peruvian shellfish in town. Save some room for the crème brûlée. The red lighting is *très chic*!

★ **Casa de Campo**   HEALTH FOOD **$$**
(📱 mobile 7199-3336; Comercio; mains B$25-75; ⊙7:30am-2pm & 5-10pm; 🐾🖥) Healthy food is the name of the game here, with all-day breakfasts, homemade pastries, vegetarian dishes, soups and salads on a breezy terrace across from El Lobo. Hospitable Adela is keen to make her guests happy (and give local hiking advice). Her 'tropical breakfast' with fresh-ground coffee and a crispy croissant is heavenly.

Beneath the restaurant – and hidden behind billowing bougainvilleas – are two comfortable **rooms** (incl breakfast US$60-65) with kitchenettes and air-con.

La Cabaña   SEAFOOD **$$**
(Costanera; mains B$40; ⊙7am-10pm Mon-Sat, to 3pm Sun) Riverfront La Cabaña grills or fries up the catch of the day.

🍷 Drinking & Nightlife

Luna Lounge   BAR
(Avaroa, near Santa Cruz; ⊙10am-2:30pm & 6pm-2am) One of Rurre's longest standing bars with a bouncing atmosphere, good pizza and great cocktails. There's also a pool table, foosball and, occasionally, live bands.

Funky Monkey Bar
and Restaurant   BAR
(Comercio, near Santa Cruz; ⊙noon-2pm) This bamboo bar is the best place for day drinking with an above-ground pool where you can laze away a sunny afternoon.

Jungle Bar Moskkito   BAR
(Vaca Diez, near Avaroa; ⊙4pm-3am) Peruvian-run, but English is spoken here. There's a positive vibe, cheery service and the foliage that hangs from the roof makes you feel like you're in the jungle, whether there are 'moskkitos' or not. Throw some darts, shoot some pool and choose your own music by request.

Bananas Pub Disco   CLUB
(cnr Comercio & Pando; incl 1 drink B$25; ⊙9:30pm-3:30am Tue-Sun) If you want to try salsa dancing or Bolivian-style grooving, this slightly sleazy club has locals shaking their booties plus gringos getting drunk and joining in. It's open into the wee hours after all other places have closed.

🛍 Shopping

La Cambita   ARTS & CRAFTS
(cambita.web.fc2.com; cnr Avaroa & Santa Cruz; ⊙8am-8pm) *Chonta*-wood plates, *jipijapa* baskets and organic coffee from Pilón Lajas are but a few of the intriguing Amazonian products on offer.

Centro Cultural Tacana   ARTS & CRAFTS
(📱892-2394; San Buenaventura; ⊙8am-noon & 2:30-6pm Mon-Fri) The Centro Cultural Tacana has a handicrafts store and celebrates the Tacana people's cosmovision. It's located on the southwest side of the main plaza in San Buenaventura.

Clothing Stalls   CLOTHING
(Pando, btwn Comercio & Avaroa; ⊙7am-9pm) The cheap clothing stalls along Pando are a good place to pick up *hamacas* (hammocks; single/double B$120/250) and finely woven cotton and synthetic *mosquiteros* (mosquito nets; from B$70).

Pampas Supermercado   DEPARTMENT STORE
(cnr Pando & Comercio; ⊙7:30am-9pm) Convenient for sun block, repellent and other jungle necessities.

ℹ Information

IMMIGRATION
For visa extensions, head to **immigration** (📱892-2241; cnr Sucre & Avaroa; ⊙8:30am-12:30pm & 2:30-6:30pm Mon-Fri).

INTERNET ACCESS
You may want to buy or top up a SIM card at **Entel** (cnr Comercio & Santa Cruz; ⊙9am-12:30pm & 3-6:30pm Mon-Fri, to 1:30pm Sat) because getting online is pricey (B$6 per hour) and often frustratingly slow. If you need a computer, **Internet Cyber Ronaldo** (Comercio, near Aniceto Arce; B$6 per hour; ⊙7am-10pm) is your best bet.

LAUNDRY
A couple of 'per kilo' laundries, including **Laundry Number One** (Avaroa, Edificio Candelaria; ⊙8am-noon & 2-8pm Mon-Sat, 11am-noon & 4-7pm Sun) and **Laundry Service Garfield**

SERERE ECO RESERVE

Rosa María Ruiz is a towering figure in Bolivian conservation and one of the key people involved in creating the park we now know as Madidi (p301). She lived in Madidi in its early years as a self-described hermit, but her outspoken criticism of Sernap – and its inability to control illegal logging and hunting – resulted in death threats, a ban from the park and, eventually, the torching of her jungle lodge. Undeterred, she set up shop three hours upriver from Rurrenabaque, creating her own private reserve: **Serere**.

Named after a bird with a blue face and punk-rock hair, this 4,000-hectare refuge has four lagoons, a week's worth of hiking trails, and enough monkeys, birds and reptiles to please the pickiest of wildlife watchers. Guides say they have more luck finding the famed Madidi wildlife here than along the increasingly crowded Río Tuichi, where nearly every other Rurrenabaque-based outfit has its jungle camps.

When you visit Serere you create your own itinerary based on your specific interests, with the help of indigenous guides. You eat organic food (much of which comes from the garden on-site) and sleep in spacious thatch-roofed cabins with screens for walls, so you feel like you're right in the thick of it when the critters saunter by. The income earned by the ecolodge gets pumped back into local conservation efforts.

The March 2000 *National Geographic* cover story that first put Madidi on the map is a great read for those who want to learn more about Ruiz and her remarkable conservation work in the face of innumerable obstacles. You can find a copy of it – and book a trip to her reserve – at the **Madidi Travel** (☑ mobile 6821-6580; www.madidi-travel.com; Comercio near Vaca Diez; all-inclusive 3-day, 2-night trip B$1899; ⊘ 8am-noon & 2-8pm) office in Rurrenabaque.

(Comercio, near Aniceto Arce; ⊘ 6am-10pm), offer a next-day service (per kilo B$8), a same-day service (per kilo B$10) and a four-hour service (per kilo, B$15) if you are in a hurry.

MEDICAL SERVICES

Clínica El Puerto (Comercio; ⊘ 24hr) is used to handling tourists with stomach problems. For anything more serious, make your way back to La Paz.

MONEY

The most convenient of the two ATMs in town is a block north of the plaza at **Banco Unión** (cnr Comercio & Vaca Diez; ⊘ 24hr). You can get cash advances at **Prodem** (cnr Avaroa & Pando; ⊘ 8am-4pm Mon-Fri, to noon Sat), but only on Visa and MasterCard (including Visa debit cards). It also does Western Union transfers and changes cash.

TOURIST INFORMATION

Workers at the **tourist office** (☑ mobile 7138-3684; cnr Vaca Diez & Comercio; ⊘ 8am-noon & 2:30-6pm Mon-Fri) are happy to answer questions and keen to advise on responsible tourism, but they're short on material. For information on Parque Nacional Madidi, head to the Sernap office (p294) in San Buenaventura.

ⓘ Getting There & Away

AIR

Rurre's **airport** is four kilometers north of town. **Amazonas** (☑ 892-2472; Comercio, near Santa

Cruz; ⊘ 7am-7pm) has daily flights to La Paz (B$480 and up) but at the time of research only one plane – you're out of luck if that's 'in maintenance.' **TAM** (☑ 892-2398; www.tam.bo; Santa Cruz) sporadically offers flights between La Paz and Rurre.

The brief flight to La Paz is an affordable way of avoiding the arduous bus journey. Flights sell out fast but are frequently cancelled during bad weather. You will be refunded only 75% of the ticket value if your flight is cancelled and you're not prepared to wait around for the next one. Be sure to reconfirm your ticket the day before flying, otherwise you may find yourself without a seat.

If you wish to fly to Riberalta or Guayaramerín, you need to go to Trinidad.

BOAT

The boat journey from Guanay to Rurre (p129) down Río Kaka and Río Beni is – for fans of slow travel – certainly the most scenic way to reach town from La Paz. Thanks to the Guayaramerín road, there's little cargo transportation further down the Río Beni to Riberalta these days. You'll need a dose of luck to find something and will have to negotiate a fair price for the boat (about B$4,000). The trip may take as long as three days.

BUS

The main **bus terminal** is across from the airport and a B$5 moto-taxi ride from town. All buses leave from here, though shared taxis to San Borja and Caranavi also depart when full from the **old terminal** by the cemetery. Prices do not vary between companies.

Several daily services make the daunting trip from Rurrenabaque to La Paz (B$70, 13 to 15 hours), via Yolosa (B$60, 12 hours), the hop-off point for Coroico. If you find the narrow, twisting Andean roads and sheer drops a harrowing experience on a bus, another option is to bus it as far as Caranavi (B$70, five to seven hours) and take a shared taxi from there, the rest of the trip being the most scary, or picturesque, depending on your point of view.

The route to Trinidad (B$130, 10 to 13 hours) via San Borja (taxi/bus B$80/50, three hours) and San Ignacio de Moxos (B$100, seven hours) was once one of the worst in the country, but is now paved for much of the way. Buses currently run year-round on this route, as well as to Riberalta (B$120, 13 to 14 hours) and Guayaramerín (B$130, 14 to 15 hours), but you need a healthy dose of stamina, insect repellent and food if you're going to attempt trips in the wet season. Departure times are erratic for these long-distance destinations and change day to day, so it's best to check at the station in advance.

❶ Getting Around

Moto-taxis around town cost B$3 per ride; there is a convenient **parada** (Taxi Stand; cnr Comercio & Santa Cruz). The **ferry** (B$1.50; ☺ 6am–11pm) across to San Buenaventura leaves from the port area every 15 minutes, though services are less frequent after 6pm.

Parque Nacional Madidi

The 1.8 million-hectare Parque Nacional Madidi is one of South America's most intact ecosystems, taking in a range of habitats from steaming lowland rainforests to 6000m Andean peaks. This little-trodden utopia is home to an astonishing variety of Amazonian wildlife: 44% of all mammals in North and South America, 38% of neotropical amphibian species and more than 1000 species of bird. Some scientists call it the most biodiverse place on earth.

The populated portions of the park along the Río Tuichi have been accorded a special Unesco designation permitting indigenous inhabitants to utilize traditional forest resources, but the park has also been named as a site for a major hydroelectric scheme. Illicit logging has damaged several areas around the perimeter and the debate continues over road building and oil exploration. With President Morales opening all Bolivian parks to oil and gas exploration, environmentalists are holding their collective breath.

🛏 Sleeping

Providing a model for responsible, sustainable ecotourism in Bolivia, the community projects in Madidi preach a respect for culture, environment and wildlife, and benefit local communities rather than private operators. You can choose from one-day tours to longer stays, incorporating walks in the rainforest with visits to indigenous communities, where you can peek into local lifestyles and traditions.

Booking offices for most of these community lodges are located in Rurrenabaque.

★ **Chalalán Ecolodge** LODGE **$$$**
(☎ 892-2419; www.chalalan.com; 4-day/3-night all-inclusive program per person US$500-544, per day US$145) ✍ This is Bolivia's oldest and most successful community-based ecotourism project. Chalalán provides the opportunity to amble through relatively untouched rainforest and appreciate the diversity of the native wildlife. The lodge's simple and elegant huts surround the idyllic oxbow lake, Laguna Chalalán. There is a booking office in Rurrenabaque (Comercio, near Campero) and also in La Paz (Galería Doryan, 2nd fl, Office 23).

Set up in the early 1990s by the inhabitants of remote San José de Uchupiamonas, it has become a lifeline for villagers, and has so far generated money for a school and a small clinic. Built entirely from natural rainforest materials by the enthusiastic San José youth, the lodge surrounds you with lovely flora and fauna. But it's the sounds that provide the magic here: the incredible bird chorus at dawn, the evening frog symphony, the collective whine of zillions of insects, the roar of bucketing tropical rainstorms and, in the early morning, the reverberating chorus of every howler monkey within a 100km radius.

Your trip starts from Rurrenabaque with a six-hour boat ride upstream on the misty Río Beni, and moves onto the smaller tributary, Río Tuichi. At Chalalán, you can go on long daytime treks or on nocturnal walks (there are 30km of trails). Boat excursions on the lake are a delight and you can see different types of monkeys who come to feed. Swimming is a must, especially at dusk when the light is heavenly.

The village of San José is another three hours upstream by boat. If you wish to visit it from Chalalán, you'll need to arrange it in advance through the ecolodge. It's especially rewarding during the week-long **fiesta** for the local patron saint around May 1.

Rates include transfers to and from the airport (if you're coming from La Paz), three great meals per day, a well-trained English-speaking guide, excursions, canoe trips on the lake, plus local taxes and a community levy.

★ **Sadiri** LODGE **$$$**
(☑ mobile 7162-2567; http://sadirilodge.com; all-inclusive per person per day US$135) ✈ One of the newest kids on the community-project block is wonderful Sadiri: six luxury cabins in dense foothill rainforest in the Serranía Sadiri. Community members staff the lodge, which has the best-trained wildlife guides in the Rurrenabaque area. Email bookings are preferred at sadirilodge@gmail.com. Rates include full board and return transfer to Rurrenabaque.

The indigenous San José de Uchupiamonas community rejected the advances of the courting forestry companies and with the assistance of local conservationists opted instead for a sustainable tourist project aimed at bringing long-term benefits to the area. The innovative lodge caters as much for serious bird-watchers and ecotravelers as it does to those who just revel in the beauty of natural areas.

What sets Sadiri apart from the other Madidi lodges is its highland location (between 500m and 950m), resulting in a much cooler temperature than in the sweaty lowlands. This means that there is a whole new set of animals and birds to enjoy, including mixed flocks filled with dozens of species of glittering tanagers, each one like a feathered jewel. Bird Bolivia (p358) organizes recommended trips.

Traditional home-cooked meals are served on a terrace flanked with hummingbird feeders, looking out over Madidi with some of the most awe-inspiring views of the national park that you could ever imagine. An office in Rurrenabaque (cnr Busch & Campero) is sometimes open.

Madidi Jungle LODGE **$$$**
(☑ mobile 7128-2697; www.madidijungle.com; 3-day/2-night all-inclusive program per person US$270) ✈ The newest community project in Madidi and the only one created and sustained 100% by the indigenous people of the park. All-inclusive trips include

bird-watching, night hikes, boat excursions, piranha fishing, handicraft workshops, river tubing and more within the 210,000-hectare stretch of land belonging to the San José de Uchupiamonas.

You'll sleep in comfortable thatch-roofed cabins set by the Río Tuichi and eat meals made with traditional rainforest ingredients. The three-hour journey to the lodge from Rurrenabaque is included in the price, as are bilingual guides.

There's a booking office (Comercio near Vaca Diez) in Rurrenabaque.

San Miguel del Bala LODGE **$$$**
(☑ 892-2394; www.sanmigueldelbala.com; per person per day B$520) ✈ A glorious community ecolodge in its own patch of paradise right on Madidi's doorstep, 40 minutes upstream by boat from Rurrenabaque. This Tacana community will be happy to show you their traditional agricultural methods, weaving and wood carving. Accommodations are in cabins with mahogany wood floors, separate bathrooms and beds covered by silky mosquito nets. The booking office is in Rurrenabaque.

❶ Getting There & Away

The easiest access point for a visit to the park in Rurrenabaque, which has great tourist infrastructure and several tour companies. You could also visit from Apolo or Pelechuco, but access is much more difficult and you'd want to consult with agencies in La Paz before setting off.

San Borja

☑ 3 / POP 40,864 / ELEV 170M (560FT)

San Borja is pretty much just a bus- and truck-stop destination, though it's a pleasant enough place with a tropical plaza and plenty of hotels and restaurants. You can easily find yourself stuck here waiting for transportation to Trinidad or Rurrenabaque during the rainy season. Those hoping to hike into Reserva de la Biosfera y Estación Biológica del Beni (p303) make an obligatory stop at the Sernap office (p304) here to plan their journey.

🛏 Sleeping & Eating

Hotel Jatata HOTEL **$**
(☑ 895-3212; Oruro 249; s/d B$100/150, with air-con B$150/200; ❄ 🛜) Two blocks off the Plaza Principal, pick-of-the-bunch Jatata offers a warm welcome, fast wi-fi, yummy

breakfasts and comfy rooms. There's also a lovely patio with drooping hammocks.

Big Burger BURGERS $
(cnr Oruro & Trinidad; burgers B$15; ⊙6-11pm Tue-Sun) Choose from five different hamburger types – American, Spanish, Italian, Mexican or Amazonian – at this popular street-side burger shack, which also serves cheap, fresh juices.

ⓘ Getting There & Away

The San Borja to Trinidad road was once one of the worst in the country, but is on its way to being completely paved by 2020. Paved does not mean no potholes, however, and it may still be a hassle in the wet season. In theory, more services to Trinidad depart from San Borja than from Rurre, so you may find yourself here whether you like it or not, stranded and waiting.

Buses pull out several times daily from the bus terminal (2km southwest of the plaza; by moto-taxi B$4) for the Reserva de la Biosfera y Estación Biológica del Beni (B$20, one hour), San Ignacio de Moxos (B$70, three to four hours for shared taxi or minivan), Trinidad (B$100/120 in the dry/rainy season, six to eight hours) and Santa Cruz (B$200, 18 hours). There are frequent *micro* (small bus) services to Rurrenabaque (B$80, three hours) on a mostly paved road, which depart when full. Taxis to Yucumo (B$30, 40 minutes) depart when full – you may need to connect there for other transport.

If you're Trinidad-bound, you'll cross the Río Mamoré on a *balsa* (raft); watch for pink river dolphins.

Reserva de la Biosfera y Estación Biológica del Beni

Created by Conservation International in 1982 as a loosely protected natural area, this 334,200-hectare **park** (☑895-3898) **FREE** was recognized by Unesco in 1986 as a 'Man & the Biosphere Reserve,' and received official recognition the following year through a pioneering debt-swap agreement with the Bolivian government. The area is home to at least 500 bird species as well as more than 100 mammals and myriad reptiles, amphibians and insects.

The ranger station at El Porvenir (p304) is the main point of entry. It's located in the *cerrado* (savanna) and quite a distance from the rainforest.

While Estación Biológica del Beni once offered decent visitor facilities, it's now best suited for intrepid travelers with sufficient Spanish-language skills. Note that before heading to El Porvenir it is essential to stop by the Sernap (p304) office in San Borja to register and plan out your trip.

◎ Sights

Laguna Normandia LAKE
This savanna lake, a 2km walk from El Porvenir, is the reserve's most popular destination. The sight of one of the world's largest populations of crawling, rare black caimans – there are at least 400 of them – is

THE MOST BIODIVERSE PLACE ON EARTH?

In June 2015 a team of (mostly Bolivian) scientists, supported by the Wildlife Conservation Society (WCS), set off on the nearly three-year Identidad Madidi expedition to survey Parque Nacional Madidi and identify as many species as possible that live within its borders. To do so, they honed in on 15 study sites spread across the mountainous puna, intermediary cloud forests and dense lowland jungles.

By the time the survey was complete in May 2018, the team had added 1,382 new plants and animals to Madidi's species lists, including 100 mammals, 41 birds, 27 reptiles, 25 amphibians, 138 fish, 440 plants and 611 butterflies (counting all the insects was deemed too difficult!). More than 120 of these are potentially new to science, including a whiptail lizard and a spiny rat.

The total number of species documented at Madidi now stands at 8,524 – including 265 mammals, 1028 birds, 105 reptiles, 109 amphibians, 314 fish, 5515 plants and 1544 butterflies. The WCS believes that this makes it the most biodiverse protected area on earth. Researchers hope Identidad Madidi will help Bolivians to better appreciate their protected lands and the need to become stewards of the globally important ecosystems in their backyards.

TCO TSIMANÉ

Adjacent to Reserva de la Biosfera y Estación Biológica del Beni lies the **TCO Tsimané**, a 1.15-million-hectare buffer zone and indigenous reserve set aside for sustainable subsistence use by the 1200 Tsimané people living within its borders.

The Tsimané reserve was threatened in 1990 when the government decided to open the area to loggers. Seven hundred Tsimané and representatives of other tribes staged a march from Trinidad to La Paz in protest. Logging concessions were changed but not altogether revoked, and the problems continue.

To learn more about the Tsimané communities, consider booking a trip to Río Maniqui.

truly astounding. Fortunately, caimans have little interest in humans, so it's generally safe to observe them (but watch out for the snakes on the hike in!).

Totaizal
VILLAGE

A stone's throw from the road and a 40-minute walk from El Porvenir is Totaizal. This friendly and well-organized village of 300 people is the closest to the reserve and it's where **Sernap** (☑ 895-3898; cnr Cuarta Sur & Trinidad; ⊘ 8am-noon & 2-6:30pm) arranges guides and horses. People living in the settlement of **Cero Ocho**, a four-hour (15km) walk from Totaizal, trudge into the village to sell bananas and other goods. You can visit the village directly, but it's best to make prior arrangements for guides through Sernap in San Borja.

🏃 Activities

The park office in San Borja organizes everything in the reserve: accommodations, food, guides and horseback riding. The best way to observe wildlife is to have them hire a guide and go for a hike, though the heat might be easier to take if you hire a horse.

For those looking to spend at least a week in the area there are also volunteer opportunities during the nesting season for Amazon river turtles (mid-August to mid-September).

 Tours

Expect to pay about B\$140 per day for a local, Spanish-speaking guide. In more remote areas of the park like Río Maniqui, the park rangers will actually work as guides for free (provided you arrange for all food and transport at the Sernap office in San Borja).

For a more high-end alternative, La Paz–based Bolivia Millenaria (p358) can organize trips to the park with English-speaking guides.

El Porvenir
WALKING TOUR, HORSEBACK RIDING

(200m off Carretera F3) Theoretically El Porvenir station can be used as a base for tours with enough notice, though these are more difficult to arrange during the wet season. Popular tours include the 2km walk to see the black caimans in Laguna Normandia (p303) and the eight-hour (20km) round-trip hike to the monkey-rich rainforests near the **Marimono ranger station**.

If you're a bird fanatic, take the **Loro tour** on foot or horseback to see the colorful spectacle of macaws and parakeets coming to roost – or you can check them out in the palms at El Porvenir, where they provide a natural 6am alarm clock.

The most interesting but also the most taxing option is the four-day **Tur Monitoreo** (per person without/with food B\$800/1080), during which visitors accompany park rangers on their wildlife monitoring rounds into the furthest reaches of the reserve. You will need your own camping gear for this and, of course, plenty of insect repellent, but you'll have a great shot at seeing monkeys, macaws and pink river dolphins.

Horse rentals are available from around B\$100 per eight-hour day.

Río Maniqui
HIKING

(tours B\$540 per person) An interesting alternative to El Porvenir is to visit the remote Tsimané communities along Río Maniqui. Two-day, one-night ranger tours operate out of the **Campamento Los Petos** ranger station, from which you can also hike up into the riparian forests or along the river to view pink dolphins and Amazonian turtles.

🛏 Sleeping & Eating

There is no food or hotel service in the park, though there is a basic **albergue** (carolavaca@hotmail.com; 200m off Carretera F3)

FREE at El Porvenir. Email to arrange a stay here or in one of the park guard's lodgings. It is also possible to camp for free.

You should tip the guards and anyone who helps you with sleeping arrangements.

ⓘ Information

The best months to visit the reserve are June and July, when there's little rain and the days are clear; bring warm clothing to protect against the occasional *surazo* (strong southerly). During the rainy season, days are hot, wet, muggy and miserable with mosquitoes, so bring plenty of repellent.

ⓘ Getting There & Away

El Porvenir is 200m off the highway, one hour east of San Borja, and is accessible via any *movilidad* (anything that moves) between Trinidad and San Borja or Rurrenabaque – ask your driver to drop you at the entrance.

Trinidad-bound buses mainly pass in the morning between 9am and 11am, those for San Borja usually in the late afternoon between 4pm and 7pm. Otherwise there's surprisingly little traffic.

San Ignacio de Moxos

♪ 3 / POP 10,050 / ELEV 145M (475FT)

San Ignacio de Moxos is a friendly, tranquil indigenous Moxos village, 92km west of Trinidad, with an ambience quite distinct from any other Bolivian town. The people speak an indigenous dialect known as *ignaciano*, and their lifestyle, traditions and food are unique. The best time to visit is during the annual festival on July 30 and 31. This is when the villagers let their hair down and get their feather headgear up, and don't stop drinking, dancing and letting off fireworks for three days.

The village was founded as San Ignacio de Loyola by the Jesuits in 1689. In 1749 it suffered pestilence and had to be shifted to its present location on healthier ground.

⦿ Sights

Iglesia Parroquial de S.I. CHURCH
(Iglesia Parroquial de San Ignacio; Main Plaza; ⊙ on request for groups) The church on the plaza was restored and rebuilt from 1995 to 2003 and adopts the familiar Jesuit style with a wide roof supported by wooden columns, though they are noticeably smooth and without decoration in this example. There's a colorful Amazonian mural on the facade,

and if you get a small group together, one of the church workers will take you around inside for a small fee.

Museo de Mojos MUSEUM
(Main Plaza; ⊙ 9am-noon & 3-6pm Mon-Sat, to noon Sun) View elements of both the Ignaciano and Moxos cultures, including the *bajones*, the immense flutes introduced by the Jesuits. You can also learn about the legacy of baroque music here at the **Archivo Musical**.

Main Plaza PLAZA
In the main plaza is a **monument** to Chirípieru, El Machetero Ignaciano, with his crown of feathers and formidable-looking hatchet, a look that's re-created extensively during the village festival. There are surely enough banana-yellow benches here to seat the entire town.

Laguna Isirere LAKE
North of town at the large Laguna Isirere, you can go fishing and swimming, observe the profuse birdlife and watch the gorgeous sunset. It's accessible on a 30-minute (2km) walk or moto-taxi (B$5) from town.

A **statue** on the shore depicts the local legend about the formation of the lake. A young boy named Isidoro was paddling in a small pool when he was swallowed up by the waters, the work of the mischievous water spirit Jichi who needed a human sacrifice in order to turn the pool into the lake it is today.

✹ Festivals & Events

In April or May of even-numbered years, a **baroque music festival** (www.festival esapac.com/musica.htm, in Spanish) takes place across more than 20 former missions, including San Ignacio.

Fiesta de Moxos RELIGIOUS
(Fiesta del Santo Patrono de Moxos; ⊙ Jul 30-31) Annually, 2pm on July 30 marks the first day of celebrations of the huge Fiesta del Santo Patrono de Moxos, held in honor of San Ignacio, the sacred protector of the Moxos. This is one of the best festivals in the Amazon and if you're in Bolivia during this time, you'd be crazy to miss it.

Strictly speaking, the festival begins on July 22 and gets off to a strange start. The small statue of Santiago from the church is paraded and worshipped each evening until July 25 (Día de la Fiesta de Santiago), after which point the same statue is then worshipped as an image of San Ignacio for the rest of the fiesta! During this time each family in the village brings an image of San Ignacio to the church and places it there in his honor. These solemn processions continue for another four days before the real festivities begin.

On July 30, a procession leaves from the church incorporating *macheteros* (local youths dressed in white with remarkable radial headdresses traditionally made from macaw feathers), *achus* (village elders with wooden masks and hats bearing fireworks) and musicians beating out the tunes of Moxos music, using drums, enormous bamboo panpipes and flutes. The procession visits every house in the village, returning the images of San Ignacio that had been deposited in the church and receiving food and drink in return. The winding route ends at the church, where the participants attend Mass, after which the festivities begin.

The evening of the first day of fiesta starts with huge fireworks let off by two rich local families outside the church, who 'compete' with each other through the lavishness of their displays. Then it's over to the *achus*, men and women wearing large, high-topped leather hats with firecrackers fizzling on the top, who run through the crowd, while everyone shrieks and runs away from them, laughing and screaming – children have a particularly good time. Fresh river fish is eaten in abundance, plenty of drinking takes place (as you'll see by the number of booze-casualties sleeping in the streets) and local *artesanía* (locally handcrafted items) is displayed around the village.

On the morning of the second day another mass is held. The small statue of San Ignacio is returned to the church and a larger statue of the same saint is extracted for the first time to lead a second procession, this time accompanied by local politicians, religious authorities, invited dignitaries and others worthy of a bigger statue. Once the formalities are dispensed with, it's party time again. The second and third days are filled with lots of dancing and bull-teasing, when the (drunk) locals attempt to get the bulls' attention. A few days later, San Ignacio goes back to its quiet life, only to go wild again the following year.

THE AMAZONIAN EL DORADO

In the Llanos de Moxos, between San Ignacio de Moxos and Loreto, the heavily forested landscape is crossed with more than 100km of canals and causeways and dotted with hundreds of *lomas* (artificial mounds), embankments and fanciful prehistoric earthworks depicting people and animals. One anthropomorphic figure measures more than 2km from head to toe – a rainforest variation on Peru's famed Nazca Lines.

The discovery of the *lomas* has caused scientists to look at the Beni region with entirely new eyes: what was previously considered to be a wilderness never touched by humans, save for a few dispersed tribes who inhabited the region, is now thought to have been an area where a vast, advanced civilization farmed, worked and lived in a highly structured society with sophisticated cities.

It is believed that the ceramic mounds came from the large numbers of people who lived on them and who ate and drank from pots, which were then destroyed and buried to improve soil stability. Archaeologists say that the sheer amount of pots indicates the complexity of this lost society.

Romantics associate the prehistoric structures of the Beni with the legendary Paitití tribe, and infer that this ancient Beni civilization was the source of the popular Spanish legends of the rainforest El Dorado known as Gran Paitití. The Paitití were said to be an Inca tribe associated with the cultural hero Inkarri who, after founding Cuzco, retired to the Amazon to found another great but mysterious civilization in an unknown location. Though some Inca fragments were found in northern Bolivia during excavations in 2003, the Inca origin of the Moxos sites remains doubtful; the most accepted theory is that if Paitití existed at all, its most likely location is Peru.

Archaeologists continue their research into this fascinating part of history, but one thing is for sure: once you know what lies here in terms of world history, you'll never look at the forests of the Beni in the same way again.

🛏 Sleeping & Eating

Hotel San Ignacio   HOTEL $
(☑482-2063; Main Plaza; r per person B$80;
❄🛜) This is the nicest option in town with
artwork on the walls, wi-fi and air-con. All
rooms are spacious and have private bathrooms, though the upstairs ones are better.

Residencial Don Joaquín   PENSION $
(☑mobile 7284-3843; Main Plaza; s/d B$80/120,
without bathroom per person B$50) At the cor-
ner of the plaza near the church, it offers a
nice patio and clean, simple rooms.

La Pascana del Gordo   BOLIVIAN $
(Santiesteban, near Sucre; mains B$20; ⊗8am-
2pm) A local favorite that specializes in traditional Moxos dishes. Worryingly, also listed
in the phone book as a disco!

ℹ Getting There & Away

San Ignacio is located smack-bang in the middle
of the notoriously poor (though increasingly
asphalted) Trinidad–San Borja road. From
April to October, it's three to four hours from
Trinidad to San Ignacio by van (B$60), including
the *balsa* crossing of the Río Mamoré, but this
route is sporadically closed during the rainy
season. San Borja–bound bus services (B$40)
pass through San Ignacio in the early afternoon
but take considerably longer. During intense
periods of rain and during the festival, flights to
Trinidad may be offered.

The tiny **Moxos airport** is at the top end of
Av Aeropuerto but you'll have to ask around for
information.

From San Borja, *micros* (small buses) to San
Ignacio (B$60, three to four hours) leave daily
when full. There are sporadic departures to
Rurrenabaque (B$80, seven to eight hours),
but it's usually easier to catch a lift to San Borja
and take one of the more frequent *micros* from
there.

EASTERN BOLIVIAN AMAZON

Trinidad

☑3 / POP 122,000 / ELEV 158M (520FT)
Trinidad is the place you'll come to if you're
after a trip down the long and deep Río
Mamoré, or on your way between Santa
Cruz and Rurrenabaque. Despite its colo-
nial architecture and colonnaded streets,
it's a modern city that is growing rapidly.
Yet, it's surprisingly easy to trade the hum of

motorbikes for the sounds of blue-throated
macaws or pink river dolphins in the surrounding wetlands.

The city of La Santísima Trinidad (the
Most Holy Trinity) was founded in 1686 by
Padre Cipriano Barace as the second Jesuit
mission in the flatlands of the southern
Beni. It was originally constructed on the
banks of the Río Mamoré, 14km from its
present location, but floods and pestilence
along the riverbanks forced relocation. In
1769 it was moved to the Arroyo de San
Juan, which now divides the city in two.

⊙ Sights

★**Santuario Chuchini**   NATURE RESERVE
(Jaguar's Lair; ☑mobile 7284 2200; www.chuchini.
org; B$20, half-day visit incl meal & boat ride B$100,
all-inclusive two-day stay from B$1120; ⊗8am-
6pm Wed-Mon) The Santuario Chuchini (Jaguar's Lair) is one of the few easily accessible
Paitití sites. This wildlife sanctuary and
camp sits on an 8-hectare *loma* (artificial
mound) of the ancient civilization. From the
camp, you can take short walks in the rainforest to lagoons with caimans, other larger
animals and profuse birdlife.

The camp has shady, covered picnic
sites, trees, children's swings and a variety
of native plants, birds and animals. There's
also an archaeological museum displaying
articles excavated from the *loma*, including bizarre statues as well as a piece that
appears to be a female figure wearing a
bikini (it's actually thought to be an iden-
tification of, and homage to, specific body
areas rather than an article of clothing).

You can volunteer here (one week minimum) and package-tour visits booked in
Trinidad may work out a bit cheaper. Further information is available from managers
Miriam and Efrem Ibis, or travel agencies in
Trinidad. Unless you organize a tour, which
will include transportation, you'll have to
negotiate with a moto-taxi driver (typically
B$20) for the 14km journey north of town.
It's also a good destination for those who've
rented their own motorcycles.

★**Museo Etnoarqueológico
Kenneth Lee**   MUSEUM
(Kenneth Lee Ethno-Archaeological Museum; Av
Ganadera; ⊗8am-noon & 2:30-6:30pm Mon-Fri)
FREE Named for the *gringo querido del
Beni*, the beloved white man of the Beni,
this small museum north of the center is
considered the city's top cultural attraction.

Trinidad

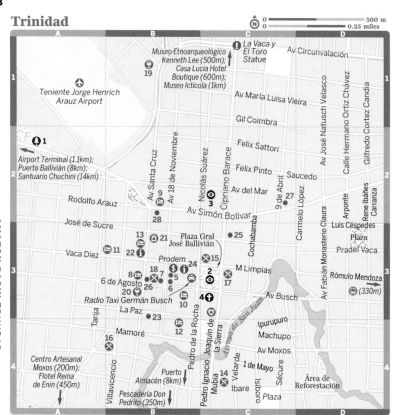

It exhibits artifacts from the Trinidad region, including traditional instruments and tribal costumes.

Parque Pantanal
PARK

(Av José Chávez Suárez; ⊙8am-noon & 2:30-6:30pm) **FREE** On the road to the airport, this wooded park no longer serves as a wildlife rehab center – the inmates got a bit feisty – but it's still a nice place to wander the pathways and check out birdlife, like the yellow-winged jacanas hopping on and off the lily pads. At the end of the park is a new **interpretation center** exploring the flora and fauna of Bolivia's wetland environments.

Museo Ictícola
MUSEUM

(Universidad Autónoma del Beni; ⊙8am-noon & 3-6pm Mon-Fri, 9am-noon Sat) **FREE** At the university 1.5km north of town along Cipriano Barace is the Museo Ictícola, an extensive aquarium featuring some of the 500 species of Amazonian fish; some are pickled and preserved, some still swimming. The electric-eel skeleton will make you think twice about jumping in the Beni. It's a B$5 moto-taxi ride.

Plazuela Natuch
PLAZA

(Plazuela Estudiante; cnr Nicolás Suárez & Av del Mar) Worth a quick look for the colorful Beni wall murals and statues of native wildlife, including a prone jaguar and a family of capybara. There are usually some stalls selling local *artesanía* (locally handcrafted items), as well as canoodling teenagers.

Plaza Gral José Ballivián
PLAZA

Trinidad's loveliest feature is Plaza Gral José Ballivián, with its tall, tropical trees, lush gardens and community atmosphere. You can spend a pleasant evening eating ice cream and listening to the rhythmic drone of hundreds of motorcycles orbiting around the square.

Trinidad

AMAZON BASIN TRINIDAD

Trinidad Cathedral   CHURCH
(Plaza Gral José Ballivián) FREE On the south
side of Plaza Gral José Ballivián, Trinidad's
mustard-yellow cathedral was built between
1916 and 1931 on the site of a Jesuit church.

👉 Tours

Several agencies run tours into the region's
hinterlands to explore the nearly 20,000
pre-Columbian *lomas* (artificial mounds),
search for macaws in the **Área Protegida
Municipal Gran Mojos**, boat with pink
river dolphins in the **Área Protegida Ibare
Mamoré** or hop on a horse and live a day in
the life of a Bolivian rancher.

★ La Ruta del Bufeo   BOATING
(ECOterra; ☑ mobile 7281-8317; https://bolivia-
natura.com/en; half-day/full-day/2-day tours from
B$195/375/690) This tour company special-
izes in *la ruta del bufeo*, a one- or two-day
boat journey through the Área Protegida
Municipal Ibare-Mamoré to view the pink
Amazon river dolphins. Departures are typically from Puerto Ballivián (8km from Trinidad). English-language guides cost extra.

Check out the informative English-
language website; it's a great resource for
planning trips in the Beni.

Rancho La Victoria   WILDLIFE WATCHING
(☑ mobile 7114-7183; www.rancholavictoria.net;
3-day all-inclusive tour from US$265) Offers

three-day trips to Rancho La Victoria, 100km
north of Trinidad, via the Jesuit missions of
San Javier and San Pedro. The tour is part
wildlife safari, part dude-ranch adventure.

**Conservación
Loros Bolivia**   WILDLIFE WATCHING
(CLB; ☑ mobile 7112-6506; https://fclbolivia.org;
18 de Noviembre 278; ◷ 8am-noon & 2-6pm Mon-
Fri, to noon Sat) 🐾 This foundation doesn't
actually sell tours, but executive director
José Antonio Díaz is so passionate about
the region and its wildlife that he can set
you up with guides (any money you pay will
serve as a donation to support CLB's conservation work). Stop by for information on
bird-watching in the Reserva Barba Azul
(p314) or Área Protegida Municipal Gran
Mojos.

Flotel Reina de Enin   BOATING
(☑ mobile 7391-2965; www.amazonasrivercruise.
com; Av Santos Noco 110; all-inclusive 3/4-day
cruise US$527/587; ◷ 8:30am-noon & 3-6:30pm
Mon-Fri) Multiday river cruises depart from
(and return to) Puerto Ballivián on the outskirts of Trinidad. You'll sleep in comfortable bunks as you glide from the sinewy Río
Ibare into the much grander Río Mamoré;
activities include looking for dolphins or
caimans and stopping for walks through
the jungle to view prehistoric *lomas*. The
boat has a top-floor hammock deck and a
river-fed 'pool.'

Bici Tour   CYCLING
(📱 mobile 7114-7183; www.facebook.com/bicitour
lyliam; Av 18 de Noviembre 278; bike rentals hr/day
B$15/80) Bike rentals and English-language
city tours. Also offers nature-focused bike
trips to Laguna Suárez, Laguna La Bomba
and destinations further afield.

Turismo Moxos   TOURS
(📱 mobile 7113-0122; www.facebook.com/moxos
viajes; Av 6 de Agosto 114; ⊙ 8am-12:30pm & 2:30-
6:30pm Mon-Fri, to 1pm Sat) Turismo Moxos
organizes one- to three-day dolphin cruises
on the Río Ibare, three-day survival courses,
visits to Sirionó villages, four-day canoe safa-
ris into the jungle and one-day horseback
trips into remote areas. English-language
guides cost extra.

🎊 Festivals & Events

Fiesta de la Santísima Trinidad   FIESTA
(⊙ May or Jun) The town's founding fiesta is
a big, loud, drunken party, and features the
climbing of greased poles for prizes and the
hocheadas de toros (teasing of bulls).

🛌 Sleeping

Hostal El Tajibo   HOTEL $
(📱 462-2324; Av Santa Cruz 423; s/d B$120/160,
with air-con B$200/260; ❄ 🛜) One of Trinidad's
better-value budget options, this hotel has
attractive, almost-stylish rooms and comfortable beds. Some rooms have balconies overlooking the street and breakfast is included
with air-con rooms. New mattresses are a
bonus, but the joint could use a coat of paint.

Nearby **Hotel Colonial** (📱 462-2864; www.
facebook.com/hotelcolonialtrinidad; Vaca Diez 306;
s/d B$200/250, ste B$250/350; ❄ 🛜 ❄) is run
by the same owners but is a step up.

Residencial Santa Cruz   PENSION $
(📱 462-0711; Av Santa Cruz 537; s/d B$80/150, s/d
without bathroom B$70/130; 🛜) A budget place
that's a bit beat up, but makes a real effort
to cheer up its rooms with colorful decor,
hand-painted wall hangings and bright bed-
clothes. Rooms on the top floor are airier. All
rooms have cable TV. Nice old couple also
offers a shared kitchen (but won't help you
cook!).

★ **Casa Lucia**
Hotel Boutique   BOUTIQUE HOTEL $$
(📱 mobile 7828-8146; www.facebook.com/Casa
LuciaHotelBoutique; El Palmar 42; s/d/tr incl break-
fast B$280/350/450; ❄ 🛜 ❄) Slightly removed
from town on a secluded residential street
near the Kenneth Lee museum (p307), this

gorgeous hideaway is Trinidad's finest, with
seven antique-filled rooms clustered around
lush gardens and a kidney-shaped pool.

Hotel Campanario   HOTEL $$
(📱 462-4733; www.hotel-campanario.com; Av 6 de
Agosto 80; s/d B$280/480, ste B$600-700; ❄ ❄)
Hotel Campanario is aiming to capitalize
on an increase in wealthy business travelers from Santa Cruz by offering a series
of high-class rooms and suites. Suites are
tastefully decorated and airy, with colorful bed spreads, and the pool access and
air-conditioning contribute towards what
should be a pleasant stay.

Hotel Jacaranda Suites   HOTEL $$
(📱 462-2400; hoteljacarandasuites@hotmail.com;
La Paz 159; s/d B$360/500; ❄ @ ❄) For a long
time taking the mantle of Trinidad's undis-
puted best hotel, this is a modern, smart
place with an upscale clientele. All rooms
are minisuites with air-con, some of which
have small balconies overlooking the leafy
courtyard. Enjoy a cocktail in the Tropical
Bar or cool off in the pool.

Hotel Aguahí   HOTEL $$
(📱 462-5569; aguahi_hotel@hotmail.com; Bolívar,
near Av Santa Cruz; s/d/tr B$320/440/560;
❄ 🛜 ❄) Feeling a bit dated and overpriced
at this point, the rooms are nevertheless
large, the beds comfortable and there is
a big, figure-of-eight pool in the spacious,
tropical garden.

🍴 Eating

Sabor Brazil   BRAZILIAN $
(www.facebook.com/saborbrasilTdd;   Av 6 de
Agosto 164; mains B$25-35; ⊙ 4-11pm Sat-Thu;
🛜) This tiny cafe is a real belly-pleaser with
its fresh juices, bountiful açaí bowls, jumbo-sized calzones and delectable desserts
(the passion-fruit cheesecake is a tropical
dream!). Oh, and it's the only place in town
with real espresso coffees. We only wish it
was open in the mornings.

★ **Churrasquería La Estancia**   STEAK $$
(www.facebook.com/ChurrasqueriaLaEstancia;
Ibare, near Velarde; mains B$45-75; ⊙ 11am-3pm
& 7pm-midnight; 🛜) Ask anybody in Trinidad
where to get a good bit of beef and you will
be sent here. With its palm roof and coal-
fire barbecue hamming up the ranch-house
setting, the succulent and juicy cuts will
make you wonder how other restaurants
even dare to call themselves *churrasquerías*
(grilled-meat restaurants).

★El Tábano   SEAFOOD **$$**
(Villavicencio, near Néstor Suárez; mains B$40-65;
⊙11:30am-2:30pm & 7pm-midnight) With cool
beers and cocktails served in the courtyard,
this grass-roofed resto-pub is a popular place
with Trinidad's young crowd on account of its
great atmosphere (thanks to live bands) and
excellent food. The menu consists of inven-
tive variations of fish and caiman dishes.

Pescadería Don Pedrito   FISH & CHIPS **$$**
(☑462-2545; Manuel Maraza, Zona Germán Busch;
mains B$60; ⊙7:30am-8pm) There's eight fish
dishes on the menu, and they all cost B$60:
fried, grilled, ceviche, whatever. Got it? Good.
The local moto-taxi drivers will tell you this
is the place to go. Chill with a beer and take
in a soccer match on the TV. The friendly
cats will patiently await your table scraps
beneath the mango trees.

La Casona   INTERNATIONAL **$$**
(Plaza Gral José Ballivián; almuerzo B$17, mains
B$25-100; ⊙9am-11pm; 🖥) Trinidad's most
popular restaurant, on the east side of the
plaza, doesn't quite live up to the hype,
though the *almuerzos* (set lunches) are

usually good and the pizzas are passable.
Give the rest of the greasy and overpriced à
la carte meals a miss.

Club Social   BOLIVIAN **$$**
(Plaza Gral José Ballivián; almuerzo B$15, mains
B$25-50; ⊙7:30am-10:30pm) Right on the
plaza, in a shady, breezy courtyard, the lovely
social club is a local family favorite. The generous two-course lunch menu includes soup,
meat, rice and veg. The dinner menu isn't
such good value.

🍷 Drinking & Nightlife

Goss   BAR, CLUB
(www.facebook.com/gossbeni; cnr Avs Armando
Llanos & Comunidad Europea; ⊙noon-1am) Feast
your eyes on this elephantine bar/disco/
karaoke/event space where the VIP area has
its very own pool. There's also an American-
style restaurant with burgers and pizzas, an
amazing gin menu and a massive projector
to watch sports. *¡Qué locura!*

Palo Diablo   BAR
(☑462-7254; Av Santa Cruz 825; ⊙6pm-1am)
Dark lights, rock videos on the flat-screen TV

AMAZON BASIN TRINIDAD

DOWN THE LAZY RIVER

River trips from Trinidad will carry you to the heart of the Bolivian Amazon along the Río
Mamoré, where you'll experience the mystique and solitude for which the rainforests are
renowned. For optimum enjoyment, visit during the dry season, which lasts roughly from
May or June until some time in October.

Although the scenery along the northern rivers changes little, the diversity of plant and
animal species along the shore picks up any slack in the pace of the journey. The longer
your trip, the deeper you'll gaze into the forest darkness and the more closely you'll scan
the riverbanks for signs of movement. Free of the pressures and demands of active travel,
you'll have time to relax and savor the passing scene.

In general, the riverboat food is decent, but meals consist mainly of *masaco* (mashed
yuca or plantains), served with *charque* (dried meat), rice, noodles, thin soup and bananas
in every conceivable form. After a couple of days you'll probably start dreaming of pizza, so
bring along some treats to supplement the daily fare. It's also wise to carry your own water
or some form of water purification.

You'll need to be quite resourceful and patient (expect to wait around a few days) to
organize your trip. Ask around at the **Capitanía** in Puerto Almacén (8km southwest of
Trinidad; moto-taxi B$20), or Puerto Ballivián, 8km to the northwest, and be sure to discuss
sleeping arrangements before setting out. Passengers must usually bring their own hammocks (available in Trinidad), but you may be allowed to sleep on deck or on the roof of the
boat. You'll also need a sleeping bag or a blanket, especially in winter, when jungle nights
can be surprisingly chilly. If you're fortunate enough to be on a boat that travels through the
night, a mosquito net isn't necessary, but on boats that tie up at night, passengers without a
mosquito net will find the experience ranges from utterly miserable to unbearable.

The Guayaramerín run takes about five days and costs around B$300 including food.
It's nearly impossible to find boats headed south to Puerto Villarroel anymore, but if you
can catch one, expect about the same duration and price for this journey.

For a plusher river affair, get on the posh hotel-boat Flotel Reina de Enin (p309).

and the largest cocktail menu in town make this the bar of choice for the karaoke-averse. There's live music on Friday and Saturday nights at 10pm.

Shopping

Chocolates Para Ti
FOOD

(cnr Av Santa Cruz & Sucre; ⊙ 9am-12:30pm & 3-7:30pm Mon-Sat) It's moved next door into the toy store, but this beloved shop still offers a wonderful selection of Sucre's most delicious chocolates, wrapped with love to take home. See if you can get back to your hotel before they melt in the Trinidad heat.

Centro Artesanal Moxos
ARTS & CRAFTS

(cnr Bopi & Santos Noco; ⊙ 8am-noon & 2-7pm Mon-Sat) Local Beni crafts, including weaving, woodwork and masks, are sold at the Centro Artesanal Moxos, 300m southwest of town by the cemetery. Look out for the *pifano*, an indigenous flute made from the wing bone of the jabiru stork using a technique more than 1000 years old – it's the staple instrument of the unique Moxos music.

ℹ️ Information

DANGERS & ANNOYANCES

Police station (Joaquín de la Sierra 70; ⊙ 24hr)

IMMIGRATION

For visa extensions, head to the **immigration office** (cnr Vaca Diez & Av Santa Cruz; ⊙ 8:30am-12:30pm & 2:30-6:30pm Mon-Fri).

INTERNET ACCESS

Internet access is typically B$3 per hour and there is a notable concentration along Av 6 de Agosto near the plaza.

LAUNDRY

There are only a handful of laundry shops, mostly on the outskirts of town. The most central option is **Lavandería Industrial Burbujas** (📱 mobile 6938-0072; La Paz 259; ⊙ 8am-noon & 2-7pm Mon-Sat), which charges B$22 per dozen stinky items.

MONEY

Several ATMs near the main plaza accept international cards – this is a good spot to get some cash before heading out to the Amazon proper.

NATIONAL TREASURE: THE BARBA AZUL MACAW

With more than 1435 bird species inhabiting the country, Bolivia is a bird-watcher's paradise. But it's not just the sheer quantity of species that makes Bolivia such an attractive destination for bird lovers; it is the quality of the birds that really makes the difference.

The gorgeous blue-throated macaw (*Ara glaucogularis*), endemic to the Beni savannas, numbers, according to the most optimistic of estimates, just 250 individuals. Known to the Bolivians as *barba azul* (bluebeard), this charismatic bird has become the focus of a number of conservation groups who are dedicated to rescuing it from the brink of extinction.

Organizations like Armonía, the Bolivian Birdlife International Partner, and Conservación Loros Bolivia, a parrot-focused nonprofit, have developed community-based conservation programs designed to protect the country's most threatened birds, principally by creating a feeling of pride among the locals. Perhaps most important of all has been the purchase of the small Reserva Barba Azul (p314) dedicated to the conservation of the bird.

Though Bolivia has 12 of the world's 19 macaw species, the blue-throated only exists in this small corner of the Beni. Intrinsic to its survival is the protection of the forest 'islands' which harbor its favored food, *motacú* palm nuts (it also digs *palma real* and *totaí* nuts). Another threat, the use of their tail feathers for ceremonial purposes, has been obviated by working with the community to fashion artificial feathers from palm fronds.

There's still much to learn about these birds: the first scientific census was taken in September 2015. They're not always easy to identify, because they fly in mixed flocks with blue-and-yellow macaws, differentiated only slightly by flight pattern, head and neck markings, and call.

Help has come from many corners. The **Parque Loro** in Tenerife funded a regional nest box program, and the bluebeards are just beginning to use them in Loreto, about an hour south of Trinidad, where the government inaugurated the 580,000-hectare Gran Mojos Protected Area in 2017. A tractor purchased with the help of a Canadian NGO has allowed for the creation of much-needed fire breaks around the Reserva Barba Azul.

Visit Armonía at its Santa Cruz office (p264) or Conservación Loros Bolivia at its Trinidad office (p309) for more information about where to see this species in the wild and how to collaborate on its conservation.

Prodem (Vaca Diez s/n; ☉8:30am-12:30pm & 2:30-6:30pm Mon-Fri, 9am-noon Sat) is just off the plaza for cash advances.

TOURIST INFORMATION

The municipal **tourist office** (📞462-1322; Vaca Diez, near 18 de Noviembre; ☉8am-12:30pm & 2:30-6:30pm Mon-Fri) offers flyers and limited info, but if you're planning a trip into the countryside you're better off chatting with English-speaking José Antonio Díaz at Conservación Loros Bolivia (p309).

❶ Getting There & Away

AIR

Departing air travelers must pay B$11 for use of the **Teniente Jorge Henrich Arauz airport** (Av José Chávez Suárez) which is just outside the northwest corner of town (taxi/moto-taxi B$20/10).

BOA (p287) has six flights weekly (not Sunday) to La Paz, and daily flights to Santa Cruz and Cochabamba. EcoJet (p287) has daily flights to Cochabamba, Guayaremerín and Riberalta, and regular flights to La Paz (three weekly) and Santa Cruz (six weekly). There are also flights to Sucre via Santa Cruz (four weekly) and Tarija via Cochabamba (two weekly). **Amazonas** (📞462-7575; www.amazonas.com; Teniente Jorge Henrich Arauz Airport, Av José Chávez Suárez; ☉7:30am-4:30pm Mon-Fri) connects Trinidad with Riberalta and Santa Cruz daily. **TAM** (📞462-2363; cnr Avs Bolívar & Santa Cruz; ☉8am-noon & 2-6:30pm Mon-Fri, to 1pm Sat) has an irregular schedule with occasional flights to Santa Cruz, Guayaremerín and Riberalta.

BUS & VAN

The rambling, disorderly **bus terminal** (Beni btwn Martiniano Fuentes & Rómulo Mendoza) is a 1km walk or B$20 taxi ride east of the center. Several *flotas* (long-distance buses) depart nightly between 6pm and 10pm for Santa Cruz (B$50, 10 to 12 hours); a bus *cama* (sleeper bus) costs B$80. A number of companies theoretically serve Rurrenabaque (B$130, 10 to 13 hours) daily via San Borja (B$80, six to eight hours), though from November to May these services can be temporarily suspended (or greatly enlarged). There are also daily departures to Riberalta (B$200) and Guayaremerín (B$200) which can take either 12 or 24 hours depending on whether they pass through Puerto Siles (when it's dry) or Rurrenabaque (when it rains).

Across from the terminal, there are a few van and car services to nearby cities which only depart when they've sold all seats. Vans depart for San Borja (B$100, six to seven hours), Rurrenabaque (B$180, nine to 11 hours) and Santa Rosa (B$230, 13 to 15 hours). Vans run to San Ignacio de Moxos (B$60, three to four hours) when full from a separate **parada** at Pedro Ignacio Muiba and Jarajorechi.

❶ Getting Around

TO & FROM THE AIRPORT

Taxis to and from the airport charge around B$20, but if you don't have much luggage, moto-taxis are cheaper (B$10) – you'll be surprised how much luggage they can accommodate with a bit of creativity.

MOTORCYCLE

Motorcycles are a great way to while the day away – for B$15 per hour or B$80 for a full day you can rent a bike and join the general public in whizzing around the square. Pick one up from **Motos de Alquiler Oscarito** (📞mobile 6896-0609; cnr Av Bolívar & 9 de Abril; per hour B$15, full-day B$80, 24-hour B$130; ☉24hr). You'll need a regular driver's license from home.

TAXI

Moto-taxis around town cost B$3 (a bit more at night), while increasingly scarce car taxis charge B$10.

For rides to outlying areas, phone **Radio Taxi Germán Busch** (📞462-0008; Plaza Gral José Ballivián), or look for one on the plaza. Bank on around B$50 per hour for up to four people, including waiting time.

NORTHERN BOLIVIAN AMAZON

Santa Ana de Yacuma

📞3 / POP 18,500 / ELEV 145M (475FT)

A real cowboy town (in the nicest possible way), populated by ranchers, farmhands and, of course, cows. Santa Ana is the main population center in this area of Beni and is proud to call itself the cattle capital of Bolivia, a title that has resulted in it having one of the highest standards of living in the Bolivian Amazon.

Unless your visit coincides with the annual **town festival** (24 July), during which cattle-related activities unsurprisingly play a starring role, there isn't much to do in town and you are only likely to land here en route to the Reserva Barba Azul (p314).

🛏 Sleeping

Hotel Mamoré HOTEL $$
(📞337-8294; Roca Suárez; s/d B$250/350; ❄🏊) Out by the airstrip, this four-star place is hands down the best in town. Bad news is that the ranchers know it too, so if you want a room you're best to book it in advance.

❶ Getting There & Away

Land routes to and from Santa Ana de Yacuma theoretically operate year-round because of the thriving local industry. However, attempting the journey in the wet season (or anytime just after it's rained) is not for the faint of heart as you can easily get stuck halfway sleeping in your transport. Frequent *trufi* (shared car or minibus) depart from the landmark La Vaca y El Toro statue (Map p308, C1) in Trinidad (B$150, four to six hours).

Once in Santa Ana, onward transport to the Reserva Barba Azul needs to be negotiated locally or arranged in advance.

Barba Azul Reserve

Thanks to the efforts of the conservation NGO Armonía (p264), the endangered blue-throated macaw or *barba azul* has become something of a regional celebrity in the Bolivian Amazon. Endemic to the unique Beni savannas, a fast-disappearing habitat found nowhere else on earth, a quarter of the world's minute population of this spectacular psittacid calls this 11,000-hectare private reserve its home.

Unlike most of the surrounding savanna, the open grasslands here are completely ungrazed and the birds can be seen relatively easily along with a plethora of other threatened birds and mammals such as maned wolves, giant anteaters and marsh deer. A new dining facility and improvements to the four existing cabins were scheduled to be completed by the end of 2018. Logistics demand a minimum three-night stay, with a memorable trip costing US$150 per person per night, including food, access to a motorboat and horseback riding.

For most of the year, by far the quickest and easiest way to get to the reserve is by chartering a plane from Trinidad or Santa Cruz. Armonía has been dealing with the local pilots for a few years so it's best to have them arrange this; the flight from Trini runs about B$580 but can be shared among three to five people. In the dry season (July to October) land transport can be arranged in Santa Ana de Yacuma; although it is only 80km away, rough roads mean that the drive will take at least three hours.

Your visit should be arranged in advance at Armonía's office in Santa Cruz, and they may be able to help with transport. Alternatively, contact Bird Bolivia (p358) or Nick's Adventures (p358) for a guided tour.

Guayaramerín

🖉 3 / POP 55,000 / ELEV 130M (426FT)

Knocking on Brazil's back door, Guayaramerín is twinned with the Brazilian town of Guajará-Mirim on the other side of the Río Mamoré. This lively town thrives on all kinds of trade (legal and illegal) with Brazil, and its streets are full of dusty motorcycle tracks and markets heaving with synthetic garments. It is now the northern terminus for river transportation along the Mamoré.

There's not a whole lot to do here except cruise down the river. North of town you can follow *la ruta de la goma* (the Rubber Trail) to Cachuela Esperanza, an old rubber-boom town that was once the grandest city in the Bolivian Amazon. Little remains of its former opulence, but it's a scenic spot near rapids of the Río Beni.

☞ Tours

Mary's Tours ⠀⠀⠀⠀⠀⠀⠀⠀⠀⠀⠀⠀⠀⠀TOURS
(🖉 855-3882, mobile 7114-2508; marytourss@gmail.com; 25 de Mayo 529; ⊙ 8:30am-noon & 2-6:30pm) Mary's Tours conducts five-hour city tours of Guayaramerín and Guajará-Mirim, as well as *la ruta de la goma* (the Rubber Trail) to Cachuela Esperanza. You can also arrange one- to four-day riverboat cruises on the Río Mamoré aboard its three-story boat, or fishing trips to Rosario del Yata. They can also help organize your flights.

🛏 Sleeping

Hotel Itauba Eco Resort ⠀⠀⠀⠀⠀RESORT $
(🖉 mobile 7828-2072; itaubaecoresort@bol.com.br; Camino a Riberalta; s/d/t/q cabins B$120/180/290/350; ❄) Situated on the edge of a private lagoon about 200m from the bus terminal, this small resort entertains guests with activities and rescued macaws. A lovely thatch-roofed restaurant is perched just above the water, while modern two-story cabins are set back in the trees.

Hotel Santa Ana ⠀⠀⠀⠀⠀⠀⠀⠀⠀HOTEL $
(🖉 855-3900; 25 de Mayo 611; s/d with fan B$70/130) The best of the cluster of hotels on this corner, with spacious rooms, all equipped with fans. Reasonable value, but be sure to avoid the windowless rooms.

✕ Eating

Asai L&L ⠀⠀⠀⠀⠀⠀⠀⠀⠀⠀⠀AMAZONIAN $
(cnr Vaca Diez & Av Federico Román; snacks B$6-15; ⊙ 7am-7pm Mon-Sat, to noon Sun) Cool down

with a bit of help from the superfruit of the Amazon at this colorful little cafe, which specializes in açaí shakes. There's also a long list of juices and fast-food staples like hamburgers, hot dogs and ham-and-cheese sandwiches.

Lina's Pizza   PIZZA **$**
(✓ mobile 7395-2015; cnr Nicolas Suárez & Reyes; slice B$10, pizza B$40-80; ⊙ 4-10:30pm Tue-Sun) A hole-in-the-wall pizza place on a quiet plaza. It's got legit pies and distinctly local toppings like *palmitos* (heart of palm) and *gusanitos* (little worms).

Restaurant El Sujal   BARBECUE **$$**
(Av Federico Román s/n; mains B$50-100; ⊙ 11:30am-3pm & 7-10pm Tue-Sun) This grandiose thatch-roofed restaurant on the main drag does 11 variations of either steak, chicken or the local *surubí* catfish. There are also a few lackluster veggie pastas.

❶ Information

EMBASSIES & CONSULATES
A block east of Plaza Hernán Roca Cazanova is the **Brazilian consulate** (✓ 855-3766; cons. guayaramerin@itamaraty.gov.br; cnr Avs Beni & 24 de Septiembre; ⊙ 8am-2pm Mon-Fri), which now takes two weeks to issue visas. You're better off applying in advance online or in La Paz.

INTERNET ACCESS
There is a decent internet connection at **Tigo Internet** (Av Alto de la Alianza s/n; internet per hr B$4; ⊙ 7am-midnight) just off Plaza Germán Bush by the market.

MONEY
Moneychangers hanging around the port area deal in US dollars, Brazilian reais and bolivianos. There are also several ATMs on Plaza Hernán Roca Cazanova.

❶ Getting There & Away

AIR
The relatively new and already dilapidated airport is about 9km from the center of town, but since the terminal has been indefinitely closed due to structural flaws, you have to check in for your flight at the airline offices on the two main plazas in town at least two hours before departure.
TAM (✓ 855-3924; www.tam.bo; Plaza Germán Bush; ⊙ vary) is operated by the Bolivian military, and while it typically offers cheaper fares, it reportedly is not held to the same strict safety standards as commercial airlines. Airplanes also tend to be less comfortable, as they

are mostly repurposed military cargo planes. Flights to Trinidad are sporadic (typically twice weekly) and the office holds irregular hours. You're better off booking with EcoJet (p287), which offers daily flights to Trinidad with onward connections to Cochabamba, La Paz, Santa Cruz, Sucre and Tarija.
A shared taxi from the airport to the center of Guayaramerín will cost B$20. The trip takes about 15 minutes.

BOAT
Cargo boats up the Río Mamoré to Trinidad (around B$300) leave very irregularly and take about six days. Ask at the port captain's office, opposite the **immigration office** (✓ 855-4413, after hours 7637-4544; cnr Avs Costanera & Federico Román; ⊙ 8am-noon & 2-7pm) for information.

BUS & TAXI
The **bus terminal** is on the south end of town, well beyond the market. Buses run to Riberalta (B$20, two hours) several times daily, while shared taxis (per person B$35, 1½ hours) leave when they have four passengers.
Vaca Diez (✓ mobile 7889-5162; Terminal de Buses) departs daily at 8am for Rurrenabaque (B$140, 10 to 12 hours) and La Paz (B$180, 30 to 40 hours) via Santa Rosa and Reyes. Do not contemplate either journey if there is even a hint of rain, or else be prepared to help pull the bus out of muddy holes every couple of hours. There are buses to Cobija (B$140, 12 to 20 hours) on Tuesday, Thursday, Saturday and Sunday. Daily buses to Trinidad (B$180) take either 12 or 24 hours, depending on whether they pass through Puerto Siles (when it's dry) or Rurrenabaque (when it rains).
Flying to most of these destinations is your best option and you will not regret the extra expense.

❶ Getting Around

Guayaramerín is small enough to walk just about anywhere. Moto-taxis and auto-rickshaws charge B$5 to anywhere in town. To explore the area, you can rent motorcycles from the two main plazas for B$15 per hour or negotiate all-day rentals – figure B$100 for 24 hours.

Riberalta

✓ 3 / POP 99,070 / ELEV 115M (377FT)
Despite being a major town in Bolivia's northern frontier region, Riberalta sees very few foreign tourists. This crumbly place is pleasant enough, even if the only thing to do is watch the orange sunsets and circling motorcycles as you enjoy an açaí shake on the plaza. According to locals of both sexes,

las riberalteñas are the most beautiful women in all of Bolivia – but they would say that, wouldn't they?

Riberalta's claim to fame is that it's one of the world's top Brazil-nut production sites. In fact, the local economy is entirely dependent on it. The other growing industry here is açaí. Those interested in agro-tourism can arrange tours to learn more about either. There are also several reserves on the periphery of town where you can observe wildlife.

◉ Sights

Area Protegida
Municipal Aquicuana   NATURE RESERVE
(B$10) This lush jungle reserve 22km north of Riberalta (B$30 by moto-taxi) is a great spot for bird-watching, wildlife watching (particularly caimans and anaconda) and fishing for giant *paiche* (a species of bonytongue). The communities of San José and Warnes run the park, and locals can be hired as guides (Spanish only). There is also an upmarket ecolodge here dedicated to traditional plant-based wellness treatments.

Tumichucuá   COMMUNITY
Tumichucuá is a small community about 25km south of town (B$30 by moto-taxi) toward 'El Triángulo' (the road junction to Cobija). There is a lake for swimming and a forested island with walking trails, plus cabins. Nobody is sure how far from Riberalta it is, as according to local legend the lake moves at night, sometimes coming to rest closer to the town, sometimes further away.

Paseo Turístico La Costanera   PARK
(Costanera) This well-maintained walking path on Riberalta's river bluff overlooks a broad, sweeping curve of the Río Beni and affords the standard Amazonian view over water and rainforest. Come at lunchtime for seafood at one of the riverfront stalls.

There's also a small **tourist information booth** here that is occasionally open on weekdays.

Cathedral   CHURCH
(Plaza de Armas) Riberalta's cathedral is a wonderful structure in classic Missionary style, wide and elegant, built using red brick and cedar. It sits on the main square in the same spot as the former, less-grandiose church and it cost more than US$500,000 to build.

☆ Activities

Club Náutico   SWIMMING
(Costanera; B$15; ⊙8am-6pm) In the paralyzing heat of the day, strenuous activity is suspended and you'll find yourself clambering into the nearest hammock. Enjoy a favorite local activity and cool down in Club Náutico's sparkling riverside pool, two blocks north of the plaza.

☞ Tours

Riberalta Tours   WILDLIFE WATCHING
(☑mobile 7126-2998; www.riberaltatours.com; Av Beni Mamoré 850; ⊙8am-12:30pm & 2:30-7pm Mon-Fri, to 12:30pm Sat) The most established agency in town, offering four- and five-day tours of the region that encompass a visit to Tumichucuá, a riverboat ride, wildlife watching, fishing and a visit to the rubber boom town of Cachuela Esperanza. Tours can also stop at Brazil-nut-processing plants or açaí-producing communities, but arranging these activities requires at least two weeks notice. English-language guides cost extra.

⊨ Sleeping

Tumichucuá Cabins   CABAÑAS $
(☑852-3432; cabins per person B$50) These red-brick and thatch-roofed cabins are in Tumichucuá, 25km south of Riberalta, next to a serene lake that's perfect for swimming, hiking and wildlife watching. Since they're part of a community-tourism project supported by the Catholic church, you'll need to book your bunk at the Vicariato Apostólico de Pando, three blocks east of the plaza in Riberalta.

Each of the cabins has five single beds and a nice deck. It's best to bring your own food and supplies.

★Hotel Colonial   HERITAGE HOTEL $$
(☑mobile 7027-9920; Plácido Méndez 745; s/d B$180/200, ste B$270-340; ❄) Riberalta's most expensive hotel is a renovated colonial home dotted with antique furniture and backed by a delightfully fresh garden where you can relax in a hammock. Rooms are elegant and spacious, while suites have their very own interior hammocks for napping.

Hotel Jomali   HOTEL $$
(www.hoteljomali.com; Av Nicolás Suárez; s/d incl breakfast B$160/210, with air-con B$220/260; ❄⊛) Popular with local business travelers, this tidy spot has spacious rooms (with tiled floors) clustered around an attractive plant-packed patio.

ⓘ CROSSING THE BORDER TO BRAZIL

Crossing to Brazil from the northern Bolivian towns of Cobija and Guayaramerín involves crossings of the Ríos Acre and Mamoré respectively.

Guayaramerín to Guajará-Mirim

Crossing into the Brazilian town of Guajará-Mirim from Bolivian Guayaramerín is really easy. *Lanchas* (small boats) across the river leave from the port when full (B$10). The immigration offices in **Guajará-Mirim** (Av Pres Dutra, Guajará-Mirim, Brazil; ⊙8am-noon & 2-6pm Mon-Fri, to noon Sat) and Guayaramerín (p315) are in the respective port areas, though the former is about three blocks inland. You'll need to show proof of a yellow-fever vaccine on both sides, and many nationalities will need visas in advance.

Cobija to Brasiléia

It's a hot slog across the bridge from Cobija to Brasiléia. Entry/exit stamps are available at **immigration in Cobija** (☑546-5760; Plaza General Germán Busch, Cobija; ⊙9am-noon & 2-5pm Mon-Fri) at the Bolivian end of the bridge (in the Prefectural building on the main plaza) and from **Brasiléia's Polícia Federal** (Av Santos Dumont, Brasiléia, Brazil; ⊙8am-noon & 2-5pm). With some negotiation, taxis will take you to the Polícia Federal in Brasiléia, wait while you clear immigration, then take you on to the bus terminal. If you need a visa, you can try and get one at the **Brazilian consulate in Cobija** (☑842-2110; Av Chelio Luna Pizarro, Cobija; ⊙8:30am-12:30pm Mon-Fri), but you're better off applying in advance online or in La Paz.

Although officials don't always check, technically everyone needs to have a yellow-fever vaccination certificate to enter Brazil. If you don't have one, head for the convenient and relatively sanitary clinic at the port at Brasiléia on the Brazilian side. For more information, check out Lonely Planet's *Brazil*.

✖ Eating

★**El Secreto de Mama**   BAKERY $
(www.facebook.com/elsecretodemama.bo; Av Gutiérrez 634; snacks B$3-5; ⊙4-7pm Mon-Fri) This pretty-in-pink bakery offers delectable local treats like empanadas, *cuñapes* (cheese and yuca balls), *bombitas* (cream-filled pastries), and *sonso* (a cheesy yuca bread). Wash them down with hot chocolate made from pure Beni-grown cacao. You'll never look at tea time the same way again!

To find it, walk three blocks east of the plaza and head south along Av Gutierrez.

Acai Life   AMAZONIAN $
(cnr Avs Natush & Martínez; snacks B$10-20; ⊙7:30am-noon & 4:30-10pm) A great spot for an energizing and antioxidant-rich breakfast with açaí bowls, fresh jungle juices, empanadas, and even proper Belgian-style waffles. The walls are as purple as your tongue will be when you leave.

Tropical   INTERNATIONAL $$$
(☑mobile 7704-0017; Oruro s/n; mains B$90-150; ⊙7-11pm Mon-Sat) This is Riberalta's most upscale restaurant, located near the airport, leading the residents to nickname it *tropicarísimo* (very expensive...). Gargantuan portions of meat, chicken and fish accompanied by salad, rice and fried manioc feed three normal-sized people. Thankfully the profusion of animal skins is now gone; the walls are decorated Christmas-tree style, full of hanging ornamentations like baskets, wooden sculptures and sombreros.

ⓘ Information

INTERNET ACCESS

There is a concentration of internet shops (mostly for kids playing games; per hour B$5) at the intersection of Nicolás Suárez and Gabriel René Moreno.

MONEY

There are several banks on the plaza with ATMs. A block to the south, **Prodem** (☑857-2212; Av Nicolás Suárez 1880; ⊙8:30am-4pm Mon-Fri, 9am-noon Sat) is the place to go for cash advances, exchanging US dollars or using Western Union.

TOURIST INFORMATION

There's a small tourist information booth on the Paseo Turístico La Costanera (p316) that is occasionally open on weekdays.

ⓘ Getting There & Away

AIR

Riberalta's airport is a 15-minute stroll south of the main plaza. Departing flights are subject to an airport tax of B$11. Flights to Cobija are by *avioneta* (light aircraft) and must be full to depart. Call **Avioneta Ariel** (☐ 852-3774, mobile 7686-3880; Av Sucre s/n) at least a day in advance and bank on paying around B$600 per person. Avioneta Ariel and **Servicios Aéreos Amazónicos** (☐ 7169-4797, mobile 7260-5890; Av Sucre s/n) both offer air-taxi services to remote parts of the Amazon and also do sightseeing flyovers on request. A few incidents/accidents in 2015 pointed to the relatively poor condition of the region's small aircraft; choose with prudence.

Both **EcoJet** (☐ 852-4837, 900-105-055; www.ecojet.bo; cnr Nicolás Suárez & Plácido Méndez; ⊙ 8am-noon & 2:30-6pm Mon-Fri, to 12:30 Sat) and **Amaszonas** (☐ 852-3933; www.amaszonas.com; cnr Chuquisaca & Sucre; ⊙ 8am-noon & 3-6:30pm Mon-Fri, to 1pm Sat) offer direct flights to Trinidad at least once daily with onward connections to Santa Cruz, La Paz and Cochabamba. EcoJet also has onward connections from Trinidad to Sucre (four times weekly) and Tarija (twice weekly). **TAM** (www.tam.bo; Chuquisaca 1146; ⊙ 7:30am-noon & 3-6pm Mon-Fri, to noon Sat) flies to Trinidad at least twice a week with onward connections to Santa Cruz, but while its prices tend to be cheaper, services are much more erratic than other airlines'.

BOAT

The Río Beni passes through countless twisting kilometers of virgin rainforest and offers Bolivia's longest single-river trip. Unfortunately, boats upriver to Rurrenabaque are now extremely rare and, in any case, they normally only run during the wet season (November to mid-April). For information on departures ask at the **Capitanía del Puerto** in the north-eastern end of town by Puerto Pila. Budget on spending B$300 to B$350 (including meals and hammock space) for the five- to eight-day trip. Lucky Peru-bound travelers may also find cargo boats to the frontier at Puerto Heath, which has onward boats to Puerto Maldonado.

BUS & TAXI

The bus terminal is 2km east of the center, along the Guayaramerín road. The road from Riberalta to Guayaramerín is a high-speed gravel track, and taxis (B$35, 1½ hours) ply the route, leaving when full from the bus terminal. Buses (B$20, 2 hours) are cheaper but slower – they depart in the morning and afternoon.

All *flotas* (long-distance buses) between Guayaramerín and Cobija (B$130, 11 to 19 hours), and the horrendously uncomfortable route via Rurrenabaque (B$120, 9 to 11 hours) to La Paz (B$180, 28 to 38 hours), stop at Riberalta. Several daily *flotas* also go to Trinidad (B$180, 12 to 24 hours).

❶ Getting Around

Moto-taxis (B$4) will take you anywhere in town. With a driver's license from home, you can rent motorcycles (per hour/day B$15/100) from *taxistas* (taxi drivers) at the corner of Nicolás Suárez and Gabriel René Moreno.

Riberalta to Cobija

The much-improved road between Riberalta and Cobija connects the once-isolated Pando department with the rest of the country. Better access means more logging and the region has now been opened up to exploitation of its natural resources with large tracts of virgin rainforest being cleared at a fast pace.

The journey requires two major *balsa* (raft) crossings, the first at Peña Amarilla, two hours outside Riberalta crossing the Río Beni. On the western bank, you can find stands selling empanadas and other snacks. The most interesting crossing on the trip, however, traverses the Río Madre de Dios. From the eastern port, the 30-minute crossing begins with a 500m cruise along a backwater tributary onto the great river itself. Along the way listen for the intriguing jungle chorus that characterizes this part of the country.

The crossing of the Río Orthon, at Puerto Rico, is by bridge. From Puerto Rico to Cobija, development has been particularly rampant. The scene is one of charred giants, a forest of stumps and smoldering bush; when something is burning, the sun looks like an egg yolk through the dense smoke.

Cobija

Capital of the remote Pando Department and Bolivia's wettest (1770mm of precipitation annually) and most humid spot, Cobija sits on a sharp bend of the Río Acre. Cobija means 'covering' and, with a climate that makes you feel as though you're being smothered with a soggy blanket, it certainly lives up to its name.

Cobija was founded in 1906 under the name 'Bahía,' and in the 1940s it boomed as a rubber-producing center. The town's fortunes dwindled with the shriveling of that industry, which has reduced it to little more than a forgotten village, albeit with a Japanese-funded hospital and a high-tech Brazil-nut-processing plant.

The town rambles over a series of hills, giving it a certain desultory charm. If you spend a day here, take a look at the remaining tropical wooden buildings in the center, and the lovely avenues of royal palms around the plaza.

Understand
Bolivia

Bolivia Today

In Bolivia, protests, poverty and inequality have long been a part of everyday life. But since Evo Morales was elected president in 2006, he has transformed Bolivia with a radical new constitution, economic reforms and social policies. What Bolivians make of Morales depends on who you ask, but to the outside observer these changes add up to one of the most interesting chapters in Bolivian history.

Best in Print

Fat Man from La Paz (Rosario Santos, editor; 2003) Excellent collection of modern fiction.

Whispering in the Giant's Ear (William Powers; 2006) Humorous and incisive look at battles over natural resources.

Turing's Delirium (Edmundo Paz Soldan; 2007) Contemporary thriller about computer hacking, code-breaking and cyber terrorism.

Best on Film

The Devil's Miner (2005) Fascinating documentary about a young boy working in Potosí's silver mine.

Cocalero (2007) A home-spun documentary on Morales' run for the presidency.

Amargo Mar (Bitter Sea; 1984) Highly regarded look at the loss of Bolivia's coastline to Chile.

Best in Music

Aguas Claras (Kalamarka; 1993) Modern Andean music at its best.

Tiempo al Tiempo (Los Kjarkas; 1985) Popular song by one of Bolivia's top folk bands, featuring traditional Bolivian instruments.

El Llanto de mi Madre (Los Jairas; 1966) The melancholic song that launched folk band Los Jairas has lyrics in Quechua and Spanish.

Economy

The nationalization of energy and mining interests was applauded by Bolivia's poor, but it has soured relations with foreign investors and some foreign governments. Bolivia has sought closer ties with Brazil, Russia, India and China (the BRIC powers) and has distanced itself more from the USA. While this has been welcomed in some parts of society, others, particularly in the Santa Cruz region, have reacted negatively.

Of the BRIC countries, it is China that has established the most powerful economic presence in Bolivia. China has lent Bolivia billions of dollars to fund the state-led transformation of Bolivia's energy and transportation infrastructure. In turn, China has become the principal contractor for projects such as the construction of new asphalt roads. The relationship is not without controversy, with tensions linked to issues such as the contamination of water sources by Chinese mining companies.

The government's hope is that with the world's largest lithium deposits, and plenty of natural gas and minerals, Bolivia can continue to see good economic progress for the foreseeable future.

Society

An improving economy has allowed for investment in social projects that have made a positive impact on poverty levels. The number of people living below the poverty line is down from 70% in 1999 to 39% in 2015 and for the time being all the progress indicators are moving in the right direction. However, whether or not these improving figures are sustainable in the event of an economic downturn remains to be seen.

These measures have succeeded in reframing Bolivia's social structure. There is now a spark of self-awareness and hope that's never been more evident among the nation's indigenous majority. And indigenous people today, especially highlands groups, are playing a significant role in politics and policy. The role of women is also slowly evolving, as they step out of their traditional roles as mothers, wives and heads of private households, emerging as business people and community leaders.

Conflict

Conflict and struggle is a way of life in a country where historically you only got what you were willing to fight for. People protest against poor working conditions, mining operations that contaminate rivers, and roads that displace communities and affect ecosystems. Protests regularly shut down Bolivia's roads and have a knock-on effect on the economy.

Moves to redistribute land and wealth have met with strong opposition from Bolivia's resource-rich eastern region, where autonomy movements occasionally rear their heads. Despite this opposition over what some perceive as weak rule of law and widespread corruption, many still expect the numerous social entitlement programs sponsored by the current government and paid for with the growing income from mining, agriculture and gas exports to keep the revolution started by Morales moving forward.

Evo Morales

In 2014 Evo Morales was reelected with a majority of 60% (more than twice that of his nearest rival) giving him power until 2020 and providing him with a strong platform to continue his social development and empowerment policies. Seeking to extend his presidency beyond 2020 with a fourth consecutive term, in 2016 Morales sought the people's permission to revise the constitution to allow him to run. The referendum had seemed like a safe bet, but in a shock result, a no vote was returned. Commentators claim the balance was tipped by a scandal that emerged in the run-up to the vote, when it was revealed that his former girlfriend, Gabriela Zapata, had played a role in securing US$500 million in government contracts for the Chinese engineering firm she worked for.

Undeterred, in 2017 Morales got the permission he needed to stand for reelection through the courts, who overruled the constitution. As things stand, Morales looks poised to run for president once again in 2019.

Internationally, Morales fomented Bolivia's links with regional partners such as Argentina, Brazil, Ecuador and Venezuela. He has also angered the US, the traditional 'big brother' of South America, by cozying up to the BRIC (Brazil, Russia, India and China) powers, and through his open criticism of capitalist ideals. But the historic polarization in Bolivia hasn't yet disappeared, and the conservative province of Santa Cruz is still his most vocal opponent, requesting more autonomy and occasionally threatening secession. The 'no' vote in 2017 was a rallying cry for the opposition.

POPULATION: **11.14 MILLION**

GDP: **US$37.82 BILLION**

INFLATION: **2.7%**

UNEMPLOYMENT: **6.9%**

····································

if Bolivia were 100 people

70 would be mestizo
20 would be indigenous
5 would be white
1 would be black
4 would be other

····································

language
(% of population)

Spanish

Quechua

Aymará

4
Other

····································

population per sq km

BOLIVIA   ARGENTINA   USA

 ≈ 3 people

History

Bolivia's history is evident in every corner of daily life – in the country's pre-Hispanic ruins, Colonial-era churches and in the museums, galleries and chaotic markets of the city centers. A cultural imprint that dates back more than 6000 years is seen in the language, dress, customs and traditions of the indigenous peoples, whose sense of identity and cultural pride has been boosted by more than a decade of rule by Evo Morales.

Prehistory

The great altiplano (which literally means high plateau), the largest expanse of arable land in the Andes, extends from present-day Bolivia into southern Peru, northwestern Argentina and northern Chile.

Cultural interchanges between the early Andean peoples occurred mostly through trade, usually between nomadic tribes in the lowlands, farmers in the Yungas, organized societies such as the Tiwanaku and Inca in the high plateau, and coastal traders in present-day Peru and Chile. These interchanges and geographic advantages around the altiplano resulted in food surpluses and eventually led to the Andes' emergence as the cradle of South America's highest cultural achievements.

Advanced civilizations first developed along the Peruvian coast and in the valleys in the early AD period. Highland civilizations developed a little later. Some archaeologists define the prehistory of the Central Andes in terms of 'horizons' – Early, Middle and Late – each of which was characterized by distinct architectural and artistic trends.

Want to know more about Bolivia's history, including the affects of geography, economics, policy and more? Check out the dense but incisive *A Concise History of Bolivia* (2011) by Herbert S Klein.

Early & Middle Horizons

The so-called Early Horizon (1400–400 BC) was an era of architectural activity and innovation, most evident in the ruins of Chavín de Huantar, on the eastern slopes of the Andes in Peru. Chavín influences resounded far and wide, even after the decline of Chavín society, and spilled over into the Early Middle Horizon (400 BC–AD 500).

By 700 BC, Tiwanaku had developed into a thriving metropolis. A highly advanced civilization for the Andes, it had an extensive system

TIMELINE	4000 BC	3200–800 BC	AD 500–900
	The first settlers arrive and begin to domesticate crops and animals, adapting slowly to high-altitude living in the altiplano. The tough conditions demand a sparse population distribution.	First traces of pottery shards in the altiplano date from around 3200 BC, indicating the formation of more structured societies. On the Peruvian coast the Chavín culture rises.	There is a food surplus and the ceremonial center of Tiwanaku, on the shores of Lake Titicaca, flourishes, developing into the religious and political capital of the altiplano.

of roads, irrigation canals and agricultural terraces. This system is believed to have supported a population of thousands in the 83-sq-km Tiwanaku Valley.

The Middle Horizon (AD 500–900) was marked by the imperial expansion of the Tiwanaku and Huari (of the Ayacucho Valley of present-day Peru) cultures. The Tiwanakans produced technically advanced work, most notably the city itself. They created impressive ceramics, gilded ornamentation, engraved pillars and slabs with calendar markings, and designs representing their bearded white leader and deity, Viracocha.

Tiwanaku was inhabited from 1500 BC until AD 1200, but its power in the region – based more on religious than economic factors – was strongest from AD 600 to around AD 900, when the civilization began the mysterious decline that lasted until the 1200s. One speculation is that Tiwanaku was uprooted by a drop in Lake Titicaca's water level, that left the lakeside settlement far from shore. Another theory postulates that it was attacked and its population massacred by the warlike Kollas (also known as the Aymará) from the west. When the Spanish arrived they were told an Inca legend about a battle between the Kollas and 'bearded white men' on an island in Lake Titicaca. These men were presumably Tiwanakans, only a few of whom were able to escape. Some researchers believe that the displaced survivors migrated southward and developed into the Chipaya people of the western Oruro department.

Late Horizon – the Inca

The period between 900 and 1475 is known as the Late Intermediate Horizon. After the fall of Tiwanaku, regionalized city-states came to power, such as Chan Chan in Peru and the Aymará Kingdoms around the southern shores of Lake Titicaca. However it was the rise and fall of the Inca empire that would truly define the pre-Columbian period.

The Inca inhabited the Cuzco region (in Peru) from the 12th century. They were renowned for their great stone cities and their skill in working with gold and silver. The Inca set up a social welfare scheme, taxed up to two-thirds of produce and worked on a system primarily based on the communal ownership of property. Through the *mita* system (where short-term forced labor was used to build public projects) they were able to build a complex road network and communication system that defied the difficult terrain of their far-flung empire.

Around 1440 the Inca started to expand their political boundaries. The eighth Inca king, Viracocha (not to be confused with the Tiwanaku deity of the same name), believed the mandate from the Sun God was

The Inca spoke Runasimi (later called Quechua by the conquistadors). They lacked a writing system but did have advanced math systems, keeping track of accounts – and perhaps other information – with knotted collections of cords known as *quipus*.

1000–1200	1440s	1520s	1531
Tiwanaku's power wanes, the population disperses and the ceremonial site is largely abandoned due to mysterious reasons – possibly climate change (drought), an earthquake or foreign invasion.	The Inca, based in Cuzco in Peru, extend their political boundaries by pushing eastward into Kollasuyo (present-day Bolivia) and assimilating local tribes by imposing taxation, religion and their own Quechua language.	Internal rivalries herald the beginning of the end for the Inca empire, a political force for less than a century. In a brief civil war, Atahualpa defeats his half brother, Huáscar, and assumes the emperor's throne.	The Spanish, led by conquistador Francisco Pizarro, arrive in Ecuador. After a quickly won fight with the Incas, they claim Alto Perú, later to become Bolivia.

not just to conquer, plunder and enslave, but to organize defeated tribes and absorb them into the realm of the benevolent Sun God.

Between 1476 and 1534 the Inca civilization was able to extend its influence over the Aymará Kingdoms around Lake Titicaca. They pushed their empire from its seat of power in Cuzco eastward into present-day Bolivia, southward to the northern reaches of modern Argentina and Chile, and northward through present-day Ecuador and southern Colombia.

The people of the Aymará Kingdoms were permitted to keep their language and social traditions, but they never truly accepted Inca rule. Today you can still see these linguistic and cultural splits in the Quechua, Aymará and myriad indigenous groups of Bolivia.

By the late 1520s internal rivalries began to take their toll on the empire with the sons of Inca Huayna Capac – Atahualpa and Huáscar – fighting a bloody civil war after the death of their father. Atahualpa (who controlled the northern reaches of the empire) won the war. While he was traveling south to Cuzco to claim his throne, he ran into the conquistador Francisco Pizarro, who captured, ransomed and eventually beheaded him. This left a power vacuum, making it easy for the Spanish to conquer the lands and peoples of the Inca empire.

Smallpox and other European diseases killed up to 90% of the indigenous population in some areas. These epidemics continued on 20-year cycles well into the 17th century.

Spanish Conquest

The Spanish conquest of South America was remarkably quick. The chaos left by the Inca Civil War helped, as did the epidemics caused by European diseases. European mastery of metallurgy for war (not ornamentation like the Inca) also played its part; so did their horses (what strange beasts they must have seemed to the Inca people), and the myth that bearded men would someday be sent by the great Viracocha.

1544	1780	1809	1822
Diego Huallpa discovers silver in Potosí's Cerro Rico (Rich Mountain), which leads to the development of the world's most prolific silver mine.	Tupac Amaru's revolt kicks off in Peru, extending later into Bolivia. The revolt is put down, and effectively dismantles the *cacique* (chieftan) structure of local indigenous government.	Bolivia proclaims its independence from Spain by establishing the first *juntas* (autonomist governments); the first in Chuquisaca (later renamed Sucre) and then in La Paz.	General Simón Bolívar succeeds in liberating Venezuela, Ecuador, Colombia and Panama from Spanish rule. He is made president of a short-lived new nation, Gran Colombia (1819–31).

Within a year of their arrival in Ecuador in 1531, Francisco Pizarro, Diego de Almagro and their bands of conquistadors arrived in Cuzco.

Alto Perú (the area we now know as Bolivia) was aligned with the defeated Huáscar during the Inca Civil War, making its conquest rather easy for Diego de Almagro. He was assassinated in 1538; three years later Pizarro suffered the same fate at the hands of mutinous subordinates. But this didn't deter the Spanish, who kept exploring and settling their newly conquered land.

During these initial stages of conquest, infighting between Spanish factions was common and the fate of Bolivia – a political backwater until the discovery of silver – was tied to the interests of the more powerful political centers in Cuzco and Lima.

The Legacy of Potosí

By the time Diego Huallpa revealed his earth-shattering discovery of silver at Cerro Rico in Potosí in 1544, Spanish conquerors had already firmly implanted their customs on the remnants of the Inca empire. Taking a page from the Inca playbook, they left the local *cacique* (chieftain) leadership and *mita* structure in place within the indigenous communities. This provided a local system of governance and an ongoing labor supply. The most powerful conquistadors were granted *encomiendas,* vast swaths of land and the peasant labor that went with it.

Potosí was officially founded in 1545, and in 1558 Alto Perú gained its autonomy from Lima with the placement of an *Audiencia* (Royal Court) in Sucre. Transportation hubs, farming communities and other support centers sprung up, centered on Potosí. And while some other Bolivian cities such as La Paz and Sucre were coming to life, the focus in the region was Potosí. Potosí's mine was the most prolific in the world and its silver underwrote Spain's international ambitions, enabling the country to conduct the Counter-Reformation in Europe, and supporting the extravagance of its monarchy for at least two centuries. But not all wealth left the region and cathedrals sprung up across the altiplano, eventually giving rise to a local school of design, and later the establishment of Bolivia's place in the fields of arts, politics and literature.

Missionaries showed up in the 18th and 19th centuries in the areas around Santa Cruz and Tarija, altering the cultural landscape of the region. Increased conflict between new Spanish arrivals and the elite of Potosí in the late 17th century triggered a broad economic decline in the 18th century.

HISTORY SPANISH CONQUEST

Between 1780 and 1782 an indigenous revolt led by Tupac Amaru extended from Peru into Bolivia. During this time, the indigenous nobility lost much of their power, creating the framework for complete domination by Spanish-descendent interests.

About eight million people have died in the Potosí mine over the years and the number rises a little every year. You can still visit the mine today (at your own risk!) or there are other interesting mine tours near Oruro.

1825	1879–84	1903	1932–38
General Sucre incites a declaration of independence for Alto Perú, and the new Republic of Bolivia is born, loosely modeled on the US, with legislative, executive and judicial branches of government.	Bolivia loses its coastline to Chile in the War of the Pacific. The loss of this transit point continues to hobble the Bolivian economy to this day.	During the rubber boom, Brazil annexes the remote Acre area, which stretched from Bolivia's present Amazonian borders to halfway up Peru's eastern border.	Bolivia enters the Chaco War against Paraguay. A ceasefire is negotiated in 1935, at which time Paraguay controls much of the region. A 1938 truce awards Paraguay three quarters of the Chaco.

Independence

In 1865 General Mariano Melgarejo drunkenly sent his army off on an overland march to aid France at the outset of the Franco-Prussian War. A sudden downpour sobered him up.

The early part of the 19th century was a time of revolution and independence in Bolivia (and much of the world for that matter). Harvest failures and epidemics severely affected the Bolivian economy between 1803 and 1805, creating fertile ground for revolution. To top it off, with the French Revolution, Napoleon's wars in Europe and British support for Latin America's independence movements, the colonists of the Americas were finally able to perceive what a world without royalty would look like.

By May 1809, Spanish America's first independence movement had gained momentum and was well underway in Chuquisaca (later renamed Sucre), with other cities fast to follow suit. This first revolutionary spark was quickly put down. Ironically, while the first shouts of revolution came from Bolivia, it would be the last country in South America to gain independence.

Here's how it played out. By the early 1820s General Simón Bolívar had succeeded in liberating both Venezuela and Colombia from Spanish domination. In 1822 he dispatched Mariscal (Field Marshall) Antonio José de Sucre to Ecuador to defeat the Royalists at the battle of Pichincha. In 1824 after years of guerrilla action against the Spanish and the victories of Bolívar and Sucre in the battles of Junín (August 6) and Ayacucho (December 9), Peru won its independence. During this time, another independence leader coming from the Río de la Plata, José de San Martín, was busy fighting battles in eastern Bolivia and liberating much of the southern corner of the continent.

With both Argentina and Peru eyeing the prize of the Potosí mines, Sucre incited a declaration of independence from Peru and, in 1825, the new Republic of Bolivia was born. Bolívar (yep, the country was named after him) and Sucre served as Bolivia's first and second presidents but, after a brief attempt by the third president Andrés Santa Cruz to form a confederation with Peru, things began to go awry. Chilean opposition eventually broke up this potentially powerful alliance, and thereafter Bolivia was relegated to a more secondary role in regional affairs with a period of caudillo rule dominating national politics until the 1880s. Thereafter Bolivia was ruled by a civilian oligarchy divided into liberal and conservative groups until the 1930s, when the traditional political system again fell apart, leading to constant military intervention until the 1952 Revolution.

Continuing Political Strife

During the early 20th century wealthy tin barons and landowners controlled Bolivian farming and mining interests, while the peasantry

1942	1952	1964	1967
Hundreds of striking trade-union laborers are shot down by government troops at a Catavi tin-mining complex. The fight for labor rights is on.	A military coup provokes a popular armed revolt by the miners, known as the April Revolution. After heavy fighting the military is defeated and Víctor Paz Estenssoro takes power.	After trying and failing for 12 years to raise the standard of living, the MNR's popularity wanes, and Víctor Paz Estenssoro's government is finally forced out by a military junta.	Argentine revolutionary Ernesto 'Che' Guevara, having failed to foment a peasant revolt in Bolivia, is executed by a US-backed military squad in the hamlet of La Higuera.

SHRINKING TERRITORY

At the time of independence Bolivia's boundaries encompassed well over 2 million sq km. But its neighbors soon moved to acquire its territory, removing coastal access and much of the area covered by its ancient Amazonian rubber trees.

The coastal loss occurred during the War of the Pacific, fought against Chile between 1879 and 1884. Many Bolivians believe that Chile stole the Atacama Desert's copper- and nitrate-rich sands and 850km of coastline from Peru and Bolivia by invading during Carnaval. Chile did attempt to compensate for the loss by building a railroad from La Paz to the ocean and allowing Bolivia free port privileges in Antofagasta, but Bolivians have never forgotten this devastating *enclaustramiento* (landlocked status).

The next major loss was in 1903 during the rubber boom when Brazil hacked away at Bolivia's inland expanse. Brazil and Bolivia had both been ransacking the forests of the Acre territory – it was so rich in rubber trees that Brazil engineered a dispute over sovereignty and sent in its army. Brazil then convinced the Acre region to secede from the Bolivian republic and promptly annexed it.

There were two separate territory losses to Argentina. First, Argentina annexed a large slice of the Chaco in 1862. Then, in 1883, the territory of Puna de Atacama also went to Argentina. It had been offered to both Chile and Argentina, the former in exchange for return of the Litoral, the latter in exchange for clarification over Bolivia's ownership of Tarija.

After losing the War of the Pacific, Bolivia was desperate to have the Chaco, an inhospitable region beneath which rich oilfields were mooted to lie, as an outlet to the Atlantic via the Río Paraguay. Between 1932 and 1935, a particularly brutal war was waged between Bolivia and Paraguay over the disputed territory (more than 80,000 lives were lost).

Though no decisive victory was reached, both nations had grown weary of fighting, and peace negotiations in 1938 awarded most of the disputed territory to Paraguay.

was relegated to *pongueaje,* a feudal system of peonage. Civil unrest brewed, with the most significant development being the emergence of the Movimiento Nacionalista Revolucionario (MNR) political party. It united the masses behind the common cause of popular reform, sparking friction between peasant miners and absentee tin bosses. Under the leadership of Víctor Paz Estenssoro, the MNR prevailed in the 1951 elections, but a last-minute military coup prevented it from actually taking power. What ensued was a period of serious combat, which ended with the defeat of the military and Paz Estensorro's rise to power in what has been called the April Revolution of 1952. He immediately nationalized the mines, evicted the tin barons, put an end to *pongueaje* and set up Comibol (Corporación Minera de Bolivia), the state entity in charge of

1975	1978	1985	1987
Operation Condor, a clandestine program to subvert communist movements and support right-wing governments in South America, gets its blackwater beginnings. Some attribute 60,000 deaths to it.	After a decade of reported human rights abuses, Hugo Banzer Suárez schedules general elections and loses. He ignores the results, but is eventually forced to step down in a coup.	Víctor Paz Estenssoro's New Economic Policy promotes spending cuts and privatization, resulting in strikes and protests by the miners' union; massive unemployment follows the crash of the price of tin.	The US begins sending Drug Enforcement Administration anti-coca squadrons into the Beni and Chapare regions, where coca generates substantial income for the growers and traffickers.

To encourage the settlement of the Amazon, Paz Estenssoro promoted road building (with Japanese aid) in the wilderness and opened up vast indigenous lands and pristine rainforest to logging interests.

mining interests. The MNR remained in power for 12 years but even with US support it was unable to raise the standard of living or increase food production substantially.

The '60s and '70s were decades of military coups, dictators, brutal regimes of torture, arrests and disappearances, as well as a marked increase in cocaine production and trafficking.

In 1982 Congress elected Hernán Siles Zuazo, the civilian left-wing leader of the Communist-supported Movimiento de la Izquierda Revolucionaria (MIR), which began one of the longest democratic periods in Bolivian history. His term was beleaguered by labor disputes, government overspending and huge monetary devaluation, resulting in a staggering inflation rate that at one point reached 35,000% annually.

When Siles Zuazo gave up after three years and called general elections, Paz Estenssoro returned to politics to become president for the fourth time. He immediately enacted harsh measures to revive the shattered economy including ousting labor unions, imposing a wage freeze and eliminating price subsidies, then deployed armed forces to keep the peace. Inflation was curtailed within weeks, but spiraling unemployment threatened the government's stability.

Chaos Prevails

The early '90s were characterized by political apathy, party politics, and the struggle between *capitalización* (the opening of state companies to international investment) and populist models. The free market won with the election of Gonzalo 'Goni' Sánchez de Lozada, the MNR leader who had played a key role in the curtailing of inflation through 'shock therapy' during the Estenssoro government.

Economic reforms saw state-owned companies and mining interests opened up to overseas investment in the hope that that privatization would bring stability and make the enterprises profitable. Overseas investors were offered 49% equity, total voting control, license to operate in Bolivia and up to 49% of the profits. The remaining 51% of the shares were distributed to Bolivians as pensions and through Participación Popular, a program meant to channel spending away from cities and into rural schools, clinics and other local infrastructure.

In late 1995 reform issues were overshadowed by violence and unrest surrounding US-directed coca eradication in the Chapare. In the late '90s the government faced swelling public discontent with the coca eradication measures, and protests in response to increasing gas prices, a serious water shortage and economic downturn in the department of Cochabamba.

Top Historic Attractions

Tiwanaku

Iskanwaya

Isla del Sol

Chullpa Tombs

El Fuerte

Potosí

Sucre

Che Trail

Choro Trek

Jesuit Mission Circuit

1993	1995	2000	2002–03
Gonzalo 'Goni' Sánchez is elected president on a center-left, free-marketeering ticket and, with his government, proceeds to introduce landmark social, economic and constitutional reforms.	Labor grievances over the new privatization policies result in a 90-day state-of-siege declaration and the arrest of 374 labor leaders. By midyear, measures are relaxed.	The Bolivian government sells Cochabamba's water utility to the private US company Bechtel. When the water rate is hiked, local people take to the streets and Bechtel is forced out.	Goni wins the presidency with only 22.5% of the vote. After massive protests against his unpopular economic policies lead to over 60 deaths, he resigns in October 2003.

Following a successful campaign advised by a team of US political consultants that he hired, 'Goni' was again appointed president in August 2002. The following year his economic policies were met with widespread demonstrations which resulted in the loss of 67 lives during a police lockdown in La Paz. In October 2003, Goni resigned amid massive popular protests and fled to the US. He currently faces charges related to the deaths during the demonstrations, both in the US and Bolivia, and a long-winded formal extradition process has been underway since 2008.

Protests, rising fuel prices and continued unrest pushed Goni's successor, Carlos Mesa, to resign in 2005.

The Morales Era

In December 2005 Bolivians elected their country's first indigenous president. A former *cocalero* (coca grower) and representative from Cochabamba, Evo Morales Ayma of Movimiento al Socialismo (MAS) won nearly 54% of the vote, having promised to change the traditional political-class system and to empower the nation's poor (mainly indigenous) majority. After the election, Morales quickly grabbed the spotlight, touring the world and meeting with Venezuela's Hugo Chávez, Cuba's Fidel Castro, Brazil's Luis Inácio Lula da Silva and members of South Africa's African National Congress. Symbolically, on May Day 2006, he nationalized Bolivia's natural gas reserves and raised taxes on energy investors in a move that would consolidate Bolivian resources in Bolivian hands. Nationalization led to an eightfold increase in revenues from natural gas by 2013.

In July 2006, Morales formed a National Constituent Assembly to set about rewriting the country's constitution. In January 2009, the new socially focused constitution was approved by 67% of voters in a nationwide referendum. The first Bolivian constitution to be approved by popular vote, it gave greater power to the country's indigenous majority, made official the role of indigenous languages and religions in the new 'plurinational' state and allowed Morales to seek a second five-year term, which he won that same year. The constitution also limited the size of landholdings in order to redistribute Bolivia's land from large ranchers and landowners to poor indigenous farmers.

As a former coca farmer Morales has made it a personal mission to highlight the difference between coca, a plant sacred to the highland indigenous cultures, and cocaine, the narcotic. This culminated in him famously holding up a coca leaf at the United Nations in 2013 and asking those present to correct the 'historical error' of its classification as

About 1.2 million kilos of coca leaf are consumed monthly in Bolivia, leading Morales to declare it an intrinsic part of Bolivia's heritage in his new constitution. Millions have been invested in alternative uses for coca.

2005	2006	2008	2009
Bolivia elects the country's first indigenous leader, Evo Morales, who wins with nearly 54% of the vote. He becomes the 80th sitting president of Bolivia's tumultuous history.	The Morales-created National Constituent Assembly sits for the first time. Its stated aim is to allow Bolivia's marginalized communities to design a new constitution for their nation.	Right-wing factions' opposition to Morales' renationalization of Bolivian gas wealth culminates in pitched street battles in Santa Cruz that leave 11 dead and more than 50 wounded.	The new constitution is approved with more than 60% support, giving greater rights to the majority indigenous population and allowing Morales to run for – and win – his second term.

a drug. Though some dismissed his performance as theater, he was successful in receiving special dispensation to legalize the traditional practices associated with coca in Bolivia. The potential uses of coca go well beyond getting high, and as the world's third-biggest coca producer, Bolivia stands to benefit enormously if wider legalization of the crop is eventually approved.

While Morales enjoys widespread support among the indigenous people of Bolivia, his radical social changes aren't without their opponents. In the eastern part of the country – the four departments known as La Media Luna (Half Moon, for their geographic shape) – where much of the natural resources lie, a strong right-wing opposition has been challenging Morales, accusing him of being an ethnocentric despot. In 2016, a referendum proposing to change the constitution to allow Morales to run for a fourth consecutive term delivered a shock no vote. Undeterred, Morales looked to the courts, who overruled the constitution, scrapping limits on terms altogether, and in 2017 Morales announced his intention to stand for reelection in 2019.

The world's largest lithium reserve is found in Bolivia, and could fuel the Bolivian economy for the next 100 years or more. While plenty of international operations are vying for a piece of the pie, the Morales administration has insisted on keeping the investment nationalized. Progress has been extremely slow.

2014	2015	2016	2017
Taking 60% of the national vote Morales receives a powerful mandate to continue with his social reforms as he is elected to a third consecutive term in office.	Pope Francis visits Bolivia and begs forgiveness for the grave sins committed against indigenous peoples of America in the name of God.	A referendum to change the constitution to allow Morales to stand for reelection in 2019 returns a shock result of no.	Bolivia's highest court overrules the constitution on the issue of electoral terms, allowing Morales to stand for reelection in 2019.

Life in Bolivia

Bolivia is a remarkably stratified society. While the hierarchies defined by 500 years of rule by Spanish descendants are slowly starting to fade thanks to the Morales-inspired *revolución indígena* (indigenous revolution), your place in society and the opportunities you will have throughout life are still largely defined by the color of your skin, the language you speak, the clothes you wear and the money you have.

The National Psyche

Attitude depends on climate and altitude. *Cambas* (lowlanders) and *kollas* (highlanders) enjoy expounding on what makes them different (ie better) than the other. Lowlanders are said to be warmer, more casual and more generous to strangers; highlanders are supposedly harder working but less open-minded. While the jesting is usually good-natured, Bolivians are acutely aware of the economic disparity between the two regions and tensions are occasionally brought to a head, when Santa Cruz threatens secession from the republic due to disagreements with the political script.

Thanks in part to Evo Morales, many Bolivians have been redefining and even questioning what it means to be Bolivian. From the beginning, Morales vigorously stressed that Bolivian identity was based on an individual's ethnic origins. Morales has been quick to espouse the status of indigenous groups, but his opponents accuse him of political manoeuvring and of further polarizing the country according to race, class and economic status. He has been seen as favoring indigenous groups over others, including mestizos who, as descendants of the Spanish colonists and indigenous people, are also proud of their Bolivian status. Others see him as simply redressing the balance after centuries of oppression and underinvestment in the highland communities. But while the political power is shifting toward the indigenous majority, the money stays in the hands of the elite.

Bolivians tend to be suspicious of politicians, and a sense of fatalism and mistrust in government simmers below the surface in a country accustomed to centuries of corruption and misrule. However Morales continues to win new supporters as his economic policies (which were much criticized by his opponents) have taken the country forward into a boom that it has never before experienced. The question is whether or not Bolivia can sustain its extraordinary growth and whether Morales' popularity will survive an economic downturn.

Lifestyle

Day-to-day life varies from Bolivian to Bolivian, mostly depending on whether they live in the city or the country, the freezing highlands or the sweaty lowlands, and whether they are rich or poor. Many *campesinos* (subsistence farmers) live without running water, heat or electricity, and some wear clothing that has hardly changed in style since the Spanish arrived. But in the cities, especially Santa Cruz (the country's richest city), La Paz, Cochabamba and Sucre, thousands enjoy the comforts of contemporary conveniences and live very modern lifestyles.

The Wiphala flag (square-shaped and consisting of 49 small squares in a grid with graduating colors of the rainbow) has been adopted as a representation of Bolivia's indigenous peoples.

Llama fetuses are used for sacrificial offerings, but llamas are not killed especially for them. About 3000 llamas are slaughtered daily on the altiplano for wool and meat; the fetuses are removed from those animals.

POPULAR PROTEST

Protests are part of everyday life in Bolivia, with people taking to the streets to mark their objections over everything from political decisions and labor disputes to economic demands and regional rivalries. These protests may take the form of *manifestaciones* (demonstrations) or marches through the street, or *bloqueos* (road blocks), preventing access to and from major cities. They are often highly organized affairs, with drums, flags and banners, and can last for weeks at a time.

Life in this fiercely self-reliant nation begins with the family. No matter what tribe or class you come from, it's likely that you have close ties to your extended family. In the highlands, the concept of *ayllu* (the traditional peasant system of communal land ownership, management and decision making) that dates back to the Inca times is still important today.

For many in Bolivia's lower class, the day is about making enough money to eat, attending church, doing chores, ensuring the children study, plus a bit of laughter and forgetting (often involving strong alcohol). For the richer city class, there are distractions that come from economic surplus such as theater, cuisine, the arts and the ever-important country club. In these circles, your last name still defines where you can get to. Young people are increasingly flaunting these rules, but it is still relatively rare to see intermarriage between people from disparate ethnic groups or economic classes.

In October 2014 Evo Morales donned a football shirt and played against a Real Madrid 'legends' team containing ex-stars like Emilio Butragueño, Fernando Hierro and Manuel Sanchis. It was to promote the sports-development program *Un gol para el desarrollo* (a goal for development), which aims to improve grassroots sport education.

Religion

Roughly 77% of Bolivia's population professes Roman Catholicism and practices it to varying degrees. The remaining 23% are Protestant, agnostic and belonging to other religions. Strong evangelical movements are rapidly gaining followers with their fire-and-brimstone messages of the world's imminent end, and in some areas are also putting paid to centuries of traditional cultural practices. Despite the political and economic strength of Christianity, it's clear that most religious activities have incorporated some Inca and Aymará belief systems. Doctrines, rites and superstitions are commonplace, and some *campesinos* still live by a traditional lunar calendar.

Sports

Like many of its Latin American neighbors, Bolivia's national sport is *fútbol* (soccer). La Paz's Bolívar and the Strongest usually participate (albeit weakly) in the Copa Libertadores, the annual showdown of Latin America's top clubs. Professional *fútbol* matches are held every weekend in big cities, and impromptu street games are always happening.

Bolivia has historically performed poorly at international sporting events, unless they are staged in the country and altitude can be used to their advantage. As a result the government has been investing considerable sums of money in a sports development program designed to provide even the most remote settlements with sports facilities, to develop the country's next generation of champions. A well-tended *cancha* (sports field) is now a feature of almost every village – and you'll be welcome to join in. Traditional communities still bar women from the field, but women's teams have started popping up in the altiplano, where they play clad in *polleras* (skirts) and jerseys.

In rural communities, volleyball is a sunset affair, with mostly adults playing a couple of times a week. Racquetball, billiards, chess and *cacho* (dice) are also popular. The unofficial national sport, however, has to be feasting and feting – the competition between dancers and drinkers knows no bounds.

Indigenous Culture

Bolivia is a multiethnic society with a remarkable diversity of linguistic, cultural and artistic traditions. In fact, the country has the largest population of indigenous peoples in South America, with most sociologists and anthropologists saying that over 60% of the population is of indigenous descent. Within these diverse indigenous communities a strong sense of cultural identity remains, evident in the use of traditional clothing and textiles, food and drink, festivals, spiritual beliefs, music and dance.

Population

Bolivia has 36 identified indigenous groups. The vast majority of those who identify as indigenous are Aymará (about 25%) and Quechua (about 30%), many of whom are located in the highlands. The remaining groups (including Guaraní and Chiquitano) are located almost entirely in the lowlands.

Mestizos (people of mixed indigenous and Spanish blood) make up a majority of the population.

Political & Social Change

Bolivia's indigenous groups historically lacked a significant political voice and made up the majority of the nation's poor. That changed with the election of Evo Morales in 2005, who implemented a new constitution reestablishing the rights of indigenous groups within a plurinational and secular state. For the first time there were numerous high-level indigenous ministers and technocrats, many of whom came from humble beginnings. This awareness is creating a growing sense of pride within indigenous communities, where centuries-old traditions of terrace farming, respect for the land and communal decision-making still play a strong role in everyday life, along with satellite TVs, cell phones, rural schools, Westernized dress and changing artistic, musical and political attitudes.

For centuries, women of indigenous descent who lived in cities were known as *cholas*. Today, many consider this term to be derogatory, and some now go with the politically correct *mestiza* moniker. The only problem is that *mestizo/a* also describes people of mixed Spanish/indigenous descent. *Indígenas* is a commonly accepted term for indigenous peoples.

Visitors to indigenous communities, especially in the altiplano where communities are especially wary of outsiders, may be turned off by the aloofness and insular nature of these people. But Bolivia has lived under a highly structured, hierarchical societal framework since the rise of Tiwanaku and a visitor is but a distraction from the daily chores of survival. Many indigenous communities are slowly embracing tourism and a stay in places such as Curahuara de Carangas can provide a unique glimpse into these communities.

The Guaraní language is wonderfully descriptive and onomatopoeic and has been adopted for numerous regional animal names, many of which you may already be familiar with. Jaguar for example is derived from *yagua* (dog or more accurately 'predator'). The Guaraní call the Jaguar *yaguareté* (very roughly 'the true predator').

Religious Life

The religious beliefs and practices of Bolivia's indigenous groups are as rich and diverse as the different cultures they represent, but the central Andean religions of the Aymará and Quechua, which are thriving, are the ones that you are most likely to encounter during your visit.

Based on animism, the Bolivian Andean indigenous religions believe in natural gods and spirits that date back to Inca times and earlier. Pachamama (Mother Earth) is the most popular recipient of sacrificial offerings, since she shares herself with human beings, helps bring forth crops and distributes riches to those she favors. She has quite an appetite for coca, alcohol and the blood of animals, particularly white llamas. If you're wondering about all the llama fetuses in the markets, they are wrapped up and buried under new constructions, especially homes, as an offering to Pachamama.

Among the Aymará and Quechua mountain gods, the *apus* and *achachilas* are important. The *apus,* mountain spirits who provide protection for travelers, are often associated with a particular *nevado* (snowcapped peak). Illimani, for example, is an *apu* who looks over inhabitants of La Paz. *Achachilas* are spirits of the high mountains; believed to be ancestors of the people, they look after their *ayllu* (loosely translated as 'tribe') and provide bounty from the earth.

Ekeko, which means 'dwarf' in Aymará, is the jolly little household god of abundance. Since he's responsible for matchmaking, finding homes for the homeless and ensuring success for businesspeople, he's well looked after, especially during the Alasitas Festival (p61) in La Paz.

One of the most bizarre and fascinating Aymará rituals is the Fiesta de las Ñatitas (Festival of Skulls), which is celebrated one week after Day of the Dead. *Ñatitas* (skulls) are presented at the cemetery chapel in La Paz to be blessed by a Catholic priest. Parish priests shy away from associating this rite with mass, but have begrudgingly recognized the custom. The skulls are adorned with offerings of flowers, candles and coca leaves, and many even sport sunglasses and a lit cigarette between their teeth. While some people own the skulls of deceased loved ones and friends (who they believe are watching over them), many anonymous craniums are believed to have been purchased from morgues and (so it is claimed) medical faculties. After the blessings, the decorated *ñatitas* are carted back to the owners' houses to bring good luck and protection. This ancient Aymará ritual was once practiced in secret but, nowadays, the chapel's head count is growing every year.

Shamans oversee religious festivals, read fortunes and provide homemade traditional cures throughout Bolivia. Your closest experiences with shamans will be near Copacabana during religious festivals, or in remote regions in the Amazon jungle where packaged-for-tourists ayahuasca healers ply their craft – be aware that ayahuasca is a powerful hallucinogenic and there have been tourist deaths related to its effects.

Stone talismans are also used in daily life to encourage prosperity or to protect a person from evil. A turtle is thought to bring health, a frog or toad carries good fortune, an owl signifies wisdom and success in school and a condor will ensure a good journey. You can buy these in La Paz's Mercado de las Brujas (p63; Witches' Market) and throughout the country.

Weaving

Bolivian textiles come in diverse patterns displaying a degree of skill resulting from millennia of artistry and tradition. The most common piece is a *manta* or *aguayo,* a square shawl made of two handwoven

In glorious celebration of the *revolución indígena* (indigenous revolution) – and in homage to the president himself – a gigantic state-of-the-art museum has been constructed in Evo Morales' home town of Orinoca, south of Oruro.

The Aymará and Quechua spiritual worlds embrace three levels: Alajpacha (the world above or eternal sky, representing light and life); Akapacha (located between the sky and hell, and between life and death); and Mankapacha (located below, symbolizing death and obscurity).

strips joined edge to edge. Also common are the *chuspa* (coca pouch), *chullo* (knitted hat), *falda* (skirt), woven belts and touristy items such as camera bags made from remnants.

Regional differences are manifested in weaving style, motif and use. Weavings from Tarabuco often feature intricate zoomorphic patterns, while distinctive red-and-black designs come from Potolo, northwest of Sucre. Zoomorphic patterns are also prominent in the wild Charazani country north of Lake Titicaca and in several altiplano areas outside La Paz, including Lique and Calamarka.

Some extremely fine weavings originate in Sica Sica, one of the many dusty and nondescript villages between La Paz and Oruro, while in Calcha, southeast of Potosí, expert spinning and an extremely tight weave – more than 150 threads per inch – produce Bolivia's finest textiles.

Vicuña fibers, the finest and most expensive in the world, are produced in Apolobamba and in Parque Nacional Sajama.

Music & Dance

While all Andean musical traditions have evolved from a series of pre-Inca, Inca, Spanish, Amazonian and even African influences, each region of Bolivia has developed distinctive musical traditions, dances and instruments.

The instrument Bolivia is most known for, and understandably proud of, is the *charango,* considered the king of all stringed instruments. Modeled after the Spanish *vihuela* and mandolin, it gained initial popularity in Potosí during the city's mining heyday. Another instrument commonplace in the gringo markets is the *quena,* a small flute made of cane, bone or ceramic. The instrument pre-dates Europeans by many centuries and the earliest examples, made of stone, were found near

The Kallawaya are strongly associated with healing and have an extraordinarily ancient history of medical practice. They were treating malaria with quinine and even performing brain surgery by AD 700, long before Western doctors dared to give it a go!

INDIGENOUS CULTURE MUSIC & DANCE

MESTIZA DRESS

The characteristic dress worn by many Bolivian indigenous women was imposed on them in the 18th century by the Spanish king and the customary center parting of the hair was the result of a decree by the Viceroy of Toledo.

This distinctive ensemble, both colorful and utilitarian, has almost become Bolivia's defining image. The most noticeable characteristic of the traditional Aymará dress is the ubiquitous dark green, black or brown bowler hat. Remarkably these are not attached with hat pins but merely balanced on the head.

The women normally braid their hair into two long plaits that are joined by a tuft of black wool known as a *pocacha.* The *pollera* skirts they wear are constructed of several horizontal pleats, worn over multiple layers of petticoats. Traditionally, only a married woman's skirt was pleated, while a single female's was not. Today, most of the synthetic materials for these brightly colored *polleras* are imported from South Korea.

The women also wear a factory-made blouse, a woolen *chompa* (sweater/jumper), a short vestlike jacket and a cotton apron, or some combination of these. Usually, they add a shawl, known as a *manta.* Fashion dictates subtleties, such as the length of both the skirt and the tassels on the shawl.

Some sling an *aguayo* (also spelled *ahuayo*), a rectangle of manufactured or handwoven cloth decorated with colorful horizontal bands, across their backs. It's used as a carryall and is filled with everything from coca or groceries to babies.

The Quechua of the highland valleys wear equally colorful, but not so universally recognized, attire. The hat, called a *montera,* is a flat-topped affair made of straw or finely woven white wool. It's often taller and broader than the bowlers worn by the Aymará. The felt *monteras* (aka *morriones*) of Tarabuco, patterned after Spanish conquistadores' helmets, are the most striking. Women's skirts are usually made of velour and are shorter in length.

Potosí. A curious instrument known as a jaguar-caller comes from the Amazon region. This hollowed-out calabash, with a small hole into which the player inserts his hand, seems to do the trick in calling the big cats to the hunt.

Traditional altiplano dances celebrate war, fertility, hunting prowess, marriage and work. With Spanish arrival came also European and African dance traditions, resulting in the hybrid dances that now characterize many Bolivian celebrations.

Oruro's Carnaval draws huge local and international crowds. Potosí is famed for its re-creations of the region's *tinku* fight tradition, while La Paz is renowned for La Morenada, which reenacts the dance of African slaves brought to the courts of Viceroy Felipe III.

UNDERSTANDING BOLIVIA'S INDIGENOUS GROUPS

Bolivia's myriad ethnic groups have remarkable linguistic, artistic and spiritual traditions.

Highlands

Aymará The Aymará culture emerged on the southern shores of Titicaca after the fall of Tiwanaku. These strong, warlike people lived in city-states and dominated the areas around the lake. Today, Aymará live in the areas surrounding the lake and in the Yungas, with La Paz's El Alto area being the capital of Aymará culture. They speak – you guessed it – Aymará.

Quechua Descended from the Inca, there are some nine to 14 million Quechua speakers in Bolivia, Peru, Ecuador, Chile, Colombia and Argentina today. These people lived across the former Inca empire. With the decline of mining in the 1980s, many Quechua speakers moved to the Chapare to harvest coca.

Chipaya Perhaps the direct descendants of Tiwanaku, the Chipaya practiced a unique and fascinating religion of ritual sacrifices and an annual digging up of the deceased to maintain a link between the living and the dead. Christian evangelization has unfortunately all but ended these traditional beliefs, resulting in the near total loss of this ancient culture.

Kallawaya A remote tribe from the mountains north of La Paz. Pre-Inca in origin, their ancient language is now dying. They are famed as a tribe of traveling healers, wandering the Andes along the ancient foot trails, collecting medicinal herbs along the way, and are welcomed by locals who present them with their sick in the hope of a cure. They have a quite remarkable history of medical innovation and specialist healers are capable of harnessing the curative effects of up to 600 different regional plant species.

Lowlands

Chiquitano Living primarily in the Chiquitania tropical savanna outside Santa Cruz, but also in Beni and into Brazil, there are about 180,000 Chiquitanos in Bolivia of whom about a quarter speak Chiquitano. Before the arrival of the Jesuits in the region there were numerous disparate ethnic groups. During the evangelization they were forced to live in small townships where a common language and dress were adopted.

Guaraní This group of hunter-gatherer tribes share a common language root with the Guaraní of Paraguay, Argentina and Uruguay and the Tupi of Brazil. You can connect with their fascinating culture at the Museo Guaraní (p258) in Santa Cruz.

Mojeño From the Beni department, this significant ethnic group was quite large before the 17th century, with over 350,000 people. Many were killed by European diseases, but the language and culture survives today. Many early European explorers believed El Dorado would be found in Mojeño territory.

Music in Bolivia

Music in Bolivia has long been an important expression of identity for its peoples, and in many ways the depths and complexities of this country might be best understood through its music. From traditional Andean folk music to the country's emerging young artists taking on social themes in their work, Bolivia is reflected in its song. Ever present (especially on the radio) is *cumbia*, with its melodramatic tales of everyday life.

Traditional Bolivian Music

Traditional music in Bolivia varies widely, and is often closely linked with dances, festivals, costumes and beliefs.

Saya

Saya originated with the African-Bolivian population of the Yungas. The genre has its roots in the drum rhythms brought by enslaved Africans from their homelands, and is sometimes accompanied by the Andean flute. The song takes the form of call and response between soloists and a chorus of musicians, accompanied by dancing. Traditionally, the song lyrics were a way of storytelling and transmitting oral history, and *saya* is viewed by African-Bolivian groups as an important expression of cultural heritage.

A *tarqueada* is a melody played using a *tarka*, a thick, angular wooden flute. The accompanying dance is one of the highlights of Oruro's Carnaval.

Tinku & Jula Jula

An Aymará cultural tradition from northern Potosí, *tinkus* (ritualized fights that are best understood as a way of releasing tensions between rival groups) are preceded by a war rhythm performed with *charangos* (a traditional string instrument made from an armadillo shell) and accompanied by female chanting. Linked to the *tinku* ritual is the playing of *jula julas:* among the most recognizable sounds of the Bolivian Andes, these melodies are played on pairs of three- and four-tube bamboo pipes. *Tinku* fights take place on May 3.

Cumbia

If you spend any time on the road in a bus or taxi in Bolivia, you're likely to hear *cumbia*. The genre is a form of folk music that originated in Colombia, with African (the rhythms and drums), indigenous (the *caña de millo* wooden flute and whistles) and Spanish (the verses) influences. Since the 1960s *cumbia* has become popular throughout South and Central America, especially in Bolivia, Agrentina, Ecuador and Peru, with *cumbia* musicians and songwriters in each country creating their own regional variations of the genre.

Festivals & Events
....
Carnaval, Oruro
....
Fiesta de Moxos
....
Fiesta de la Cruz
....
Fiesta de la Virgen de Urkupiña
....
Feria del Charango

Cumbia Boliviana

In Bolivia, *cumbia* is particularly influenced by *cumbia chicha* from Peru, with sentimental lyrics that narrate the emotional dramas of everyday life; themes usually concern falling in and out of love, but there are other more humdrum topics, such as an ode to beer. The 1980s were marked by the emergence of a new strand of *cumbia* in Bolivia: techno *cumbia*. Names to look out for are Wally Zeballos, Miguel Orías, Jorge Eduardo y los 4:40, David Castro, Los Brothers, Los Ronisch and FM y Silvana.

BOLIVIA'S BAROQUE MUSIC

The Jesuit priests who arrived in the jungles of the Chiquitania region in the 17th century left an important legacy in the mission towns they established: the baroque music tradition. Music was viewed as a tool for evangelism by the Jesuits, who also valued education, and they taught local people to play, make their own instruments and compose scores. Baroque music continues to be played and performed by orchestras and choirs and is taught in music schools in the Bolivian lowlands. An international festival held every two years in the Chiquitanía region attracts more than 50 baroque ensembles from within Bolivia and beyond.

Techno *cumbia* is still popular today, but there are other contemporary forms emerging that combine *cumbia* with various musical genres. Andrek Ortiz is a musician from La Paz and the man behind Villa Victoria Sound System, a project that mixes *cumbia* and electronica. Originally from Cochabamba, Pablo Pachacutik is a music producer whose work combines Andean folk music, *cumbia* and reggae. Sweden-based Bolivian DJ Jallallalacumbia produces mash-ups of *cumbia* and hip-hop, while Las Florecitas de Mizque is a group of three female singers whose sound is a purer form of Andean *cumbia*.

Folk

Perhaps Bolivia's most well-known band is Los Kjarkas, a legendary Andean folk ensemble who have toured internationally. The band was formed by guitarist and songwriter Gonzalo Hermosa González and his two brothers in 1965, and has been releasing records ever since, with a rotating cast of band members.

Founded in La Paz in 1984, K'ala Marka is considered one of Bolivia's most important folk bands. Their music uses a wide range of traditional Bolivian rhythms.

Wara is a folk-rock band from the shores of Lake Titicaca, whose first album *El Inca* was released in 1973; the band uses a mix of traditional instruments such as *charangos* and *zapoñas* (pan pipes) as well as guitars, bass, drums and synthesizers. Their lyrics capture the Bolivian landscape.

Rock & Metal

Rock band Lou Kass was popular in the 1990s; founding members Llegas and Krauss now have solo careers. Hailing from La Paz, iconic rock-band Atajo has had hits with songs portraying the struggles of everyday life in their native city. Almost 20 years after their first album was released, in 2017 they announced they were to split. Look out for solo projects by band member Pinchi Maldonado. Also from La Paz is metal-band Alcoholika. Their 1990s hits have heavily influenced some of Bolivia's emerging young musicians.

Bolivian Music Today

Today Bolivia's music scene is diverse, with plenty of exciting new artists emerging in a wide range of genres. There aren't many female hip-hop artists in South America, but Imilla MC is one worth looking up for her soulful melodies and message of female empowerment and social change in Bolivia; check out her song 'Criaturas'. Octavia is a pop-rock band from La Paz, whose catchy hit about their native city, 'La ciudad que habita en mi' (The City that Lives in Me), will stay in your head for days. Querembas (the Guaraní word for warriors) is a metal band from Santa Cruz, with a unique sound that combines industrial metal, symphonic metal and new metal. Reggae artist Matamba's lyrics have a strong social message; his song 'Alerta roja' gives a flavor of his work. Look out too for Avionica, a band from Cochabamba headed by rocker José Mrochek.

Bolivian folk band Los Kjarkas's most famous song is 'Llorando se fue', released in 1981. The melody will no doubt be familiar, but you might be recognizing the 1989 megahit 'Lambada' by French-Brazilian band Kaoma. Los Kjarkas successfully sued the group for plagiarism in 1990.

The Natural World

When people think of Bolivia they generally conjure up images of somewhere high (La Paz), dry (altiplano) or salty (Uyuni salt plains). While this may be true for large areas of the country, there's so much more to the Bolivian landscape. The range of altitude – 130m in the jungles of the Amazon Basin to 6542m on the peaks of the rugged Andes – has resulted in a huge variety of ecological and geological niches supporting a bewildering variety of nature.

Natural Assets

Environmentally, Bolivia is one of the most diverse countries on the continent. The country has 1415 bird species and 5000 described plant species, some of the highest numbers in the world. It's also among the neotropical countries with the highest level of endemism (species which exist only in Bolivia), with 21 birds, 28 reptiles, 72 amphibians and 25 mammals found nowhere else on earth.

But while it may seem obvious that Bolivia's natural resources are one of its greatest assets, not everybody values assets that don't have a direct monetary value. From the lush tropical forests of Amboró National Park to the wetlands of the Pantanal, the scrub that obscures the Chaco gas fields and the Polylepis woodlands of the Andes, the Bolivian environment is under constant threat from destruction by economic exploitation.

As the Bolivian economy keeps on growing, and the expectations of the newly empowered populace continue to rise, the country is struggling to balance the tireless demand for progress with the need to implement a sustainable and responsible exploitation of its natural resources. With the uncertain effects of climate change thrown into the mix, the Bolivian environment is facing its biggest challenges in millennia and its populace, albeit unwittingly, is dependent on a positive outcome.

Lago Poopó was Bolivia's second-largest lake, but in 2015 it dried out completely, leaving swaths of dead fish on the cracked ground once covered by water.

The Land

Two Andean mountain chains define the west of the country, with many peaks above 6000m. The western Cordillera Occidental stands between Bolivia and the Pacific coast. The eastern Cordillera Real runs southeast, then turns south across central Bolivia, joining the other chain to form the southern Cordillera Central.

The haunting altiplano (altitude 3500m to 4000m) is boxed in by these two great cordilleras. It's an immense, nearly treeless plain punctuated by mountains and solitary volcanic peaks. At the altiplano's northern end, straddling the Peruvian border, Lake Titicaca is one of the world's highest navigable lakes. In the far southwestern corner, the land is drier and less populated. The salty remnants of two vast ancient lakes, the Salar de Uyuni and the Salar de Coipasa, are there as well.

East of the Cordillera Central are the Central Highlands, a region of scrubby hills, valleys and fertile basins with a Mediterranean-like climate. North of the Cordillera Real, the rainy Yungas form a transition zone between arid highlands and humid lowlands.

At 1,083,300 sq km, landlocked Bolivia is South America's fifth-largest country, 3½ times the size of the British Isles.

More than half Bolivia's total area is in the Amazon Basin, with sweaty tropical rainforest in the western section, and flat *cerrado* savannas and extensions of the Pantanal wetland in the east. In the country's southeastern corner is the nearly impenetrable scrubland of the Gran Chaco, an arid, thorny forest that experiences the highest temperatures in the country.

Animals

More than 40% of the Bolivian territory is affected by desertification caused by climate change, population increase and indiscriminate forest felling.

Bolivia is one of the best places on the continent to observe wildlife and even seasoned wildlife watchers will be impressed by the diversity on show.

The distribution of wildlife is dictated by the country's geography and varies considerably from region to region. The altiplano is home to vicuñas, flamingos and condors; the Chaco to secretive jaguars, pumas and peccaries; the Pantanal provides refuge for giant otters, marsh deer and waterbirds; and the Amazon Basin contains the richest density of species on earth, featuring an incredible variety of reptiles, parrots, monkeys, hummingbirds, butterflies, fish and bugs (by the zillion!).

Of course the animals that steal the show are the regional giants: the majestic jaguar, the continent's top predator; the elephant-nosed tapir *(anta)* and the lolloping giant anteater. The ostrichlike rhea or *piyo,* the continent's biggest bird, is here too and it can be surprisingly common in some areas. You may even be lucky enough to spot the breathtaking Andean condor – revered by the Inca – soaring on mountain thermals.

River travelers are almost certain to see capybaras (like giant aquatic guinea pigs), caiman (alligators) and river dolphins. It's not unusual to see anacondas in the rivers of the department of Beni (an endemic species hangs out here, the Beni anaconda) and a spot of piranha fishing is virtually an obligation for anybody spending time in the Amazon.

Overland travelers frequently see armadillos, foxes, *jochis* (agoutis) and the domesticated camelids of the altiplano, the bad-tempered llama and the fuzzy alpaca. Similar, but more delicately proportioned, is the smaller vicuña, once mercilessly hunted for its woolly coat but now recovering well.

With massive government investment in the road network, getting around Bolivia is now easier than ever, and the country is experiencing a minor revolution as an exotic bird-watching destination, with more remote areas becoming newly accessible. This is thanks in no small measure to a series of gloriously charismatic endemics such as the blue-throated and red-fronted macaws, which have the star power to pull twitchers halfway across the globe for the chance to tick them.

ENVIRONMENTAL ISSUES

Environmental issues are becoming an increasingly pressing issue in Bolivia. Environmentalists are concerned that accelerating economic growth is not being tempered by the necessary measures to maintain a sound ecological balance.

Besides extensive land clearing for agricultural monocultures (particularly soybean), ranching and hydrocarbon exploration, there are also concerns about the future of freshwater supplies, with glaciers melting and the rivers increasingly polluted, especially in areas where mining is the major industry.

Many local nonprofit groups are working on countrywide environmental conservation efforts.

Threatened Species

Though anteaters and jaguars get all the headlines, these species are widespread throughout South America and the most threatened members of the Bolivian fauna are not necessarily the most conspicuous or famous. There are exceptions of course: the endangered Chaco peccary, an enormous piglike creature known only from fossil remains until 1976; the elusive spectacled bear; or the Golden Palace titi monkey, which hit the world headlines when a Canadian casino paid a fortune for the rights to name it.

The Andean condor, one of the world's heaviest flying birds, has a 3m wingspan and can effortlessly drag a 20kg carcass.

Among the most threatened wildlife in the highlands are the little known deer, the North Andean huemul, the Andean hairy armadillo and the endemic short-tailed chinchilla, sought after for its luxurious fur. The windswept lakes of the Southern Altiplano are the exclusive habitat of the rare James flamingo, while the charming Cochabamba mountain finch has a total range of just 3500 sq km, perilously close to the city of Cochabamba.

The Amazon Basin may be famous for its pink river dolphins, but rather less well known is the blue-throated macaw *(barba azul)* a species considered critically endangered and thought to number fewer than 300 individuals. The mythical unicorn bird of the Yungas, more properly known as the horned curassow, is critically endangered and can only be found in Bolivia. This is also the haunt of the wondrously colored Palkachupa Cotinga, gilded with gold and black.

In the Pantanal region the golden spear-nosed bat lives only in a handful of caves, while the hyacinth macaw has suffered for its comical appearance through capture for the pet trade. Another eye-catching parrot, the green, red and yellow red-fronted macaw of the dry inter-Andean valleys around Vallegrande, is also on the brink of extinction, with fewer than 4000 remaining.

Some of Bolivia's most remarkable threatened species aren't so pretty. Consider the bizarre marsupial frogs of the genus *Gastrotheca,* which includes five species in Bolivia that are all threatened with extinction, and the Jabba the Hutt–like Titicaca giant frog, confined to Bolivia's most famous lake. The latter can weigh up to 400g and is under extreme pressure because of a local belief that drinking the juice from the liquidized amphibian has aphrodisiac properties. More information is online at www.bolivianamphibianinitiative.org.

Plants

Because of its enormous range of altitudes, Bolivia enjoys a wealth and diversity of flora rivaled only by its Andean neighbors. No fewer than 895 plants are considered endemic to the country, including 16 species of passion-fruit vines and at least three genera of orchids.

In the overgrazed highlands, the only remaining vegetable species are those with some defense against grazing livestock or those that are unsuitable for firewood. Much of what does grow in the highlands grows slowly and is endangered, including the globally threatened genus of *Polylepis* shrubs which form dense, low forests at altitudes of up to 5300m, making them the highest growing arborescent plants in the world.

The national flower of Bolivia is the *kantuta;* not only is it aesthetically beautiful, but it also reflects the color of the country's national flag.

The lower elevations of the temperate highland hills and valleys support vegetation superficially reminiscent of that of Spain or California. The area around Samaipata is particularly rich in endemic plants, including the cactus *Samaipaticereus* and the bromeliad *Tillandsia samaipatensis,* while the gigantic Bolivian mountain coconut

EL CHAQUEO: THE BIG SMOKE

Each dry season, from July through September, Bolivia's skies fill with a thick pall of smoke, obscuring the air, occasionally canceling flights, aggravating allergies and causing respiratory strife. This is all the result of *el chaqueo*, the slashing and burning of the savannas (and some forest) for agricultural and grazing land. A prevailing notion is that the rising smoke forms rain clouds and ensures good rains for the coming season. In reality the hydrological cycle, which depends on transpiration from the forest canopy, is interrupted by the deforestation resulting in diminished rainfall.

Ranchers in the Beni department have long set fire to the savannas annually to encourage the sprouting of new grass. These days, however, the most dramatic defoliation is occurring along the highways in the country's east, the new agricultural frontier. Here the forest is being consumed by expanding cattle ranches and pristine natural habitat is being replaced by seemingly endless monocultures. Although the burned vegetable matter initially provides rich nutrients for crops, those nutrients aren't replenished. After two or three years the land is exhausted and it takes 15 years to become productive again. That's too long for most farmers to wait; most just pull up stakes and burn larger areas.

As the rural population increases, so do the effects of *el chaqueo*. Despite the fact that this burning is prohibited by Bolivian forestry statutes, the law has proved impossible to enforce in the vast Bolivian lowlands. The long-term implications aren't yet known but international pressure to reduce the negative effects of the burning has seen the Bolivian government implement a program encouraging lowland farmers to minimize *el chaqueo* in favor of alternatives that don't drain the soil of nutrients.

Parajubaea torallyi of the inter-Andean valleys is the world's highest growing palm.

The moist upper slopes of the Yungas are characterized by dwarf forest. Further down the slopes stretches the cloud forest, where the trees grow larger and the vegetation thicker. Northern Bolivia's lowlands consist of islands of true rainforest dotted with vast wetlands and endangered *cerrado* savannas, while the Amazon Basin contains the richest botanical diversity on earth.

National Parks & Reserves

In 2017, Evo Morales signed a law reversing the 'untouchable' status of TIPNIS, allowing the construction of a much disputed highway through the center of the park.

Bolivia has protected 18% of its total land by declaring 22 national protected areas and additional regional reserves under what is known as the Sistema Nacional de Áreas Protegidas (SNAP). The system is one of the most extensive on the continent, but despite covering much of Bolivia's most amazing landscapes, the reality is that most reserves are only nominally protected. Pressure continues to build on the protected areas system as the remote frontiers of the country are opened up to development, and the age-old technique of protection through inaccessibility is becoming less effective.

Management of the system of protected areas is by the government-run administrative body Servicio Nacional de Áreas Protegidas (p79). To try to address the chronic financial and staffing issues that this body faces, local and international NGOs have worked with Sernap to create innovative ways to preserve select habitats, with varying degrees of success.

Such projects have typically aimed to encourage local involvement and comanagement of protected areas in an effort to attract tourists to community-based, ecotourism experiences, as well as to produce commercially viable natural products, including medicinal patents.

Survival Guide

Directory A–Z

Accessible Travel

The sad fact is that Bolivia's infrastructure is ill equipped for travelers with disabilities. You will, however, see locals overcoming myriad obstacles and challenges while making their daily rounds. If you encounter difficulties yourself, you'll likely find locals willing to go out of their way to lend a hand. Download Lonely Planet's free Accessible Travel guides from http://lptravel.to/AccessibleTravel.

Accommodations

Bolivian accommodations are among South America's cheapest.

➡ *alojamientos* (basic accommodations) The cheapest places are usually found around the bus and train stations

➡ *residenciales* (simple accommodations)

➡ *casas de huéspedes* (family-run guesthouses)

➡ *posadas* (inns) Increasingly a *posada* is a small, often upmarket hotel

➡ *hostales* (hostels) Note that *hostales* are not necessarily hostels as you might normally think; some are in fact upmarket hotels

➡ *hoteles* (hotels)

Booking Ahead

Room availability is only a problem at popular weekend getaways such as Coroico and during fiestas (especially Carnaval in Oruro and festivals in Copacabana), when prices double.

Camping

➡ Bolivia offers excellent camping, especially along trekking routes and in remote mountain areas. Remember that highland nights are often freezing.

➡ There are few organized campsites, but you can pitch a tent almost anywhere outside population centers. It's always a good idea to ask for permission if possible.

➡ Gear (of varying quality) is easily rented in La Paz and at

popular trekking base camps such as Sorata.

➡ Theft and assaults have been reported in some areas – always ask locally about security before heading off to set up camp.

Hostels

➡ **Hostelling International** (HI; www.hostellingbolivia.org) is affiliated with a network of accommodations in different parts of Bolivia.

➡ Most hostels have common areas, bunk beds in shared rooms, shared bathrooms with or without hot water, book exchanges and wi-fi. Some even have pubs and hot tubs.

➡ You can often get cheaper accommodations at low-end hotels, but you'll miss out on the traveler culture.

Hostales & Hotels

➡ Bolivia has pleasant midrange places and five-star luxury resorts, although these are generally limited to larger cities and popular vacation and weekend resort destinations.

➡ Standard hotel amenities include breakfast, private bathrooms with 24/7 hot showers (gas- or electric-heated), phones, wi-fi and color TV, usually with cable.

➡ Save big by booking ahead online.

➡ A good breakfast is nearly always included.

BOOK YOUR STAY ONLINE

For more accommodations reviews by Lonely Planet authors, check out http://lonelyplanet.com/hotels/. You'll find independent reviews, as well as recommendations on the best places to stay. Best of all, you can book online.

PROPANE HEATER WARNING

Readers have alerted us to improper use of propane heaters in Bolivia. These are sometimes offered in cheaper accommodations but are not meant to be used in enclosed spaces so refrain from using them if supplied.

Posadas, Alojamientos, Residenciales & Casas de Huéspedes

➡ The accommodations at the cheapest end of the scale can be pretty bad and are best avoided. At worst they can be smelly, dirty, with dangerous electrics and a suspicious clientele.

➡ The terms *residenciales, alojamientos, posadas* etc are often used interchangeably, but a quick look around will tell you all you need to know about standards.

➡ Communal bathrooms are most common (check cleanliness!), heating and hot water are usually absent.

➡ When there is hot water it's usually in the form of an electric shower. To avoid electric shock, don't touch the shower while the water is running and wear rubber sandals.

➡ *Casas de huéspedes* sometimes offer a more midrange, B&B-like atmosphere.

➡ Ask to see a couple of rooms before committing, keep your valuables in a safe when available and check the sheets for bedbugs.

SLEEPING PRICE RANGES

The following price ranges refer to a double room with bathroom.

$ less than B$180

$$ B$180–500

$$$ more than B$500

Consulates & Embassies

Argentinian Embassy (Map p54; 241-7737; www.ebolv. cancilleria.gov.ar; Aspiazu 475, Sopocachi; 8:30am-1:30pm Mon-Fri)

Argentinian Consulate (Map p256; 03-332-4153; www. cscrs.cancilleria.gov.ar; Junín 22, 3rd fl; 8:30am-5pm Mon-Fri)

Australian Consulate (Map p61; mobile 7676-8787; https://dfat.gov.au/about-us/ our-locations/missions/Pages/ australian-consulate-in-la-paz-bolivia.aspx; Av Montenegro 961, Torre Olimpo, San Miguel; 9am-noon Mon-Fri)

Brazilian Embassy (Map p54; 244-1273; http://lapaz. itamaraty.gov.br/pt-br; Av Arce s/n, Edificio Multicentro, Sopocachi; 9am-1pm & 2-5pm Mon-Fri)

Brazilian Consulate (03-344-7575; http://santacruz. itamaraty.gov.br; Av Banzer 334; 8am-2pm Mon-Fri)

Canadian Embassy (Map p54; 241-5141; www.international. gc.ca; Victor Sanjinés 2678, 2nd fl, Sopocachi; 8:30am-1:30pm Mon-Fri)

Ecuadorian Embassy (Map p61; 211-5869; https://bolivia. embajada.gob.ec; Calle 14 No 8136, Calacoto; 9am-5pm Mon-Fri)

French Embassy (214-9900; https://bo.ambafrance.org; Calle 8 No 5390, Obrajes; 8:30am-12:30pm Mon-Fri)

German Embassy (Map p54; 244-0066; www.la-paz.diplo. de; Av Arce 2395, Sopocachi; 9am-noon Mon-Fri)

Irish Honorary Consul (2241-3949, 2242-1408; consulbolivia

@gmail.com; Pasaje Gandarillas 2667, cnr Macario Pinilla, Sopocachi, La Paz)

Italian Embassy (mobile 7155-4805; www.amblapaz. esteri.it; cnr Av Hernando Siles & Calle 5, Obrajes; 8:30am-noon Mon-Thu)

Japanese Embassy (Map p54; www.bo.emb-japan.go.jp; cnr Av Sánchez Lima & Gutiérrez; 8:30-11:30am & 1:30-5pm Mon-Fri)

Netherlands Consulate General (Map p54; 2242-2542; lapaz@ nlconsulate.com; 7th fl, Edificio, Rosario, Sopocachi, Av Sanchez Lima 2061, La Paz; 3:30-6pm Mon & Wed)

Paraguayan Embassy (Map p54; 243-2201; Pedro Salazar 351, Edificio Illimani II, Sopocachi; 9am-4pm Mon-Fri)

Peruvian Embassy (Map p54; 244-1250; www. embaperubolivia.com; Fernando Guachalla 300, Sopocachi; 9:30am-1:30pm & 3:30-6:30pm Mon-Fri)

Spanish Embassy (Map p54; 243-4180; www.exteriores. gob.es/Embajadas/LaPaz; Av 6 de Agosto 2827, Sopocachi; 9am-1pm Mon-Fri)

Spanish Consulate (Map p256; 03-312-1349; cnr Av Cañoto & Perú; 8:30am-12:30pm Mon-Fri)

UK Embassy (Map p54; 243-3424; www.gov.uk/ world/bolivia; Av Arce 2732, Sopocachi; 8:30am-12:30pm & 1:30-5pm Mon-Thu, 8:30am-12:30pm Fri)

UK Honorary Consulate (3-353-5035; silvanag@scis-bo. com; Santa Cruz International School)

US Embassy (Map p54; 216-8000; https://bo.usembassy. gov; Av Arce 2780, Sopocachi; 8am-5pm Mon-Thu, 9am-12:30pm Fri)

US Consulate (3-351-3477; Radial Castilla, 3ero anillo, in front of Santo Tomas School soccer field; 8am-3pm Mon & Tue, from 8:30am Wed & Thu, 9am-noon Fri)

Discount Cards

The **International Student Travel Confederation** (ISTC; www.isic.org) is an international network of specialist student travel organizations and the body behind the International Student Identity Card (ISIC), which gives carrier discounts on a few services in Bolivia.

Electricity

Type A
230V/50Hz

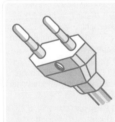

Type C
230V/50Hz

Food

Bolivia's cities are home to some excellent eating options (p17). In remote, rural areas, restaurant choices are often limited. It's not usually necessary (and often impossible) to book ahead.

Markets The cheapest and most adventurous place to eat.

Comedores (simple restaurants) The most common type of restaurant in rural areas.

Restaurants Bolivia's restaurants range from homey places to fine dining.

Cafes Found only in Bolivia's more cosmopolitan towns and cities.

Hotels Remote lodges and hotels have restaurants where you can dine on-site.

Insurance

A good travel-insurance policy to cover theft, loss and medical mishaps is important. A wide variety of policies is available: shop around and scrutinize the fine print. Some policies specifically exclude 'dangerous activities,' which can include skiing, motorcycling, mountain biking and even trekking. Check that the policy covers ambulances and emergency airlift evacuations.

Worldwide travel insurance is available at www.lonelyplanet.com/travel-insurance. You can buy, extend and claim online anytime – even if you're already on the road.

Internet Access

➡ Nearly every corner of Bolivia has a cyber cafe and wi-fi is now standard in most midrange and top-end hotels (and many cafes).

➡ Rates run from B$4 to B$6 per hour.

➡ In remote areas, internet access is sometimes only possible via a cell-phone

signal. Consider buying a local chip/SIM with data.

Language Courses

➡ Language courses are offered in Cochabamba, Coroico, La Paz, Oruro and Sucre.

➡ Including a homestay will greatly expand your cultural exposure and increase your learning curve.

Legal Matters

➡ The biggest legal problems affecting travelers include trafficking and possession of cocaine and other drugs, minor traffic violations and sex-related crimes.

➡ If you are arrested, contact your embassy immediately. Note however that they don't have the power to resolve the legalities (or illegalities) if you break the law.

➡ Be aware that incidences of fake police have been on the rise.

LGBT+ Travelers

➡ Bolivia's 2009 constitution is one of the first in the world to expressly ban discrimination on the basis of sexual orientation or gender identity. However homosexuality is still not widely accepted by the populace and gay marriage and same-sex unions are illegal.

➡ LGBT+ bars and venues are limited to larger cities,

especially Santa Cruz and La Paz (check out **Open Mind Club** (Map p50; www.facebook.com/omc.openmindclub; Cochabamba 100, Rosario; ⏰9pm-4am Fri & Sat), but these are still somewhat clandestine affairs. Sharing a room is no problem – but discretion is suggested.

➡ LGBT+ rights lobby groups are active in La Paz, Cochabamba and most visibly in progressive Santa Cruz, which held Bolivia's first Gay Pride march in 2001.

➡ La Paz is known for La Familia Galán, the capital's most fabulous group of cross-dressing queens who aim to educate Bolivians around issues of sexuality and gender through theater performances.

➡ Mujeres Creando (www.mujerescreando.org) is a feminist activist group based in La Paz that promotes the rights of oppressed groups.

Maps

Maps are available through Los Amigos del Libro in **La Paz** (Map p50; Ballivián 1273; ⏰9am-12:30pm & 3-7:30pm Mon-Fri, 9:30am-12:30pm Sat), Cochabamba and **Santa Cruz** (Map p256; ☎336-0709; Ballivián 145; ⏰9am-1pm & 3-10pm Mon-Sat) and some bookstores. Government 1:50,000 topographical and specialty sheets are available from the **Instituto Geográfico Militar** (IGM; Map p50; Av Diagonal Juan XXIII No 100, Edificio Murillo, San Pedro; ⏰8:30am-12:30pm & 2:30-6:30pm Mon-Thu, 8:30am-12:30pm Fri), with offices in most major cities.

Money

➡ Bolivia uses the boliviano (B$), divided into 100 centavos.

➡ Most prices are pegged to the US dollar.

➡ Often called pesos (the currency was changed from pesos to bolivianos in 1987).

➡ Only crisp US dollar bills are accepted (they are the currency for savings).

➡ Boliviano notes: 10, 20, 50, 100 and 200.

➡ Coins: one, two and five bolivianos as well as 10, 20 and 50 centavos.

➡ Bolivianos are extremely difficult to unload outside the country. Change them before you leave.

ATMs

➡ All sizeable towns have *cajeros automáticos* (ATMs) – usually Banco Nacional de Bolivia, Banco Fassil, Banco Mercantil Santa Cruz and Banco Unión.

➡ They dispense bolivianos in 50 and 100 notes (sometimes US dollars as well) on Visa, MasterCard, Plus and Cirrus cards.

➡ In smaller towns, the local bank Prodem is a good option for cash advances on Visa and MasterCard (3% to 6% commission charged) but the service is sometimes unreliable.

➡ Don't rely on ATMs; always carry some cash with you, especially if venturing into rural areas.

Counterfeits

➡ Counterfeit bolivianos and US dollars are less common than they used to be, but it still happens more often than you'd like.

➡ If a bill looks excessively tatty don't accept it, because nobody else will.

➡ Torn notes are still legal tender, but unless both halves of a repaired banknote bear identical serial numbers, the note is worthless.

Credit Cards

➡ Brand-name plastic – such as Visa, MasterCard and (less often) American Express – may be used in larger cities at the better

hotels, restaurants and tour agencies.

Exchanging Money

➡ Currency may be exchanged at *casas de cambio* (exchange bureaux) and at some banks in larger cities. Occasionally travel agencies, hotels and sometimes tourist stores will change money, but at a price.

➡ Visitors fare best with US dollars; it's hard to change euros or British pounds, and rates are poor.

➡ *Cambistas* (street money changers) operate in most cities but only change cash dollars, paying roughly the same as *casas de cambio*. They're convenient but beware of rip-offs and counterfeit notes.

➡ The rate for cash doesn't vary much from place to place, and there is no black-market rate.

➡ Currencies of neighboring countries may be exchanged in border areas and at *casas de cambio* in La Paz.

International Transfers

To transfer money from abroad use the following:

Western Union (www.westernunion.com).

MoneyGram (www.moneygram.com).

Your bank can also wire money to a cooperating Bolivian bank; it may take a couple of business days.

PayPal (www.paypal.com) Increasingly used to make bank transfers to pay for hotels.

Opening Hours

Take care of business on weekdays. Nearly all businesses close for lunch, usually from noon to 2:30pm.

Banks Standard hours 9am–4pm or 6pm Monday to Friday, and 10am–noon or 5pm Saturday.

PRACTICALITIES

Addresses In addresses s/n means *sin numero,* or no street number. In smaller cities, landmarks are preferred to street names to get around.

Newspapers International periodicals are sold in bigger cities. Popular reads include *La Razón* (www.la-razon.com), the nation's biggest daily newspaper; *El Correo del Sur* (www.correodelsur.com) in Sucre; *El Deber* (www.eldeber.com.bo) in Santa Cruz.

Radio Try *Bolivia Web Radio* (www.boliviaweb.com/radio) for a 24/7 stream of Andean artists or *Radio Panamericana* (www.panamericana.bo).

Television A decent grasp of at least Spanish is required to watch the local TV. Cable TV with international stations is available in most upmarket hotels.

Smoking Banned in certain public spaces, including on public transportation, in health-care facilities and government offices, but there is no law against smoking in restaurants, cafes, bars or offices. Many hotels forbid smoking in rooms.

Weights & Measures The metric system is used.

Shops Weekdays 10am–7pm but sometimes close for lunch noon–2pm. Open 10am–noon or 5pm Saturdays.

Restaurants Hours vary, but are generally open for breakfast (8am–10am), lunch (noon–3pm) and dinner (6pm–10pm or 11pm) daily.

Photography

Lonely Planet's Guide to Travel Photography is full of helpful tips for photography while on the road.

➡ Some Bolivians are willing photo subjects; others may be suspicious of your camera and/or your motives. Ask permission to photograph if a shot avoiding people can't be made; if permission is denied, you should neither insist nor snap a picture. Be sensitive to the wishes of locals.

➡ Many children will ask for payment, often after you've taken their photo. A few bolivianos will suffice.

➡ Avoid taking photographs of political rallies, military facilities or police – they are not noted for their sense of humor or understanding.

➡ La Paz is generally the best place to buy equipment and to look for repairs.

Post

In 2018 the Bolivian post service Ecobol (Empresa Correos de Bolivia) was closed (with a backlog of post left undelivered) and the government created the Agencia Nacional de Correos (www.oopp.gob.bo/agbc). Mail sent from bigger cities is more reliable than that sent from small towns. Expect delays!

➡ To mail an international parcel take it open to the post office so that the contents can be inspected. After inspection close it yourself (take what you need with you) before handing it over.

➡ You may be asked to fill in some official forms detailing the contents of the package. Avoid being too detailed, and don't explicitly mention items that might be attractive to thieves.

➡ The cost of sending the package depends on its weight. If you are offered the chance to 'register' the package for a small cost, take it; it doesn't guarantee much, but at least it gives you some kind of leg to stand on if it subsequently disappears.

➡ Avoid sending anything valuable by standard mail. Use an international courier, such as DHL (www.dhl.com). It's more expensive, but it will get to where you send it.

Public Holidays

Public holidays vary from province to province. The following are celebrated nationally.

Año Nuevo (New Year's Day) January 1

Día del Estado Plurinacional (Celebrates new constitution) January 22

Carnaval February/March

Semana Santa (Good Friday) March/April

Día del Trabajo (Labor Day) May 1

Corpus Christi May/June

Año Nuevo Andino Amazónico y del Chaco (Andean New Year) June 21

Día de la Independencia (Independence Day) August 6

Día de los Muertos (All Souls' Day) November 2

Navidad (Christmas) December 25

Departmental Holidays

Not about to be outdone by its neighbors, each department has its own holiday.

Oruro February 10

Tarija April 15

Chuquisaca May 25

La Paz July 16

Cochabamba September 14

Santa Cruz September 24

Pando October 11

Potosí November 10

Beni November 18

Safe Travel

➡ Crime against tourists is on the increase in Bolivia, especially in La Paz and, to a lesser extent, Cochabamba, Copacabana and Oruro.

➡ There is a strong tradition of social protest in Bolivia and demonstrations are a regular occurrence. While generally peaceful, they can turn threatening in nature: agitated protesters throw stones and rocks and police occasionally use force and tear gas to disperse crowds.

➡ Note that the mine tours in Potosí, bike trips outside La Paz and 4WD excursions around Salar de Uyuni can be dangerous. Some agencies are willing to forgo safety, so choose carefully.

Scams

Scams are commonplace and fake police, false tourist police and 'helpful' locals are on the rise. Be aware, too, of circulating counterfeit banknotes.

Bribes

Bribes are illegal in Bolivia, but common. People stopped for minor traffic violations or more serious infractions sometimes ask if they can 'pay the fine now.' Watch out for false police – authentic police officers will always wear a uniform and will never force you to show them your passport, insist you get in a taxi with them, or search you in public.

Protests

Bloqueos (roadblocks) and strikes by transportation workers often lead to road closures and long delays. When there is an ongoing dispute, bus services between certain towns may be canceled indefinitely. Keep an eye on the news and ask around to find out if there are any trouble spots that might disrupt your travel plans. Be careful using taxis during transportation strikes – you may end up at the receiving end of a rock, pelted by protesters at those who are not in sympathy with them.

Flooding

The rainy season means flooding, landslides and road washouts, which in turn means more delays. Getting stuck overnight behind a landslide can happen; you'll be a happier camper with ample food, drink and warm clothes on hand.

Shopping

Each town or region has its own specialty *artesanía* (locally handcrafted items). You'll find a range of reasonably priced artwork from all over the country in La Paz, Copacabana and Santa Cruz, but prices are generally lower at the point of original production. Many articles are made by cooperatives or profit companies with ecofriendly and culturally responsible practices.

Telephone

Local SIM cards should work in cell phones that are not tied to a single network. Make sure your phone has triband network capabilities. Roaming rates can be high. Kiosks often have telephones that charge B$1 for brief local calls.

Dialing in to the Telephone Network

Numbers *Líneas fijas* (landlines) have seven digits; cellular numbers have eight digits.

Area codes Each department (region) has its own single-digit area code which must be used when dialing from another region or to another city, regardless of whether it's the same area code as the one you're in. The department codes are as follows.

La Paz, Oruro, Potosí	☎2
Santa Cruz, Beni, Pando	☎3
Cochabamba, Chuquisaca, Tarija	☎4

Public phones Dialing landlines from public phones (often located in small convenience stores and kiosks, or local call centers known as *puntos*) is easy; ask the cashier for help.

Placing calls To make a call to another landline within the same city, simply dial the seven-digit number. If you're calling another region, dial ☎0 plus the single-digit area code followed by the seven-digit number, eg ☎02-123-4567. If calling a cell phone, ask the cashier for instructions; most *puntos* have different phones for calls to mobiles and landlines, so you may have to swap cabins if calling both.

International calls For international calls, you must first dial ☎00 followed by a country code, area code (without the first 0) and the telephone number.

GOVERNMENT TRAVEL ADVICE

The following government websites offer travel advisories and information on current hot spots.

Australian Department of Foreign Affairs (www.smartraveller.gov.au)

British Foreign Office (www.gov.uk/foreign-travel-advice)

Canadian Department of Foreign Affairs (travel.gc.ca)

US State Department (www.travel.state.gov)

International Calls

Bolivia international dialing code	☑591
International access code	☑00

Internet Calls

Most internet places have Skype installed, which you can use at no extra cost – you just have to pay for the time online. WhatsApp messages and calls can be a convenient (and free) way to communicate and even make hotel and tour reservations.

Mobile Phones

➡ Cellular SIM cards are cheap, include credit and are available from larger carrier outlets as well as small private phone shops.

➡ Make sure your phone has triband network capabilities.

Time

Bolivian time is four hours behind Greenwich Mean Time (GMT), and an hour ahead of the US Eastern Standard Time. The 24-hour clock is commonly used. Some examples of global times are given in the table below.

La Paz	noon
San Francisco	8am
New York	11am
London	4pm
Sydney	2am (next day)
Auckland	4am (next day)

Toilets

➡ Toilet humor becomes the norm in Bolivia. First and foremost, you'll have to learn to live with the fact that facilities are nonexistent on nearly all buses (except for a few of the luxury ones).

➡ Smelly, poorly maintained *baños públicos* (public toilets) abound and charge about B$1 in populated areas and B$5 in the wilderness, such as near the Salar de Uyuni.

➡ Carry toilet paper with you wherever you go, at all times!

➡ Toilet paper isn't flushed down any Bolivian toilet – use the wastebaskets provided.

➡ Use the facilities at your hotel before heading out.

➡ Some budget hotels and hostels can be stingy with toilet paper. It's best to always come armed with your own.

Tourist Information

➡ Bolivian tourism has really taken off in recent years, but the industry and its associated infrastructure is still in its formative stages.

➡ InfoTur (www.visitbolivia.org) offices are found in most of the major tourist destinations. The amount of printed material available and the level of attention from staff can vary from place to place, and from visit to visit. Don't expect a lengthy conversation if you go just before lunch for example. Note that the posted opening hours are not always followed.

➡ The **Ministerio de Culturas y Turismo** (Map p50; ☑2-220-0910; www.minculturas.gob.bo; Palacio Chico, cnr Ayacucho & Potosí, La Paz; ⊙8:30am-6:30pm Mon-Fri) provides a register of official operators in the tourist industry.

➡ There is plenty of competition between tourist operators in the most popular destinations and this is often reflected in their website content, which often features abundant information to make the company more attractive.

This can be a useful research tool, provided you remember the context the information is provided in!

Visas

US citizens need a visa to visit Bolivia. Citizens of Australia, Canada, New Zealand and most European countries do not need a visa.

Entry Requirements

➡ Your passport must be valid for six months beyond the date of entry.

➡ Charging of unofficial 'administration fees,' particularly at remote borders, is not unusual. The path of least resistance is to just pay and go.

➡ US citizens need a visa to visit Bolivia (a 90-day visa valid for 10 years costs US$160). Theoretically it is possible to obtain the visa upon arrival in Bolivia, but some airlines will not let you board your flight without one and the US embassy advises to get a visa before traveling.

➡ Citizens of Australia, Canada, New Zealand, most European countries and most South American countries do not need a visa and will be granted an entry stamp valid for 30 days.

➡ If you want to stay longer, you can get a free 30-day extension at the immigration office in any major city. The maximum time travelers are permitted to stay is 90 days.

➡ Overstayers can be forced to pay a fine – payable at the immigration office or airport – and may face ribbons of red tape at the border or airport when leaving the country.

➡ In addition to a valid passport and visa, citizens of some African, Middle Eastern and Asian countries may require 'official permission' from the Bolivian Ministry of Foreign Affairs before a visa will be issued.

⇒ Personal documents – passports and visas – must be carried at all times, especially in lowland regions. It's safest to carry photocopies rather than originals, but if you are going anywhere near a border area (even if you don't actually cross) you should have your real passport with you.

Volunteering

⇒ There are hundreds of voluntary and nongovernmental organizations (NGOs) working in Bolivia, making this a popular spot to volunteer.

⇒ Many of the opportunities follow the pay-to-volunteer model, and often include room and board, costing anywhere from US$200 to US$1000 per month. Options to do free volunteer work are more limited.

⇒ Research your placement carefully. Be aware that some profit organizations offer 'internship' or 'volunteer' opportunities, when in reality it's unpaid work in exchange for free trips or activities.

⇒ Government-sponsored organizations or NGOs offer longer-term programs for which you receive an allowance, predeparture briefings and ongoing organizational support.

⇒ Church-affiliated or religious organizations offer short-term opportunities, often on a group basis.

⇒ Smaller volunteer organizations (sometimes profit-based) offer independent travelers the opportunity to work on community projects. These usually have a two- or four-week minimum for which you pay.

Animales SOS (☏230-8080; www.animalessos.org; Av Chacaltaya 1759, Achachicala) An animal-welfare group caring for mistreated or abused stray animals.

Sustainable Bolivia (☏423-3783; www.sustainablebolivia. org; Julio Arauco Prado 230) Cochabamba-based not-for-profit with a variety of volunteering programs, both short- and long-term, through 22 local organizations. Also offers Spanish language classes.

Volunteer Bolivia (Map p182; ☏7171-2491; www. volunteerbolivia.org; Ecuador E-0342) Arranges short- and long-term volunteer work, Spanish language classes in Cochabamba and homestay programs throughout Bolivia.

WWOOF Latin America (www. wwooflatinamerica.com) Sets you up with volunteer opportunities on organic farms.

Work

⇒ Teachers can try for private-school positions with the greatest demand in maths, science or social studies. New or unqualified teachers must forfeit two months' salary in return for their training.

⇒ Other travelers find work in bars, hostels or with tour operators.

⇒ For paid work, qualified English-language teachers can try the professionally-run **Centro Boliviano-Americano** (www.cba.edu. bo) in La Paz, with branches in other cities. Accredited teachers can expect to earn up to US$500 per month for a full-time position.

Transportation

GETTING THERE & AWAY

A landlocked country, Bolivia has numerous entry/exit points, and you can get here by boat, bus, train, plane, bike and on foot. Some places are easier to travel through and more accessible than others.

Flights, cars and tours can be booked online at lonely planet.com/bookings.

Entering the Country

If you have your documents in order and are willing to answer a few questions about the aim of your visit, entering Bolivia should be a breeze. If crossing at a small border post, you may be asked to pay an 'exit fee.' In most cases, such fees are strictly unofficial, but it's easier just to pay them anyway.

Note that more remote Bolivian border opening times can be unreliable at best and it is worth checking with a *migración* (immigration) office in the nearest major town. If you plan to cross the border outside the stated hours, or at a point where there is no border post, you can usually obtain an exit/entry stamp from the nearest *migración* office on departure or arrival.

Air

There are direct services to most major South American cities and the flights to/from Chile and Peru are the cheapest. Santa Cruz is an increasingly popular entry point from European hubs. Due to altitude-related costs, it is more expensive to fly into La Paz than Santa Cruz. High season for most fares is from early June to late August, and from mid-December to mid-February.

Airports & Airlines

Bolivia's principal international airports are La Paz's **El Alto International Airport** (LPB; Héroes Km 7), formerly known as John F Kennedy Memorial, Santa Cruz's **Viru-Viru International Airport** (☑338-5000) and Cochabamba's **Jorge Wilstermann International Airport** (☑412-0400; Av Killman s/n).

The national airline is the state-owned **Boliviana de Aviación** (BOA; ☑901-105-010; www.boa.bo), which has international flights to Madrid, Barcelona and Miami.

Aerolíneas Argentinas (☑800-100-242; www.aerolineas.com.ar) Daily flights from Santa Cruz to Buenos Aires.

Amaszonas (☑901-105-500; www.amaszonas.com) Flights to Asunción, Buenos Aires, Cuzco, Iquique and Montevideo.

American Airlines (☑800-100-541; www.aa.com) Daily flights from Santa Cruz to Miami.

CLIMATE CHANGE & TRAVEL

Every form of transport that relies on carbon-based fuel generates CO_2, the main cause of human-induced climate change. Modern travel is dependent on airplanes, which might use less fuel per mile per person than most cars but travel much greater distances. The altitude at which aircraft emit gases (including CO_2) and particles also contributes to their climate change impact. Many websites offer 'carbon calculators' that allow people to estimate the carbon emissions generated by their journey and, for those who wish to do so, to offset the impact of the greenhouse gases emitted with contributions to portfolios of climate-friendly initiatives throughout the world. Lonely Planet offsets the carbon footprint of all staff and author travel.

Avianca (☎1-866-998-3357; www.avianca.com) Flights from La Paz to Bogotá and Lima.

Copa (☎800-102-672; www.copaair.com) Flights from Santa Cruz to Panama, with onward connections.

Gol (☎800-122-201; www.voegol.com.br) Flights from Santa Cruz to Rio de Janeiro and other destinations.

Land & River

Border Crossings

Bolivia has land borders with Argentina (at Villazón, Yacuiba and Bermejo); Brazil (via Quijarro on the main highway from Santa Cruz, and a smaller crossing at San Matías), Chile (at Tambo Quemado, Hito Cajón and Ollagüe); Paraguay (the trans-Chaco crossing) and Peru (at Kasani and Desaguadero).

US citizens and citizens of a number of other countries need a visa (p350) to enter Bolivia.

ARGENTINA

There are three overland crossings between Argentina and Bolivia.

Villazón/La Quiaca (p178), with connections by bus and train north to Tupiza and Uyuni in Bolivia and south to Salta in Argentina.

Yacuiba/Pocitos, in the Chaco region (p251). Buses traveling further into Argentina leave every couple of hours.

Bermejo/Aguas Blancas (p248), south of Tarija, at an international bridge that leads on to a highway going further into Argentina. Bus companies from Tarija to Salta in Argentina use this crossing.

BRAZIL

Note that proof of yellow-fever vaccination is usually needed when crossing into Brazil. If you don't have one, you can get a shot at the border (in relatively sanitary conditions).

DEPARTURE TAX

Departure tax is included in the ticket price for international and domestic flights from La Paz El Alto, Santa Cruz and Cochabamba airports. Other airports charge a small fee of varying amounts.

Quijarro/Corumbá (p284) The main border crossing to Brazil, at the end of the train line from Santa Cruz.

San Matías/Cáceres (p284) A more adventurous, minor crossing, connected by dirt road to San Ignacio on the Jesuit mission circuit.

CHILE

Note that meat, fruit and food produce (including coca leaves) cannot be taken from Bolivia into Chile and will be confiscated at the border.

Tambo Quemado/Chungará (p156) The most popular route between Chile and Bolivia is by bus from La Paz to Arica, via the crossing at Tambo Quemado.

Hito Cajón/San Pedro (p167) A convenient alternative for those doing the 4WD Southwest Circuit tour is to be dropped off on the last day at Hito Cajón (8am to 11pm, although it's wise to be there before 6pm) and head for San Pedro, Chile (many tour operators now offer transfers). From here, you can pick up a bus. Note the one-hour trip between the Bolivian border and San Pedro – it's better to arrange transport for this in advance, in case there aren't any taxis.

Ollagüe/Avaroa (p167) A crossing can be made by road from Uyuni to Calama, where the border crossing is in Ollagüe (8am to 8pm).

PARAGUAY

Trans-Chaco crossing This bus trip between Santa Cruz in Bolivia and Asunción in Paraguay is a daily service. This is a notorious smuggling route, so expect to be lined up with your bags while customs officials and sniffer dogs rifle through your possessions.

PERU

Kasani–Yunguyo (p98) Bolivia is normally reached overland from Peru via Lake Titicaca and the crossing at Kasani–Yunguyo.

Desaguadero (p98) A quicker, but less appealing route is via Desaguadero on the southern side of the lake.

La Paz–Puno An efficient alternative is to catch a tourist bus from La Paz to Puno via Copacabana (from B$60) or vice versa; some deals allow you a couple of days' stay in Copacabana.

Bus

Depending on which country you enter from, some intercountry buses booked through an agency might

---

US STOPOVERS

Some fares include a stopover in the USA. Note if you're traveling through New York (JFK) or Miami you must pass through American immigration procedures, even if you aren't visiting the USA. That means you'll either need to have a US visa or be eligible for the Visa Waiver Program, which is open to Australians, New Zealanders and most Western Europeans, unless you're traveling on a nonaccredited airline (which includes most Latin American airlines).

TRANSPORTATION LAND & RIVER

cover your entire route; at other times you'll switch to an associated bus company once you cross the border. If traveling by local bus, you'll usually need to catch onward buses once you've made your border crossing.

Car & Motorcycle

You can enter Bolivia by road from any of the neighboring countries. The Trans-Chaco road from Paraguay is in a dreadful state, especially beyond the town of Mariscal Estigarribia, and should be considered only if you are driving a 4WD. The main routes from Argentina, Brazil, Chile and Peru pose no significant problems.

Foreigners entering Bolivia from another country need a *hoja de ruta* (circulation card, www.dgsc.gob.bo/hoja-ruta.php), available from the Servicio Nacional de Tránsito/Aduana at the border. This document must be presented and stamped at all police posts – variously known as *trancas, tránsitos* or *controles* – which are found along highways and just outside major cities. *Peajes* (tolls) are often charged at these checkpoints and vehicles may be searched for contraband.

GETTING AROUND

Air

Air travel within Bolivia is inexpensive and the quickest and most reliable way to reach out-of-the-way places. It's also the only means of transportation that isn't washed out during the wet season. When weather-related disruptions occur, planes eventually get through, even during summer flooding in northern Bolivia. Schedules tend to change often and cancellations are frequent, so plan ahead.

Airlines in Bolivia

Amaszonas (901-105-500; www.amaszonas.com) Domestic connections to La Paz, Santa Cruz, Uyuni, Sucre, Cochabamba, Rurrenabaque, Trinidad and Riberalta.

Boliviana de Aviación (BOA; 901-105-010; www.boa.bo) Flights to La Paz, Santa Cruz, Cochabamba, Potosí, Sucre, Oruro, Uyuni, Tarija, Trinidad, Chimore, Cobija and Yacuiba.

TAM (2-268-1111; www.tam.bo) Flights to La Paz, Santa Cruz, Tarija, Rurrenabaque, Riberalta, Sucre, Cochabamba and Cobija.

Bicycle

For cyclists who can cope with the challenges of cold winds, poor road conditions, high altitudes and steep terrain, Bolivia is a paradise. Mountain bikes are common on Bolivia's large number of dirt roads. While traffic isn't a serious problem (though cliffs are), intimidating buses and *camiones* (flatbed trucks) can leave cyclists in clouds of dust or embedded in mud. Finding supplies may prove difficult, so cyclists in remote areas must carry ample food and water. Given these challenges, many prefer to leave the work to a tour company.

If you're considering any biking in Bolivia, make sure you purchase a comprehensive travel insurance policy.

Bolivia has its fair share of inexpensive bikes, which are mostly supermarket beaters from China. Quality new wheels are rarer. Your best bet for purchasing a used, touring-worthy stead is through agencies in La Paz. Try **Gravity Assisted Mountain Biking** (Map p50; 231-0218, mobile 7721-9634; www.gravitybolivia.com; Linares 940, Rosario; 9am-7pm Mon-Fri, 10am-3pm Sat, 2-6pm Sun) for spare parts and help with repairs. Bringing your own

bicycle into the country is generally hassle-free.

Boat
Ferry

The only public ferry service in Bolivia operates between San Pedro and San Pablo, across the narrow Estrecho de Tiquina (Straits of Tiquina) on Lake Titicaca. You can travel by launch or rowboat to any of Lake Titicaca's Bolivian islands. Boats and tours are available from Huatajata to the Huyñaymarka islands in the lake's southernmost extension.

River Boat

There's no scheduled passenger service on the Amazon, so travelers almost invariably wind up on some sort of cargo vessel. The most popular route is from Guanay to Rurrenabaque. Thanks to the Guayaramerín road, there's little cargo transportation further down the Río Beni to Riberalta these days.

Bus

Bus travel is cheap and relatively safe in Bolivia, but can also be quite uncomfortable and nerve-wracking at times. Buses are the country's most popular type of transport, and come in various forms.

Types Long-distance bus services are called *flotas*, large buses are known as *buses*, three-quarter (usually older) ones are called *micros*, and minibuses are just that.

Terminals If looking for a bus terminal, ask for *la terminal terrestre* or *la terminal de buses*. Each terminal charges a small fee (a couple of bolivianos), which you pay to an agent upon boarding or when purchasing a ticket at the counter.

Theft There have been numerous reports of items disappearing from buses' internal overhead compartments and luggage holds. Put any valuables into your day pack and keep them close to you in the bus. Try to watch as your luggage is loaded – there have been instances of bags becoming 'lost' or 'disappearing.' You will be given a baggage tag, which you must show when reclaiming your bag. A lock is a good idea: very occasionally belongings are stolen from within bags while they are in the hold!

Departures Except on the most popular runs, most companies' buses depart at roughly the same time to the same destinations, regardless of how many companies are competing for the same business. Between any two cities, you should have no trouble finding at least one daily bus. On the most popular routes,

TOP TIPS FOR GETTING AROUND

Transportation to most places in Bolivia is covered by small bus, boat, train and airline companies. Over the past few years Bolivia's roads have vastly improved as the government has invested in paving major roads. However road closures caused by protests, construction or landslides are common, as are flooded roads and rivers with too little water to traverse. Air transit is also getting easier and slightly more cost effective and prevalent, especially in the lowlands.

Air

Save time by flying Flights will save you days of travel, but can add to your overall budget. In the Amazon, flying is now much preferred to boat or road travel.

Reconfirm Cancellations are common. Call ahead to make sure you are still booked. You may need to wait until the next day, and if not you may be able to get a 70% refund.

Carry heavy stuff Weight limits are often 15kg for checked bags.

Save money online Book online or with the airline office.

Bus

Go direct Direct *cama* (reclining seat), *semicama* (partially reclining seat) and tourist-class services cost more but can save several hours.

Safeguard valuables Keep them with you on the bus (not in the overhead bin). You should padlock your bag if it's going on top.

Stay warm Bring warm clothes and even a sleeping bag if going anywhere in the altiplano.

Bring snacks Roadside vendors offer snacks along the way, but bring some just in case, as well as some water.

Be patient Times may change; expect transit times to vary by up to three hours. Getting stranded overnight is not hugely uncommon.

Stay safe If your driver is drunk, don't get on board. Accidents caused by drunk bus drivers are all too common in Bolivia. Daytime driving is the safest.

Boat

Don't rely on boats Boat services are less common in the lowlands than they used to be. Adventurous spirits will find unique experiences if they are willing to seek services out, but it's not always cheap.

Protect valuables Keep them padlocked.

Bring creature comforts Such as hammock, book and mosquito repellent.

Car & Motorcycle

Speak Spanish Only drive or ride if you speak Spanish moderately well.

Expect delays There might be speed traps, potholes and closures on the road.

Bring supplies Bring a GPS, a good map, extra food and water, sleeping bag and clothes.

Don't drive at night Stick to daytime travel.

Train

Expect delays Timetables are more like guidelines than strict schedules.

Plan for comfort Bring snacks, games and sleeping bags.

Stay alert Pickpockets and bag snatchers often lurk at stops.

you can choose between dozens of daily departures.

Safety It's always a good idea to check the vehicles of several companies before purchasing your ticket. Some buses are ramshackle affairs with broken windows, cracked windshields and worn tires; it's best to stay away from these and look for a better vehicle, even if it means paying a little more. Don't try to save on safety.

Classes & Costs

The only choices you'll have to make are on major, long-haul routes, where the better companies offer *coche* (or '*bus*'), *semicama* (half-sleeper, with seats that recline a long way and footrests) and *cama* (sleeper) services. The cost can be double for sleeper service, but is often worth it for the comfort. Tourist buses to major destinations such as Copacabana and Uyuni are twice the price of standard buses, but are safer and more comfortable.

The DVD player on the newest buses will be in better shape than the reclining seats (expect Van Damme all night), heaters *may* function, snacks *may* be served and toilets (yes, toilets) *may* work. Be prepared.

Prices vary according to the different standard of bus (from the more luxurious *bus cama* service to the ancient Bluebird-style buses) and the length of trip (whether overnight or short day hop).

Reservations

To be certain, reserve bus tickets at least several hours in advance. Many buses depart in the afternoon or evening and arrive at their destination in the small hours of the morning. On most major routes there are also daytime departures.

Car & Motorcycle

The advantages of a private vehicle include flexibility, access to remote areas and the chance to seize photo opportunities. Most major roads have now been paved but some (especially in the Amazon) are in varying stages of decay, making high-speed travel impossible and inadvisable.

Preparation The undaunted should prepare their expeditions carefully. Bear in mind that spare parts are a rare commodity outside cities. A high-clearance 4WD vehicle is essential for off-road travel. You'll need tools, spare tires, a puncture repair kit, extra gas and fluids, and as many spare parts as possible. For emergencies, carry camping equipment and plenty of rations. You'll also need to purchase a good travel insurance policy back home (check with your credit card to see if it covers rental insurance in Bolivia).

Fuel types Low-grade (85-octane) gasoline *(nafta)* and diesel fuel *(gasoil)* is available at *surtidores* (gas stations) in all cities and major towns, but in more remote areas these can sometimes run out. Before embarking on any long journeys make sure you know where you can get fuel and, if necessary, take it with you. Gasoline costs about B$8.68 per liter for foreigners (the price of fuel is subsidized for Bolivians, who pay about half the price) and more in remote areas.

Motorcycles In lowland areas where temperatures are hot and roads are scarce, motorbikes are popular for zipping around the plazas, as well as exploring areas not served by public transportation. They can be rented from about B$100 per day from moto-taxi stands. Note that many travel insurance policies will not cover you for injuries arising from motorbike accidents.

Driver's License

Most Bolivian car-rental agencies will accept your home driver's license, but if you're doing a lot of driving, it's wise to back it up with an International Driver's License.

Bolivia doesn't require special motorcycle licenses, but neighboring countries do. All that is normally required for motorcycle and moped rentals is a passport.

Private Drivers

Hiring a driver can be a more comfortable and efficient alternative to being squashed in a bus for long periods on bad roads. Alternatively, many people just want transportation to trailheads or base camps, rather than a tour.

Private 4WD service with a driver costs about B$250 to B$300 per hour for the entire car (four to six people). Private taxi service and/or driver service costs B$80 to B$150 per hour.

You can hire drivers through car-rental companies and tour operators. Private taxi drivers may also be hired.

Rental

Few travelers in Bolivia rent self-driven vehicles and with high-mountain passes and potholes, not to mention other drivers to contend with, driving in the country is challenging. Only the most reputable agencies service their vehicles regularly, and insurance purchased from rental agencies may cover only accidental damage – breakdowns may be considered the renter's problem. Check ahead and make sure your credit card covers incidentals.

You must be aged over 25, have a driver's license from your home country and provide a major credit card or cash deposit (typically around US$1000). You'll be charged a daily rate and a per-kilometer rate (some agencies allow some free kilometers). They'll also want you to leave a copy of your passport.

To save money, book online or through an aggregator. Weekly rentals will save you more. Daily rates are about US$50 for small cars, while 4WDs cost upwards of US$100 per day.

Road Rules

Traffic regulations are similar to those in North America or Europe. Speed limits are infrequently posted, but in most cases the state of the road would prevent you from exceeding them anyway. If stopped, you should show your driver's license rather than your passport. If your passport is requested, only show a copy. Bribes are common here.

Bolivians keep to the right. When two cars approach an uncontrolled intersection from different directions, the driver who honks (or gets there first) tends to have the right of way if passing straight through – but this can be somewhat hit and miss. In La Paz, those going uphill have right of way at an intersection. When two vehicles meet on a narrow mountain road, the downhill vehicle must reverse until there's room for the other to pass.

Hitchhiking

Thanks to relatively easy access to *camiones* and a profusion of buses, hitchhiking isn't really necessary or popular in Bolivia. Still, it's not unknown and drivers of *movilidades* – *coches* (cars), *camionetas* (pickup trucks), NGO vehicles, gas trucks and other vehicles – are usually happy to pick up passengers when they have room. Always ask the price, if any, before climbing aboard, even for short distances. If they do charge, it should amount to about half the bus fare for the same distance.

Hitching is never entirely safe, and we don't recommend it. Travelers who hitch should understand that they are taking a small but potentially serious risk.

Local Transportation

Camión

Prior to today's expansive bus network, *camiones* (flatbed trucks) were often the only way for travelers to venture off the beaten track. These days, in the more populated areas you might consider a *camión* trip more for the novelty value than necessity.

Camiones generally cost about half the bus fare. You'll need time and a strong constitution, as travel can be excruciatingly slow and rough, depending on the cargo and number of passengers. A major plus is the raw experience, including the best views of the countryside.

On any *camión* trip, especially in the highlands by day or night, be sure to take plenty of warm clothing as night temperatures can plunge below freezing and at best they can be chilly.

To get on a *camión*, wait on the side of the road and flag it down as it passes.

Micros, Minibuses & Trufis

Micros (half-size buses) are used in larger cities and are Bolivia's least expensive form of public transportation. They follow set routes, with the route numbers or letters usually marked on a placard behind the windshield. There is also often a description of the route, including the streets taken to reach the end of the line. They can be hailed anywhere along their route, though bus stops are starting to pop up in some bigger cities. When you want to disembark, move toward the front and tell the driver or assistant where you want them to stop.

Minibuses and *trufis* (which may be cars, vans or minibuses), also known as *rapiditos* or *colectivos*, are prevalent in larger towns and cities, and follow set routes that are numbered and described on placards. They are always cheaper than taxis and nearly as convenient if you can get the hang of them. As with *micros*, you can board or alight anywhere along their route.

Taxis

In cities and towns, taxis are relatively inexpensive. Few are equipped with meters, but in most places there are standard per-person fares for short hauls. In some places, taxis are collective and behave more like *trufis*, charging a set rate per person. However, if you have three or four people all headed for the same place, you may be able to negotiate a reduced rate for the entire group.

Tours

Many organized tours run out of La Paz or towns closest to the attractions you're likely to wish to visit. Tours are a convenient way to visit a site when you are short of time or motivation, and are frequently the easiest way to visit remote areas. They can also be relatively cheap, depending on the number of people in your group and the mode of transport.

There are scores of companies offering trekking, mountain-climbing and rainforest-adventure packages around Bolivia. For climbing in the Cordilleras, operators offer customized expeditions and can arrange anything from guide and transportation to equipment, porters and a cook. Some also rent trekking equipment.

It's best to check an agency's website first, before making contact and bookings.

America Tours (Map p54; ☑237-4204; www.america-ecotours.com; Av 16 de Julio 1490, Oficina No 9, Prado;

⊙9am-5pm Mon-Fri) This warmly recommended English-speaking agency offers a wide range of community-based eco-tourism projects and tailor-made tours around La Paz and Bolivia.

Andean Expeditions Dirninger (Map p50; ☑241-4235, mobile 7755-0226; www.andean-expeditions.com; Sagárnaga 189, Galería Doryan, 3rd fl, Oficina 32, Rosario; ⊙9am-12:30pm & 2-5:30pm Mon-Fri) An Austrian-founded company that offers mountain treks in Bolivia and neighboring countries, and uses guides certified by the International Federation of Mountain Guides Associations (IFMGA). More than 10 years in Bolivia, and not the same old run-of-the-mill tours.

Bird Bolivia (☑356-3636; www.birdbolivia.com) Professional birding and wildlife tours with expert guides for those with a special interest in nature. Based in Santa Cruz but without a public office; arrange tours by phone or email.

Bolivia Millenaria (Map p54; ☑241-4753; www.mille nariantours.com; Av Sánchez Lima 2193, Sopocachi; ⊙9am-3pm Mon-Fri) This agency offers tailor-made tours around Bolivia with a focus on remote parks and cultural interactions.

Bolivian Journeys (Map p50; www.bolivianjourneys.org; Sagárnaga 363, Rosario; ⊙9am-7pm Mon-Fri, to noon Sat) This company specialising in climbing, mountaineering and trekking organizes guided climbs to Huayna Potosí. Equipment rental is available, with maps and gas for MSR stoves for sale.

Bolivia Specialist (Map p202; ☑643-7389; www.boliviaspecialist.com; Audiencia 80; ⊙8:30am-noon & 2:30-7pm Mon-Fri, 8:30am-noon Sat) All-purpose travel agency that can book flights, buses and organized tours all over Bolivia as well as in the region around Sucre, including Cordillera de los Frailes hikes.

Fremen Tours (Map p54; ☑242-1258; www.andes-amazonia.com; Av 20 de Octubre 2396, Sopocachi;

⊙9am-noon & 2:30-6pm Mon-Fri) Upmarket agency specializing in soft adventure in the Amazon and Chapare.

Inca Land Tours (Map p50; ☑231-6760; www.incalandtours.com; Sagárnaga 233, Oficina No 3, Rosario; ⊙7:30am-8pm) An established Peruvian budget operation specializing in tours out of Rurrenabaque and Coroico.

Madidi Travel (Map p50; ☑231-8313; www.madidi-travel.com; Linares 947, Rosario; ⊙9am-7pm Mon-Fri, to 5pm Sat & Sun) Specializing in trips to Madidi, this tour operator's 4000-hectare private reserve east of the park (Eco Reserve Serere) adds another layer of protection.

Magri Turismo (Map p54; ☑244-2727; www.magritur ismo.com; Capitán Ravelo 2101, Sopocachi; ⊙8:30am-12:30pm & 2:30-6:30pm Mon-Fri, 9am-noon Sat) A large, well-established agency with a range of tours organized around Bolivia.

Misional Tours (☑332-7709; www.misionaltours.com; Av Beni, 9th fl, Edificio Top Center, office 9-E; ⊙9am-12:30pm & 2-7pm Mon-Fri, 9am-1pm Sat) One of Santa Cruz's most well-organized and reliable tour operators. Specializes in the Mission Circuit, but just as good for other attractions across Bolivia.

Nick's Adventures (☑334-1820; www.nicksadventures bolivia.com; Celia Salmón, Edificio Isuto, office 208) Excellent tour company with a strong ethos of social responsibility and promoting conservation through tourism. Especially good for wildlife tours, including tours to the San Miguelito Jaguar Reserve and the Pantanal.

Terra Andina (Map p54; ☑241-9932; www.bolivia-travels.com; Av Ecuador 2682, Sopocachi; ⊙9am-6:30pm Mon-Fri) Tailor-made trekking, climbing and 4WD tours across Bolivia in English, French or German.

Turisbus (Map p50; ☑279-8786; www.turisbus.com; Hotel Rosario, Illampu 704, Rosario) A

large range of day and multiday tours organized for groups and individuals around Bolivia.

Tusoco Travel (Map p50; ☑mobile 7220-7682; www.tusoco.com; Sagárnaga 227, Rosario; ⊙9:30am-1:30pm & 3:30-7:30pm Mon-Fri, 10am-2pm Sun) Supports 22 indigenous communities across Bolivia by offering tours that provide them a sustainable income while promising travelers meaningful cultural interactions.

Train

Train fares range from B$11 to B$240, depending on the class and distance. Prices are competitive with bus fares and trains are more comfortable, but typically they are quite a bit slower.

Empresa Ferroviaria Andina (www.fca.com.bo) Operates the western network from Oruro to Villazón on the Argentinian border. Note that at research time trains were not running south of Uyuni due to track damage.

Ferroviaria Oriental (www.fo.com.bo) Covers eastern Bolivia, operating a line from Santa Cruz to the Brazilian frontier at Quijarro, where you can cross to the Pantanal. An infrequently used service goes south from Santa Cruz to Yacuiba on the Argentine border.

Tren Turístico Guaraní (www.ferroviaria-andina.com.bo/tren_turistico_fca) A tourist service departing every second Sunday of the month between El Alto and Tiwanaku.

Reservations

It's a good idea to buy your tickets in advance, which you can do at the train station. At smaller stations, tickets may not be available until the train has arrived and intermediate stations along major routes are allotted only a few seat reservations. Careful planning is needed to avoid disappointment.

When buying tickets, make sure you have a passport for each person for whom you're buying a ticket.

Health

BEFORE YOU GO

The only required vaccine for Bolivia is yellow fever, and that's only if you're arriving from a high-yellow-fever-risk country. Though some countries may require you to have a yellow-fever certificate to re-enter after visiting Bolivia.

Vaccines that are usually recommended are hepatitis A and tetanus. Other vaccines to consider are diphtheria, hepatitis B, rabies and typhoid.

Insurance

➡ If your health insurance does not cover you for medical expenses abroad, consider supplemental insurance.

➡ Find out in advance if your insurance plan will make payments directly to providers or reimburse you later for overseas health expenditures. Most private-practice providers in Bolivia expect cash payment and should provide receipts for your insurance company claims and reimbursement.

➡ Credit cards are usually not accepted for medical services.

IN BOLIVIA

Healthcare

➡ Good medical care is available in the larger cities, but may be difficult to find in rural areas.

➡ Many doctors and hospitals expect payment in cash, regardless of whether you have travel health insurance. Note that a taxi may get you to the emergency room faster than an ambulance.

➡ If you develop a life-threatening medical problem, you'll probably want to be evacuated to a country with state-of-the-art medical care. Since this may cost tens of thousands of dollars, be sure you have insurance to cover this before you depart.

➡ Bolivian pharmacies offer most of the medications available in other countries. In general it's safer to buy pharmaceuticals made by international manufacturers than local companies.

➡ Buy the brand name prescribed by your doctor, not the generic-brand drugs that may be offered at lower prices. These medications may be out of date or have no quality control from the manufacturer.

Infectious Diseases

Cholera

➡ Cholera is an intestinal infection acquired through ingestion of contaminated food or water. The main symptom is profuse, watery diarrhea, which may be so severe that it causes life-threatening dehydration.

➡ Cholera sometimes occurs in Bolivia, but it's rare among travelers.

➡ A cholera vaccine is no longer required. There are effective vaccines, but they're not available in many countries and are only recommended for those at particularly high risk.

➡ The key treatment is drinking oral rehydration solution. Antibiotics are also given, usually tetracycline or doxycycline, though quinolone antibiotics such as ciprofloxacin and levofloxacin are also effective.

Dengue Fever

➡ Dengue fever is a viral infection found throughout South America. Dengue causes flu-like symptoms, including fever, muscle aches, joint pains, headache, nausea and vomiting, often followed by a rash.

➡ The body aches may be quite uncomfortable, but most cases resolve uneventfully in a few days. Severe cases usually occur in children under age 15 who are experiencing their second dengue infection.

➡ Dengue is transmitted by aedes mosquitoes, which bite preferentially during the daytime and are usually found close to human habitation, often indoors.

They breed in artificial water containers, such as jars, barrels, cans, cisterns, metal drums, plastic containers and discarded tires.

➡ Dengue is most common in densely populated, urban environments.

➡ There is no specific antivirus treatment for dengue fever except to take analgesics such as acetaminophen/paracetamol (Tylenol) and drink plenty of fluids. Severe cases may require hospitalization for intravenous fluids and supportive care. There is no vaccine. The cornerstone of prevention is insect control.

Hepatitis A

➡ Hepatitis A is the second most common travel-related infection (after traveler's diarrhea). The illness occurs throughout the world, but the incidence is higher in developing nations.

➡ It's a viral infection of the liver that is usually acquired by ingestion of contaminated water, food or ice, or by direct contact with infected persons.

➡ Symptoms may include fever, malaise, jaundice, nausea, vomiting and abdominal pain. Most cases resolve without complications, though hepatitis A occasionally causes severe liver damage.

➡ There is no treatment.

Malaria

➡ Malaria occurs in nearly every South American country but is rare. It's transmitted by mosquito bites at night.

➡ The main symptom is high spiking fever, which may be accompanied by chills, sweats, headache, body aches, weakness, vomiting or diarrhea. Severe cases may involve the central nervous system and lead to seizures, confusion, coma and death.

➡ Taking malaria pills is only recommended for areas below 2500m (8202ft) in the departments of Beni and Pando, where the risk is highest, though it is absent in the cities. Falciparum malaria, which is the most dangerous kind, occurs in Beni and Pando.

➡ There is a choice of three malaria pills, all of which work about equally well. Mefloquine (Lariam) is taken once weekly in a dosage of 250mg, starting one to two weeks before arrival, and continuing through the trip and for four weeks after return. The problem is that a certain percentage of people (the number is controversial) develop neuropsychiatric side effects, which may range from mild to severe. Stomachache and diarrhea are also common. Atovaquone/proguanil (Malarone) is taken once daily with food, starting two days before arrival and continuing daily until seven days after departure. Side effects are typically mild. Doxycycline is relatively inexpensive and easy to obtain, but it is taken daily and can cause an exaggerated sunburn reaction.

➡ For longer trips it's probably worth trying mefloquine; for shorter trips, Malarone will be the drug of choice for most people.

➡ Protecting yourself against mosquito bites is just as important as taking malaria pills, since none of the pills are 100% effective.

➡ If you might not have access to medical care while traveling, you should bring along additional pills for emergency self-treatment, which you should take if you can't reach a doctor and you develop symptoms that suggest malaria, such as high spiking fevers. One option is to take four tablets of Malarone once daily for three days. However, Malarone should not be used for treatment if you're already taking it for prevention. An alternative is to take 650mg quinine three times daily and 100mg doxycycline twice daily for one week. If you start self-medication, see a doctor at the earliest possible opportunity.

➡ If you develop a fever after returning home, see a physician, as malaria symptoms may not occur for months.

TAP WATER

Tap water is not safe to drink. Bottled mineral water is cheap and freely available. Use it for everything and if you are going anywhere remote take a good supply with you.

Should you find yourself desperate, thirsty and with nowhere to buy water, then try the following:

Boiling Vigorous boiling for one minute is the most effective means of water purification. At altitudes greater than 2000m (6500ft), boil for three minutes.

Purification pills Disinfect water with purification tablets, available at most pharmacies.

Filters Filters with smaller pores (reverse osmosis filters) provide the broadest protection, but they are relatively large and are readily plugged by debris. Those with larger pores (microstrainer filters) are ineffective against viruses, although they remove other organisms. Manufacturers' instructions must be carefully followed.

Typhoid Fever

➡ Typhoid fever is caused by the ingestion of food or water contaminated by a species of salmonella known as *Salmonella typhi.*

➡ Fever occurs in virtually all cases. Other symptoms may include headache, malaise, muscle aches, dizziness, loss of appetite, nausea and abdominal pain. Either diarrhea or constipation may occur. Possible complications include intestinal perforation, intestinal bleeding, confusion, delirium or (rarely) coma.

➡ A typhoid vaccine is a good idea. It's usually given orally, but is also available as an injection. Neither vaccine is approved for use in children under age two.

➡ It is not a good idea to self-treat for typhoid fever as the symptoms may be indistinguishable from malaria. If you show symptoms for either, see a doctor immediately – treatment is likely to be a quinolone antibiotic such as ciprofloxacin (Cipro) or levofloxacin (Levaquin).

Yellow Fever

➡ Yellow fever is a life-threatening viral infection transmitted by mosquitoes in forested areas. Taking measures to protect yourself from mosquito bites is an essential part of preventing yellow fever.

➡ The illness begins with flu-like symptoms, such as fever, chills, headache, muscle aches, backache, loss of appetite, nausea and vomiting. These symptoms usually subside in a few days, but one person in six enters a second, toxic phase characterized by recurrent fever, vomiting, listlessness, jaundice, kidney failure and hemorrhage, leading to death in up to half of the cases.

➡ There is no treatment except for supportive care.

➡ Yellow fever vaccine is strongly recommended for all those visiting areas where yellow fever occurs, which includes the departments of Beni, Cochabamba, Santa Cruz and La Paz. For the latest information on which areas in Bolivia are reporting yellow fever, see the website of Centers for Disease Control & Protection (CDC, www.cdc.gov).

➡ Proof of vaccination is required from all travelers arriving from a high-yellow-fever-risk country in Africa or the Americas.

➡ The yellow-fever vaccine is given only in approved yellow-fever vaccination centers, which provide validated International Certificates of Vaccination (yellow booklets). The vaccine should be given at least 10 days before any potential exposure to yellow fever, and remains effective for approximately 10 years.

➡ Reactions to the vaccine are generally mild and may include headaches, muscle aches, low-grade fevers, or discomfort at the injection site. Severe, life-threatening reactions have been described but are extremely rare. In general

MEDICAL CHECKLIST

Bring medications in their original containers, clearly labeled, and a signed, dated letter from your physician describing all medical conditions and medications. If carrying syringes or needles, carry a physician's letter documenting their medical necessity.

➡ acetaminophen (eg Tylenol) or aspirin

➡ acetazolamide (Diamox) for altitude sickness

➡ adhesive or paper tape

➡ antibacterial ointment (eg Bactroban) for cuts and abrasions

➡ antibiotics

➡ antidiarrheal drugs (eg loperamide)

➡ antihistamines (for hay fever and allergic reactions)

➡ anti-inflammatory drugs (eg ibuprofen)

➡ bandages, gauze, gauze rolls

➡ DEET-containing insect repellent for the skin

➡ iodine tablets (for water purification)

➡ oral rehydration salts

➡ permethrin-containing insect spray for clothing, tents and bed nets

➡ pocket knife

➡ scissors, safety pins, tweezers

➡ sunblock

➡ steroid cream or cortisone (for poison ivy and other allergic rashes)

➡ syringes and sterile needles

➡ thermometer

the risk of becoming ill from the vaccine is far less than the risk of becoming ill from yellow fever, and you're strongly encouraged to get the vaccine.

Other Infections

➡ A number of rare but serious diseases are carried by insects and rodents, such as bartonellosis, Bolivian hemorrhagic fever, Chagas' disease, leishmaniasis, typhus and the plague. Rabies is also a concern, especially in the southeastern part of the country.

➡ Do not attempt to pet, handle or feed any animal. Any bite or scratch by any mammal should be promptly and thoroughly cleansed with large amounts of soap and water, followed by application of an antiseptic such as iodine or alcohol.

➡ The local health authorities should be contacted immediately for possible post-exposure rabies treatment, whether or not you've been immunized against rabies. It may also be advisable to start an antibiotic, since wounds caused by animal bites and scratches frequently become infected. Or use one of the newer quinolones, such as levofloxacin (Levaquin), which many travelers carry in case of diarrhea.

Traveler's Diarrhea

You are almost certain to get a bout at some stage, but you can put it off for as long as possible by observing some simple rules.

➡ Avoid tap water unless it has been boiled, filtered or chemically disinfected (with iodine tablets).

➡ Only eat fresh fruits or vegetables if peeled or cooked.

➡ Be wary of dairy products that might contain unpasteurized milk.

➡ Be highly selective when eating food from street vendors. If it looks, smells or tastes iffy, don't eat it!

➡ If you develop diarrhea, be sure to drink plenty of fluids, preferably an oral rehydration solution containing lots of salt and sugar. A few loose stools doesn't require treatment but if you start having more than four or five stools a day you should start taking an antibiotic (usually a quinolone drug) and an antidiarrheal agent (such as loperamide).

➡ If diarrhea is bloody, or persists for more than 72 hours, or is accompanied by fever, shaking chills or severe abdominal pain, you should seek medical attention.

Environmental Hazards

Altitude Sickness

➡ Altitude sickness may develop in those who ascend rapidly to altitudes greater than 2500m (8100ft). In Bolivia this includes La Paz (altitude 4000m). The risk increases with faster ascents, higher altitudes and greater exertion.

➡ Symptoms may include headache, nausea, vomiting, dizziness, malaise, insomnia and loss of appetite. Severe cases may be complicated by fluid in the lungs (high-altitude pulmonary edema) or swelling of the brain (high-altitude cerebral edema).

➡ Being physically fit offers no protection.

➡ Those who have experienced altitude sickness in the past are prone to future episodes.

➡ The best treatment for altitude sickness is descent. If you are exhibiting symptoms, do not ascend. If symptoms are severe or persistent, descend immediately.

➡ To protect yourself against altitude sickness, take 125mg or 250mg acetazolamide (Diamox) twice or three times daily, starting 24 hours before ascent and continuing for 48 hours after arrival at altitude. Possible side effects include increased urinary volume, numbness, tingling, nausea, drowsiness, myopia and temporary impotence. Acetazolamide should not be given to pregnant women or anyone with a history of sulfa allergy.

➡ For those who cannot tolerate acetazolamide, the next best option is 4mg dexamethasone taken four times daily, best with medical supervision. Unlike acetazolamide, dexamethasone must be tapered gradually on arrival at altitude if taken for longer than 10 days, since there is a risk that altitude sickness will occur as the dosage is reduced. Dexamethasone is a steroid, so it should not be given to diabetics or anyone for whom steroids are contraindicated. A natural alternative is gingko, which helps some people.

➡ When traveling to high altitudes, it's also important to avoid overexertion, eat light meals and abstain from alcohol.

➡ If your symptoms are more than mild or don't resolve promptly, see a doctor immediately. Altitude sickness should be taken seriously; it can be life-threatening.

Snake Bites

In Bolivia there are two families of poisonous snakes: vipers (including rattlesnakes) and coral snakes. It is extremely rare to be bitten by a venomous snake, but in the event that it does occur, place the victim at rest, keep the bitten area immobilized and move the victim to the nearest medical facility immediately.

Avoid tourniquets, which are no longer recommended.

Insect Bites & Stings

➡ To prevent mosquito bites, wear long sleeves, long pants, hats and shoes (rather than sandals).

➡ Don't sleep with the window open unless there is a screen.

➡ If sleeping outdoors or in accommodations that allow entry of mosquitoes, use a fine-mesh bed net, preferably treated with permethrin, with edges tucked in under the mattress. If the sleeping area is not protected, use a mosquito coil, which will fill the room with insecticide through the night.

➡ Bring along a good insect repellent, preferably one containing DEET, which should be applied to exposed skin and clothing, but not to eyes, mouth, wounds or irritated skin. Products containing lower concentrations of DEET are as effective, but for shorter periods of time.

➡ In general, adults and children over 12 should use preparations containing 25% to 35% DEET, which usually lasts about six hours. Children between two and 12 years of age should use preparations containing no more than 10% DEET, applied sparingly, which will usually last about three hours. Neurologic toxicity has been reported from DEET, especially in children, but appears to be rare and related to overuse. DEET-containing compounds should not be used on children under age two.

➡ Insect repellents containing certain botanical products, including eucalyptus oil and soybean oil, are effective but last only 1½ to two hours. DEET-containing repellents are preferable for areas where

there is a high risk of malaria or yellow fever. Products based on citronella and repellent-impregnated wristbands are not effective.

➡ For additional protection you can apply permethrin to clothing, shoes, tents and bed nets. Permethrin treatments are safe and remain effective for at least two weeks, even when items are laundered, but do not apply it directly to skin.

Sunburn & Heat Exhaustion

You should protect yourself from excessive sun exposure.

➡ Stay out of the midday sun.

➡ Drink plenty of fluids.

➡ Avoid strenuous exercise in high temperatures.

➡ Wear sunglasses.

➡ Wear a wide-brimmed sun hat.

➡ Apply sunscreen with SPF 15 or higher, with both UVA and UVB protection. Sunscreen should be generously applied to all exposed parts of the body approximately 30 minutes before sun exposure and should be reapplied after swimming or vigorous activity.

Water

Ground water has been polluted by mining in many areas of the altiplano, and some cities, such as Trinidad, are known for having a toxic water supply that will have you regretting that little sip out of the tap in the middle of the hot sweaty Amazonian night.

HEALTH ENVIRONMENTAL HAZARDS

Language

Latin American Spanish pronunciation is easy, as most sounds have equivalents in English. Read our colored pronunciation guides as if they were English, and you'll be understood. Note that kh is a throaty sound (like the 'ch' in the Scottish loch), v and b are like a soft English 'v' (between a 'v' and a 'b'), and r is strongly rolled, although you may hear some Bolivians pronounce it as the 's' in 'pleasure' at the beginning of a word or after l, n or s. There are some variations in spoken Spanish across Latin America, the most notable being the pronunciation of the letters ll and y. In our guides they are represented with y because they are pronounced as the 'y' in 'yes' in Bolivia, as is the case in most parts of Latin America. In some parts of the continent they sound like the 'lli' in 'million'. The stressed syllables are in italics in our pronunciation guides.

The polite form is used in this chapter; where both polite and informal options are given, they are indicated by the abbreviations 'pol' and 'inf'. Where necessary, both masculine and feminine forms of words are included, separated by a slash and with the masculine form first, eg perdido/a (m/f).

BASICS

Hello.	*Hola.*	o·la
Goodbye.	*Adiós.*	a·dyos
How are you?	*¿Qué tal?*	ke tal
Fine, thanks.	*Bien, gracias.*	byen gra·syas
Excuse me.	*Perdón.*	per·don

WANT MORE?

For in-depth language information and handy phrases, check out Lonely Planet's *Latin American Spanish Phrasebook*. You'll find it at **shop.lonelyplanet.com**, or you can buy Lonely Planet's iPhone phrasebooks at the Apple App Store.

Sorry.	*Lo siento.*	lo *syen*·to
Please.	*Por favor.*	por fa·*vor*
Thank you.	*Gracias.*	*gra*·syas
You are welcome.	*De nada.*	de *na*·da
Yes.	*Sí.*	see
No.	*No.*	no

My name is ...
Me llamo ...　　　　me *ya*·mo ...

What's your name?
¿Cómo se llama Usted? ko·mo se ya·ma oo·*ste* (pol)
¿Cómo te llamas? ko·mo te ya·mas (inf)

Do you speak English?
¿Habla inglés? a·bla een·*gles* (pol)
¿Hablas inglés? a·blas een·*gles* (inf)

I don't understand.
Yo no entiendo. yo no en·*tyen*·do

ACCOMMODATIONS

I'd like a single/double room.
Quisiera una kee·*sye*·ra oo·na
habitación a·bee·ta·*syon*
individual/doble. een·dee·vee·*dwal/do*·ble

How much is it per night/person?
¿Cuánto cuesta por kwan·to kwes·ta por
noche/persona? no·che/per·so·na

Does it include breakfast?
¿Incluye el desayuno? een·*kloo*·ye el de·sa·yoo·no

campsite	*terreno de*	te·*re*·no de
	cámping	*kam*·peeng
guesthouse	*pensión*	pen·*syon*
hotel	*hotel*	o·*tel*
youth hostel	*albergue*	al·*ber*·ge
	juvenil	khoo·ve·*neel*
air-con	*aire acondi-*	*ai*·re a·kon·dee·
	cionado	syo·*na*·do

bathroom	baño	ba·nyo
bed	cama	ka·ma
window	ventana	ven·ta·na

DIRECTIONS

Where's ...?
¿Dónde está ...? — don·de es·ta ...

What's the address?
¿Cuál es la dirección? — kwal es la dee·rek·syon

Could you please write it down?
¿Puede escribirlo, — pwe·de es·kree·beer·lo
por favor? — por fa·vor

Can you show me (on the map)?
¿Me lo puede indicar — me lo pwe·de een·dee·kar
(en el mapa)? — (en el ma·pa)

at the corner	en la esquina	en la es·kee·na
at the traffic lights	en el semáforo	en el se·ma·fo·ro
behind ...	detrás de ...	de·tras de ...
in front of ...	enfrente de ...	en·fren·te de ...
left	izquierda	ees·kyer·da
next to ...	al lado de ...	al la·do de ...
opposite ...	frente a ...	fren·te a ...
right	derecha	de·re·cha
straight ahead	todo recto	to·do rek·to

EATING & DRINKING

Can I see the menu, please?
¿Puedo ver el menú, — pwe·do ver el me·noo
por favor? — por fa·vor

What would you recommend?
¿Qué recomienda? — ke re·ko·myen·da

Do you have vegetarian food?
¿Tienen comida — tye·nen ko·mee·da
vegetariana? — ve·khe·ta·rya·na

I don't eat (red meat).
No como (carne roja). — no ko·mo (kar·ne ro·kha)

That was delicious!
¡Estaba buenísimo! — es·ta·ba bwe·nee·see·mo

Cheers!
¡Salud! — sa·loo

The bill, please.
La cuenta, por favor. — la kwen·ta por fa·vor

I'd like a table for ...	Quisiera una mesa para ...	kee·sye·ra oo·na me·sa pa·ra ...
(eight) o'clock	las (ocho)	las (o·cho)
(two) people	(dos) personas	(dos) per·so·nas

KEY PATTERNS

To get by in Spanish, mix and match these simple patterns with words of your choice:

When's (the next flight)?
¿Cuándo sale — kwan·do sa·le
(el próximo vuelo)? — (el prok·see·mo vwe·lo)

Where's (the station)?
¿Dónde está — don·de es·ta
(la estación)? — (la es·ta·syon)

Where can I (buy a ticket)?
¿Dónde puedo — don·de pwe·do
(comprar un billete)? — (kom·prar oon bee·ye·te)

Do you have (a map)?
¿Tiene (un mapa)? — tye·ne (oon ma·pa)

Is there (a toilet)?
¿Hay (servicios)? — ai (ser·vee·syos)

I'd like (a coffee).
Quisiera (un café). — kee·sye·ra (oon ka·fe)

I'd like (to hire a car).
Quisiera (alquilar — kee·sye·ra (al·kee·lar
un coche). — oon ko·che)

Can I (enter)?
¿Se puede (entrar)? — se pwe·de (en·trar)

Could you please (help me)?
¿Puede (ayudarme), — pwe·de (a·yoo·dar·me)
por favor? — por fa·vor

Do I have to (get a visa)?
¿Necesito — ne·se·see·to
(obtener — (ob·te·ner
una visa)? — oo·na vee·sa)

Key Words

appetisers	aperitivos	a·pe·ree·tee·vos
bottle	botella	bo·te·ya
bowl	bol	bol
breakfast	desayuno	de·sa·yoo·no
children's menu	menú infantil	me·noo een·fan·teel
(too) cold	(muy) frío	(mooy) free·o
dinner	cena	se·na
food	comida	ko·mee·da
fork	tenedor	te·ne·dor
glass	vaso	va·so
hot (warm)	caliente	kal·yen·te
knife	cuchillo	koo·chee·yo
lunch	comida	ko·mee·da
main course	segundo plato	se·goon·do pla·to
plate	plato	pla·to

restaurant	restaurante	res·tow·ran·te
spoon	cuchara	koo·cha·ra
with	con	kon
without	sin	seen

Meat & Fish

beef	carne de vaca	kar·ne de va·ka
chicken	pollo	po·yo
duck	pato	pa·to
fish	pescado	pes·ka·do
lamb	cordero	kor·de·ro
pork	cerdo	ser·do
turkey	pavo	pa·vo
veal	ternera	ter·ne·ra

Fruit & Vegetables

apple	manzana	man·sa·na
apricot	albaricoque	al·ba·ree·ko·ke
artichoke	alcachofa	al·ka·cho·fa
asparagus	espárragos	es·pa·ra·gos
banana	plátano	pla·ta·no
beans	judías	khoo·dee·as
beetroot	remolacha	re·mo·la·cha
cabbage	col	kol
carrot	zanahoria	sa·na·o·rya
celery	apio	a·pyo
cherry	cereza	se·re·sa
corn	maíz	ma·ees
cucumber	pepino	pe·pee·no
fruit	fruta	froo·ta
grapes	uvas	oo·vas
lemon	limón	lee·mon
lentils	lentejas	len·te·khas
lettuce	lechuga	le·choo·ga
mushroom	champiñón	cham·pee·nyon
nuts	nueces	nwe·ses
onion	cebolla	se·bo·ya
orange	naranja	na·ran·kha
peach	melocotón	me·lo·ko·ton
peas	guisantes	gee·san·tes
(red/green) pepper	pimiento (rojo/verde)	pee·myen·to (ro·kho/ver·de)
pineapple	piña	pee·nya
plum	ciruela	seer·we·la
potato	papa	pa·pa
pumpkin	calabaza	ka·la·ba·sa

spinach	espinacas	es·pee·na·kas
strawberry	fresa	fre·sa
tomato	tomate	to·ma·te
vegetable	verdura	ver·doo·ra
watermelon	sandía	san·dee·a

Other

bread	pan	pan
butter	mantequilla	man·te·kee·ya
cheese	queso	ke·so
egg	huevo	we·vo
honey	miel	myel
jam	mermelada	mer·me·la·da
oil	aceite	a·sey·te
pasta	pasta	pas·ta
pepper	pimienta	pee·myen·ta
rice	arroz	a·ros
salt	sal	sal
sugar	azúcar	a·soo·kar
vinegar	vinagre	vee·na·gre

Drinks

beer	cerveza	ser·ve·sa
coffee	café	ka·fe
(orange) juice	jugo (de naranja)	khu·go (de na·ran·kha)
milk	leche	le·che
red wine	vino tinto	vee·no teen·to
sparkling wine	vino espumoso	vee·no es·poo·mo·so
tea	té	te
(mineral) water	agua (mineral)	a·gwa (mee·ne·ral)
white wine	vino blanco	vee·no blan·ko

SIGNS

Abierto	Open
Cerrado	Closed
Entrada	Entrance
Hombres/Varones	Men
Mujeres/Damas	Women
Prohibido	Prohibited
Salida	Exit
Servicios/Baños	Toilets

EMERGENCIES

Help!	*¡Socorro!*	so·*ko*·ro
Go away!	*¡Vete!*	*ve*·te
Call ...!	*¡Llame a ...!*	*ya*·me a ...
a doctor	*un médico*	oon *me*·dee·ko
the police	*la policía*	la po·lee·*see*·a

I'm lost.
Estoy perdido/a. es·*toy* per·*dee*·do/a (m/f)

I'm ill.
Estoy enfermo/a. es·*toy* en·*fer*·mo/a (m/f)

I'm allergic to (antibiotics).
Soy alérgico/a a soy a·*ler*·khee·ko/a a
(los antibióticos). (los an·tee·*byo*·tee·kos) (m/f)

Where are the toilets?
¿Dónde están los *don*·de es·*tan* los
baños? *ba*·nyos

SHOPPING & SERVICES

I'd like to buy ...
Quisiera comprar ... kee·*sye*·ra kom·*prar* ...

I'm just looking.
Sólo estoy mirando. *so*·lo es·*toy* mee·*ran*·do

Can I look at it?
¿Puedo verlo? *pwe*·do *ver*·lo

I don't like it.
No me gusta. no me *goos*·ta

How much is it?
¿Cuánto cuesta? *kwan*·to *kwes*·ta

That's too expensive.
Es muy caro. es mooy *ka*·ro

Can you lower the price?
¿Podría bajar un po·*dree*·a ba·*khar* oon
poco el precio? *po*·ko el *pre*·syo

There's a mistake in the bill.
Hay un error ai oon e·*ror*
en la cuenta. en la *kwen*·ta

ATM	*cajero automático*	ka·*khe*·ro ow·to·*ma*·tee·ko
credit card	*tarjeta de crédito*	tar·*khe*·ta de *kre*·dee·to
internet cafe	*cibercafé*	see·ber·ka·*fe*
market	*mercado*	mer·*ka*·do
post office	*correos*	ko·*re*·os
tourist office	*oficina de turismo*	o·fee·*see*·na de too·*rees*·mo

TIME & DATES

What time is it?	*¿Qué hora es?*	ke *o*·ra es
It's (10) o'clock.	*Son (las diez).*	son (las dyes)
It's half past (one).	*Es (la una) y media.*	es (la *oo*·na) ee *me*·dya

NUMBERS

1	*uno*	*oo*·no
2	*dos*	dos
3	*tres*	tres
4	*cuatro*	*kwa*·tro
5	*cinco*	*seen*·ko
6	*seis*	seys
7	*siete*	*sye*·te
8	*ocho*	*o*·cho
9	*nueve*	*nwe*·ve
10	*diez*	dyes
20	*veinte*	*veyn*·te
30	*treinta*	*treyn*·ta
40	*cuarenta*	kwa·*ren*·ta
50	*cincuenta*	seen·*kwen*·ta
60	*sesenta*	se·*sen*·ta
70	*setenta*	se·*ten*·ta
80	*ochenta*	o·*chen*·ta
90	*noventa*	no·*ven*·ta
100	*cien*	syen
1000	*mil*	meel

morning	*mañana*	ma·*nya*·na
afternoon	*tarde*	*tar*·de
evening	*noche*	*no*·che
yesterday	*ayer*	a·*yer*
today	*hoy*	oy
tomorrow	*mañana*	ma·*nya*·na
Monday	*lunes*	*loo*·nes
Tuesday	*martes*	*mar*·tes
Wednesday	*miércoles*	*myer*·ko·les
Thursday	*jueves*	*khwe*·ves
Friday	*viernes*	*vyer*·nes
Saturday	*sábado*	*sa*·ba·do
Sunday	*domingo*	do·*meen*·go
January	*enero*	e·*ne*·ro
February	*febrero*	fe·*bre*·ro
March	*marzo*	*mar*·so
April	*abril*	a·*breel*
May	*mayo*	*ma*·yo
June	*junio*	*khoon*·yo
July	*julio*	*khool*·yo
August	*agosto*	a·*gos*·to
September	*septiembre*	sep·*tyem*·bre

October	octubre	ok·too·bre
November	noviembre	no·vyem·bre
December	diciembre	dee·syem·bre

TRANSPORTATION

Public Transportation

boat	barco	bar·ko
bus	autobús	ow·to·boos
plane	avión	a·vyon
taxi	taxi	tak·see
train	tren	tren

first	primero	pree·me·ro
last	último	ool·tee·mo
next	próximo	prok·see·mo

A ... ticket, please.	Un billete de ..., por favor.	oon bee·ye·te de ... por fa·vor
1st-class	primera clase	pree·me·ra kla·se
2nd-class	segunda clase	se·goon·da kla·se
one-way	ida	ee·da
return	ida y vuelta	ee·da ee vwel·ta

airport	aeropuerto	a·e·ro·pwer·to
aisle seat	asiento de pasillo	a·syen·to de pa·see·yo
bus stop	parada de autobuses	pa·ra·da de ow·to·boo·ses
cancelled	cancelado	kan·se·la·do
delayed	retrasado	re·tra·sa·do
platform	plataforma	pla·ta·for·ma
ticket office	taquilla	ta·kee·ya
timetable	horario	o·ra·ryo
train station	estación de trenes	es·ta·syon de tre·nes
window seat	asiento junto a la ventana	a·syen·to khoon·to a la ven·ta·na

I want to go to ...
Quisiera ir a ...   kee·sye·ra eer a ...

Does it stop at ...?
¿Para en ...?   pa·ra en ...

What stop is this?
¿Cuál es esta parada?   kwal es es·ta pa·ra·da

What time does it arrive/leave?
¿A qué hora llega/sale?   a ke o·ra ye·ga/sa·le

How?	¿Cómo?	ko·mo
What?	¿Qué?	ke
When?	¿Cuándo?	kwan·do
Where?	¿Dónde?	don·de
Who?	¿Quién?	kyen
Why?	¿Por qué?	por ke

Please tell me when we get to ...
¿Puede avisarme cuando lleguemos a ...?   pwe·de a·vee·sar·me kwan·do ye·ge·mos a ...

I want to get off here.
Quiero bajarme aquí.   kye·ro ba·khar·me a·kee

Driving & Cycling

I'd like to hire a ...	Quisiera alquilar ...	kee·sye·ra al·kee·lar ...
4WD	un todo-terreno	oon to·do·te·re·no
bicycle	una bicicleta	oo·na bee·see·kle·ta
car	un coche	oon ko·che
motorcycle	una moto	oo·na mo·to

child seat	asiento de seguridad para niños	a·syen·to de se·goo·ree·da pa·ra nee·nyos
diesel	petróleo	pet·ro·le·o
gas	gasolina	ga·so·lee·na
helmet	casco	kas·ko
hitchhike	hacer dedo	a·ser dey·do
mechanic	mecánico	me·ka·nee·ko
service station	gasolinera	ga·so·lee·ne·ra
truck	camión	ka·myon

Is this the road to ...?
¿Se va a ... por esta carretera?   se va a ... por es·ta ka·re·te·ra

(How long) Can I park here?
¿(Cuánto tiempo) Puedo aparcar aquí?   (kwan·to tyem·po) pwe·do a·par·kar a·kee

The car has broken down (at ...).
El coche se ha averiado (en ...).   el ko·che se a a·ve·rya·do (en ...)

I had an accident.
He tenido un accidente.   e te·nee·do oon ak·see·den·te

I have a flat tyre.
Tengo un pinchazo.   ten·go oon peen·cha·so

I've run out of gas.
Me he quedado sin gasolina.   me e ke·da·do seen ga·so·lee·na

AYMARÁ & QUECHUA

The few phrases in Aymará and Quechua included here will be useful for those traveling in the Bolivian highlands. Travelers interested in learning more will find language courses in La Paz, Cochabamba and Sucre. Dictionaries and phrasebooks are available through Los Amigos del Libro and larger bookstores in La Paz, but to use them you'll first need a sound knowledge of Spanish.

In the following phrases, Aymará is given first, Quechua second. The principles of pronunciation for both languages are similar to those found in Spanish. An apostrophe (') represents a glottal stop, which is the 'nonsound' that occurs in the middle of 'uh-oh.'

Hi.	Laphi.	Raphi.
Hello.	Kamisaraki.	Napaykullayki.
Please.	Mirá.	Allichu.
Thank you.	Yuspagara.	Yusulipayki.
Yes.	Jisa.	Ari.
No.	Janiwa.	Mana.

It's a pleasure.		
Take chuima'hampi.	Tucuy sokoywan.	
How do you say ...?		
Cun sañasauca'ha ...?	Imainata nincha chaita ...?	
It's called ...		
Ucan sutipa'h ...	Chaipa'g sutin'ha ...	
Please repeat that.		
Uastata sita.	Ua'manta niway.	
Where is ...?		
Kaukasa ...?	Maypi ...?	
How much?		
K'gauka?	Maik'ata'g?	

distant	haya	caru
downhill	aynacha	uray
father	auqui	tayta

food	manka	mikíuy
lodging	korpa	pascana
mother	taica	mama
near	maka	kailla
river	jawira	mayu
snowy peak	kollu	riti-orko
trail	tapu	chakiñan
very near	hakítaqui	kaillitalla
water	uma	yacu

1	maya	u'
2	paya	iskai
3	quimsa	quinsa
4	pusi	tahua
5	pesca	phiska
6	zo'hta	so'gta
7	pakalko	khanchis
8	quimsakalko	pusa'g
9	yatunca	iskon
10	tunca	chunca
100	pataca	pacha'g
1000	waranka	huaranca

GLOSSARY

abra – opening; refers to a mountain pass, usually flanked by steep high walls

achachilas – *Aymará* mountain spirits, believed to be ancestors who look after their people and provide bounty from the earth

aduana – customs office

aguayo – colorful woven square used to carry things on one's back, also called a *manta*

albergue – basic guesthouse

alcaldía – municipal/town hall

Altiplano – High Plain; the largest expanse of level (and, in places, arable) land in the Andes, extending from Bolivia into southern Peru, northwestern Argentina and northern Chile

Alto Perú – the Spanish colonial name for the area now called Bolivia

anillos – literally 'rings'; the name used for main orbital roads around some Bolivian cities

apacheta – mound of stones on a mountain peak or pass; travelers carry a stone from the valley to place on top of the heap as an offering to the *apus;* the word may also be used locally to refer to the pass itself

api – a local drink made of maize

apu – mountain spirit who provides protection for travelers and water for crops, often associated with a particular *nevado*

arenales – sand dunes

artesanía – locally handcrafted items, or a shop selling them

Aymará – indigenous people of Bolivia; 'Aymará' also refers to the language of these people; also appears as 'Aymara' or *Kolla*

azulejos – decorative tiles, so named because most early Iberian *azulejos* were blue *(azul)* and white

bajones – immense flutes introduced by the Jesuits to the lowland indigenous communities; they are still featured in festivities at San Ignacio de Moxos

balsa – raft; in the Bolivian Amazon, *balsas* are used to ferry cars across rivers that lack bridges

barranquilleros – wildcat gold miners of the Yungas and Alto Beni regions

barrio – district or neighborhood

bloqueo – roadblock

bodega – boxcar, carried on some trains, in which 2nd-class passengers can travel; also wine cellar

boliche – nightclub

bolivianos – Bolivian people; also the Bolivian unit of currency

bus cama – literally 'bed bus'; a bus with fully reclining seats that is used on some international services, as well as a few longer domestic runs; it's often substantially more expensive than normal services

cabaña – cabin

camarín – niche in which a religious image is displayed

camba – a Bolivian from the Eastern Lowlands; some highlanders use this term for anyone from the Beni, Pando or Santa Cruz departments

cambista – street money-changer

camino – road, path, way

camión – flatbed truck; a popular form of local transportation

camioneta – pickup truck, used as local transportation in the Amazon Basin

campesino – subsistence farmer

cancha – open space in an urban area, often used for market activities; also soccer field

cerrado – sparsely forested scrub savanna, an endangered habitat that may be seen in Parque Nacional Noel Kempff Mercado

cerro – hill; this term is often used to refer to mountains, an understatement given their altitudes

cha'lla – offering

chalanas – ferries

chapacos – residents of Tarija; used proudly by *tarijeños* and in misguided jest by other Bolivians

(el) chaqueo – annual burning of Amazonian rainforest to clear agricultural and grazing land; there's a mistaken belief that the smoke from *el chaqueo* forms clouds and ensures good rains

charango – a traditional Bolivian ukulele-type instrument

chicha – fermented corn

chichería – bar specializing in *chicha*

cholo/a (m/f) – Quechua or Aymará person who lives in the city but continues to wear traditional dress

chompa – sweater/jumper

chullo – traditional pointed woolen hat, usually with earflaps

chullpa – funerary tower, normally from the Aymará culture

cocalero – coca grower

cochabambinos – Cochabamba locals

colectivo – minibus or collective taxi

Colla – alternative spelling for *Kolla*

comedor – dining hall

Comibol – Corporación Minera de Bolivia (Bolivian Mining Corporation), now defunct

cooperativos – small groups of miners who purchase temporary rights

cordillera – mountain range

corregidor – chief magistrate

cruce – turnoff

cruceños – Santa Cruz locals

DEA – Drug Enforcement Agency, the US drug-offensive body sent to Bolivia to enforce coca-crop substitution programs and to apprehend drug magnates

edificio – building

Ekeko – household god of abundance; the name means 'dwarf' in Aymará

Entel – Empresa Nacional de Telecomunicaciones (Bolivian national communications commission)

entrada – entrance procession

esquina – street corner, often abbreviated *esq*

estancia – extensive ranch, often a grazing establishment

feria – fair, market

ferrobus – passenger rail bus

flota – long-distance bus company

fútbol – soccer

guardaparque – national park ranger

hechicería – traditional Aymará witchcraft

helados – ice creams

hoja de ruta – circulation card

hornecinos – niches commonly found in Andean ruins, presumably used for the placement of idols and/or offerings

huemul – Andean deer

iglesia – church

Inca – dominant indigenous civilization of the Central Andes at the time of the Spanish conquest

ingenio – mill; in Potosí, it refers to silver smelting plants along the Ribera, where metal was extracted from low-grade ore by crushing it with a mill wheel in a solution of salt and mercury

jardín – garden

jefe de la estación – stationmaster

jipijapa – the fronds of the cyclanthaceae fan palm (*Carludovica palmata*)

jochi – agouti, an agile, long-legged rodent of the Amazon Basin; it's the only native animal that can eat the Brazil nut

Kallahuayas – itinerant traditional healers and fortune-tellers of the remote Cordillera Apolobamba; also spelled 'Kallawaya'

koa – sweet-smelling incense bush (*Senecio mathewsii*), which grows on Isla del Sol and other parts of the Altiplano and is used as an incense in Aymará ritual; also refers to a similar-smelling domestic plant *Mentha pulegium*, which was introduced by the Spanish

Kolla – the name used by the Aymará to refer to themselves; also spelt 'Colla'

Kollasuyo – Inca name for Bolivia, the 'land of the Kolla,' or Aymará people; the Spanish knew the area as Alto Perú, 'upper Peru'

La Diablada – Dance of the Devils, frequently performed at festivals

lago – lake

laguna – lagoon; shallow lake

lancha – motorboat

lavandería – laundry

licuado – fruit shake made with either milk or water

llanos – plains

loma – artificial mounds

Manco Capac – the first Inca emperor

manta – shawl, also called an *aguayo*

mariguí – a small and very irritating biting fly of the Amazon lowlands; the bite initially creates a small blood blister and then itches for the next two weeks, sometimes leaving scars

mate – herbal infusion of coca, chamomile, or similar

mercado – market

mestizo – person of mixed Spanish and indigenous parentage or descent; also architectural style incorporating natural-theme designs

micro – small bus or minibus

mirador – lookout

moto-taxi – motorbike taxi, a standard means of public transportation in the Eastern Lowlands and Amazon Basin

movilidades – anything that moves (in terms of transportation)

mudéjar – Spanish name for architecture displaying Moorish influences

ñandu – rhea, a large, flightless bird also known as the South American ostrich

nevado – snowcapped mountain peak

orureño/a (m/f) – Oruro local

paceño/a (m/f) – La Paz local

Pachamama – the Aymará and Quechua goddess or 'Mother Earth'

pahuichi – straw-thatched home with reed walls; a common dwelling in the Beni department

paja brava – spiky grass of the high Altiplano

parrilla – barbecue

parrillada – plate of mixed grilled meats

peajes – tolls sometimes charged at a *tranca* or toll station

peña – folk-music program

piso – floor

plata – silver (also slang for money)

pollera – traditional *chola* skirt

pongueaje – feudal system of peonage inflicted on the Bolivian peasantry; abolished after the April Revolution of 1952

pullman – 'reclining' 1st-class rail or bus seat; it may or may not actually recline

puna – high open grasslands of the Altiplano

punto – privately run phone office

quebrada – ravine or wash, usually dry

Quechua – highland (Altiplano) indigenous language of Ecuador, Peru and Bolivia; language of the former Inca empire

quena – simple reed flute

queñua – dwarf shaggy-barked tree (*Polylepis tarapana*) that grows at higher altitudes than any other tree in the world; it can survive at elevations of over 5000m

quinoa – highly nutritious grain similar to sorghum, used to make flour and thicken stews; grown at high elevations

quirquincho – armadillo carapace used in the making of *charangos;* nickname for a resident of Oruro

radiales – 'radials', the streets forming the 'spokes' of a city laid out in *anillos,* or rings; the best Bolivian example of this is in Santa Cruz

refugio – mountain hut

río – river

roca – rock

salar – salt pan or salt desert

salteña – pastry shell filled with meat and vegetables

saya – Afro-Bolivian dance that recalls the days of slavery in Potosí; it's featured at festivities

seringueros – rubber tappers in the Amazon region

SERNAP – Servicio Nacional de Áreas Protegidas, government-run environment agency

singani – a distilled grape spirit (local firewater)

soroche – altitude sickness, invariably suffered by newly arrived visitors to highland Bolivia

surazo – cold wind blowing into lowland Bolivia from Patagonia and Argentine pampa

surtidores de gasolina – gas dispensers/stations

tambo – wayside inn, market and meeting place selling staple domestic items

tarijeños – Tarija locals

taxista – taxi driver

termas – hot springs

terminal terrestre – long-distance bus terminal

thola – small desert bush

tienda – small shop, usually family-run

tinku – traditional festival that features ritual fighting, taking place mainly in the north of the department of Potosí; any bloodshed during these fights is considered an offering to Pachamama

totora – type of reed, used as a building material around Lake Titicaca

tranca – highway police post, usually found at city limits

tranquilo – 'tranquil', the word often used by locals to describe Bolivians' relatively safe and gentle demeanor; it's also used as an encouragement to slow down to the local pace of life

trufi – collective taxi or minibus that follows a set route

vicuña – a small camelid of the high *puna* or Altiplano; a wild relative of the llama and alpaca

viscacha – small, long-tailed rabbit-like rodent *(Lagidium viscaccia)* related to the chinchilla; inhabits rocky outcrops on the high Altiplano

Wara Wara – slow train on the Red Occidental that stops at most stations

yatiri – traditional Aymará healer or witch doctor

zampoña – pan flute made of hollow reeds of varying lengths, lashed together side by side; it's featured in most traditional music performances

FOOD GLOSSARY

ají – chili condiments

anticuchos – beef-heart shish kebabs

api – syrupy form of *chicha* made from sweet purple corn, lemon, cinnamon and white sugar

brazuelo – shoulder

buñuelo – sticky type of doughnut dipped in sugar syrup

cabrito – goat

camote – sweet potato

carne – beef

carne de chancho – pork

cerveza – beer; Taquiña is the best, Huari the fizziest

chairo – mutton or beef soup with *chuños*, potatoes and *mote*

chajchu – beef with *chuño*, hard-boiled egg, cheese and hot red-pepper sauce

chanko – chicken with yellow pepper and a tomato and onion sauce; a Tarija specialty

chaque – like *chupe* but much thicker and contains more grain

charque – meat jerky (often llama meat); the source of the English word 'jerky'

charquekan – meat jerky served with *choclo*, potato and boiled egg

chicha – popular beverage that is often alcoholic and made from fermented corn

chicharrón de cerdo – fried pork

chirimoya – custard apple; a green scaly fruit with creamy white flesh

choclo – large-grain corn (maize)

chuños – freeze-dried potatoes

chupe – thick meat, vegetable and grain soup with a clear broth flavored with garlic, *ají*, tomato, cumin or onion

churrasco – steak

cordero – lamb or mutton

cuñape – cassava and cheese roll

despepitado – (aka *mocachinchi*) a dried and shriveled peach in a boiled cane-sugar and cinnamon liquid

empanada – meat or cheese pasty

escabeche – vinegar-pickled vegetables

fricasé – pork soup; a specialty from La Paz

fritanga – spicy-hot pork with mint and hominy

haba – bean of the palqui plant found on the Altiplano, similar to fava beans

huminta – (aka *humita*) like a *tamale* but filled with cheese only and normally quite dry

kala purkha – soup made from corn that is cooked in a ceramic dish by adding a steaming chunk of heavy pumice; a Potosí and Sucre specialty

lawa – (aka *lagua*) meat-stew broth thickened with corn starch or wheat flour

licuado – fruit shake made with either milk or water

llajhua – spicy-hot tomato sauce

llaucha paceña – a doughy cheese bread

locoto – small, hot pepper pods

lomo – loin (of meat)

maní – peanuts

maracuyá – a sweet and delicious fruit (aka passion fruit); also see *tumbo*

masaco – *charque* served with mashed plantain, yuca and/or corn; a Bolivian Amazonian staple sometimes served with cheese

mate – herbal infusion of coca, chamomile, or similar

milanesa – a fairly greasy type of beef or chicken schnitzel (see *silpancho*)

mote – freeze-dried corn

oca – tough edible tuber similar to a potato

papas rellenas – mashed potatoes stuffed with veggies or

meat and fried; especially tasty when piping hot and served with hot sauce

parrillada – meat grill or barbecue

pastel – a deep-fried *empanada;* may be filled with chicken, beef or cheese

pescado – generic term for fish

pollo – chicken

pomelo – large, pulpy-skinned grapefruit

pucacapa – circular *empanada* filled with cheese, olives, onions and hot pepper sauce, and baked in an earth oven

queso – cheese

quinoa – nutritious grain similar to sorghum

saíce – hot meat and rice stew

salteña – delicious, juicy meat and vegetable pasty; a popular mid-morning snack

silpancho – a schnitzel pounded till very thin and able to absorb more grease than a *milanesa* (a properly prepared *silpancho* is said to be perfect to use when viewing a solar eclipse!)

tallarines – long, thin noodles

tamale – cornmeal dough filled with spiced beef, vegetables and potatoes, then wrapped in a corn husk and fried, grilled or baked

tarhui – legume from Sucre

thimpu – spicy lamb and vegetable stew

tomatada de cordero – lamb stew with tomato sauce

tucumana – *empanada*-like pastry stuffed till bursting with meat, olives, eggs, raisins and other goodies; originated in Tucumán, Argentina

tumbo – a variety of passion fruit

tuna – prickly pear cactus

witu – beef stew with pureed tomatoes

yuca – cassava (manioc) tuber

Behind the Scenes

SEND US YOUR FEEDBACK

We love to hear from travelers – your comments keep us on our toes and help make our books better. Our well-traveled team reads every word on what you loved or loathed about this book. Although we cannot reply individually to postal submissions, we always guarantee that your feedback goes straight to the appropriate authors, in time for the next edition. Each person who sends us information is thanked in the next edition – the most useful submissions are rewarded with a selection of digital PDF chapters.

Visit **lonelyplanet.com/contact** to submit your updates and suggestions or to ask for help. Our award-winning website also features inspirational travel stories, news and discussions.

Note: We may edit, reproduce and incorporate your comments in Lonely Planet products such as guidebooks, websites and digital products, so let us know if you don't want your comments reproduced or your name acknowledged. For a copy of our privacy policy visit lonelyplanet.com/privacy.

OUR READERS

Many thanks to the travellers who used the last edition and wrote to us with helpful hints, useful advice and interesting anecdotes: Alain Verhasselt, Aleksandra Urbanowska, Dennis Hamann, Eileen Finkelstein, Filip Vandamme, Gaëtan Coatanroch, Hannako Bakker, Iris Bos, Jeanne Marie Thomas, Johanna Grau, Kim de Oude, Laura Halbach, Lucie Dabos, Mariska Helmus, Michael Bech, Nicolas Combremont, Ole Brederlau, Olga Cirera, Peter Dullnig, Ramón de la Rosa Steinz, Robert Martyniecki, Sean Romero, Siu-yin Cheung, Stela Prodanovic, Susan Spronk, Tim Laslavic

WRITER THANKS

Isabel Albiston

Huge thanks to everyone who helped me on the road, especially Juan Carlos Vargas, Natasha Gamboa, Daniel Cahill, Paula Nina, Leo Lino, Gonzalo Sandoval, Goyo Surriable, Sandra Gilbert, Inez Daza, Javier Huarachi and Nick, and the many others whose names I don't recall. *Gracias* also to Bailey Freeman, Michael Grosberg and Mark Johanson. It was a great project to work on!

Michael Grosberg

I'm so grateful to all of the many people who helped me along the road, including Hector, Jaime and Edith in Tarija; Daniel, Zulma and Bismark from Condor Trekkers in Sucre; Rene from El Mundo Verde Travel in Cochabamba; and Vincent and Julia from Valle de los Condores; as well as other travelers along the road. And always to Rosie and Carly and Boone for their support.

Mark Johanson

Muchas gracias to all the Bolivian people who warmed my heart and filled my belly. Thanks to Felipe Bascuñán for allowing me to be gone from home for so many weeks and to Tomas Sivila, María Fernanda Alandia, Alex Villca Limaco, Raul Mendoza, Augusto Aruquipa Coromi, Rosa Maria Ruiz and Jose Antonio Diaz for being fountains of knowledge along the way.

ACKNOWLEDGMENTS

Climate map data adapted from Peel MC, Finlayson BL & McMahon TA (2007) 'Updated World Map of the Köppen-Geiger Climate Classification', *Hydrology and Earth System Sciences*, 11, 1633–44.

Cover photograph: Murals and women wearing traditional clothing, Aldo Pavan/4Corners ©

THIS BOOK

This 10th edition of Lonely Planet's *Bolivia* guidebook was researched and written by Isabel Albiston, Michael Grosberg and Mark Johanson. The previous edition was written by Michael Grosberg, Brian Kluepfel and Paul Smith. The 8th edition was written by Greg Benchwick and Paul Smith, and Professor Henry S Klein

was a contributing author. This guidebook was produced by the following:

Destination Editor
Bailey Freeman

Senior Product Editor
Saralinda Turner

Regional Senior Cartographer Corey Hutchison

Product Editor
Hannah Cartmel

Book Designer
Jessica Rose

Assisting Editors
Janet Austin, Michelle Bennett, Jacqueline Danam, Kellie Langdon, Jodie Martire, Susan Paterson, Maja Vatrić

Assisting Cartographers
Laura Bailey, Anita Banh

Cover Researcher
Naomi Parker

Thanks to Shona Gray, Anne Mason, Jenna Myers, Kathryn Rowan

Index

Map Legend

Sights

- Beach
- Bird Sanctuary
- Buddhist
- Castle/Palace
- Christian
- Confucian
- Hindu
- Islamic
- Jain
- Jewish
- Monument
- Museum/Gallery/Historic Building
- Ruin
- Shinto
- Sikh
- Taoist
- Winery/Vineyard
- Zoo/Wildlife Sanctuary
- Other Sight

Activities, Courses & Tours

- Bodysurfing
- Diving
- Canoeing/Kayaking
- Course/Tour
- Sento Hot Baths/Onsen
- Skiing
- Snorkeling
- Surfing
- Swimming/Pool
- Walking
- Windsurfing
- Other Activity

Sleeping

- Sleeping
- Camping
- Hut/Shelter

Eating

- Eating

Drinking & Nightlife

- Drinking & Nightlife
- Cafe

Entertainment

- Entertainment

Shopping

- Shopping

Information

- Bank
- Embassy/Consulate
- Hospital/Medical
- Internet
- Police
- Post Office
- Telephone
- Toilet
- Tourist Information
- Other Information

Geographic

- Beach
- Gate
- Hut/Shelter
- Lighthouse
- Lookout
- Mountain/Volcano
- Oasis
- Park
- Pass
- Picnic Area
- Waterfall

Population

- Capital (National)
- Capital (State/Province)
- City/Large Town
- Town/Village

Transport

- Airport
- Border crossing
- Bus
- Cable car/Funicular
- Cycling
- Ferry
- Metro station
- Monorail
- Parking
- Petrol station
- Subway/Subte station
- Taxi
- Train station/Railway
- Tram
- Underground station
- Other Transport

Routes

- Tollway
- Freeway
- Primary
- Secondary
- Tertiary
- Lane
- Unsealed road
- Road under construction
- Plaza/Mall
- Steps
- Tunnel
- Pedestrian overpass
- Walking Tour
- Walking Tour detour
- Path/Walking Trail

Boundaries

- International
- State/Province
- Disputed
- Regional/Suburb
- Marine Park
- Cliff
- Wall

Hydrography

- River, Creek
- Intermittent River
- Canal
- Water
- Dry/Salt/Intermittent Lake
- Reef

Areas

- Airport/Runway
- Beach/Desert
- Cemetery (Christian)
- Cemetery (Other)
- Glacier
- Mudflat
- Park/Forest
- Sight (Building)
- Sportsground
- Swamp/Mangrove

Note: Not all symbols displayed above appear on the maps in this book

OUR STORY

A beat-up old car, a few dollars in the pocket and a sense of adventure. In 1972 that's all Tony and Maureen Wheeler needed for the trip of a lifetime – across Europe and Asia overland to Australia. It took several months, and at the end – broke but inspired – they sat at their kitchen table writing and stapling together their first travel guide, *Across Asia on the Cheap*. Within a week they'd sold 1500 copies. Lonely Planet was born.
Today, Lonely Planet has offices in Franklin, London, Melbourne, Oakland, Beijing and Delhi, with more than 600 staff and writers. We share Tony's belief that 'a great guidebook should do three things: inform, educate and amuse'.

OUR WRITERS

Isabel Albiston
Southern Altiplano, Santa Cruz & Gran Chiquitania
After six years working for the *Daily Telegraph* in London, Isabel left to spend more time on the road. A job as writer for a magazine in Sydney, Australia, was followed by a four-month overland trip across Asia and five years living and working in Buenos Aires, Argentina. Isabel started writing for Lonely Planet in 2014 and has contributed to 10 guidebooks. She's currently based in Madrid, Spain. Isabel also wrote the Plan, Understand and Survival Guide chapters.

Michael Grosberg
Central Highlands, South Central Bolivia & the Chaco
Michael has worked on over 50 Lonely Planet guidebooks. Other international roles have included development work on Rota in the western Pacific, and teaching in Quito, Ecuador. He has also worked in South Africa, where he investigated and wrote about political violence, and trained newly elected government representatives. He received a Masters in Comparative Literature, and has taught literature and writing as an adjunct professor.

Mark Johanson
Lake Titicaca, The Cordilleras & Yungas, La Paz & Around, Amazon Basin
Mark Johanson grew up in Virginia and has called five different countries home over the last decade while circling the globe reporting for British newspapers (*The Guardian*), American magazines (*Men's Journal*) and global media outlets (CNN, BBC). When not on the road, you'll find him gazing at the Andes from his current home in Santiago, Chile. Follow his adventures at www.markjohanson.com

WITHDRAWN

Published by Lonely Planet Publications Pty Ltd
ABN 36 005 607 983
10th edition – June 2019
ISBN 978 1 786574 732
© Lonely Planet 2019   Photographs © as indicated 2019
10 9 8 7 6 5 4 3 2 1
Printed in China